Prentice Hall

MANAGEMENT INFORMATION SYSTEMS TITLES

MIS:

Jessup/Valacich, *Information Systems Today 2/e* © 2006
Laudon/Laudon, *Management Information Systems 9/e* © 2006
Laudon/Laudon, *Essentials of Business Information Systems 7/e* © 2007
Luftman et al., *Managing the IT Resource* © 2004
Malaga, *Information Systems Technology* © 2005
Martin et al., *Managing IT 5/e* © 2005
McLeod/Schell, *Management Information Systems 10/e* © 2007
McNurlin/Sprague, *Information Systems Management In Practice 7/e* © 2006
Miller, *MIS: Decision Making with Application Software (Cases) 3/e* © 2007
Senn, *Information Technology 3/e* © 2004

Database Management:

Bordoloi/Bock, *Oracle SQL* © 2004
Bordoloi/Bock, *SQL for SQL Server* © 2004
Frost/Day/VanSlyke, *Database Design and Development: A Visual Approach* © 2006
Hoffer/Prescott/McFadden, *Modern Database Management 8/e* © 2007
Kroenke, *Database Concepts 3/e* © 2007
Kroenke, *Database Processing 10/e* © 2006
Perry/Post, *Introduction to Oracle 10g* © 2007
Perry/Post, *Introduction to SQL 2005* © 2007

Systems Analysis and Design:

Hoffer/George/Valacich, *Modern Systems Analysis and Design 4/e* © 2005
Kendall/Kendall, *Systems Analysis and Design 6/e* © 2005
Valacich/George/Hoffer, *Essentials of Systems Analysis and Design 3/e* © 2006

Object-Oriented Systems Analysis and Design:

Stumpf/Teague, *Object-Oriented Systems Analysis and Design with UML* © 2005
George/Batra/Valacich/Hoffer, *Object-Oriented Systems Analysis and Design 2/e* © 2007

Decision Support Systems:

Turban/Aronson/Liang, *Decision Support and Business Intelligence Systems 8/e* © 2007
Marakas, *Decision Support Systems 2/e* © 2003
Marakas, *Modern Data Warehousing, Mining, and Visualization* © 2003

Data Communications & Networking:

Dooley, *Business Data Communications* © 2005
Panko, *Business Data Networks and Telecommunications 6/e* © 2007

Electronic Commerce:

Turban/King/Lee/Viehland, *Electronic Commerce 4/e* © 2006
Awad, *Electronic Commerce 3/e* © 2007

Project Management:

Fuller/Valacich/George, *Information Systems Project Management: A Process and Team Approach* © 2008

Enterprise Resource Planning:

Sumner, *Enterprise Resource Planning* © 2005

IS Communications:

Liebowitz/Agresti/Djavanshir, *Communicating as IT Professionals* © 2006

Knowledge Management:

Awad/Ghaziri, *Knowledge Management* © 2004
Becerra-Fernandez/Gonzalez/Sabherwal, *Knowledge Management* © 2004

Corporate Security:

Panko, *Corporate Computer and Network Security* © 2004
Volonino/Robinson, *Principles and Practice of Information Security* © 2004

For more information on these titles and the rest of Prentice Hall's best-selling Management Information Systems list, please visit www.prenhall.com/mis.

Object-Oriented Systems Analysis and Design

SECOND EDITION

Object-Oriented Systems Analysis and Design

SECOND EDITION

Joey F. George
Florida State University

Dinesh Batra
Florida International University

Joseph S. Valacich
Washington State University

Jeffrey A. Hoffer
University of Dayton

PEARSON

Prentice
Hall

Upper Saddle River, New Jersey 07458

Library of Congress Cataloging-in-Publication Data

George, Joey F.
Object-oriented systems analysis and design / Joey F. George. -- 2nd ed.
   p. cm.
Includes bibliographical references and index.
ISBN 0-13-227900-2
1. Object-oriented programming (Computer science) 2. System design. 3. System
analysis. I. Title.
   QA76.64.G45 2007
   005.1'17--dc22

                                                        2006028800

AVP/Executive Editor: Bob Horan
VP/Editorial Director: Jeff Shelstad
Manager, Product Development: Pamela Hersperger
Assistant Editor: Ana Jankowski
Associate Director, Production Editorial: Judy Leale
Senior Managing Editor: Cynthia Zonneveld
Production Editor: Denise Culhane
Permissions Coordinator: Charles Morris
Associate Director, Manufacturing: Vinnie Scelta
Manufacturing Buyer: Diane Peirano
Cover Design: Bruce Kenselaar
Cover Illustration/Photo: Getty Images – Photonica Amana America, Inc.
Composition/Full-Service Project Management: Carlisle Communications, Ltd.—Ann Imhof,
   Project Manager
Printer/Binder: Courier - Westford
Typeface: 10/12 Palatino

Credits and acknowledgments borrowed from other sources and reproduced, with permission, in this textbook appear on appropriate page within text.

Photo Credit p. 33, Ted Thai/Getty Images, Inc.

Microsoft® and Windows® are registered trademarks of the Microsoft Corporation in the U.S.A. and other countries. Screen shots and icons reprinted with permission from the Microsoft Corporation. This book is not sponsored or endorsed by or affiliated with the Microsoft Corporation.

Pearson Education LTD.
Pearson Education Singapore, Pte. Ltd
Pearson Education, Canada, Ltd
Pearson Education–Japan

Pearson Education Australia PTY, Limited
Pearson Education North Asia Ltd
Pearson Educación de Mexico, S.A. de C.V.
Pearson Education Malaysia, Pte. Ltd.

10 9 8 7 6 5 4 3 2 1
ISBN: 0-13-227900-2

To Karen, Evan, and Caitlin,
for your love, support, and patience.

—Joey

To Neema, Neha, and Rohan
for your love and support.

—Dinesh

To Jackie, Jordan, James, and the rest
of my family—your love and support
are my greatest inspirations.

—Joe

To Dillon, Nick, Anna, and Emma—and the
rest of the next generation
of analysts.

—Jeff

BRIEF CONTENTS

CONTENTS

PART II: PROJECT MANAGEMENT AND PLANNING 51

PART III: SYSTEM ANALYSIS   130

PREFACE

OUR APPROACH

Today's business environment is dynamic, turbulent, and global. Information systems have moved from back-office technologies understood by only a few to pervasive, essential support technologies that touch all aspects of business and all players in the game. As the role of information technology in business has changed, so have the underlying technologies and the manner in which systems are developed. Long predicted to be the next big thing, object orientation has finally arrived. The adoption of object orientation has not resulted in the dramatic paradigm shift that also was predicted for so long. Instead, we are witnessing the emergence of a hybrid approach to systems and their development—an approach that encompasses some aspects of traditional systems development and some aspects of object orientation. Although this book focuses on object-oriented systems analysis and design and it adheres to UML standards, it contains elements from other approaches, such as elements of relational database system design, that remain a part of systems development in business organizations today.

Among the four of us, we have more than 80 years of combined teaching experience in systems analysis and design, including teaching database management and object-oriented approaches. We have used that experience to create *Object-Oriented Systems Analysis and Design*, Second Edition. As was true in the first edition, we provide a clear presentation of the concepts, skills, and techniques students need to become effective systems analysts who work with others to create information systems for businesses. We continue to use a systems development cycle model as an organizing tool throughout the book to provide students with a strong conceptual and systematic framework. Internet coverage is provided in each chapter via an integrated, extended illustrative case (Pine Valley WebStore) and an end-of-chapter case (Broadway Entertainment Company, Inc.).

Many systems analysis and design courses involve lab work and outside reading. This means that lecture time can be limited. Based on market research and our own teaching experience, we understand the importance of using a book that combines depth of coverage with brevity. We have created a 14-chapter book that covers key object-oriented systems analysis and design (OOSAD) content without overwhelming students with unnecessary detail. The book is a compromise between briefer approaches to OOSAD and larger, more comprehensive volumes.

Object-Oriented Systems Analysis and Design, Second Edition is characterized by the following themes:

1. **Systems development is firmly rooted in an organizational context.** The successful systems analyst needs a broad understanding of organizations, organizational culture, and operation.
2. **Systems development is a practical field.** Coverage of current practices as well as accepted concepts and principles is essential in a textbook.
3. **Systems development is a profession.** Standards of practice, a sense of continuing personal development, ethics, and a respect for and collaboration with the work of others are general themes in the textbook. These principles are constant, regardless of the technical approach to development.

4. **Systems development has changed significantly with the explosive growth in the adoption of object-oriented approaches to systems development.** In many organizations, traditional tools that support systems development, such as data flow diagrams, have been replaced with object-oriented tools such as use-case diagrams, sequence diagrams, and analysis class diagrams. Pure relational database management approaches have been replaced with object-relational approaches. Our approach in this book focuses exclusively on diagrams and techniques associated with OOSAD.

5. **Success in systems analysis and design requires not only skills in methodologies and techniques but also in the management of time, resources, and risks.** Thus, learning systems analysis and design requires a thorough understanding of the process as well as the techniques and deliverables of the profession. Our approach to process emphasizes a systems development cycle as an organizing principle and the focus on development iterations prevalent in object-oriented analysis and design.

Given these themes, this textbook emphasizes the following:

- A business rather than a technology perspective.
- The role, responsibilities, and mindset of the systems analyst as well as the systems project manager, rather than those of the programmer or business manager.
- The methods and principles of systems development rather than the specific tools or tool-related skills of the field.

NEW TO THE SECOND EDITION

1. **UML 2 compliant:** The text is now UML 2 compliant throughout. Coverage of each UML diagram has been improved. Adequate coverage of UML diagrams is important for prospective systems analysts. A recent study shows that systems developers routinely rely on these diagrams in their work (Lang, 2006). Almost all, 97 percent, use screen prototypes, with the proportions using other analysis and design diagrams as follows: 95 percent use activity diagrams; 74 percent use entity relationship diagrams; 72 percent rely on use-case diagrams; 62 percent use class diagrams; and 50 percent use state diagrams. All of these diagram types are covered in the book.

2. **Agile methodologies:** While the first edition included limited coverage of eXtreme programming, the text now contains much more extensive treatment of agile methodologies, including but not limited to eXtreme programming. Coverage extends across several chapters, including Chapters 1, 5, and 14.

3. **Use cases:** Chapter 6 now features a more extensive treatment of use cases and of differing levels of perspective from which use cases can be written.

4. **OCL:** The object constraint language (OCL) is introduced to express business rules in Chapter 9.

5. **Patterns:** In Chapter 12, patterns are used to convert sequence diagrams from the analysis to the design stage.

6. **BEC case:** The Broadway Entertainment Company case has been updated and improved, both to be more current, in business terms, and to feature more object-oriented systems analysis and design in the case.

AUDIENCE

Object-Oriented Systems Analysis and Design is written with the assumption that students have taken an introductory course on computer systems and have experience writing programs in at least one programming language, preferably an object-oriented language. We review basic system principles for those students who have not been exposed to the material on which systems development methods are based. We also assume that students have a solid background in computing literacy and a general understanding of the core elements of a business, including basic terms associated with the production, marketing, finance, and accounting functions.

ORGANIZATION

The overall organization of the book is the same as it was in the first edition. The outline of the book begins with basic foundational material and then follows a systems development cycle, which allows for a logical progression of topics. This cycle is designed to be high level and consists of four steps: planning, analysis, design, and implementation. The book, then, has five parts:

- Part I, "Foundations for Object-Oriented Systems Development," gives an overview of systems development and previews the remainder of the book.
- Part II, "Project Management and Planning," covers how to assess project feasibility and build the baseline project.
- Part III, "Systems Analysis," covers determining system requirements, process modeling, conceptual modeling, and determining the best design.
- Part IV, "Systems Design," covers how to design the human interface and databases.
- Part V, "System Implementation and Operation," covers system implementation, operation, closedown, and system maintenance.

DISTINCTIVE FEATURES

Some of the distinctive features of the second edition of *Object-Oriented Systems Analysis and Design* are:

1. **System Development Cycle (SDC) Framework**—A systems development methodology is central in the development of an information system. The generic methodology used here is a four-step systems development cycle. Each chapter, except Chapter 2, opens with an SDC figure and shows how each step of the SDC builds on the previous step.
2. **Object-Oriented (OO) definitions chapter**—Chapter 2 is devoted to definitions of key OO terms and examples of them. The chapter serves as a key reference as students progress through the book.
3. **Standard Unified Modeling Language (UML) terminology and diagrams**—All of the terminology and diagrams are UML compliant. Diagrams include use case, sequence, state transition, and so on.
4. **Running case: The Pine Valley Furniture WebStore case**—The PVF case is used throughout the text as an example of OOSAD development. The case shows how a team of analysts work together to develop, propose, implement, and maintain Internet-based applications.
5. **Broadway Entertainment Company, Inc.**—This end-of-chapter case illustrates how a fictional video and record retailer develops an object-oriented application. This case first appears at the end of Chapter 2 and concludes at the end of Chapter 14.
6. **Communication**—The book includes extensive coverage of oral and written communication skills including systems documentation, project management, team management, and a variety of systems development and acquisition strategies.

7. **Managerial focus**—Throughout the book, the treatment of systems development and implementation is always within the context of management of change, conversion strategies, and organizational factors in systems acceptance.
8. **Database approach**—Unique approach to data using object-relational database management systems (DBMSs) featuring Oracle10g.
9. **Diagrams**—The diagrams used throughout the text were developed using the Rational Rose CASE tool, Microsoft's Visio, and Microsoft's Project.

Illustrative Fictional Cases

Pine Valley Furniture (PVF) This case is introduced in Chapter 4 and revisited throughout the book. As key systems development cycle and object-oriented concepts are presented, they are applied and illustrated with this case. A margin icon identifies the location of the case. PVF is a furniture company, founded in 1980, and management has decided to explore electronic commerce as an avenue to increase its market share. A case problem related to PVF is included in the end-of-chapter material for many of the chapters.

Broadway Entertainment Company, Inc. (BEC) This fictional video rental and music company is used as an extended case at the end of each chapter, beginning with Chapter 2. Designed to bring the chapter concepts to life, this case illustrates how a company initiates, plans, models, designs, and implements a Web-based customer relationship management system using an object-oriented systems development approach. Discussion questions are included to promote critical thinking and class participation. Suggested solutions to the discussion questions are provided in the Instructor's Resource Manual located in the Faculty area of the Website: http://www.prenhall.com/george.

End-of-Chapter Material

We have developed an extensive selection of end-of-chapter material designed to accommodate various learning and teaching styles.

Key Points Review This repeats the learning objectives that appear at the opening of the chapter and summarizes the key points related to the objectives.

Key Terms Checkpoint This is designed as a self-test feature. Students match each key term in the chapter with its definition.

Review Questions These questions test students' understanding of key concepts.

Problems and Exercises These problems and exercises test students' analytical skills and require them to apply key concepts.

Discussion Questions These questions promote class participation and discussion.

Case Problems These problems require students to apply the concepts of the chapter to three fictional cases from various industries. The illustrative case from the book—Pine Valley Furniture—is revisited. Other cases are from various fields such as medicine, agriculture, and technology. Solutions are provided in the Instructor's Manual located in the Faculty area of the Website: http://www.prenhall.com/george.

Margin Term Definitions Each of the key terms and their definitions appear in the margins. A glossary of terms appears at the back of the book.

References Located at the end of the text, references organized by chapter list more than 100 books and journals that can provide students and faculty with additional coverage of topics.

SOFTWARE PACKAGING OPTIONS

- Visible Analyst
- Microsoft Visio
- Microsoft Project
- Oracle10g

To enhance the hands-on learning process, Prentice Hall offers the option to package this text with a choice of Visible Analyst, Microsoft Visio, Microsoft Project, or Oracle10g software. Your Prentice Hall sales representative can provide additional information on pricing and ordering.

INSTRUCTOR'S RESOURCE CENTER

The Instructor's Resource Center found on the catalog page is a password protected Faculty site that contains instructor supplements for download.

1. *PowerPoint presentation slides feature lecture notes that highlight key text terms and concepts.*
2. *The **Instructor's Resource Manual** is secured in the password-protected Faculty area. It contains teaching suggestions and answers to all text review questions, problems, exercises, and case problems.*
3. *The **Test Item File** also is secured in the Faculty area. It is available in Microsoft Word, converted WebCT, and BlackBoard files.*
4. *An **Image Library** is provided in the Faculty area. This is a collection of figures and tables from the text to enhance class lectures and PowerPoint slides.*

ACKNOWLEDGMENTS

The authors have been blessed by considerable assistance from many people on all aspects of preparation of this text and its supplements. We are, of course, responsible for what eventually appears between the covers, but the insights, corrections, contributions, and proddings of others have greatly improved our manuscript. The people we recognize here all have a strong commitment to students, to the IS field, and to excellence. Their contributions have stimulated us and frequently rejuvenated us during periods of waning energy for this project.

We would like to recognize the efforts of the many faculty and practicing systems analysts who served as reviewers for this book. We have tried to deal with each reviewer comment, and although we did not always agree with specific points (within the approach we wanted to take with this book), all reviewers made us stop and think carefully about what and how we were writing. The reviewers were:

Richard Allen, Richland Community College
Allen Corbett, University of South Carolina-Columbia
Terry Fox, Baylor University
Marilyn Griffin, Virginia Polytechnic Institute
Russ Hanna, Johnson County Community College
David James Howe, Augusta Technical College

Robert Josefek, University of Southern California, Marshall School of
   Business
Leonardo Legorreta, California State University-Sacramento
Mary Beth Zak Lohse, Ohio State University
Trevor Moores, University of Nevada, Las Vegas
Alan Graham Peace, West Virginia State University
Vladimir V. Riabov, Rivier College
Toru Sakaguchi, Northern Kentucky University
Carl Scott, University of Houston
Eileen Sellers, Maryville University
Deborah Smith, University of Nevada-Las Vegas
Ron Sones, James Madison University
Tei Wei Wang, FIU-University Part Campus
Heinz Weistroffer, Virginia Commonwealth University
Connie Wells, Roosevelt University
Elaine Weltz, Seattle Pacific University
Robert Wrembel, Poznan University of Technology
H. R. Weistroffer, Virginia Commonwealth University

We have been fortunate to work with a large number of creative and insightful people at Prentice Hall, who have added much to the development, format, and production of this text. We have been thoroughly impressed with their commitment to this text and to the IS education market. These people include Robert Horan, Executive Editor; Debbie Clare, Marketing Manager; Ana Jankowski, Assistant editor; Denise Culhane, Production editor; [designer]; and Laura Cirigliano, Marketing Assistant. We also want to thank Ann Imhof and the folks at Carlisle Communications, Ltd., for their hard work in getting this book ready for production.

Thanks also go to our faculty colleagues Fred McFadden (University of Colorado-Colorado Springs), Mary Prescott (University of Tampa), and Dean Joyce Elam (Florida International University).

We extend a special note of thanks to Jeremy Alexander of Web-X.com. Jeremy was instrumental in conceptualizing and writing the Pine Valley WebStore feature that appears throughout the book. Jeremy also built the installation procedures on the Website for Oracle, and Saonee Sarker of Washington State University developed the Oracle tutorial modules.

The writing of this text has involved thousands of hours of time from the authors and from all of the aforementioned people. Although our names will be visibly associated with this book, we know that much of the credit goes to the individuals and organizations listed here for any success this book might achieve. It is important for the reader to recognize all the individuals and organizations that have been committed to the preparation and production of this book.

ABOUT THE AUTHORS

Joey F. George is professor and Thomas L. Williams Jr. Eminent Scholar in Information Systems in the College of Business at Florida State University. Dr. George earned his bachelor's degree at Stanford University in 1979 and his Ph.D. in management at the University of California at Irvine in 1986. He was previously the Edward G. Schlieder Chair of Information Systems in the E. J. Ourso College of Business Administration at Louisiana State University. He also served at Florida State University as chair of the Department of Information and Management Sciences from 1995 to 1998.

Dr. George has published many articles in such journals as *Information Systems Research, Communications of the ACM, MIS Quarterly, Journal of MIS*, and *Communication Research*. His research interests focus on the use of information systems in the workplace, including computer-based monitoring, computer-mediated deceptive communication, and group support systems.

Dr. George, along with Joseph Valacich and Jeffrey Hoffer, is coauthor of the textbooks *Modern Systems Analysis and Design*, fifth edition, published in 2007 by Prentice Hall, and *Essentials of Systems Analysis and Design*, third edition, copyright 2006 by Prentice Hall. He is also the editor of *Computers and Society: Privacy, Ethics, and the Internet*, copyright 2004 by Prentice Hall. Dr. George is currently the Editor-in-Chief for the journal *Communications of the AIS*. In the past, he has served as a senior editor and an associate editor for the journal *MIS Quarterly* and an associate editor for the journal *Information Systems Research*. He has also served on various other journal editorial boards. Dr. George was the conference co-chair for the 2001 ICIS, held in New Orleans, Louisiana, and he was the co-chair of the doctoral consortium for the 2003 ICIS, held in Seattle, Washington.

Dinesh Batra is professor at the Department of Decision Sciences and Information Systems in the College of Business Administration at the Florida International University. He earned his B.Tech. from the Indian Institute of Technology at Delhi in 1979, M.B.A. from Southern Illinois University at Carbondale in 1985, and Ph.D. from Indiana University at Bloomington in 1989. After his bachelor's degree and during the period 1979–1983, he worked for four years in a consulting company conducting process and design of large engineering projects.

Dr. Batra has published over 25 articles in such journals as *Management Science, Communication of the ACM, Journal of MIS, International Journal of Human Computer Studies, Data Base, European Journal of Information Systems, Journal of Database Management, Communications of the AIS, Decision Support Systems, Computers and OR,* and *Information & Management*. His research interests focus on usability issues in systems and database analysis and design. He has served as an associate editor in the journal Data Base, and is on the editorial board of the *Journal of Database Management* and *Information Systems Management*. He has also served as the director of the MS in MIS program at the Florida International University. He is currently the president of the AIS Special Interest Group on Systems Analysis & Design (SIGSAND).

Joseph S. Valacich, The George and Carolyn Hubman Distinguished Professor in MIS and the inaugural Marian E. Smith Presidential Endowed Chair, joined the faculty at Washington State University in 1996. He was previously an associate professor with tenure (early) at Indiana University, Bloomington, and was named the Sanjay Subhedar Faculty Fellow. He has had visiting faculty appointments at the University of Arizona, City University of Hong Kong, Buskerud College (Norway), Riga Technical University (Latvia), and the Helsinki School of Economics and Business. He received the Ph.D. degree from the University of Arizona (MIS), and the M.B.A. and B.S. (computer science) degrees from the University of Montana. His teaching interests include systems analysis and design, collaborative computing, project management, and management of information systems. Professor Valacich served on the national task forces to design *IS '97* and *2002: The Model Curriculum and Guidelines for Undergraduate Degree Programs in Information Systems,* as well as *MSIS 2000* and *2006: The Master of Science in Information Systems Model Curriculum.* He also served on the Executive Committee, funded by the National Science Foundation, to define the *IS Program Accreditation Standards* and on the Board of Directors for CSAB (formally, the Computing Sciences Accreditation Board), representing the Association for Information Systems (AIS). He was the general conference co-chair for the 2003 International Conference on Information Systems (ICIS) in Seattle and was the vice-chair of ICIS 1999 in Charlotte, NC.

Jeffrey A. Hoffer is the Sherman-Standard Register Professor of Data Management in the Department of MIS, Operations Management, and Decision Sciences in the School of Business Administration at the University of Dayton. He also taught at Indiana University and Case Western Reserve University. Dr. Hoffer earned his A.B. from Miami University in 1969 and his Ph.D. from Cornell University in 1975.

Dr. Hoffer has published four other college textbooks: *Modern Systems Analysis and Design*, fifth edition, with Joey George and Joseph Valacich; *Essentials of Systems Analysis and Design*, third edition, with Joseph Valacich and Joey George; *Modern*

Database Design, eighth edition, with Mary Prescott and Fred McFadden; and *Information Technology for Managers: What Managers Need to Know*, fourth edition, with Carol Brown, Daniel DeHayes, E. Wainright Martin, and William Perkins, all published by Prentice Hall. His research articles have appeared in numerous journals, including *MIS Quarterly Executive, Journal of Database Management, Small Group Research, Communications of the ACM,* and *Sloan Management Review*. He has received research and equipment grants from IBM Corporation, U.S. Department of the Navy, and NCR Teradata division.

Dr. Hoffer is cofounder of the International Conference on Information Systems and the Association for Information Systems. He has served as a guest lecturer at Catholic University of Chile, Santiago, and the Helsinki School of Economics and Business in Mikkeli, Finland. Dr. Hoffer is currently an associate director of the Teradata University Network.

Joey F. George,
Florida State University

Dinesh Batra,
Florida International University

Joseph S. Valacich,
Washington State University

Jeffrey A. Hoffer,
University of Dayton

REFERENCE

Lang, M. 2006. "An Empirical Study of Processes, Methods, and Techniques for Web/Hypermedia Systems Design. *Information Systems Management.*

Object-Oriented Systems Analysis and Design

SECOND EDITION

Chapter

1

The Object-Oriented Systems Development Environment

Chapter Objectives

After studying this chapter, you should be able to:

➤ Define information systems analysis and design.

➤ Explain the basics about systems.

➤ Describe the information systems development cycle (SDC).

➤ Describe three types of information systems: transaction processing systems, management information systems, and decision support systems.

➤ Describe the organizational role of the systems analyst in information systems development.

➤ Recount the evolution of systems development methodologies.

Chapter Contents

The key to success in business is the ability to gather, organize, and interpret information. The Object-Oriented Systems Analysis and Design (OOSAD) approach for developing information systems is gaining popularity quickly. As is true of other approaches to systems analysis and design, the person most involved in OOSAD is the systems analyst. As a systems analyst, you will enjoy a rich career path that will enhance your computer, organizational, analytical, and interpersonal skills.

Although OOSAD is based on object-oriented concepts and is different from the still-popular structured analysis methodology developed in the 1970s, the overall focus on the development of effective information systems is the same. The four major steps involved in developing systems are the foundation for all approaches to systems analysis and design: (1) project management and planning, (2) systems analysis, (3) systems design, and (4) systems implementation and operation. These steps represent a basic problem-solving approach for systems development. They include such basic development activities as evaluating economic and technical feasibility; understanding user requirements; evaluating design alternatives; determining the best alternative; converting design specifications to code; and integrating and testing the hardware, software, and data communications components. The actual methods might vary from one approach to another and from one organization to another, and advances in development might facilitate more design choices; however, the essential steps remain the same. This systems development cycle is illustrated in Figure 1.1. Most chapters of this book include an updated version of the systems development cycle, highlighting which steps have been covered and which steps remain.

This text requires a general understanding of computer-based information systems as provided in an introductory information systems course. Chapter 1 previews OOSAD and lays the groundwork for the rest of the book.

Figure 1.1 The Systems Development Cycle

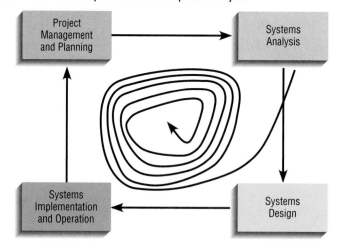

WHAT IS INFORMATION SYSTEMS ANALYSIS AND DESIGN?

Information systems analysis and design
The process of developing and maintaining an information system.

Information systems analysis and design is a method used by companies ranging from IBM to Pepsi to Amazon.com to create and maintain information systems that perform basic business functions such as keeping track of customer names and addresses, processing orders, and paying employees. The main goal of systems analysis and design is to improve organizational systems, typically by applying software that can help employees accomplish key business tasks more easily and efficiently. A systems analyst is at the center of developing this software. The analysis and design of information systems are based on the following:

Systems analyst
The organizational role most responsible for the analysis and design of information systems.

- An understanding of the organization's objectives, structure, and processes.
- Knowledge of how to exploit information technology for advantage.

To be successful in this endeavor, it is essential to follow a systematic approach such as the four-step approach shown in Figure 1.1 to identifying, analyzing, designing, and implementing an information system. This book details a methodology for developing systems based on object-oriented systems analysis and design. First, some core concepts pertaining to systems analysis and design are described.

SYSTEMS ANALYSIS AND DESIGN: CORE CONCEPTS

Application software
Software designed to process data and support users in an organization. Examples of application software include spreadsheets, word processors, payroll systems, and inventory management systems.

The major goal of systems analysis and design is to improve organizational systems. Often this involves developing or acquiring application software and training employees to use it. Application software, also called a system, is designed to support a specific organizational function or process, such as inventory management, payroll, or market analysis. The goal of application software is to turn data into information. For example, software developed for the inventory department at a bookstore may keep track of the number of books in stock for the latest best-seller. Software for the payroll department might keep track of the changing pay rates of employees. For office automation needs, a variety of off-the-shelf application software, such as Microsoft Office or another office suite, can be purchased. For enterprise-wide needs, a large, integrated, off-the-shelf software package configured to an organization's needs might address a variety of organizational functions, such as inventory management, accounting, and logistics. However, off-the-shelf software might not always satisfy the specific needs of a particular organization, and so the organization might choose to develop its own system. In developing its own system, an organization can deploy components that are purchased from vendors for a part of the overall system and code the remaining part.

In addition to application software, the information system includes the following:

- The hardware and systems software on which the application software runs. Note that the system software helps the computer function, whereas the application software helps the user perform tasks such as generating an invoice, preparing a spreadsheet, and linking to the Internet.

- Documentation and training materials, which are materials created by the systems analyst to help employees use the software they've helped create.

- The specific job roles associated with the overall system, such as the people who run the computers and keep the software operating.

- Controls and security mechanisms, which are parts of the software written to help prevent fraud and theft.

- The people who use the software in order to do their jobs.

The components of a computer-based information systems application are summarized in Figure 1.2. We address all the dimensions of the overall system, with particular emphasis on application software development, which is the primary responsibility of a systems analyst.

Figure 1.2
Components of a
Computer-Based
Information Systems
Application

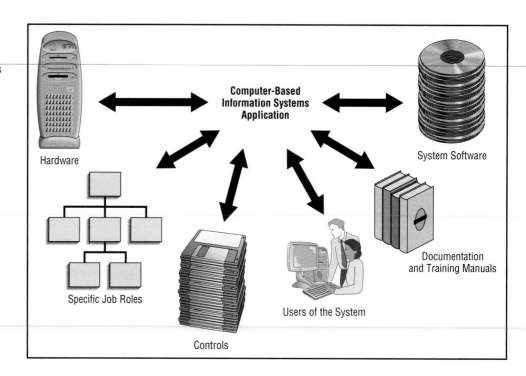

Our goal is to help you understand and follow the systems development process that leads to the creation of information systems. As shown in Figure 1.3, proven methodologies, techniques, and tools are central to systems development processes (and to this book).

Methodologies are a sequence of step-by-step approaches that help in the development of the final product: the information system. Most methodologies incorporate several development techniques, such as direct observations and interviews with users of the current system.

Techniques are processes that analysts follow to help ensure that their work is well thought out, complete, and comprehensible. Techniques provide support for a wide range of tasks including conducting thorough interviews with current and future users of the information systems to determine what the system should do, planning and managing the activities in a systems development project, diagramming how the system will function, and designing the reports, such as invoices, that the system will generate for its users to perform their jobs.

Tools are computer programs, such as computer-aided software engineering (CASE) tools, that make it easy to use specific techniques. These three elements—methodologies, techniques, and tools—work together to form an organizational approach to systems analysis and design.

The rest of this chapter covers approaches to systems development—the data-, process-, and object-oriented approaches. Although the data- and process-oriented

Figure 1.3 The
Software Development
Process Uses
Methodologies,
Techniques, and Tools

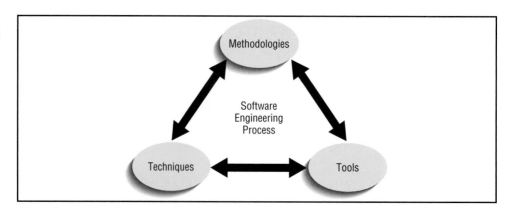

approaches are not the focus of this book, a rudimentary understanding of these approaches is important not only because they are still being used, but also because they provide a historical context for the currently popular object-oriented approach. This book also identifies the various people who develop systems and the different types of systems they develop. Included as well is a brief introduction to the Unified Modeling Language (UML), a widely accepted standard for representing object-oriented systems designs. The bulk of the next chapter is devoted to introducing object-oriented concepts. Before covering information systems for business, let's briefly discuss what the word *system* means.

SYSTEMS

The key term used most frequently in this book is system. Understanding systems and how they work is critical to understanding systems analysis and design.

Definitions of a System and Its Parts

System
Group of interrelated procedures used for a business function, with an identifiable boundary, working together for some purpose.

A system is an interrelated set of business procedures, objects, or components used within one business unit, working together for some purpose. For example, a system in the payroll department keeps track of checks, whereas an inventory system keeps track of supplies. The two systems are separate. A system has nine characteristics, seven of which are shown in Figure 1.4. A detailed explanation of each characteristic follows, but the figure shows that a system exists within a larger world—an environment. A boundary separates the system from its environment. The system takes input from the environment, processes it, and sends the resulting output back to its environment. The arrows in the figure show this interaction between the system and the world outside of it.

1. System components
2. Interrelationships

Figure 1.4 Seven Characteristics of a System

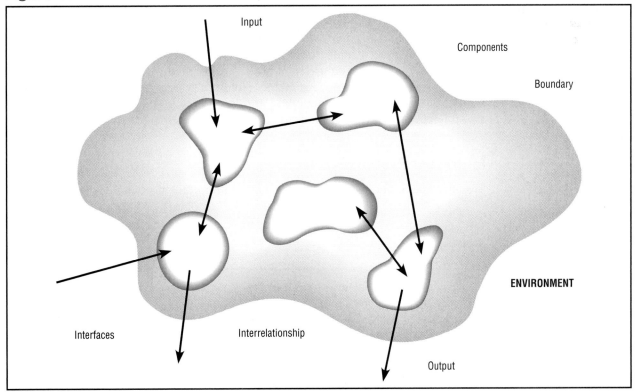

3. Boundary
4. Purpose
5. Environment
6. System interfaces
7. Input
8. Output
9. Constraints

System component
An irreducible part or aggregation of parts that makes up a system; also called a subsystem.

Interrelated components
Dependence of one part of the system on one or more other system parts.

Boundary
The line that marks the inside and outside of a system and that sets off one system from other systems in the organization.

Purpose
The overall goal or function of a system.

Environment
Everything external to a system that interacts with the system.

System interface
Point of contact where a system meets its environment or where subsystems meet each other.

Constraint
A limit to what a system can accomplish.

A system is made up of components. A system component is either an irreducible part or an aggregate of parts, also called a subsystem. The simple concept of a component is powerful. For example, just as with an automobile or a stereo system that is designed properly, the system can be repaired or upgraded by changing individual components without having to make changes throughout the entire system. The components are interrelated; that is, the function of one is tied to the functions of the others. For example, the work of one component, such as a sales order, might depend on another component, such as a shopping cart. A system has a boundary within which all of its components are contained and that establishes the limits of a system, separating it from other systems. Components within the boundary can be changed, whereas systems outside the boundary cannot be changed. All of the components work together to achieve some overall purpose for the larger system: the system's reason for existing.

A system exists within an environment, which is everything outside the system's boundary that influences the system. For example, the environment of a state university includes prospective students, foundations and funding agencies, and the news media. Usually, the system interacts with its environment. A university interacts with prospective students by having open houses and recruiting from local high schools. An information system interacts with its environment by receiving data (raw facts) and information (data processed in a useful format). Figure 1.5 shows how a university can be seen as a system. The points at which the system meets its environment are called system interfaces, and system interfaces also exist between subsystems.

A system must face constraints in its functioning because of limitations (in terms of capacity, speed, or capabilities) to what it can do and how it can achieve its purpose within its environment. Some of these constraints are imposed inside the system (e.g., a limited number of staff available), and others are imposed by the environment (e.g., due dates or regulations). A system takes input from its environment in order to function. People, for example, take in food, oxygen, and water from the environment as input. You are constrained from breathing fresh air if you're in an elevator with someone who is smoking. Finally, a system returns output to its environment as a result of its functioning and thus achieves its purpose. The system is constrained if electrical power is cut.

Important Systems Concepts

Systems analysts need to know several other important systems concepts:

- Decomposition
- Modularity
- Coupling
- Cohesion

Decomposition
The process of breaking down a system into smaller constituents, which may be subsystems or terminal units.

Decomposition is the process of breaking down a system into smaller constituents, which may be subsystems or terminal units. The subsystems are themselves systems and can be broken down recursively until only terminal units remain. A terminal unit is an irreducible part; that is, a piece that cannot or need not be broken down further. How does decomposition aid understanding of a system? It results in smaller and less complex pieces that are easier to understand than larger,

Figure 1.5 A University as a System

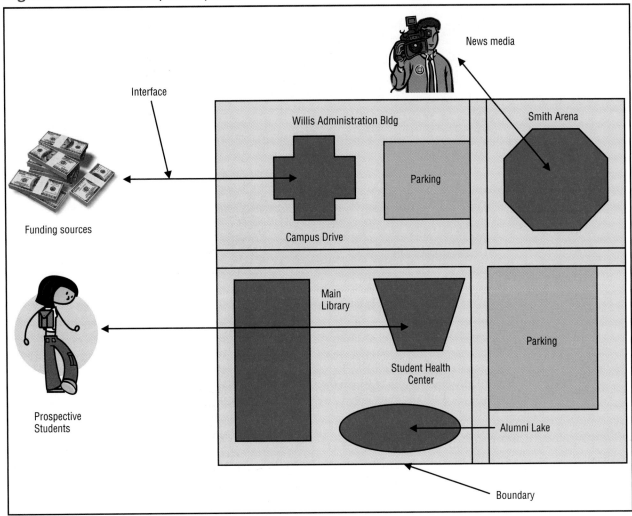

complicated pieces. Decomposing a system also allows us to focus on one particular part of a system, making it easier to think of how to modify that one part independently of the entire system. Decomposition is a technique that allows the systems analyst to do the following:

• Break a system into small, manageable, and understandable subsystems.
• Focus attention on one area (subsystem) at a time without interference from other areas.
• Concentrate on the part of the system pertinent to a particular group of users without confusing users with unnecessary details.
• Build different parts of the system at independent times and have the help of different analysts.

Figure 1.6 shows the decomposition of a USB flash drive. Decomposing the system into components reveals the system's inner workings. Each of the eight components identified in the figure has a separate function. The USB connector allows the flash drive to interact with a computer system, so the connector is also an interface. The flash memory chip is where the data are stored. The LED is on when the flash drive is successfully connected and is operating appropriately. The other components have their own jobs to perform as well. Breaking a system, such as a flash drive, down into its components reveals even more about the system's inner workings and greatly enhances our understanding of how the overall system works.

Figure 1.6
**A USB-Flash Drive
System Is
Decomposed into
Eight Components**

Source: http://en.wikipedia.
org/wiki/USB_flash_drive,
accessed 9/28/05. (Used by
permission.)

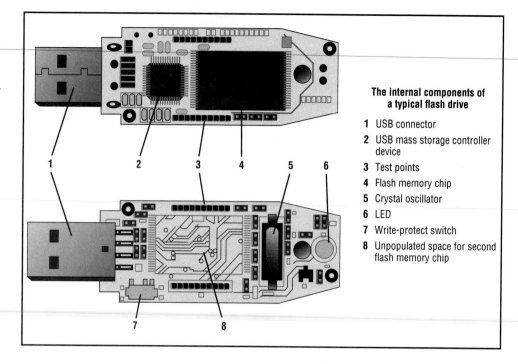

**The internal components of
a typical flash drive**

1 USB connector
2 USB mass storage controller
   device
3 Test points
4 Flash memory chip
5 Crystal oscillator
6 LED
7 Write-protect switch
8 Unpopulated space for second
   flash memory chip

Modularity
Dividing a system into
smaller chunks or modules.

Modularity is a direct result of decomposition. It refers to dividing a system into smaller chunks or modules. Modules can represent a system simply, making it easier to understand and easier to redesign and rebuild. For example, each of the separate components in the flash drive system in Figure 1.6 can be considered a module in order to show how decomposition makes it easier to understand the overall system.

Coupling
The extent to which subsystems depend on each other.

Coupling means that subsystems are dependent on each other. Subsystems should be as independent as possible. If one subsystem fails and other subsystems are highly dependent on it, the others either will fail themselves or have problems functioning. Looking at Figure 1.6, we would say the components of a flash drive are tightly coupled. The USB connector, the USB mass storage controller, and the flash memory chip must all be working correctly for any data to be moved from a computer to the drive or from the drive to a computer. If one of these components fails, the flash drive must be repaired (or thrown away in favor of buying a new one, given how inexpensive they are). In a home computer system, the components are more loosely coupled than in a flash drive. If a hard drive in a home computer fails, it can be pulled from the computer and repaired or easily replaced. The entire computer does not have to be repaired or thrown away. In a home computer, many of the components, such as the central processor, core memory, hard drives, CD and DVD drives, and modems, are typically physically separate and function independently.

Cohesion
The extent to which a system or subsystem performs a single function.

Cohesion is the extent to which a subsystem performs a single function. In the flash drive example, the LED performs a single function of being on when the drive is connected to a computer and being off otherwise.

This brief discussion of systems should provide preparation for thinking about computer-based information systems and how they are built. Many of the same principles that apply to systems in general apply to information systems, as well. (For example, the generic term interrelated, which deals with the dependency of components on each other, corresponds to certain information systems constructs, such as association and aggregation.) Interfaces, components, inputs, and outputs are important in the analysis and design of information systems. We now explain the steps in information systems analysis and design in more detail and provide a history of systems analysis, which includes the process-, data-, and object-oriented approaches.

In the preview section in this chapter, we listed four steps in information systems development (see Figure 1.1). We now define these four steps with special emphasis on analysis and design.

Step One: Project Management and Planning

Project management and planning
The first step in systems development in which an organization's total information systems needs are analyzed and arranged, and in which a potential information systems project is identified and an argument for continuing or not continuing with the project is presented.

The first step in a systems development project, project management and planning, has two primary activities. First, someone identifies the need for a new or enhanced system. Information needs of the organization are examined and projects to meet these needs are identified. The organization's information systems needs can result from the following:

- Requests to deal with problems in current procedures.
- The desire to perform additional tasks.
- The realization that information technology could be used to capitalize on an existing opportunity.

The systems analyst prioritizes and translates the needs into a written plan for the information systems (IS) department, including a schedule for developing new major systems. Requests for new systems spring from users who need new or enhanced systems. During the systems planning and selection phase, an organization determines whether or not resources should be devoted to the development or enhancement of each information system under consideration. A *feasibility study* is conducted to determine the economic and organizational impact of the system.

The second task in the systems planning and selection phase is to investigate the system and determine the proposed system's scope. The team of systems analysts then produces a specific plan for the proposed project for the team to follow. This baseline project plan specifies the time and resources needed for its execution. The formal definition of a project is based on the likelihood that the organization's IS department is able to develop a system that will solve the problem or exploit the opportunity and determine whether the costs of developing the system outweigh the possible benefits. The final presentation of the plan for proceeding with the subsequent project phases usually is made by the project leader and other team members to the organization's management.

Step Two: Systems Analysis

Systems analysis
The second step in systems development in which the current system is studied and alternative replacement systems are proposed.

Use case
A depiction of a system's behavior or functionality under various conditions as the system responds to requests from users.

The dictionary definition of *analyze* is: "to separate into parts or basic principles so as to determine the nature of the whole; examine methodically" (*American Heritage Dictionary, 4th ed.*). An organization's functions can be analyzed into tasks such as order processing, shipping, payroll, and so on. During systems analysis, the analyst thoroughly studies the organization's current procedures and the information systems used to perform tasks such as general ledger, shipping, order processing, machine scheduling, and payroll. Within a high-level task such as payroll, smaller manageable analysis units called use cases can be employed. A use case is a description of a set of sequences of actions that a system performs that yield an observable result of value to a particular actor.

Analysis includes several steps, the first of which involves determining the requirements of the system. For this step, analysts work with users to determine what the users want from a proposed system. This step involves a careful study of any current systems, manual and computerized, that might be replaced or enhanced as part of this project. In the second step of analysis, the analyst studies the requirements and structures them according to their interrelationships, eliminating any redundancies. The requirements are represented in analysis models, which focus on data, interface, and process specifications. The third step involves generating alternative initial designs to match the requirements. Analysts compare these alternatives to determine which best meets the requirements of the cost, labor, and technical levels the organization is willing to commit to the development process. The output of analysis is a description of the alternative solution recommended by the analysis team. Once the recommendation is accepted by the organization, the analyst can make plans to acquire any hardware and system software necessary to build or operate the system as proposed.

Step Three: Systems Design

Systems design
The third step in systems development in which the system chosen for development in systems analysis is first described independent of any computer platform (logical design) and is then transformed into technology-specific details (physical design) from which all programming and system construction can be accomplished.

Systems design is concerned mainly with *how*, as opposed to systems analysis, which is concerned mainly with *what*. In other words, systems design specifies how the recommended alternative solution that results from the analysis phase is translated into detailed logical and then physical systems specifications. These specifications can be used for coding and deployment during implementation. In the initial stages of design, the analysis classes are refined and expanded. This includes interface details such as input and output screens, reports, databases, and computer processes. Because the difference between analysis and initial design is in the amount of detail, a sharp line usually does not divide the two stages of design.

Logical design is not tied to any specific hardware and systems software platform. Theoretically, the systems the analyst designs could be implemented using any hardware and systems software. Like analysis, logical design concentrates on the business aspects of the system; it differs from analysis in the amount of detail.

In physical design, the analyst turns the logical design into physical, or technical, specifications. During physical design, the analysis team decides which programming languages the computer instructions will be written in; which database systems and file structures will be used for the data; and which hardware platform, operating system, and network environment the system will run under. Further, the team needs to identify subsystems that can be addressed by readily available components either inside or outside the organization. These decisions finalize the hardware and software plans initiated at the end of the analysis phase. At this point, any new technology not already present in the organization can be acquired. The final product of the design phase is the physical systems specifications, presented in a form, such as a diagram or written report, ready to be turned over to programmers and other systems builders for coding.

Step Four: Systems Implementation and Operation

Systems implementation and operation
The final step of systems development in which the information system is coded, tested, and installed in the organization, and in which the information system is repaired and improved systematically.

During systems implementation and operation, the analyst turns systems specifications into a working system that is tested and then put into use. Implementation includes coding, testing, and installation. During coding, programmers write the programs that make up the systems. If previously coded components are being used, coding will be reduced but still required to integrate the component into the systems. During testing, programmers and analysts test individual programs and the entire system in order to find and correct errors. During installation, the new system becomes part of the daily activities of the organization. Application software is installed, or loaded, on existing or new hardware; then users are introduced to the new system and trained. Begin planning for testing and installation as early as the project planning and selection phase, because they require extensive analysis in order to develop exactly the right approach.

Systems implementation activities also include initial user support such as the finalization of documentation, training programs, and ongoing user assistance. Note that documentation and training programs are finalized during implementation; documentation is produced throughout the systems development cycle, and training (and education) occurs from the initiation of a project. Systems implementation can continue for as long as the system exists because ongoing user support is also part of implementation. However, despite the best efforts of analysts, managers, and programmers, installation is not always a simple process. Note that even a well-designed system can fail if implementation is not well managed. Because the management of systems implementation usually is done by the project team, implementation issues are stressed throughout this book.

After implementation comes operation. Once a system is operating in an organization, users sometimes find problems and often think of improvements. During operation, analysts and programmers make the changes that users ask for and modify the system to reflect changing business conditions. These upgrades and improvements are considered part of maintaining the system. These changes are necessary to keep the system running and useful. However, the time inevitably comes when an information system is no longer performing as desired, when the costs of keeping a system running become prohibitive, or when an organization's needs have changed substantially. Such problems indicate that it is time to begin designing the system's replacement, thereby completing the loop and starting the cycle again.

The loop from the implementation to systems planning also can occur if an incremental, iterative approach is used. Such an approach entails development in increments, where each increment can involve all four phases of planning, analysis, design, and implementation. The later increments might not include planning and sometimes not even analysis. Generally, the more critical and risky aspects of the system are developed and implemented first. The incremental, iterative approach is discussed later in this chapter.

TYPES OF INFORMATION SYSTEMS AND SYSTEMS DEVELOPMENT

Given the broad range of people and interests represented in organizations, it could take several different types of information systems to satisfy all of an organization's information systems needs. Until now we have talked about information systems in generic terms, but several different types or classes of information systems exist. These classes are distinguished from each other on the basis of what the system does or by the technology used to construct the system. Part of a systems analyst's job is to determine which kind of system will best address the organizational problem or opportunity in a given situation. In addition, different classes of systems might require different methodologies, techniques, and tools for development.

Systems analysts working as part of a team might work with various classes of information systems such as the following:

- Transaction processing systems.
- Management information systems.
- Decision support systems (for individuals, groups, and executives).

These systems types are represented graphically in Figure 1.7. Although each of these major systems types is explained in more detail in the following sections, Figure 1.7 shows some contrasts between them. The diagram for transaction processing systems shows that the major focus is capturing transaction data, which are then sent to a computerized database of all transactions. The icons of the man with the cash register and the woman taking orders represent the capture of transaction data. The arrows from the icons to the computer represent moving the data to a database for storage. The picture in Figure 1.7 that illustrates management information systems shows a manager using transaction data to make a report about last month's sales. Management information systems are designed to process transaction data into standard reports. The next picture in Figure 1.7 shows a decision support system. Decision support systems help managers make decisions by analyzing data in different ways. Managers can make changes to their data, like changing interest rates, and see how those changes affect the parts of the business they manage. In the picture in Figure 1.7, the manager tries to determine what it takes to turn a downward trend into an upward trend. The following sections briefly highlight how systems analysis and design methods differ across various types of systems.

Figure 1.7
Depictions of Classes
of Information
Systems: TPS, MIS,
DSS

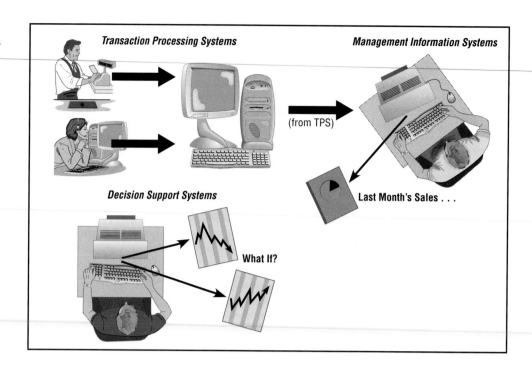

Transaction Processing Systems

Transaction processing systems (TPSs) automate the handling of data about business activities or transactions. For example, a bank's TPS captures information about withdrawals from and deposits to customer accounts. Data about each transaction are captured, transactions are verified and accepted or rejected, and validated transactions are stored. Reports can be produced immediately to provide summaries of transactions, and transactions can be moved from process to process in order to handle all aspects of the business activity.

The analysis and design of a TPS requires the analyst to focus on the firm's current procedures for processing transactions. How does the organization track, capture, process, and output data? The goal of TPS development is to improve transaction processing by speeding it up, enhancing worker productivity, improving efficiency and accuracy, integrating it with other organizational information systems, improving customer service, or providing information not previously available.

Management Information Systems

A *management information system (MIS)* is a computer-based system that takes the raw data available through a TPS and converts them into a meaningful, aggregated form. For example, a transaction processing system keeps track of sales, and a management information system can pinpoint which items are selling slowly and which are selling quickly. As a result, the MIS can direct the manufacturing department regarding what to produce when. Developing an MIS calls for a good understanding of what kind of information managers require and how managers use information in their jobs. Sometimes managers themselves might not know precisely what they need or how they will use information. Thus, the analyst also must develop a good understanding of the business and the transaction processing systems that provide data for an MIS.

Management information systems often require data from several transaction processing systems (e.g., customer order processing, raw material purchasing, and employee timekeeping). Therefore, development of an MIS can benefit from a data orientation in which data are considered an organization resource separate from the TPS in which they are captured. Because it is important to be able to draw on data from various subject areas, developing a comprehensive and accurate model of data is essential in building an MIS.

Decision Support Systems

Decision support systems (DSSs) are designed to help decision makers with decisions. Whereas an MIS produces a report, a DSS provides an interactive environment in which decision makers can manipulate data and models of business operations quickly. A DSS has three parts. The first part is composed of a database (which can be extracted from a TPS or an MIS). The second part consists of mathematical or graphical models of business processes. The third part is made up of a user interface (or dialogue module) that provides a way for the decision maker to communicate with the DSS. A DSS might use historical data as well as judgments (or "what if" analysis) about alternative histories or possible futures. An executive information system (EIS) is a DSS that allows senior management to explore data starting at a high level of aggregation and selectively drill down into specific areas where more detailed information is required. A DSS is characterized by less structured and less predictable use. DSS software supports certain decision-making activities (from problem finding to choosing a course of action).

The systems analysis and design for a DSS often concentrates on the three main DSS components: database, model base, and user dialogue. As with an MIS, a data orientation is used most often for understanding user requirements. The systems analysis and design project will document carefully the mathematical rules that define interrelationships among different data. These relationships are used to predict future data or to find the best solutions to decision problems. Decision logic must be understood and documented carefully. Also, because a decision maker typically interacts with a DSS, the design of easy-to-use yet thorough user dialogues and screens is important.

A special kind of DSS is a data warehouse, which may be defined as a "subject-oriented, integrated, time-variant, and nonvolatile collection of data used in support of management decision making" (Inmon & Hackathorn, 1994). A data mart is a data warehouse that is limited in scope. A knowledge management system is similar to a data warehouse but involves less structured data, which are collated from internal as well as external sources. An example of a knowledge management system is an enterprise information portal (EIP), which also is called a corporate portal. An EIP provides users with a one-point access to knowledge and application sources through the familiar Web browser interface.

THE ANALYST'S ROLE IN SYSTEMS DEVELOPMENT

Although many people in organizations are involved in systems analysis and design, the systems analyst has the primary responsibility. A career as a systems analyst allows a person to have a significant impact on how the organization operates. The primary role of a systems analyst is to study the problems and needs of an organization in order to determine how people, methods, and information technology can best be combined to bring about improvements in the organization. A systems analyst helps system users and other business managers define their requirements for new or enhanced information services.

Let's consider an example of the type of organizational problems one could face as a systems analyst, using the information systems department of a major magazine company for the scenario. The company is having problems keeping an updated and accurate list of subscribers, and some customers are getting two magazines instead of one. The company will lose money and subscribers if this continues. To create a more efficient tracking system, the users of the current computer system as well as financial managers submit their problem to the systems analyst and other colleagues in the information systems department.

Figure 1.8 An Organizational Chart for a Typical Information Systems Department

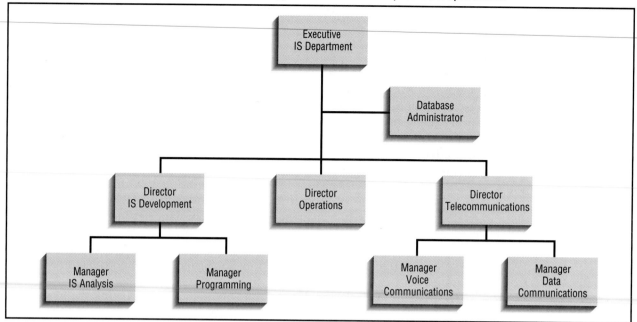

When developing information systems to deal with problems such as these, an organization and its systems analysts have several options: They can use an in-house staff to develop the system, they can buy the system off-the-shelf, they can implement an enterprise-wide system from a company like SAP, they can hire a company to develop and run the software on its own computers, or they can go to a consulting company such as Accenture or EDS to have the system developed for them.

Several types of jobs are involved in an organization with its own in-house staff. Medium to large organizations such as Procter & Gamble or Caterpillar usually have a separate information systems (IS) department. The IS department might be an independent department reporting to the organization's top manager, or it might be part of another functional department, such as finance. IS departments might even be part of several major business units. In any of these cases, the manager of an IS department is involved in systems development. If the department is large enough, a separate division might be established for systems development, which would be home base for systems analysts, and another division might be set up for programming, where programmers would be based. Figure 1.8 highlights an organizational chart for a typical information systems department. Systems are designed to help people in functional departments do their jobs. These people are called end users. The end users often request new or modified software applications, test and approve applications, and may serve on project teams as business experts.

Systems development is a team effort. Systems analysts work together in a team, usually organized on a project basis. A good team has the following characteristics, as described in Table 1-1:

- A diverse team has representation from all the different groups interested in a system. For example, the team might consist of people from the database administration area and the group responsible for training, as well as the marketing department (future systems users). The representation of these groups on the team increases the likelihood of acceptance of the changes a new system will cause.
- Diversity exposes team members to new and different ideas—ideas they might never think of if all team members were from the same background with the same skills and goals. Someone in the data administration area would have a different view than someone in the marketing department. These different views could add new information.

End users

Non-information-systems (IS) professionals in an organization. End users often request new or modified software applications, test and approve applications, and may serve on project teams as business experts.

TABLE 1-1
Characteristics of
Successful Teams.

Diversity in backgrounds, skills, and goals
Tolerance of diversity, uncertainty, and ambiguity
Clear and complete communication
Trust
Mutual respect and putting one's own views second to the team
Reward structure that promotes shared responsibility and accountability

- New and different ideas can help a team generate better solutions to its problems.
- Team members must be open to new ideas without being overly critical and without dismissing new ideas out of hand simply because they are new.
- Team members must be able to deal with ambiguous information as well as with complexity. They must learn to play a role on a team (and different roles on different teams) so that the talents of all team members can be utilized to the fullest.

A good team must communicate clearly and completely with its members. Team members will communicate more effectively if they trust each other. Trust, in turn, is built on mutual respect and an ability to place one's own goals and views secondary to the goals and views of the group. To help a team work well together, management needs to develop a reward structure that promotes shared responsibility and accountability. Rewards could include a financial bonus or special company acknowledgment. In addition to rewards for individual efforts, team members must be rewarded by IS managers for their output as members of an effective work unit.

Team success depends not only on how a team is assembled or the efforts of the group but also on the management of the team. In addition to a reward system, effective project management is another key element of successful teams. Project management includes the following:

- Devising a feasible and realistic work plan and schedule.
- Monitoring progress against this schedule.
- Coordinating the project with executives who sponsor the system.
- Allocating resources to the project.
- Sometimes even deciding whether and when a project should be terminated before completing the system.

The characteristics of each systems analysis and design project will dictate which types of individuals should be on the project team. In general, those involved in systems development include IS managers, systems analysts, programmers, end users, and business managers, as well as additional IS managers, technicians, and specialists such as security analysts. These persons or roles are related directly to the project and are considered stakeholders, that is, people or organization entities who or which have a vested interest in the behavior of the system under discussion. Other stakeholders can be internal or external to the system, such as the owner of the system, the company's board of directors, or regulatory government and professional bodies.

The role being addressed here, however, is that of systems analyst.

SYSTEMS ANALYSTS IN THE SYSTEMS DEVELOPMENT PROCESS

Systems analysts are key to the systems development process. To succeed as a systems analyst, one needs to develop four types of skills: *analytical, technical, managerial,* and *interpersonal*. Analytical skills enable a person to understand the organization and its functions, to identify opportunities and problems, and to analyze and solve problems. One of the most important analytical skills is systems thinking, or the ability to see organizations and information systems as systems. Systems thinking provides a

Simon & Taylor, Inc., an optical goods manufacturer, has an immediate opening for a systems analyst in its Vermont-based office.

The ideal candidate will have:

1. A bachelor's degree in MIS, CIS, or Computer Science
2. Experience with Object-Oriented Analysis and Design and Rational Rose
3. Working knowledge of Oracle and VisualBasic or Java
4. Familiarity with distribution and manufacturing concepts
5. Strong analytical and organizational skills
6. Ability to work in a team

We offer a competitive salary, relocation assistance, and the challenges of working in a state-of-the-art IT environment.

E-mail your resume and a list of references to human_resources@simontaylor.com

framework from which to see the important relationships among information systems, the organizations they exist in, and the environment in which the organizations themselves exist. Systems thinking can lead to improvement of business processes, which is critical to improvement of organizational productivity. Technical skills help one understand the potential and the limitations of information technology. Analysts must be able to envision an information system that will help users solve problems and that will guide the system's design and development. An analyst might be required to have database design skills and experience with database management systems (DBMSs) such as Oracle, DB2, or SQL server; system modeling skills such as UML and Rational Rose; ERP systems such as SAP R/3; programming language skills such as Java; various operating systems such as Windows and Linux; and new technologies such as XML, J2EE, .NET, and security software. It would be impossible to expect one person to have all these technical skills so it is wise to concentrate on a subset and try to have a working knowledge of others.

Management skills help the analyst manage projects, resources, risk, and change. Note that a successful system implies that the completed project meets the users' needs, is completed in time, and is completed within budget. Although the analyst might not be the project manager, an awareness of the managerial issues is critical to the project's success. Interpersonal skills help one work with end users as well as with other analysts and programmers. Systems analysts play a major role as a liaison among users, programmers, and other systems professionals. It is essential that analysts have effective written and oral communication skills, including competence in leading meetings, interviewing end users, and listening. Effective analysts successfully combine these four types of skills, as Figure 1.9, a typical advertisement for a systems analyst position, illustrates.

THE EVOLUTION OF SYSTEMS DEVELOPMENT METHODOLOGIES

It might seem odd to be discussing the evolution and history of systems development, which is probably less than 50 years old. Yet, this is a fast-evolving field that has seen significant changes over these years.

Information systems development started in the 1950s. Development during the 1950s and for the greater part of the 1960s was synonymous with programming. Hardware was a constraint, and the effective developer was the efficient developer, that is, someone who could do creative programming tricks on limited hardware. However, as systems grew in size, developers realized that systems development was more than mere programming; the project had to be managed, and a methodology was required to govern the project from concept to commissioning.

The output-input–based methodology emerged in the late 1960s. It was based on the notion that by examining the fields appearing in outputs such as reports, one can trace the output to inputs such as forms and determine the data fields and the processing required. Although nothing was inherently wrong with this approach, because outputs are an important source of user requirements, the approach was deficient in several respects. The focus was on outputs and inputs instead of data and processes. The approach did not provide a representation for understanding and improving the system. It was not based on a database approach, and there was redundancy in the system. Further, artifacts such as reports are not particularly stable over a period of time. Thus, the maintenance overhead was excessive, and the time required to address changes to the system was unduly long. As years passed, the size of systems grew larger and larger, and a new approach was required to understand, develop, and manage systems.

Systems Development Life Cycle (SDLC)

Systems development life cycle (SDLC)
The series of steps used to mark the phases of development for an information system in the structured analysis and design approach.

Sometime in the 1970s and especially during the 1980s, the systems development life cycle (SDLC) became popular. The SDLC considers systems development as a single cycle of sequential steps; there might be other cycles during the operation/maintenance of the system. The organization that will use the system decides to devote the necessary resources to acquiring it. A careful study is done of how the organization currently handles the work the system will support. Professionals develop a strategy for designing the new system, which is then either built or purchased. Once complete, the system is installed in the organization, and after proper training, the users begin to incorporate the new system into their daily work. Every organization uses a slightly different life cycle model to model these steps, with anywhere from three to almost 20 identifiable phases. One SDLC approach is to divide it into four steps: (1) planning and selection, (2) analysis, (3) design, and (4) implementation and operation.

The advantage of SDLC is in its emphasis on planning and analysis. The majority of errors in a project can be traced to errors in determining user requirements, which occur during the early phases of a systems development project. SDLC forces analysts to spend a significant amount of time on analysis, thereby understanding the problem thoroughly before designing and coding the system. User requirements are determined and documented in detail before embarking on the risk of design and implementation.

However, SDLC suffers from several limitations. Users might not be able to articulate requirements accurately. Even when they can, the analysts who do not have the functional knowledge might not be able to understand them. Further, although any life cycle appears at first glance to be a sequentially ordered set of phases, it is not. User requirements might change as time passes, and it is usually difficult to revisit early steps in the process as necessitated by the changes. Finally, project risk cannot be estimated until the later stages of the project. By this time, significant resources might have been consumed.

Despite the limitations, SDLC presents a useful sequencing of project phases. It emphasizes that requirements need to be understood and analyzed, and these requirements need to be detailed and mapped into design before implementation can proceed.

Structured Analysis and Design

Structured analysis and design
A methodology based on decomposition of processes and data flow diagrams using an SDLC approach.

The structured analysis and design methodology is essentially a process modeling–based SDLC methodology. Process modeling involves graphically representing the processes, or actions, that capture, manipulate, store, and distribute data between a system and its environment and among components within a system. A common form of a process model is a data flow diagram (DFD). A data flow diagram is a

Figure 1.10
A Data Flow Diagram

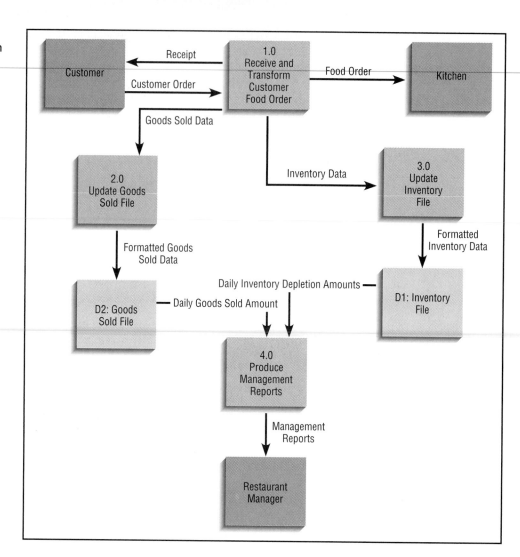

graphic that illustrates the movement of data between external entities and the processes and data stores within a system (Figure 1.10).

The structured approach also is based on the decomposition concept. A business process is decomposed into smaller processes, which in turn are decomposed into still smaller pieces, and the decomposition continues until a process of a size appropriate for the problem at hand is obtained. For example, if the systems analyst has a meeting with senior managers, a high-level diagram might be appropriate. If the analysis is being done to develop a detailed DFD, which will serve as the basis for design, then the decomposition needs to be done to processes that are fine grained enough to translate into functions and procedures.

DFDs were the common mechanism for systems analysis during the 1980s. Although companies still use DFDs, especially because of the huge amount of legacy code, they seldom are used in new applications. DFDs are excellent representation tools for studying processes, and a systems analyst should not ignore them merely because they are not the latest fad in the market.

Despite the success of the structured analysis and design methodology and the DFD tool, practitioners have pointed out several limitations. The structured approach is tuned for process modeling. However, processes are not as stable as data, and changes in processes can lead to substantial maintenance. The structured approach has a minimal focus on data modeling and does not lend itself easily to DBMS-based systems. The lack of data focus can lead to file-based systems and "islands of automation," that is, smaller systems that are not fully integrated.

Data-Oriented Methodologies

Another popular approach during the 1980s used principles similar to structured analysis and design but provided more emphasis on data. Database management systems (DBMSs) started becoming popular toward the end of the 1970s. Around this time, relational-model–based DBMSs were making swift inroads into the market. Further, in 1976, the entity-relationship (ER) model was proposed (Chen, 1976), which provided a graphical view of data and allowed easy translation into the relational model. Analysts quickly realized that the ER model could be used to represent data for a large-scale application, thereby providing more business focus on data and facilitating implementation using the relational technology. Further, it helped analysts communicate more effectively with users on data requirements. These factors led to methodologies such as information engineering (IE), which were data oriented but process sensitive. The data-oriented methodologies prescribed modeling of data before processes on the premise that data are inherently more stable than processes.

The Object-Oriented Methodology

During the 1990s, several researchers and practitioners were working on a new approach based on the notion of an object. The methodologies mentioned so far separated data and processes. Analysts found this division unnatural because a real-world object has properties (akin to data) and behavior (akin to processes). Using this perspective, there was no reason to separate the two in the information systems world. The separation mitigated reuse, a concept that is detailed later in this chapter. In an attempt to facilitate reuse and improve development productivity, the object-oriented systems analysis and design approach (OOSAD) was proposed. The growing popularity of OOSAD coincided with the emergence of Unified Modeling Language (UML).

The Unified Modeling Language (UML) is the language that has been adopted by the Object Management Group (OMG), which includes some of the largest software vendors in the world. It is expected that UML will be the standard language in the future. UML unifies features from some of the leading proponents of OOSAD, especially those of Grady Booch, James Rumbaugh, and Ivar Jacobson, who are fondly known as "the three amigos" of the object modeling approach. You will read more about UML in Chapter 2.

Agile Methodologies

Many other approaches to systems analysis and design have been developed over the years. Out of the object-oriented approach emerged the latest view of systems development, collectively called the agile methodologies. In February 2001, many of the proponents of these alternative approaches met in Utah and reached a consensus on many of the underlying principles their various approaches contained. This consensus turned into a document they called "The Agile Manifesto." The agile methodologies share three key principles: (1) A focus on adaptive rather than predictive methodologies, (2) a focus on people rather than roles, and (3) a self-adaptive process.

The agile methodologies group argues that software development methodologies adapted from engineering generally do not fit well the reality of developing software. In the engineering disciplines, such as civil engineering, requirements tend to be well understood. Once the creative and difficult work of design is completed, construction becomes very predictable. In addition, construction may account for as much as 90 percent of the total project effort. For software, on the other hand, requirements are rarely understood well, and they change continually during the lifetime of the project. Construction may account for as little as 15 percent of the total project effort, leaving design to constitute as much as 50 percent of the project effort. Applying techniques that work well for predictable, stable projects, like building a bridge, tend not to work

---

Data-oriented methodologies
Data-centered but process-sensitive methodologies that attempt to minimize redundancy of data in an organization.

Object-oriented systems analysis and design approach (OOSAD)
An analysis and design approach based on notion of an object, which captures the data and processes of a thing in a single construct.

Unified Modeling Language (UML)
A notation that allows the modeler to specify, visualize, and construct the artifacts of software systems, as well as business models.

Agile methodologies
Current approaches to systems development that focus on adaptive methodologies, people instead of roles, and an overall self-adaptive development process.

well for fluid, design-heavy projects like writing software, say the agile methodology proponents. What is needed are methodologies that embrace change and that are able to deal with a lack of predictability. One mechanism for dealing with a lack of predictability, which all agile methodologies share, is iterative development. Iterative development, which will be discussed in more detail later in this chapter, focuses on the frequent production of working versions of a system that have a subset of the total number of required features. Iterative development provides feedback to customers and developers alike.

Second, the focus on people in agile methodologies is a focus on individuals rather than on the roles that people perform. The roles that people fill, of systems analyst or tester or manager, are not as important as the individuals who fill those roles. Some have argued that the focus on engineering principles applied to systems development has resulted in a view of people as interchangeable units instead of a view of people as talented individuals, each of whom has something unique to bring to the development team. Third, the agile methodologies also promote a self-adaptive software development process. As software is developed, the process used to develop it should be refined and improved. Development teams can do this through a review process, often associated with the completion of iterations. The implication is that, as processes are adapted, you would not expect to find a single monolithic methodology within a given corporation or enterprise. Instead, you would find many variations of the methodology, each of which reflects the particular talents and experience of the team using it.

Many different individual methodologies come under the umbrella of agile methodologies. Fowler (2003) lists the Crystal family of methodologies, Adaptive Software Development, Scrum, Feature Driven Development, and others as Agile Methodologies. Perhaps the best known of these methodologies is eXtreme Programming. You will read more about eXtreme Programming in later sections of this book.

Whether a systems development project is organized in terms of agile or more traditional methodologies depends on many different considerations. If a project is considered to be high risk, highly complex, and has a development team made up of hundreds of people, then more traditional methods will apply. Less risky, smaller, and simpler development efforts lend themselves more to agile methods. Other determining factors include organizational practice and standards, and the extent to which different parts of the system will be contracted out to others to develop. Obviously, the larger the proportion of the system that will be farmed out, the more detailed the design specifications will need to be so subcontractors can understand what is needed.

WHY SHOULD WE USE OBJECT-ORIENTED SYSTEMS ANALYSIS AND DESIGN (OOSAD)?

The object-oriented systems analysis and design (OOSAD) approach has found enthusiastic reception in the market and is gradually replacing the structured approach for conducting user requirements, analysis, and design for many types of systems. The structured methodology is introduced in this chapter. Several excellent textbooks have been written on structured analysis for the interested reader. To distinguish OOSAD from structured analysis, one needs to first understand the key features of the latter approach.

The key tenet of the structured methodology is to separate data and processes. For example, if there is a "business item," say a sales order, to be modeled, the attributes of the sales order such as order number and order date are considered data, and its processes such as display details and calculated total are considered processes; the two are logically separated. However, researchers and practitioners find this separation unnatural. The disapproval can be traced to several factors. First, it is abnormal from an ontology perspective. Ontology issues consider the mapping of real-world "things" into

Figure 1.11
A Systems Development Life Cycle

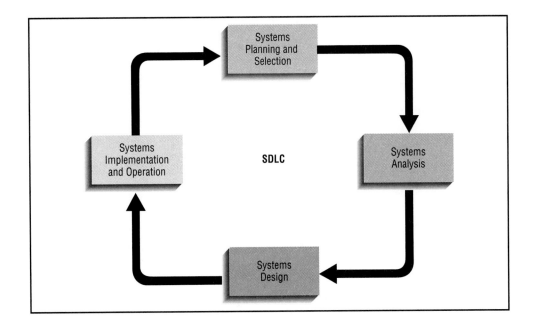

representation constructs. The separation also mitigates reuse of the representation of the thing. In the real world, the data aspects of a thing (e.g., a DVD player) and its behavior or process aspects usually are not considered separately. For example, it is not natural to think of the attributes of a DVD player such as make, model, and price, and its behavior such as play, fast forward, and show subtitles as logically separate items.

The structured methodology is based on the systems development life cycle (SDLC). The SDLC is a four-phased approach to identify, analyze, design, and implement information systems. The four phases are: (1) systems planning and selection, (2) systems analysis, (3) systems design, and (4) systems implementation and operation (Figure 1.11). The transition from one phase to another might overlap but is otherwise linear. The method can be effective if certain conditions are met. However, the method suffers from several shortcomings. First, the SDLC is not receptive to changes in user requirements; going backward in this life cycle is generally difficult and expensive. If the system is at the implementation stage, for example, a change in user requirements might result in the waste of a considerable amount of effort. Further, the user usually does not get to try the system until it is almost complete. The user might discover during the initial trials that the system is substantially different from what was intended. This is a risky proposition for developers, users, managers, and owners.

Another serious criticism of the structured analysis methodology is the disconnection between analysis and design. The diagrams and representations from the analysis do not readily map into design constructs. In the structured methodology, the data flow diagrams are transformed to a hierarchically structured chart. This transformation is erratic, and it is not easy to trace a module in a structured chart to a DFD. The problem is acute because changes in user requirements are inevitable, which alters analysis constructs, which in turn needs to be mapped constantly to structured charts.

Some of the key differences between the structured analysis and design methodology and the object-oriented approach are featured in Table 1-2. The OOSAD methodology is based on the notion of object, which encapsulates data and processes. This results in a representation that is closer to our view of the real world. Because the essential data and process features are encapsulated in an object, they can be reused easily. The analysis constructs can be mapped into design constructs in a fairly seamless fashion, thereby increasing understanding and productivity. The recommended development approach for OOSAD is the phased iterative development, which reduces risk by focusing on critical pieces first, enables early user feedback, and is more receptive to changing user requirements. These features of OOSAD will be detailed in this and subsequent chapters.

Table 1-2
Key Differences
Between
Structured
Analysis and
Design and
Object-Oriented
Analysis and
Design.

CHARACTERISTICS	STRUCTURED ANALYSIS AND DESIGN	OBJECT-ORIENTED SYSTEMS ANALYSIS AND DESIGN
Methodology	SDLC	Iterative/Incremental
Focus	Processes	Objects
Risk	High	Low
Reuse	Low	High
Maturity	Mature and widespread	Emerging
Suitable for:	Well-defined projects with stable user requirements	Risky large projects with changing user requirements

ITERATIVE AND INCREMENTAL DEVELOPMENT

Methodologies are a sequence of step-by-step approaches that help develop an information system. The purpose of the incremental development methodology is to reduce the risk of large projects that have a significant element of uncertainty. In modern times, this would include the majority of projects. The SDLC has a single cycle of planning, analysis, design, and implementation. The outcome of the SDLC project is not completely known until implementation takes place. By this time, the user requirements might have changed, and the project might be declared a failure even if it meets the original requirements. Further, the user, analyst, developer, and other stakeholders might not see the product until a number of years have passed. In the meantime, there could be turnover of these stakeholders. Competitors also might introduce alternative software products that reduce the usefulness of the project under development. In other words, SDLC projects can be fraught with risk unless the requirements are stable and the developers have developed similar projects in the past.

The iterative and incremental methodology mitigates risk by developing the most critical and risky aspects of the project before addressing the less critical and less risky aspects. Further, users have a chance to start experiencing the product early in the development period. If the project needs to be abandoned, it usually will be done early in the development phase, thereby minimizing loss. If an aspect of the project proves unusually difficult, it can be completed in several iterations. If requirements change after users experience an initial release and discover that they had been wrong in providing these requirements, the project is only minimally affected. Testing can be done after each release, ensuring that no surprises crop up at the end.

The iterative and incremental approach to development has become a key part of the agile methodologies, as you read earlier. Perhaps the most popular realization of this approach is the Rational Unified Process (RUP), which is based on an iterative, incremental approach to systems development. We now provide a brief description of the RUP methodology.

Iterative methodology
Development of a piece by growing, improving, and refining over several time periods.

Incremental methodology
Development in pieces, which are progressively tested and integrated.

Rational Unified Process (RUP)
An object-oriented program development methodology. RUP establishes four phases of development: in the inception phase, developers define the scope of the project and its business case; in the elaboration phase, developers analyze the project's needs in greater detail; in the construction phase, developers create the application design and source code; and in the transition phase, developers deliver the system to users.

RUP's Iterative, Incremental Approach to OOSAD

Earlier sections of this chapter addressed the four basic steps in any systems development approach: (1) planning and selection, (2) analysis, (3) design, and (4) implementation and orientation. One aspect of object-oriented systems analysis and design is that these steps are performed again and again, in iterative and incremental fashion, throughout the development process. This iterative, incremental development is what we are implying through the spiral in Figure 1.1 that runs between analysis and design and implementation and operation.

The preferred approach to the development of an efficient information system using the OOSAD approach is this iterative, incremental, and phased process. The four phases typically associated with OOSAD-based development are: *inception, elaboration, construction,* and *transition* (see Figure 1.12). Although these terms are part of

Figure 1.12
Phases of
OOSAD-Based
Development.

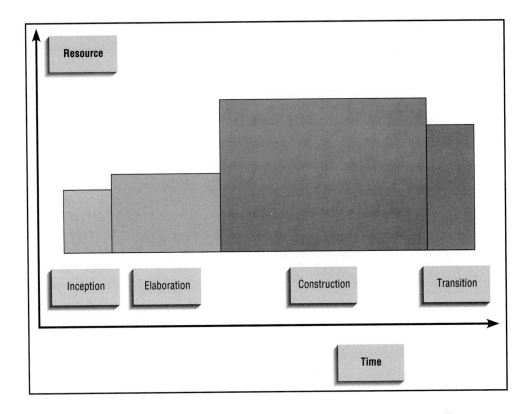

the Rational Unified Process (RUP) methodology, they are widely used even outside the RUP methodology.

The inception phase includes defining the scope, determining the feasibility of the project, understanding user requirements, and preparing a software development plan. In the elaboration phase, detailed user requirements and a baseline architecture are developed. Analysis and design activities constitute the bulk of the elaboration phase. In the construction phase, the software is coded, tested, and documented. In the transition phase, the system is deployed and the users are trained and supported. As is evident from Figure 1.12, the construction phase is generally the longest and the most resource intensive. The elaboration phase is also long but less resource intensive. The transition phase is resource intensive but short. The inception phase is short and the least resource intensive. The area of the rectangles in the figure provides an estimate of overall resources allocated to each phase.

What is the relationship between these four phases and the conventional systems development steps of planning and selection, analysis, design, and implementation and orientation? A phase represents a period of time; the end of a phase represents achievement of a major milestone. Terms such as *requirements, analysis,* and *design* are called workflows in RUP and suggest activities as defined in this chapter; we call them steps in a systems development cycle. A phase typically will involve several workflows (see Figure 1.13). For example, at the inception phase, the main tasks involve business modeling and determining user requirements although a prototype might be built and tested to demonstrate the viability of the project. Further, as the system is constructed, we will be involved primarily in coding although, as a better understanding of the system to be built is established, we may continue to conduct further analysis and designs.

Iteration

A time-bound minor milestone within a phase.

Each phase can be divided further into iterations. An iteration is a time-bound minor milestone within a given phase, and is generally of a duration of about two to eight weeks. The software is developed incrementally as a series of iterations. The critical pieces of the system are addressed in earlier iterations. An executable is released at the end of each iteration. This mitigates risk because the success or failure of the system is determined at an early stage. As the project is developed, everyone

Figure 1.13
Iterative Development:
Mapping of Phases to
Workflows

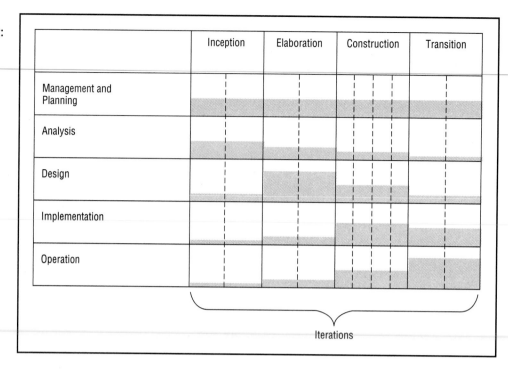

	Inception	Elaboration	Construction	Transition
Management and Planning				
Analysis				
Design				
Implementation				
Operation				

Iterations

gains a better understanding of the system, which reduces the risk of failure. Each and every aspect of analysis and design does not need to be completed before the first line of code is written.

The inception phase generally entails a single iteration. The scope and feasibility of the project is determined at this stage. Preliminary cost estimates are made. The most critical use cases of the project are identified, and a few prototypes might be completed. A successful implementation of the most critical piece also can reinforce the feasibility of the project. Note that the implementation may just be minimal and lack features such as an attractive user interface or security, which can be added in future iterations.

The elaboration phase may have one or two iterations and generally is considered the most critical of the four phases (Kruchten, 2000). The elaboration phase is mainly about systems analysis and design, although other activities also are involved. It is evident from Figure 1.12 that the major expenditure occurs during the construction phase. Therefore, at the end of the elaboration phase, cost estimates need to be accurate. This may entail design activities such as comparing design alternatives. Some of the critical pieces will be analyzed, designed, and implemented so that project risk is virtually eliminated. At the end of the elaboration phase, the architecture of the project should have been developed. This means that the UML diagrams of about 80 percent of the use cases are complete. The architecture includes a vision of the product, an executable demonstration of the critical pieces, a detailed glossary and a preliminary user manual, a detailed construction plan, and a revised estimate of planned expenditure. This book is mainly about the inception and elaboration phases.

Although the construction phase primarily involves coding, which is accomplished in several iterations, revised user requirements could require analysis and design. The components are developed or purchased and used in the code. As each executable is ready, it is tested and integrated. Because the construction phase is cost intensive, cost monitoring and control are important project management activities. Also, quality assurance is critical. The user manuals are written throughout the phase. At the end of the construction phase, a beta version of the project is released. A beta version promises initial operational capability.

The transition phase entails correcting problems, beta testing, user training, and conversion of the product. The software product is released to the users. If a legacy system is in place, the beta system might need to be run in parallel so that the product can be tested in the real environment. Users can put their learning to the test. The phase serves as a final dress rehearsal to remove last-minute bugs. The transition phase is complete when the project objectives meet the acceptance criteria. The product can then be released for distribution.

OUR APPROACH TO OBJECT-ORIENTED SYSTEMS ANALYSIS AND DESIGN

Our approach to object-oriented systems analysis and design is based on the four steps—planning, analysis, design, and implementation—indicative of any systems analysis and design effort in an incremental development environment. We employ the modeling language UML to represent the object-oriented constructs typically encountered in business applications. Because business applications invariably have a database component, we devote a separate chapter to conceptual and logical database design, which are considered in an object-relational environment. We do not consider a pure object-oriented database environment because the market is dominated by object-relational DBMSs such as Oracle, DB2, SQL Server, and Informix. The UML diagrams included in this book can be drawn conveniently using a CASE tool such as Rational or Visio.

We have provided a step-by-step approach that offers fairly seamless transition from requirements to analysis, and analysis to design. However, because of the realities of the market, some mapping will be required from design to implementation. That said, this is not a book on object-oriented programming or detailed implementation issues. We provide a brief plan of the book now.

Chapter 2 is an introduction to object orientation. Here we define key terms and concepts important to object orientation, and we provide examples to help make these ideas clearer. If this is your first time studying object orientation, this chapter will serve as a handy reference for you as you move through the rest of the book.

Chapter 3 addresses issues related to managing a systems development project based on an OOSAD methodology. Although primarily related to the planning step of SDC, it also peripherally addresses analysis and design issues. We provide descriptions of project management practices that are generic, as well as those that are specific to an incremental development environment. We stress issues such as managing risk, controlling costs, managing instead of avoiding changes in user requirements, testing and documenting on an ongoing basis, and deploying components whenever possible.

Chapter 4 covers the first step of the SDC, that is, systems planning and selection for an OOSAD project. The main task in this step is to identify and select projects. The feasibility of the project is addressed from multiple angles. We introduce the Rational Unified Process (RUP) as a basis for systems planning.

Chapter 5 leads us into systems analysis. The chapter deals with the important topic of determining user requirements. It provides various strategies for eliciting user requirements such as interviewing users, administering questionnaires, observing users, and using prototyping to discover user needs. The chapter has detailed sections on JAD and on prototyping.

Chapter 6 continues with analysis and provides a way to structure requirements by employing use cases, which are now accepted as the most common method of specifying requirements. Use cases are not the only documents capturing requirements, and the systems analyst can elaborate on the requirements with commonly available software such as word processors and spreadsheets.

Chapter 7 introduces UML data modeling. The focus of the chapter is conceptual data modeling, moving from requirements to the creation of a high-level set of object classes and their relationships. In this chapter, we go beyond the traditional relational concepts and present concepts pertaining to object data modeling such as generalization, aggregation, object identifiers, multivalued attributes, and so on.

Chapter 8 describes conceptual and logical data modeling for object-relational databases. The focus of the chapter is object extensions to the relational data model, including the translation of class diagrams into object relations.

Chapter 9 addresses analysis classes, which in OOSAD are the end product of the analysis step. Based on use cases descriptions (Chapter 6) and the availability of entity classes (Chapter 7), we illustrate how sequence diagrams can be developed. The sequence diagrams show how messages are passed to assign responsibilities among three kinds of classes: entity, control, and boundary classes. From sequence diagrams, we can derive analysis class diagrams (which later become design class diagrams). We also cover collaboration diagrams and activity charts, which are important artifacts in analysis.

Chapter 10 leads us into design. At this stage, decisions have to be made regarding selecting a design strategy from proposed alternatives. We address several issues such as outsourcing, off-the-shelf software, enterprise software, component-based development, and hardware and network issues.

Chapter 11 is about physical database design. Its topics include designing fields, choosing data types, denormalization, and file organization, especially indexed file organization.

Chapter 12 discusses the transformation of analysis classes into design elements. This requires deciding how analysis classes will map into design elements. Design classes are then grouped logically into packages. The chapter includes an extensive introduction to components and design architecture.

Chapter 13 addresses interfaces: user, component, and legacy interfaces. User or human interfaces pertain to screen and report design. The discussion on component interfaces addresses issues pertaining to integrating the system software with components via their operations. The discussion on legacy interfaces addresses using middleware that maps the messages from the system to legacy systems.

The final chapter, Chapter 14, is about the last step in systems development—systems implementation and operation. This final step also lasts the longest of any step. Implementation is the point at which the system is coded and installed. Operation is the production phase of the systems life, during which it works to do what it was designed to do. During operation, the system will evolve to handle new requirements and changes in the business environment.

KEY POINTS REVIEW

1. **Define information systems analysis and design.**
   Systems analysis and design is the complex organizational process whereby computer-based information systems are developed and operated.

2. **Explain the basics of systems.**
   A system is an interrelated set of business procedures, objects, or components used within one business unit, working together for some purpose. A system has nine characteristics: (1) system components, (2) interrelationships, (3) boundary, (4) purpose, (5) environment, (6) system interfaces, (7) input, (8) output, and (9) constraints. A system exists within a larger world, an environment. A boundary separates the system from its environment. The system takes input from the environment, processes it, and sends the resulting output back to its environment.

3. **Describe the information systems development cycle (SDC).**
   The systems development cycle used in this book has four major steps: (1) project management and planning, (2) systems analysis, (3) systems design, and (4) systems implementation and operation. In the first step, project management and planning, analysts make detailed road maps of the systems development project. In analysis, analysts work to solve the business problem being studied. In design, the solution to the problem is built. Finally, in the last step, the system is given to users and maintained.

4. **Describe three types of information systems: transaction processing systems, management information systems, and decision support systems.**

Many different kinds of information systems are used in organizations. These include transaction processing systems, management information systems, and decision support systems. Transaction processing systems (TPS) automate the handling of data about business activities or transactions. Management information systems (MIS) are computer-based systems that take the raw data available through a TPS and convert them into meaningful aggregated form. Decision support systems (DSS) are designed to help decision makers with decisions. Development techniques vary with system type.

5. **Describe the organizational role of the systems analyst in information systems development.**

Systems analysts play a key organizational role in systems development. They act as liaisons between business users on one hand, and technical personnel on the other. Analysts need to develop four sets of skills in order to succeed: analytical, technical, managerial, and interpersonal.

6. **Recount the evolution of systems development methodologies.**

Various approaches to systems development have emerged over time. They include process-oriented methodologies, as represented by the systems development life cycle, data-oriented methodologies, object-oriented methodologies, and agile methodologies. Important aspects of the object-oriented methodologies include the Unified Modeling Language (UML) and the Rational Unified Process (RUP).

KEY TERMS CHECKPOINT

Here are the key terms from the chapter. The page where each term is first explained is in parentheses after the term.

a. Agile methodologies (p. 19)
b. Application software (p. 2)
c. Boundary (p. 6)
d. Cohesion (p. 8)
e. Constraint (p. 6)
f. Coupling (p. 8)
g. Data-oriented methodologies (p. 19)
h. Decomposition (p. 6)
i. End user (p. 14)
j. Environment (p. 6)
k. Incremental methodology (p. 22)
l. Information systems analysis and design (p. 3)

m. Interrelated components (p. 6)
n. Iteration (p. 22)
o. Iterative methodology (p. 22)
p. Modularity (p. 8)
q. Object-oriented systems analysis and design approach (OOSAD) (p. 19)
r. Project management and planning (p. 9)
s. Purpose (p. 6)
t. Rational Unified Process (RUP) (p. 22)
u. Structured analysis and design (p. 17)

v. System (p. 5)
w. System component (p. 6)
x. System interface (p. 7)
y. Systems analysis (p. 9)
z. Systems analyst (p. 3)
aa. Systems design (p. 10)
bb. Systems development life cycle (SDLC) (p. 17)
cc. Systems implementation and operation (p. 10)
dd. Unified Modeling Language (UML) (p. 19)
ee. Use case (p. 9)

Match each of the key terms above with the definition that best fits it.

1. The process of developing and maintaining an information system.
2. The organizational role most responsible for the analysis and design of information systems.
3. Software designed to process data and support users in an organization. Examples of application software include spreadsheets, word processors, payroll system, and inventory management system.
4. Group of interrelated procedures used for a business function, with an identifiable boundary, working together for some purpose.
5. An irreducible part or aggregation of parts that makes up a system; also called a subsystem.
6. Dependence of one part of the system on one or more other system parts.

7. The line that marks the inside and outside of a system and that sets off one system from other systems in the organization.
8. The overall goal or function of a system
9. Everything external to a system that interacts with the system.
10. Point of contact where a system meets its environment or where subsystems meet each other.
11. A limit to what a system can accomplish.
12. The process of breaking down a system into smaller constituents, which may be subsystems or terminal units.
13. Dividing a system into smaller chunks or modules.
14. The extent to which subsystems depend on each other.
15. The extent to which a system or subsystem performs a single function.

16. The first step in systems development, in which an organization's total information system needs are analyzed and arranged, and in which a potential information systems project is identified and an argument for continuing or not continuing with the project is presented.

17. The second step in systems development, in which the current system is studied and alternative replacement systems are proposed.

18. The third step in systems development, in which the system chosen for development in systems analysis is first described, independent of any computer platform (logical design), and is then transformed into technology-specific details (physical design) from which all programming and system construction can be accomplished.

19. The final step of systems development, in which the information system is coded, tested, and installed in the organization, and in which the information system is systematically repaired and improved.

20. Non-information-systems professionals in an organization. End users often request new or modified software applications, test and approve applications, and might serve on project teams as business experts.

21. The series of steps used to mark the phases of development for an information system in the structured analysis and design approach.

22. A methodology based on decomposition of processes and data flow diagrams using an SDLC approach.

23. Data-centered but process-sensitive methodologies that attempt to minimize redundancy of data in an organization.

24. An analysis and design approach based on notion of an object, which captures the data and processes of a thing in a single construct.

25. A notation that allows the modeler to specify, visualize, and construct the artifacts of software systems, as well as business models.

26. Development in pieces that are progressively tested and integrated.

27. Development of a piece by growing, improving, and refining over several time periods.

28. A time-bound minor milestone within a phase.

29. An object-oriented program development methodology with four phases of development: inception, elaboration, construction, and transition phase.

30. Current approaches to systems development that focus on adaptive methodologies, people instead of roles, and an overall self-adaptive development process.

31. A depiction of a system's behavior or functionality under various conditions as the system responds to requests from users.

REVIEW QUESTIONS

1. What skills are needed by a systems analyst?
2. What is systems thinking? How is it useful for thinking about computer-based information systems?
3. What is decomposition? Coupling? Cohesion?
4. What factors increase the risk of an information systems project? How does the iterative, incremental methodology mitigate risk?
5. What are the characteristics of successful systems development teams?
6. Explain how systems analysis and design has changed from 1950 to the present day.
7. What is meant by an agile methodology? How does an agile method differ from other methods?

PROBLEMS AND EXERCISES

1. Why is it important to use object-oriented analysis and design methodologies when building a system? Why not just build the system in whatever way seems to be quick and easy? What value is provided by using an engineering approach?

2. Describe your university or college as a system. What is the input? The output? The boundary? The components? Their interrelationships? The constraints? The purpose? The interfaces? The environment? Draw a diagram of this system.

3. A car is a system with several subsystems, including the braking subsystem, the electrical subsystem, the engine, the fuel subsystem, the climate-control subsystem, and the passenger subsystem. Draw a diagram of a car as a system and label all of its system characteristics.

4. Your personal computer is a system. Draw and label a personal computer as a system as you did for a car in Problem and Exercise 3.

5. How would you organize a project team of students to work with a small-business client? How would you organize a project team if you were working for a professional consulting organization? How might these two methods of organization differ? Why?

6. Changes in user requirements can increase the cost and time estimate of a project. As a project manager, should you ask users to sign off on requirements so you are not blamed for an escalation in costs or an increase in completion period?

7. At what points should you test your system?

8. What are the similarities between construction of a house and the development of an information system? What are the differences?

1. If someone at a party asked you what a systems analyst is and why anyone would want to be one, what would you say? Support your answer with evidence from this chapter.
2. Explain how a computer-based information system designed to process payroll is a specific example of a system. Be sure to account for all nine components of any system in your explanation.
3. How does the Internet, and more specifically the World Wide Web, fit into the picture of object-oriented analysis and systems development drawn in this chapter?
4. What do you think object-oriented analysis and design will look like in the next decade? What changes might occur in the next 10 years?

CASE PROBLEMS

1. Pine Valley Furniture

Alex Schuster began Pine Valley Furniture (PVF) as a hobby. Initially, Alex would build custom furniture in his garage for friends and family. As word spread about the quality of his craftsmanship, he began taking orders. The hobby has since evolved into a medium-sized business, employing more than 50 workers.

Over the years, increased demand has forced Alex to relocate several times, increase his sales force, expand his product line, and renovate Pine Valley Furniture's information systems. As the company began to grow, Alex organized the company into functional areas—manufacturing, sales, orders, accounting, and purchasing. Originally, manual information systems were used; however, as the business began to expand rapidly, a minicomputer was installed to automate applications.

In the beginning, a process-oriented approach was utilized. Each separate application had its own data files. The applications automated the manual systems on which they were modeled. In an effort to improve its information systems, PVF has recently renovated them, resulting in a company-wide database and applications that work with this database. Pine Valley Furniture's computer-based applications are primarily in the accounting and financial areas. All applications have been built in-house, and when necessary, new information systems staff are hired to support Pine Valley Furniture's expanding information systems.

a. How did Pine Valley Furniture go about developing its information systems? Why do you think the company chose this option? What other options were available?
b. One option available to Pine Valley Furniture was an enterprise-wide system. What features does an enterprise-wide system, such as SAP, provide? What is the primary advantage of an enterprise-wide system?
c. Pine Valley Furniture will be hiring two systems analysts next month. Your task is to develop a job advertisement for these positions. Locate several Web sites or newspapers that have job advertisements for systems analysts. What skills are required?
d. What types of information systems are currently utilized at Pine Valley Furniture? Provide an example of each.

2. Hoosier Burger

As college students in the 1970s, Bob and Thelma Mellankamp often dreamed of starting their own business. While on their way to an economics class, Bob and Thelma drove by Myrtle's Family Restaurant and noticed a "For Sale" sign in the window. Bob and Thelma quickly made arrangements to purchase the business, and Hoosier Burger Restaurant was born. The restaurant is moderately sized, consisting of a kitchen, dining room, counter, storage area, and office. Currently, all paperwork is done by hand. Thelma and Bob have discussed the benefits of purchasing a computer system; however, Bob wants to investigate alternatives and hire a consultant to help them.

Perishable food items such as beef patties, buns, and vegetables are delivered daily to the restaurant. Other items such as napkins, straws, and cups are ordered and delivered as needed. Bob Mellankamp receives deliveries at the restaurant's back door and then updates a stock log form. The stock log form helps Bob track inventory items. The stock log form is updated when deliveries are received and also nightly after daily sales have been tallied.

Customers place their orders at the counter and are called when their orders are ready. The orders are written on an order ticket, totaled on the cash register, and then passed to the kitchen where the orders are prepared. The cash register is not capable of capturing point-of-sale information. Once an order is prepared and delivered, the order ticket is placed in the order ticket box. Bob reviews these order tickets nightly and makes adjustments to inventory.

In the past several months, Bob has noticed several problems with Hoosier Burger's current information systems, especially with the inventory control, customer ordering, and management reporting systems. Because the inventory control and customer ordering systems are paper based, errors occur frequently, often impacting delivery orders received from suppliers and the taking of customer orders. Bob has often wanted to have electronic access to forecasting information, inventory usage, and basic sales information. This access is impossible because of the paper-based system.

    a. Apply the SDC approach to Hoosier Burger.
    b. Using the Hoosier Burger scenario, identify an example of each system characteristic.
    c. Decompose Hoosier Burger into its major subsystems.
    d. Briefly summarize the approaches to systems development discussed in this chapter. Which approach do you feel should be used by Hoosier Burger?

3. Natural Best Health Food Stores

Natural Best Health Food Stores is a chain of health food stores serving Oklahoma, Arkansas, and Texas. Garrett Davis opened his first Natural Best Health Food Store in 1975 and has since opened 15 stores in three states. Initially, he sold only herbal supplements, gourmet coffees and teas, and household products. In 1990, he expanded his product line to include personal care, pet care, and grocery items.

In the past several months, many of Garrett Davis's customers have expressed the desire to purchase prepackaged meals, such as chicken, turkey, fish, and vegetarian, and have these prepackaged meals automatically delivered to their homes weekly, biweekly, or monthly. Garrett feels that this is a viable option, because Natural Best has an automatic delivery system in place for its existing product lines.

With the current system, a customer can subscribe to the Natural Best Delivery Service (NBDS) and have personal care, pet care, gourmet products, and grocery items delivered on a weekly, biweekly, or monthly basis. The entire subscription process takes approximately five minutes. The salesclerk obtains the customer's name, mailing address, credit card number, desired delivery items and quantity, delivery frequency, and phone number. After the customer's subscription has been processed, delivery usually begins within a week. As customer orders are placed, inventory is updated automatically.

The NBDS system is a client/server system. Each store is equipped with a client computer that accesses a centralized database housed on a central server. The server tracks inventory, customer activity, delivery schedules, and individual store sales. Each week the NBDS generates sales summary reports, low-in-stock reports, and delivery schedule reports for each store. The information contained on each of these individual reports is then consolidated into master sales summary, low-in-stock, and forecasting reports. Information contained in these reports facilitates restocking, product delivery, and forecasting decisions. Garrett has an Excel worksheet that he uses to consolidate sales information from each store. He then uses this worksheet to make forecasting decisions for each store.

    a. Identify the different types of information systems used at Natural Best Health Food Stores. Provide an example of each. Is an expert system currently used? If not, how could Natural Best benefit from the use of such a system?
    b. Figure 1.4 identifies seven characteristics of a system. Using the Natural Best Health Food Stores scenario, provide an example of each system characteristic.
    c. What type of computing environment does Natural Health Food Stores have?

Chapter

2

Introduction to Object Orientation

Chapter Objectives

After studying this chapter, you should be able to:

➤ Define an object.
➤ Understand the terms *class, attribute,* and *operations.*
➤ Explain generalization, polymorphism, and inheritance.
➤ Define association.
➤ Describe modeling and the Unified Modeling Language.

Chapter Contents

➤ Chapter Preview
➤ Object Orientation
➤ Systems Modeling

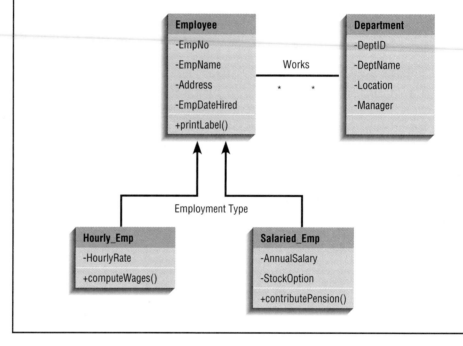
OBJECT ORIENTATION

During the 1990s, several researchers and practitioners were working on a new approach based on the notion of an object. Prior approaches to programming computers separated data and processes, but many analysts found this division unnatural. A real-world object, whether natural or human-made, has properties (akin to data) and behavior (akin to processes) combined. From this perspective, it seemed logical to combine data and process in computer programming as well. This approach is object orientation. To understand this approach, we must start with a definition of objects.

Object
An entity that encapsulates properties and behavior.

Property
A characteristic trait that serves to describe its possessor.

Behavior
The observable effects of an operation.

What Is an Object?

An object has properties and behavior. A cordless drill is an object. It has properties such as voltage, weight, and charge time, and behavior like rotating in either direction. A cellular phone is an object since it has properties such as model and price, and

Figure 2.2
A DVR

behavior such as dialing a number and receiving a call. However, a sales order is also an object since it has properties such as order number and date, and behavior such as calculating tax and calculating total. Let us study some important concepts related to OOSAD by using a familiar example.

Consider a DVR as an example of an object (Figure 2.2). The DVR is *uniquely identified* by a serial number. It has data properties such as manufacturer name (e.g., Panasonic), model number (e.g., PC D4744S), color, disc capacity, playback formats, VCR capability, and so on. Further, this object has behavior. The DVR can play a DVD, VCR tape, record a program, forward or reverse a disc, and so on. To enable the DVR to play a disc, a message needs to be sent. This can be sent by a remote control, which is another object, or by pressing the play button, which is part of the DVR interface. The user expects the DVR to perform such operations but doesn't have to know details of the implementation of the operations. The implementation is *hidden* from the user, which would be called encapsulation for an object. A change in implementation of an operation (e.g., the playback mechanism) should not affect the interface.

If certain conditions are met (e.g., the DVR has a disc, the power is on, etc.), the pressing of the play button will lead to a successful scenario, and the DVR will behave as expected. However, if a condition is not satisfied, then, if possible, the DVR might signal an error. For example, if the disc is not present, the DVR could return a message prompting the user to provide a disc.

The DVR can send messages to other objects. For example, a DVR has an interface that can connect it to other audio and video components. A cable can be used to connect a DVR to a receiver. The DVR can send an audio/video signal (i.e., a message) to the receiver, which can amplify the audio signal and send it to speakers as well as send the video signal to a television, which can then produce a high-quality picture and sound (Figure 2.3). Each stage involves the notions of object, message, interface, implementation, and behavior.

Thus, one may assemble an audio/video sound system using components. Note that an audio/video receiver supports plug-and-play; that is, a Panasonic DVR can be replaced by a JVC DVR, and a similar performance will result. Thus, the Panasonic DVR and the JVC DVR are polymorphic. In a similar fashion, different speakers might plug into the same port on a computer and provide similar performance; therefore, they are polymorphic. In a business setting, different vendors might provide different versions of the software component *shopping cart* that realize the same interfaces. Similarly, different vendors can provide front-end components for composing structured query language (SQL) queries in visual mode. The functionality is similar when one component is replaced by another.

Class

A class is different from an object. A class is abstract, and an object is concrete. Sometimes an object is also called an *instance*. A DVR object can be identified by a code such as D1IE93833. Several such DVR objects may define a class called DVR with additional attributes such as modelNo, disc capacity, playback formats, and so on.

Message
The passing of information from one object to another.

Interface
A named set of operations that characterize the behavior of a class or component.

Implementation
A definition of how something is constructed.

Encapsulation
Hiding data and behavior behind a public interface.

Operation
A specification that can be used to invoke behavior in an object by passing a message.

Component
A replaceable part of a system that provides a clearly defined function through a set of interfaces.

Plug-and-play
The ability to substitute one class or component with another without affecting the overall functionality of the system.

Polymorphic
Different classes or components implementing the same interfaces.

Class
A set of objects that share the same attributes, operations, relationships, and semantics.

Figure 2.3 Audio and video components.

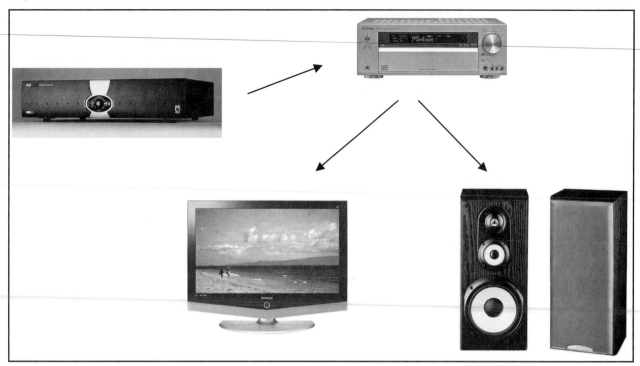

Let us now consider a business object such as SalesOrder, which is a transaction to record sales of items or services to a customer. This example will provide a better introduction to the OOSAD concepts. We will use the Unified Modeling Language (UML) notations.

Note that multiple sales orders are possible. Different sales orders can have the same attributes (e.g., order date) and operations (e.g., calculate order total), and can be involved in the same relationships to other objects (e.g., customer). The collection of such objects constitutes the SalesOrder class (Figure 2.4). A class is commonly represented using a rectangle. Orders identified by numbers 10056, 12890, 19834, and so on, can be the objects of the class SalesOrder. The notation for a generic object of class SalesOrder "is: SalesOrder."?

Attribute

Attribute
A named property of an object that describes a range of values that instances of the attribute might hold.

A class has attributes. Thus, SalesOrder might have attributes such as orderNo, orderDate, deliveryDate, and orderTerms (Figure 2.5). The state of an object is described by the values of its attributes. To distinguish an attribute name from a class name, the initial letter of a class is capitalized, and the initial letter of an attribute is in lowercase. Class and attribute names are generally nouns.

Operation

Method
The implementation of an operation.

A class also has operations, which describe the behavior of the class. An operation is sometimes called a method, although strictly speaking the method is limited to the implementation of the operation and does not include the signature of the operation.

Figure 2.4 An Illustration of a Class

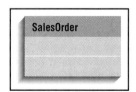

SalesOrder

Figure 2.5   A Class
with Attributes

Figure 2.6
An Operation with
Signature and Method
Written in PL/SQL

```
create or replace procedure add_order
            (v_custid ord.custid%type      ⎤
            )                              ⎬ Signature
                                           ⎦
as

begin
        if valid_cust(v_custid) then                            ⎤
                    insert into ord(ordid, orderdate, custid, shipdate)
                    values (ord_seq.nextval, sysdate, v_custid, sysdate+60);
        else                                                    ⎬ Method
                    raise_application_error (-20002, 'cust not valid');
        end if;

end add_order;                                                  ⎦
/
```

Signature
The name, parameters, and
return type of an operation.

The signature of an operation provides the name, parameters, and return type. The operation, in a sense, is the sum of the signature and the method, where the method is the code part that describes the logic required to achieve the behavior promised by the operation. For example, if an operation add_order creates a new order when given a customer number, the signature of the operation will be add_Order (CustNo Number), and the method will be code that creates the order. The method will include the referential integrity check for CustNo, the insert statement, and the code that checks for errors. Figure 2.6 shows the operation add_order with its signature and method written in PL/SQL.

An operation is usually a verb. Figure 2.7 shows two operations: calcTotal() and changeDelivDate(). An operation such as calcTotal is an inquiry, and the object :SalesOrder can send messages to other objects to calculate the total. The operation changeDelivDate() will change the value of the deliveryDate attribute, thus altering the state of the object. Other objects can invoke such operations by sending messages to :SalesOrder.

Encapsulation

The object :SalesOrder encapsulates data (attributes) and processes (operations). The object that calls the operation calcTotal() does not need to know the implementation of the operation. Therefore, the implementation of operations is hidden from other

Figure 2.7
A Class with
Attributes and
Operations

objects. Similarly, the data are hidden from unexpected changes by providing operations such as get and set. Data and processes are thus protected inside a capsule (hence the term *encapsulation*).

Object Identity

Each SalesOrder object or Customer object needs to be uniquely identified. Two customers might have the same name; thus, customerName is unlikely to distinguish these customers. Even the Social Security number might not always uniquely distinguish individuals. An information system needs to observe that each object has a distinctive identity. In some implementations, this is accomplished by using an attribute that serves to distinguish the objects. In others, a system-generated identifier may be used.

Generalization

Next, we illustrate the concepts of generalization and inheritance. An animal database generally has a hierarchy of classes with specialized classes inheriting the data and behavior of the more general classes. Thus, a more general class, Mammal, may be used to capture data and behavior common to animals such as cat, dog, ape, and man, while the specialized classes capture the distinguishing data and behavior. The ape class will inherit all data and behavior associated with the general class mammal. A detailed database will have several layers of classes with each specialized class inheriting from the more general classes in its hierarchy.

Consider the same concept in a business setting. Suppose the sales order can be paid by check or credit card. If the sales order is paid by check, the check number and other data pertaining to the check should be recorded. In the case of credit cards, the credit card number and expiration date need to be recorded, and this information must be verified by the bank. Other mechanisms for payment also are possible.

In Figure 2.8, the classes SalesOrderCheckPmt and SalesOrderCreditPmt are called subclasses of SalesOrder. The class SalesOrder is called the superclass of SalesOrderCheckPmt and SalesOrderCreditPmt. The relationship between a class and its subclass (or superclass) is called generalization or specialization. Subclasses

Identity
The property of an object that makes it distinct even if the state is the same as that of another object.

Generalization
A relationship between a more general (or a parent) class and a more specific (or a child) class; the more specific class has additional attributes and operations.

Inheritance
The mechanism by which the more specific class includes the attributes and operations of the more general class.

Figure 2.8
An Example of
Generalization

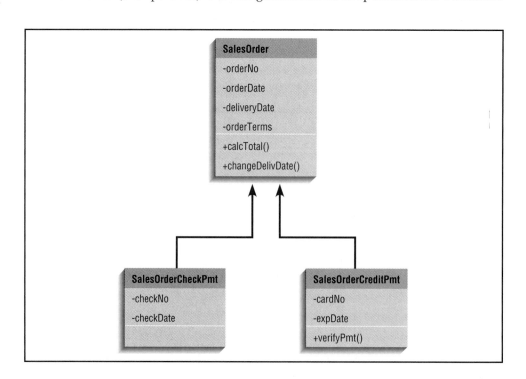

inherit attributes and operations from their class. A subclass has its own additional attributes and operations. For example, the class SalesOrderCreditPmt inherits the attributes orderNo, orderDate, deliveryDate, and orderTerms and the methods calcTotal and changeDelivDate. In this case, the class SalesOrder is the generalized class, and SalesOrderCheckPmt and SalesOrderCreditPmt are the specialized classes.

A generalization is a relationship between a general thing (called the superclass or parent) and a more specific kind of that thing (called the subclass or child). Generalization typically is verified by using the "is a kind of" or "is a type of" rule. For example, SalesOrderCheckPmt *is a kind of* SalesOrder, a full-time employee *is a kind of* employee, and a centrifugal pump *is a type of* pump, which in turn *is a type of* equipment. A subclass typically inherits from only one parent class. When a subclass inherits from more than one class, the generalization relationships result in multiple inheritance. Some software do not support multiple inheritance, which can create ambiguous situations.

Polymorphism

Earlier it was mentioned that a DVR and a DVD player that respond similarly but differently to the same message are polymorphic. Polymorphism means "having many forms." In the context of OOSAD, polymorphism means that the same message can invoke similar but different behavior. Thus, a message that invokes the operation calcTotal() of a :SalesOrder object will result in the sales order total calculation; a message that invokes the operation calcTotal() of a PurchaseOrder object will result in a purchase order total calculation. The implementation of the operations in the respective classes will be different.

This ability facilitates easier development. Consider a class called Vehicle. Suppose NewVehicle and UsedVehicle are both kinds of vehicles and are specified as specialization classes of Vehicle (Figure 2.9). The price of a new vehicle is itemized and calculated by summing up the base price of the vehicle, the costs of its options, and miscellaneous charges, such as destination charge, along with taxes. Assume that the price of a used vehicle is not itemized but stated as a lump-sum figure and calculated by summing this price with the taxes. Thus, the implementation of the operation calcPrice() for NewVehicle is different from that of UsedVehicle. However, it isn't necessary to use operation names like calcNewVehiclePrice() and calcUsedVehiclePrice().

In OOSAD, polymorphism has another significant use. It provides the ability to hide different implementations behind an interface and is a vital requirement for component-based development.

Figure 2.9
An Example of
Polymorphism

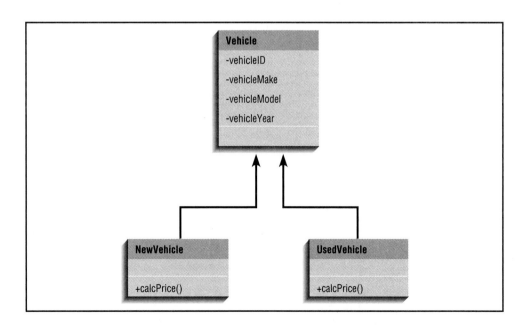

Interface

The structure of an operation has already been discussed. Each operation has a signature and an implementation. If a class wants to invoke the operation, it needs only the signature. The concept is no different than being able to fast-forward a DVD player without having to know the details of its implementation. Similarly, it should be possible to find out the total amount from the SalesOrder class by invoking the operation calcTotal(p_orderNo), where the p_orderNo is the parameter that has the value of the order number. The object invoking the operation by sending a message is not concerned with the implementation of the operation as long as the correct answer is delivered.

A class will not be useful if it provides only one operation. Typically, a class will provide a number of operations. The signatures of these operations form the *interface* of the class. Note that providing a public interface while keeping the implementation private enables us to change the implementation without affecting the messages from the calling objects. Further, by applying polymorphism to interfaces, one can allow plug-and-play ability and enable component-based development. Different classes that realize the same interface are polymorphic to each other. Thus, one class can be replaced by another if both realize the same set of operations. The ability to replace one part with another leads to the definition of a component.

Component

A software component is just like a physical component. In a personal computer, one can replace the DVD drive with one made by any manufacturer as long as the replacement component can physically fit in the space and provide a standard interface to the electronic and electrical connections. The component includes the implementation of its interfaces. An interface of a DVD will include a certain size socket for the power supply, which must meet certain specifications of voltage and current. In the same sense, a software component provides a set of interfaces. For example, a shopping cart component can be used in an application that involves selling over the Web (Figure 2.10). The same application can use a credit card authorization component and a debit card component. As a service to customers, the application might provide a component that allows users to build simple queries on their order information. Another component might manage user name and password creation and maintenance.

The premise of component-based development is that software development can be accelerated considerably if reliable, tested parts are available for assembly and do not have to be coded from scratch. A component also is replaceable because the developer who deploys these components is interested in the interface, not in its implementation.

Figure 2.10
An EC System with
Four Components

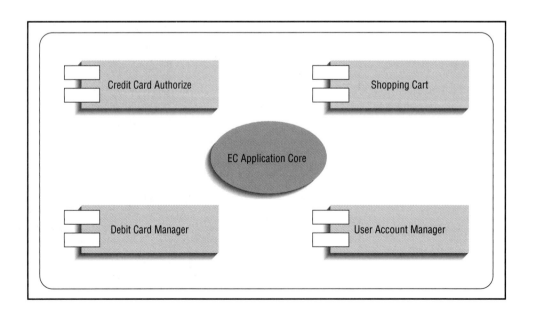

Figure 2.11
An Example of
a Package

Package

Package
A logical grouping of
related analysis or design
elements.

A package is a logical grouping of related analysis or design elements. A development project can have a large number of models, which also are called artifacts. A package normally includes related artifacts, such as sales artifacts (Figure 2.11). Note that a package is different from a component, which has a clearly defined function. A package clusters related classes and components into a named mechanism. Its primary purpose is to identify the main units in a system. In this sense, a package is also a subsystem. However, a subsystem with a clearly defined function and interface is called a component.

Association

Association
A relationship or link
between instances (or
objects) of classes.

A sales order is related to a customer, a student is related to a section, and a course is related to its prerequisites, and so on. An association is a relationship between instances (or objects) of classes. It also can be a relationship between objects of the same class.

Figure 2.12 shows an association between the classes Customer and SalesOrder. Even though an association is realized at the object level, the abstract representation shows it as a link between classes. The Customer class has the role Client, and the SalesOrder has the role Transaction. The multiplicity of Customer is 1 and that of SalesOrder is 0..*. This means that a Customer object can relate to several SalesOrder objects or may not relate to any SalesOrder. However, a :SalesOrder must relate to one and only one :Customer.

Aggregation
An association that models
a whole-part relationship
between an aggregate,
which is called the whole,
and its parts. It is a strong
form of association in
which the aggregate has no
meaning without parts.

A stronger form of association is aggregation, which also is called a whole-part relationship. For example, a team consists of players. The team is "whole" or "aggregate," and the player is "part" in this relationship. If there are no players, then generally it is meaningless to talk about a team. In aggregation, the whole has no meaning without parts, but parts may or may not exist without the whole. If a team can exist without players, then the relationship is better modeled as an association. Some analysts prefer to model an aggregation by using an association that shows minimum cardinality has 1, that is, the whole must have at least one part.

Composition
A strong form of aggrega-
tion in which the aggregate
is meaningless without
parts, and the parts are
meaningless without the
aggregate.

An even stronger case of aggregation is called composition. In composition, the aggregate is meaningless without parts, and a part is meaningless without an aggregate. For example, a DVD is composed of parts. If the parts are removed, the DVD has no existence; conversely, if the DVD is lost, the parts are considered lost, too. Similarly, it is generally meaningless to talk about a sales order without its line items, and a line item is meaningless without its sales order. Thus, if a sales order is created, then its line items must be created, too. SalesOrder and LineItem can be considered to participate in a composition relationship. Depending on the semantics of a given application, a developer selects whether a relationship will be an association, an aggregation, or a composition.

Figure 2.12
An Example of an
Association between
Two Objects

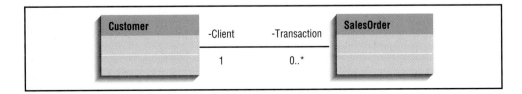

That is the basic terminology involved in OOSAD applications. The next questions are: What do I do with these concepts? Is there an approach that ties these terms together so an OOSAD application can be developed? To accomplish this, these terms and concepts need to be employed in a methodology. The dominant aspect of the methodology is to be able to model the system using a commonly accepted notation.

SYSTEMS MODELING

Systems modeling
Creating an abstraction of a system.

A systems analyst needs to be well versed in systems development methodologies. Systems modeling is a key aspect of most systems development methodologies. The IS industry has had about 35 years of experience in formal development methodologies, and it is important for a student to understand the evolution and history of systems development.

What Is Modeling?

Abstraction
Focusing on the relevant aspects and ignoring other details.

To develop an effective information system, the system needs to be examined from various perspectives and its features need to be modeled. The larger the project is, the more important the modeling is. A model is an abstraction of a system. Abstraction means focusing on the aspects relevant to a particular situation and ignoring other details. A model is like a blueprint. Depending on the need, a model can be abstract or detailed. Models typically are represented by diagrams.

One model is likely to be inadequate to describe a system. If one is building a wooden table, one diagram might be sufficient. If one is building a house, several blueprints/models are necessary. However, in building a refinery, hundreds or thousands of models might be needed. The piping alone might require dozens of models. Similarly, a large information system might require hundreds or thousands of models. The information system needs to be modeled from various aspects such as structural and dynamic. The models can help users, developers, and stakeholders communicate with each other as well as among themselves. The models should allow a new person in a project to comprehend quickly the essentials of the system relevant to that person. Thus, the models should serve as aids to documentation. Finally, a model should help detail and construct the system.

To represent these models, a modeling language is needed. The language should be able to address the system from various perspectives, preferably in visual representations. Further, the language should be standard or at least accepted by a large segment of the information systems practitioners. In recent years, the Unified Modeling Language (UML) has emerged as a popular language for developing information systems based on OOSAD. However, the road to UML has been long and fraught with numerous IS development failures. Further, UML might just be another milestone as the field makes further progress. UML will be covered in more detail next.

What Is Unified Modeling Language (UML)?

As discussed in Chapter 1, the Unified Modeling Language (UML) is the language that has been adopted by Object Management Group (OMG). UML unifies features from some of the leading proponents of OOSAD, especially those of Grady Booch, James Rumbaugh, and Ivar Jacobson. However, many others contributed to the effort, and it might be useful to read a brief history of OOSAD and the emergence of UML.

The first object-oriented programming language, SIMULA, was proposed as early as the mid-1960s. However, the language Smalltalk, developed by Xerox PARC in the 1970s, popularized object-oriented programming. In the 1980s, C++ emerged and quickly became popular. The success of object-oriented programming paved the way for object-oriented analysis and design. Several researchers and practitioners came up with ideas, methods, and notations for advancing OOSAD. In addition to the three amigos, these include Sally Shlaer, Steve Mellor, Rebecca Wirf-Brock, Kent Beck, Ward Cunningham, Peter Coad, Jim Odell, and several others. Once Rumbaugh and Jacobson joined Booch at Rational Software, a standard modeling language emerged. In January 1997, Rational Software released UML version 1.0. Since then, enhancements have appeared regularly, and UML version 2 was adopted in 2003. In this book, unless specified otherwise, UML will denote the UML version 2, also called UML 2.

Although OOSAD seems to have origins in programming, a close examination of UML shows its database roots. In fact, one of the most important UML diagrams, the class diagram, has a strong structural similarity with the ER diagram. This is also evident from the terminology employed for class diagrams. The dominant type of class in a class diagram is the entity class.

At this stage, it appears that OOSAD will be the leading methodology for the next decade. This is evident by the evolutionary trend in the database market, which is becoming object relational. All leading DBMS products such as Oracle, Informix, DB2, and SQL Server have object-relational features. Object-oriented programming languages such as Java and C++ have been popular for some time, and students enrolled in MIS and CIS programs are now required to take one or more programming courses using such languages. In other words, the stage is set for adoption of OOSAD.

The following is a discussion of the kinds of diagrams UML 2 supports, many of which will be important in the OOSAD process presented in this book. The UML 2 language supports 11 kinds of diagrams:

1. Use-case diagram
2. Sequence diagram
3. Communication diagram
4. Class diagram
5. Object diagram
6. Activity diagram
7. State diagram
8. Composite structure diagram
9. Package diagram
10. Component diagram
11. Deployment diagram

A brief description of each follows. Note that the class, object, package, composite structure, component, and deployment diagrams focus mainly on the structure or the building blocks, and are therefore called structural diagrams. The use-case, sequence, communication, activity, and state diagrams focus mainly on the behavior or the interaction and flow among objects, and are therefore called behavioral diagrams.

A *use-case diagram* includes a set of use cases and actors, and the relationships among them. A use case is a description of a set of sequences of actions that a system performs that yields an observable result of value to a particular actor. An actor is a role that a user plays with respect to the system.

A *sequence diagram* shows the interactions among objects in a time-ordered manner. An interaction shows the passing of a message from one object to another. If the interactions are shown without the time-ordering of messages, the representation is called a *communication diagram*, which focuses on the messages passed among objects. A sequence diagram can be translated into a communication diagram, and if a communication diagram has time-ordered message numbers, it can be translated into a sequence diagram.

A *class diagram* shows a set of classes and the relationships (such as association, generalization, and aggregation) among the classes. An object diagram shows a set of objects and the relationships among the objects. An *object diagram* is used to illustrate a specific instance of a class diagram.

An *activity diagram* shows the flow from one activity to another. An activity diagram can also be used to capture the workflow among objects.

A *state diagram* shows the transitioning of an object from state to state in response to various events. A state diagram captures the dynamic aspects of a system.

A *composite structure diagram* is used to show how a composite whole is made from its parts.

A *package diagram* is used to show logically grouped analysis or design elements.

A *component diagram* shows the software components or modules and their dependencies.

A *deployment diagram* shows the configuration of run-time processing nodes and the components that live on them.

KEY POINTS REVIEW

This short chapter consisted primarily of new terms and definitions. However, for those who have never studied objects and object orientation, this may be one of the most important chapters in this book. Those not previously familiar with objects probably will revisit this chapter many times during their OOSAD course to refresh their memory about the many new terms one needs to know and understand to work with objects. It is also important to know what the Unified Modeling Language (UML) is and why it exists. This chapter provided a brief introduction to UML; it will be built upon in the remainder of the book.

1. **Define an object.**

   An object is something intelligible or perceptible by the mind. It has properties and behavior. Technically, an object is an entity that encapsulates data and behavior. Basically, that means an object is a thing that contains data and instructions for acting on those data.

2. **Understand the terms *class, attribute, and operations.***

   An object is a specific thing, and a class is a collection of objects with the same properties. An object is specific, but a class is much more general and abstract. A plumber named John Smith is an object, and Plumber is a class. Attributes are the characteristics of the class and can be translated into data. The technical definition of an attribute is "a named property of a class that describes a range of values that instances of the attribute may hold." Operations are the instructions that the class can follow. The technical definition of an operation is "specification that can be used to invoke behavior in an object by passing a message."

3. **Explain generalization, polymorphism, and inheritance.**

   A class is more general than an object, but there can be many levels of generalization. A class can be general, such as a class called Animal. It is possible to have more specific classes within the class Animal, such as Bird, Reptile, and Mammal. If the class Animal can be thought of as the parent class, the other classes can be thought of as children. The children have many things in common with the parent, but they all have their own distinguishing features. Inheritance refers to the passing of characteristics from the parent to the child, or technically, inheritance is "the mechanism by which the more specific class includes the attributes and operations of the more general class." Polymorphism means "many forms," or "different classes or components implementing the same interfaces."

4. **Define association.**

   An association is a relationship among instances of classes. It also can be a relationship among objects of the same class. An association is a relationship or link among instances (or objects) of classes.

5. **Describe modeling and the UML.**

   To develop an effective information system, the system needs to be examined from various perspectives and its features need to be modeled. The larger the project is, the more important the modeling is. A model is an abstraction of a system. UML stands for the Unified Modeling Language. It unifies features from some of the leading proponents of OOSAD, especially those of Grady Booch, James Rumbaugh, and Ivar Jacobson.

KEY TERMS CHECKPOINT

Here are the key terms from the chapter. The page where each term is first explained is in parentheses after the term.

a. Abstraction (p. 40)
b. Aggregation (p. 39)
c. Association (p. 39)
d. Attribute (p. 34)
e. Behavior (p. 32)
f. Class (p. 33)
g. Component (p. 33)
h. Composition (p. 39)

i. Encapsulation (p. 33)
j. Generalization (p. 36)
k. Identity (p. 36)
l. Implementation (p. 33)
m. Inheritance (p. 36)
n. Interface (p. 33)
o. Message (p. 33)
p. Method (p. 34)

q. Object (p. 32)
r. Operation (p. 33)
s. Package (p. 39)
t. Plug-and-play (p. 33)
u. Polymorphic (p. 33)
v. Property (p. 32)
w. Systems modeling (p. 40)

Match each of the key terms above with the definition that best fits it.

1. An entity that encapsulates data and behavior.
2. Hiding data and behavior behind a public interface.
3. The observable effects of an operation.
4. A specification that can be used to invoke behavior in an object by passing a message.
5. The passing of information from one object to another.
6. A named set of operations that characterize the behavior of a class or component.
7. A definition of how something is constructed.
8. The implementation of an operation.
9. A replaceable part of a system that provides a clearly defined function through a set of interfaces.
10. Different classes or components implementing the same interfaces.
11. The ability to substitute one class or component with another without affecting the overall functionality of the system.
12. A set of objects that share the same attributes, operations, relationships, and semantics.
13. An attribute is a named property of a class that describes a range of values that instances of the attribute may hold.

14. The property of an object that makes it distinct even if the state is the same as that of another object.
15. A relationship between a more general (or a parent) class and a more specific (or a child) class, where the more specific class has additional attributes and operations.
16. The mechanism by which the more specific class includes the attributes and operations of the more general class.
17. A logical grouping of related analysis or design elements.
18. An association that models a whole-part relationship between an aggregate, which is called the whole, and its parts. It is a strong form of association in which the aggregate has no meaning without parts.
19. A strong form of aggregation in which the aggregate is meaningless without parts and the parts are meaningless without the aggregate.
20. Creating an abstraction of a system.
21. Focusing on the relevant aspects and ignoring other details.
22. A relationship or link between instances (or objects) of classes.

REVIEW QUESTIONS

1. What is an object? Give some examples.
2. Name and describe several of the characteristics of an object.
3. What does it mean to say an object has operations?
4. What does it mean for an object to have attributes?
5. What is polymorphism? What are some advantages of polymorphism?
6. What is a class? Give examples.
7. What is generalization? What are the advantages of generalization?
8. What is an interface?
9. Define package.
10. What is a component? What are the advantages of components?
11. Explain what is meant by objects having associations. Give examples.
12. Give an example of aggregation and of composition.
13. What is modeling?
14. What is UML?
15. Briefly name and describe the nine types of diagrams provided for in UML.

PROBLEMS AND EXERCISES

1. Provide some examples of aggregation and composition. Do you find it difficult in certain cases to distinguish association, aggregation, and composition? (Several experts are not finicky about the subtle differences in exceptional cases.)
2. Many of the examples of objects and their characteristics provided in this chapter are based on consumer electronics. Think of other common, everyday things that could be used to explain objects and their characteristics.
3. Ask friends or family members who work in the information technology industry about objects and object orientation. Ask them for examples of objects they work with or have created as part of their jobs. Use these examples to demonstrate the characteristics of objects discussed in this chapter.

DISCUSSION QUESTIONS

1. How do objects and object orientation differ from the traditional approaches to data and processes you have learned about in other MIS courses? What are the advantages and disadvantages of each? Make a table that compares the two approaches.
2. Why do you think Booch and colleagues developed UML? What purpose does it serve? Do you think it is important for an IT person to know about UML? Why or why not?
3. What do you think the role of system modeling is in systems development? Why can't developers just sit down and start writing code when they develop a system?

CASE: BROADWAY ENTERTAINMENT COMPANY, INC.

Company Background

Case Introduction

Broadway Entertainment Company, Inc. (BEC) is a fictional company in the video rental and recorded music retail industry, but its size, strategies, and business problems (and opportunities) are comparable to those of real businesses in this highly competitive industry.

In this section, we introduce the company, the people who work for it, and the company's information systems. At the end of each subsequent chapter, we revisit BEC to illustrate the phase of the life cycle discussed in that chapter. Our aim is to provide a realistic case example of how object-oriented systems development moves through its steps and how analysts, managers, and users work together to develop an information system. This example provides practice in working on tasks and discussing issues related to each activity in an ongoing systems development project.

The Company

As of January 2006, Broadway Entertainment Company owned 2,403 outlets across the United States, Canada, Mexico, and Costa Rica. There is at least one BEC outlet in every state and each Canadian province. Canada has 58 stores, Mexico has 10, and Costa Rica has 5. The company currently is struggling to open a retail outlet in Japan and plans to expand into the European Union (EU) within two years. In the United States, Broadway is headquartered in Spartanburg, South Carolina; Canadian operations are headquartered in Vancouver, British Columbia; and Latin American operations are based in Mexico City.

Each BEC outlet offers for sale two product lines: recorded music (on CDs) and video games. Each outlet also rents two product lines: recorded videos (on DVDs) and video games. In calendar year 2005, music sales and video rentals together accounted for nearly 80 percent of Broadway's U.S. revenues (see BEC Table 2.1). Foreign operations added another $21.5 million to company revenues.

BEC Table 2.1 BEC Domestic Revenue by Category (calendar year 2005).

CATEGORY	REVENUE (IN $000s)	PERCENT
Sales Revenue		
Music Sales	$572,020	34%
Video Sales (DVD)	$154,000	9%
Video Game Sales	$92,760	5%
Rental Revenue		
Video Rentals	$742,080	44%
Video Game Rentals	$139,140	8%
Total	$1,700,000	100%

The home video and music retail industries are strong and growing, domestically and internationally, in spite of the growth in music and video on demand delivered via the Internet. For several years, home video has generated more revenue than either theatrical box offices or movie pay-per-view.

To get a good idea of the industry in which Broadway competes, we look at five key elements of the home video and music retail industries:

1. **Suppliers**—all of the major distributors of recorded music (e.g., Matsushita, Sony, Time Warner), video games (e.g., Microsoft, Nintendo, Sega, Sony), and recorded videos (e.g., CBS, Fox, Sony, Viacom).
2. **Buyers**—individual consumers.
3. **Substitutes**—television (broadcast, cable, and satellite), subscription entertainment (such as HBO and Showtime), first-run movies, pay-per-view, video-on-demand services, Internet-based multimedia, theater, radio, concerts, and sporting events.
4. **Barriers to entry**—few barriers and many threats, including alliances between telecommunications and entertainment companies to create cable television and Web-based TV, which lets consumers choose from a large number and variety of videos, music, and other home entertainment products from a computerized menu system in their homes.
5. **Rivalries among competing firms**—large music chains (such as Musicland and Tower Records, all smaller than BEC) and large video chains (such as Blockbuster Entertainment, which is larger and more globally competitive than BEC), and online movie rental service providers (such as Blockbuster, Netflix, and Wal-Mart, which are larger and more competitive than BEC).

Company History

The first BEC outlet opened in the Westgate Mall in Spartanburg, South Carolina, in 1977, as a music (record) sales store. The first store sold recorded music exclusively, primarily in vinyl format, but also stocked cassette tapes. Broadway's founder and current chairman of the board, Nigel Broad, had immigrated to South Carolina from his native Great Britain in 1968. After nine years of playing in a band in jazz clubs, Nigel used the money he had been left by his mother, formed Broadway Entertainment Company, Inc., and opened the first BEC outlet.

Sales were steady and profits increased. Soon Nigel was able to open a second outlet and then a third. Predicting that his BEC stores had met Spartanburg's demand for recorded music already, Nigel decided to open his fourth store in nearby Greenville in 1981. At about the same time, he added a new product line—Atari video game cartridges. Atari's release of its Space Invaders game cartridge resulted in huge profits for Nigel. The company continued to grow, and Broadway expanded beyond South Carolina into neighboring states.

In the early 1980s, Nigel saw the potential in videotapes. A few video rental outlets had opened in some of Broadway's markets, but they were all small, independent operations. Nigel saw the opportunity to combine video rentals with music sales in one place. He also decided that he could rent more videos to customers if he changed some of the typical video store rules, such as eliminating the heavy membership fee and allowing customers to keep videos for more than one night. Nigel also wanted to offer the best selection of videos anywhere.

Nigel opened his first joint music and video store at the original BEC outlet in Spartanburg in 1985. Customer response was overwhelming. In 1986, Nigel decided to turn all 17 BEC outlets into joint music and video stores. To move into the video rental business in a big way, Nigel and his chief financial officer, Bill Patton, decided to have a public offering. They were happily surprised when all 1 million shares sold at $7 per share. The proceeds also allowed Broadway to revive the dying video game line by dropping Atari and adding the newly released Nintendo game cartridges.

Profits from BEC outlets continued to grow throughout the 1980s, and Broadway further expanded by acquiring existing music and video store chains including Music World. From 1987 through 1993, the number of BEC outlets roughly doubled each year. The decision to go international, made in 1991, resulted in 12 Canadian stores that year. The initial three Latin American stores were opened in mid-1994. Throughout the rest of the 1990s, steady growth occurred as this industry matured.

During 2003, the home video game industry continued to expand. Nigel noticed an emerging trend when analyzing the video game sales figures. Whenever a new hardware platform or game is introduced, there is a significant growth in sales, but the sales volume tapers down after a while as consumers hold back their purchases in expectations of new platforms or games. Nigel realized that BEC could take advantage of this cyclical nature of the home video game industry by implementing a game-trading model in the outlets, where consumers are able to exchange games for new ones, or other used games if they can get a fair value for them. This initiative resulted in increased revenue from video game sales.

In 2005, Nigel recognized that in order for the company to remain competitive in the movie rental industry, BEC will need to implement an online rental subscription service. The major player in this new industry, Netflix, Inc., already has a significant market share, as does Blockbuster and newcomer Wal-Mart. To remain competitive in the changing marketplace, and to provide wider product distribution at a relatively low cost, Nigel strongly feels that BEC must quickly move into the online rental market for both DVD movies and video games.

From its beginnings in 1977, with 10 employees and $398,000 in revenues, Broadway Entertainment Company, Inc., grew to 24,225 employees and worldwide revenues of $1.7 billion by January 1, 2006.

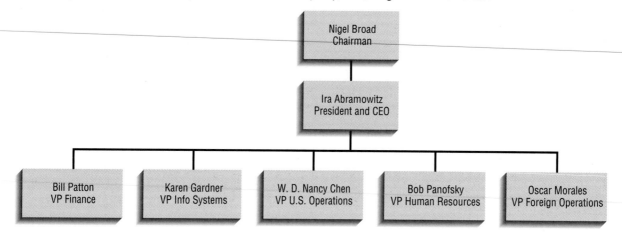

Company Organization

In 1992, when the company opened its one thousandth store, Nigel decided that he no longer wanted to be chief executive officer of the company. He took the position of chairman, and promoted his close friend Ira Abramowitz to the offices of president and CEO (see BEC Figure 2.1).

Most of Broadway's other senior officers also have been promoted from within. Bill Patton, the chief financial officer, started as the fledgling company's first bookkeeper and accountant. Karen Gardner had been part of the outside consulting team that built Broadway's first information system in 1986 and 1987. She became the vice president in charge of information systems (IS) for BEC in 1990. Bob Panofsky, the vice president for human resources, has been with the company since 1981. An exception to the promote-from-within tendency, W. D. Nancy Chen, the vice president for domestic operations, was recruited from Music World in 1991, shortly before the chain was purchased by Broadway. Oscar Morales was hired in 1992 from Blockbuster Entertainment, where he had been in charge of Latin American expansion.

Development of Information Systems

Broadway Entertainment Company operated from 1977 until 1984 without any computer-based information systems support. As the company grew, ledgers, files, and customer account information became unruly. Like many businesses this size, the owner did not have the expertise or the capital for developing the company's own information systems. For example, Bill Patton managed inventory by hand until he bought an IBM AT in 1984. Computerizing the company made the expansion to 10 stores in 1984 much easier. In 1985, BEC had nobody who was trained in information systems on staff, and all the BEC managers were busy coping with the business expansion. Nigel and Bill considered hiring a small staff of experienced IS professionals, but they did not know how to manage such a group, how to select quality staff, or what to expect from such employees. Nigel and Bill realized that computer software could be complicated, and building systems for a rapidly changing organization could be a challenge. They also knew that building information systems required dis-

cipline. So Nigel, after talking with leaders of several other South Carolina businesses, contacted the information consulting firm of Fitzgerald McNally, Inc., about designing and building a custom, computer-based information system for Broadway. In 1985, no prewritten programs were available to help run the still relatively new business of video and music rental and sales stores.

Nigel and Bill wanted the new system to perform accounting, payroll, and inventory control. Nigel wanted the system to be readily expandable because he was planning for Broadway's rapid growth. At the operational level, Nigel realized that the video rental business would require unique features in its information system. For one thing, rental customers would not only be taking product from the store, they also would be returning it at the end of the rental period. Further, customers would be required to register with Broadway and attach some kind of deposit to their account in order to help ensure that videos would be returned.

At the managerial level, Nigel wanted the movement of videos in and out of the stores and all customer accounts computerized. He also wanted to be able to search through the data on the rental habits of Broadway's customers. He wanted to know which videos were the most popular, and he wanted to know who Broadway's most frequent customers were, not only in South Carolina but also in every location where Broadway did business.

Fitzgerald McNally, Inc., was happy to get Broadway's account. Karen Gardner was assigned to head the development team. Karen led a team of her own staff of analysts and programmers, along with several BEC managers, in a thorough analysis and design study using what was considered to be the most modern development techniques at that time, following structured analysis and design methods. The methodology applied in this study provided the discipline needed for such a major systems development effort. The methodology began with information planning and continued through all phases of the systems development life cycle.

Karen and her team delivered and installed the system at the end of the two-year project. The system was centralized, with an IBM 4381 mainframe installed at headquarters in Spartanburg and three terminals, three light pens, and three dot-matrix printers installed in each BEC outlet. The light pens recorded, for example, when the tapes were rented and when they were returned by reading the bar code on the cassette. The light pens also were used to read the customer's account number, which was recorded in a bar code on the customer's BEC account card. The printers generated receipts. In addition, the system included a small personal computer and printer to handle a few office functions such as the ordering and receiving of goods. The software monitored and updated inventory levels. Another software product generated and updated the customer database, whereas other parts of the final software package were designed for accounting and payroll.

In 1990, Karen Gardner left Fitzgerald McNally and joined Broadway as the head of its information systems group. Karen led the effort to expand and enhance Broadway's information systems as the company grew to more than 2,000 company-owned stores in 1995. Broadway now uses a client/server network of computers at headquarters and in-store, point-of-sale (POS) computer systems to handle the transaction volume generated by millions of customers at all BEC outlets.

Information Systems at BEC Today BEC has two systems development and support groups, one for in-store applications and the other for corporate, regional, and country-specific applications. The corporate development group has liaison staff with the in-store group, because data in many corporate systems feed or are fed by in-store applications (e.g., market analysis systems depend on transaction data collected by the in-store systems). BEC creates one-year and three-year IS plans that encompass store and corporate functions. After more than 15 years of experience with many new systems and now stable enhancements, BEC's IS staff members are skilled at systems development and enhancement using structured methods; in fact, BEC is considered an information systems leader in the home entertainment industry.

The functions of the original in-store systems at BEC have changed little since they were installed in 1987; for example, customer and inventory tracking are still done by pen-based, bar code scanning of product labels and membership cards. Rentals and returns, sales, and other changes in inventory as well as employee time in and out are all captured at the store in electronic form via a local POS computer system. These data are transmitted in batches at night using modems and regular telephone connections to corporate headquarters, where all records are stored in a network of IBM AS/400 computers (see BEC Figure 2.2).

As shown in BEC Figure 2.2, each BEC store has an NCR POS server that serves as a host for a number of POS termi-

BEC Figure 2.2 BEC Hardware and Network Architecture

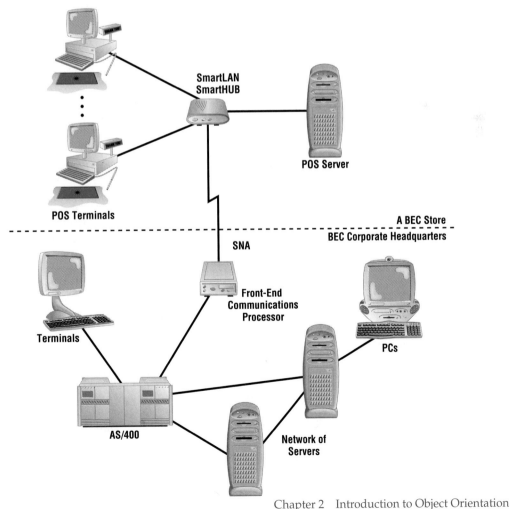

BEC Table 2.2 List of BEC In-Store (entertainment tracker) Applications.

System Name	Description
Membership	Supports enrollment of new members, issuing membership cards, reinstatement of inactive members, and local data management for transient members.
Rental	Supports rentals and returns of all products and outstanding rental reports.
Sales	Supports sales and returns of all products (including videos, music, snack food, BEC apparel, and gift certificates).
Inventory control	Supports all changes in rental and sales inventory that are not sales based (e.g., receipt of a new tape for rental, rejection of goods damaged in shipment, and transfer of an item from rental to sales categories).
Employee	Supports hiring and terminating hourly employees, as well as all time-reporting activities.

nals at checkout counters and is used for generating reports. Some managers also have learned how to use spreadsheet, word processing, and other packages to handle functions not supported by systems provided by BEC. The front-end communications processor offloads traffic from the IBM AS/400 network so that the servers can concentrate on data processing applications. BEC's communication protocol is System Network Architecture (SNA), an IBM standard. Corporate databases are managed by IBM's relational DBMS DB2. BEC uses a variety of programming environments, including C, COBOL, SQL (as part of DB2), and code generators.

Inventory control and purchasing are done centrally, and employees are paid by the corporation. Each store has electronic records of only its own activity, including inventory and personnel. Profit and loss, balance sheets, and other financial statements are produced for each store by centralized systems. The following sections review the applications that exist in the stores and at the corporate level.

In-Store Systems BEC Table 2.2 lists the application systems installed in each store. BEC has developed a turnkey package of hardware and software (called Entertainment Tracker—ET), which is installed in each store worldwide. Besides English, the system also works in Spanish and French.

As can be seen from BEC Table 2.2, all of these applications are transaction-processing systems. In fact, the POS terminals have a master screen from which each ET application is activated. These systems work off of a local decentralized database, and each store has a similarly structured database. Various batched data transfers occur between corporate and store systems at night (store transactions, price and membership data updates, etc.). The local database contains data on members, products, sales, rentals, returns, employees, and work assignments. The database contains only current data; the history of customer sales and rentals is retained in a corporate database. Thus, local stores do not retain any customer sales and rental activity information (except for open rentals).

Data for those members who have had no activity at a local store for more than one year are purged from the local database. When members use a BEC membership card and no member record exists in the local database, members are

asked to provide a local address and phone number where they can be contacted.

All store employees, except the store manager who is on salary, are paid on an hourly basis, so clock-in and clock-out times are entered as a transaction, using employee badges with a bar code strip, on the same POS terminal that is used for member transactions. Paychecks are delivered by express mail twice a month. Employee reports (e.g., attendance, payroll, and productivity) are produced by corporate systems and sent to store managers.

All other store record keeping is manual, and corporation offices handle accounts receivable and payable. The local store manager is responsible for contacting, via phone or mail, members who are late in returning rented items. Each night a file of delinquent members is transmitted to each store. If a member tries to use a delinquent membership, the member is asked to return all outstanding rentals before renting any more items, and the current transaction is invalidated. When terminated members try to use their cards, a BEC store clerk keeps the membership card and members are given a printed form that explains their rights at that point. Stolen membership cards are handled similarly, except that the store manager deals personally with people using cards that have been reported stolen.

Corporate Systems Corporate systems run on IBM servers using IBM's DB2 relational database management system, although some run on PCs. Application software is written in COBOL, C, SQL (a database processing language), and several 4GLs, and all systems are developed by BEC. Clerks and managers use PCs for interactive access into corporate systems as well as for stand-alone, end-user applications such as word processing, spreadsheets, specialized databases, and business graphics.

More than 20 major corporate systems exist with more than 350 programs and approximately 500,000 lines of code. There are many more specialized systems, often developed for individual managers, projects, or special events. BEC Table 2.3 lists some of the most active and largest of the major corporate systems.

One interesting aspect of the banking application is that because stores have no financial responsibilities, BEC

BEC Table 2.3   List of BEC Corporate Applications.

SYSTEM NAME	DESCRIPTION
Human resources	Supports all employee functions, including payroll, benefits, employment and evaluation history, training, and career development (including a college scholarship for employees and dependents).
Accounts receivable	Supports notification of overdue fees and collection of payment from delinquent customers.
Banking	Supports interactions with banking institutions, including account management and electronic funds transfers.
Accounts payable, purchasing, and shipping	Supports ordering products and all other purchased items used internally and resold/rented, distribution of products to stores, and payment to vendors.
General ledger and financial accounting	Supports all financial statement and reporting functions.
Property management	Supports the purchasing, rental, and management of all properties and real estate used by BEC.
Member tracking	Supports record keeping on all BEC members and transmits and receives member data between corporate and in-store systems.
Inventory management	Supports tracking inventory of items in stores and elsewhere and reordering those items that must be replenished.
Sales tracking and analysis	Supports a variety of sales analysis activities for marketing and product purchasing functions based on sales and rental transaction data transmitted nightly from stores.
Store contact	Supports transmittal of data between corporate headquarters and stores nightly, and the transfer of data to and from corporate and store systems.
Fraud	Supports monitoring abuse of membership privileges.
Shareholder services	Supports all shareholder activities, including recording stock purchases and transfers, disbursement of dividends, and reporting.
Store and state analysis	Supports the activity and profit analysis of stores and the analysis of potential sites for stores.

uses a local bank only for daily deposits and getting change. BEC's corporate bank, Bank of America (BoA), arranges correspondent banking relationships for BEC so that local deposits are transferred electronically to BEC's corporate accounts with BoA.

BEC's applications are still expanding, and they are under constant revision. For example, in cooperation with several hotel and motel chains that provide VCRs for rental, BEC is undertaking a new marketing campaign aimed at frequent travelers. At any one time, there are approximately 10 major system changes or new systems under development for corporate applications. More than 250 change requests are received annually, covering requirements from minor bug fixes to reformatting or creating new reports to whole new systems. The systems development workload is, at times, overwhelming for the IS development staff. For example, they believe that too often they duplicate prior systems development work and build applications from scratch rather than being able to reuse and evolve prior system components.

Status of Systems   A rapidly expanding business, BEC has created significant growth for the information systems group managers. Karen Gardner is considering reorganizing her staff to provide more focused attention on the international area. BEC still uses the services of Fitzgerald McNally when Karen's resources are fully committed. Karen's department includes 33 developers (programmers, analysts, and other specialists in database, networking,

etc.) plus the data center staff, which is now large and technically skilled enough to handle almost all requests. Given how experienced Karen's staff members are, they have become experts on the techniques and technologies they have been using, but they have had little time to learn new techniques and technologies they do not need on the job.

Karen's current challenge in managing the IS group is keeping her staff current in the skills they need to support the systems successfully in a rapidly changing and competitive business environment. In addition, Karen's staff members need to be excellent project managers, to understand the business completely, and to exhibit excellent communication with clients and each other. Karen also is concerned about information systems literacy among BEC management and that technology is not being as thoroughly exploited as it could be.

To deal with this situation, Karen is considering several initiatives. First, she has requested a sizable increase in her training budget, including expanding the benefits of the college tuition reimbursement program. Second, Karen is considering instituting a development program that will better develop junior staff members and will involve user departments. As part of this program, BEC personnel will rotate in and out of the IS group as part of their normal career progression. This program should greatly improve relationships with user departments and increase end-user understanding of technology. The development of this set of technical, managerial, business, and interpersonal skills in and outside IS is a critical success factor for Karen's group in responding to the significant demands and opportunities of the IS area.

Recently, Karen has read a lot about object-oriented systems development methods, a rather significant departure from how BEC has been developing systems. Karen certainly cannot switch cold turkey to these new methods, even if she were convinced that they are better than the proven methods BEC has been using. However, she would like to experiment with object-oriented methods if the right kind of project came along.

Case Summary

Broadway Entertainment Company is a $1.7 billion international chain of music, video, and game rental and sales outlets. BEC started with one store in Spartanburg, South Carolina, in 1977, and has grown through astute management of expansion and acquisitions into more than 2,000 stores in four countries.

BEC's hardware and software environment is similar to that used by many national retail chains. Each store has a computer system with point-of-sale terminals that run mainly sales and rental transaction-processing applications, such as product sales and rental, membership, store-level inventory, and employee pay activities. Corporate systems are executed on a network of computers at a corporate data center. Corporate systems handle all accounting, banking, property, sales and member tracking, and other applications that involve data from all stores.

BEC is a rapidly growing business with significant demand for information services. To build and maintain systems, BEC has divided its staff into functional area groups for domestic and international needs. BEC uses modern database management and programming language technologies. The BEC IS organization is challenged by keeping current in business and technology areas. Case studies in subsequent chapters will show how BEC responds to a request for a new system within this business and technology environment.

CASE QUESTIONS

1. What qualities have led to BEC's success so far? Do these qualities have anything to do with the type of information systems development methods they have used?
2. Is the IS organization at BEC poised to undertake significant systems development in the near future?
3. Is the IS organization at BEC poised to utilize object-oriented systems development effectively in the near future? If not, what would they need to do to be ready to utilize these new methods?
4. What benefits might BEC gain from using object-oriented systems development methods? What risks might they encounter in using such newer methods?
5. What retraining would BEC IS professionals need if they were to find a project with which they could experiment with object-oriented development methods?
6. Do corporate and in-store systems seem to be tightly or loosely related at BEC? Why do you think this is so?
7. What challenges and limitations will affect what and how systems are developed in the future at BEC?
8. Study the description of BEC and its information systems closely. Based on your understanding of BEC so far, provide examples of the following object-oriented terms within the BEC environment: class, object, method, and association.
9. Is BEC ready to use the Internet to deliver information systems to employees and customers? Explain.

Chapter *3*

Managing the Object-Oriented Information Systems Project

Chapter Objectives

After studying this chapter, you should be able to:

➤ Describe the skills required to be an effective project manager.

➤ Describe the unique characteristics of an OOSAD project.

➤ List and describe the skills and activities of a project manager during project initiation, project planning, project execution, and project closedown.

➤ Explain what critical path scheduling means and describe the process of creating Gantt Charts and Network Diagrams.

➤ Explain how commercial project management software packages can be used to assist in representing and managing project schedules.

Chapter Contents

➤ Chapter Preview

➤ Managing an OOSAD Project

➤ Representing and Scheduling Project Plans

➤ Constructing a Gantt Chart and Network Diagram for an OOSAD Project in Microsoft Project

51

The prior chapters introduced the four phases of the systems development cycle (SDC) and explained how an information system project repeatedly moves through those four phases. This chapter focuses on the systems analyst's role as project manager of information systems projects. Throughout the SDC, the project manager is responsible for initiating, planning, executing, and closing down the systems development project. Figure 3.1 illustrates these four functions. The next section describes the project manager's role and the project management process. The subsequent section examines techniques for reporting project plans using Gantt Charts and Network Diagrams. The chapter concludes by demonstrating how to represent a project plan in Microsoft Project, a popular project management software tool.

Figure 3.1   Project Management Occurs throughout the Systems Development Cycle (SDC).

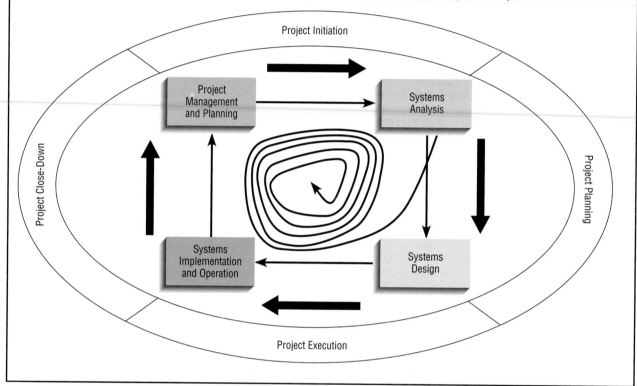

MANAGING AN OOSAD PROJECT

Project manager
A systems analyst with a diverse set of skills—management, leadership, technical, conflict management, and customer relations—who is responsible for initiating, planning, executing, and closing down a project.

Project
A planned undertaking of related activities to reach an objective that has a beginning and an end.

Project management is an important aspect of the development of information systems and an important skill for a systems analyst to master. The focus of project management is to assure that systems development projects meet customer expectations and are delivered within budget and time constraints.

The project manager is often a systems analyst with a diverse set of skills—management, leadership, technical, conflict management, and customer relations—who is responsible for initiating, planning, executing, and closing down a project. A proj-ect manager's environment is one of continual change and problem solving. In some organizations, the project manager is an experienced systems analyst; in others, junior and senior analysts are expected to take on this role, managing parts of a proj-ect or actively supporting a more senior colleague who is assuming this role. Understanding the project management process is a critical skill for future success.

Creating and implementing successful projects requires managing resources, activities, and tasks needed to complete the information systems project. A project is a planned undertaking of a series of related activities to reach an objective that has a beginning and an end. The first question to consider is where projects come from.

After considering all the different things that a project manager could be asked to work on within an organization, the project manager must determine which projects to address. The ways in which each organization answers these questions vary. Typically, a request is made to a project review board (or some other decision-making authority) that selects and prioritizes projects. Most organizations use a formal report, called a Systems Service Request (SSR), to make a project request. Figure 3.2 shows an

Figure 3.2 A Systems Service Request Includes Name and Contact Information of the Person Requesting the System, a Statement of the Problem, and the Name and Contact Information of the Liaison and Sponsor

Pine Valley Furniture: *Systems Service Request*

REQUESTED BY ___ Jackie Judson ___ DATE ___ October 1, 2007 ___

DEPARTMENT ___ Marketing ___

LOCATION ___ Headquarters, 570c ___

CONTACT ___ Tel: 4-3290   FAX: 4-3270   e-mail: jjudson@pinevalleyfurniture.com ___

TYPE OF REQUEST   URGENCY

[X]   New System   [   ]   Immediate—Operations are impaired or opportunity lost

[   ]   System Enhancement   [   ]   Problems exist, but can be worked around
[   ]   System Error Correction   [X]   Business losses can be tolerated until new system installed

PROBLEM STATEMENT

The Internet has become an important sales channel for many organizations. Beyond sales, the Internet provides opportunities for companies to enhance internal communications as well as to enhance communication and coordination with suppliers and customers. In order to provide a sales channel that is being requested by a growing number of our customers, we need to immediately begin the development of a corporate Web site to support online sales. This site will allow customers—corporate, home office, and students—to more easily shop for PVF products. It will also open new markets for PVF. Our biggest and most immediate opportunity is in the corporate sales area. Although we have many loyal customers, we are hearing more and more grumbling by this market segment that we do not have a Web-based sales outlet. We will likely redirect some sales away from our existing direct marketing and sales efforts by the creation of an online Web site; however, failure to move into this new channel could have severe long-term consequences for PVF. Additionally, this Web site will provide a foundation for the development of a broad range of Internet-based applications.

SERVICE REQUEST

I request a thorough analysis of our current sales methods and customer purchasing activity with the intent to design and build a completely new information system that will allow customers to buy PVF products over the Internet using a standard Web browser. This system should handle all customer purchasing activity, including viewing the catalog and prices, order tracking, returns, and so on. The system will also provide critical information to management on sales activity and trends, as well as tie into inventory, manufacturing, and other relevant systems. The development of this system will help PVF to continue to be profitable in an increasingly complex and competitive business environment. I feel that such a system will improve that competitiveness of PVF, particularly in our ability to better serve our customers.

IS LIAISON ___ Jim Woo   Tel: 4-6207   FAX: 4-6200   e-mail: jwoo@pinevalleyfurniture.com ___
SPONSOR ___ Jackie Judson, Vice President Marketing ___

------------------------- TO BE COMPLETED BY SYSTEMS PRIORITY BOARD -------------------------

[   ]   Request approved   Assigned to _____
                                      Start date _____

[   ]   Recommend revision
[   ]   Suggest user development
[   ]   Reject for reason _____

_____
_____

example of an SSR. This form includes the name and contact information of the person requesting the system, a statement of the problem, and the name and contact information of the liaison and sponsor. Once the SSR is created, the board reviews it.

Because all organizations have limited time and resources, not all project requests can be approved. Consequently, the review board is used to evaluate all project requests in relation to the business problems or opportunities the system will solve or create. These boards also consider how the proposed project fits within the organization's information systems architecture and long-range development plans. In short, the review board selects those projects that best meet overall organizational goals. (Organizational goals and project selection are covered in more detail in Chapter 4, Selecting and Planning Projects.)

Feasibility study
Determines if the information system makes sense for the organization from an economic and operational standpoint.

Once selected, the project manager examines the project more carefully to see if it makes sense for the organization from an economic and operational standpoint. This examination is called a feasibility study. Most organizations require that this detailed study take place before the system is constructed. Figure 3.3 presents a graphical view of the steps typically followed during the project initiation process.

In summary, systems development projects are undertaken for two primary reasons: to take advantage of business opportunities and to solve business problems. Taking advantage of an opportunity might mean providing an innovative service to customers through the creation of a new system. For example, an organization might want to create a Web site so that customers can access its catalog and place orders online easily. Solving a business problem could involve modifying how an existing system processes data so that more accurate or timely information is provided to users. For example, an organization might create a password-protected Intranet site that contains important announcements and budget information to enhance employee productivity.

Projects are not always initiated for the aforementioned rational reasons (taking advantage of business opportunities or solving business problems). For example, in some instances organizations and governments undertake projects to spend resources, attain or pad budgets, keep people busy, or help train people and develop their skills. Our focus in this chapter is not on how and why organizations identify projects, but on the management of projects once they have been identified.

Figure 3.3
A Graphical View of the Steps Followed during Project Initiation

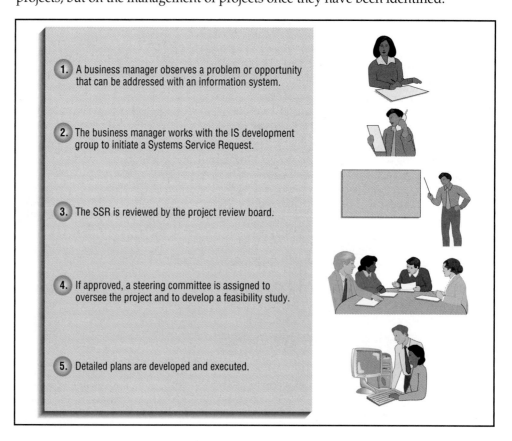

1. A business manager observes a problem or opportunity that can be addressed with an information system.

2. The business manager works with the IS development group to initiate a Systems Service Request.

3. The SSR is reviewed by the project review board.

4. If approved, a steering committee is assigned to oversee the project and to develop a feasibility study.

5. Detailed plans are developed and executed.

Figure 3.4
A Project Manager
Juggles Numerous
Activities

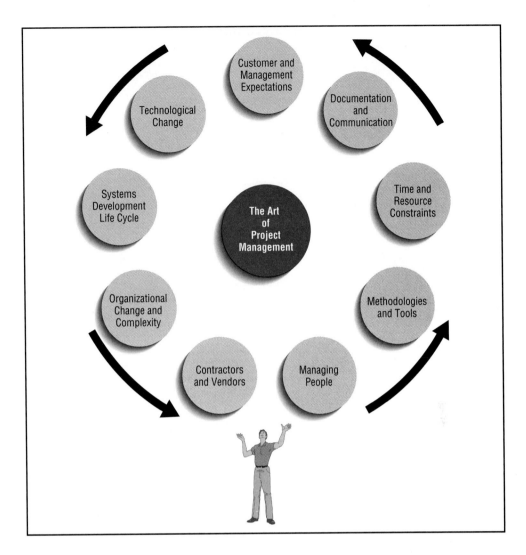

Once a potential project has been identified, an organization must determine the resources required for its completion. This is done by analyzing the scope of the project and determining the probability of successful completion. After getting this information, the organization can determine whether taking advantage of an opportunity or solving a particular problem is feasible within the time and resource constraints. If deemed feasible, a more detailed project analysis is conducted. The ability to determine the size, scope, and resource requirements for a project is just one of the many skills that a project manager must possess. A project manager often is referred to as a juggler keeping many balls aloft; the balls reflect the various aspects of a project's development, as depicted in Figure 3.4.

To orchestrate the construction of a complex information system successfully, a project manager must have interpersonal, leadership, and technical skills. Table 3-1 lists the project manager's common skills and activities. Note that many of the skills are related to personnel or general management; they are not simply technical skills. In addition to requiring an excellent manager, object-oriented systems analysis and design (OOSAD) projects have several unique characteristics that have important ramifications; these are discussed next.

Characteristics of the OOSAD Project

Chapter 1 reviewed and contrasted systems development approaches where OOSAD was described as an iterative and incremental development process. This means that over the duration of the project, a portion of the final system is constructed during each iteration phase. In this way, the system evolves incrementally

Table 3-1 Common Activities and Skills of a Project Manager.

ACTIVITY	DESCRIPTION	SKILL
Leadership	Influencing the activities of others toward the attainment of a common goal through the use of intelligence, personality, and abilities	Communication; liasion between management, users, and developers; assigning activities; monitoring progress
Management	Getting projects completed through the effective utilization of resources	Delining and sequencing activities, communicating expectations; assigning resources to activities; monitoring outcomes
Customer relations	Working closely with customers to assure project deliverables meet expectations	Interpreting system requests and specifications; site preparation and user training; contact point for customers
Technical problem solving	Designing and sequencing activities to attain project goals	Interpreting system requests and specifications; defining activities and their sequence; making trade-offs between alternative solutions; designing solutions to problems
Conflict management	Managing conflict within a project team to assure that conflict is not too high or too low	Problem solving; smoothing out personality differences; compromising; goal setting
Learn management	Managing the project team for effective team performance	Communication within and between teams; peer evaluations; conflict resolution; team building; self-management
Risk and change management	Identifying, assessing, and managing the risks and day-to-day changes that occur during a project	Environmental scanning; risk and opportunity identification and assessment; forecasting; resource redeployment

so that by the last iteration of the project, the entire system is completed (see Figure 3.5). In order for the system to evolve in this manner, the project manager must understand several unique characteristics of an OOSAD project. For more information on managing OOSAD projects, see "Software Project Management" (Royce, 1998).

Define the System as a Set of Components

In order to manage the project as a series of iterations, the project manager must subdivide the overall system into a set of components; when combined, this set will yield the entire system (see Figure 3.6). Each of these separate system components often is referred to as a "vertical slice" of the overall system; this is a key feature of the system that can be demonstrated to users (see Chapter 2). Alternatively, each slice should not be a subsystem that spans "horizontally" throughout the entire system because these horizontal slices typically do not focus on a specific system feature, nor are they typically good for demonstration to users. Basically, each vertical slice represents a use case of the system (see Chapter 6 for more information on use-case diagrams). Also, note in Figure 3.6 that project management and planning is an activity that continues throughout the life of the project.

One outcome of defining the overall system as a collection of components is the likelihood that the components constructed earlier in the project will require greater rework than those developed later in the project. For example, during the early stages of the project, missing components or a lack of understanding of key architectural features will require that components developed early in the project be modified substantially as the project moves forward, in order to integrate these components into a single, comprehensive system successfully. This means that rework is a natural part of an OOSAD project and that one should not be overly concerned when this occurs. It is simply a characteristic of the iterative and incremental development process of OOSAD.

Figure 3.5
During the OOSAD Process, the System Evolves Incrementally over the Life of the Project

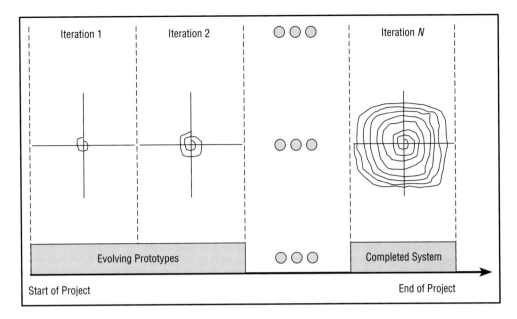

Complete Hard Problems First

Another characteristic of the OOSAD approach is that it tackles the hard problems first. In classic structured systems development, a hard problem, such as choosing the physical implementation environment, is addressed late in the development process. As a result, following a classic systems development approach tends to result in putting off the making of some of the key systems architectural decisions until late in the project. This approach is problematic because such decisions often determine whether a project is a success or a failure. On the other hand, addressing hard problems as early as possible allows the difficult problems to be examined before substantial resources have been expended. This mitigates project risk.

Figure 3.6 Object-Oriented Development Projects Are Developed Using Ongoing Management and Evolving System Functionality

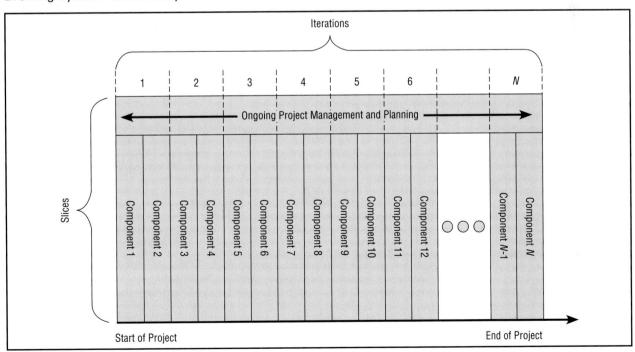

Figure 3.7 The Focus and Ordering of System Components Change over the Life of the Project

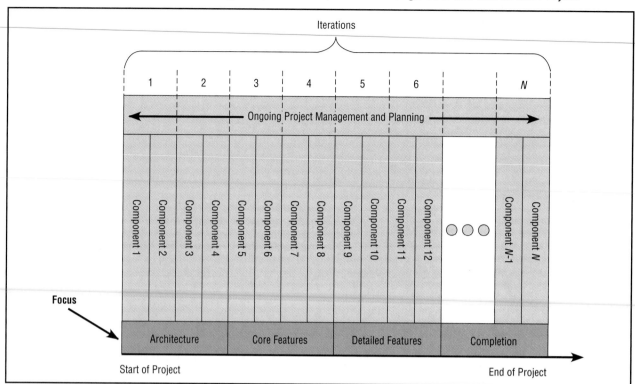

In addition, completing the harder problems associated with the systems architecture as early as possible helps in completing all subsequent components, because most will build upon these basic architectural capabilities. (With some projects, the hardest components depend upon simpler components. In these cases, one must complete the simpler slices first before moving to the harder ones. Nonetheless, focus should be placed on the hard problems as soon as possible.) From a project planning perspective, this means that there is a natural progression and ordering of components over the life of the project. The initial iteration or two must focus on the system architecture, such as the database or networking infrastructure. Once the architecture is completed, core system capabilities such as creating and deleting records are implemented. After the core system components are completed, detailed system features are implemented that help to fine-tune key system capabilities. During the final iteration phases, the primary focus is on activities that bring the project to a close (e.g., interface refinement, user manuals, and training see Figure 3.7).

Using Iterations to Manage the Project

During each project iteration, all systems development cycle activities are performed (see Figure 3.8). This means that each project iteration has management and planning, analysis, design, and implementation and operation activities. For each iteration, the inputs to the process are the allocated project components—vertical slices or use cases—to perform during this iteration and the results from the prior iteration. The results of this iteration are then used as inputs to the next iteration. For example, as components are designed and implemented, much is learned about how subsequent components will need to be implemented. The learning that occurs during each iteration helps the project manager gain a better understanding about how subsequent components will be designed, what problems might occur, what resources are needed, and how long and complex a component will be to complete. As a result, most experienced project managers believe that it is a mistake to make project plans too detailed early in the project when much is still unknown.

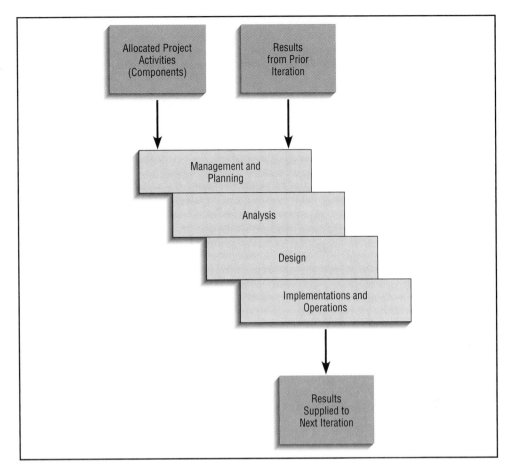

Don't Plan Too Much Up Front

During each iteration, more and more will be learned about how subsequent components will need to be designed, how long each might take to complete, and so on. Therefore, it is a mistake to make highly detailed plans far into the future because it is likely that these plans will be wrong. In OOSAD, as each iteration is completed, the goal is to learn more about the system being constructed, the capabilities of the development team, the complexity of the development environment, and so on. As this understanding is gained over the course of the project, the project manager is able to make better and better predictions and plans. As a result, making highly detailed plans for all project iterations is likely to result in a big waste of time. The project manager should be concerned only with making highly detailed plans for the next iteration or two. As the project manager learns over the course of the project, he or she will be able to continually refine schedules, time estimates, and resource requirements with better and better estimates (see Figure 3.9). This topic will be discussed in more detail later in the chapter.

How Many and How Long Are Iterations?

One question that many people have when first experiencing OOSAD has to do with the number and duration of iterations. Iterations are designed to be a fixed length of time, typically from two to eight weeks, but they can be as short as one week (especially for smaller projects). During a single iteration, multiple components (use cases) can be completed. However, it is important not to try to pack the development of too many components into a single iteration. Experience has shown that having more iterations with fewer components to be completed is better than having only a few iterations with many components needing to be completed. It is only by iterating—completing a full systems development cycle—that significant learning can occur to help the project manager better plan subsequent iterations.

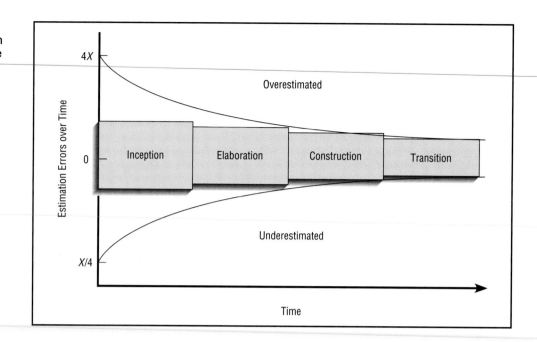

The inception phase generally will entail one iteration, but it is not uncommon for this to require two or more iterations in large, complex projects. Likewise, elaboration often is completed in one or two iterations, but again system complexity and size can influence this. Construction can range from two to several iterations, and transition typically occurs over one or two iterations. Thus, experienced OOSAD project managers typically use from six to nine iterations when designing and constructing a system (see Figure 3.10). Note that all completed components are integrated into a comprehensive system at the conclusion of each iteration. During the first iteration, it is likely that simple component prototypes will be created such as file opening, closing, and saving. However, as the project progresses, the prototypes become increasingly sophisticated until the entire system is completed (see Figure 3.11).

Figure 3.10
An OOSAD Project
Typically has 6 to 9
Iterations

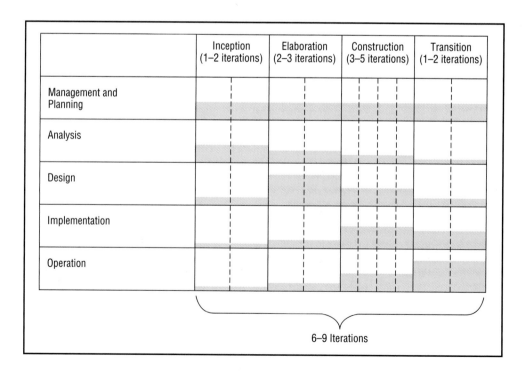

Figure 3.11
As the Project
Evolves, System
Functionality Evolves

Source: Adapted from Royce,
1998.

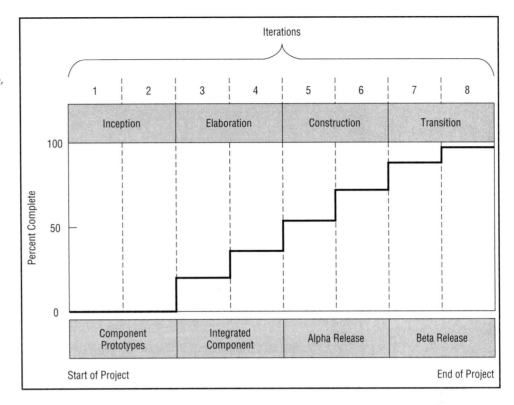

Project Activity Focus Changes over the Life of a Project

Over the life of a project, the project manager moves from iteration to iteration, beginning with inception and ending with the transition phase. Additionally, during all project iterations the manager engages in all phases of the systems development cycle. However, the level of activity in each phase changes over the life of the project (see Figure 3.12). For example, throughout the life of the project, management and planning is an ongoing and important element. Additionally, during inception the primary focus is analysis, during elaboration the primary focus is design, during construction the primary focus is implementation, and during transition the primary focus is making the system operational. In sum, although all project life cycle activities are employed during every project iteration, the mix and focus of these activities change over time.

Figure 3.12
The Level and Focus
of Activity across the
Systems Development
Process Change from
the Start to the End of
the Project

	Inception (1–2 iterations)	Elaboration (2–3 iterations)	Construction (3–5 iterations)	Transition (1–2 iterations)
Management and Planning				
Analysis				
Design				
Implementation				
Operation				

Start of Project ⟶ End of Project

Project management
A controlled process of initiating, planning, executing, and closing down a project.

This section briefly describes some of the unique characteristics of managing an OOSAD project. The remainder of this section will focus on the project management process, which involves four phases:

1. Initiating the project.
2. Planning the project.
3. Executing the project.
4. Closing down the project.

Several activities must be performed during each of these four phases. Following this formal project management process greatly increases the likelihood of project success.

Initiating the Project

Project initiation
The first phase of the project management process in which activities are performed to assess the size, scope, and complexity of the project and to establish procedures to support later project activities.

During project initiation, the project manager performs several activities that assess the size, scope, and complexity of the project, and establishes procedures to support subsequent activities. Depending on the project, some initiation activities might be unnecessary and some might be very involved. The types of activities the project manager will perform when initiating a project are summarized in Figure 3.13 and described next.

1. **Establishing the project initiation team.** This activity involves organizing an initial core of project team members to assist in accomplishing the project initiation activities. Typically, initiation teams consist of at least one user representative and one member of the IS development group.
2. **Establishing a relationship with the customer.** A thorough understanding of the customer builds stronger partnerships and higher levels of trust. Often, organizations try to foster strong working relationships between business units (like purchasing) and the IS development group by assigning a specific individual to work as a liaison between both groups.
3. **Establishing the project initiation plan.** This step defines the activities required to organize the initiation team while it is working to define the scope of the project. For example, the project manager can work with the customer to better translate business requirements into a written project request. This typically requires the collection, analysis, organization, and transformation of a lot of information. These steps eventually lead to the creation of a Systems Service Request (SSR see Chapter 4).
4. **Establishing management procedures.** Successful projects require the development of effective management procedures. In general, when establishing procedures, the project manager is concerned with developing team communication and reporting procedures, job assignments and roles, project change procedures, and determining how project funding and billing will be handled.

Figure 3.13 Six Project Initiation Activities

```
                    Project Initiation

   1.  Establishing the Project Initiation Team

   2.  Establishing a Relationship with the Customer

   3.  Establishing the Project Initiation Plan

   4.  Establishing Management Procedures

   5.  Establishing the Project Management
       Environment and Project Workbook

   6.  Developing the Project Charter
```

Figure 3.14
The Project Workbook Can Be a Hard-Copy or an Electronic Document

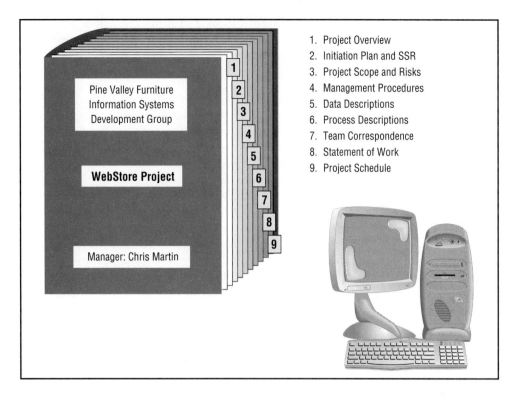

1. Project Overview
2. Initiation Plan and SSR
3. Project Scope and Risks
4. Management Procedures
5. Data Descriptions
6. Process Descriptions
7. Team Correspondence
8. Statement of Work
9. Project Schedule

Pine Valley Furniture
Information Systems
Development Group

WebStore Project

Manager: Chris Martin

Project workbook
An online or hard-copy repository for all project correspondence, inputs, outputs, deliverables, procedures, and standards that is used for performing project audits, orienting new team members, communicating with management and customers, identifying future projects, and performing post-project reviews.

5. **Establishing the project management environment and project workbook.** The focus of this activity is to collect and organize the tools that will be used while managing the project and to construct the project workbook. For example, most diagrams, charts, and systems descriptions provide much of the project workbook contents. Thus, the project workbook serves as a repository for all project correspondence, inputs, outputs, deliverables, procedures, and standards established by the project team (see Figure 3.14). The project workbook can be stored as an online electronic document or in a large, three-ring binder. The project workbook is used by all team members and is useful for project audits, orientation of new team members, communication with management and customers, identifying future projects, and performing post-project reviews. The establishment and diligent recording of all project information in the workbook are two of the most important activities that the project manager performs.

   Many project teams keep their project workbooks on the Web. A Web site can be created so that project members can access all project documents easily. This Web site can be a simple repository of documents or an elaborate site with password protection and security levels. The best feature of using the Web as the repository is that it allows project members and customers to review a project's status and related information continually.

Project charter
A short, high-level document prepared for both internal and external stakeholders to formally announce the establishment of the project and to briefly describe its objectives, key assumptions, and stakeholders.

6. **Developing the project charter.** The project charter is a short (typically one-page) high-level document prepared for both internal and external stakeholders to formally announce the establishment of the project and to briefly describe its objectives, key assumptions, and stakeholders. The project charter ensures that both you and your customer gain a common understanding of the project. It is also a very useful communication tool; it helps to announce to the organization that a particular project has been chosen for development.

Project initiation is complete after these six activities have been performed. Before moving to the next phase of the project, the work performed during project initiation is reviewed at a meeting attended by management, customers, and project team members. An outcome of this meeting is a decision to continue the project, modify it, or abandon it. If the scope of the project is modified, it might be necessary to return to project initiation activities and collect additional information. Once a decision is made to continue the project, a much more detailed project plan is developed during the project planning phase.

Planning the Project

Project planning

The second phase of the project management process, which focuses on defining clear, discrete activities and the work needed to complete each activity within a single project.

The next step in the project management process is project planning. Project planning involves defining clear, discrete activities and the work needed to complete each activity within a single project. It often requires numerous assumptions about the availability of resources such as hardware, software, and personnel. It is much easier to plan nearer-term activities than those occurring in the future. In actual fact, the project manager often has to construct longer-term plans that are more general in scope and nearer-term plans that are more detailed. As discussed, the repetitive nature of the project management process requires that plans be monitored constantly throughout the project and be updated repeatedly (usually after each project iteration) based upon the most recent information available.

Figure 3.15 illustrates the principle that nearer-term plans are typically more specific and firmer than longer-term plans. For example, it is virtually impossible to plan rigorously for activities late in the project without first completing earlier activities. Also, the outcome of activities performed earlier in the project is likely to have an impact on later activities. This means that it is difficult, and likely inefficient, to try to plan detailed solutions for activities that will occur far into the future.

As with the project initiation process, varied and numerous activities must be performed during project planning. Also, depending upon the size of the project, the amount of planning can vary greatly. For a small project, a 10-page plan might be adequate, whereas a project plan for a large system could be several hundred pages in length. The types of activities that can be performed during project planning are summarized in Figure 3.16 and are described next.

1. *Describing project scope, alternatives, and feasibility.* The purpose of this activity is to understand the content and complexity of the project. During this activity, the project manager should work with the customer to reach agreement on the following questions:

   - What problem or opportunity does the project address?
   - What are the quantifiable results to be achieved?
   - What needs to be done?
   - How will success be measured?
   - How will we know when we are finished?

After defining the scope of the project, the next objective is to identify and document general alternative solutions for the current business problem or opportunity. The project manager must then assess the feasibility of each alternative solution and choose which to consider during subsequent systems development phases. In some

Figure 3.15
The Level of Project Planning Detail Should Be High in the Short Term, with Less Detail for Activities That Are Taking Place in the Longer Term

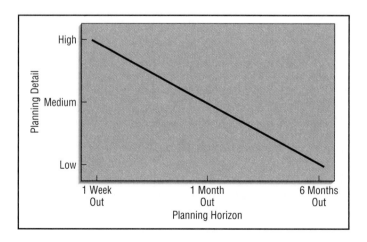

Figure 3.16
Ten Project Planning Activities

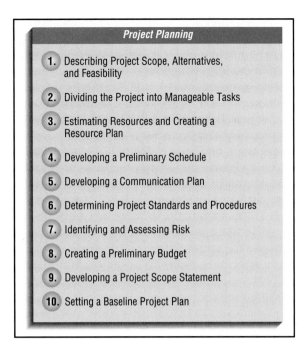

Project Planning

1. Describing Project Scope, Alternatives, and Feasibility

2. Dividing the Project into Manageable Tasks

3. Estimating Resources and Creating a Resource Plan

4. Developing a Preliminary Schedule

5. Developing a Communication Plan

6. Determining Project Standards and Procedures

7. Identifying and Assessing Risk

8. Creating a Preliminary Budget

9. Developing a Project Scope Statement

10. Setting a Baseline Project Plan

Work breakdown structure (WBS)
The process of dividing the project into manageable tasks and logically ordering them to ensure a smooth evolution between tasks.

Deliverable
An end product in a phase of the SDC.

Gantt Chart
A graphical representation of a project that shows each task as a horizontal bar whose length is proportional to its time for completion.

instances, off-the-shelf software can be found. It is also important that any unique problems, constraints, and assumptions about the project be stated clearly.

2. *Dividing the project into manageable tasks.* This is a critical activity during the project planning process. At this point, the project manager must divide the entire project into manageable tasks and then logically order them to ensure a smooth evolution between tasks. The definition of tasks and their sequence is referred to as the work breakdown structure (WBS). Some tasks can be performed in parallel, whereas others must follow one another sequentially. Task sequence depends on which tasks produce deliverables needed in other tasks, when critical resources are available, the constraints placed on the project by the client, and the process outlined in the SDC.

For example, suppose the project manager is working on a new development project and needs to collect system requirements by interviewing users of the new system and reviewing reports they currently use to do their job. A work breakdown for these activities is represented in a Gantt Chart in Figure 3.17. A Gantt Chart is a

Figure 3.17
Gantt Chart Showing Project Tasks, duration Times for Those Tasks, and Predecessors

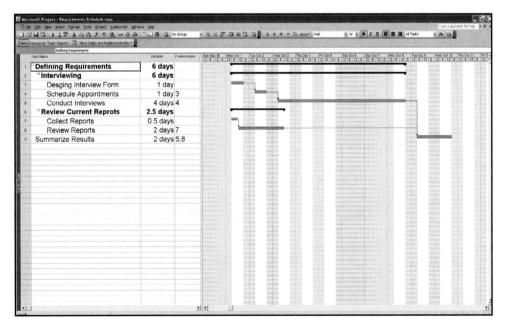

graphical representation of a project that shows each task as a horizontal bar whose length is proportional to its time for completion. Different colors, shades, or shapes can be used to highlight each kind of task. For example, those activities on the critical path (defined in the following text) could be in red, and a summary task could have a special bar. Note that the black horizontal bars—rows 1, 2, and 8 in Figure 3.17—represent summary tasks. Planned versus actual times or progress for an activity can be compared by parallel bars of different colors, shades, or shapes. Gantt Charts do not always show how tasks must be ordered (precedence) but simply show when an activity should begin and end. In Figure 3.17, the task duration is shown in the second column by days, and necessary prior tasks are noted in the third column as predecessors. Most project management software tools support a broad range of task durations including minutes, hours, days, weeks, and months. As will be discussed later in this chapter, creating the WBS for an OOSAD project should follow the iteration phases underlying this methodology. In general, creating a work breakdown structure requires the decomposition of phases into activities—summary tasks—and activities into specific tasks. For example, Figure 3.17 shows that the activity Interviewing consists of three tasks: design interview form, schedule appointments, and conduct interviews.

Network Diagram
A diagram that depicts project tasks and their interrelationships.

The schedule also can be represented as a Network Diagram, as illustrated in Figure 3.18. A Network Diagram is a graphical depiction of project tasks and their interrelationships. As with a Gantt Chart, each type of task can be highlighted by different features on the Network Diagram. The distinguishing feature of a Network Diagram is that the ordering of tasks is shown by connecting tasks—depicted as rectangles or ovals—with their predecessor and successor tasks. However, the relative size of a node (representing a task) or a gap between nodes does not imply the task's duration. Both types of diagrams are described later in this chapter.

Defining tasks in too much detail will make the management of the project unnecessarily complex. The characteristics of a task are as follows:

- Can be done by one person or a well-defined group.
- Has a single and identifiable deliverable. (The task, however, is the process of creating the deliverable.)
- Has a known method or technique.
- Has well-accepted predecessor and successor steps.
- Is measurable so that percent completed can be determined.

Figure 3.18
A Network Diagram Illustrates Tasks with Rectangles (or ovals) and the Relationships and Sequences of Those Activities

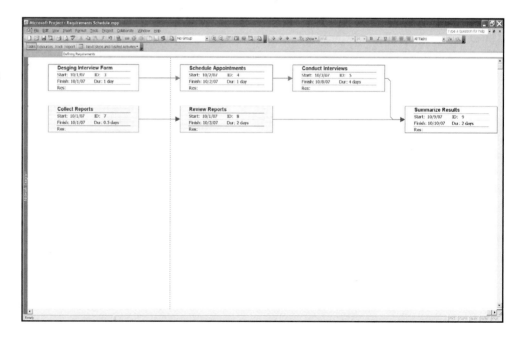

The project manager will develop the skill of discovering the optimal level of detail for representing tasks through experience. For example, it might be difficult to list tasks that require less than one hour of time to complete in a final work breakdown structure. Alternatively, choosing tasks that are too large in scope (e.g., several weeks long) will not provide a clear sense of the status of the project or of the interdependencies between tasks.

3. *Estimating resources and creating a resource plan.* The goal of this activity is to estimate resource requirements for each project activity and use this information to create a project resource plan. The resource plan helps assemble and deploy resources in the most effective manner. For example, the project manager would not want to bring additional programmers onto the project at a rate faster than work could be prepared for them. Project managers use a variety of tools to assist in making estimates of project size and costs. The most widely used method is called COCOMO (**CO**nstructive **CO**st **MO**del) which uses parameters that were derived from prior projects of differing complexity (Boehm et al., 2000). COCOMO uses these different parameters to predict human resource requirements for basic, intermediate, and very complex systems (see Figure 3.19).

People are the most important, and expensive, part of project resource planning. Project time estimates for task completion and overall system quality are influenced significantly by the assignment of people to tasks. It is important to give people tasks that allow them to learn new skills. It is equally important to make sure that project members are not in over their heads or working on a task that is not well suited to their skills. Resource estimates might need to be revised based upon the skills of the actual person (or people) assigned to a particular activity. Figure 3.20 indicates the relative programming speed versus the relative programming quality of three programmers. The figure suggests that Carl should not be assigned tasks in which completion time is critical and that Brenda should be assigned to tasks in which high quality is most vital.

One approach to assigning tasks is to assign a single task type (or only a few task types) to each worker for the duration of the project. For example, one worker could be assigned to create all computer displays and another to create all system reports.

Figure 3.19
COCOMO is Used By Many Project Managers to Estimate Project Resources

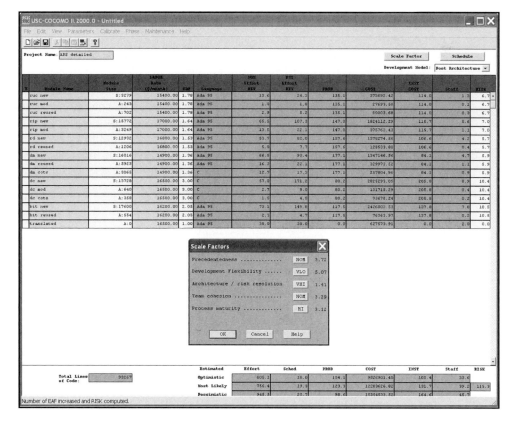

Figure 3.20
Trade-Offs between the Quality of the Program Code versus the Speed of Programming Are Decisions Project Managers Must Make

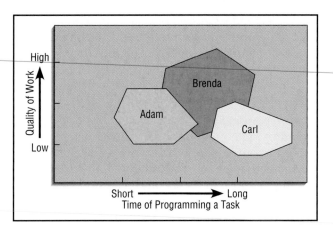

Such specialization ensures that both workers become efficient at their own particular tasks. A worker might become bored if the task is too specialized or is long in duration, so workers could be assigned to a wider variety of tasks. However, this approach might lead to lowered task efficiency. A middle ground would be to make assignments with a balance of specialization and task variety. Assignments depend upon the size of the development project and the skills of the project team. Regardless of the manner in which tasks are assigned, each team member should work on only one task at a time. Exceptions to this rule can occur when a task occupies only a small portion of a team member's time (e.g., testing the programs developed by another team member), or during an emergency.

4. *Developing a preliminary schedule.* During this activity, the information on tasks and resource availability is used to assign time estimates to each activity in the work breakdown structure. These time estimates allow the creation of target starting and ending dates for the project. Target dates can be revisited and modified until a schedule is produced that is acceptable to the customer. Determining an acceptable schedule might require that you find additional or different resources or that the scope of the project be changed.

5. *Developing a communication plan.* The goal of this activity is to outline the communication procedures among management, project team members, and the customer. The communication plan includes when and how written and oral reports will be provided by the team, how team members will coordinate work, what messages will be sent to announce the project to interested parties, and what kinds of information will be shared with vendors and external contractors involved with the project. It is important that free and open communication occurs among all parties, with respect for proprietary information and confidentiality with the customer. When developing a communication plan, numerous questions must be answered in order to assure that the plan is comprehensive and complete, including:

- Who are the stakeholders for this project?
- What information does each stakeholder need?
- When, and at what interval, does this information need to be produced?
- What sources will be used to gather and generate this information?
- Who will collect, store, and verify the accuracy of this information?
- Who will organize and package this information into a document?
- Who will be the contact person for each stakeholder, should any questions arise?
- What format will be used to package this information?
- What communication medium will be most effective for delivering this information to the stakeholder?

Once these questions are answered for each stakeholder, a comprehensive communication plan can be developed. In this plan, a summary of communication documents,

Figure 3.21
The Project
Communication
Matrix Provides a
High Level Summary
of the Communication
Plan

Stakeholder	Document	Format	Team Contact	Date Due
Team Members	Project Status Report	Project Intranet	Juan Kim	First Monday of Month
Management Supervisor	Project Status Report	Hard Copy	Juan Kim	First Monday of Month
User Group	Project Status Report	Hard Copy	James Kim	First Monday of Month
Internal IT Staff	Project Status Report	Email	Jackie James	First Monday
IT Manager	Project Status Report	Hard Copy	Juan Jeremy	First Monday of Month
Contract Programmers	Software Specifications	Email / Project	Jordan Kim	October 1, 2007
Training Subcontractor	Implementation and Training Plan	Intranet Hard Copy	Jordan James	January 7, 2008

work assignments, schedules, and distribution methods will be outlined. Additionally, a project communication matrix can be developed which provides a summary of the overall communication plan (see Figure 3.21). This matrix can be easily shared among team members, and stakeholders outside the project team can verify that the right people are getting the right information at the right time, and in the right format.

6. *Determining project standards and procedures.* During this activity, the project manager specifies how various deliverables are to be produced and tested. For example, the team must decide on which tools to use, how the standard development processes might be modified, documentation styles (e.g., type fonts and margins for user manuals), how team members will report the status of their assigned activities, and terminology. Setting project standards and procedures for work acceptance is a way to assure the development of a high-quality system. Also, it is much easier to train new team members when clear standards are in place. Organizational standards for project management and conduct make the determination of individual project standards easier and the interchange or sharing of personnel among different projects feasible.

7. *Identifying and assessing risk.* The goal of this activity is to identify sources of project risk and to estimate the consequences of those risks. Risks might arise from the use of new technology, prospective users' resistance to change, availability of critical resources, competitive reactions or changes in regulatory actions due to the construction of a system, or team member inexperience with technology or the business area. The project manager should try continually to identify and assess project risk. The OOSAD principle of putting the hard problems first also could be stated as putting the risky problems first. Risk will be discussed in more detail in Chapter 4.

8. *Creating a preliminary budget.* During this phase, a preliminary budget is created that outlines the planned expenses and revenues associated with the project. The project justification will demonstrate that the benefits are worth these costs. Figure 3.22 shows a cost-benefit analysis for a new development project. This analysis shows net present value calculations of the project's benefits and costs, as well as a return on investment and cash flow analysis. Project budgets are discussed fully in Chapter 4.

9. *Developing a Project Scope Statement.* An important activity that occurs near the end of the project planning phase is the development of the Project Scope Statement. Developed primarily for the customer, this document outlines work that will be done and clearly describes what the project will deliver. The Project Scope Statement is useful to make sure that you, the customer, and other project team members have a clear understanding of the intended project size, duration, and outcomes.

Figure 3.22
A Financial Cost-Benefit Analysis for a Systems Development Project

Microsoft Excel - Project Feasibility Analysis.xls

Economic Feasibility Analysis

	Years from Today						
	0	1	2	3	4	5	TOTALS
Build New System	$0	$85,000	$85,000	$85,000	$85,000	$85,000	
Discount Rate (12%)	1.0000	0.8929	0.7972	0.7118	0.6355	0.5674	
PV of Benefits	$0	$75,893	$67,761	$60,501	$54,019	$48,231	
NPV of Building New System	$0	$75,893	$143,654	$204,156	$258,175	$306,406	$306,406
One-time COSTS	($75,000)						
Continue Maintaining Existing System							
Recurring Costs		($35,000)	($35,000)	($35,000)	($35,000)	($35,000)	
Discount Rate (12%)	1.0000	0.8929	0.7972	0.7118	0.6355	0.5674	
PV of Recurring Costs	$0	($31,250)	($27,902)	($24,912)	($22,243)	($19,860)	
NPV of All COSTS	($75,000)	($106,250)	($134,152)	($159,064)	($181,307)	($201,167)	($201,167)
Overall NPV							$105,239
ROI = Overall NPV / NPV of Costs							52.31%

Year of Project	0	1	2	3	4	
Break-Even Analysis						
Yearly NPV Cash Flow	($75,000)	$44,643	$39,860	$35,589	$31,776	$28,371
Overall NPV Cash Flow	($75,000)	($30,357)	$9,503	$45,092	$76,867	$105,239

Break-Even Ratio = (yearly NPV cash flow - general NPV cash flow) / yearly NPV cash flow
Break Even occurs in 1.8 years

Note: All dollar values have been rounded to the nearest dollar

10. *Setting a Baseline Project Plan.* After all of the prior project planning activities have been completed, a Baseline Project Plan can be developed. This baseline plan provides an estimate of the project's tasks and resource requirements and is used to guide the next project phase—execution. As new information is acquired during project execution, the baseline plan is updated continually.

At the end of the project planning phase, a review of the Baseline Project Plan is conducted to double-check all the information in the plan. As with the project initiation phase, it might be necessary to modify the plan, which means returning to prior project planning activities before proceeding.

Executing the Project

Project execution
The third phase of the project management process in which the plans created in the prior phases (project initiation and planning) are put into action.

Project execution puts the Baseline Project Plan into action. The five key activities of project execution are summarized in Figure 3.23 and described in the remainder of this section:

1. *Executing the Baseline Project Plan.* The project manager oversees the execution of the baseline plan. This means initiating the execution of project activities, acquiring and assigning resources, orienting and training new team members, keeping the project on schedule, and assuring the quality of project deliverables. This is a formidable task, but a task made much easier through the use of sound project management techniques. For example, as tasks are completed during a project, they can be

Figure 3.23
Five Project Execution Activities

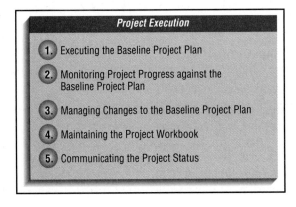

Project Execution

1. Executing the Baseline Project Plan
2. Monitoring Project Progress against the Baseline Project Plan
3. Managing Changes to the Baseline Project Plan
4. Maintaining the Project Workbook
5. Communicating the Project Status

Figure 3.24
Gantt Chart with Tasks
3 and 7 Completed

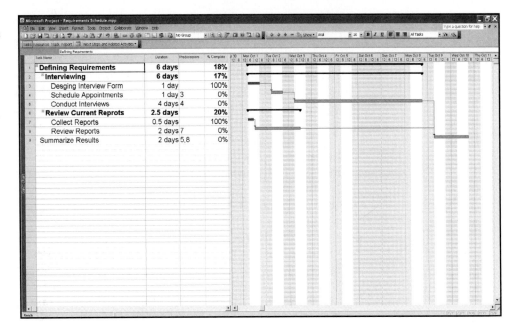

marked as completed on the project schedule. In Figure 3.24, tasks 3 and 7 are marked as completed by showing 100 percent in the % Complete" column. Members of the project team will come and go. The project manager is responsible for initiating new team members by providing them with the resources they need and helping them assimilate into the team. The project manager might want to plan social events, regular team project status meetings, team-level reviews of project deliverables, and other group events to mold the group into an effective team.

2. *Monitoring project progress against the Baseline Project Plan.* While executing the Baseline Project Plan, the project manager should monitor progress. If the project gets ahead of (or behind) schedule, resources, activities, and budgets might have to be adjusted. Monitoring project activities can result in modifications to the current plan. Measuring the time and effort expended on each activity helps lead to an improvement in the accuracy of estimations for future iterations and projects. It is possible with project schedule charts, like Gantt, to show progress against a plan, and it is easy with Network diagrams to understand the ramifications of delays in an activity. Monitoring progress also means that the team leader must evaluate and appraise each team member, occasionally change work assignments or request changes in personnel, and provide feedback to the employee's supervisor.

3. *Managing changes to the Baseline Project Plan.* The project manager will encounter pressure to make changes to the baseline plan. At many organizations, policies dictate that only approved changes to the project specification can be made, and all changes must be reflected in the baseline plan and project workbook, including all charts and design diagrams. For example, to make a significant design change, a formal change request must be submitted and approved. This request should explain why changes are desired and describe all possible impacts on prior and subsequent activities, project resources, and the overall project schedule. Such information allows a project steering committee to evaluate more easily the costs and benefits of a significant midcourse change.

In addition to changes occurring through formal request, changes also can be needed because of events outside the project manager's control. In fact, numerous events might initiate a change to the Baseline Project Plan, including the following possibilities:

- A slipped completion date for an activity.
- A bungled activity that must be redone.

- The identification of a new activity that becomes evident later in the project.

- An unforeseen change in personnel due to sickness, resignation, or termination.

When an event occurs that delays the completion of an activity, two choices typically are possible: Devise a way to get back on schedule or revise the plan. Devising a way to get back on schedule is the preferred approach because no changes to the plan will have to be made. The ability to head off and smoothly work around problems is a critical skill that must be mastered.

As will be discussed later in this chapter, project schedule charts are helpful in assessing the impact of change. Using such charts, one can quickly see if the completion time of other activities will be affected by changes in the duration of a given activity or if the whole project completion date will change. Often the activities will have to be rearranged somehow because the ultimate project completion date might be rather fixed. A penalty to the organization (or even legal action) might result if the expected completion date is not met.

4. *Maintaining the project workbook.* As in all project phases, maintaining complete records of all project events is necessary. The workbook provides the documentation new team members require to assimilate project tasks quickly. It explains why design decisions were made and is a primary source of information for producing all project reports.

5. *Communicating the project status.* The project manager is responsible for keeping all stakeholders—systems developers, managers, and customers—abreast of the project status. In other words, communicating the project status focuses on the *execution* of the project communication plan and the response to any ad hoc information requests by stakeholders. There are a broad variety of methods that can be used to distribute information, each with strengths and weakness. Some methods are easier for the information sender, but more difficult or less convenient for the receiver. With the maturing of digital networks and the Internet, more and more digital communication is being exchanged. Procedures for communicating project activities vary from formal meetings to informal hallway discussions. Some procedures are useful for informing others of project status, others for resolving issues, and others for keeping permanent records of information and events. Two types of information are routinely exchanged throughout the project: *work results*—the outcomes of the various tasks and activities that are performed to complete the project; and the *project plan*—the formal comprehensive document that is used to execute the project; it includes numerous items including the project charter, project schedule, budgets, risk plan, and so on. Table 3-2 lists numerous communication procedures, their level of formality, and most likely use. Whichever procedure is used, frequent communication helps assure project success.

This section outlined the role of the project manager during the execution of the Baseline Project Plan. The ease with which the project can be managed is influenced significantly by the quality of prior project phases. If a high-quality project plan is developed, it is much more likely that the project will be executed successfully. The next section describes the project manager's role during project closedown, the final phase of the project management process.

Closing Down the Project

Project closedown
The final phase of the project management process that focuses on bringing a project to and end.

The focus of project closedown is to bring the project to an end. Projects can conclude with a natural or an unnatural termination. A natural termination occurs when the requirements of the project have been met; the project has been completed and is a success. An unnatural termination occurs when the project is stopped before completion. Several events can cause an unnatural termination to a project. For example, perhaps the assumption used to guide the project proved to be false, or the performance of the system or development group was somehow inadequate, or the requirements are no longer relevant or valid in the customer's business environment.

Table 3-2
Project Team
Communication
Methods.

PROCEDURE	FORMALITY	USE
Project workbook	High inform	Permanent record
Meetings	Medium to high	Resolve issues
Seminars and workshops	Low to medium	Inform
Project newsletters	Medium to high	Inform
Status reports	High	Inform
Specification documents	High	Inform
		Permanent record
Minutes of meetings	High	Inform
		Permanent record
Bulletin boards		Low inform
Memos	Medium to high	Inform
Brown bag lunches	Low	Inform
Hallway discussions	Low	Inform
		Resolve issues

The most likely reasons for the unnatural termination of a project relate to running out of time, money, or both. Regardless of the project termination outcome, several activities must be performed: closing down the project, conducting post-project reviews, and closing the customer contract. Figure 3.25 summarizes the project close-down activities that are described more fully in the remainder of this section:

1. *Closing down the project.* During closedown, several diverse activities are performed. For example, if several team members are working with the project manager, project completion might signify job and assignment changes for some members. The project manager will likely be required to assess each team member and provide an appraisal for personnel files and salary determination. Other potential activities include providing career advice to team members, writing letters to superiors praising special accomplishments of team members, and sending thank-you letters to those who helped but were not team members. The project manager must be prepared to handle possible negative personnel issues such as job termination, especially if the project was not successful. When closing down the project, it is also important to notify all interested parties that the project has been completed and to finalize all project documentation and financial records so that a final review of the project can be conducted. The accomplishments of the team also should be celebrated. Some teams will hold a party, and each team member may receive memorabilia (e.g., a T-shirt with "I survived the X project"). The goal is to celebrate the team's effort to bring a difficult task to a successful conclusion.

2. *Conducting post-project reviews.* Once the project is closed down, final reviews of the project should be conducted with management and customers. The objective of these reviews is to determine the strengths and weaknesses of project deliverables, the processes used to create them, and the project management process. It is important that everyone understands what went right and what went wrong in order to improve the process for the next project. Remember, the systems development methodology adopted by an organization is a living guideline that must undergo continual improvement.

3. *Closing the customer contract.* The focus of this final activity is to ensure that all contractual terms of the project have been met. A project governed by a contractual

Figure 3.25
Three Project
Closedown Activities

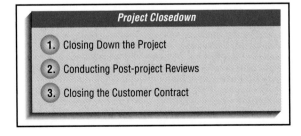

agreement typically is not completed until agreed to by both parties, often in writing. Thus, it is of paramount importance to gain agreement from the customer that all contractual obligations have been met and that further work is either their responsibility or covered under another or contract.

Closedown is an important activity. A project is not complete until it is closed, and it is at closedown that projects are deemed a success or failure. Completion also signifies the chance to begin a new project and apply what has been learned. Now that the project management process has been explained, the next section describes specific techniques used in systems development for representing and scheduling activities and resources.

REPRESENTING AND SCHEDULING PROJECT PLANS

A project manager has a wide variety of techniques available for depicting and documenting project plans. These planning documents can take the form of graphical or textual reports, although graphical reports have become more popular for this use. The most commonly used methods are Gantt Charts and Network Diagrams. Because Gantt Charts do not always show how tasks must be ordered (precedence) but simply show when a task should begin and when it should end, they are often more useful for depicting relatively simple projects or subparts of a larger project, showing the activities of a single worker, or monitoring the progress of activities compared to scheduled completion dates (see Figure 3.26[a]). Recall that a Network Diagram shows the ordering of activities by connecting a task to its predecessor and successor tasks (see Figure 3.26[b]). Sometimes a Network Diagram is preferable; other times a Gantt Chart more easily shows certain aspects of a project. Here are the key differences between these two representations.

- A Gantt Chart visually shows the duration of tasks, whereas a Network Diagram visually shows the sequence dependencies between tasks.
- A Gantt Chart visually shows the time overlap of tasks, whereas a Network Diagram does not show time overlap; a Network Diagram does show which tasks could be done in parallel.
- Some forms of Gantt Charts visually show slack time available within an earliest start and latest finish duration. A Network Diagram shows this by data within activity rectangles.

Figure 3.26a
Graphical Diagrams
That Depict Project
Plans: A Gantt Chart

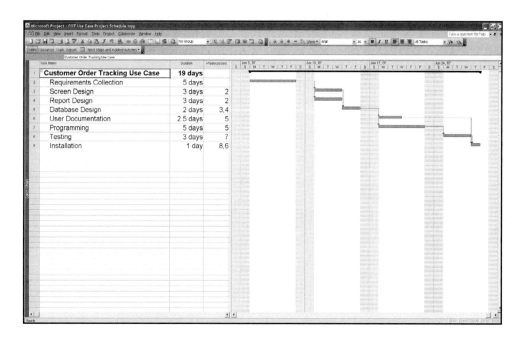

Figure 3.26b
Graphical Diagrams
That Depict Project
Plans: A Network
Diagram

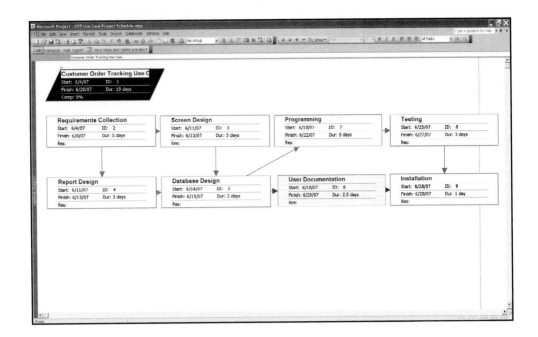

Project managers also use textual reports that depict resource utilization by tasks, complexity of the project, and cost distributions to control activities. For example, Figure 3.27 shows a screen from Microsoft Project for Windows that summarizes all project activities, their durations in days, and their scheduled starting and ending dates. Most project managers use computer-based systems to help develop their graphical and textual reports. Later in this chapter, these automated systems are discussed in more detail.

A project manager periodically will review the status of all ongoing project task activities to assess whether the activities will be completed early, on time, or late. If early or late, the duration of the activity, depicted in column 2 of Figure 3.27, can be updated. Once changed, the scheduled start and finish times of all subsequent tasks also will change. Making such a change also will alter a Gantt Chart or Network Diagram used to represent the project tasks. The ability to make changes to a project easily is a powerful feature of most project management environments. It allows the

Figure 3.27
A Screen from
Microsoft Project That
Summarizes All
Project Activities,
Their Durations in
Days, and Their
Scheduled Starting
and Ending Dates

	Task Name	Duration	Predecessors	Start	Finish	Total Slack	Early Finish	Late Finish
1	**Customer Order Tracking Use Case**	**19 days**		**Mon 6/4/07**	**Thu 6/28/07**	**0 days**	**Thu 6/28/07**	**Thu 6/28/07**
2	Requirements Collection	5 days		Mon 6/4/07	Fri 6/8/07	0 days	Fri 6/8/07	Fri 6/8/07
3	Screen Design	3 days	2	Mon 6/11/07	Wed 6/13/07	0 days	Wed 6/13/07	Wed 6/13/07
4	Report Design	3 days	2	Mon 6/11/07	Wed 6/13/07	0 days	Wed 6/13/07	Wed 6/13/07
5	Database Design	2 days	3,4	Thu 6/14/07	Fri 6/15/07	0 days	Fri 6/15/07	Fri 6/15/07
6	User Documentation	2.5 days	5	Mon 6/18/07	Wed 6/20/07	5.5 days	Wed 6/20/07	Wed 6/27/07
7	Programming	5 days	5	Mon 6/18/07	Fri 6/22/07	0 days	Fri 6/22/07	Fri 6/22/07
8	Testing	3 days	7	Mon 6/25/07	Wed 6/27/07	0 days	Wed 6/27/07	Wed 6/27/07
9	Installation	1 day	8,6	Thu 6/28/07	Thu 6/28/07	0 days	Thu 6/28/07	Thu 6/28/07

project manager to determine easily how changes in task duration impact the project completion date. It is also useful for examining the impact of "what if" scenarios of adding or reducing resources, such as personnel, for an activity.

Understanding the Critical Path of a Network Diagram

Resource
Any person, group of people, piece of equipment, or material used in accomplishing an activity.

Critical path scheduling
A scheduling technique whose order and duration of a sequence of task activities directly affects the completion date of a project.

Project scheduling and management require that time, costs, and resources be controlled. Resources are any person, group of people, piece of equipment, or material used in accomplishing an activity. Network diagramming is a critical path scheduling technique used for controlling resources. A critical path refers to a sequence of task activities whose order and durations directly affect the completion date of a project. A Network Diagram is one of the most widely used and best-known scheduling methods. A major strength of Network diagramming is its ability to show how changes to completion times impact the overall schedule. Because of this, it is used more often than Gantt Charts to manage projects such as information systems development where variability in the duration of activities is the norm. A Network Diagram would be used when tasks:

- Are well-defined and have a clear beginning and end point.
- Can be worked on independently of other tasks.
- Are ordered.
- Serve the purpose of the project.

To better understand critical path scheduling, assume that you have been assigned to work on a small project defining the major steps for a key feature within a larger system. We will call this project the *Key Feature Project*. For this particular project, you identify seven major activities, and from your experience with similar projects, you make time estimates and order these activities as follows:

Activity	Time Estimate (in days)	Preceding Activity
1. Collect Requirements	1	–
2. Design Screens	2	1
3. Design Database	2	1
4. Coding	3	2, 3
5. Documentation	2	4
6. Testing	3	4
7. Integration	1	5, 6

With this information defined, you are now able to draw a Network Diagram. Recall that Network Diagrams are composed of circles or rectangles representing activities and connecting arrows showing required workflows, as illustrated in Figure 3.28. The critical path of a Network Diagram is represented by the sequence of connected activities that produce the longest overall time period. All nodes and activities within this sequence are referred to as being "on" the critical path. The critical path represents the shortest time in which a project can be completed. In other words, any

Critical path
The shortest time in which a project can be completed.

Figure 3.28
A Network Diagram for the *Key Feature Project* Showing Activities (represented by circles) and Sequences of Those Activities (represented by arrows)

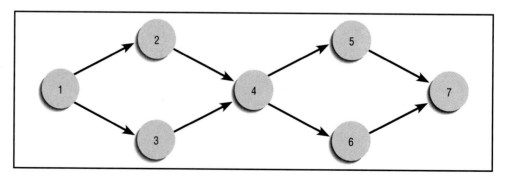

Figure 3.29
A Network Diagram for the *Key Feature Project* Showing Estimated Times for Each Activity and the Earliest and Latest Expected Completion Time for Each Activity

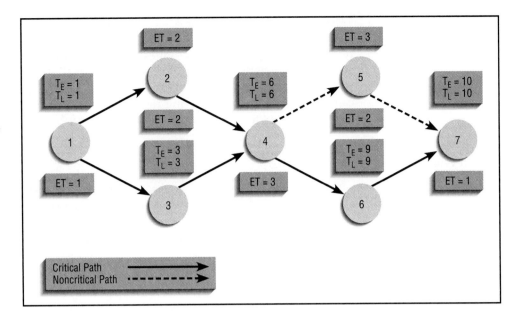

Slack time
The amount of time that an activity can be delayed without delaying the project.

activity on the critical path that is delayed in completion delays the entire project. Nodes not on the critical path, however, can be delayed (for some amount of time) without delaying the final completion of the project. Nodes not on the critical path contain slack time and allow some flexibility in scheduling.

To determine the critical path and the expected completion time for the *Key Feature Project*, you must calculate the earliest and latest expected completion time for each activity (see Figure 3.29). To do this, you must first calculate the earliest expected completion time (T_E) for each activity by summing the estimated time (ET) for each activity from left to right (i.e., in precedence order), starting at activity 1 and working toward activity 7. In this case, T_E for activity 7 is equal to 10 days. If two or more activities precede an activity, the largest expected completion time of these activities is used in calculating the new activity's expected completion time. For example, because activity 7 is preceded by both activities 5 and 6, the largest expected completion time between 5 and 6 is 9, so T_E for activity 7 is 9 + 1, or 10. The earliest expected completion time for the last activity of the project represents the amount of time the project should take to complete. Because the time of each activity can vary, however, the projected completion time represents only an estimate. The project may, in fact, require more or less time for completion.

The latest expected completion time (T_L) refers to the time in which an activity can be completed without delaying the project. To find the values for each activity's T_L, start with activity 7 and set T_L equal to the final T_E (10 days). Next, work right to left toward activity 1 and subtract the expected time for each activity. The slack time for each activity is equal to the difference between its latest and earliest expected completion times ($T_L - T_E$). The slack time calculations for all activities of the *Key Feature Project* are as follows:

Activity	T_E	T_L	Slack $T_L - T_E$	On Critical Path?
1	1	1	0	Yes
2	3	3	0	Yes
3	3	3	0	Yes
4	6	6	0	Yes
5	8	9	1	No
6	9	9	0	Yes
7	10	10	0	Yes

Note that all activities with a slack time equal to zero are on the critical path. Thus, all activities except 5 are on the critical path. Also, the diagram in Figure 3.29 shows two critical paths, between activities 1-2-4 and 1-3-4, because both of these parallel activities have zero slack. In addition to the possibility of having multiple critical paths, two types of slack are possible. *Free slack* refers to the amount of time a task can be delayed without delaying the early start of any immediately following task. *Total slack* refers to the amount of time a task can be delayed without delaying the

Figure 3.30
Default Work Breakdown Structure for an OOSAD Project

Source: Adapted from Royce, 1998.

1. Management and Planning
   1.1. Inception phase management and planning
      1.1.1. Business case development
      1.1.2. Elaboration phase release specifications
      1.1.3. Elaboration phase WBS baseline
      1.1.4. Software development plan
      1.1.5. Inception phase project control and status assessments
   1.2. Elaboration phase management and planning
      1.2.1. Construction phase planning
      1.2.2. Construction phase release specifications
      1.2.3. Construction phase WBS baseline
      1.2.4. Elaboration phase project control and status assessments
   1.3. Construction phase management and planning
      1.3.1. Deployment phase planning
      1.3.2. Deployment phase WBS baseline
      1.3.3. Construction phase project control and status assessments
   1.4. Transition phase management and planning
      1.4.1. System maintenance planning
      1.4.2. Transition phase project control and status assessments
2. Analysis
   2.1. Inception phase requirements development
      2.1.1. Vision specifications
      2.1.2. Use case modeling
   2.2. Elaboration phase requirements refinement
      2.2.1. Vision refinement
      2.2.2. Use case refinement
   2.3. Construction phase requirements refinement
   2.4. Transition phase requirements refinement
3. Design
   3.1. Inception phase architecture prototyping
   3.2. Elaboration phase architecture refinement
      3.2.1. Architecture design modeling
      3.2.2. Design demonstration
      3.2.3. Software architecture description
   3.3. Construction phase design
      3.3.1. Architecture design modeling
      3.3.2. Component design modeling
   3.4. Transition phase design refinement
4. Implementation
   4.1. Inception phase implementation
      4.1.1. Component prototyping
      4.1.2. Assessment planning
   4.2. Elaboration phase component implementation
      4.2.1. Critical component coding
      4.2.2. Component assessment
      4.2.3. Critical component demonstration
   4.3. Construction phase component integration
      4.3.1. Initial release component coding and testing
      4.3.2. Alpha release component coding and testing
      4.3.3. Beta release component coding and testing
      4.3.4. Component maintenance
      4.3.5. Transition phase component maintenance
5. Operations
   5.1. Inception phase operations planning
   5.2. Elaboration phase operation planning
   5.3. Construction phase operations
   5.4. Transition phase operations
      5.4.1. System transition to user

Figure 3.31
Level of Planning
Detail in the Work
Breakdown Structure
throughout the
Systems Development
Process

Source: Adapted from Royce,
1998.

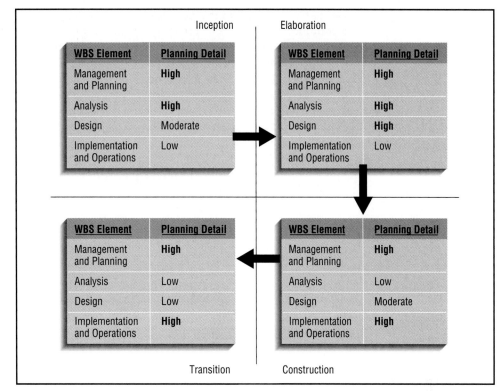

completion of the project and it is what we have calculated in the *Key Feature Project*. Understanding free and total slack allows the project manager to better identify where trade-offs can be made if changes to the project schedule need to be made. For more information on slack and how it can be used to manage tasks, see Information Systems Project Management (Fuller, Valacich, & George, 2007).

Defining the Work Breakdown Structure for OOSAD Projects

When creating the work breakdown structure for an OOSAD project, the major planning elements should be organized to follow the systems development cycle, with each phase containing elements for inception, elaboration, construction, and transition. For example, Figure 3.30 shows a default work breakdown structure (WBS) for an OOSAD project. The level of detail needed for a given project will reflect the size of the project and the number of iterations. The lowest-level elements within the WBS typically reflect tasks that produce specific project deliverables such as a program, a test result, or a document.

Throughout the life of the project, the level of detail within each major area of the WBS will evolve (see Figure 3.31). For example, during project inception, greater planning detail will be needed for analysis-related activities. Likewise, during transition, great detail will be required for implementation and operations activities. Note that the SDC activity project management and planning requires a high level of consideration throughout the entire life of the project.

Calculating Expected Time Durations Using the Program Evaluation Review Technique (PERT)

Program Evaluation Review Technique (PERT)
A technique that uses optimistic, pessimistic, and realistic time estimates to calculate the expected time for a particular task.

One of the most difficult and most error-prone activities when constructing a project schedule is the determination of the time duration for each task within a work breakdown structure. It is particularly problematic to make these estimates when a high degree of complexity and uncertainty surround a task. Program Evaluation Review Technique (PERT) is a technique that uses optimistic, pessimistic, and realistic time estimates to calculate the *expected time* for a particular task to be completed. This technique helps the project manager obtain a better time estimate when some uncertainty arises regarding how much time a task will require.

The optimistic *(o)* and pessimistic *(p)* times reflect the minimum and maximum possible periods of time for an activity to be completed. The realistic time *(r)*, or most likely time, reflects the project manager's best guess of the amount of time the activity will require for completion. After each of these estimates is made for an activity, an expected time *(ET)* can be calculated. Because the expected completion time should be close to the realistic time *(r)*, it typically is weighted four times more than the optimistic *(o)* and pessimistic *(p)* times. Once these values are added together, the sum must be divided by 6 to determine the *ET*. This equation is shown in the following formula.

$$ET = \frac{o + 4r + p}{6}$$

where

ET = expected time for the completion for an activity
o = optimistic completion time for an activity
r = realistic completion time for an activity
p = pessimistic completion time for an activity

For example, suppose that your instructor asked you to calculate an expected time for the completion of an upcoming programming assignment. For this assignment, you estimate an optimistic time of two hours, a pessimistic time of eight hours, and a most likely time of six hours. Using PERT, the expected time for completing this assignment is 5.67 hours. Commercial project management software like Microsoft Project can offer assistance in using PERT to make expected time calculations. In addition, many commercial tools allow the customization of the weighing of optimistic, pessimistic, and realistic completion times.

CONSTRUCTING A GANTT CHART AND NETWORK DIAGRAM FOR AN OOSAD PROJECT IN MICROSOFT PROJECT

A wide variety of automated project management tools are available to help manage a development project. New versions of these tools are being developed and released continuously by software vendors. Most of the available tools have a common set of features that include the ability to define and order tasks, assign resources to tasks, and modify tasks and resources easily. Project management tools are available to run on Windows-compatible personal computers, the Macintosh, and larger mainframe and workstation-based systems. These systems vary in the number of task activities supported, the complexity of relationships, system processing and storage requirements, and cost. Prices for these systems can range from a few hundred dollars for personal computer–based systems to more than $100,000 for large-scale multiproject systems. Yet a lot can be done with systems like Microsoft Project as well as public domain and shareware systems. For example, numerous shareware project management programs (e.g., MinuteMan, Delegator, or Project KickStart) can be downloaded from the World Wide Web (e.g., www.download.com). Because these systems are changing continuously, comparison shopping is an important step before choosing a particular package.

We now illustrate the types of activities a project manager performs when using project management software. Microsoft Project for Windows is a project management system that has had consistently high marks in computer publication reviews (see www.microsoft.com and search for "project"—also, if you search the Web, there are many very useful tutorials for improving your Microsoft Project skills). When using this system to manage a project, one needs to perform at least the following activities:

- Establish a project starting or ending date.
- Enter tasks and assign task relationships.
- Select a scheduling method to review project reports.

Establishing a Project Starting Date

Assume you have been assigned to design, develop, and implement a new corporate Intranet Web site for the personnel director of your company. You have been given 12 weeks to complete this system called *InfoNet*. The vision for *InfoNet* is to create a Web portal for employees, providing information on corporate performance, news, benefits plans, training programs, job postings, corporate policies, and so on. The personnel director also wants *InfoNet* to be interactive so that employees can, for example, change insurance plans or register for training courses using an online interface.

A first step in using Microsoft Project to represent a project schedule is to enter the project starting date into the system. Starting (or ending) dates are used to schedule future activities or backdate others based upon their duration and relationships to other activities. To set the starting date for the *InfoNet* project as November 5, 2007, follow the steps shown in Figure 3.32.

Entering Tasks and Assigning Task Relationships

The next step in defining a project is to define project tasks, their duration, and sequence. Given the 12-week schedule, you discuss with your colleagues how many iterations should be used for this project given its scope and complexity. Because a two-week iteration is the typical iteration cycle within your development group, you decide to design a schedule using six two-week iterations. Also, using the OOSAD principle of working on the hard problems first as a guide, you sequence the components as shown in the table. (Note that during iteration 6, all 10 days are not consumed; it is often desirable to reserve some time at the end of the project for wrapping up details, fine-tuning the system, finishing up documentation and training, etc.)

Figure 3.32
Establishing a Project Starting Date in Microsoft Project for the *InfoNet* Project

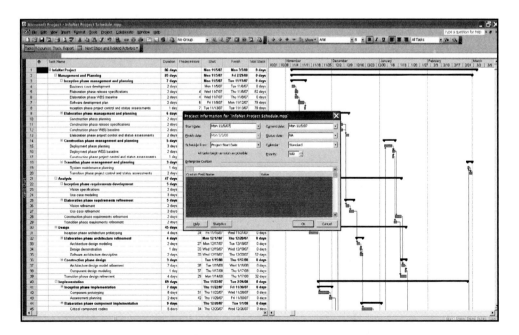

Iteration	Component	Duration (days)	Total Days
1	Employee Benefit Inquiry or Change	10	10
2	Employee Training Inquiry or Registration	10	20
3	Employee Retirement Planning Inquiry	6	26
	Employee Job Inquiry or Application	4	30
4	Corporate Policy Inquiry	4	34
	Corporate News Inquiry	3	37
	Corporate Performance Inquiry	3	40
5	Management Benefit Posting	3	43
	Management Training Posting	3	46
	Management Job Posting	2	48
	Management Corporate Policy Posting	2	50
6	Management Corporate News Posting	2	52
	Management Corporate Performance Posting	2	54

Now that the high-level components for the *InfoNet* system have been defined, you can begin entering tasks into Microsoft Project. The task entry screen, shown in Figure 3.33, is similar to a financial spreadsheet program. The user moves the cursor to a cell with arrow keys or the mouse and then simply enters a textual Name, a numeric Duration for each activity, and task predecessors. Scheduled Start and Scheduled Finish are entered automatically based upon the project start date and the duration entered previously. To set a task precedent relationship, the task number (or numbers) that must be completed before the start of the current task is entered into the Predecessors column. The project management software uses this information to construct Gantt Charts, Network Diagrams, and other project-related reports.

Selecting a Scheduling Method to Review Project Reports

As you enter more and more task information into Microsoft Project, it is easy to review the information in a variety of graphical and textual formats. For example, Figure 3.34 shows the current project information in a Gantt Chart format, and Figure 3.35 shows a Network Diagram. How you view the information can be changed easily by making a selection from menu options on the left side of the screen.

Figure 3.33
Entering Tasks and Assigning Task Relationships in Microsoft Project for the *InfoNet* Project

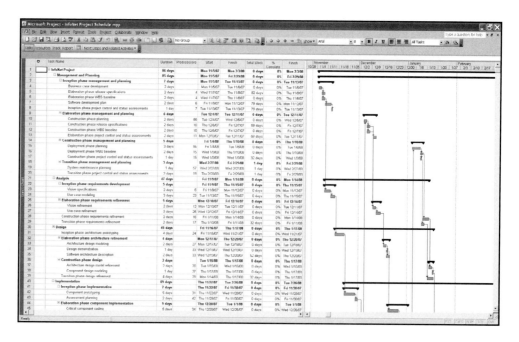

Figure 3.34
Gantt Chart of the
InfoNet Project

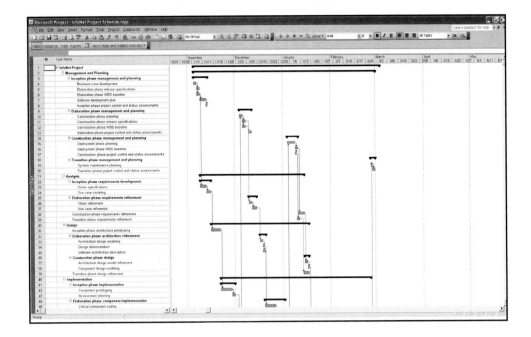

This brief introduction to project management software has only scratched the surface to show the power and the features of these systems. Other features widely available and especially useful for multiperson projects relate to resource usage and utilization. Resource-related features allow one to define characteristics such as standard costing rates and daily availability via a calendar that records holidays, working hours, and vacations. These features are particularly useful for billing and estimating project costs. Often, resources are shared across multiple projects, which could significantly affect a project's schedule. Depending upon how projects are billed within an organization, assigning and billing resources to tasks is a time-consuming activity for most project managers. The features provided in these powerful tools can greatly ease the planning and managing of projects so that project and management resources are utilized effectively.

Figure 3.35
Network Diagram of
the *InfoNet* Project

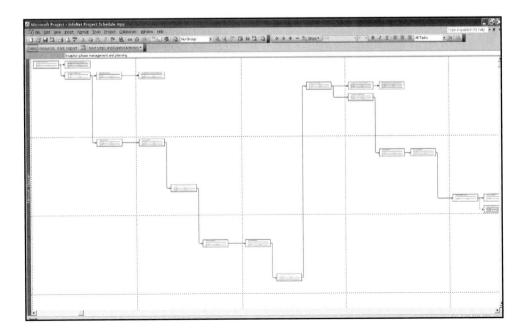

KEY POINTS REVIEW

1. **Describe the skills required to be an effective project manager.**

   A project manager has technical and managerial skills, and is ultimately responsible for determining the size, scope, and resource requirements for a project. Once a project is deemed feasible by an organization, the project manager ensures that the project meets the customer's needs and is delivered within budget and time constraints.

2. **Describe the unique characteristics of an OOSAD project.**

   When managing an OOSAD project, the project manager must define the project as a set of components. Once defined, these components can be analyzed and ordered so that the most difficult components are implemented first. An OOSAD project is managed by a series of iterations, and each iteration contains all phases of the systems development cycle. Over each iteration, more and more of the system is created (component by component), and more and more is learned about the system being constructed, the capabilities of the development team, and the complexity of the development environment. As this learning increases over time, the project manager is better able to plan project activities more accurately. Therefore, it is not good practice to plan long-range activities in great detail; detailed planning should occur only for the current and subsequent iteration. Most projects have six to nine iterations, but large projects could have several more. An iteration is a fixed time period, usually about two weeks, but it can be shorter or longer, depending upon the characteristics of the project.

3. **List and describe the skills and activities of a project manager during project initiation, project planning, project execution, and project closedown.**

   To manage the project, the project manager must execute four primary activities: project initiation, project planning, project execution, and project closedown. The focus of project initiation is on assessing the size, scope, and complexity of a project and establishing procedures to support later project activities. The focus of project planning is on defining clear, discrete activities and the work needed to complete each activity. The focus of project execution is on putting the plans developed in project initiation and planning into action. Project closedown focuses on bringing the project to an end.

4. **Explain what is meant by critical path scheduling, and describe the process of creating Gantt Charts and Network Diagrams.**

   Critical path scheduling refers to planning methods whereby the order and duration of the project's activities directly affect the completion date of the project. Gantt Charts and Network Diagrams are powerful graphical techniques used in planning and controlling projects. Gantt and Network diagramming scheduling techniques require that a project have the following characteristics: activities with a clearly defined beginning and end, which can be worked on independently of each other; activities that are ordered; and activities partitioned such that their completion signifies the end of the project. Gantt Charts use horizontal bars to represent the beginning, duration, and ending of an activity. Network diagramming is a critical path scheduling method that shows the interrelationships among activities. These charts show when activities can begin and end, which activities cannot be delayed without delaying the whole project, how much slack time each activity has, and progress against planned activities. The fact that Network diagramming can use probability estimates in determining critical paths and deadlines makes it a widely used technique for complex projects.

5. **Explain how commercial project management software packages can be used to assist in representing and managing project schedules.**

   A wide variety of automated tools for assisting the project manager is available. Most tools have common features including the ability to define and order tasks, assign resources to tasks, and modify tasks and resources. Systems vary regarding the number of activities supported, the complexity of relationships, processing and storage requirements, and cost.

KEY TERMS CHECKPOINT

Here are the key terms from this chapter. The page where each term is first explained is in parentheses after the term.

a. Critical path (p. 76)
b. Critical path scheduling (p. 76)
c. Deliverable (p. 65)
d. Feasibility study (p. 54)
e. Gantt Chart (p. 65)
f. Network Diagram (p. 66)
g. Program Evaluation Review Technique (PERT) (p. 79)
h. Project (p. 52)
i. Project charter (p. 63)
j. Project closedown (p. 72)
k. Project execution (p. 70)
l. Project initiation (p. 62)
m. Project management (p. 62)
n. Project manager (p. 52)
o. Project planning (p. 64)
p. Project workbook (p. 63)
q. Resource (p. 76)
r. Slack time (p. 77)
s. Work breakdown structure (WBS) (p. 65)

Match each of the key terms with the definition that best fits it.

1. An online or hard-copy repository for all project correspondence, inputs, outputs, deliverables, procedures, and standards that is used for performing project audits, orientation of new team members, communication with management and customers, scoping future projects, and performing post-project reviews.
2. An end product in a phase of the SDC.
3. Determines if the information system makes sense for the organization from an economic and operational standpoint.
4. A controlled process of initiating, planning, executing, and closing down a project.
5. The third phase of the project management process in which the plans created in the prior phases (project initiation and planning) are put into action.
6. The first phase of the project management process in which activities are performed to assess the size, scope, and complexity of the project and to establish procedures to support later project activities.
7. A diagram that depicts project tasks and their interrelationships.
8. A planned undertaking of related activities to reach an objective that has a beginning and an end.
9. The amount of time that an activity can be delayed without delaying the project.
10. The process of dividing the project into manageable tasks and logically ordering them to ensure a smooth evolution between tasks.
11. The final phase of the project management process that focuses on bringing a project to an end.
12. A graphical representation of a project that shows each task activity as a horizontal bar whose length is proportional to its time for completion.
13. Any person, group of people, piece of equipment, or material used in accomplishing an activity.
14. A scheduling technique whereby the order and duration of a sequence of activities directly affect the completion date of a project.
15. An individual with a diverse set of skills—management, leadership, technical, conflict management, and customer relationship—who is responsible for initiating, planning, executing, and closing down a project.
16. The second phase of the project management process, which focuses on defining clear, discrete activities and the work needed to complete each activity within a single project.
17. The shortest time in which a project can be completed.
18. A technique that uses optimistic, pessimistic, and realistic time estimates to calculate the expected time for a particular task.
19. A short, high-level document prepared for both internal and external stakeholders to formally announce the establishment of the project and to briefly describe its objectives, key assumptions, and stakeholders.

REVIEW QUESTIONS

1. Discuss the reasons why organizations undertake information systems projects.
2. List and describe the common skills and activities of a project manager. Which skill do you think is most important? Why?
3. Describe the unique characteristics of OOSAD projects that have ramifications for how these projects are managed.
4. What is a project iteration, and how many iterations does a typical project have?
5. Describe the activities performed by the project manager during project initiation.
6. Describe the activities performed by the project manager during project planning.
7. Describe the activities performed by the project manager during project execution.
8. List various project team communication methods, and describe an example of the type of information that might be shared among team members using each method.
9. Describe the activities performed by the project manager during project closedown.
10. What characteristics must a project have in order for critical path scheduling to be applicable?

11. Describe the steps involved in making a Gantt Chart.
12. Describe the steps involved in making a Network Diagram.
13. In which phase of the systems development cycle does project management occur?
14. What are some reasons why one activity might have to be completed before the next activity can begin? In other words, what causes precedence relationships between project activities?

PROBLEMS AND EXERCISES

1. Why should project managers complete hard problems first in an OOSAD project?
2. Why is too much up-front planning a mistake in an OOSAD project?
3. Which of the four phases of the project management process do you believe is most challenging? Why?
4. What are some sources of risk in a systems analysis and design project, and how does a project manager cope with risk during the stages of project management?
5. Search computer magazines or the Web for recent reviews of project management software. Which packages seem to be most popular? What are the relative strengths and weaknesses of each system? What advice would you give to someone intending to buy project management software for a PC? Why?
6. How are information systems projects similar to other types of projects? How are they different? Are the project management packages you evaluated in Problem and Exercise 5 suited for all types of projects or for particular types of projects? Which package is best suited for information systems projects? Why?
7. If given the chance, would you become the manager of an information systems project? If so, why? Prepare a list of the strengths that you would bring to the project as its manager. If not, why not? What would it take for you to feel more comfortable managing an information systems project? Prepare a list and timetable for the necessary training you would need to feel more comfortable about managing an information systems project.
8. Calculate the expected time for the following tasks.

Task	Optimistic Time	Most Likely Time	Pessimistic Time	Expected Time
A	3	7	11	
B	5	9	13	
C	1	2	9	
D	2	3	16	
E	2	4	18	
F	3	4	11	
G	1	4	7	
H	3	4	5	
I	2	4	12	
J	4	7	9	

9. A project has been defined to contain the following list of activities along with their required times for completion.

Activity No.	Activity	Time (weeks)	Immediate Predecessors
1	Collect requirements	2	—
2	Analyze processes	3	1
3	Analyze data	3	2
4	Design processes	7	2
5	Design data	6	2
6	Design screens	1	3,4
7	Design reports	5	4,5
8	Program	4	6,7
9	Test and document	8	7
10	Install	2	8,9

a. Draw a Network Diagram for the activities.
b. Calculate the earliest expected completion time.
c. Show the critical path.
d. What would happen if activity 6 were revised to take six weeks instead of one week?

10. Construct a Gantt Chart for the project defined in Problem and Exercise 9.
11. Look again at the activities outlined in Problem and Exercise 9. Assume that your team is in its first week of the project and has discovered that each of the activity duration estimates is wrong. Activity 2 will take only two weeks to complete. Activities 4 and 7 each will take three times longer than anticipated. All other activities will take twice as long to complete as previously estimated. In addition, a new activity, number 11, has been added. It will take one week to complete, and its immediate predecessors are activities 10 and 9. Adjust the Network Diagram and recalculate the earliest expected completion times.
12. Construct a Gantt Chart and a Network Diagram for a project you are or will be involved in. Choose a project of sufficient depth from work (although a project from home or school could also be used if complex enough). Identify the activities to be completed; determine the sequence of the activities; and construct a diagram reflecting the starting, ending, duration, and precedence (Network Diagram only) relationships among all activities. For your Network Diagram, use the procedure in this chapter to determine time estimates for each activity and calculate the expected time for each activity. Now determine the critical path, and the early and late starting and finishing times for each activity. Which activities have slack time?
13. For the project you described in Problem and Exercise 12, assume that the worst has happened. A key team

member has dropped out of the project and has been assigned to another project in another part of the country. The remaining team members are having personality clashes. Key deliverables for the project are now due much earlier than expected. In addition, you have just determined that a key phase in the early life of the project will take much longer than you originally expected. To make matters worse, your boss absolutely will not accept that this project cannot be completed by this new deadline. What will you do to account for these project changes and problems? Begin by reconstructing your Gantt Chart and Network Diagram and determining a strategy for dealing with the specific changes and problems described. If new resources are needed to meet the new deadline, outline the rationale that you will use to convince your boss that these additional resources are critical to the success of the project.

14. Assume you have a project with seven activities labeled A–G, as shown. Derive the earliest completion time (or early finish—EF), the latest completion time (or late finish—LF), and slack for each of the following tasks (begin at time = 0). Which tasks are on the critical path? Draw a Gantt Chart for these tasks.

Task	Preceding Event	Expected Duration	EF	LF	Slack	Critical Path?
A	—	5				
B	A	3				
C	A	4				
D	C	6				
E	B,C	4				
F	D	1				
G	D,E,F	5				

15. Draw a Network Diagram for the tasks shown in Problem and Exercise 14. Highlight the critical path.

16. Assume you have a project with 10 activities labeled A–J. Create a Network Diagram that connects the activities. Derive the earliest completion time (or early finish—EF), the latest completion time (or late finish—LF), and slack for each of the following tasks (begin at time = 0). Which tasks are on the critical path? Highlight the critical path on your Network Diagram.

Activity	Preceding Event	Expected Duration	EF	LF	Slack	Critical Path?
A	—	4				
B	A	5				
C	A	6				
D	A	7				
E	A,D	6				
F	C,E	5				
G	D,E	4				
H	E	3				
I	F,G	4				
J	H,I	5				

17. Draw a Gantt Chart for the tasks shown in Problem and Exercise 16.

18. Assume you have a project with 11 activities labeled A–K, as shown. Derive the earliest completion time (or early finish—EF), the latest completion time (or late finish—LF), and slack for each of the following tasks (begin at time = 0). Which tasks are on the critical path? Draw a Gantt Chart and a Network Diagram for these tasks, and make sure you highlight the critical path on your Network Diagram.

Activity	Preceding Event	Expected Duration	EF	LF	Slack	Critical Path?
A	—	2				
B	A	3				
C	B	4				
D	C	5				
E	C	4				
F	D,E	3				
G	F	4				
H	F	6				
I	G,H	5				
J	G	2				
K	I,J	4				

19. Make a list of the tasks that you performed when designing your schedule of classes for this term. Develop a table showing each task, its duration, preceding event(s), and expected duration. Develop a Network Diagram for these tasks. Highlight the critical path on your Network Diagram.

DISCUSSION QUESTIONS

1. You interview for a job and the employer asks you if the project management process for systems development should be a structured, formal process. What will be your answer?

2. Do you agree that breaking down projects into small, manageable tasks is an important part of managing a project? What are the pros and cons of doing this?

3. What are the strengths and weaknesses of using a Gantt Chart for representing a project plan? When using a Network Diagram? Is one method better than the other?

4. When completing a project, some tasks are independent of others, whereas others are interdependent on others. What does this mean with regard to slack? How are slack and the critical path related?

CASE PROBLEMS

1. Pine Valley Furniture

In an effort to better serve the various departments at Pine Valley Furniture (PVF), the information systems department assigns one of its systems analysts to serve as a liaison to a particular business unit. Chris Martin is currently the liaison to the purchasing department.

After graduating from Valley State University, Chris began working at PVF. He began his career there as a programmer/analyst I. This job assignment required him to code and maintain financial application systems in COBOL. In the six years he has been at PVF, he has been promoted several times; his most recent promotion was to a junior systems analyst position. During his tenure at PVF, Chris has worked on several important projects, including serving as a team member on a project that developed a five-year plan that would renovate the manufacturing information systems.

Chris enjoys his work at Pine Valley Furniture and wishes to continue moving up the information systems ladder. Over the last three years, Chris often has thought about becoming certified by the Project Management Institute. In the last three years, he has taken several courses toward his MBA; has attended three technology-related seminars; and has helped the local Feed the Hungry chapter develop, implement, and maintain its computerized information system.

a. While eating lunch one day, Juanita asked Chris about the benefits of becoming a project management professional. Briefly make a case for becoming a project management professional.

b. What are the project management professional eligibility criteria for Chris? What documentation must he provide?

c. Assume Chris has obtained his certification. What are PDUs, and how many must Chris acquire over a three-year period?

d. Several activity categories are listed as qualifying for PDUs on the Project Management Institute's Web site. Identify these categories. In which categories would you place Chris's experience?

2. Hoosier Burger

Bob and Thelma Mellankamp have come to realize that the current problems with their inventory control, customer ordering, and management reporting systems are having a serious impact on Hoosier Burger's day-to-day operations. At the close of business one evening, Bob and Thelma decide to hire the Build a Better System (BBS) consulting firm. Harold Parker and Lucy Chen, two of BBS's owners, are frequent Hoosier Burger customers. Bob and Thelma are aware of the excellent consulting service BBS is providing in the Bloomington, Indiana, area.

Build a Better System is a medium-sized consulting firm based in Bloomington. Six months ago, BBS hired you as a junior systems analyst for the firm. Harold and Lucy were impressed with your résumé, course work, and systems analysis and design internship. During your six months with BBS, you have had the opportunity to work alongside several senior systems analysts and observe the project management process.

On a Friday afternoon, you learn that you have been assigned to the Hoosier Burger project and that the lead analyst on the project is Juan Rodriquez. A short while later, Juan stops by your desk and mentions that you will be participating in the project management process. Mr. Rodriquez has scheduled a meeting with you for 10:00 a.m. on Monday to review the project management process with you. You know from your brief discussion with Mr. Rodriquez that you will be asked to prepare various planning documents, particularly a Gantt Chart and a Network Diagram.

a. In an effort to learn more about project management, you decide to research this topic over the weekend. Locate an article(s) that discusses project management. Summarize your findings.

b. At your meeting on Monday, Mr. Rodriquez asks you to prepare a Gantt Chart for the Hoosier Burger project. Using the following information, prepare a Gantt Chart.

Activity No.	Activity	Time (weeks)	Immediate Predecessors
1	Requirements collection	1	—
2	Requirements structuring	2	1
3	Alternative generation	1	2
4	Logical design	2	3
5	Physical design	3	4
6	Implementation	2	5

c. Using the information provided in part b, prepare a Network Diagram.

d. After reviewing the Gantt Chart and a Network Diagram, Mr. Rodriquez feels that alternative generation should take only half of a week and that implementation might take three weeks. Modify your charts to reflect these changes.

3. Lilly Langley's Baking Goods Company

In 1919, Lionel Langley opened his first bakery store, which he named after his wife Lilly. Initially, he sold only breads, cakes, and flour to his customers. Through the years, the business expanded rapidly by opening additional bakeries, acquiring flour mills, and acquiring food-processing companies. After 81 years in business, the company is now a well-known, highly reputable, international corporation. Lilly Langley's Baking Goods Company (LLBGC) has more than 15,000 employees, operates in 50 countries, and offers a wide variety of products.

Frederica Frampton, LLBGC's chief information officer, has just returned from a meeting with Chung Lau, LLBGC's director of operations. They discussed the many problems the company is having with getting supplies and distributing products. In essence, the end users of the current operations/manufacturing systems are demanding information that the current system just cannot provide. The current information systems are inflexible. The problems include the following:

- Combining data housed in separate plant databases is difficult, if not impossible.
- End users have difficulty generating ad hoc reports.
- Scheduling the production lines is becoming tedious.

Costs to enhance the systems are becoming unwieldy, so it is now time to consider renovating these systems. Due to a top management directive, the systems must be operational within nine months.

Frederica Frampton recognizes the importance of the LLBGC operations/manufacturing systems renovation. She decides to assemble a team of her best systems analysts to develop new operations/manufacturing systems for LLBGC. You are assigned as a member of this team.

a. Lorraine Banderez, the project manager, has asked you to investigate how other companies have used project management software, particularly Microsoft Project. Investigate two companies and provide a brief summary of how each has used project management software.

b. Part of your responsibility is to assist in the preparation of the planning documents. Using the information provided in the table, prepare a Gantt Chart.

Activity No.	Activity	Time (weeks)	Immediate Predecessors
1	Requirements collection	3	—
2	Requirements structuring	4	1
3	Process analysis	3	2
4	Data analysis	3	2
5	Logical design	5	3,4
6	Physical design	5	5
7	Implementation	6	6

c. Using the information from part b, prepare a Network Diagram. Identify the critical path.

d. After reviewing your planning documents, Lorraine decides to modify several of the activity times. Revise your Gantt Chart and Network Diagram to reflect the following modifications.

Activity Time	(weeks)
Requirements collection	4
Requirements structuring	3
Process analysis	4
Data analysis	4.5
Logical design	5
Physical design	5.5
Implementation	7

CASE: BROADWAY ENTERTAINMENT COMPANY, INC.

Managing an Object-Oriented Information Systems Project

Case Introduction

Broadway Entertainment Company, Inc. (BEC), is considered a leader in information systems (IS) within the video rental and recorded music retail industry. Karen Gardner, vice president for IS at BEC, wants her organization to remain in this leadership position. She constantly is looking for new ways to improve the efficiency and quality of the information systems her staff develops.

In this section, we introduce the thinking Karen and her staff are doing as they consider introducing object-oriented systems development methods to associates who are highly proficient in structured systems development.

Seeking Improvements in IS Development Methods

Although the systems analysts and other IS staff at BEC have become proficient at information systems development, they realize that the IS field is changing, and new and improved methods, techniques, and tools are available nearly every month. By themselves, these innovations are not useful unless they solve some problems or provide new opportunities. Over the years, BEC's IS staff members have tried to be leaders but not bleeders. To give BEC a competitive edge, Karen has introduced many innovations but usually in the second wave of adoption. This has allowed BEC staff to learn from the mistakes made in other organizations but still introduce innovations in time to be early to market with improvements.

Another key element of the IS strategy has been to invest in experimentation—essentially research and development on small, noncritical projects. These initial projects allow the staff to become familiar with an innovation; make mistakes when they don't matter too much; manage change so that other BEC staff members are not intimidated; and develop support from early, limited successes.

Several issues are bothering Karen and her staff, and she is seeking ways to address these issues. First, the pressures of modern business mean that people want results faster. BEC corporate management and in-store staff are not as patient in waiting for a systems project to be completed. They want results yesterday. The structured systems development methods BEC has used have resulted in high-quality systems, but the cycle time from idea to deployment has become frustrating for some BEC managers and IS staff members.

Second, many of the information systems BEC needs are already in place, but they must be enhanced and extended frequently, either to improve system features or to replace old technologies. BEC now spends more for information systems maintenance than it does for new systems development. In addition, these changes take considerable time, in part because one change often requires many other system component changes and because the impact of change must be studied carefully across all systems. The careful, structured methods and techniques that BEC has used for systems development have created systems that have fairly tightly coupled components, even with an attempt to modularize.

Finally, even though BEC uses CASE tools and code libraries as a means to share prior systems development work products, previously developed system design elements and programs are not reusable in new situations. More often than not, too much work goes into trying to modify previous, excellent work so it can be used for new reports, similar but slightly different business procedures, or new users. A system feature developed for one group of users can be peculiar to other users.

Karen and her staff think that object-oriented systems development, with associated tools and techniques, might provide an approach that will help them overcome these persistent issues. Karen wants her staff to experiment with this approach, which will be a rather radical change from their prior practices. To keep things simple and low risk, Karen wants her staff to develop an information system that she personally can use. This kind of project will not possess all the features to prove the value of object-oriented systems development (e.g., reusability of design elements), but at least her staff can see how difficult the transition from structured to object-oriented methods might be.

Karen wants a system that stands alone from other existing systems. The goal is to practice object-oriented development, not to develop a high-impact system. Karen is an avid reader, and she subscribes to many information systems and other magazines; she also buys books about management and technology topics, and derives active pleasure in reading publications. She also seems to be the department's librarian (her middle name is Marian), because she is constantly loaning out her latest publications to colleagues. Therefore, her idea is to have a few of her staff develop a simple publication-lending application.

Planning the Publication-Lending Application

Karen has read (in one of the books in her personal library) that one key to managing an object-oriented project is to define the system as a set of components or vertical slices. Karen envisions the system having the following few components that she will see once the system is complete:

1. Receiving a new publication into the library.
2. Lending a publication from the library.
3. Returning a publication to the library.
4. Deleting a publication from the library (due to obsolescence, loss, or lack of space).

Karen also has read that object-oriented projects are unique because they are iterative, meaning, in part, that features developed in the early stages of the project will require rework as other components are developed and understood more fully. In reaction to this, another suggestion from the literature is to work on the most difficult or complex parts of the project first, which facilitates work on subsequent parts. However, Karen is uncertain whether there are more iterations than just the four she has identified. Certainly, these four are the core components or uses of the system, but more iterative steps might be necessary.

Karen knows from experience that no matter how an information systems development project is run, work has to be planned; requirements have to be analyzed; system capabilities have to be designed; and finally a working system has to be tested, documented, and deployed into the operation. People must also be trained. With an object-oriented approach, these activities are repeated, to some degree, across the project in each iteration. In addition, in the object-oriented approach, people think in terms of organizing iterations into phases called inception, elaboration, construction, and transition. Karen is glad to start with such a low-key project; many new things will have to be dealt with that have not been a part of their successful systems development methods.

What is appealing about the object-oriented approach is that it is based on a learning paradigm within a project as well as across projects, whereas structured methods rely on learning only from one project to the next. Structured methods, to be successful, also require a significant investment in planning activities up front in the early stages of a project; however, Karen has read that detailed planning is done only on an iteration-by-iteration basis in object-oriented methods (looking ahead only one or two iterations at a time).

Case Summary

Karen Gardner wants her staff to experiment with what, for them, will be a new systems development approach, an object-oriented systems development methodology. None of her staff members have used object-oriented techniques before, so she wants them to get their feet wet with a low-risk project—a publication-lending library application for her personal library, which also serves largely as the department's library. She has been lending her object-oriented publications to her staff members, who will be the guinea pigs for this new approach to systems development for BEC. Karen has identified four key functional features for the system.

CASE QUESTIONS

1. What does it mean to be a leader but not a bleeder in using new systems development methods, techniques, and technologies?

2. Based on what you have learned so far about object-oriented systems development, will object-oriented methods provide the solution to the issues Karen has outlined for systems development at BEC? Justify your answer.

3. Do you think the department library lending application is a good choice for experimenting with object-oriented systems development at BEC? Justify your answer.

4. What management and communication skills and what organization knowledge will Karen's staff members need to work on this project?

5. Microsoft Project is a popular, generic project management tool, which is illustrated in and which BEC uses as its standard project charting and management tool. You might have been introduced to another tool for use in your course. Evaluate Microsoft Project or the software you are to use as a tool for helping BEC to manage the publication-lending systems development project. In particular, evaluate how this software handles the iterative nature of an object-oriented project.

6. What might you anticipate to be the most difficult transitions the BEC systems analysts will have to make in order to adopt an object-oriented approach to systems development? Why?

7. Develop a project schedule for the publication-lending application. What features are the subjects of each iteration? Why? How many iterations do you have, and if you have more than four, why?

8. Because the publication-lending application is an experimental project, do you suggest some special, atypical project closedown activities? What are these and what are the purposes of these activities?

Chapter 4

Selecting and Planning Projects

Chapter Objectives

After studying this chapter, you should be able to:

➤ Describe the steps involved when identifying and selecting projects, as well as those for initiating, planning, and executing projects.

➤ Explain the need for, and the contents of, a Project Scope Statement and Baseline Project Plan.

➤ List and describe various methods for assessing project feasibility.

➤ Describe the differences between tangible and intangible benefits and costs, and the differences between one-time and recurring costs.

➤ Perform cost-benefit analysis and describe what is meant by the time value of money, present value, discount rate, net present value, return on investment, and break-even analysis.

➤ Describe the activities and participant roles within a structured walkthrough.

Chapter Contents

➤ Chapter Preview

➤ Identifying and Selecting OOSAD Projects

➤ Initiating, Planning, and Executing OOSAD Projects

➤ Pine Valley Furniture Company Background

➤ Assessing Economic Feasibility

➤ Building and Reviewing the Baseline Project Plan

Chapter Preview

The acquisition, development, and maintenance of information systems consume substantial resources for most organizations. Organizations can benefit from following a formal process for identifying, selecting, initiating, planning, and executing projects. The first phase of the systems development cycle—project management and planning—deals with this issue. As shown in Figure .1, this phase includes two primary activities. The next section discusses the first activity of project management and planning: a general method for identifying and selecting projects and the deliverables and outcomes from this process. Next, we briefly describe the second activity: project initiation, planning, and execution. After completing these overviews of the project management and planning step, we present several techniques for assessing project feasibility. The information uncovered during feasibility analysis is organized into a document called a Baseline Project Plan. Once this plan is developed, a formal review of the project can be conducted. The process of building this plan is discussed next. As the project evolves, the project plan must be refined and reviewed. The final section of this chapter provides an overview of the project review process.

Figure 4.1 Systems Development Cycle. Step 1, Project Management and Planning: Step 1 Activities Are Project Identification and Selection, and Project Initiation, Planning, and Execution

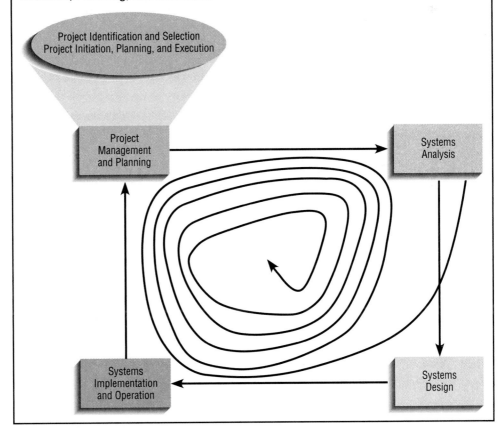

IDENTIFYING AND SELECTING OOSAD PROJECTS

The first activity of the project management and planning phase of the SDC is project identification and selection. During this activity, a senior manager, a business group, an IS manager, or a steering committee identifies and assesses all possible systems development projects that a business unit could undertake. Next, those projects deemed

Figure 4.2
Three Key Sources for
Information Systems
Projects

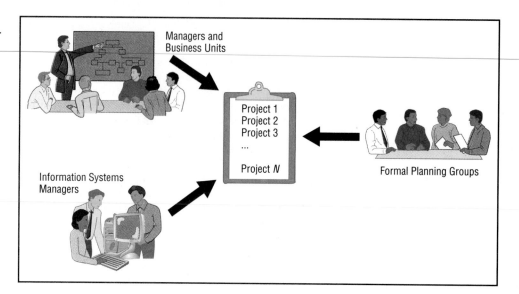

most likely to yield significant organizational benefits, given available resources, are selected. Organizations vary in their approach to identifying and selecting projects. In some organizations, project identification and selection is a formal process in which projects are outcomes of a larger overall planning process. For example, a large organization might follow a formal project identification process that involves rigorously comparing all competing projects. Alternatively, a small organization might use informal project selection processes that allow the highest-ranking IS manager to select projects independently or allow individual business units to decide on projects after agreeing on funding.

Requests for information systems development can come from three key sources, as depicted in Figure 4.2.

1. Managers and business units that want to replace or extend an existing system in order to gain needed information or to provide a new service to customers.
2. Managers who want to make a system more efficient and less costly to operate, or who want to move a system to a new operating environment.
3. Formal planning groups that want to improve an existing system in order to help the organization meet its corporate objectives, such as providing better customer service.

Regardless of how an organization executes the project identification and selection process, a common sequence of activities occurs. The following sections describe a general process for identifying and selecting projects and producing the deliverables and outcomes of this process.

The Process of Identifying and Selecting OOSAD Projects

Project identification and selection consists of three primary activities: identifying potential development projects, classifying and ranking projects, and selecting projects for development. Each of these activities is described next.

1. **Identifying potential development projects.** Organizations vary as to how they identify projects. This process can be performed by any of the following:
   - A key member of top management, either the CEO of a small- or medium-sized organization or a senior executive in a larger organization.
   - A steering committee composed of a cross section of managers with an interest in systems.
   - User departments, in which either the head of the requesting unit or a committee from the requesting department decides which projects to submit (systems analysts help users prepare such requests).
   - The development group or a senior IS manager.

Each identification method has strengths and weaknesses. For example, projects identified by top management have a strategic organizational focus. Alternatively, projects identified by steering committees reflect the diversity of the committee and therefore have a cross-functional focus. Projects identified by individual departments or business units have a narrow, tactical focus. The development group identifies projects based on the ease with which existing hardware and systems will integrate with the proposed project. Other factors, such as project cost, duration, complexity, and risk, also influence the people who identify a project. Table 4-1 summarizes the characteristics of each selection method.

Of all the possible project sources, those identified by top management and steering committees most often reflect the broader needs of the organization. These groups have a better understanding of overall business objectives and constraints. Therefore, projects identified by top management or by a diverse steering committee are referred to as coming from a top-down source.

Projects identified by a functional manager, a business unit, or the information systems development group often are designed for a particular business need within a given business unit and might not reflect the overall objectives of the organization. This does not mean that projects identified by individual managers, business units, or the IS development group are deficient; only that they might not consider broader organizational issues. Project initiatives stemming from managers, business units, or the development group are referred to as coming from a bottom-up source. Systems analysts provide ongoing support for users of these types of projects and are involved early in the life cycle. They help managers describe their information needs and the reasons for doing the project. These descriptions are evaluated in selecting which projects will be approved to move into the project initiation, planning, and execution activities.

In sum, projects are identified by top-down and bottom-up initiatives. The formality of identifying and selecting projects can vary substantially across organizations. Because limited resources preclude the development of all proposed systems, most organizations have some process of classifying and ranking each project's merit. Those projects deemed to be inconsistent with overall organizational objectives, redundant in functionality to some existing system, or unnecessary will not be considered.

2. **Classifying and ranking IS development projects.** Assessing the merit of potential projects is the second major activity in the project identification and selection activities. As with project identification, classifying and ranking projects can be performed by top managers, a steering committee, business units, or the IS development group. The criteria used to assign the merit of a given project can vary based on the size of the organization. Table 4-2 summarizes the criteria commonly used to evaluate projects. In any given organization, one or several criteria might be used during the classifying and ranking process.

As with project identification, the criteria used to evaluate projects will vary by organization. If, for example, an organization uses a steering committee, it might choose to meet monthly or quarterly to review projects and use a wide variety of evaluation criteria. At these meetings, new project requests are reviewed relative to projects already identified, and ongoing projects are monitored. The relative ratings of projects are used to guide the final activity of this identification process—project selection.

Table 4-1 Common Characteristics of Alternative Methods for Making Information Systems Identification and Selection Decisions.

Project Source	Cost	Duration	Complexity	System Size	Focus
Top management	Highest	Longest	Highest	Largest	Strategic
Steering committee	High	Long	High	Large	Cross-functional
User department	Low	Short	Low	Small	Departmental
Development group	Low–high	Short–long	Low–high	Small–large	Integration with existing systems

Table 4-2 Possible Evaluation Criteria When Classifying and Ranking Projects.

EVALUATION CRITERIA	DESCRIPTION
Value chain analysis	Extent to which activities add value and costs when developing products and/or services: information systems projects providing the greatest overall benefits will be given priority over those with fewer benefits.
Strategic alignment	Extent to which the project is viewed as helping the organization achieve its strategic objectives and long-term goals.
Potential benefits	Extent to which the project is viewed as improving profits, customer service, etc., and the duration of these benefits.
Resource availability	Amount and type of resources the project requires and their availability.
Project size/duration	Number of individuals and the length of time needed to complete the project.
Technical difficulty/risks	Level of technical difficulty to complete the project successfully within given time and resource constraints.

3. **Selecting IS development projects.** The selection of projects is the final step during project identification and selection. The short- and long-term projects most likely to achieve business objectives are considered. As business conditions change over time, the relative importance of any single project could change substantially. Thus, the identification and selection of projects is an important and ongoing activity.

Numerous factors must be considered when selecting a project, as illustrated in Figure 4.3. These factors are:
- Perceived needs of the organization.
- Existing systems and ongoing projects.
- Resource availability.
- Evaluation criteria.
- Current business conditions.
- Perspectives of the decision makers.

This decision-making process can lead to numerous outcomes. Projects can be accepted or rejected. Acceptance of a project usually means that funding to conduct the next SDC activity has been approved. Rejection means that the project no longer will be considered for development. However, projects also can be accepted conditionally, or they can be accepted pending the approval or availability of needed resources or the demonstration that a particularly difficult aspect of the system can be developed. Projects also can be returned to the original requesters, who are told to develop or purchase the requested system themselves. Finally, the requesters of a project might be asked to modify and resubmit their request after making suggested changes or clarifications.

Figure 4.3
Numerous Factors
Must Be Considered
When Selecting a
Project. Decisions Can
Result in One of
Seven Outcomes

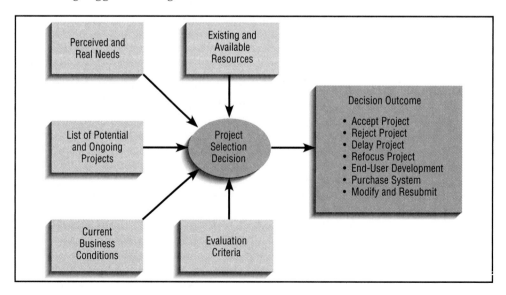

Figure 4.4
Information Systems
Development Projects
Come from Top-Down
and Bottom-Up
Initiatives

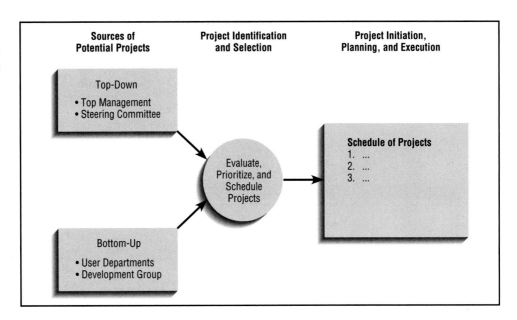

Deliverables and Outcomes

The primary deliverable, or end product, from project identification and selection is a schedule of specific IS development projects. These projects come from top-down and bottom-up sources, and once selected they move into the second activity within this SDC phase—project initiation, planning, and execution. This sequence of events is illustrated in Figure 4.4. An outcome of this activity is the assurance that people in the organization gave careful consideration to project selection and clearly understood how each project could help the organization reach its objectives. Due to the principle of incremental commitment, a selected project does not necessarily result in a working system. Incremental commitment means that after each subsequent SDC activity, the systems analyst, other members of the project team, and organization officials will reassess the project. This reassessment will determine whether the business conditions have changed or whether a more detailed understanding of a system's costs, benefits, and risks would suggest that the project is not as worthy as previously thought. Several techniques for gaining a thorough understanding of a development project are discussed later in this chapter.

Incremental commitment
A strategy in systems
analysis and design in
which the project is
reviewed after each phase
and continuation of the
project is rejustified in
each of these reviews.

INITIATING, PLANNING, AND EXECUTING OOSAD PROJECTS

After a project has been selected, it moves to project initiation, planning, and execution. Project initiation is performed once at the beginning of the project, whereas project planning and execution are ongoing activities that occur throughout the duration of the project. Once initiated, proper and insightful project planning and execution—including determining project scope, feasibility, and identification of project activities—can reduce the time needed to complete subsequent project activities and minimize organizational risk. For example, a careful feasibility analysis during planning could lead to rejecting a project and saving a considerable expenditure of resources. If a project is not rejected, it is important that the project manager makes refinements in project plans and feasibility analyses throughout the duration of the project. Most successful project managers spend a considerable amount of time planning and managing a project. The actual amount of time expended is affected by the size and complexity of the project, as well as by the experience of the organization in building similar systems. A rule of thumb is that between 10 percent and 20 percent of the entire development effort should be expended on project management and planning activities.

Figure 4.5
The Systems Analyst Transforms a Vague Systems Request into a Tangible Project Description during Project Management and Planning

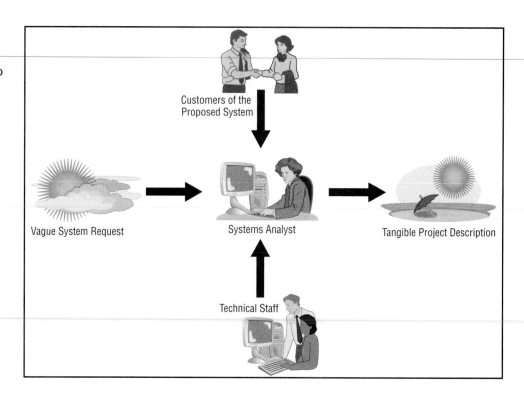

Customers of the Proposed System

Vague System Request

Systems Analyst

Tangible Project Description

Technical Staff

Most organizations assign an experienced systems analyst, or a team of analysts for large projects, to perform project initiation, planning, and execution. The analyst will work with the proposed customers—managers and users in a business unit—of the system and other technical development staff in preparing project planning documents. Experienced analysts, working with customers who well understand their information services needs, should be able to perform a detailed analysis with relatively little effort. Less experienced analysts, with customers who only vaguely understand their needs, likely will expend more effort in order to be certain that the project scope and work plan are feasible.

The initial objective of project initiation, planning, and execution is to transform a vague systems request document into a tangible project description, as illustrated in Figure 4.5. Effective communication among the systems analyst, users, and management is crucial to the creation of a meaningful project plan. Getting all parties to agree on the direction of a project might be difficult for cross-department projects when different parties have different business objectives. Projects at large, complex organizations require systems analysts to take more time to analyze the current and proposed systems. The ongoing objective of project initiation, planning, and execution is to refine project plans continuously as project iterations are completed.

The Process of Initiating, Planning, and Executing OOSAD Projects

As its name implies, three major activities occur during project initiation, planning, and execution. During project initiation, the focus is on activities that will help organize a team to conduct project planning. During initiation, one or more analysts are assigned to work with a customer to establish work standards and communication procedures. Additionally, a project charter (defined in Chapter 3) is prepared for both internal and external stakeholders to provide a high-level overview of the project. A project charter typically contains the following:

- Project title and date of authorization.
- Project manager name and contact information.
- Customer name and contact information.

- Projected start and completion dates.
- Key stakeholders, project role, and responsibilities.
- Project objectives and description.
- Key assumptions or approach.
- Signature section for key stakeholders.

The project charter is a useful communication tool that helps to assure that the organizations and other stakeholders understand the initiation of a project. A sample project charter is shown in Figure 4.6. Table 4-3 summarizes six activities performed during project initiation.

Figure 4.6 A Project Charter for the WebStore at Pine Valley Furniture

Pine Valley Furniture	Prepared: September 24, 2007
Project Charter	

Project Name:	WebStore System
Project Manager:	Jim Woo (jwoo@pvf.com)

Customer:	Marketing
Project Sponsor:	Jackie Judson (jjudson@pvf.com)
Project Start/End (projected):	10/1/07–2/1/08

Project Overview:

This project will implement an Internet-based product ordering system. The purpose of this system is to automate the ... to increase sales, to access new markets and customers, to serve as a platform for additional Internet applications, to save employee time, to reduce errors, to have more timely information.

Objectives:
- Increase sales
- Access new customers
- ...

Key Assumptions:
- System will be built in-house
- Interface will be a Web-Browser
- System will access product and customer database
- ...

Stakeholders and Responsibilities

Stakeholders	**Role**	**Responsibility**	**Signatures**
Jackie Judson	VP Marketing	Project Vision, Resources	*Jackie Judson*
Alex Datta	CIO	Monitoring, Resources	*Alex Datta*
Jim Woo	Project Manager	Plan, Monitor, Execute Project	*Jim Woo*
James Jordan	Director of Sales	System Functionality	*James Jordan*
Mary Shide	VP Human Resources	Staff Assignments	*Mary Shide*

Table 4-3

Activities Performed during Project Initiation.

- Establishing the project initiation team
- Establishing a relationship with the customer
- Establishing the project initiation plan
- Establishing management procedures
- Establishing the project management environment and project workbook
- Developing the project charter

The second activity, project planning, focuses on defining clear, discrete tasks and the work needed to complete each task. The objective of the project planning process is to produce two documents: a Baseline Project Plan (BPP) and the Project Scope Statement (PSS). The BPP becomes the foundation for the remainder of the development project. It is an internal document used by the development team but not shared with customers. The Project Scope Statement outlines the objectives and constraints of the project for the customer. The BPP and PSS are discussed further in the following text. As with the project initiation process, the size, scope, and complexity of a project dictate the comprehensiveness of the project planning process and resulting documents. Further, numerous assumptions about resource availability and potential problems will have to be made. Analysis of these assumptions and system costs and benefits forms a business case. Table 4-4 lists the activities performed during project planning.

The focus of the third activity, project execution, is on putting the plans created during project planning into action. Specifically, the Baseline Project Plan is executed. In addition to completing planned project activities, during execution the project manager must monitor progress, manage change, maintain documentation, and communicate project status. Table 4-5 summarizes the activities performed during project execution.

Business case

A written report that outlines the justification for an information system. The report highlights economic benefits and costs, and the technical and organizational feasibility of the proposed system.

Baseline Project Plan (BPP)

The major outcome and deliverable from the project initiation and planning phase. It contains an estimate of the project's scope, benefits, costs, risks, and resource requirements.

Deliverables and Outcomes

The major outcomes and deliverables from project initiation, planning, and execution are the Project Charter, Baseline Project Plan, and Project Scope Statement. The Baseline Project Plan (BPP) contains all information collected and analyzed during the project initiation and planning. The plan reflects the best estimate of the project's scope, benefits, costs, risks, and resource requirements given the current understanding of the project. As the project evolves, the BPP is refined to reflect improved

Table 4-4

Activities Performed during Project Planning.

- Describing the project scope, alternatives, and feasibility
- Dividing the project into manageable tasks
- Estimating resources and creating a resource plan
- Developing a preliminary schedule
- Developing a communication plan
- Determining project standards and procedures
- Identifying and assessing risk
- Creating a preliminary budget
- Developing a Project Scope Statement
- Setting a Baseline Project Plan

Table 4-5

Activities Performed during Project Execution.

- Executing the Baseline Project Plan
- Monitoring project progress against the Baseline Project Plan
- Managing charges to the Baseline Project Plan
- Maintaining the project workbook
- Communicating the project status

understanding and the results of prior activities. The BPP specifies detailed project activities for the next project phases and less detail for later project phases (see Chapter 2). Similarly, benefits, costs, risks, and resource requirements will become more specific and quantifiable as the project progresses. The project selection committee uses the BPP to help decide whether to continue, redirect, or cancel a project as it evolves. When initially selected, the BPP becomes the foundation document for all subsequent SDC activities and is updated as new information is learned. Techniques for constructing the BPP are examined later in this chapter.

Throughout the remainder of this book, a fictional company—Pine Valley Furniture—is used to help illustrate key SDC concepts. Icons appear in the margins to make references to this company easy to spot. The next section provides background on Pine Valley Furniture (PVF), a manufacturing company.

PINE VALLEY FURNITURE COMPANY BACKGROUND

Pine Valley Furniture (PVF) Company manufactures high-quality wood furniture and distributes it to retail stores in the United States. Its product lines include dinette sets, stereo cabinets, wall units, living room furniture, and bedroom furniture. In the early 1980s, PVF's founder, Alex Schuster, started to make and sell custom furniture in his garage. Alex managed invoices and kept track of customers by using file folders and a filing cabinet. By 1984, business expanded and Alex had to rent a warehouse and hire a part-time bookkeeper. PVF's product line had multiplied, sales volume had doubled, and staff had increased to 50 employees. By 1990, PVF moved into its third and present location. Due to the added complexity of the company's operations, Alex reorganized the company into the following functional areas:

*   Manufacturing (further subdivided into three separate functions—fabrication, assembling, and finishing)
*   Sales
*   Orders
*   Accounting
*   Purchasing

Alex and the heads of the functional areas established manual information systems, such as accounting ledgers and file folders, which worked well for a time. Eventually, however, PVF selected and installed a network server to automate invoicing, accounts receivable, and inventory control applications. When the applications were first computerized, each separate application had its own individual data files tailored to the needs of each functional area. As is typical in such situations, the applications closely resembled the manual systems on which they were based.

The computer-based applications at PVF have been designed to support its business processes. When customers order furniture, their orders must be processed appropriately: Furniture must be built and shipped to the right customer, and the right invoice must be mailed to the right address. Employees have to be paid for their work. Given these tasks, most of PVF's computer-based applications are located in the accounting and financial areas. The applications include order filling, invoicing, accounts receivable, inventory control, accounts payable, payroll, and general ledger. Today, all systems are designed and integrated successfully through a company-wide database where data are organized around entities, or subjects, such as customers, invoices, and orders.

PVF, like many firms, decided to develop its application software in-house; that is, it hired staff and bought computer hardware and software necessary to build application software suited to its own needs. Although PVF is continuing to grow at a rapid rate, market conditions are becoming extremely competitive, especially with the advent of the Internet and the World Wide Web. Most businesses have discovered the power of Internet-based electronic commerce as a means to communicate efficiently with customers and to extend their marketing reach. Consequently, PVF's management is considering alternative channels for marketing and selling furniture. The initiation, planning, and execution of the PVF WebStore are described throughout the remainder of the book.

Identification and Selection of the WebStore

The PVF board of directors has requested that a project team be created to explore the opportunity to develop an electronic commerce system. Specifically, market research has revealed a good opportunity for online furniture sales, especially in the following areas:

- Corporate furniture
- Home office furniture
- Student furniture

The board wants to incorporate all three target markets into its long-term plan but wants to focus initially on the corporate furniture buying system. The board believes that this segment has the greatest potential to provide an adequate return on investment and would be a good building block for moving into the customer-based markets. Because the corporate furniture-buying system will be targeted specifically to the business furniture market, it will be easier to define the system's operational requirements. In addition, this electronic commerce system should integrate nicely with two currently existing systems, purchasing fulfillment and customer tracking. Together, these attributes make it an ideal candidate for initiating PVF's Web strategy.

Initiating and Planning the WebStore

Given the high priority of this project, Jackie Judson, vice president of marketing, and Jim Woo, senior systems analyst, were assigned to work on this project. As described earlier in this chapter, their first job was to begin the project's initiation and planning activities. Consequently, over the next few days, Jim and Jackie met several times to initiate and plan the proposed system. At the first meeting, they agreed that WebStore would be the proposed system project name. Throughout the remainder of this chapter, we will outline how they completed the first iteration of the project management and planning phase of the SDC.

Assessing Project Feasibility

Most information systems projects have budgets and deadlines. Assessing project feasibility is a required task that can be a large undertaking because it requires the systems analyst to evaluate a wide range of factors. Although the specifics of a given project will dictate which factors are most important, most feasibility factors fall into the following six categories:

- Economic
- Operational
- Technical
- Schedule
- Legal and contractual
- Political

The analysis of these six factors forms the business case that justifies the expenditure of resources on the project. The remainder of this section examines various feasibility studies, beginning with economic feasibility. In order to provide a solid understanding of the feasibility assessment process, we examine the WebStore project at Pine Valley Furniture. As a first step in this process, Jackie and Jim prepared a Systems Service Request (SSR), illustrated in Figure 4.7, to develop the WebStore. If

Figure 4.7 Systems Service Request (SSR) for a WebStore at Pine Valley Furniture: The SSR Includes Contact Information, a Problem Statement, a Service Request Statement, and Liaison Contact Information

Pine Valley Furniture: *Systems Service Request*

REQUESTED BY ___Jackie Judson___ DATE ___October 15, 2007___

DEPARTMENT ___Marketing___

LOCATION ___Headquarters, 570c___

CONTACT ___Tel: 4-3290   FAX: 4-3270   e-mail: jjudson@pinevalleyfurniture.com___

TYPE OF REQUEST   URGENCY

[X] New System   [   ] Immediate—Operations are impaired or opportunity lost

[   ] System Enhancement   [   ] Problems exist, but can be worked around
[   ] System Error Correction   [X] Business losses can be tolerated until new system installed

PROBLEM STATEMENT

The Internet has become an important sales channel for many organizations. Beyond sales, the Internet provides opportunities for companies to enhance internal communications as well as to enhance communication and coordination with suppliers and customers. In order to provide a sales channel that is being requested by a growing number of our customers, we need to immediately begin the development of a corporate Web site to support online sales. This site will allow customers—corporate, home office, and students—to more easily shop for PVF products. It will also open new markets for PVF. Our biggest and most immediate opportunity is in the corporate sales area. Although we have many loyal customers, we are hearing more and more grumbling by this market segment that we do not have a Web-based sales outlet. We will likely redirect some sales away from our existing direct marketing and sales efforts by the creation of an online Web site; however, failure to move into this new channel could have severe long-term consequences for PVF. Additionally, this Web site will provide a foundation for the development of a broad range of Internet-based applications.

SERVICE REQUEST

I request a thorough analysis of our current sales methods and customer purchasing activity with the intent to design and build a completely new information system that will allow customers to buy PVF products over the Internet using a standard Web browser. This system should handle all customer purchasing activity, including viewing the catalog and prices, order tracking, returns, and so on. The system will also provide critical information to management on sales activity and trends, as well as tie into inventory, manufacturing, and other relevant systems. The development of this system will help PVF to continue to be profitable in an increasingly complex and competitive business environment. I feel that such a system will improve that competitiveness of PVF, particularly in our ability to better serve our customers.

IS LIAISON   Jim Woo   Tel: 4-6207   FAX: 4-6200   e-mail: jwoo@pinevalleyfurniture.com

SPONSOR   Jackie Judson, Vice President Marketing

------------------------- TO BE COMPLETED BY SYSTEMS PRIORITY BOARD -----------------------

[   ] Request approved   Assigned to _____
                           Start date _____
[   ] Recommend revision
[   ] Suggest user development
[   ] Reject for reason _____
       _____
       _____

implemented, Jackie feels that the WebStore would provide many benefits to PVF. Specifically, she believes that the WebStore would help improve revenue (a tangible benefit) and would make it easier for customers to do business with PVF (an intangible benefit).

Economic feasibility
A process of identifying the financial benefits and costs associated with a development project.

A study of economic feasibility is required for the Baseline Project Plan. The purpose of assessing economic feasibility is to identify the financial benefits and costs associated with the development project. Economic feasibility often is referred to as cost-benefit analysis. During project initiation and planning, it will be impossible to define precisely all the benefits and costs related to a particular project. Yet, it is important to identify and quantify benefits and costs or it will be impossible to conduct a sound economic analysis and determine if one project is more feasible than another. Next, we review worksheets that can be used to record costs and benefits, and techniques for making cost-benefit calculations. These worksheets and techniques are used after each SDC phase to decide whether to continue, redirect, or kill a project.

Determining Project Benefits

An information system can provide many benefits to an organization. For example, a new or renovated IS can automate monotonous jobs; reduce errors; provide innovative services to customers and suppliers; and improve organizational efficiency, speed, flexibility, and morale. These benefits are tangible and intangible. A tangible benefit is an item that can be measured in dollars and with certainty. Examples of tangible benefits include reduced personnel expenses, lower transaction costs, or higher profit margins. It is important to note that not all tangible benefits can be quantified easily. For example, a tangible benefit that allows a company to perform a task 50 percent of the time might be difficult to quantify in terms of hard dollar savings. Most tangible benefits fit in one or more of the following categories:

Tangible benefit
A benefit derived from the creation of an information system that can be measured in dollars and with certainty.

- Cost reduction and avoidance.
- Error reduction.
- Increased flexibility.
- Increased speed of activity.
- Improvement of management planning and control.
- Opening new markets and increasing sales opportunities.

Determining WebStore Benefits

Jim and Jackie identified several tangible benefits of the WebStore at PVF and summarized them in a worksheet, shown in Figure 4.8. Jackie and Jim collected information from people in PVF's sales department in order to create the worksheet. They first interviewed the sales manager and several clerks. From these interviews, they gathered estimates on the potential for increased sales and efficiency benefits derived from automating the ordering process. Jackie and Jim also interviewed existing and potential customers; the results of these interviews suggested that customers would be more likely to shop a WebStore given the convenience of online access. They learned

Figure 4.8
Tangible Benefits Worksheet for the Pine Valley Furniture WebStore

Tangible Benefit Worksheet *WebStore Project*	
	Years 1–5
A. Cost reduction or avoidance	$ 4,500
B. Error reduction	2,500
C. Increased flexibility	7,500
D. Increased speed of activity	10,500
E. Improvement in management planning or control	0
F. Increase sales	25,000
TOTAL tangible benefits	**$50,000**

that cost reduction or avoidance benefits could be gained with better inventory management. Also, they believed that increased operational flexibility would occur from a reduction in the time normally taken to enter and process data. Further, improvements in management planning or control should result from a broader range of analyses provided by the data captured by the new system. This analysis forecasts that benefits from the system would amount to approximately $50,000 per year.

Jim and Jackie also identified some intangible benefits of the system. Although they could not quantify these benefits—first to market, foundation for broader Web-based information systems, simplicity for customers—they still will be described in the final BPP. Intangible benefits refers to items that cannot be measured easily in dollars or with certainty. Intangible benefits might have direct organizational benefits, such as the improvement of employee morale, or they might have broader societal implications, such as the reduction of waste creation or resource consumption. Potential tangible benefits might have to be considered intangible during the early stages of a project because it might not be possible to quantify them in dollars or with certainty at this stage in the life cycle. During later stages, such intangibles can become tangible benefits as the ramifications of the system being designed are better understood. Intangible benefits include:

- Competitive necessity.
- Increased organizational flexibility.
- Increased employee morale.
- Promotion of organizational learning and understanding.
- More timely information.

After determining project benefits, project costs must be identified.

Determining Project Costs

Like benefits, an information system can have tangible and intangible costs. A tangible cost refers to an item that can be measured in dollars easily and with certainty. From a systems development perspective, tangible costs include items such as hardware costs, labor costs, and operational costs from employee training and building renovations. Alternatively, an intangible cost refers to an item that cannot be measured in terms of dollars easily or with certainty. Intangible costs can include loss of customer goodwill, employee morale, or operational inefficiency.

Besides tangible and intangible costs, systems-related development costs can be distinguished as either one-time or recurring. A one-time cost refers to a cost associated with project initiation, systems development, and the start-up of the system. These costs typically encompass the following activities:

- System development.
- New hardware and software purchases.
- User training.
- Site preparation.
- Data or system conversion.

When conducting an economic cost-benefit analysis, a worksheet should be created for capturing these expenses. This worksheet can be a two-column document or a multicolumn spreadsheet. For large projects, one-time costs can be staged over one or more years. In these cases, a separate one-time cost worksheet should be created for each year. This separation makes it easier to perform present-value calculations (see the following). A recurring cost refers to a cost resulting from the ongoing evolution and use of the system. Examples of these costs typically include:

- Application software maintenance.
- Incremental data storage expense.
- Incremental communications.
- New software and hardware leases.
- Consumable supplies and other expenses (e.g., paper, forms, data center personnel).

Intangible benefit
A benefit derived from the creation of an information system that cannot be measured in dollars easily or with certainty.

Tangible cost
A cost associated with an information system that can be measured in dollars easily and with certainty.

Intangible cost
A cost associated with an information system that cannot be measured in terms of dollars easily or with certainty.

One-time cost
A cost associated with project start-up and development, or system start-up.

Recurring cost
A cost resulting from the ongoing evolution and use of a system.

Table 4-6 Unknowns That Must Be Dealt with When Designing and Building Internet Applications.

User	Concern: Who is the user?
	Examples: Where is the user located? What is his/her expertise, education, or expectations?
Connection Speed	Concern: What is the speed of the connection and what information can be effectively displayed?
	Examples: cable, satellite, broadband, cellular.
Access Method	Concern: What is the method of accessing the Internet?
	Examples: Web browser, personal digital assistant (PDA), Web-enabled cellular phone, Web-enabled television.

One-time and recurring costs can consist of items that are fixed or variable in nature. Fixed costs refer to costs that are billed or incurred at a regular interval and usually at a fixed rate. A facility lease payment is an example of a one-time cost. Variable costs refer to items that vary in relation to usage. Long-distance phone charges are variable costs.

When developing an Internet application for exclusive use within an organization, developers know who the users are, what applications will be used, the speed of the network connection, and the type of communication devices (e.g., Web browsers like Internet Explorer, personal digital assistants like a Palm Pilot, or a Web-enabled cellular phone like a PocketPC). On the other hand, when developing an Internet electronic commerce application, developers have to discern countless unknowns in order to build a useful system. Table 4-6 lists several unknowns the systems analyst and the project team might deal with when designing and building an electronic commerce application. These unknowns could result in making trade-offs based on a careful analysis of who the users are likely to be, where they are likely to be located, and how they are likely to be connected to the Internet. Even with all these difficulties to contend with, Internet Web sites are springing up all across the world.

Determining WebStore Costs

Jim and Jackie next identified one-time and recurring costs for the WebStore project. Figure 4.9 shows that this project will incur a one-time cost of $42,500. Figure 4.10 shows a recurring cost of $28,500 per year. One-time costs were established by discussing the system with Jim's boss, who felt that the system would require approximately four months to develop (at $5,000 per month). To run the new system effectively, the sales department would need to upgrade at least five of its current workstations (at $3,000 each). In addition, the Internet service setup fee, the domain registration, and software licenses would cost an additional one-time amount of $5,000. Finally, user training would be required for several people throughout the company (10 users at $250 each).

Figure 4.9
One-Time Costs
Worksheet for the
Pine Valley Furniture
WebStore

One-Time Costs Worksheet *WebStore Project*	
	Year 0
A. Development costs	$20,000
B. New hardware	15,000
C. New (purchased) software, if any:	
1. Packaged applications software	4,000
2. Internet site registration	1,000
D. User training	2,500
E. Site preparation	0
F. Other _____	0
TOTAL one-time costs	**$42,500**

Recurring Costs Worksheet
Customer Tracking System Project

	Years 1–5
A. Application software maintenance	$25,000
B. Incremental data storage required: 20 MB × $50	1,000
(estimated cost/MB = $50)	
C. Internet communications	2,000
D. New software or hardware leases	0
E. Supplies	500
F. Other _____	0
TOTAL recurring costs	**$28,500**

As you can see from Figure 4.10, Jim and Jackie estimate that the proposed system will require, on average, five months of annual maintenance, primarily for enhancements that users will expect from the system (at $5,000 per month). Other ongoing expenses such as Internet service hosting fees, software upgrades, and ongoing support also should be expected. Intangible costs identified included the unknown value of reducing face-to-face customer contact and the fact that not all customers use the Internet.

This section presented the types of benefit and cost categories associated with an information systems project. The next section addresses the relationship between time and money.

The Time Value of Money

Time value of money (TVM)
The process of comparing present cash outlays to future expected returns.

Most techniques used to determine economic feasibility encompass the concept of the time value of money (TVM). TVM refers to comparing present cash outlays to future expected returns. As discussed, the development of an information system has one-time and recurring costs. Furthermore, benefits from systems development likely will occur sometime in the future. Because many projects might be competing for the same investment dollars and might have different useful life expectancies, all costs and benefits must be viewed in relation to their present rather than future value when comparing investment options.

A simple example will help explain the concept of TVM. Suppose you want to buy a used car from an acquaintance, and she asks that you make three payments of $1,500 for three years, beginning next year, for a total of $4,500. If she would agree to a single lump-sum payment at the time of sale (and if you had the money), what amount do you think she would agree to? Should the single payment be $4,500? Should it be more or less? To answer this question, one must consider the time value of money. Most people would gladly accept $4,500 today rather than three payments of $1,500, because $1 today (or $4,500 for that matter) is worth more than $1 tomorrow or next year, because money can be invested. The interest rate at which money can be borrowed or invested, the cost of capital, is called the discount rate for TVM calculations. Suppose the seller could put the money received for the sale of the car in the bank and receive a 10 percent return on her investment. A simple formula can be used when figuring out the present value of the three $1,500 payments:

Discount rate
The interest rate used to compute the present value of future cash flows.

Present value
The current value of a future cash flow.

$$PV_n = Y \times \frac{1}{(1 + i)^n}$$

where PV_n is the present value of Y dollars n years from now when i is the discount rate.

From our example, the present value of the three payments of $1,500 can be calculated as

$$PV_1 = 1,500 \times \frac{1}{(1 + .10)^1} = 1,500 \times .9091 = 1,363.65$$

$$PV_2 = 1,500 \times \frac{1}{(1 + .10)^2} = 1,500 \times .8264 = 1,239.60$$

$$PV_3 = 1,500 \times \frac{1}{(1 + .10)^3} = 1,500 \times .7513 = 1,126.95$$

where PV_1, PV_2, and PV_3 reflect the present value of each $1,500 payment in year 1, 2, and 3, respectively.

Performing an Economic Feasibility Analysis for the WebStore

Now that the relationship between time and money is known, the next step in performing the economic analysis is to create a summary worksheet that reflects the present values of all benefits and costs. PVF's Systems Priority Board feels that the useful life of many information systems might not exceed five years. Therefore, all cost-benefit analysis calculations will be made using a five-year time horizon as the upper boundary on all time-related analyses. In addition, the management of PVF has set its cost of capital to be 12 percent (i.e., PVF's discount rate). The worksheet constructed by Jim is shown in Figure 4.11.

Cell H11 of the worksheet displayed in Figure 4.11 summarizes the NPV of the total tangible benefits from the project over five years ($180,239). Cell H19 summarizes the NPV of the total costs from the project. The NPV for the project, indicated in cell H22 ($35,003), shows that benefits from the project exceed costs.

The overall return on investment (ROI) for the project also is shown on the worksheet in cell H25 (0.24). Because alternative projects likely will have different benefit and cost values, and possibly different life expectancies, the overall ROI value is useful for making project comparisons on an economic basis. This example shows ROI for the overall project over five years. An ROI analysis could be calculated for each year of the project.

Break-even analysis
A type of cost-benefit analysis to identify at what point (if ever) benefits equal costs.

The last analysis shown on line 34 in Figure 4.11 is a break-even analysis. The objective of the break-even analysis is to discover at what point (if ever) cumulative benefits equal costs (i.e., when breakeven occurs). To conduct this analysis, the NPV of the yearly cash flows is determined. Here, the yearly cash flows are calculated by

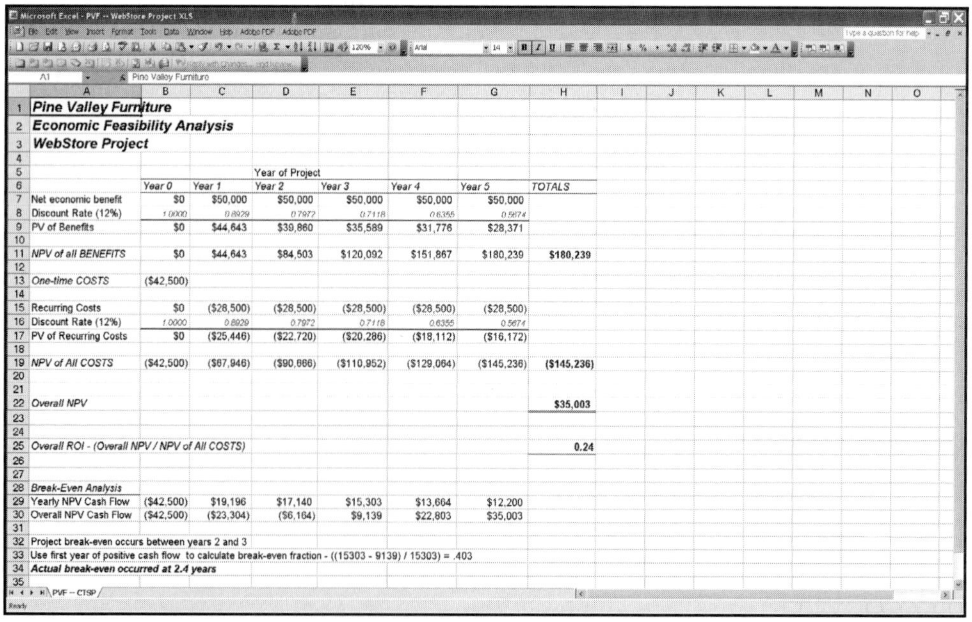

	A	B	C	D	E	F	G	H
1	Pine Valley Furniture							
2	Economic Feasibility Analysis							
3	WebStore Project							
5				Year of Project				
6		Year 0	Year 1	Year 2	Year 3	Year 4	Year 5	TOTALS
7	Net economic benefit	$0	$50,000	$50,000	$50,000	$50,000	$50,000	
8	Discount Rate (12%)	1.0000	0.8929	0.7972	0.7118	0.6355	0.5674	
9	PV of Benefits	$0	$44,643	$39,860	$35,589	$31,776	$28,371	
11	NPV of all BENEFITS	$0	$44,643	$84,503	$120,092	$151,867	$180,239	$180,239
13	One-time COSTS	($42,500)						
15	Recurring Costs	$0	($28,500)	($28,500)	($28,500)	($28,500)	($28,500)	
16	Discount Rate (12%)	1.0000	0.8929	0.7972	0.7118	0.6355	0.5674	
17	PV of Recurring Costs	$0	($25,446)	($22,720)	($20,286)	($18,112)	($16,172)	
19	NPV of All COSTS	($42,500)	($67,946)	($90,666)	($110,952)	($129,064)	($145,236)	($145,236)
22	Overall NPV							$35,003
25	Overall ROI - (Overall NPV / NPV of All COSTS)							0.24
28	Break-Even Analysis							
29	Yearly NPV Cash Flow	($42,500)	$19,196	$17,140	$15,303	$13,664	$12,200	
30	Overall NPV Cash Flow	($42,500)	($23,304)	($6,164)	$9,139	$22,803	$35,003	
32	Project break-even occurs between years 2 and 3							
33	Use first year of positive cash flow to calculate break-even fraction - ((15303 - 9139) / 15303) = .403							
34	Actual break-even occurred at 2.4 years							

Figure 4.11
Worksheet Reflecting the Present Value Calculations of All Benefits and Costs for the Pine Valley Furniture WebStore: This Worksheet Indicates That Benefits from the Project over 5 Years Exceed Its Costs by $35,003

Figure 4.12
Break-Even Analysis
for the Pine Valley
Furniture WebStore

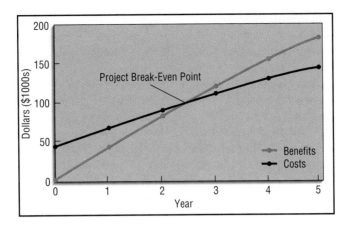

subtracting the one-time cost and the present values of the recurring costs from the present value of the yearly benefits. The overall NPV of the cash flows reflects the total cash flows for all preceding years. Line 30 of the worksheet shows that breakeven occurs between years 2 and 3. Because year 3 is the first year in which the overall NPV cash flows figure is nonnegative, the point when breakeven occurs can be derived as follows:

$$\text{Break-Even Ratio} = \frac{\text{Yearly NPV Cash Flow} - \text{Overall NPV Cash Flow}}{\text{Yearly NPV Cash Flow}}$$

Using data from Figure 4.11,

$$\text{Break-Even Ratio} = \frac{15{,}303 - 9{,}139}{15{,}303} = .403$$

Project breakeven occurs at approximately 2.4 years. A graphical representation of this analysis is shown in Figure 4.12. Using the information from the economic analysis, PVF's Systems Priority Board will be in a much better position to understand the potential economic impact of the WebStore. Without this information, it would be virtually impossible to know the cost benefits of a proposed system and impossible to make an informed decision on approving or rejecting the service request.

Many techniques can be used to compute a project's economic feasibility. Because most information systems have a useful life of more than one year and will provide benefits and incur expenses for more than one year, most techniques for analyzing economic feasibility employ the concept of the time value of money, TVM. Table 4-7 describes three commonly used techniques for conducting economic feasibility analysis. (For a more detailed discussion of TVM or cost-benefit analysis techniques in general, the interested reader is encouraged to review an introductory finance or managerial accounting textbook.)

To be approved for continuation, a systems project might not have to achieve breakeven or have a return on investment (ROI) greater than estimated during

Table 4-7 Commonly Used Economic Cost-Benefit Analysis Techniques: Net Present Value, Return on Investment, and Break-Even Analysis.

ANALYSIS TECHNIQUE	DESCRIPTION
Net present value (NPV)	NPV uses a discount rate determined from the company's cost of capital to establish the present value of a project. The discount rate is used to determine the present value of both cash receipts and outlay.
Return on investment (ROI)	ROI is the ratio of the net cash receipts of the project divided by the cash outlays of the project. Trade-off analysis can be made among projects compelling for investment by comparing their representative ROI ratios.
Break-even analysis (BEA)	BEA finds the amount of time required for the cumulative cash flow from a project to equal its initial and ongoing investment.

project initiation and planning. Because it might not be possible to quantify many benefits or costs at this point in a project, such financial hurdles for a project might be unattainable. In this case, simply doing as thorough an economic analysis as possible, including producing a long list of intangibles, might be sufficient for the project to progress. One other option is to run the type of economic analysis shown in Figure 4.11 using pessimistic, optimistic, and expected benefit and cost estimates during project initiation and planning. This range of possible outcomes, along with the list of intangible benefits and the support of the requesting business unit, often will be enough to allow the project to continue to the analysis phase. It is critical, however, to be as precise as possible with the economic analysis, especially when investment capital is scarce. In this case, it might be necessary to conduct some typical analysis phase activities during project initiation and planning in order to identify clearly any inefficiencies and shortcomings with the existing system and to explain how a new system will overcome these problems.

Assessing Technical Feasibility

Technical feasibility
The process of assessing the development organization's ability to construct a proposed system.

The purpose of assessing technical feasibility is to gain an understanding of the organization's ability to construct the proposed system. This analysis should include an assessment of the development group's understanding of the possible target hardware, software, and operating environments to be used, as well as system size, complexity, and the group's experience with similar systems. This section discusses a framework that can be used for assessing the technical feasibility of a project in which a level of project risk can be determined after answering a few fundamental questions.

It is important to note that all projects have risk and that risk is not necessarily something to avoid. Yet it is also true that because organizations typically expect a greater return on their investment for riskier projects, understanding the sources and types of technical risks proves to be a valuable tool when assessing a project. Also, risks need to be managed in order to be minimized; therefore, it is important to identify potential risks as early as possible in a project. The potential consequences of not assessing and managing risks can include the following outcomes:

1. Failure to attain expected benefits from the project.
2. Inaccurate project cost estimates.
3. Inaccurate project duration estimates.
4. Failure to achieve adequate system performance levels.
5. Failure to integrate the new system adequately with existing hardware, software, or organizational procedures.

Risk on a project can be managed by changing the project plan to avoid risky factors, assigning project team members to manage the risky aspects carefully, and setting up monitoring methods to determine whether or not potential risk is, in fact, materializing.

The amount of technical risk associated with a given project is contingent on four primary factors: project size, project structure, the development group's experience with the application and technology area, and the user group's experience with development projects and application area. Aspects of each of these risk areas are summarized in Table 4-8. Using these factors for conducting a technical risk assessment, four general rules emerge:

1. **Large projects are riskier than small projects.** Project size relates to the relative project size that the development group is familiar with. A small project for one development group might be relatively large for another. The types of factors that influence project size are listed in Table 4-8.
2. **A system in which the requirements are easily obtained and highly structured will be less risky than one in which requirements are messy, ill structured, ill defined, or subject to the judgment of an individual.** For example, the development of a payroll system has requirements that might be easy to

Table 4-8 Project Risk Assessment Factors.

RISK FACTOR	EXAMPLES
Project Size	Number of members on the project team
	Project duration time
	Number of organizational departments involved in project
	Size of programming effort (e.g., hours, function points)
Project Structure	New system or renovation of existing system(s)
	Organizational, procedural, structural, or personnel changes resulting from system
	User perceptions and willingness to participate in effort
	Management commitment to system
	Amount of user information in system development effort
Development Group	Familiarity with target—hardware, software development environment, tools, and operating system
	Familiarity with proposed application area
	Familiarity with building similar systems of similar size
User Group	Familiarity with information systems development process
	Familiarity with proposed application area
	Familiarity with using similar systems

Source: Adapted from Applegate and McFarlan, 1999.

obtain due to legal reporting requirements and standard accounting procedures. On the other hand, the development of an executive support system would need to be customized to the particular executive's decision style and critical success factors of the organization, thus making its development more risky (see Table 4-8).

3. **The development of a system employing commonly used or standard technology will be less risky than one employing novel or nonstandard technology.** A project has a greater likelihood of experiencing unforeseen technical problems when the development group lacks knowledge related to some aspect of the technology environment. A less risky approach is to use standard development tools and hardware environments. It is not uncommon for experienced systems developers to talk of the difficulty of using leading-edge (or in their words, bleeding edge) technology (see Table 4-8).

4. **A project is less risky when the user group is familiar with the systems development process and application area than if unfamiliar.** Successful IS projects require active involvement and cooperation between the user and development groups. Users who are familiar with the application area and the systems development process are more likely to understand the need for their involvement and how this involvement can influence the success of the project (see Table 4-8).

A project with high risk still might be conducted. Many organizations look at risk as a portfolio issue: Considering all projects, it is okay to have a reasonable percentage of high-, medium-, and low-risk projects. Given that some high-risk projects will get into trouble, an organization cannot afford to have too many of these. On the other hand, having too many low-risk projects might not be an aggressive enough approach to make major breakthroughs in innovative uses of systems. Each organization must decide on its acceptable mix of projects of varying risk. A matrix for assessing the relative risks related to the aforementioned general rules is shown in Figure 4.13.

Operational feasibility
The process of assessing the degree to which a proposed system solves business problems or takes advantage of business opportunities.

Assessing Other Feasibility Concerns

Other feasibility studies might need to be considered when formulating the business case for a system during project planning. Operational feasibility is the process of examining the likelihood that the project will attain its desired objectives. The goal of this study is to understand the degree to which the proposed system likely will solve

Figure 4.13
Effects of Degree of
Project Structure,
Project Size, and
Familiarity with
Application Area on
Project
Implementation Risk

*Source: The Challenges of
Managing in the Information
Age, 5e,* F 11.1, p. 284, by L.
M. Applegate and F. W.
McFarlan. © 1999. The
McGraw-Hill Companies.

		Low Structure	High Structure
High Familiarity with Technology or Application Area	Large Project	(1) Low risk (very susceptible to mismanagement)	(2) Low risk
	Small Project	(3) Very low risk (very susceptible to mismanagement)	(4) Very low risk
Low Familiarity with Technology or Application Area	Large Project	(5) Very high risk	(6) Medium risk
	Small Project	(7) High risk	(8) Medium-low risk

the business problems or take advantage of the opportunities outlined in the Systems Service Request or project identification study. In other words, assessing operational feasibility requires a clear understanding of how an information system will fit into the current day-to-day operations of the organization.

Schedule feasibility considers the likelihood that all potential time frames and completion date schedules can be met and that meeting these dates will be sufficient for dealing with the needs of the organization. For example, a system might have to be operational by a government-imposed deadline, by a particular point in the business cycle (such as the beginning of the season when new products are introduced), or at least by the time a competitor is expected to introduce a similar system.

Assessing legal and contractual feasibility requires an understanding of any potential legal and contractual ramifications due to the construction of the system. Considerations might include copyright or nondisclosure infringements, labor laws, antitrust legislation (which might limit the creation of systems to share data with other organizations), foreign trade regulations (for example, some countries limit access to employee data by foreign corporations), and financial reporting standards, as well as current or pending contractual obligations. Typically, legal and contractual feasibility is a greater consideration if an organization historically has used an outside organization for specific systems or services that the organization now is considering handling itself. Assessing political feasibility involves understanding how key stakeholders within the organization view the proposed system. Because an information system might affect the distribution of information within the organization, and thus the distribution of power, the construction of an IS can have political ramifications. Those stakeholders not supporting the project could take steps to block, disrupt, or change the project's intended focus.

In addition to the financial analysis, Jim and Jackie also identified several feasibility concerns for the PVF WebStore project (see Table 4-9). It is crucial that a broad feasibility analysis be conducted early in the life of a project. This analysis should consider economic, operational, technical, schedule, legal, contractual, and political issues related to the project. In addition to these considerations, issues beyond those discussed here might influence project selection by an organization. For example, projects might be selected for construction despite high costs and high technical risk if the system is viewed as a strategic necessity; that is, a project viewed by the organization as being critical to its survival. Alternatively, projects might be selected because they will require few resources and have little risk. Projects also can be selected due to the power or persuasiveness of the manager proposing the system.

Schedule feasibility
The process of assessing the degree to which the potential time frame and completion dates for all major activities within a project meet organizational deadlines and constraints for affecting change.

Legal and contractual feasibility
The process of assessing potential legal and contractual ramifications due to the construction of a system.

Political feasibility
The process of evaluating how key stakeholders within the organization view the proposed system.

Table 4-9

PVF WebStore:
Feasibility Concerns.

Feasibility Concern	Description
Operational	Online store open 24/7/365
	Returns/customer support
Technical	New skill set for development, maintenance, and operation
Schedule	Must be open for business by Q3
Legal	Credit card fraud
Political	Traditional distribution channel loses business

This means that project selection can be influenced by factors beyond those discussed here and beyond items that can be analyzed. The role of a systems analyst is to provide a thorough examination of the items that can be assessed so that a project review committee can make informed decisions. The next section covers how project plans typically are constructed.

BUILDING AND REVIEWING THE BASELINE PROJECT PLAN

All the information collected during project initiation and planning is collected and organized into a document called the *Baseline Project Plan*. Once the BPP is completed, a formal review of the project can be conducted with customers. This presentation, a walkthrough, is discussed later in this chapter. The focus of the walkthrough is to verify all information and assumptions in the Baseline Project Plan before moving ahead with the project.

Building the Baseline Project Plan

As mentioned previously, the project size and organizational standards will dictate the comprehensiveness of the Baseline Project Plan. Yet, most experienced systems developers have found project planning and a clear and comprehensive project plan to be invaluable to project success. An outline of a BPP, shown in Figure 4.14, contains four major sections:

1. Introduction.
2. System description.
3. Feasibility assessment.
4. Management issues.

Introduction Section of the Baseline Project Plan

The purpose of the *introduction* is to provide a brief overview of the entire document and outline a recommended course of action for the project. The introduction is often limited to only a few pages. Although it is sequenced as the first section of the BPP, it is often the final section to be written. It is only after performing most of the project planning activities that a clear overview and recommendation can be created. One initial activity that should be performed is the definition of project scope—its range—which is an important part of the BPP's introduction section.

When defining scope for the WebStore at PVF, Jim Woo first needed to gain a clear understanding of the project's objectives. Jim interviewed Jackie Judson and several of her colleagues to gain a good idea of their needs. He also reviewed existing sales procedures and data-use requirements. In addition, several existing PVF customers and potential customers of the WebStore were interviewed (see Chapter 5 for more information on collecting system requirements). These activities provided him with the information needed to define the project scope and to identify possible alternative solutions. Alternative system solutions can relate to different

Figure 4.14 An Outline of a Baseline Project Plan Contains Four Major Sections: Introduction, System Description, Feasibility Assessment, and Management Issues

---

Baseline Project Plan Report

1.0 Introduction

A. Project Overview—Provides an executive summary that specifies the project's scope, feasibility, justification, resource requirements, and schedules. Additionally, a brief statement of the problem, the environment in which the system is to be implemented, and constraints that affect the project are provided.

B. Recommendation—Provides a summary of important findings from the planning process and recommendations for subsequent activities.

2.0 System Description

A. Alternatives—Provides a brief presentation of alternative system configurations.

B. System Description—Provides a description of the selected configuration and a narrative of input information, tasks performed, and resultant information.

3.0 Feasibility Assessment

A. Economic Analysis—Provides an economic justification for the system using cost-benefit analysis.

B. Technical Analysis—Provides a discussion of relevant technical risk factors and an overall risk rating of the project.

C. Operational Analysis—Provides an analysis of how the proposed system solves business problems or takes advantage of business opportunities in addition to an assessment of how current day-to-day activities will be changed by the system.

D. Legal and Contractual Analysis—Provides a description of any legal or contractual risks related to the project (e.g., copyright or nondisclosure issues, data capture or transferring, and so on).

E. Political Analysis—Provides a description of how key stakeholders within the organization view the proposed system.

F. Schedules, Timeline, and Resource Analysis—Provides a description of potential time frame and completion date scenarios using various resource allocation schemes.

4.0 Management Issues

A. Team Configuration and Management—Provides a description of the team member roles and reporting relationships.

B. Communication Plan—Provides a description of the communication procedures to be followed by management, team members, and the customer.

C. Project Standards and Procedures—Provides a description of how deliverables will be evaluated and accepted by the customer.

D. Other Project-Specific Topics—Provides a description of any other relevant issues related to the project uncovered during planning.

---

system scopes, platforms for deployment, or approaches to acquiring the system. During project initiation and planning, the most crucial element of the design strategy is the system's scope. Scope depends on the answers to these questions:

- Which organizational units (business functions and divisions) might be affected by or use the proposed system or system change?
- With which current systems might the proposed system need to interact or be consistent, or which current systems might be changed due to a replacement system?
- Who inside and outside the requesting organization (or the organization as a whole) might care about the proposed system?
- What range of potential system capabilities is to be considered?

Figure 4.15 Statement of Project Scope for the Pine Valley Furniture WebStore

---

Pine Valley Furniture   Prepared by: Jim Woo
Project Scope Statement   Date: October 22, 2007

General Project Information:
> **Project Name:**   WebStore
> **Sponsor:**   Jackie Judson, VP Marketing
> **Project Manager:**   Jim Woo

Problem/Opportunity Statement:
> The Internet has become an important sales channel for our current and future customers. The creation of the WebStore will allow customers to review products, place orders, and receive customer support over the Internet using a standard Web browser. The creation of this system is required in order to reach company objectives.

Project Objectives:
> To enable customers to effectively and efficiently place product orders with PVF. The creation of this system will also provide a platform for the develpment of additional Internet-based applications.

Project Description:
> A new information system will be constructed that will allow customers to complete all sales activities over the Internet using a standard Web browser. The project will follow PVF's systems develpment cycle.

Business Benefits:
> - Increased sales
> - Improved understanding of customer buying patterns
> - Improved utilization of marketing and sales personnel

Project Deliverables:
> - WebStore system analysis and design
> - WebStore system programs
> - WebStore system documentation
> - WebStore transition and training procedures

Estimated Project Duration:
> 6 months

Project scope statement
A document prepared for the customer that describes what the project will deliver and outlines, generally at a high level, all work required to complete the project.

The statement of project scope for the WebStore project at PVF is shown in Figure 4.15. A project scope statement is a short document that is prepared primarily for the customer to clearly describe what the project will deliver and outline all the work required for completing the project. It is therefore a very useful communication tool. The project scope statement ensures that both you and your customer gain a common understanding of the project size, duration, and outcomes. The project scope statement is a very easy document to create because it typically consists of a high-level summary of the Baseline Project Plan (BPP) information (described next).

Depending upon your relationship with your customer, the role of the project scope statement may vary. At one extreme, the project scope statement can be used as the basis of a formal contractual agreement outlining firm deadlines, costs, and specifications. At the other extreme, it can simply be used as a communication vehicle to outline the current best estimates of what the project will deliver, when it will be completed, and the resources it may consume. A contract programming or consulting firm, for example, may establish a very formal relationship with a customer and use a proj-ect charter that is more extensive and formal. Alternatively, an internal development group may develop a project scope statement that is shorter and less formal as it will be intended to inform customers rather than to set contractual obligations and deadlines.

For the WebStore, project scope was defined using only textual information. However, it is not uncommon to define project scope using use-case or sequence diagrams. The other items in the introduction section of the BPP are simply executive summaries of the other sections of the document.

System Description Section of the Baseline Project Plan

The second section of the BPP is the *system description*, which includes an outline of possible alternative solutions to the one deemed most appropriate for the given situation. Note that this description is highly detailed and mostly narrative in form. Alternatives can be stated as simply as this:

1. Web-based online system.
2. Mainframe with central database.
3. Local area network with decentralized databases.
4. Batch data input with online retrieval.
5. Purchasing of a prewritten package.

If the project is approved for construction or purchase, the systems analyst will need to collect and structure information in a more detailed and rigorous manner during the systems analysis phase, and evaluate in greater depth these and other alternatives for the system.

When Jim and Jackie were considering system alternatives for the WebStore, they focused on two primary issues. First, they discussed how the system would be acquired and considered three options: (1) purchase the system if one could be found that met PVF's needs, (2) outsource the development of the system to an outside organization, or (3) build the system within PVF. Next, Jim and Jackie defined the comprehensiveness of the system's functionality. To complete this task, Jackie wrote a series of statements listing the types of tasks that she believed customers would be able to accomplish when using the WebStore. This list became the basis of the system description and was instrumental in helping them make the acquisition decision. After considering the unique characteristics of the system, they decided that the best decision was to build the system within PVF.

Feasibility Assessment Section of the Baseline Project Plan

In the third section of the BPP, *feasibility assessment*, the systems analyst outlines project costs and benefits and technical difficulties. This is also the section where high-level project schedules are specified using network diagrams and Gantt charts. Recall from Chapter 3 that this process is referred to as a work breakdown structure. Little value is gained by specifying task and activity estimates in great detail at this point in the project. An accurate work breakdown can be done only for the next one or two iterations. Nonetheless, after defining the primary tasks for the project, an estimate of the resource requirements can be made. As with defining tasks and activities, this activity involves obtaining estimates of the human resources requirements, because people are typically the most expensive resource element of a project. Once the major tasks and resource requirements are defined, a preliminary schedule can be developed. Defining an acceptable schedule might involve finding additional or different resources, or indicate that the scope of the project be changed. The greatest amount of project planning effort typically is expended on feasibility assessment activities.

Management Issues Section of the Baseline Project Plan

The final section of the BPP, *management issues*, outlines the concerns that management has about the project. This will be a short section if the proposed project is going to be conducted exactly as prescribed by the organization's standard systems development methodology. Most projects, however, have some unique characteristics that require minor to major deviation from the standard methodology. In the team configuration and management portion, the following is identified: the types of people to work on the project, who will be responsible for which tasks, and how work will be supervised and reviewed. The communications plan portion explains how the user will be kept informed about project progress, such as periodic review meetings or even a newsletter, and which mechanisms will be used to foster sharing of ideas among team members, such as a computer-based conference facility. An example of the type of information contained in the project standards and procedures portion would be procedures for submitting and approving project change requests and any other issues deemed important for the project's success.

This section has explained how a BPP is constructed and the types of information it contains. Its creation is not meant to be a project in and of itself, but rather a step in the overall systems development process. Developing the BPP has two primary objectives. First, it helps assure that the customer and development group share a common understanding of the project. Second, it helps provide the sponsoring organization with a clear idea of the scope, benefits, and duration of the project. Meeting these objectives creates the foundation for a successful project.

Reviewing the Baseline Project Plan

Before completing the first iteration of the project management and planning phase of the SDC, the users, management, and development group must review and approve the Baseline Project Plan. This review takes place before the BPP is submitted or presented to some project approval body, such as an IS steering committee or the person who must fund the project. The objective of this review is to assure that the proposed system conforms to organizational standards and to make sure that all relevant parties understand and agree with the information contained in the Baseline Project Plan. A common method for performing this review is called a walkthrough. Walkthroughs, also called *structured walkthroughs*, are peer group reviews of any product created during the systems development process. They are widely used by professional development organizations, such as Microsoft, IBM, Xerox, and the U.S. government, and have proven effective in ensuring the quality of an information system. Systems analysts are frequently involved in walkthroughs.

Walkthrough
A peer group review of any product created during the systems development process; also called a structured walkthrough.

Although walkthroughs are not rigidly formal or exceedingly long in duration, they have a specific agenda that highlights what is to be covered and the expected completion time. Individuals attending the meeting have specific roles. These roles can include the following:

- *Coordinator.* This person, who plans the meeting and facilitates discussions, can be the project leader or a lead analyst responsible for the current life cycle step.
- *Presenter.* The job of the presenter is to describe the work product to the group. The presenter is usually an analyst who has done all or some of the work being presented.
- *User.* The user (or group) makes sure that the work product meets the needs of the project's customers. This user usually would be someone who is not on the project team.
- *Secretary.* This person takes notes and records decisions or recommendations made by the group. This can be a clerk assigned to the project team or one of the analysts on the team.
- *Standard-bearer.* Ensuring that the work product adheres to organizational technical standards is the job of the standard-bearer. Many larger organizations have staff groups within the unit responsible for establishing standard procedures, methods, and documentation formats. For example, within Microsoft, user interface standards are developed and rigorously enforced on all development projects. As a result, all systems have the same look and feel to users. These standard-bearers validate the work so that others can use it in the development organization.

- *Maintenance oracle.* This person reviews the work product in terms of future maintenance activities. The goal is to make the system and its documentation easy to maintain.

Walkthroughs are used throughout the duration of the project for briefing team members and external stakeholders. These presentations can provide many benefits to the team, but, unfortunately, are often not well done. With the proliferation of computer technology and the availability of powerful software to assist in designing and delivering presentations, making an effective presentation has never been easier. Microsoft's PowerPoint has emerged as the de facto standard for creating computer-based presentations. Although this program is relatively easy to use, it can also be misused such that the "bells and whistles" added to a computer-based presentation actually detract from the presentation. Like any project, to make an effective presentation, it must be planned, designed, and delivered. Planning and designing your presentation is equally important to delivering it. If your slides are poorly laid out, hard to read, or inconsistent, it won't matter how good your delivery is; your audience will think more about the poor quality of the slides than about what you are saying. Fortunately, with a little work it is easy to design a high-quality presentation if you follow a few simple steps that are outlined in Table 4-10.

Table 4-10 Guidelines for Making an Effective Presentation.

Presentation Planning	
Who is the audience?	To design the most effective presentation, you need to consider the audience (e.g., What do they know about your topic? What is their education level?).
What is the message?	Your presentation should be designed with a particular objective in mind.
What is the presentation environment?	Knowledge of the room size, shape, and lighting is valuable information for designing an optimal presentation.
Presentation Design	
Organize the sequence	Organize your presentation so that like elements or topics are found in one place instead of scattered throughout the material in random fashion.
Keep it simple	Make sure that you don't pack too much information onto a slide so that it is difficult to read. Also, work to have as few slides as possible; in other words, only include information that you absolutely need.
Be consistent	Make sure that you are consistent in the types of fonts, font sizes, colors, design approach, and backgrounds.
Use variety	Use both textual and graphical slides to convey information in the most meaningful format.
Don't rely on the spell checker alone	Make sure you carefully review your presentation for typographical and wording errors.
Use bells and whistles sparingly	Make sure that you use familiar graphical icons to guide and enhance slides: don't lose sight of your message as you add bells and whistles. Also, take great care when making transitions between slides and elements so that "special effects" don't take away from your message.
Supplemental materials	Take care when using supplemental materials so that they don't distract the audience. For example, don't provide handouts until you want the audience to actually read this material.
Have a clear beginning and end	At the beginning, introduce yourself and your teammates (if any), thank your audience for being there, and provide a clear outline of what will be covered during the presentation. At the conclusion, have a concluding slide so that the audience clearly sees that the presentation is over.
Presentation Delivery	
Practice	Make sure that you thoroughly test your completed work on yourself and others to be sure it covers your points and presents them in an effective manner within the time frame required.
Arrive early and cue up your presentation	It is good practice, when feasible, to have your presentation ready to go prior to the arrival of the audience.
Learn to use the "special" software keys	Using special keys to navigate the presentation will allow you to focus on your message and not on the software.
Have a backup plan	Have a backup plan in case technology fails or your presentation is lost when traveling.
Delivery	To make an effective presentation, you must become an effective public speaker through practice.
Personal appearance	Your appearance and demeanor can go a long way toward enhancing how the audience receives your presentation.

Reviewing the Baseline Project Plan for the PVF WebStore

After Jim and Jackie completed their BPP for the WebStore, Jim approached his boss and requested that a walkthrough meeting be scheduled and a walkthrough coordinator be assigned to the project. PVF provides the coordinator with a Walkthrough Review Form, shown in Figure 4.16. Using this form, the coordinator can more easily make sure that a qualified individual is assigned to each walkthrough role; that each member has been given a copy of the review materials; and that each member knows the agenda,

Figure 4.16 Walkthrough Review Form for the Pine Valley Furniture WebStore

Pine Valley Furniture
Walkthrough Review Form

Session Coordinator:

Project/Segment:

Coordinator's Checklist:

1. Confirmation with producer(s) that material is ready and stable: _____
2. Issue invitations, assign responsibilities, distribute materials: [ ] Y   [ ] N
3. Set date, time, and location for meeting:

   Date: ____ / ____ / ____   Time: _____ A.M. / P.M. (circle one)

   Location: _____

Responsibilities	*Participants*	*Can Attend*	*Received Materials*
Coordinator	_____	[ ] Y [ ] N	[ ] Y [ ] N
Presenter	_____	[ ] Y [ ] N	[ ] Y [ ] N
User	_____	[ ] Y [ ] N	[ ] Y [ ] N
Secretary	_____	[ ] Y [ ] N	[ ] Y [ ] N
Standards	_____	[ ] Y [ ] N	[ ] Y [ ] N
Maintenance	_____	[ ] Y [ ] N	[ ] Y [ ] N

Agenda:
_____ 1. All participants agree to follow PVF's Rules of a Walkthrough
_____ 2. New material: Walkthrough of all material
_____ 3. Old material: Item-by-item check-off of previous action list
_____ 4. Creation of new action list (contribution by each participant)
_____ 5. Group decision (see below)
_____ 6. Deliver copy of this form to the project control manager

Group Decision:
_____ Accept product as-is
_____ Revise (no further walkthrough)
_____ Review and schedule another walkthrough

Signatures		

Figure 4.17 Walkthrough Action List for Pine Valley Furniture

Pine Valley Furniture *Walkthrough Action List*	
Session Coordinator:	
Project/Segment:	
Date and Time of Walkthrough: Date: ___ / ___ / ___ Time: _____ A.M. / P.M. (circle one)	
Fixed (✓)	*Issues raised in review:*

date, time, and location of the meeting. At the meeting, Jim presented the BPP and Jackie added comments from a user perspective. Once the walkthrough presentation was completed, the coordinator polled each representative for his or her recommendation concerning the work product. The results of this voting may result in validation of the work product, validation pending changes suggested during the meeting, or a suggestion that the work product requires major revision before being presented for approval. In this latter case, substantial changes to the work product usually are requested, after which another walkthrough must be scheduled before the project can be proposed to the Systems Priority Board (steering committee). In the case of the WebStore, the BPP was supported by the walkthrough panel pending some minor changes to the duration estimates of the schedule. These suggested changes were recorded by the secretary on a Walkthrough Action List, shown in Figure 4.17, and given to Jim to incorporate into a final version of the baseline plan presented to the steering committee.

Walkthrough meetings are a common occurrence in most systems development groups. In addition to reviewing the BPP, these meetings can be used for the following activities:

- System specifications.
- Logical and physical designs.
- Code or program segments.
- Test procedures and results.
- Manuals and documentation.

One of the key advantages to using a structured review process is to ensure that formal review points occur during the project. At each subsequent phase of the project, a formal review should be conducted (and shown on the project schedule) to make sure that all aspects of the project are accomplished satisfactorily before assigning additional resources to the project. This conservative approach of reviewing each major project activity with continuation contingent on successful completion of the prior phase is called incremental commitment. It is much easier to stop or redirect a project at any point when using this approach.

KEY POINTS REVIEW

1. **Describe the steps involved when identifying and selecting projects as well as those for initiating, planning, and executing projects.**

   Project identification and selection consists of three primary activities: identifying potential development projects, classifying and ranking projects, and selecting projects for development. A variety of organizational members or units can be assigned to perform this process including top management, a diverse steering committee, business units and functional managers, the development group, or the most senior IS executive. Potential projects can be evaluated and selected using a broad range of criteria such as value chain analysis, alignment with business strategy, potential benefits, resource availability and requirements, and risks. At this point, projects are accepted for development, rejected as infeasible, or redirected. Project initiation, planning, and execution are critical and ongoing activities in the life of a project. Project initiation includes forming the project initiation team, establishing customer relationships, developing a plan to get the project started, setting project management procedures, and creating an overall project management environment. After project initiation, project planning focuses on assessing numerous feasibility issues associated with the project in order to create a clear project plan and scope statement. The objective of this process is to transform a vague system request into a tangible system description, clearly outlining the objectives, feasibility issues, benefits, costs, and time schedules for the project. Project execution focuses on putting the plans created during project planning into action. Specific activities include performing planned project activities, monitoring project progress, managing change, maintaining documentation, and communicating project status.

2. **Explain the need for and the contents of a project scope statement and a baseline project plan.**

   A Project Scope Statement and a Baseline Project Plan are created during project initiation and planning. The Project Scope Statement is a short document prepared for the customer that describes what the project will deliver and outlines all work required to complete the project; it assures that the systems analyst and the customer gain a common understanding of the project. The Baseline Project Plan contains an introduction, a high-level description of the proposed system or system change, an outline of the various feasibilities, and an overview of management issues specific to the project. Before the development of an information system can begin, the users, management, and development group must review and agree on this specification.

3. **List and describe various methods for assessing project feasibility.**

   Assessing project feasibility can include an examination of economic, operational, technical, schedule, legal and contractual, and political aspects of the project. This assessment is influenced by the project size, the type of system proposed, and the collective experience of the development group and potential customers of the system. High project costs and risks are not necessarily bad; rather, it is more important that the organization understands the costs and risks associated with a project and with the portfolio of active projects before proceeding.

4. **Describe the differences between tangible and intangible benefits and costs and the differences between one-time and recurring costs.**

   Tangible benefits can be measured easily in dollars and with certainty. Intangible benefits cannot be measured easily in dollars or with certainty. Tangible costs can be measured easily in dollars and with certainty. Intangible costs cannot be measured easily in terms of cost or with certainty. One-time costs are associated with project start-up and development. Recurring costs result from the ongoing evolution and use of a system.

5. **Perform cost-benefit analysis, and describe what is meant by the time value of money, present value, discount rate, net present value, return on investment, and break-even analysis.**

   The time value of money refers to comparing present cash outlays to future expected returns. Thus, the present value represents the current value of a future cash flow. The discount rate refers to the rate of return used to compute the present value of future cash flows. The net present value uses a discount rate to gain the present value of a project's overall benefits and costs. The return on investment is the ratio of the cash benefits of a project divided by the cash costs; trade-off analysis can be made among projects by comparing their representative ROI ratios. Break-even analysis is used to determine the amount of time required for the cumulative incoming cash flow (the benefits) from a project to equal its initial and ongoing investment (the costs).

6. **Describe the activities and participant roles within a structured walkthrough.**

   A walkthrough assesses the merits of the project and assures that the project, if accepted for development, conforms to organizational standards and goals. An objective of this process also is to make sure that all relevant parties understand and agree with the information contained in the project before subsequent development activities begin. Several individuals participate in a walkthrough, including the coordinator, presenter, user, secretary, standards-bearer, and maintenance oracle. Each plays a specific role to make sure that the walkthrough is a success. Walkthroughs are used to assess all types of project deliverables, including system specifications, logical and physical designs, code and program segments, test procedures and results, and manuals and documentation.

KEY TERMS CHECKPOINT

Here are the key terms from the chapter. The page where each term is first explained is in parentheses after the term.

a. Baseline Project Plan (BPP) (p. 100)
b. Break-even analysis (p. 108)
c. Business case (p. 100)
d. Discount rate (p. 107)
e. Economic feasibility (p. 104)
f. Incremental commitment (p. 97)
g. Intangible benefit (p. 105)
h. Intangible cost (p. 105)

i. Legal and contractual feasibility (p. 112)
j. One-time cost (p. 105)
k. Operational feasibility (p. 111)
l. Political feasibility (p. 112)
m. Present value (p. 107)
n. Project scope statement (p. 115)
o. Recurring cost (p. 105)

p. Schedule feasibility (p. 112)
q. Tangible benefit (p. 104)
r. Tangible cost (p. 105)
s. Technical feasibility (p. 110)
t. Time value of money (TVM) (p. 107)
u. Walkthrough (p. 117)

Match each of the key terms above with the definition that best fits it.

1. The process of evaluating how key stakeholders within the organization view the proposed system.

2. A document prepared for the customer that describes what the project will deliver and outlines generally at a high level all work required to complete the project.

3. The justification for an information system, presented in terms of the economic benefits and costs, and the technical and organizational feasibility of the proposed system.

4. A process of identifying the financial benefits and costs associated with a development project.
5. A strategy in systems analysis and design in which the project is reviewed after each phase and continuation of the project is rejustified in each of these reviews.
6. A cost resulting from the ongoing evolution and use of a system.
7. The interest rate used to compute the present value of future cash flows.
8. A benefit derived from the creation of an information system that cannot be measured easily in dollars or with certainty.
9. The process of assessing the degree to which the potential time frame and completion dates for all major activities within a project meet organizational deadlines and constraints for affecting change.
10. A cost associated with an information system that can be measured easily in dollars and with certainty.
11. A peer group review of any product created during the systems development process.
12. A process of assessing the development organization's ability to construct a proposed system.

13. A cost associated with project start-up and development, or system start-up.
14. The current value of a future cash flow.
15. A benefit derived from the creation of an information system that can be measured in dollars and with certainty.
16. The process of assessing potential legal and contractual ramifications due to the construction of a system.
17. A cost associated with an information system that cannot be measured easily in terms of dollars or with certainty.
18. The major outcome and deliverable from the project initiation and planning phase; contains the best estimate of the project's scope, benefits, costs, risks, and resource requirements.
19. The process of assessing the degree to which a proposed system solves business problems or takes advantage of business opportunities.
20. The process of comparing present cash outlays to future expected returns.
21. A type of cost-benefit analysis to identify at what point (if ever) benefits equal costs.

REVIEW QUESTIONS

1. Describe the project identification and selection process.
2. Describe several project evaluation criteria.
3. List and describe the steps in the project initiation, planning, and execution processes.
4. What is contained in a Baseline Project Plan? Are the content and format of all baseline plans the same? Why or why not?
5. Describe three commonly used methods for performing economic cost-benefit analysis.
6. List and discuss the different types of project feasibility factors. Is any factor most important? Why or why not?

7. What are the potential consequences of not assessing the technical risks associated with an information systems development project?
8. What are the types or categories of benefits from an IS project?
9. What intangible benefits might an organization obtain from the development of an IS?
10. Describe the concept of the time value of money. How does the discount rate affect the value of $1 today versus one year from today?
11. Describe the structured walkthrough process. What roles need to be performed during a walkthrough?

PROBLEMS AND EXERCISES

1. The economic analysis carried out during project management and planning is rather superficial. Why is this? Consequently, what factors do you think tend to be most important for a potential project to survive this first project assessment?
2. Consider your use of a PC at home or at work and list tangible benefits from an information system. Based on this list, does your use of a PC seem to be beneficial? Why or why not?
3. Consider, as an example, buying a network of PCs for a department at your workplace, or alternatively, consider outfitting a laboratory of PCs for students at a university. Make sure you estimate the one-time and the recurring costs.
4. Assuming monetary benefits of an information system at $85,000 per year, one-time costs of $75,000, recurring

costs of $35,000 per year, a discount rate of 12 percent, and a five-year time horizon, calculate the net present value of the costs and benefits of an information system. Also calculate the overall return on investment of the project and then present a break-even analysis. At what point does breakeven occur?
5. Choose as an example one of the information systems you described in Problem and Exercise 3, either buying a network of PCs for a department at your workplace or outfitting a laboratory of PCs for students at a university. Estimate the costs and benefits of your system, and calculate the net present value and return on investment and present a break-even analysis. Assume a discount rate of 12 percent and a five-year time horizon.
6. Use the outline for the Baseline Project Plan provided in Figure 4.14 to present the system specifications for

the information system you chose for Problems and Exercises 3 and 5.

7. Change the discount rate for Problem and Exercise 4 to 10 percent and redo the analysis.
8. Change the recurring costs in Problem and Exercise 4 to $40,000 and redo the analysis.
9. Change the time horizon in Problem and Exercise 4 to three years and redo the analysis.
10. Assume monetary benefits of an information system of $50,000 the first year and increasing benefits of $5,000 a year for the next four years (year 1 = $50,000; year 2 = $55,000; year 3 = $60,000; year 4 = $65,000; year 5 = $70,000). One-time development costs were $90,000, and recurring costs beginning in year 1 were $40,000 over the duration of the system's life. The discount rate for the company was 10 percent. Using a five-year horizon, calculate the net present value of these costs and benefits. Also calculate the overall return on investment of the project and then present a break-even analysis. At what point does breakeven occur?
11. Change the discount rate for Problem and Exercise 10 to 12 percent and redo the analysis.
12. Change the recurring costs in Problem and Exercise 10 to $60,000 and redo the analysis.

13. For the system you chose for Problems and Exercises 3 and 5, complete section 1.0.A, the project overview, of the Baseline Project Plan report. How important is it that this initial section of the Baseline Project Plan report be done well? What could go wrong if this section is incomplete or incorrect?
14. For the system you chose for Problems and Exercises 3 and 5, complete section 2.0.A, the alternatives, of the Baseline Project Plan report. Without conducting a full-blown feasibility analysis, what is your gut feeling regarding the feasibility of this system?
15. For the system you chose for Problems and Exercises 3 and 5, complete section 3.0.A–F, the feasibility analysis, of the Baseline Project Plan report. How does this feasibility analysis compare with your gut feeling from the previous question? What might go wrong if you rely on your gut feeling in determining system feasibility?
16. For the system you chose for Problems and Exercises 3 and 5, complete section 4.0.A–C, management issues, of the Baseline Project Plan report. Why might people sometimes believe that these additional steps in the project plan are a waste of time? What could you say to convince them that these steps are important?

DISCUSSION QUESTIONS

1. Imagine that you are the chief information officer (CIO) of a company and are responsible for making all technology investment decisions. Would you ever agree to build an information system that had a negative net present value? If so, why? If not, why not? How would you justify your decision?
2. Imagine that you are interviewing for a job and the interviewer asks you which cost-benefit analysis technique is best for assessing a project's economic feasibility. What would be your response?

3. Imagine that you are working at a company and a new project idea has been assigned to you. After getting this assignment, you have a conversation with your customer who says, "This project management and planning stuff takes too much time. Let's get on with it and start building the system!" What would be your response?
4. Of the six methods for assessing project feasibility, which is the most important? In which situation is each method more or less important?

CASE PROBLEMS

1. Pine Valley Furniture

Pine Valley Furniture recently implemented a new internship program and has begun recruiting interns from nearby university campuses. As part of this program, interns have the opportunity to work alongside a systems analyst. This shadowing opportunity provides invaluable insights into the systems analysis and design process. Recently you were selected for a six-month internship at Pine Valley Furniture, and Jim Woo has been assigned as your supervisor.

At an initial meeting with Jim Woo, he explains that Pine Valley Furniture currently is involved with two important systems development projects: the Customer Tracking

System and WebStore. The purpose of the Customer Tracking System is to enable the PVF marketing group to track customer purchase activity and sales trends better. The WebStore project will help move the company into the twenty-first century by facilitating online furniture purchases, with an initial focus on corporate furniture buying. During your meeting with Mr. Woo, he reviews the documentation assembled for both systems. Mr. Woo hands you a copy of the Customer Tracking System's economic feasibility analysis. He mentions that he would like to modify the spreadsheet to reflect the information provided in the following table. Because you are familiar with a spreadsheet product, you volunteer to make the modifications for him.

	Year 0	Year 1	Year 2	Year 3	Year 4	Year 5
Net Economic Benfits	$0	$50,000	$55,000	$55,000	$60,000	$60,000
One-time costs	$47,500					
Recurring costs		$30,000	$30,000	$30,000	$30,000	$30,000

a. How were Pine Valley Furniture's projects initiated? What is the focus for each of the new systems?

b. Modify the Customer Tracking System's economic feasibility analysis to reflect the modifications mentioned in this case problem. Use a discount rate of 10 percent. After the changes are made, what are the new overall NPV, ROI, and BEA?

c. Modify the worksheet created in part b using discount rates of 12 percent and 14 percent. What impact do these values have on the overall NPV, ROI, and BEA?

d. Jim Woo would like to investigate how other online stores are targeting the business furniture market. Identify and evaluate two online stores that sell business furniture. Briefly summarize your findings.

Hoosier Burger

The Hoosier Burger project development team has met several times with Bob and Thelma Mellankamp. During these meetings, Bob has stressed the importance of improving Hoosier Burger's inventory control, customer ordering, and management reporting systems. Demand for Hoosier Burger food is at an all-time high, and this increased demand is creating problems for Hoosier Burger's staff, creating stock-out problems and impacting sales.

During rush periods, customers sometimes wait 15 minutes to place an order and might wait an additional 25 minutes to receive their order. Low-in-stock inventory items often are not reordered in a timely fashion, thus creating problems with the food preparation. For instance, vanilla ice cream is used to prepare vanilla malts, an item that accompanies the Hoosier Burger Special. Last week, Bob did not order enough vanilla ice cream, resulting in a last-minute dash to the grocery store.

Bob and Thelma have expressed their feelings that a new information system will be beneficial in the areas of inventory management, marketing, customer service, and food preparation. In addition, the project team discussed with Bob and Thelma the possibility of implementing a point-of-sale system as an alternative design strategy.

a. How was the Hoosier Burger project identified and selected? What focus will the new system have?

b. Identify the Hoosier Burger project's scope.

c. Using the six feasibility factors presented in this chapter, assess the Hoosier Burger project's feasibility.

d. Using Figure 4.6 as a guide, develop a Statement of Work for the Hoosier Burger project.

Golden Age Retirement Center

The Golden Age Retirement Center is a retirement village designed for adults over age 60 who want to "get away from it all." Golden Age leases apartments; sells condominiums; and provides housekeeping, basic utilities, cable television, and recreational activities for its residents. The retirement village is locally owned and managed; however, a residents' advisory board has significant input when changes or recommendations to the retirement village are contemplated.

Golden Age Retirement Center's manager, Mary Lou Tobias, approached you recently for help with the retirement center's outdated information system. Currently, the retirement office has five employees, including Ms. Tobias. She explains that all data concerning residents, financial matters, suppliers, employees, and recreational activities are kept manually. The management office does have a Pentium II computer running Windows 95 and Office 97 software. Currently, the computer is used only to prepare a weekly newsletter that is sent to current residents. Ms. Tobias would like to have a system that automates the aforementioned areas. She also would like to establish a network where any employee can access information. This new system must be implemented within six months.

After an initial analysis, you make the following estimations. You will use these data as part of your initial feasibility assessment.

	Year 0	Year 1	Year 2	Year 3	Year 4	Year 5
Net Economic Benfits	$0	$25,000	$25,000	$25,000	$25,000	$25,000
One-time costs	$40,000					
Recurring costs		$15,000	$15,000	$15,000	$15,000	$15,000

a. Identify several benefits and costs associated with implementing this new system.

b. Using the feasibility factors identified in this chapter, assess the new system's feasibility.

c. Using Figure 4.11 as a guide, prepare an economic feasibility analysis worksheet for Ms. Tobias. Using a discount rate of 10 percent, what are the overall NPV and ROI? When will breakeven occur?

d. Modify the spreadsheet developed for part c to reflect discount rates of 11 percent and 14 percent. What impact will these new rates have on the economic analysis?

CASE: BROADWAY ENTERTAINMENT COMPANY, INC.

Initiating and Planning a Web-Based Customer Relationship Management System

Case Introduction

Carrie Douglass graduated from St. Claire Community College with an associate's degree in business marketing. Among the courses Carrie took at St. Claire were several on information technology in marketing, including one on electronic commerce. While at St. Claire, Carrie worked part-time as an assistant manager at the Broadway Entertainment Company (BEC) store in Centerville, Ohio, a suburb of Dayton. After graduation, she was recruited by BEC for a full-time position because of her excellent job experience at BEC and her outstanding record in classes and student organizations at St. Claire. Carrie immediately entered the BEC Manager Development Program, which consisted of three months of training, observation of experienced managers at several stores, and work experience.

The first week of training was held at the BEC regional headquarters in Columbus, Ohio. Carrie learned about company procedures and policies, trends in the home entertainment industry, and personnel practices used in BEC stores. It was during this week that Carrie was introduced to the BEC Blueprint for the Decade, a vision statement for the firm, as shown in BEC Figure 4.1.

The blueprint, as it is called, seemed rather abstract to Carrie while in training. Carrie saw a video in which Nigel Broad, BEC's chairman, explained the importance of the blueprint. Nigel was sincere and clearly passionate about BEC's future hinging on every employee finding innovative ways for the company to achieve the vision outlined in the blueprint.

After the three-month development program was over, Carrie was surprised to be appointed manager of the Centerville store. The previous manager was promoted to a marketing position in Columbus, which created this opportunity. Carrie started her job with enthusiasm, wanting to apply what she had learned at St. Claire and in the Manager Development Program.

The Idea for a New System

Although confident in her skills, Carrie believes that learning never stops. So, she logged onto the Amazon.com Web site one night from her home computer to look for some books on trends in retail marketing. While on the Web site, Carrie saw that Amazon.com was selling some of the same products BEC sells and rents in its stores. She had visited the BEC Web site often. Although it was a rich source of information about the company (she had found her first job with BEC from a job posting on the company's Web site), BEC was not engaged in electronic commerce with customers. All of a sudden, the words of the BEC Blueprint for the Decade started to come to life for Carrie. The blueprint said that "BEC will be a leader in all areas of our business—human resources, technology, operations, and marketing." And, "BEC will be innovative in the use of technology . . . to provide better service to our customers." These statements caused Carrie to recall a conversation she had had in the store just that day with a mother of several young children.

The mother, a frequent BEC customer, had complimented Carrie on the cleanliness of the store and the efficiency of checkout. The mother added, however, that she wished BEC better understood all of her needs. For example, she allowed her children to pick out movies and games, but she found that the industry rating system was not always consistent with her wishes. It would be great if she and other parents could submit and view comments about videos and games. This way, parents would be more aware of the content of the products and the reactions of other children to these products. Carrie wondered why this kind of information couldn't be placed on a Web site for anyone to use. The comments made by parents shopping at the Centerville store would probably be different from those of parents shopping at other stores, so it seemed to make sense that this information service should be a part of the local store operations.

One of the books Carrie found on Amazon.com discussed customer relationship management. This seemed exactly what the mother wanted from BEC. The mother didn't want just products and services; rather, she wanted a store that understood and supported all of her needs for home entertainment. She wanted the store to relate to her, not just sell and rent products to her and her children.

As a new store manager, Carrie was busy, but she was excited to do something about her idea. She still did not

Blueprint for the Decade

Foreword
> This blueprint provides guidance to Broadway Entertainment Corporation (BEC) for this decade. It shows our vision for the firm—our mission, objectives, and strategy fit together—and provides direction for all individuals and decisions of the firm.

Our Mission
> BEC is a publicly held, for-profit organization focusing on the home entertainment industry that has a global focus for operations. BEC exists to serve customers with a primary goal of enhancing shareholders' investment through the pursuit of excellence in everything we do. BEC will operate under the highest ethical standards; will respect the dignity, rights, and contributions of all employees; and will strive to better society.

Our Objectives
> 1. BEC will strive to increase market share and profitability (prime objective).
> 2. BEC will be a leader in all areas of our business—human resources, technology, operations, and marketing.
> 3. BEC will be cost-effective in the use of all resources.
> 4. BEC will rank among industry leaders in both profitability and growth.
> 5. BEC will be innovative in the use of technology to help bring new products and services to market faster than our competition and to provide better service to our customers.
> 6. BEC will create an environment that values diversity in gender, race, values, and culture among employees, suppliers, and customers.

Our Strategy
> BEC will be a *global* provider of home entertainment products and services by providing the highest-quality *customer service*, the *broadest range of products and services*, at the *lowest possible price*.

understand how all aspects of BEC worked (e.g., the Manager Development Program had not discussed how to work with BEC's information systems (IS) organization), and she especially believed that without a more thorough plan for her idea about a customer information service, she would not be able to get BEC management to pay attention to it. Carrie knew a way, however, to better develop her idea while still giving all the necessary attention to her new job. If she made just one phone call, she thought her idea could take shape.

Requesting the Project

Carrie's call was to Professor Martha Tann, head of the computer information systems (CIS) program at St. Claire Community College. Carrie had taken Professor Tann's course on business information systems, which was required of all business students at St. Claire. Professor Tann also teaches a two-quarter capstone course for CIS majors in which student teams work in local organizations to analyze and structure the requirements for a new or replacement information system. Carrie's idea was to have a CIS student team develop a prototype of the system and use this prototype to sell the concept of the system to BEC management.

Over the next few weeks, Carrie and Professor Tann discussed Carrie's idea and how projects are conducted by CIS students. Students in the course indicate which projects they want to work on among a set of projects submitted for the course by local organizations. More requests are always submitted by local organizations than can be handled by the course, just like most organizations have more demand for information systems than can be satisfied by the available resources. Projects are presented to the students via a Systems Service Request form, typical of what would be used inside an organization for a user to request the IS group to undertake a systems development project. Once a group of students is assigned by Professor Tann to a project of their choice, the student team proceeds as if they were a group of systems analysts employed by the sponsoring organization. Within any limitations imposed by the sponsoring organization, the students can conduct the project using any methodology or techniques appropriate for the situation.

The initial Systems Service Request that Carrie submitted for review by Professor Tann appears in BEC Figure 4.2. This request appears in a standard format used for all project

Systems Service Request
St. Claire Community College
Capstone CIS Project Course

REQUESTED BY _____ Carrie Douglass _____ DATE _____ August 12, 2007 _____

DEPARTMENT _____ Broadway Entertainment Company, Store OH-84 _____

LOCATION _____ 4600 S. Main Street _____

CONTACT _____ Tel: 422-7700   FAX: 422-7760   e-mail: CarrieDoug@aol.com _____

TYPE OF REQUEST   URGENCY

[X]   New System   [   ]   Immediate—Operations are impaired or opportunity lost
[   ]   System Enhancement   [   ]   Problems exist, but can be worked around
[   ]   System Error Correction   [X]   Business losses can be tolerated until new system installed

PROBLEM STATEMENT

Today, Broadway Entertainment Company (BEC) sells and rents videos, music, and games to customers. BEC is profitable and growing. Increased competition from existing and emerging competitors requires BEC constantly to consider better ways to meet the needs of its customers. Increasingly, customers want information services as well as products as part of the relationship with our store. Customers want us to be aware of their likes, dislikes, and preferences, and want us to create a sense of community for the exchange of information among customers. The vision of BEC is to be a market leader in the use of technology to provide the highest-quality customer service with the broadest range of products and services. Even though providing information services as part of our relationship with our customers is consistent with this vision, no such services are provided today. The purpose of the proposed project is to prove (or disprove) that such customer information services will improve customer satisfaction and lead to increased revenue and potentially increased market share. A sustainable competitive advantage would be desirable, but is not necessary at this stage.

Specifically, the proposed system will provide information services such as (1) ability for customers to submit unstructured and structured comments about movies, music, and games they have bought or rented; (2) submit requests for new products for sale and rent; (3) check on due dates for a customer's outstanding rentals; (4) extend a rental without penalty for a minor fee to be applied when the item is returned; (5) review the inventory of items carried in the store; (6) parents can monitor (see a list of) items rented or purchased by their children. This project should conduct a thorough analysis of such information services desired by customers, design a Web-based system to provide such services, and implement and test a prototype of this system.

SERVICE REQUEST

I request a thorough analysis of this idea be conducted. I need a working prototype of the system that could be tested with a selected group of actual customers. The prototype should include major system functions. A survey of users should be conducted to gather evidence to support (or possibly not support) my subsequent request to BEC to build such a system for all stores.

IS LIAISON _____ Student team leader, assigned when a team is selected for this project _____

SPONSOR _____ Carrie Douglass, Manager BEC Store OH-84 _____

---------------------- TO BE COMPLETED BY SYSTEMS PRIORITY BOARD ----------------------

[   ]   Request approved   Assigned to _____
                            Start date _____
[   ]   Recommend revision
[   ]   Suggest user development
[   ]   Reject for reason _____
        _____

submissions for the CIS project course at St. Claire Community College. Professor Tann reviews initial requests for understandability by the students and gives submitters guidance on how to make the project more appealing to students.

When selecting among final Systems Service Requests, the students look for the projects that will give them the best opportunity to learn and integrate the skills needed to manage and conduct a systems analysis and design project. Professor Tann also asks the students to pretend to be a steering committee (sometimes called a systems priority board) to select projects that appear to be well justified and of value to the sponsoring organization. So, Carrie knew that she would have to make the case for the project succinctly and persuasively, even before a preliminary study of the situation could be conducted. Her project idea would have to compete with other submissions, just as it will when she proposes it later within BEC. At least by then, she will have the experience from the prototype to prove the value of her ideas—if the students at St. Claire accept her request.

Case Summary

Ideas for new or improved information systems come from a variety of sources or are generated for a variety of reasons, including the need to fix a broken system, the need to improve the performance of an existing system, competitive pressures, new or changed government regulations, requirements generated from top-down organizational initiatives, and creative ideas by individual managers. The request for a Web-based customer information system submitted by Carrie Douglass is an example of this common, last category. Often an organization is overwhelmed by such requests. An organization must determine which ideas are the most worthy and what action should be taken in response to each request.

Carrie's proposal creates an opportunity for students at St. Claire Community College to engage in an actual systems development project. Although Carrie is not expecting a final, professional, and complete system, a working prototype that will be used by actual customers can serve as an example of the type of system that could be built by Broadway Entertainment. The project, as proposed, requests that all the typical steps in the analysis and design of an information system be conducted. Carrie Douglass could be rewarded for her creativity if the system proves to be worthwhile, or her idea could flop. The success of her idea depends on the quality of the work done by the students at St. Claire.

CASE QUESTIONS

1. The Systems Service Request (SSR) submitted by Carrie Douglass (BEC Figure 4.2) has not been reviewed by Professor Tann. If you were Professor Tann, would you ask for any changes to the request as submitted? If so, what changes, and if no changes, why? Remember, an SSR is a call for a preliminary study, not a thorough problem statement.

2. If you were a student in Professor Tann's class, would you want to work on this project? Why or why not?

3. If you were a member of BEC's steering committee, what action would you recommend for this project request? Justify your answer.

4. If you were assigned to a team of students responsible for this project, identify a preliminary list of tangible and intangible costs you think would be incurred for this project and ultimately for the system. At this point, no tangible benefits have been computed, so all potential benefits are intangible. What intangible benefits do you anticipate for this system?

5. What do you consider to be the risks of the project as you currently understand it? Is this a low-, medium-, or high-risk project? Justify your answer. From your position as a member of a student team conducting this project, would you have any particular risks? What risks does Carrie Douglass have given that a team of students is conducting this project?

6. If you were assigned to a team of students responsible for this project, how would you utilize the concept of incremental commitment in the design of the Baseline Project Plan?

7. If you were assigned to a team of students responsible for this project, when in the project schedule (in what phase or after which activities are completed) do you think you could develop an economic analysis of the proposed system? What economic feasibility factors do you think would be relevant?

8. If you were assigned to a team of students responsible for this project, what activities would you conduct in order to prepare the details for the Baseline Project Plan? Explain the purpose of each activity and show a time line or schedule for these activities.

9. From the explanation in this case study, you have only a general idea of the system Carrie wants. However, even from this brief explanation, you probably have some idea of the system features that will influence the iterations of an object-oriented project. List these features.

10. In Case Question 5, you analyzed the risks associated with this project. Once deployed, what are the potential operational risks of the proposed systems? How do you factor operational risks into a systems development project?

Chapter

5

Determining Object-Oriented Systems Requirements

Chapter Objectives

After studying this chapter, you should be able to:

➤ Describe options for designing and conducting interviews and develop a plan for conducting an interview to determine system requirements.

➤ Explain the advantages and pitfalls of observing workers and analyzing business documents to determine system requirements.

➤ Participate in and help plan a Joint Application Design session.

➤ Use prototyping during requirements determination.

➤ Describe agile approaches to requirements determination.

➤ Select the appropriate methods to elicit system requirements.

Chapter Contents

➤ Chapter Preview
➤ Performing Requirements Determination
➤ Traditional Methods for Determining Requirements
➤ Modern Methods for Determining System Requirements
➤ PVF WebStore Determining System Requirements

Chapter Preview

Determining how a current information system in an organization functions is the part of the systems development cycle called systems analysis. The next thing that must be assessed is what users would like to see in a new system. Analysis has three parts: determining requirements, structuring requirements, and selecting the best alternative design strategy. Figure 5.1 illustrates these three parts and highlights the focus of this chapter—determining system requirements.

Requirements determination is a key issue in systems analysis regardless of which methodology is being followed: structured or object-oriented. We first study the more traditional requirements determination methods, which include interviewing, observing users in their work environment, and collecting procedures and other written documents. We then discuss more modern methods for collecting system requirements. The first of these methods is joint application design (JAD). The second method is prototyping. The third method involves two techniques from agile methodologies: Agile Usage-Centered Design, and the Planning Game from eXtreme Programming. Requirements determination continues to be a major part of systems analysis and design, even for object-oriented development and for developing Internet applications.

Figure 5.1 Systems Analysis Has Three Parts: Requirements Determination, Requirements Structuring, and Alternative Generation and Selection

✔ **Requirements Determination (Ch. 5)**
Requirements Structuring (Chs. 6–9)
Alternative Generation and Selection (Ch. 10)

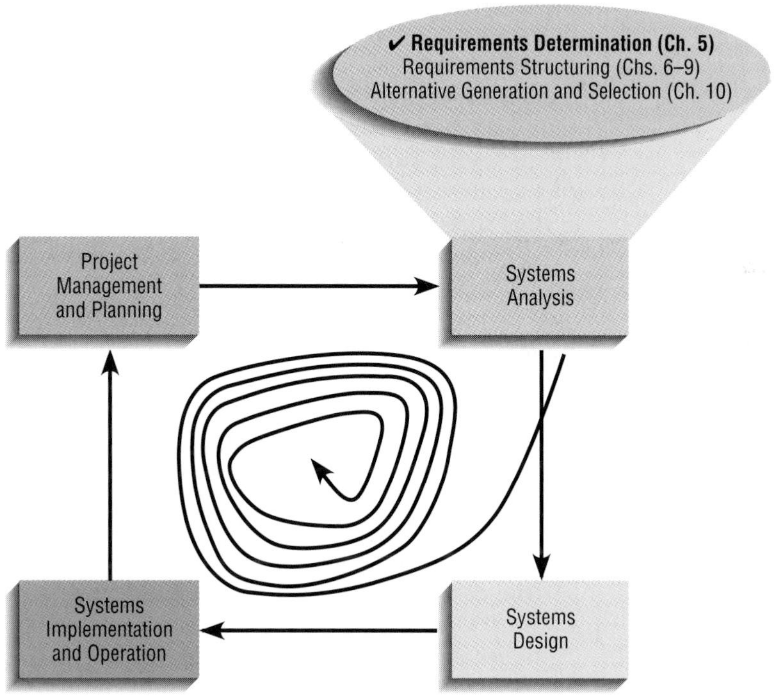

PERFORMING REQUIREMENTS DETERMINATION

Systems analysis has three parts: determining requirements (this chapter), structuring requirements (Chapters 6 through 9), and selecting the best alternative design strategy (Chapter 10). We address these as three separate steps, but these steps should be considered somewhat parallel and repetitive. For example, as some aspects of the current and desired system(s) are outlined, the systems analyst begins to structure these requirements or build prototypes to show users how a system might behave. Inconsistencies and deficiencies discovered through structuring and prototyping lead to further exploration of the operation of the current system(s) and the future needs of the organization. Eventually, the systems analyst's ideas and discoveries merge into a thorough and accurate depiction of current operations and the requirements for the new system. We will discuss how to begin the requirements determination process, but first we need to talk about what is meant by a requirement for an object-oriented system.

What Is a Requirement?

A requirement describes what a system is supposed to do, not how the system is supposed to do it. Think about requirements in terms of what the users of the system need the system to do. Requirements, then, typically focus on functions the system can or will perform. However, requirements also will identify the objects that must be included in the system and the various states those objects will assume over time. A systems analyst also needs to determine the attributes each object needs and to figure out how the objects and their states relate to system functions. As part of determining requirements, the systems analyst also will gather information about the constraints that govern the behavior of the system and the objects that are part of it.

The Process of Determining Requirements

At the end of the systems planning, management, and selection phase of the systems development cycle, management can grant permission to pursue development of a new system. A project is initiated and planned (as described in Chapter 4), and a determination is made regarding what the new system should do. During requirements determination, the analysts gather information from as many sources as possible on how the system should function. Such sources include users of the current system, reports, forms, and procedures. All of the system requirements are documented carefully and made ready for structuring. Structuring means taking the system requirements found during requirements determination and ordering them into diagrams, such as use-case and class diagrams, which make them easier to translate into technical system specifications. Structuring is discussed in detail in Chapters 6 through 9.

In many ways, gathering system requirements is like conducting any investigation. The characteristics needed to enjoy solving mysteries and puzzles are the same ones needed to be a good systems analyst during requirements determination. These characteristics include:

- *Impertinence.*   Question everything. Ask questions such as "Are all transactions processed the same way?" "Could anyone be charged something other than the standard price?" "Might we someday want to allow and encourage employees to work for more than one department?"
- *Impartiality.*   The role of the systems analyst is to find the best solution to a business problem or opportunity. It is not, for example, to find a way to justify the purchase of new hardware or to insist on incorporating what users think they want into the new system requirements. The systems analyst must consider issues raised by all parties and try to find the best organizational solution.
- *Relaxing of constraints.*   Assume anything is possible and eliminate the infeasible. For example, the systems analyst should not accept this statement: "We've always done it that way, so we have to continue the practice." Traditions are different from rules and policies. Traditions probably started for a good reason, but as the organization and its environment change, they might turn into habits rather than sensible procedures.
- *Attention to details.*   Every fact must fit with every other fact. One element that is out of place means the ultimate system will fail at some time. For example, an imprecise definition of who a customer is might mean purging customer data when a customer has no active orders, yet these past customers might be vital contacts for future sales.

- *Reframing.* Analysis is, in part, a creative process. The systems analyst must be challenged to look at the organization in new ways and to consider how users view their requirements. They should be careful not to jump to this conclusion: "I worked on a system like that once; this new system must work the same way as the one I built before."

Deliverables and Outcomes

The primary deliverables from requirements determination are the types of information gathered during the determination process. The information can take many forms: transcripts of interviews; notes from observation and analysis of documents; sets of forms, reports, job descriptions, and other documents; and computer-generated output such as system prototypes. In short, anything that the analysis team collects as part of determining system requirements is included in these deliverables. Table 5-1 lists examples of some specific information that might be gathered at this time.

The deliverables summarized in Table 5-1 contain the information needed for systems analysis. In addition, the following components of an organization must be understood:

- The business objectives that drive what and how work is done.
- The information people need to do their jobs.
- The data handled within the organization to support the jobs.
- The sequence and other dependencies among different data-handling activities and among functions.
- The rules governing how data are handled and processed.
- Policies and guidelines that describe the nature of the business and the market and environment in which it operates.
- Key events affecting data values and when these events occur.
- Key events affecting system states and when these events occur.

Such a large amount of information must be organized in order to be useful. This is the purpose of the next part of systems analysis—requirements structuring.

Requirements Structuring

The amount of information gathered during requirements determination could be huge, especially if the scope of the system under development is broad. The time required to collect and structure a great deal of information can be extensive and, because it involves so much human effort, expensive. Too much analysis is not productive, and the term *analysis paralysis* has been coined to describe a project that has been bogged down in an abundance of analysis work. This is especially true for object-

Table 5-1 Deliverables for Requirements Determination.

TYPES OF DELIVERABLES	SPECIFIC DELIVERABLES
Information collected from conversations with users	Interview transcripts
	Notes from observations
	Meeting notes
Existing documents and files	Business mission and strategy statement
	Sample business forms and reports and computer displays
	Procedure manuals
	Job descriptions
	Training manuals
	Flowcharts and documentation of existing systems
	Consultant reports
Computer-based information	Results from Joint Application Design sessions
	Reports of existing systems
	Displays and reports from system prototypes

oriented analysis, where a premium is placed on speed and iteration. Because of the dangers of excessive analysis, today's systems analysts focus more on the system to be developed than on the current system. Later in this chapter, Joint Application Design (JAD) and prototyping will be addressed; these techniques were developed to keep the analysis effort at a minimum yet still effective. Traditional fact-gathering techniques must be understood before one can fully appreciate alternative approaches.

TRADITIONAL METHODS FOR DETERMINING REQUIREMENTS

Collection of information is at the core of systems analysis. At the outset, the systems analyst must collect information about the information systems that are currently in use. It is important to find out how users would like to improve the current systems and organizational operations with new or replacement information systems. One of the best ways to get this information is to talk to those directly or indirectly involved in the different parts of the organizations affected by the possible system changes. Another way is to gather copies of documentation relevant to current systems and business processes. This chapter presents traditional ways to get information directly from those who have the information needed: interviews and direct observation. It also discusses collecting documentation on the current system and organizational operation in the form of written procedures, forms, reports, and other hard copy. These traditional methods of collecting system requirements are listed in Table 5-2.

Interviewing and Listening

Interviewing is one of the primary ways analysts gather information about an information systems project. Early in a project, an analyst might spend a large amount of time interviewing people about their work, the information they use to do it, and the types of information processing that might supplement their work. Others are interviewed to understand organizational direction, policies, and expectations that managers have on the units they supervise. During interviewing, facts, opinions, and speculations are gathered, and body language, emotions, and other signs of what people want and how they assess current systems are observed.

Interviewing someone effectively can be done in many ways, and no one method is necessarily better than another. Some guidelines to keep in mind when interviewing are summarized in Table 5-3 and discussed next.

First, the systems analyst should prepare thoroughly before the interview. An appointment should be set up at a time and for a duration that is convenient for the interviewee. The general nature of the interview should be explained to the interviewee in advance. The interviewee can be asked to think about specific questions or issues or to review certain documentation to prepare for the interview. The interviewer should spend some time thinking about what needs to be learned and writing down questions. The interviewer should not assume that all possible questions can be anticipated though. The interview should be natural and, to some degree, spontaneous as it is discovered what expertise the interviewee brings to the session.

Table 5-2 Traditional Methods of Collecting System Requirements.

TRADITIONAL METHOD	ACTIVITIES INVOLVED
Interviews with individuals	Interview individuals informed about the operation and issues of the current system and the need for systems in future organizational activities.
Observations of workers	Observe workers at selected times to see how data are handled and what information people need to do their jobs.
Business documents	Study business documents to discover reported issues, policies, rules, and directions as well as concrete examples of the use of data and information in the organization

Table 5-3 Guidelines for Effective Interviewing.

GUIDELINES	WHAT IS INVOLVED
Plan the interview	Prepare the interviewee by making an appointment and explaining the purpose of the interview. Prepare a checklist, an agenda, and questions.
Be neutral	Avoid asking leading questions.
Listen and take notes	Give your undivided attention to the interviewee and take notes and/or tape record the interview (if permission is granted).
Review notes	Review your notes within 48 hours of the meeting. If you discover follow-up questions or need additional information, contact the interviewee.
Seek diverse views	Interview a wide range of people, including potential users and managers.

The systems analyst should prepare an interview guide or checklist so that it is clear in which sequence questions should be asked and how much time should be spent in each area of the interview. The checklist might include some probing questions to ask as follow-up if certain anticipated responses are received. To some degree, the interview guide can be integrated with the notes taken during the interview, as depicted in a sample guide in Figure 5.2. This same guide can serve as an outline for a summary of what is discovered during an interview.

Figure 5.2 A Typical Interview Guide

Interview Outline

Interviewee: *Name of person being interviewed*	Interviewer: *Name of person leading interview*
Location/Medium: *Office, conference room, or phone number*	Appointment Date: Start Time: End Time:
Objectives: *What data to collect* *On what to gain agreement* *What areas to explore*	Reminders: *Background/experience of interviewee* *Known opinions of interviewee*

Agenda:	Approximate Time:
Introduction	1 minute
Background on Project	2 minutes
Overview of Interview	
Topics to Be Covered	1 minute
Permission to Tape Record	
Topic 1 Questions	5 minutes
Topic 2 Questions	7 minutes
...	...
Summary of Major Points	2 minutes
Questions from Interviewee	5 minutes
Closing	1 minute

General Observations:
    Interviewee seemed busy—probably need to call in a few days for follow-up questions because he gave only short answers. PC was turned off—probably not a regular PC user.

Unresolved Issues, Topics Not Covered:
    He needs to look up sales figures from 2001. He raised the issue of how to handle returned goods, but we did not have time to discuss.

(continues on next page)

Figure 5.2 Continued.

Interviewee:	Date:
Questions:	Notes:

When to ask question, if conditional
Question number: 1
 	
    Have you used the current sales tracking system? If so, how often?
	Answer
	        Yes, I ask for a report on my product line weekly.
	
	Observations
	        Seemed anxious—may be overestimating usage frequency.

If yes, go to Question 2	

Question: 2
 	
    What do you like least about this system?
	Answer
	        Sales are shown in units, not dollars.
	
	Observations
	        System can show sales in dollars, but user does not know this.

The first page of the sample interview guide contains a general outline of the interview. Besides basic information on who is being interviewed and when, the analyst should list major objectives for the interview. These objectives typically cover the most important data needed, a list of issues on which agreement must be reached (e.g., content for certain system reports), and which areas need to be explored. Also included should be reminder notes on key information about the interviewee (e.g., job history, known positions taken on issues, and role with current system). This information helps the interview remain personal, shows that the analyst considers the interviewee important, and might assist in interpreting some answers later. Also included is an agenda with approximate time limits for different sections of the interview. The time limits do not need to be followed precisely, but the schedule helps make sure that all areas are covered during the time the interviewee is available. Space also is allotted for general observations that do not fit under specific questions and for notes taken during the interview about topics skipped or issues raised that could not be resolved.

On subsequent pages, specific questions can be listed. The sample form in Figure 5.2 includes space for taking notes on these questions. Because the interviewee might provide information that was not expected, the guide might not be followed in sequence. However, it is wise to check off questions that have been asked and to write reminders to return to or skip other questions as the interview takes place.

Choosing Interview Questions

Open-ended question
An interview question that has no prespecified answer.

The systems analyst needs to decide on the mix and sequence of open-ended and closed-ended questions to ask. Open-ended questions usually are used to probe for information when all possible responses cannot be anticipated or when the precise questions to ask are unknown. The person being interviewed is encouraged to talk about whatever interests him or her within the general bounds of the question. An example is: "What would you say is the best thing about the information system you currently use to do your job?" or "List the three most frequently used menu options." The analyst must react quickly to answers and determine whether or not any follow-up questions are needed for clarification or elaboration. Sometimes body language will suggest that a user has given an incomplete answer or is reluctant to provide certain information. This is where a follow-up question might result in more information. One advantage of open-ended questions is that previously unknown information can surface. The systems analyst can then continue exploring along unexpected lines of inquiry to reveal even more new information. Open-ended questions also often put the interviewees at ease because they are able to respond in their own words using their own structure. Open-ended questions give interviewees more of a sense of involvement and control in the interview. A major disadvantage of open-ended questions is the length of time it can take for the questions to be answered. They also can be difficult to summarize.

Closed-ended question
An interview question that asks respondents to choose from among a set of specified responses.

Closed-ended questions provide a range of answers from which the interviewee can choose. Here is an example: "Which of the following would you say is the one best thing about the information system you currently use to do your job?" (Pick only one.)

- Having easy access to all of the data you need.
- The system's response time.
- The ability to run the system concurrently with other applications.

Closed-ended questions work well when the major answers to questions that are well known. Another plus is that interviews based on closed-ended questions do not necessarily require a large time commitment; more topics can be covered. Closed-ended questions also can be an easy way to begin an interview and to determine which line of open-ended questions to pursue. An "other" option can be included to encourage the interviewee to add unexpected responses. A major disadvantage of closed-ended questions is that useful information that does not quite fit the defined answers might be overlooked as the respondent tries to make a choice instead of providing the best answer.

Closed-ended questions, like objective questions on an examination, can follow several forms, including these choices:

- True or false.
- Multiple choice (with only one response or selecting all relevant choices).
- Rating a response or idea on some scale, say from bad to good or strongly agree to strongly disagree. Each point on the scale should have a clear and consistent meaning to each person, and a neutral point usually is included in the middle of the scale.
- Ranking items in order of importance.

Interview Guidelines

First, with either open- or closed-ended questions, the interviewer should not phrase a question in a way that implies a right or wrong answer. Respondents must feel free to state their true opinions and perspectives, and trust that their ideas will be considered. The interviewer should avoid questions such as, "Should the system continue to provide the ability to override the default value, even though most users now do not like the feature?" because such wording predefines a socially acceptable answer.

Second, the analyst must listen carefully to what is being said. Careful notes should be taken or, if possible, the interview should be recorded on a tape recorder (with permission). The answers might contain extremely important information for the project. Also, this might be the only chance the analyst has to get information from this particular person. If the interviewer runs out of time and still needs more information from the person being interviewed, a follow-up interview can be requested.

Third, once the interview is over, the interviewer should go back to the office and key in the notes within 48 hours with a word-processing program such as Microsoft Word. For numerical data, a spreadsheet program such as Microsoft Excel can be used. If the interview was recorded, the recording can be used to verify notes. After 48 hours, the memory of the interview will fade quickly. While typing and organizing notes, the interviewer should write down any additional questions that might arise from lapses in the notes or ambiguous information. Facts should be separated from opinions and interpretations. A list should be made of unclear points that need to be clarified. The person can be contacted to get answers to these new questions. In addition, the phone call can be used as an opportunity to verify the accuracy of the notes. It is also wise to send a written copy of the notes to the interviewee to check them for accuracy. Finally, the interviewer should thank the person for his or her time. It is always possible that more information will be needed from the respondent later. If the interviewee will be a user of the system or is involved in some other way in the system's success, it is important to leave a good impression.

Fourth, the interviewer should be careful during the interview not to set expectations about the new or replacement system unless these features definitely will be part of the delivered system. The interviewee should know that the project includes many steps and that many people will have to be interviewed. Choices must be made from among many technically possible alternatives. Respondents should be made aware that their ideas will be considered carefully. However, due to the repetitive nature of the systems development process, it is premature for the analyst to say at this point exactly what the ultimate system will or will not do.

Fifth, a variety of perspectives should be sought from the interviews. Lots of different people should be interviewed: potential users of the system, users of other systems that might be affected by this new system, managers and superiors, information systems staff, and others. People can be encouraged to think about current problems and opportunities and what new information services might better serve the organization. The systems analyst wants to understand all possible perspectives so that later the information will be available on which to base a recommendation or design decision that everyone can accept.

Directly Observing Users

All the methods of collecting information that we have discussed involve getting people to recall and convey information they have about organizational processes and the information systems that support them. People, however, are not always reliable, even when they try to be and say what they think is the truth. As odd as it might sound, people often do not have a completely accurate appreciation of what they do or how they do it. This is especially true concerning infrequent events, issues from the past, or issues for which people have considerable passion. Because people cannot always be trusted to interpret and report their own actions reliably, what people tell the analyst can be supplemented by watching what they do in work situations.

For example, one possible view of how hypothetical managers do their jobs is that managers carefully plan their activities, work long and consistently on solving problems, and control the pace of their work. Managers might tell the interviewer that is how they spend their day. Several studies have shown, however, that a manager's day is punctuated by many, many interruptions. Managers work in a fragmented manner, focusing on a problem or a communication for only a short time before they are interrupted by phone calls or visits from subordinates and other managers. An information system designed to fit the work environment described by the hypothetical manager would not effectively support the actual work environment in which that manager finds himself or herself.

As another example, consider the difference between what other employees might tell the interviewer about how much they use electronic mail and how much electronic mail use the interviewer might discover through more objective means. Employees might say they are swamped with e-mail messages and spend a significant proportion of time responding to e-mail messages. However, if the interviewer were able to check electronic mail records, he or she might find that employees receive only three e-mail messages per day on average, and that the most messages a particular employee has ever received during one 8-hour period is 10. In this case, the analyst was able to obtain an accurate behavioral measure of how much e-mail this employee copes with without having to watch the employee read the e-mail.

The intent behind obtaining system records and direct observation is the same, however, and that is to obtain more firsthand and objective measures of employee interaction with information systems. In some cases, behavioral measures will reflect reality more accurately than what employees themselves believe. In other cases, the behavioral information will substantiate what employees have told the analyst directly. Although observation and obtaining objective measures are desirable ways to collect pertinent information, such methods are not always possible in real organizational settings. Thus, these methods are not totally unbiased, just as no one data-gathering method is unbiased.

For example, observation can cause people to change their normal operating behavior. Employees who know they are being observed might be nervous and make more mistakes than normal. On the other hand, employees under observation might follow exact procedures more carefully than they typically do. They might work faster or slower than normal. Because observation typically cannot be continuous, the interviewer receives only a snapshot image of the person or task being observed. Such a view might not include important events or activities. Due to time constraints, the analyst will observe for only a limited time, a limited number of people, and a limited number of sites. Observation yields only a small segment of data from a possibly vast variety of data sources. Exactly which people or sites to observe is a difficult selection problem. The analyst needs to pick typical and atypical people and sites and observe during normal and abnormal conditions and times to receive the richest possible data from observation.

Analyzing Procedures and Other Documents

As noted, interviewing people who use a system every day or who have an interest in a system is an effective way to gather information about current and future systems. Observing current system users is a more direct way of seeing how an existing system operates. However, interviewing and observing have limitations. Methods for determining system requirements can be enhanced by examining system and organizational documentation to discover more details about current systems and the organization they support.

We discuss several important types of documents that are useful in understanding system requirements, but our discussion is not necessarily exhaustive. In addition to the few specific documents we mention, some other documents are important to locate and consider. These include organizational mission statements, business plans, organization charts, business policy manuals, job descriptions, internal and external correspondence, and reports from prior organizational studies.

What can the analysis of documents tell the analyst about the requirements for a new system? In documents, information is available about the following:

- Problems with existing systems (e.g., missing information or redundant steps).
- Opportunities to meet new needs if only certain information or information processing were available (e.g., analysis of sales based on customer type).

- Organizational direction that can influence information system requirements (e.g., trying to link customers and suppliers more closely to the organization).
- Titles and names of key individuals who have an interest in relevant existing systems (e.g., the name of a sales manager who has led a study of buying behavior of key customers).
- Values of the organization or individuals who can help determine priorities for different capabilities desired by different users (e.g., maintaining market share even if it means lower short-term profits).
- Special information processing circumstances that occur irregularly and that might not be identified by any other requirements determination technique (e.g., special handling needed for a few large-volume customers and that requires use of customized customer ordering procedures).
- The reason why current systems are designed as they are, which can suggest features left out of current software that might now be feasible and desirable (e.g., data about a customer's purchase of a competitor's products that were not available when the current system was designed; these data now might be available from several sources).
- Data, rules for processing data, and principles by which the organization operates that must be enforced by the information system (e.g., each customer is assigned exactly one sales department staff member as a primary contact if the customer has any questions).

One type of useful document is a written work procedure for an individual or a work group. The procedure describes how a particular job or task is performed, including data and information used and created in the process of performing the job. For example, the procedure shown in Figure 5.3 includes data (a list of features and advantages, drawings, inventor name, and witness names) required to prepare an invention disclosure. It also indicates that besides the inventor, the vice president for research and the department head and dean must review the material, and that a witness is required for any filing of an invention disclosure. These insights clearly affect what data must be kept, to whom information must be sent, and the rules that govern valid forms.

Procedures are not trouble-free sources of information, however. Sometimes an analysis of several written procedures reveals a duplication of effort in two or more jobs. The analyst should call such duplication to the attention of management as an issue to be resolved before system design can proceed. That is, it might be necessary to redesign the organization before the redesign of an information system can achieve its full benefits. Another problem the analyst might encounter is a missing procedure. Again, it is not the analyst's job to create a document for a missing procedure—that is up to management. A third and common problem happens when the procedure is out of date. The analyst might realize this in an interview of the person responsible for performing the task described in the procedure. Once again, the decision to rewrite the procedure so that it matches reality is made by management, but the analyst might make suggestions based upon an understanding of the organization. A fourth problem often encountered is that the formal procedures might contradict information collected from interviews and observation about how the organization operates and what information is required. As in the other cases, resolution rests with management.

All of these problems illustrate the difference between formal systems and informal systems. A formal system is one an organization has documented; an informal system is the way in which the organization actually works. Informal systems develop because of inadequacies of formal procedures, individual work habits and preferences, and resistance to control. It is important to understand formal and informal systems because each provides insight into information requirements and what is necessary to convert from present to future systems.

Formal system
The official way a system works as described in organizational documentation.

Informal system
The way a system actually works.

Figure 5.3 Example of a Written Work Procedure for an Invention Disclosure

Guide for Preparation of Invention Disclosure
(See faculty and staff manuals for detailed patent policy and routing procedures.)

1. Disclose Only One Invention per Form.

2. Prepare Complete Disclosure.

   The disclosure of your invention is adequate for patent purposes *only* if it enables a person skilled in the art to understand the invention.

3. Consider the Following in Preparing a Complete Disclosure:

   a. All essential elements of the invention, their relationship to one another, and their mode of operation

   b. Equivalents that can be substituted for any elements

   c. List of features believed to be new

   d. Advantages this invention has over the prior art

   e. Whether the invention has been built and/or tested

4. Provide Appropriate Additional Material.

   Drawings and descriptive material should be provided as needed to clarify the disclosure. Each page of this material must be signed and dated by each inventor and properly witnessed. A copy of any current and/or planned publication relating to the invention should be included.

5. Indicate Prior Knowledge and Information.

   Pertinent publications, patents or previous devices, and related research or engineering activities should be identified.

6. Have Disclosure Witnessed.

   Persons other than co-inventors should serve as witnesses and should sign each sheet of the disclosure only after reading and understanding the disclosure.

7. Forward Original Plus One Copy (two copies if supported by grant/contract) to Vice President for Research via Department Head and Dean.

A second type of document useful to systems analysts is a business form, illustrated in Figure 5.4. Forms are used for all types of business functions, from recording an order to acknowledging the payment of a bill to indicating what goods have been shipped. Forms are important for understanding a system because they explicitly indicate what data flow in or out of a system. In the sample invoice form in Figure 5.4, space is provided for data such as the customer identification code, the "ship to" address, the quantity of items ordered, their descriptions, discounts, and unit prices.

A printed form may correspond to a computer display that the system will generate for someone to use to enter and maintain data or to display data for online

Figure 5.4
An Example of a
Business Form—An
Invoice Form for
QuickBooks, from
jnk.btobsource.com.
Reprinted by
permission

Source: http://jnk.
btobsource.com/NASApp/
enduser/products/
product_detail.jsp?
pc=13050M#.

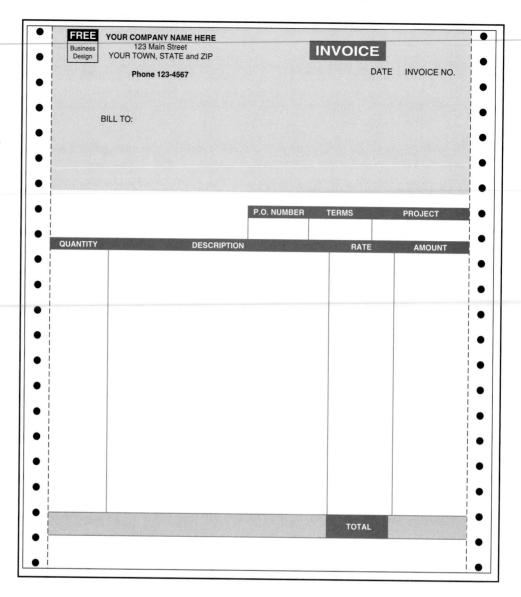

users. The most useful forms contain actual organizational data, as this allows the analyst to determine the data characteristics used by the application. The ways in which people use forms change over time, and data that were needed when a form was designed may no longer be required.

A third type of useful document is a report generated by current systems. As the primary output for some types of systems, a report enables the analyst to work backward from the information on the report to the data that must have been necessary to generate it. Figure 5.5 presents an example of a common financial accounting report, the consolidated balance sheet. Every number listed on the balance sheet is an aggregated amount, based on the accumulation of millions of individual business transactions. Such reports are analyzed to determine which data need to be captured over what time period and what manipulation of these raw data is necessary to produce each field on the report.

If the current system is computer-based, a fourth set of useful documents is those that describe the current information systems—how they were designed and how they work. Many different types of documents fit this description, including flowcharts, data dictionaries, and user manuals. An analyst who has access to such documents is fortunate because many in-house-developed information systems lack complete documentation.

Figure 5.5 An Example of a Report. An Accounting Balance Sheet Reprinted from www.corning.com (accessed September 28, 2005)

Source: Reprinted with permission of Corning Incorporated

Consolidated Balance Sheets	*Corning Incorporated and Subsidiary Companies*	
		December 31,
(In millions, except share and per share amounts)	**2004**	2003
Assets		
Current assets:		
Cash and cash equivalents	**$ 1,009**	$ 1,079
Short-term investments, at fair value	**872**	715
Total cash, cash equivalents and short-term investments	**1,881**	1,266
Trade accounts receivable, net of doubtful accounts and allowances - $30 and $38	**585**	525
Inventories (Note 5)	**535**	467
Deferred income taxes (Note 6)	**92**	242
Other current assets	**188**	194
Total current assets	**3,281**	2,694
Investments (Note 7)	**1,484**	1,045
Property, net of accumulated depreciation - $3,532 and $3,415 (Note 8)	**3,941**	3,620
Goodwill and other intangible assets, net (Note 9)	**398**	1,901
Deferred income taxes (Note 6)	**440**	1,225
Other assets	**166**	267
Total assets	**$ 9,710**	**$10,752**
Liabilities and Shareholders' Equity		
Current liabilities:		
Short-term borrowings, including current portion of long-term debt (Note 11)	**$ 478**	$ 146
Accounts payable	**682**	333
Other accrued liabilities (Note 10)	**1,176**	1,074
Total current liabilities	**2,336**	1,553
Long-term debt (Note 11)	**2,214**	2,668
Postretirement benefits other than pensions (Note 12)	**600**	619
Other liabilities (Note 10)	**715**	412
Total liabilities	**5,865**	5,252
Commitments and contingencies (Note 13)		
Minority interests	**29**	35
Shareholders' equity (Note 14):		
Preferred stock – Par value $100.00 per share: Shares authorized: 10 million		
Series C mandatory convertible perferred stock – Shares issued: 5.75 million;		
Shares outstanding: 637 thousand and 854 thousand	**64**	85
Common stock – Par value $0.50 per share; Shares authorized: 3.8 billion		
Shares issued: 1,424 million and 1,401 million	**712**	701
Additional paid-in capital	**10,363**	10,298
Accumulated deficit	**(7,309)**	(5,144)
Total shareholders' equity	**3,816**	5,464
Total liabilities and shareholders' equity	**$9,710**	**$10,752**

See accompanying notes to condensed statements.

Table 5-4 Comparison of Observation and Document Analysis.

CHARACTERISTIC	OBSERVATION	DOCUMENT ANALYSIS
Information richness	High (many channels)	Low (passive) and old
Time required	Can be extensive	Low to moderate
Expense	Can be high	Low to moderate
Chance for follow-up and probing	Good: Probing and clarification questions can be asked during or after observation	Limited: Probing is possible only if original author is available
Confidentiality	Observee is known to interviewer; observee may change behavior when observed	Depends on nature of document; does not change simply by being read
Involvement of subject	Interviewees may or may not be involved and committed depending on whether they know if they are being observed	None; no clear commitment
Potential audience	Limited numbers and limited time (snapshot) of each	Potentially biased by which documents were kept or because document not created for this purpose

Analysis of organizational documents and observation, along with interviewing, are the methods used most for gathering system requirements. Table 5-4 summarizes the comparative features of observation and analysis of organizational documents.

MODERN METHODS FOR DETERMINING SYSTEM REQUIREMENTS

Even though we called interviews, observation, and document analysis traditional methods for determining a system's requirements, all of these methods are still very much used by analysts to collect important information. Today, however, additional techniques are used to collect information about the current system, the organizational area requesting the new system, and what the new system should be like. This section presents three modern information-gathering techniques for analysis: Joint Application Design (JAD), prototyping, and techniques used in agile methodologies. All of these techniques can support effective information collection and structuring while reducing the amount of time required for analysis.

Joint Application Design

JAD started in the late 1970s at IBM as a means to bring together the key users, managers, and systems analysts involved in the analysis of a current system. Since the 1970s, JAD has spread throughout many companies and industries. For example, it is popular in the insurance industry. The primary purpose of using JAD in the analysis phase is to collect systems requirements simultaneously from the key people involved with the system. The result is an intense and structured but highly effective process. Having all the key people together in one place at one time allows analysts to see the areas of agreement and the areas of conflicts.

JAD sessions usually are conducted in a location away from where the people involved normally work. This is to keep participants away from as many distractions as possible so that they can concentrate on systems analysis. A JAD might last anywhere from 4 hours to an entire week and can consist of several sessions. Meeting with all these important people for more than a week of intense sessions allows the analyst the opportunity to resolve conflicts or at least to understand why a conflict might not be simple to resolve. A JAD employs thousands of dollars of corporate resources, the most expensive of which is the time of the people involved. Other expenses include the costs associated with flying people to a remote site, and putting them up in hotels and feeding them for several days.

The typical participants in a JAD include the following:

- *JAD session leader.* The JAD session leader organizes and runs the JAD. This person has been trained in group management and facilitation, as well as in systems analysis. The JAD leader sets the agenda and sees that it is met. He or she remains neutral on issues and does not contribute ideas or opinions, but rather concentrates on keeping the group on the agenda, resolving conflicts and disagreements, and soliciting all ideas.
- *Users.* The key users of the system under consideration are vital participants in a JAD. They are the only ones who clearly understand what it means to use the system on a daily basis.
- *Managers.* Managers of the work groups who use the system in question provide insight into new organizational directions, motivations for and organizational impacts of systems, and support for requirements determined during the JAD.
- *Sponsor.* As a major undertaking, due to its expense, a JAD must be sponsored by someone at a relatively high level in the company such as a vice president or chief executive officer. If the sponsor attends any sessions, it is usually only at the beginning or the end.
- *Systems analysts.* Members of the systems analysis team attend the JAD although their participation might be limited. Analysts are there to learn from users and managers, not to run or dominate the process.
- *Scribe.* The scribe takes notes during the JAD sessions, usually on a desktop PC or laptop.
- *IS staff.* Besides systems analysts, other IS staff such as programmers, database analysts, IS planners, and data center personnel might attend the session. Their purpose is to learn from the discussion and possibly to contribute their ideas on the technical feasibility of proposed ideas or on the technical limitations of current systems.

JAD sessions usually are held in special-purpose rooms where participants sit around horseshoe-shaped tables, as in Figure 5.6. These rooms typically are equipped with whiteboards (possibly electronic, with a printer to make copies of what is written on the board). Other audiovisual tools can be used, such as transparencies and overhead projectors, magnetic symbols that can be rearranged easily on a whiteboard, flip charts, and computer-generated displays. Flip chart paper typically is used for keeping track of issues that cannot be resolved during the JAD or for those issues requiring additional information that can be gathered during breaks in the proceedings. Computers can be used to create and display forms or report designs, or to diagram existing or replacement systems. In general, however, most JADs do not benefit much from computer support.

The end result of a completed JAD is a set of documents that detail the workings of the current system and the features of a replacement system. Depending on the exact purpose of the JAD, analysts may gain detailed information on what is desired of the replacement system.

Taking Part in a JAD

Imagine that you are a systems analyst taking part in your first JAD. What might participating in a JAD be like? Typically, JADs are held off-site, in comfortable conference facilities. On the first morning of the JAD, you and your fellow analysts walk into a room that looks much like the one depicted in Figure 5.6. The JAD facilitator is already there. She is finishing writing the day's agenda on a flip chart. The scribe is seated in a corner with a laptop, preparing to take notes on the day's activities. Users and managers begin to enter in groups and seat themselves around the U-shaped table. You and the other analysts review your notes describing what you have learned so far about the information system you are all there to discuss. The session leader opens the meeting with a welcome and a brief rundown of the agenda. The first day will be devoted to a general overview of the current system and major problems associated with it. The

Figure 5.6 A Typical Room Layout for a JAD Session

Source: Adapted from Wood & Silver, 1989.

next 2 days will be devoted to an analysis of current system screens. The last 2 days will be devoted to analysis of reports.

The session leader introduces the corporate sponsor, who talks about the organizational unit, the current system related to the systems analysis study, and the importance of upgrading the current system to meet changing business conditions. He leaves and the JAD session leader takes over. She yields the floor to the senior analyst, who begins a presentation on key problems with the systems that have been identified already. After the presentation, the session leader opens the discussion to the users and managers in the room.

After a few minutes of talk, a heated discussion begins between two users from different corporate locations. One user, who represents the office that served as the model for the original systems design, argues that the system's perceived lack of flexibility is really an asset, not a problem. The other user, who represents an office that was part of another company before a merger, argues that the current system is so inflexible as to be virtually unusable. The session leader intervenes and tries to help the users isolate particular aspects of the system that might contribute to the system's perceived lack of flexibility.

Questions arise about the intent of the original developers. The session leader asks the analysis team about their impressions of the original system design. Because these questions cannot be answered during this meeting, as none of the original designers are present nor are the original design documents readily available, the session leader assigns the question about intent to the "to-do" list. This becomes the first question on a flip chart sheet of to-do items, and the session leader gives you the assignment of finding out about the intent of the original designers. She writes your name next to the to-do item on the list and continues with the session. Before the end of the JAD, you must get an answer to this question.

The JAD will continue like this for its duration. Analysts will make presentations, help lead discussions of form and report design, answer questions from users and managers, and take notes on what is being said. After each meeting, the analysis team will meet, usually informally, to discuss what has occurred that day and to consolidate what they have learned. Users will continue to contribute during the meetings, and the session leader will facilitate, intervening in conflicts, seeing that the group follows the agenda. When the JAD is over, the session leader and her assistants must prepare a report that documents the findings in the JAD and circulate it among users and analysts.

Using Prototyping during Requirements Determination

Prototyping is a repetitive process in which analysts and users build a rudimentary version of an information system based on user feedback (Figure 5.7). In this section, we see how prototyping can augment the requirements determination process.

To establish requirements for prototyping, the analyst still has to interview users and collect documentation. Prototyping, however, allows the analyst to convert basic requirements into a working, though limited, version of the desired information system quickly. The user then views and tests the prototype. Typically, seeing verbal descriptions of requirements converted into a physical system prompts the user to modify existing requirements and generate new ones. For example, in the initial interviews, users might have said they wanted all relevant utility billing information on a single computer display form, such as the client's name and address, the service record, and payment history. Once the same users see how crowded and confusing such a design would be in the prototype, they might change their minds and instead ask for the information to be organized on several screens but with easy transitions from one screen to another. They also might be reminded of some important requirements (data, calculations, etc.) that had not surfaced during the initial interviews.

The analyst would then redesign the prototype to incorporate the suggested changes. Once modified, users would again view and test the prototype. Once again, the analyst would incorporate their suggestions for change. Through such a repetitive process, the chances are good that the analyst will be able to better capture a system's requirements. The goal with using prototyping to support requirements determination is to develop concrete specifications for the ultimate system, not to build the ultimate system.

Figure 5.7
The Prototyping
Method

Source: Copyright © 1992 by the Management Information Systems Research Center (MISRC) of the University of Minnesota and the Society of Information Management (SIM). Reprinted by permission.

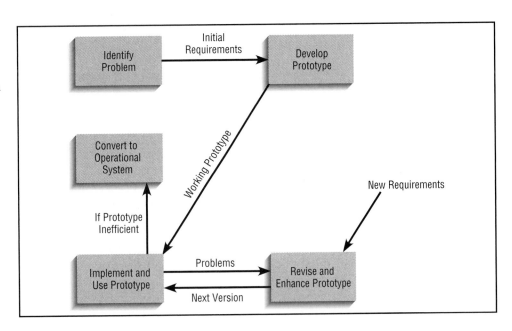

Prototyping is most useful for requirements determination when:

- User requirements are not clear or well understood, which is often the case for totally new systems or systems that support decision making.
- One or a few users and other stakeholders are involved with the system.
- Possible designs are complex and require concrete form to evaluate fully.
- Communication problems have existed in the past between users and analysts, and both parties want to be sure that system requirements are as specific as possible.
- Tools (such as form and report generators) and data are readily available to build working systems rapidly.

Prototyping also has some drawbacks as a tool for requirements determination. These drawbacks include:

- A tendency to avoid creating formal documentation of system requirements, which can then make the system more difficult to develop into a fully working system.
- Prototypes can become idiosyncratic to the initial user and difficult to diffuse or adapt to other potential users.
- Prototypes are often built as stand-alone systems, thus ignoring issues of sharing data and interactions with other existing systems.
- Checks in the SDC are bypassed so that some more subtle, but still important, system requirements might be forgotten (e.g., security, some data entry controls, or standardization of data across systems).

Using Agile Methodologies during Requirements Determination

New methods and techniques to determine the requirements for a system are constantly being developed. Two more requirements determination techniques used in agile methodologies are presented in this section. The first is approach is a JAD-like process called Agile Usage-Centered Design. The second technique is the Planning Game, which was developed as part of eXtreme Programming.

Agile Usage-Centered Design

Continual user involvement in systems development is an excellent way to ensure that requirements are captured accurately and immediately implemented in system design. However, such constant interaction works best when the development team is small. Also, it is not always possible to have continual access to users for the duration of a development project. To address these issues, agile developers have come up with techniques for effectively involving users in the requirements determination process. One such method is called Agile Usage-Centered Design, originally developed by Larry Constantine (Constantine, 2002) and adapted for agile methodologies by Jeff Patton (Patton, 2002). Patton describes the process in nine steps, which we have adapted and presented as eight steps in Table 5-5.

Notice how similar the overall process is to a JAD meeting. All of the experts are gathered together and work with the help of the facilitator. What's unique about the Agile Usage-Centered Design is the process that supports it, with a focus on user roles, user goals, and the tasks necessary to achieve those goals. Then tasks are grouped and turned into paper-and-pencil prototypes before the meeting is over. Requirements captured from users and developers are captured as prototyped system screens. Patton (2002) believes the two most effective aspects of this approach are the venting session, which lets everyone get their complaints out in the open, and the use of 3x5 cards, which serve as very effective communication tools. As with any analysis and design process or technique, however, Agile Usage-Centered Design will not work for every project or every company.

Table 5-5 The Steps in the Agile Usage-Centered Design Method for Requirements Determination.

1) Gather a group of people, including analysts, users, programmers, and testing staff, and sequester them in a room to collaborate on this design. Include a facilitator who knows this process.

2) Give everyone a chance to vent about the current system and to talk about the features everyone wants in the new system. Record all of the complaints and suggestions for change on white boards or flip charts for everyone to see.

3) Determine what the most important user roles would be. Determine who will be using the system and what their goals for using the system. Write the roles on 3x5 cards. Sort the cards so that similar roles are close to each other. Patton (2002) calls this a role model.

4) Determine what tasks user roles will have to complete in order to achieve their goals. Write these down on 3x5 cards. Order tasks by importance and then by frequency. Place the cards together based on how similar the tasks are to each other. Patton calls this a task model.

5) Task cards will be clumped together on the table based on their similarity. Grab a clump of cards. This is called an interaction context.

6) For each task card in the interaction context, write a description of the task, directly on the task card. List the steps that are necessary to complete the task. Keep the descriptions conversational to make them easy to read. Simplify.

7) Treat each clump as a tentative set of tasks to be supported by a single aspect of the user interface, such as a screen, page or dialog, and create a paper-and-pencil prototype for that part of the interface. Show the basic size and placement of the screen components.

8) Take on a user role and step through each task in the interation context as modeled in the paper-and-pencil prototype. Make sure the user role can achieve its goals by using the prototype. Refine the prototype accordingly.

The Planning Game from eXtreme Programming

eXtreme Programming was mentioned in Chapter 1 as one of the best-known agile methodologies. It is an approach to software development put together by Kent Beck (2000). eXtreme Programming is distinguished by its short cycles, its incremental planning approach, its focus on automated tests written by programmers and customers to monitor the process of development, and its reliance on an evolutionary approach to development that lasts throughout the lifetime of the system. One of the key emphases of eXtreme Programming is its use of two-person programming teams and having a customer on-site during the development process. The relevant parts of eXtreme Programming that relate to requirements determination are (1) how planning, analysis, design, and construction are all fused together into a single phase of activity; and (2) its unique way of capturing and presenting system requirements and design specifications. All phases of the life cycle converge together into a series of activities based on the basic processes of coding, testing, listening, and designing.

What is of interest here, however, is the way requirements and specifications are dealt with. Both of these activities take place in what Beck calls the "Planning Game." The Planning Game is really just a stylized approach to development that seeks to maximize fruitful interaction between those who need a new system and those who build it. The players in the Planning Game, then, are Business and Development. Business is the customer and is ideally represented by someone who knows the processes to be supported by the system being developed. Development is represented by those actually designing and constructing the system. The game pieces are what Beck calls "Story Cards." These cards are created by Business and contain a description of a procedure or feature to be included in the system. Each card is dated and numbered and has space on it for tracking its status throughout the development effort.

The Planning Game has three phases: exploration, commitment, and steering (Figure 5.8). In exploration, Business creates a Story Card for something it wants the new system to do. Development responds with an estimation of how long it would take to implement the procedure. At this point, it may make sense to split a Story Card into multiple Story Cards, as the scope of features and procedures becomes more clear during discussion. In the commitment phase, Business sorts Story Cards into three stacks: one for essential features, one for features that are not essential but would still add value, and one for features that would be nice to have. Development then sorts Story Cards according to risk, based on how well they can estimate the time needed to develop each feature. Business then selects the cards that will be included in the next release of the product. In the final phase, steering, Business has a chance to see how the

Figure 5.8 eXtreme Programming's Planning Game

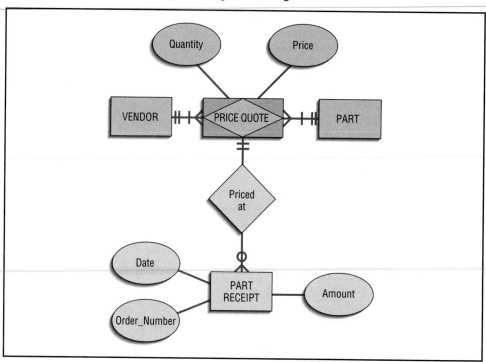

development process is progressing and to work with Development to adjust the plan accordingly. Steering can take place as often as once every three weeks.

The Planning Game between Business and Development is followed by the Iteration Planning Game, played only by programmers. Instead of Story Cards, programmers write Task Cards, which are based on Story Cards. Typically, several Task Cards are generated for each Story Card. The Iteration Planning Game has the same three phases as the Planning Game: exploration, commitment, and steering. During exploration, programmers convert Story Cards into Task Cards. During commitment, they accept responsibility for tasks and balance their workloads. During steering, the programmers write the code for the feature, test it, and if it works, they integrate the feature into the product being developed. The Iteration Planning Game takes place during the time intervals between steering phase meetings in the Planning Game.

You can see how the Planning Game is similar in some ways to Agile Usage-Centered Design. Both rely on participation by users, rely on cards as communication devices, and focus on tasks the system being designed is supposed to perform. Although these approaches differ from some of the more traditional ways of determining requirements, such as interviews and prototyping, many of the core principles are the same. Customers, or users, remain the source for what the system is supposed to do. Requirements are still captured and negotiated. The overall process is still documented, although the extent and formality of the documentation may differ. Given the way requirements are identified and recorded and broken down from stories to tasks, design specifications can easily incorporate the characteristics of quality requirements: completeness, consistency, modifiability, and traceability.

PVF WEBSTORE: DETERMINING SYSTEM REQUIREMENTS

Determining system requirements for an Internet-based electronic commerce application is no different than the process followed for other applications. Chapter 4 told how Pine Valley Furniture's management began the WebStore project to sell furniture products over the Internet. Here we examine the process followed by PVF to determine system requirements and highlight some of the issues and capabilities that should be considered when developing an Internet-based application.

Determining System Requirements for Pine Valley Furniture's WebStore

To collect system requirements as quickly as possible, Jim Woo and Jackie Judson decided to hold a 3-day JAD session. In order to get the most out of these sessions, they invited a broad range of people, including representatives from Sales and Marketing, Operations, and Information Systems. Additionally, they asked an experienced JAD facilitator, Cheri Morris, to conduct the session. Together with Cheri, Jim and Jackie developed an ambitious and detailed agenda for the session. Their goal was to collect requirements on the following items:

- System layout and navigation characteristics.
- WebStore and site management system capabilities.
- Customer and inventory information.
- System prototype evolution.

The remainder of this section briefly highlights the outcomes of the JAD session.

System Layout and Navigation Characteristics

As part of the process of preparing for the JAD session, all participants were asked to visit several established retail Web sites, including www.amazon.com, www.landsend.com, www.sony.com, and www.pier1.com. At the JAD session, participants were asked to identify characteristics of these sites that they found appealing and those they found cumbersome; this allowed participants to identify and discuss those features that they wanted the WebStore to possess. The outcomes of this activity are summarized in Table 5-6.

WebStore and Site Management System Capabilities

After agreeing to the general layout and navigational characteristics of the WebStore, the session participants then turned their focus to the basic system capabilities. To assist in this process, systems analysts from the Information Systems Department developed a draft skeleton of the WebStore based on the types of screens and capabilities of popular retail Web sites. For example, many retail Web sites have a "shopping cart" feature that allows customers to accumulate multiple items before checking out rather than buying a single item at a time. After some discussion, the participants agreed that the system structure shown in Table 5-7 would form the foundation for the WebStore system.

In addition to the WebStore capabilities, members of the Sales and Marketing Department described several reports that would be necessary to manage customer accounts and sales transactions effectively. In addition, the department wants to be able to conduct detailed analyses of site visitors, sales tracking, and so on. Members of the Operations Department expressed a need to update the product catalog easily. These collective requests and activities were organized into a system design structure, called the Site Management System, summarized in Table 5-7. The structures of

Table 5-6
Desired Layout and Navigation Feature of WebStore.

LAYOUT AND DESIGN
Navigation menu and logo placement should remain consistent throughout the entire site (this allows users to maintain familiarity while using the site and minimizes users who get "lost" in the site).
Graphics should be lightweight to allow for quick page display.
Text should be used over graphics whenever possible.
NAVIGATION
Any section of the store should be accessible from any other section via the navigation menu.
Users should always be aware of what section they are currently in.

Table 5-7 System Structure of the WebStore and Site Management Systems.

WEBSTORE SYSTEM	SITE MANAGEMENT SYSTEM
Main page	User profile manager
Product line (catalog)	Order maintenance manager
• Desks	Content (catalog) manager
• Chairs	Reports
• Tables	• Total hits
• File cabinets	• Most frequent page views
Shopping cart	• Users/time of day
Checkout	• Users/day of week
Account profile	• Shoppers not purchasing (used shopping cart—did not check out)
Order status/history	• Feedback analysis
Customer comments	
Company information	
Feedback	
Contact information	

the WebStore and Site Management Systems will be given to the Information Systems Department as the baseline for further analysis and design activities.

Customer and Inventory Information

The WebStore will be designed to support the furniture purchases of three distinct types of customers:

- Corporate customers.
- Home office customers.
- Student customers.

To track the sales to these different types of customers effectively, the system must capture and store distinct information. Table 5-8 summarizes this information for each customer type identified during the JAD session. Orders reflect the range of product information that must be specified to execute a sales transaction. Thus, in addition to capturing the customer information, product and sales data also must be captured and stored; Table 5-8 lists the results of this analysis.

System Prototype Evolution

As a final activity, the JAD participants discussed, along with extensive input from the Information Systems staff, how the system implementation should evolve. After completing analysis and design activities, they agreed that the system implementation should progress in three main stages so that requirements changes could be identified and implemented more easily. Table 5-9 summarizes these stages and the functionality incorporated at each one.

Table 5-8 Customer and Inventory Information for WebStore.

CORPORATE CUSTOMER	HOME OFFICE CUSTOMER	STUDENT CUSTOMER	INVENTORY INFORMATION
Company name	Name	Name	SKU
Company address	Doing business as (company name)		School name
Company phone		Address	Description
Company fax	Address	Phone	Finished product size
Company preferred	Phone	E-mail	Finished product weight
shipping method	Fax		Available materials
Buyer name	E-mail		Available colors
Buyer phone			Price
Buyer e-mail			Lead time

Table 5-9
Stages of System
Implementation of
WebStore.

STAGE 1 (BASIC FUNCTIONALITY)
Simple catalog navigation; 2 products per section—limited attribute set.
25 sample users.
Simulated credit card transaction.
Full shopping cart functionality.
STAGE 2 (LOOK AND FEEL)
Full product attribute set and media (images, video)—commonly referred to as "product data catalog."
Full site layout.
Simulated integration with Purchasing Fulfillment and Customer Tracking systems.
STAGE 3 (STAGING/PREPRODUCTION)
Full integration with Purchasing Fulfillment and Customer Tracking systems.
Full credit card processing integration.
Full product data catalog.

At the conclusion of the JAD session, all the participants felt good about the progress that had been made and the clear requirements that had been identified. With these requirements in hand, Jim and the Information Systems staff could begin to turn these lists of requirements into formal analysis and design specifications. To show how information flows through the WebStore, Jim and his staff will produce use-case diagrams (Chapter 6). To show a conceptual model of the data used within WebStore, they will generate class diagrams (Chapter 7).

KEY POINTS REVIEW

The three parts to the systems analysis phase of the systems development life cycle are: determining requirements, structuring requirements, and selecting the best alternative design strategy. This chapter focuses on requirements determination, the gathering of information about current systems, and the need for replacement systems. Chapters 6 through 9 address techniques for structuring the information discovered during requirements determination. Chapter 10 closes Part III of the book by explaining how analysts generate alternative design strategies for replacement systems and choose the best one.

1. **Describe options for designing and conducting interviews, and develop a plan for conducting an interview to determine system requirements.**
   Interviews can involve open-ended and closed-ended questions. In either case, the analyst must be precise in formulating a question in order to avoid ambiguity and to ensure a proper response. Making a list of questions is just one activity necessary to prepare for an interview. The interviewer also must create a general interview guide (see Figure 5.2) and schedule the interview.

2. **Explain the advantages and pitfalls of observing workers and analyzing business documents to determine system requirements.**
   During observation, the systems analyst must try not to intrude or interfere with normal business activities so that the people being observed do not modify their activities from normal processes. Observation can be expensive because it is so labor intensive. Analyzing documents typically is much less expensive, but any insights gained will be limited to what is available, based on the reader's interpretation. Often the creator of the document is not there to answer questions.

3. **Describe how to help plan and participate in a Joint Application Design session.**
   Joint Application Design (JAD) begins with the idea of the group interview and adds structure and a JAD session leader to it. Typical JAD participants include the session leader, a scribe, key users, managers, a sponsor, systems analysts, and IS staff members. Many of these roles are very specialized, and the session leader will have the primary responsibility for planning a JAD. Everyone who participates helps plan the JAD by identifying key issues

to be examined during the meetings. JAD sessions usually are held off-site and may last as long as one week.

4. **Explain how prototyping can be used during requirements determination.**

   Information systems can support requirements determination with prototyping. As part of the prototyping process, users and analysts work closely together to determine requirements that the analyst then builds into a model. The analyst and user then work together on revising the model until it is close to what the user desires. Through such a repetitive process, the chances are good that the analyst will be able to better capture a system's requirements. The goal with using prototyping to support requirements determination is to develop concrete specifications for the ultimate system, not to build the ultimate system.

5. **Describe agile approaches to requirements determination.**

   Agile requirements determination techniques are another contemporary approach to figuring out what a new or improved system is supposed to do. Agile Usage-Centered Design and the Planning Game rely on novel interactions between users and developers to uncover basic tasks and features the new system should include.

6. **Explain the appropriate methods that can be used to elicit system requirements.**

   For requirements determination, the traditional sources of information about a system include interviews, observation, procedures, forms, and other useful documents. Often many or even all of these sources are used to gather perspectives on the adequacy of current systems and the requirements for replacement systems. Each form of information collection has its advantages and disadvantages, which were summarized in Table 5-4. Selecting the methods to use depends on the need for rich or thorough information, the time and budget available, the need to probe deeper once initial information is collected, the need for confidentiality for those providing assessments of system requirements, the desire to get people involved and committed to a project, and the potential audience from which requirements should be collected.

KEY TERMS CHECKPOINT

Here are the key terms from the chapter. The page where each term is first explained is in parentheses after the term.

a. Closed-ended question (p. 137)
b. Formal system (p. 140)
c. Informal system (p. 140)
d. JAD session leader (p. 145)
e. Open-ended question (p. 137)
f. Scribe (p. 145)

Match each of the key terms above with the definition that best fits it.

1. The person who makes detailed notes of the happenings at a Joint Application Design session.
2. The way a system actually works.
3. The official way a system works as described in organizational documentation.
4. An interview question that asks respondents to choose from among a set of specified responses.
5. An interview question that has no prespecified answer.
6. The trained individual who plans and leads Joint Application Design sessions.

REVIEW QUESTIONS

1. Describe systems analysis and the major activities that occur during this phase of the systems development life cycle.
2. What are some useful character traits for an analyst involved in requirements determination?
3. Describe four traditional techniques for collecting information during analysis. When might one be better than another?
4. What are the general guidelines for conducting interviews?
5. What are the general guidelines for collecting data through observing workers?
6. What are the general guidelines for collecting data through analyzing documents?
7. Compare collecting information through observation and through document analysis. Describe a hypothetical situation in which each of these methods would be an effective way to collect information system requirements.
8. What is JAD? How is it better than traditional information-gathering techniques? What are its weaknesses?
9. Describe how prototyping can be used during requirements determination. How is it better or worse than traditional methods?
10. Explain the techniques for requirements determination used in some of the agile methodologies. How do they differ from traditional techniques such as interviewing and observing?

1. One of the potential problems (mentioned in this chapter) with gathering information requirements by observing potential system users is that people might change their behavior when observed. What could you do to overcome this potential confounding factor in accurately determining information requirements?

2. Summarize the problems with the reliability and usefulness of analyzing business documents as a method for gathering information requirements. How could you cope with these problems to use business documents effectively as a source of insights on system requirements?

3. Suppose you were asked to lead a JAD session. List 10 guidelines you would follow in playing the proper role of a JAD session leader.

4. Prepare a plan, similar to Figure 5.2, for an interview with your academic adviser to determine which courses you should take to develop the skills you need to be hired as a programmer/analyst.

5. Write at least three closed-ended questions to use in an interview of users of a word processing package in order to develop ideas for the next version of the package. Test these questions by asking a friend to answer them; then interview your friend to determine why she responded as she did. From this interview, determine if she misunderstood any of your questions and, if so, rewrite the questions to be less ambiguous.

6. Figure 5.2 shows part of a guide for an interview. How might an interview guide differ when a group interview is to be conducted?

7. JADs are powerful ways to collect system requirements, but special problems arise during group requirements collection sessions. Summarize these special interviewing and group problems, and suggest ways that you, as a group facilitator, might deal with them.

DISCUSSION QUESTIONS

1. All of the methods of data collection discussed in this chapter take a lot of time. What are some ways analysts can still collect the information they need for systems analysis but also save time? What methods can you think of that would improve upon traditional and newer techniques?

2. Some of the key problems with information systems that show up later in the systems development life cycle can be traced back to inadequate work during requirements determination. How might this be avoided?

3. Survey the literature on JAD in the academic and popular press and determine the "state of the art." How is JAD being used to help determine system requirements? Is using JAD for this process beneficial? Why or why not? Present your analysis to the IS manager at your workplace or at your university. Does your analysis of JAD fit with his or her perception? Why or why not? Is he or she currently using JAD, or a JAD-like method, for determining system requirements? Why or why not?

CASE PROBLEMS

Pine Valley Furniture

Jackie Judson, vice president of marketing, and Jim Woo, a senior systems analyst, have been involved with Pine Valley Furniture's Customer Tracking System since the beginning of the project. After receiving project approval from the Systems Priority Board, Jim and his project development team turned their attention toward analyzing the Customer Tracking System.

During a Wednesday afternoon meeting, Jim and his project team members decide to utilize several requirements determination methods. Because the Customer Tracking System will facilitate the tracking of customer purchasing activity and help identify sales trends, various levels of end users will benefit from the new system.

Therefore, the project team believes it is necessary to collect requirements from these potential end users. The project team will use interviews, observations, and JAD sessions as data-gathering tools.

Jim assigns you the task of interviewing Stacie Walker, a middle manager in the marketing department; Pauline McBride, a sales representative; and Tom Percy, assistant vice president of marketing. Tom is responsible for preparing the sales forecasts. In addition, Jim assigns Pete Polovich, a project team member, the task of organizing the upcoming JAD sessions.

a. Because this is Pete Polovich's first time organizing a JAD session, he would like to locate additional information about organizing and conducting a JAD session. Visit one of the Web sites recommended in the textbook or locate a site on your own. After visiting this site, provide Pete with several recommendations for conducting and organizing a JAD session.

b. When conducting your interviews, what guidelines should you follow?

c. As part of the requirements determination process, what business documents should be reviewed?

d. Is prototyping an appropriate requirements determination method for this project?

Hoosier Burger

Juan Rodriquez has assigned you the task of requirements determination for the Hoosier Burger project. You are looking forward to this opportunity because it will allow you to meet and interact with Hoosier Burger employees. Besides interviewing Bob and Thelma Mellankamp, you decide to collect information from Hoosier Burger's servers, cooks, and customers.

Mr. Rodriquez suggests that you formally interview Bob and Thelma Mellankamp and perhaps observe them performing their daily management tasks. You decide that the best way to collect requirements from the servers and cooks is to interview and observe them. You realize that discussing the order-taking process with Hoosier Burger employees and then observing them in action will provide you with a better idea of where potential system improvements can be made. You also decide to interview some of Hoosier Burger customers.

a. What types of questions would you ask customers? Prepare five questions that you would ask.

b. What types of questions would you ask the servers? What types of questions would you ask the cooks? Prepare five questions that you would ask each group.

c. What types of documents are you likely to obtain for further study? What types of documents will most likely not be available? Why?

d. What modern requirements determination methods are appropriate for this project?

Clothing Shack

The Clothing Shack is an online retailer of men's, women's, and children's clothing. The company has been in business for 4 years and makes a modest profit from its online sales. However, in an effort to compete successfully against online retailing heavyweights, the Clothing Shack's marketing director, Makaya O'Neil, has determined that the Clothing Shack's marketing information systems need improvement.

Ms. O'Neil believes that the Clothing Shack should begin sending out catalogs to its customers, keep better track of its customers' buying habits, perform target marketing, and provide a more personalized shopping experience for its customers. Several months ago, Ms. O'Neil submitted a Systems Service Request to the Clothing Shack's steering committee. The committee unanimously approved this project. You were assigned to the project at that time and have since helped your project team successfully complete the project initiation and planning phase. Your team is now ready to move into the analysis phase and begin identifying requirements for the new system.

a. Whom would you interview? Why?

b. What requirements determination methods are appropriate for this project?

c. Based on the answers provided for part b, which requirements determination methods are appropriate for the individuals identified in part a?

d. Identify the requirements determination deliverables that will likely result from this project.

CASE: BROADWAY ENTERTAINMENT COMPANY, INC.

Determining Requirements for the Web-Based Customer Relationship Management System

Case Introduction

Carrie Douglass, manager of the Broadway Entertainment Company store in Centerville, Ohio, was pleased when the computer information system (CIS) students at St. Claire Community College accepted her request to design a customer information system. The students saw the development of this system as a unique opportunity. This system deals with one of the hottest topics in business today—customer relationship management—and is a simple form of one of the most active areas of information systems development—electronic commerce. Many of the CIS students wanted to work on this project, but Professor Tann limits each team to four members. Professor Tann selected

a team that included Tracey Wesley, John Whitman, Missi Davies, and Aaron Sharp to work on the BEC project. The BEC student team had never worked together before; in fact, the members did not know each other. This is not uncommon at St. Claire, because many students attend part-time and take classes around work and family obligations. Also, none of the team members had ever worked in a store like those operated by BEC, although all of them were regular BEC customers. Tracey, John, and Missi have children and, hence, have some personal interest in an information system such as Carrie has proposed. Professor Tann selected Tracey, John, Missi, and Aaron, in part, for their diversity. Tracey is a full-time COBOL computer programmer, who spent several busy years working on Y2K conversions for the local electric utility company. John works full-time for the Dayton Public Schools as a computer applications trainer. Missi wants to return to the workforce after her first child enters first grade; Missi worked in customer service at a local department store before her 6-year break from working outside the home. Aaron recently graduated from the local high school tech prep program and began taking CIS classes at St. Claire while in this high school program. Aaron was in charge of the Web site for his high school and has done Web site consulting with several small businesses in the Dayton area. Missi and Aaron are full-time St. Claire students.

Getting Started on Requirements Determination

The first step for the student team was to meet Carrie at a project kickoff meeting (see BEC Figure 5.1). BEC stores do not have a meeting room, so the team visited Carrie's

BEC Figure 5.1 Interview Outline for Initial Interview with Carrie Douglass

Interview Outline	
Interviewee: *Carrie Douglass* *Manager, BEC Store OH-84* *Centerville, Ohio*	**Interviewers:** *Missi Davies* *Aaron Sharp* *Tracey Wesley* *John Whitman*
Location/Medium: *Centerville BEC store* *and nearby restaurant*	**Appointment Date:** Start Time: *3:00* P.M. End Time: *4:30* P.M.
Objectives: *Develop rapport with client* *Obtain client's orientation to project*	**Reminders:** *Show enthusiasm for project* *Pay for food and beverages*

Agenda:
Introduce one another
Tour store
Go to restaurant and order food/drinks
Explain course requirements and systems
  development methodology
Describe team member backgrounds/goals
Have client explain her background
Discuss updates to SSR
  Ask for new ideas
  Ask for client concerns
Identify business and personal client goals
Ask client about project expectations
  Discover if employees know about it
  Ask about letter to employees
Request computer system description
Summarize meeting and set follow-up time
	Approximate Time:
	1 minute
	10 minutes
	10 minutes
	10 minutes
	
	10 minutes
	10 minutes
	
	10 minutes
	10 minutes
	5 minutes
	5 minutes
	2 minutes
	1 minute
	1 minute
	5 minutes

General Observations:	
Notes on Questions:	

store for a tour and to meet a few store employees, and then the team and Carrie got a table at a nearby restaurant for their discussion. The team shared with Carrie information about their project course requirements, including a tentative schedule of when the team was expected to submit interim reports to Professor Tann. These reports document the results at the end of inception, elaboration, construction, and transition project phases, and possibly at other key milestones pertinent to each project. Each team member explained his or her background and skills, and stated personal goals for the project. Carrie explained her background. The team members were surprised to discover that Carrie had only recently graduated from St. Claire, and they felt they had found a kindred spirit for a project sponsor.

This preliminary meeting at the start of the project was a transition meeting from the project initiation and planning phase to the analysis phase. The Systems Service Request (see BEC Figure 4.2 at the end of Chapter 4) provided the team with a basic background. Before developing a plan for the detailed steps of the analysis phase, the team wanted to determine whether anything had changed in Carrie's mind since she submitted the request.

Carrie, not too surprisingly, had been busy since she submitted the request and had only a few new ideas. First, Carrie had become even more excited about the system she proposed. She explained that after the project started, she probably would generate new ideas every day. The team explained that they planned to use a systems development method that, to some extent, allowed evolutionary development of requirements. Carrie would see a prototype of her system at multiple intermediate points in the project, at which time she could react, suggest improvements, and elaborate her expectations for the next few features to be developed. The object-oriented approach they would use allows some revision of previous features as new ones are incrementally included; however, revisions mean extra work, and less total progress might be accomplished if many revisions are requested. Second, Carrie raised a concern about what would happen once the course was over and an initial system was built. How would she get any further help? The team suggested that it would consider how follow-up might be handled. Missi offered the option that if Carrie thought the final product of the project was good enough, it might be time to involve BEC corporate IS people near the end of the project in a handoff meeting. Carrie suggested that this would be an alternative to readdress later in the project.

Third, Carrie asked how the team would interact with her during the project. The team responded by saying that they would provide to Carrie in the next 2 weeks a detailed schedule for the first phase of the project (called inception) and a general idea of subsequent steps. Along with this schedule would be a statement of when face-to-face review meetings would take place, the nature of written status reports, and other elements of a communication plan for the project. Finally, Carrie had one new idea about the requirements for the system. She suggested that a useful feature would be a page that would change weekly with comments from a store employee concerning his or her favorite picks for the week in several categories: adventure, mystery, documentary, children's, and so on. Carrie emphasized that she wanted to provide these comments from her own employees, not from outside sources that provide links to outside movie and music review Web sites.

Conducting Requirements Determination

The St. Claire team of students was almost ready to develop a detailed plan for the inception phase and a general plan for the whole project. Carrie's comments had been helpful; however, they had a few more questions they needed to ask to help them determine how to conduct the requirements determination portion of the analysis phase. First, they asked Carrie what business goals she had for herself and her store. Carrie explained that each BEC store had three main goals: (1) to increase dollar income volume by at least 1.5 percent each month, (2) to increase profit by at least 1 percent each month, and (3) to maintain customer overall satisfaction above 95 percent. The store manager receives bonus pay for achieving these objectives. Customer satisfaction is measured monthly by random telephone calls placed by an independent market research firm. Samples of customers from each store and in each area where a BEC store is located are contacted and asked to answer a list of 10 questions about their experience at BEC or competing stores. Personally, Carrie wants to perform as an above-average store manager during her first year, which means that she expects to clearly beat the goals given to her by BEC. She also wants to be viewed as an innovative store manager, and someone with potential for more significant positions later in her career. She likes working for BEC and sees a long-term career within the organization.

Second, the team asked Carrie what expectations she had about how the project would be conducted. Carrie expects the team to act independently without much direction or supervision from her; she does not have the time to work closely with them. She also expects that they will ask any questions of her or her employees and that everyone will cooperate with the project. The team asked if Carrie had told all of the store employees about the project. Carrie said that she had mentioned it to a few employees, but no formal announcement had been made. The team then asked if it could draft a note for Carrie to send to each employee explaining the nature of the project and requesting their assistance. Carrie agreed, but reserved the right to edit the note before sending it.

Next, Carrie asked about the time line for the project. The team members replied that their project plan would outline this but that their course included 18 more weeks of work over the following 20 calendar weeks. Finally, Carrie expects there to be minimal project expenses. The team said that it would develop and submit a cost estimate as part of the detailed project plan for the analysis phase.

At the end of the meeting, the team members asked Carrie for a description of the computer capabilities available to them through in-store technology. Carrie agreed to send them a copy of an overview of the BEC information systems she obtained in the training program (see the BEC case at the end of Chapter 2). If they need more details, they should ask for specific information, and Carrie will try to get those details from corporate staff.

Case Summary

The St. Claire team of students is off to an enthusiastic start with the BEC customer relationship management system project. The initial meeting with the client went well. The team members liked Carrie, and she seemed to like them and spoke frankly to them. However, the project also showed some signs of risk. First, Carrie might be overly enthusiastic and naïve about the system. As an inexperienced store manager, she might not have well-seasoned or definitive ideas. Second, other store employees, many of whom are part-time help with no long-term commitment to BEC, have not been involved in the development of the

project's ideas. The team will have to assess whether the employees or other people are critical stakeholders in the project. Third, Carrie needs to have the project conducted with minimal costs. Until the team can develop a clear understanding of the system requirements and the available technology in the store, additional costs are unclear. Certainly the team can develop the design and proof-of-concept prototype of a system on computers at St. Claire, but if the system is to be used in the store, significant start-up costs might be incurred. Finally, the team is a little concerned about Carrie's reluctance to involve the corporate IS staff in the project. Carrie seemed hesitant about the hand-off meeting as a way to provide follow-up after the team's work is done, and she wants to be a buffer with corporate about IS details.

The team members agree that the project looks like a great learning experience. Original analysis and design work need to be done. The project schedule and techniques to be used are wide open as long as they fall within the constraints of their course requirements. Some interesting stakeholder issues need to be handled. The benefits of the system are still vague, as are the costs for a complete implementation. In addition, the team is diverse, with a variety of skills and experience, but with the unknowns of how members will react and work together when critical deadlines must be met.

CASE QUESTIONS

1. From what you know so far about the customer relationship management system project at BEC, whom do you consider to be the stakeholders in this system? How would you suggest involving each stakeholder in the project in order to gain the greatest insights during requirements determination and to achieve success for the project?

2. Develop a detailed project schedule for the inception phase and a general project schedule for subsequent phases of this project. This schedule should be established from answers to questions in BEC cases from prior chapters and from any class project guidelines given to you by your instructor. Be prepared to suggest a different overall schedule than the 18 work weeks indicated in the case if your available project time is different from this project length. For example, it might not be possible to complete the project through the entire transition phase. If you are having difficulty developing a specific project schedule after inception, you should at least prepare a generic schedule for subsequent phases and explain what else you will need to learn in order to make the generic steps specific. Also, prepare a budget for the project as you would conduct it. What resources do you anticipate the team will need to conduct the project as you outline it? How might these resources be acquired?

3. Probably an early activity you outlined in your answer to Question 2 is to distribute the project announcement to employees, as discussed in this case. The BEC team offered to write a draft of this note. What are the critical items to communicate in this letter? Draft the letter for Carrie Douglass's approval.

4. Your answer to Question 2 likely included review points with Carrie and other stakeholders. These review points are part of the project's overall communication plan. Explain the overall communication activities you would suggest for this project. How should team members communicate questions, findings, and results to one another? How should the team communicate with stakeholders?

5. In this case, the BEC student team asked for details on the in-store computing environment. What other documents or documentation should the team collect during requirements determination? Why?

6. The initial meeting with Carrie Douglass in this BEC case was not intended to be a formal interview as part of requirements determination. Prepare a detailed interview plan for the first interview you would hold with Carrie to explore the needs she sees for a customer relationship management system. Recall the structure of an object-oriented systems development project, including its iterative nature. Pay close attention to the objectives for this interview. As part of this

interview plan, consider any opportunities that might exist for reengineering current customer relationship business processes.

7. How would you propose involving BEC store customers (actual and potential) in requirements determination? Do they need to be involved? If not, why not? If so, prepare a plan for interviews, a focus group or JAD session, observation, or whatever means you suggest using to elicit their requirements for the system.

8. How would you propose involving BEC store employees in requirements determination? Do they need to be involved? If not, why not? If so, prepare a plan for interviews, a focus group or JAD session, observation, or whatever means you suggest using to elicit their requirements for the system.

9. Visit the Web sites of at least three companies that sell or rent merchandise in physical stores. From reviewing these Web sites, what features would you suggest for the BEC customer relationship management system? How would you determine whether BEC needs these features for its Web site? What features and other system characteristics appear to be the hard problems that will have to be addressed early in the project?

Chapter

6

Structuring System Requirements: Use-Case Description and Diagrams

Chapter Objectives

After studying this chapter, you should be able to:

➤ Understand how to structure system requirements with use-case diagrams.

➤ Explain the basics of use-case construction using UML standards.

➤ Construct use-case diagrams.

➤ Write text-based use cases.

Chapter Contents

➤ Chapter Preview

➤ Use Cases

➤ Use-Case Diagrams

➤ Written Use Cases

The last chapter covered various methods that systems analysts use to collect the information they need to determine systems requirements. In this chapter, we continue our focus on the systems analysis part of the SDC, which is highlighted in Figure 6.1. Note that analysis has three parts: determining requirements, structuring requirements, and selecting the best alternative design strategy. In this chapter, we focus on a technique that has become a standard for object-oriented analysis and design: use cases. Use cases illustrate a system's behavior or functionality. Use case diagrams are graphic illustrations of the use cases in a system and how they are related to each other. However, they do not provide much detail on the steps necessary to complete each function. Therefore, each use case also requires a textual description that lists the steps for the function. This chapter discusses how to draw use case diagrams, including the basic symbols and a set of rules for drawing them, and how to write use cases. We will develop the use case diagram of the Pine Valley Furniture WebStore example, which we first introduced in Chapter 3. From this diagram, we will detail a few use cases.

Figure 6.1 The Systems Development Cycle, Showing the Different Aspects of Systems Analysis

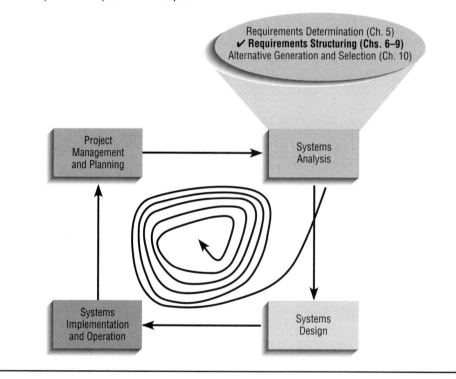

USE CASES

Functional requirements
Desired system characteristics that deal with system behavior, with what the system must be capable of performing

Use-case modeling is applied to analyze the functional requirements of a system. Functional requirements refer to the behavior of a system, to what the system must be able to do. Systems also have nonfunctional requirements, which refer to system qualities that go beyond behavior and include such things as accuracy, performance, efficiency, cost, maintainability, quality, security, and modifiability. Use-case modeling is designed to capture functional requirements. It is done in the early stages of system development, during the analysis phase, to help developers understand the functional requirements of the system without worrying about how those requirements will be implemented. The process is inherently iterative; developers need to involve the users in discussions throughout the model development process and finally come to an agreement on the requirements specification.

What Is a Use Case?

A use case shows the behavior or functionality of a system. It consists of a set of possible sequences of interactions between a system and a user in a particular environment and related to a particular goal. A use case describes the behavior of a system under various conditions as the system responds to requests from principal actors. A principal actor initiates a request of the system related to a goal, and the system responds. A use case can be stated as a present-tense verb phrase containing the verb (what the system is supposed to do) and the object of the verb (what the system is to act on). For example, use-case names would include "Enter sales data," "Compute commission," and "Generate quarterly report." Use cases do not collect all of the requirements and need to be augmented by documents that detail requirements such as business rules, data fields and formats, and complex formulae.

A use-case–driven design, in which use cases control the formation of all other models, promotes traceability among the different models used in object-oriented development. If user requirements change during the development life cycle, those changes are first made in the use-case model. Changes to the use cases then dictate what changes need to be made in the other models. Therefore, the models are traceable. For example, it is possible to trace a set of requirements specified in a use case to elements in the other analysis, design, and test models. It is also possible to trace backwards. For instance, the systems analyst could see what effects, if any, a design change has on the use-case model. Traceability is an important aspect of system documentation, as it allows an analyst to see how different models are interconnected, making later maintenance and modification of the system easier. However, traceability does require the use of a superior CASE tool.

A use-case model consists of actors and use cases. An actor is an external entity that interacts with the system. It is someone or something that exchanges information with the system. For the most part, a use case represents a sequence of related actions initiated by an actor to accomplish a specific goal; it is a specific way of using the system (Jacobson et al., 1992). Note that an actor and a user are not the same thing. A user is anyone who uses the system. An actor, on the other hand, represents a role that a user can play. The actor's name should indicate that role. An actor is a type or class of users; a user is a specific instance of an actor class playing the actor's role. Note that the same user can play multiple roles. For example, if William Alvarez plays two roles, one as an instructor and the other as an advisor, he can be represented as an instance of an actor called Instructor and as an instance of another actor called Advisor.

Because actors are outside the system, they do not need to be described in detail. The advantage of identifying actors is that it helps the analyst identify the use cases they carry out.

For identifying use cases, Jacobson et al. (1992) recommend asking the following questions:

- What are the main tasks performed by each actor?
- Will the actor read or update any information in the system?
- Will the actor have to inform the system about changes outside the system? Does the actor have to be informed about unexpected changes?

Deliverables and Outcomes

Table 6-1 lists the progression of deliverables that result from studying and documenting a system's behavior. First, the systems analyst will produce a use-case diagram or series of diagrams. These diagrams show multiple use cases, the relationships among

Table 6-1 Use-
Case Deliverables.

Use-case diagrams.
Written descriptions of use-case contents.

them, and the actors involved in them. As use cases are generated in developing diagrams, the analyst will begin to write the use cases themselves. This involves writing descriptions of how the functionality represented by each use case can be achieved. A written use case is basically a list of steps necessary to carry out the use-case function. Depending on the situation and the size of the project team, it can be written informally or in a detailed format.

USE-CASE DIAGRAMS

Use cases help capture the functional requirements of a system. As discussed in Chapter 5, during the requirements analysis stage the analyst sits down with the intended users of a system and makes a thorough analysis of what functions they desire from the system. When it comes time to structure these requirements, the identified system functions are represented as use cases. For example, a university registration system has a use case for class registration and another for student billing. These use cases, then, represent the typical interactions the system has with its users.

A use-case diagram, drawn according to Unified Modeling Language (UML) standards, is depicted diagrammatically as shown in Figure 6.2. This use-case diagram is for a university registration system, which is shown as a box. Outside the box are four actors—Student, Registration Clerk, Instructor, and Bursar's Office—that interact with the system. An actor is shown using a stick figure symbol with its name below. Inside the box are four use cases—"Register for classes," "Register for special class," "Identify prereq courses not completed," and "Bill student"—which are shown as ellipses with their names underneath. These use cases are performed by the actors outside the system.

Typically, a use case is initiated by an actor. For example, "Bill student" is initiated by the bursar's office. A use case can interact with actors other than the one that initiated it. The "Bill student" use case, although initiated by the bursar's office, interacts with the students by mailing them tuition invoices. Another use case, "Register for classes," is carried out by two actors, Student and Registration Clerk.

Use-case diagram
A picture showing system behavior along with the key actors that interact with the system.

Figure 6.2
A Use-Case Diagram for a University Registration System

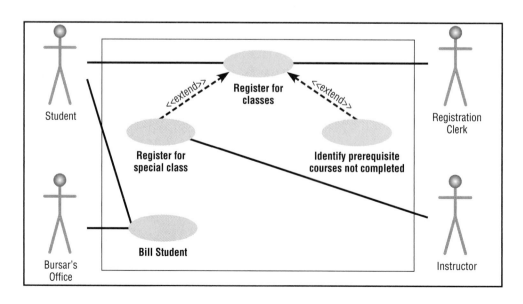

This use case performs a series of related actions aimed at registering a student for a class. Although use cases typically are initiated by actors, there are circumstances in which a use case is initiated by another use case. A use case initiated by another use case is called an abstract use case, discussed in more detail later in this chapter.

A use case represents complete functionality. An individual action that is part of an overall function should not be represented as a use case. For example, although submitting a registration form and paying tuition are two actions performed by users (students) in the university registration system, they are not shown as use cases because they do not specify a complete course of events; each of these actions is executed only as part of an overall function or use case. "Submit registration form" can be thought of as one of the actions of the "Register for classes" use case, and "Pay tuition" can be considered one of the actions of the "Bill student" use case. Note that the "complete functionality" criterion depends on the context. At times, you may find that a transaction that handles a service like registration is considered as completed when a client is billed. Here "Make Payment" may be a separate functionality, and you would then separate the payment use case from the billing use case.

Definitions and Symbols

Use-case diagramming is relatively simple in that it involves only a few symbols. However, like many relatively simple diagramming tools, these few symbols can be used to represent complex situations. Mastering use-case diagramming takes lots of practice. The key symbols in a use-case diagram are illustrated in Figure 6.2 and explained next.

- *Actor:* As explained previously, an actor is a role, not an individual. Individuals are instances of actors. One particular individual can play many roles simultaneously. An actor role is involved with the functioning of a system at some basic level. Actors are represented with stick figures.
- *Use case:* Each use case is represented an as ellipse. Each use case represents a single system function. The name of the use case can be listed inside the ellipse or just below it.
- *System boundary:* The system boundary is represented as a box that includes all of the relevant use cases. Note that actors are outside the system boundary.
- *Connections:* In Figure 6.2, note that actors are connected to use cases through lines, and that use cases are connected to each other through arrows. A solid line connecting an actor to a use case shows that the actor is involved in that particular system function. The solid line does not necessarily mean that the actor is sending data to or receiving data from the use case, although it is certainly possible. Note that not all actors in a use-case diagram are involved in all the use cases in the system. The dotted-line arrows that connect use cases also have labels (an <<extend>> label is found on the arrows in Figure 6.2). These use-case connections and their labels are explained next. Note that use cases do not have to be connected to other use cases. The arrows between use cases do not illustrate data or process flows.

Extend relationship
An association between two use cases where one adds new behaviors or actions to the other.

- *Extend Relationship:* An extend relationship extends a use case by adding new behaviors or action. It is shown as a dotted-line arrow pointing toward the use case that has been extended and labeled with the <<extend>> symbol. The dotted-line arrow does not indicate any kind of data or process flow between use cases. In Figure 6.2, for example, the "Register for special class" use case extends the "Register for classes" use case by capturing the additional actions that need to be performed in registering a student for a special class. Registering for a special class requires prior permission of the instructor, in addition to the other steps carried out for a regular registration. Think of "Register for classes" as the basic course, which is always performed—independent of whether the extension is performed or not—and "Register for special class" as an alternative course, which is performed only under special circumstances.

Note also that the Instructor actor is needed for "Register for special class." The Instructor is not needed for "Register for classes," which involves the Student and Registrar actors only. The reason for not including the Instructor for normal registration but including that actor for registering for special classes is that certain additional actions are required from the Instructor for a special class. The Instructor's approval is likely needed just to create an instance of a special class, and other special requirements might need to be met for the class to be created. None of these special arrangements are necessary for normal registration, so the Instructor is not needed under normal circumstances.

Another example of an extend relationship is that between the "Identify prereq courses not completed" and "Register for classes" use cases. The former extends the latter in situations where a student registering for a class has not taken the prerequisite courses.

- *Include Relationship:* Another kind of relationship between use cases is include relationship, which arises when one use case uses another use case. An include relationship also is shown diagrammatically as a dotted-line arrow pointed toward the use case that is being used. The line is labeled with the <<include>> symbol. The dotted-line arrow does not indicate any kind of data or process flow between use cases. An include relationship implies that the use case where the arrow originates uses the use case where the arrow ends while it is executing. Typically, the use case that is "included" represents a generic function that is common to many business functions. Rather than reproduce that functionality within every use case that needs it, the functionality is factored into a separate use case that can then be used by other use cases. This facilitates reuse, which in the long run improves the quality and speed of the systems development process. Note that reuse can and should be considered during the analysis stage because reuse is as much a business concept as it is an implementation concept. Too often, reuse is considered only at the implementation stage. An example of an include relationship is shown in Figure 6.3.

Figure 6.3 shows a generic use-case diagram for any business that needs to reorder supplies on a regular basis, such as a retail establishment or a restaurant. Because this is a generic use-case diagram, the use cases it includes are high level. Three different use cases are identified in the figure: "Reorder supplies," "Produce management reports," and "Track sales and inventory data." Two actors have been identified: Supplier and Manager. "Reorder supplies" involves the Manager and Supplier actors. A manager initiates the use case, which then sends requests to suppliers for various items. The "Produce management reports" use case involves only the Manager actor. In Figure 6.3, the include relationship between the "Reorder supplies" and "Track sales and inventory data" use cases implies that the former uses the latter while executing. Simply put, when a manager reorders supplies, the sales and inventory data are tracked. The same data also are tracked when management

Include relationship
An association between two use cases where one use case uses the functionality contained in the other.

Figure 6.3 An Example of an Include Relationship between Use Cases

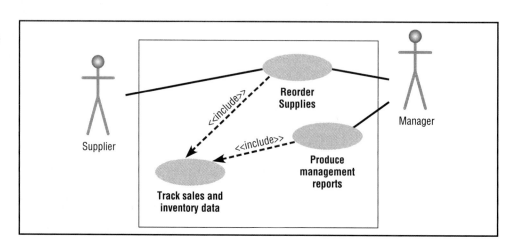

Figure 6.4 A Use-Case Diagram for a University Registration System Represented with Microsoft's Visio

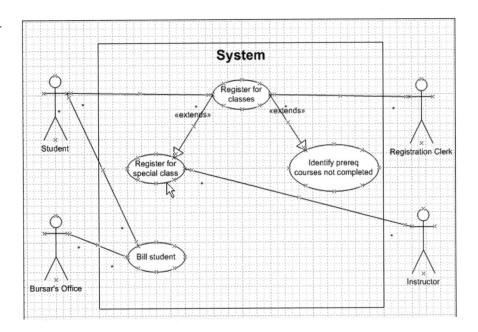

reports are produced, so another include relationship is found between the "Produce management reports" and "Track sales and inventory data" use cases.

The "Track sales and inventory data" is a generalized use case, representing the common behavior among the specialized use case, "Reorder supplies" and "Produce management reports." When "Reorder supplies" or "Produce management reports" is performed, the entire use case "Track sales and inventory data" is used. Note, however, that it is used only when one of the specialized use cases is performed. Such a use case, which is never performed by itself, is called an abstract use case (Eriksson & Penker, 1998; Jacobson et al., 1992). An abstract case does not interact directly with an actor.

Given that use-case diagrams have so few symbols, they are easy to draw by hand. However, many software tools are available that support use-case diagramming. Some tools are part of sophisticated computer-assisted software engineering packages, such as Rational Rose. Others are stand-alone diagramming tools, such as Microsoft's Visio, which includes a special set of templates for UML diagrams. Figure 6.2 is redrawn as Figure 6.4 using Visio. Visio puts the names of the use cases inside the ellipses, which is also common practice in other books you might read about use cases and on Web sites you might access. In this book, we place the use-case names outside the ellipse because that is how it is done in Rational Rose and because this approach avoids writing use-case names that fit the ellipse instead of fitting the use case. Visio uses solid lines with empty triangles at the end for arrows, and Visio uses <<extends>> instead of <<extend>> and <<uses>> instead of <<include>>. However, the general thrust of the diagram is the same, as is clear when comparing Figures 6.2 and 6.4. You may need to check your workplace standards regarding the preferred convention.

Developing Use-Case Diagrams: Three Examples

The first example involves a use-case diagram for a reservation system (Figure 6.5). Many different organizations offer reservations, from hotels to airlines to movie theaters to convention centers and arenas. The central idea from a user perspective is to search for the availability of a desired service and, if it is available, to reserve it for use as some specified day and time and location. There are four primary functions in such an activity: (1) search for availability, (2) make the reservation, (3) pay for the service, and (4) receive the service or some token that lets the user claim the service at the time of consumption. Each of these functions corresponds to a use case, and they

Figure 6.5 A Use-Case Diagram for a Reservations System

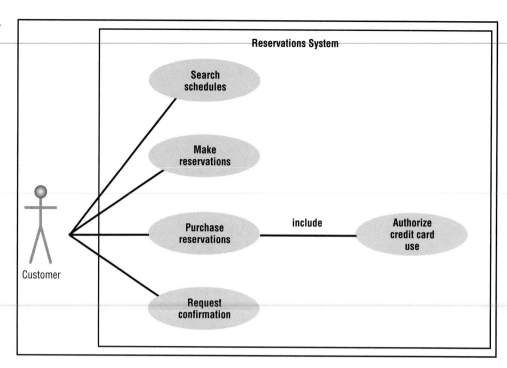

are all shown in Figure 6.5. All four functions would be initiated by an actor called Customer. The use cases in the diagram would all need to be present for a reservations transaction that took place online or at a ticket counter or box office. At the latter two locations, the Customer actor would initiate each use case through an intermediary such as a ticket agent.

In Figure 6.5 there is also an include relationship, as the "Purchase Reservations" use case calls the "Authorize credit card use" use case. Every time a customer makes a purchase with a credit card, something like "Authorize credit card use" is used. Whether the transaction is conducted online or in person, the reservations system must connect to the credit card issuer in order to get authorization to charge the purchase to the customer's card. If there is not enough credit in the customer's account, or if the credit card has been cancelled, the transaction will not go through. Getting credit authorization is a common task in most purchasing activity, and getting authorization is fairly separate from, and independent of, the actual purchasing process. "Authorize credit card use," then, is a good candidate for an abstract use case.

In a second example, Figure 6.6 shows a use-case diagram for a retail sales system. This is the type of system that would be in place on the cash registers at the checkout station for most retail stores. The two actors are the Customer and the Sales Clerk. This example has two specialized use cases, "Return item" and "Make purchase," and each of these would be initiated by the Customer actor. Not every register at checkout in a given store would be able to handle returns, at least not most of the time, as this would create bottlenecks for customers trying to make purchases. However, some registers in a store have to be able to handle returns all the time, and these registers also can handle purchases, so both functionalities are included in this example.

Notice that three abstract use cases also are included in the example in Figure 6.6. Two of these abstract use cases have include relationships with an abstract use case, and one has an extend relationship with a use case. When a Customer actor initiates "Return item," he or she expects either to get a new item in exchange for the one being returned, a cash refund for the value of the item if cash or a check was paid initially, or a credit on the credit card account if the item was paid for with a credit card. The process of getting a credit is captured in the use case "Credit customer account." Crediting a customer account has been factored out of the "Return item" use case, as it could be used by other use cases in addition to "Return item." For example, assume the

Figure 6.6 A Use-Case Diagram of a Retail Sales System, Featuring Insert Relations and an Extend Relation

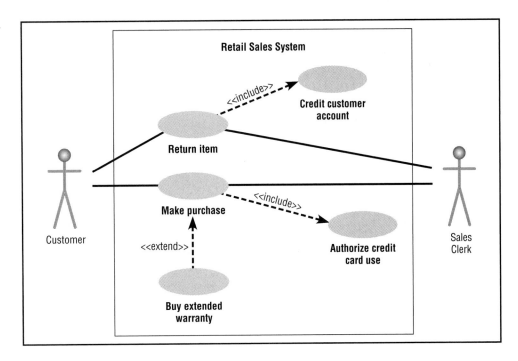

store has a policy about refunding part of the purchase price of an item if the customer finds the same item at a lower price at a competitor's store. The policy might call for the refund to be in the form of a credit to a customer account, so a "Grant refund" use case also would have an include relationship with the "Credit customer account" use case.

The second include relationship is between "Make purchase" and "Authorize credit card use." You saw this before in Figure 6.5. The principle is the same. The store where the purchase is made makes a connection to the credit card issuer to get authorization to charge the purchase to the customer's card. If the customer has maxed out his or her credit card limit, the store won't be able to make the charge. Getting authorization is a common task at retail stores, much as it is in a transaction for making reservations.

Finally, Figure 6.6 also contains an extend relationship between "Make purchase" and "Buy extended warranty." Every time an electronics item is purchased, from a computer to an MP3 player, the salesclerk has probably asked the customer to buy an extended warranty to protect the item once its manufacturer's warranty expires. Creating such an extended warranty is not something that would occur for every item sold at a retail store, so it would not be an integral part of the use case "Make purchase." "Buy extended warranty" does, however, expand the functionality of "Make purchase" without changing the "Make purchase" use case. If at some point the store's management decided not to sell extended warranties anymore, they simply could eliminate the extend relationship, and the "Make purchase" use case would not be affected.

In the third example, Figure 6.7 shows a use-case model for different types of credit applications at a bank. The credit applications include those for home equity loans, home mortgage loans, auto loans, and credit cards. Therefore, from the bank's perspective the customers are home owners, home buyers, auto buyers, and credit card applicants. Figure 6.7 shows those different customer classes as actors—Home Owner, Home Buyer, Auto Buyer, and Credit Card Applicant—generalized into an actor called Customer, which represents the class of all customers. Each of the four relationships between a specialized actor and Customer, shown by an arrow pointing toward the more general actor, is a generalization relationship.

To process most credit card applications, the bank needs to check the applicant's credit history, based on a report from the credit bureau. Therefore, a use case called "Check credit history" is established, which is used by three use cases relating to credit applications: "Process home mortgage loan application," "Process auto loan application," and "Process credit card application." The

Figure 6.7
Examples of
Generalized Use
Cases and Include
Relationships

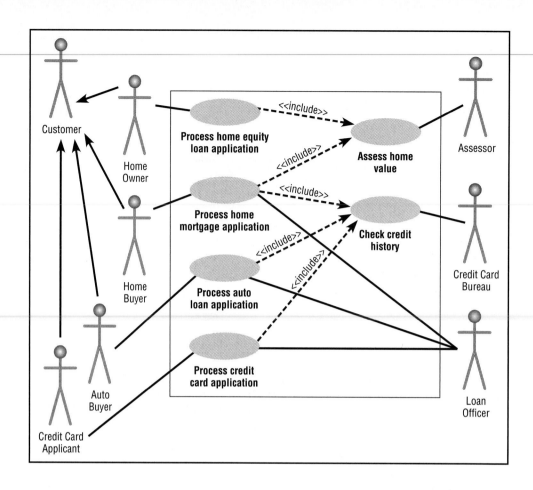

"Assess home value" use case models the common behavior among the "Process home mortgage loan application" and "Process home equity loan application" use cases. For both types of loans, the bank summons an assessor to assess the property value before making a decision.

In situations in which it is unclear whether to employ extend or include to model a given relationship between two use cases, consider the following criteria suggested by Jacobson. If the intent is to model an extension to, or a variation of, a complete use case that exists in its own right, employ extend. In Figure 6.2, for example, "Register for classes" is a complete use case. It is totally independent of the extension use cases—"Register for special class" and "Identify prerequisite courses not completed"—that were inserted to model alternatives to its basic behavior. On the other hand, if the intent is to factor the common behavior among two or more use cases into a single generalized use case, then the include relationship should be employed. The common behavior described by the generalized use case must be inserted into a specialized use case to complete it. For example, to carry out the "Process home equity loan application" or "Process home mortgage loan application" use case (see Figure 6.7), the "Assess home value" use case must also be performed.

Although a use-case diagram shows all the use cases in the system, it does not describe how those use cases are carried out by the actors. The contents of a use case normally are described in plain text. When describing a use case, the focus should be on its external behavior, that is, how it interacts with the actors, rather than how the use case is performed inside the system (Eriksson & Penker, 1998). For example, the "Register for classes" use case can be described as follows:

1. A student completes a registration form by entering the following information: courseNumber, sectionNumber, term, year.

2. The student then takes the completed registration form to his or her advisor for a signature. After checking the entries, the advisor signs the form.
3. The student then submits the form to a clerk at the registration office, who enters the information into the computer.
4. The clerk provides the student with a computer printout of the classes in which he or she is successfully registered.

Note that the description includes the following three components:

1. The objective of the use case, which is to register the student for a class.
2. The actor (Student) who initiates the use case.
3. The exchange of information between the actors (Student and Registration Clerk) and the use case.

In this section, we have shown how to develop a use-case model that captures the functional requirements of a system. A use-case diagram is an invaluable vehicle for communication between developers and end users. It also promotes modifiability by allowing the systems analyst to trace the effects of changes made in the use-case model on other models.

Developing Use Cases for Pine Valley Furniture's WebStore

After completing the JAD session, Senior Systems Analyst Jim Woo went to work on translating the WebStore system structure into a use-case diagram. He carefully examined the outcomes of the JAD session that focused on defining the system, and identified five high-level functions that would be included in his use-case diagram. Jim made a table that listed the main characteristics of the WebStore Web site in one column and the corresponding system functions in another column (Table 6-2). Note how these functions correspond to the major Web site characteristics listed in the system structure. These functions represented the "work" or "action" parts of the Web site. Jim noted that the functions listed in his table all involved the customer, so Jim realized Customer would be a key actor in his use-case diagram.

In looking at the table, however, Jim realized that one of the key functions identified in the JAD, "Fill order," was not represented in his table. He had to include it in the use-case diagram, but it was clear to him that it was a behind-the-scenes or back-office function and required adding another actor to the use-case diagram. This actor would be the Shipping Clerk. Jim added Shipping Clerk to the right-hand side of his use-case diagram. The finished diagram is shown in Figure 6.8.

Table 6-2 System Structure of WebStore and Corresponding Functions.

WEBSTORE SYSTEM	FUNCTIONS
Main Page	
• Product line (catalog)	Browse catalog
• Desks	
• Chairs	
• Tables	
• File cabinets	
• Shopping cart	Place order
• Checkout	Place order
• Account profile	Maintain account
• Order status/history	Check order
• Customer comments	
Company information	
Feedback	
Contact information	

Figure 6.8
WebStore Use
Case Diagram

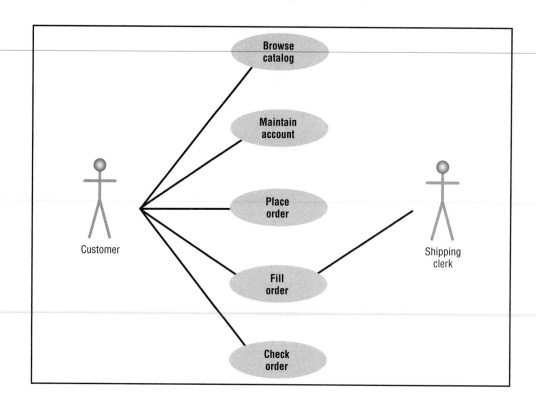

WRITTEN USE CASES

Use-case diagrams can represent the functionality of a system by showing use-case names and the actors who are involved with them. As explained previously, the names of the use cases alone do not provide much of the information that is necessary to continue with analysis and to move on to the design phase. We also need to know what goes on inside each use case. The contents of a use case can be written in simple text, as was explained before for the "Register for classes" use case in Figure 6.2. Others recommend templates that force consideration of all of the important information one needs to have about use cases.

Cockburn (2001) recommends a specific template for writing use cases (Figure 6.9). Templates can be simpler or more complicated than the one Cockburn recommends. The point is not the format of the template so much as it is how the template encourages analysts to write complete use cases. Each heading reminds the analyst of the information that needs to be provided. In the template in Figure 6.9, it should be clear what information is being sought. The use-case title and the name of the primary actor role, both of which were featured in the discussion of use-case diagrams, can be found on the use-case diagram. The other information asked for in the template is new and will be discussed in more detail. The next section will deal exclusively with an important concept, the *level* of the use case. The following section will deal with the rest of the terms in the template.

Level

Level

Perspective from which a use-case description is written, typically ranging from high level to extremely detailed.

Level has to do with the level of detail at which the use case is being described. Level can range from high to low, where high is general and abstract and low is detailed. Cockburn suggests five different levels of detail:

- White: As seen from the clouds, as if flying in a plane at 35,000 feet.
- Kite: Still in the air so still general, but more detail than at cloud level.
- Blue: Also known as sea level.

Figure 6.9
A Template for Writing
Use Cases

Source: Writing Effective Use
Cases by A. Cockburn, ©
2001. Adapted by permis-
sion of Pearson Education,
Inc., Upper Saddle River, NJ
07458.

- Fish: This is below sea level with a lot of detail. The detail increases deeper down, just like air pressure.
- Black: This is the bottom of the sea where the maximum amount of detail is provided.

Both the white and kite levels provide a summary of the use-case goals. These goals are at a very high level. Goals at the white level would be enterprise-wide, while at the kite level the goals would be those of a single business unit. Use cases at the white and kite levels are sometimes called summary use cases. Summary use cases do not include functional requirements. Use cases written at the blue level, or sea level, focus on user goals: What is the user trying to achieve in interacting with the system? Use cases written at the fish and black levels (sometimes called the clam level) are much more detailed and focus on subfunction goals. To think about how the levels relate to each other, think about the view of the Caribbean Sea you would get if you were flying over it in a big plane like a 757. You can't see the bottom of the sea, and at this altitude you can't even see much detail about the surface of the water. This would be the white level. Then think about how the same stretch of the Caribbean would look from about 100 feet up. This is the kite level. From here, you would be able to see a lot more detail on the surface, compared to being in the 757, but you still can't see a lot of detail on the sea bottom, even with the water as clear as it is in a lot of the Caribbean. Now imagine the view of the same place from a rowboat. This is the user goal or sea level view. You can see the bottom much more clearly now, but it's still not completely clear. Now dive under the water and go down about 50 feet. You are a lot closer to the bottom—the fish level—and so now you can see a lot more detail on the bottom of the sea. But you don't see the most detail possible until you are sitting on the bottom itself—the black or clam level.

To put all this into a business function perspective, let's imagine five levels of use cases written for the Ford Motor Company. The white level use cases would serve an enterprise-wide goal ("Buy parts to build cars"), while a kite level use case would serve one business unit ("Buy parts to build Volvos"). If a system user has the role of procurement manager for Volvo, the user goals at sea level might be "Order Volvo parts from suppliers" and "Pay bills." A fish level goal for the procurement system might include "Choose supplier for a part." A black or clam level goal for the same system might include "Establish a secure connection." Figure 6.10 graphically shows the relationships among the levels.

The Rest of the Template

Stakeholder
Person who has a vested
interest in the system being
developed.

Next in the use-case template is the list of stakeholders. Stakeholders are those people who have some key interest in the development of the system. They would include the system's users as well as the manager, other managers in the company, customers, stockholders, the vendors that supply the company, and so on. Stakeholders are

Figure 6.10 Use-Case Levels Add Detail When Moving from Top to Bottom

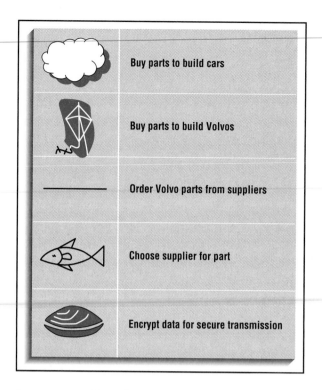

important to identify as they typically have some impact on what the system does and on how it is designed. It should be obvious that some stakeholders have more of a stake than others, and the most involved stakeholders are the ones that probably should be listened to first.

Continuing through the list of terms in Cockburn's template (Figure 6.8), the next term is preconditions. Preconditions refer to those things the system must ensure are true before the use case can start. For example, in Figure 6.6, for the use case "Check credit history," there would have to be a valid login to the system used to check a client's credit history before the process would be allowed. "Valid login" would be listed under "Preconditions" for "Check credit history" in its written use-case template.

Next is minimal guarantee. According to Cockburn, the minimal guarantee is the least amount promised by the use case to the stakeholder. One way to determine what this should be is to ask, "What would make the stakeholder unhappy?" For some use cases, the minimal guarantee might be simply "Nothing happens." The stakeholder would be unhappy because the system does not do what it is supposed to. However, no detrimental effects result either; no bad data are entered into the system, no data are lost, and the system does not crash. For many use cases, the best thing to offer for a minimal guarantee is to roll back the transaction to its original starting place; nothing is gained but no harm is done either.

A success guarantee lists what it takes to satisfy stakeholders if the use case is completed successfully. For example, in Figure 6.6, for the use case "Assess home value," a success guarantee would involve the successful collection of the data necessary to estimate a house's appraised value, the correct operation of the formula used for the assessment, the return of value for the house, and the successful saving of the transaction record. This does not imply that the stakeholder is *happy* with the result; he or she might think the assessed value is too high or too low. What is important is that the use case functioned correctly and achieved its goals.

Next is the slot in the template for trigger. A trigger is the thing that initiates the use case. A trigger could be a phone call, a letter, or even a call from another use case. In the example of "Assess home value," the trigger could be a request from a customer, a mortgage broker, a tax official, or some other stakeholder to have an assessment done.

The last item in Cockburn's written use-case template is extensions. Maybe the best way to think about an extension is as the "else statement" that follows an "if statement." An extension is invoked only if its associated condition is encountered.

Preconditions
Things that must be true before a use case can start.

Minimal guarantee
The least amount promised to the stakeholder by a use case.

Success guarantee
What a use case must do effectively in order to satisfy stakeholders.

Trigger
Event that initiates a use case.

Extension
The set of behaviors or functions in a use case that follow exceptions to the main success scenario.

In a written use case, the conditions that invoke extensions usually refer to some type of system failure. For example, if a use case involves access through the Internet and a network failure occurs so that the Internet connection is lost, what happens? If the system requires a login and the user provides the wrong account name, what happens? If the user provides the wrong password, what happens? All of the actions that would follow these conditions would be listed in the use-case template as extensions.

Figure 6.11 shows a finished written use case, based on the reservation use-case diagram in Figure 6.5. This use-case description is written at the kite or summary level, which means that it shows only the user goals rather than the functional requirements. You'll notice that five user goals are described, four of which are carried out by the customer, and this reflects the content of the use-case diagram in Figure 6.5. While

Figure 6.11   Kite Level Written Use Case for Making a Hotel Room Reservation

Use-Case Title: Making a Hotel Room Reservation

Primary Actor: Customer

Level: Kite (summary)

Stakeholders: Customer, credit bureau

Precondition: Customer accesses the hotel Web site

Minimal Guarantee: Rollback of any uncompleted transaction

Success Guarantee: Reservation held with one night's deposit

Trigger: Customer accesses hotel homepage

Main Success Scenario:

1. Customer searches for hotel location and room availability for desired time period.
2. Customer makes reservation for desired room for desired time period.
3. Customer holds reservation by authorizing a deposit for one night's stay.
4. Credit bureau verifies that customer has necessary credit for deposit.
5. Customer requests confirmation of reservations.

Extensions:

1.a. Hotel property search function is not available.
    1.a.1. Customer quits site.
1.b. Specific hotel room not available for desired time period.
    1.b.1. Customer quits site.
    1.b.2. Customer searches for different hotel for desired time period.
    1.b.3. Customer searches for same hotel for different time period.
2.a. Making reservation transaction is interrupted.
    2.a.1. Transaction rolled back. Customer starts again.
    2.a.2. Transaction rolled back. Customer quits site.
3.a. Holding reservation transaction is interrupted.
    3.a.1. Transaction rolled back. Customer starts again.
    3.a.2. Transaction rolled back. Customer quits site.
4.a. Credit bureau cannot verify that customer has necessary credit.
    4.a.1. Customer notified of issue. Transaction rolled back. Customer quits site.
    4.a.2. Customer notified of issue. Transaction rolled back. Customer begins reservation
        process again with different credit card.
5.a. Confirmation of transaction is interrupted.
    5.a.1. Customer seeks other means of confirmation.
    5.a.2. Customer quits site.

Figure 6.5 is generic to any system that handles reservations, the written use case in Figure 6.11 is specific to hotel reservations. For hotel reservations made on the Web, certain simplifying assumptions particular to hotel reservations have been made, such as customers being required to provide one night's deposit in order to hold the reservation. You'll also notice that there is a list of extensions at the end of the written use case. There is at least one extension for each user goal, although the first function, searching for a room for a desired time period at a specific hotel, has two extensions. There is no set number of extensions required for a user goal. In fact, there is no requirement that a user goal has an extension at all.

Writing Use Cases for Pine Valley Furniture's WebStore

Jim Woo was pleased with the use-case diagram he created for WebStore (Figure 6.8). Now that he had identified all of the use cases necessary (he thought), he was ready to go back and start writing the use cases. The management in Pine Valley's Information Systems Department had mandated that analysts use a standard template for writing use cases. Given his use-case diagram, Jim decided to create two types of written use cases. The first would deal with the entire process of buying a PVF product on WebStore, as depicted in Jim's use-case diagram. This written use

Figure 6.12 Jim Woo's Kite Level Written Use Case for Buying a Product at PVF's WebStore

Use-Case Title: Buying a PVF Product at WebStore

Primary Actor: Customer

Level: Kite (summary)

Stakeholders: Customer, shipping clerk

Precondition: Customer accesses the WebStore Web site

Minimal Guarantee: Rollback of any uncompleted transaction

Success Guarantee: Order filled

Trigger: Customer accesses WebStore homepage

Main Success Scenario:

1. Customer browses catalog.
2. Customer places order for desired product(s).
3. Shipping clerk fills order.
4. Customer checks status of order.

Extensions:

1.a. Catalog is not available.
    1.a.1. Customer quits site.
    1.a.2. Customer takes action to gain access to catalog.
2.a. Order transaction is interrupted.
    2.a.1. Transaction rolled back. Customer starts again.
    2.a.2. Transaction rolled back. Customer quits site.
3.a. Item is out of stock.
    3.a.1. Shipping clerk notifies customer. Customer waits for stock to be replenished.
    3.a.2. Shipping clerks notifies customer. Customer cancels order.
4.a. Order status is not available.
    4.a.1. Customer quits site.
    4.a.2. Customer takes action to gain access to order status.

case would be at the kite level. It would be a summary use case and not include functional requirements. The finished product is shown in Figure 6.12.

After finishing the kite level use case, Jim went on to create a couple of written use cases for individual use cases in his diagram. Jim wanted to write these use cases at the sea level or user goal level. He started with the first use case in his diagram, "Browse catalog." Figure 6.13 shows the template Jim completed for this first use case.

Jim was amazed at how much detail he could generate for something as seemingly simple as a customer browsing a Web catalog. Yet he knew that he had left out

Figure 6.13 Jim Woo's Completed Template for PVF's "Browse Catalog" Use Case

Use-Case Title: Browse Catalog
Primary Actor: Customer
Level: Sea level (user goal)
Stakeholders: Customer
Precondition: Customer must be online with Web access
Minimal Guarantee: Rollback of any uncompleted transaction; system logs progress until failure
Success Guarantee: Files customer desires load correctly
Trigger: Customer accesses WebStore homepage

Main Success Scenario:

1. Cookie created on customer hard drive.
2. Customer selects category of item to view from list (e.g., home, office, patio).
3. Customer selects subcategory of item to view from list (e.g., home is subdivided into kitchen, dining room, bedroom, living room, den, etc.).
4. Customer selects specific item from list in subcategory to view (e.g., TV stand in den).
5. Customer selects specific item from list of products (e.g., Smith & Wesson TV stand).
6. Customer clicks on thumbnail photo of item to get regular-sized photo to view.
7. Customer selects "Product Specifications" to get detailed information on product.
8. Customer uses Web browser "Back" button to go back to see other products or other rooms or other types of furniture.
9. Customer selects from choices on menu bar to go elsewhere, either "Other Types of Furniture," "WebStore Home," or "PVF Home."

Extensions:

1.a. Cookie cannot be created.
  1.a.1. Message created indicates to customer that browsing is not possible because his or her Web browser does not allow for the creation of cookies.
  1.a.2. Customer either adjusts the browser's cookie settings and tries again or leaves the site.
6.a. Full-sized photo does not load.
  6.a.1. Customer gets a broken-link symbol.
  6.a.2. Customer hits the refresh button and the photo loads successfully.
  6.a.3. Customer hits the refresh button and the photo does not load successfully; customer leaves the site.
2-7.a. The requested Web page does not load or cannot be found.
  2-7.a.1. Customer gets a "page not found" error page in browser.
  2-7.a.2. Customer hits the refresh button and the requested page loads successfully.
  2-7.a.3. Customer hits the refresh button and the requested page does not load successfully; customer leaves the site.

many details, details that could be specified in a use case as different levels, such as fish level or below. Still, Jim was happy with the progress he had made on this use case for catalog browsing. Now he turned his attention to the "Place order" use case. Jim's use-case description for "Place order" is shown in Figure 6.14.

Figure 6.14 Jim Woo's Written Use Case for Placing an Order at PVF's WebStore

Use-Case Title: Place Order

Primary Actor: Customer

Level: Sea level (user goal)

Stakeholders: Customer, shipping clerk

Precondition: Customer has invoked "Browse catalog" use case

Minimal Guarantee: Rollback of any uncompleted transaction; system logs progress until failure

Success Guarantee: Customer successfully completes order; pick slip created; credit card charged; receipt created

Trigger: Customer selects "Add Item to Shopping Cart"

Main Success Scenario: Customer selects "Browse Catalog":

1. An order is created for this transaction.
2. Line item for order is created for item added to shopping cart. Customer receives confirmation of item being added to shopping cart.
3. Customer adds additional items to shopping cart, line items created, with each addition confirmed.
4. Customer selects "Review Order."
5. Customer receives the order with each line item, cost total, tax, and shipping charges. Customer selects "Place Order."
6. Customer invokes the "Login" use case.
7. Customer selects "Submit Order." Customer, order, and shopping cart data are updated.
8. Customer credit card is charged.
9. Pick slip for shipping clerk is created.
10. Customer receipt is created and sent to customer for display on Web browser. Receipt data is sent as e-mail to customer's e-mail account address.

Extensions:

2.a. Line item cannot be created as the item is out of stock.
    2.a.1. Customer receives the out-of-stock message. Customer back-orders the item.
    2.a.2. Customer receives the out-of-stock message. Customer continues shopping for a substitute.
    2.a.3. Customer receives the out-of-stock message. Customer exits the use case.
6.a. "Login" use-case failure.
    6.a.1. Customer is told the account information invalid. Customer provides the valid information and logs in successfully.
    6.a.2. Customer is told the account is invalid. Customer is taken to the customer service site.
8.a. Customer credit card account is not charged successfully.
    8.a.1. Customer experiences credit card problems. Customer is asked for a new credit card account.
    8.a.2. Credit card vendor is experiencing problems. Customer is told to try again later.
1-10.a. Internet connection is broken.
    1-10.a.1. System rolls back to the pretransaction position for the customer.
1-10.b. Customer suddenly exits the system at any point.
    1-10.b.1. System rolls back to the pretransaction position for the customer.

When Jim was satisfied with his "Place order" use case, he turned his attention to the other four use cases he had identified for WebStore (Figure 6.8) and wrote sea level use cases for them. Once he was finished, he called a couple of other analysts at PVF so they could review his work.

Developing Use Cases

When developing use cases for a system, it is important to represent as much of the functionality as possible. The systems analyst will want to have the functionality of the system as well defined as possible before beginning to design and code, so that the system being built is as close as possible to the system the customer wants and needs.

Achieving this goal of completeness can be attempted in several ways. One way is to work with the customer to continue to develop functional requirements even as use cases are being written. All of a system's functional requirements do not need to be identified before use cases are written. In fact, the review of a series of use cases by a customer can generate other use cases. Another way to find additional and to correct existing use cases is through rapid prototyping with users. As users work through a mock-up of the system, they should be able to determine quickly which functions are captured by the prototype and which are not. Existing use cases should drive the design of the prototype; new ones identified in the process can be built into the next mock-up. Rosenberg and Scott (1999) suggest writing a user manual first in order to determine if the set of use cases is complete. A user manual, even though the system has not been built yet, should list every function that a user would want the system to perform. From the lists of how to do things that typically fill user manuals, one can generate a reasonable set of list cases.

Remember that use cases are the primary UML models for structuring the system requirements you uncovered in the first part of the analysis process. As such, use cases are important tools for communication, so it is important that they be written carefully and clearly. You can improve your ability to write good use cases by following some simple rules. One set of guidelines for writing good use cases is presented in Table 6-3. Most of these guidelines focus on keeping things simple:

- choose a good name with a strong verb phrase
- represent a complete behavior and name the use case accordingly
- only model one behavior
- describe the behavior from the actor's point of view, not the system's; and if the use case models behavior that changes the state of the system, write another use case that returns the system to its prior state.

Following these simple guidelines will help you write use cases that help you communicate requirements clearly with your customers and your fellow developers.

Table 6-3 Guidelines for Good Use Cases.

Choose a good name	Name a use case with a verb phrase since it represents behavior. Include a noun that refers to the class of objects the behavior affects.
Illustrate a complete behavior	The use case must be a complete behavior that begins with initiation by the actor and ends when the user goal has been met. Each use case must be capable of standing alone and not depending on something else to return a useful result.
Identify a completable behavior	The use case must complete in order to fulfill a goal and to achieve a result. Use a verb phrase that indicates completion, such as "Register for class," not "Registering for class."
Provide "inverse" use cases	If a use case changes a state in the system when it completes, then also include a use case that lets the system revert to the earlier state. A use case "Enroll in class" should be balanced with a use case "Drop class."
Limit each use case to one behavior	To avoid confusion, have the use case do only one thing.
Represent the actor's point of view	Write the use case from the perspective of the actor, not the system. For example, in Figure 6.5, the last use case in the diagram is titled "Request confirmation," not "Send confirmation."

Source: Adapted from Chonoles & Schardt, 2002. Copyright Wiley Publishing Inc., used by permission.

Remember that iteration is an important part of OOSAD, and having customers review use cases and having users evaluate prototypes to generate new use cases are both examples of this iterative process. Further, while the quest for completeness goes on, the systems analyst should be refining existing textual use cases. The job is done when the analyst is confident that he or she has defined all of the system's functionality and when all of the textual use cases are complete.

KEY POINTS REVIEW

1. **Explain how to structure system requirements with use-case diagrams.**
   Use cases are representations of a system's functionality and behavior. In a use-case diagram, each use case is depicted as an ellipse, and any relationships among use cases are depicted with arrows. The key users of the use cases in a diagram, called actors, are shown on the left and right sides of a use-case diagram. Their relationships with the use cases are shown with lines. Although these diagrams are helpful for identifying use cases and showing how they are related to each other and to key actors, the diagrams provide little detail of each use case's contents.

2. **Explain what a use-case diagram is and the kinds of relationships it can show.**
   In addition to the actors and use cases, use-case diagrams are used to show relationships between use cases. One such relationship is an extend relationship, in which the functionality of one use case extends the functionality of another. Another type of relationship is an include relationship, whereby one use case uses the functionality of another. The use case that is being used typically does not stand alone but exists only to be called by other use cases.

3. **Explain what text-based use cases are.**
   To more completely show the functionality of a use case, text descriptions can be written. These written descriptions have no set template of contents. Cockburn recommends a written use case that addresses the level at which it is written, the important people the use case affects, preconditions for starting the use case, minimal and success guarantees, the event that initiates the use case, a detailed description of the use case's behavior, and a set of actions that should be followed when exceptions to expected behavior arise. Determining and listing all of this information might be time-consuming, but it makes downstream activities in analysis much easier.

KEY TERMS CHECKPOINT

Here are the key terms from the chapter. The page where each term is first explained is in parentheses after the term.

a. Actor (p. 163)
b. Extend relationship (p. 165)
c. Extension (p. 174)
d. Functional requirements (p. 162)
e. Include relationship (p. 166)
f. Level (p. 172)
g. Minimal guarantee (p. 174)
h. Nonfunctional requirements (p. 163)
i. Preconditions (p. 174)
j. Stakeholder (p. 173)
k. Success guarantee (p. 174)
l. Trigger (p. 174)
m. Use case (p. 163)
n. Use-case diagram (p. 164)

Match each of the key terms above with the definition that best fits it.

1. A picture showing system behavior along with the key actors that interact with the system.
2. Things that must be true before a use case can start.
3. Person who has a vested interest in the system being developed.
4. An association between two use cases where one adds new behaviors or actions to the other.
5. Desired system characteristics describe not what the software will do but how it will do it.
6. An association between two use cases where one use case uses the functionality contained in the other.
7. The set of behaviors or functions in a use case that follows exceptions to the main success scenario.
8. Event that initiates a use case.
9. An external entity that interacts with a system.
10. Desired system characteristics that deal with system behavior.

11. Perspective from which a use-case description is written, typically ranging from high level to extremely detailed.
12. A depiction of a system's behavior or functionality under various conditions as the system responds to requests from users.
13. What a use case must do effectively in order to satisfy stakeholders.
14. The least amount promised to the stakeholder by a use case.

REVIEW QUESTIONS

1. What is a use case? What are the differences among a use case, a use-case diagram, and a written use case?
2. What is the role of use-case diagrams in systems analysis?
3. Explain what an extend relationship is.
4. Explain what an include relationship is.
5. What can a written description of a use case provide that a use-case diagram cannot?
6. Describe Cockburn's template for a written use case.
7. List and explain the five levels from which use case descriptions can be written.
8. What is the difference between a minimal guarantee and a success guarantee?
9. What are extensions?

PROBLEMS AND EXERCISES

1. Develop a use-case diagram for using an ATM machine to withdraw cash.
2. Develop a written use case for using an ATM machine to withdraw cash.
3. Choose a transaction that you are likely to encounter, perhaps ordering a cap and gown for graduation, and develop a use-case diagram for it.
4. Choose a transaction that you are likely to encounter and develop a written use case for it.
5. The diagram in Figure 6.8 includes five use cases. In this chapter, Jim Woo wrote descriptions for two of them, "Browse catalog" and "Place order." Prepare written descriptions for the other three use cases in Figure 6.8.
6. Rewrite the use-case description in Figure 6.12 at a higher level (white) and at a lower level (fish).
7. Rewrite the use-case description in Figure 6.13 at a higher level (white) and at a lower level (fish).
8. Draw a use-case diagram for the following situation: Maximum Software is a developer and supplier of software products to individuals and businesses. As part of its operations, Maximum provides an 800 telephone number help desk for clients with questions about software purchased from Maximum. When a call comes in, an operator inquires about the nature of the call. For calls that are not truly help desk functions, the operator redirects the call to another unit of the company (such as order processing or billing). Because many customer questions require in-depth knowledge of a product, help desk consultants are organized by product. The operator directs the call to a consultant skilled on the software that the caller needs help with. Because a consultant is not always immediately available, some calls must be put into a queue for the next available consultant. Once a consultant answers the call, the consultant determines whether this is the first call from this customer about this problem. If so, he or she creates a new call report to keep track of all information about the problem. If not, the consultant asks the customer for a call report number, and retrieves the open call report to determine the status of the inquiry. If the caller does not know the call report number, the consultant collects other identifying information such as the caller's name, the software involved, or the name of the consultant who has handled the previous calls on the problem in order to conduct a search for the appropriate call report. If a resolution of the customer's problem has been found, the consultant informs the client what that resolution is, indicates on the report that the customer has been notified, and closes out the report. If resolution has not been discovered, the consultant finds out whether the consultant handling this problem is on duty. If so, the call is transferred to the other consultant (or it is put into the queue of calls waiting to be handled by that consultant). Once the proper consultant receives the call, he or she records any new details the customer has. For continuing problems and for new call reports, the consultant tries to discover an answer to the problem by using the relevant software and looking up information in reference manuals. If the problem can be resolved, the consultant tells the customer how to deal with the problem and closes the call report. Otherwise, the consultant files the report for continued research and tells the customer that someone at Maximum will get back to him or her, or if the customer discovers new information about the problem, to call back identifying the problem with a specified call report number.
9. Write use-case descriptions for all of the use cases you identified in Problem 8. Write them at sea level.

1. Discuss the importance of diagramming tools for modeling a system's behavior. Without such tools, what would an analyst do to model behavior?
2. Compare use-case diagrams to written use cases. Which one is better? Why?
3. Determining the level at which a use-case description should be written is not easy. For example, should the level be high or low? What makes it too high or too low? What things do you think need to be considered to determine the appropriate level?

CASE PROBLEMS

Pine Valley Furniture

As a Pine Valley Furniture intern, you have gained valuable insights into the systems development process. Jim Woo has made it a point to discuss with you the WebStore and the Customer Tracking System projects. The data requirements for both projects have been collected and are ready to be organized into use-case diagrams and written use cases. Jim has prepared use-case diagrams and written use cases for the WebStore; however, he has requested your help in preparing these documents for the Customer Tracking System.

You recall that Pine Valley Furniture distributes its products to retail stores, sells directly to customers, and is in the process of developing its WebStore, which will support online sales in the areas of corporate furniture buying, home office furniture purchasing, and student furniture purchasing. You also know that the Customer Tracking System's primary objective is to track and forecast customer buying patterns.

Information collected during the requirements determination activity suggests that the Customer Tracking System should collect customer purchasing activity data. Customers will be tracked based on a variety of factors, including customer type, geographic location, type of sale, and promotional item purchases. The Customer Tracking System should support trend analysis, facilitate sales information reporting, enable managers to generate ad hoc queries, and interface with the WebStore.

a. Create a use-case diagram for the Customer Tracking System. How many use cases should you include? How many actors should there be?
b. Using the template in Figure 6.9, create a written use-case description for at least one of the use cases in the diagram you created for part a.
c. Exchange your use-case diagram and written use-case description with a classmate. Compare and contrast your work with your classmate's. Focus on areas where your work differs and try to figure out why.

Hoosier Burger

As one of Build a Better System's lead analysts on the Hoosier Burger project, you have spent significant time discussing the current and future needs of the restaurant with Bob and Thelma Mellankamp. In one of these conversations, Bob and Thelma mentioned that they were in

the process of purchasing the empty lot next to Hoosier Burger. In the future, they would like to expand Hoosier Burger to include a drive-through, build a larger seating area in the restaurant, include more items on the Hoosier Burger menu, and provide delivery service to Hoosier Burger customers. After several discussions and much thought, the decision was made to implement the drive-through and delivery service and wait on the activities requiring physical expansion. Implementing the drive-through service will require only minor physical alterations to the west side of the Hoosier Burger building. Many of Hoosier Burger's customers work in the downtown area, so Bob and Thelma think a noon delivery service will offer an additional convenience to their customers.

One day, while having lunch at Hoosier Burger with Bob and Thelma, you discuss how the new delivery and drive-through services will work. Customer order taking via the drive-through window will mirror in-house dining operations. Therefore, drive-through window operations will not require information system modifications. Until a new system is implemented, the delivery service will be operated manually; each night, Bob will enter necessary inventory data into the current system.

Bob envisions the delivery system operating as follows. When a customer calls and places a delivery order, a Hoosier Burger employee records the order on a multiform order ticket. The employee captures such details as customer name, business or home address, phone number, order placement time, items ordered, and amount of sale. The multiform document is sent to the kitchen where it is separated when the order is ready for delivery. Two copies accompany the order; a third copy is placed in a reconciliation box. When the order is prepared, the delivery person delivers the order to the customer, removes one order ticket from the food bag, collects payment for the order, and returns to Hoosier Burger. Upon arriving at Hoosier Burger, the delivery person gives the order ticket and the payment to Bob. Each evening, Bob reconciles the order tickets stored in the reconciliation box with the delivery payments and matching order tickets returned by the delivery person. At the close of business each evening, Bob uses the data from the order tickets to update the goods sold and inventory files.

a. Create a use-case diagram for Hoosier Burger's delivery system. How many use cases should you include? How many actors should there be?

b. Using the template in Figure 6.9, create a written use-case description for at least one of the use cases in the diagram you created for part a.

c. Exchange your use-case diagram and written use-case description with a classmate. Compare and contrast your work with your classmate's. Focus on areas where your work differs and try to figure out why.

Evergreen Nurseries

Evergreen Nurseries offers a wide range of lawn and garden products to its customers, and conducts wholesale and retail operations. Although the company serves as a wholesaler to nurseries all over the United States, its founder and president has restricted its retail operations to California, the company's home state. The company is situated on 150 acres and wholesales its bulbs, perennials, roses, trees, shrubs, and Evergreen Accessory products. Evergreen Accessory products include a variety of fertilizers, plant foods, pesticides, and gardening supplies.

In the past 5 years, the company has seen phenomenal sales growth. Unfortunately, its information systems have been left behind. Although many of Evergreen Nurseries' processing activities are computerized, these activities require reengineering. You are part of the project team hired by Seymour Davis, the company's president, to renovate its wholesale division. Your project team was

hired to renovate the billing, order taking, and inventory control systems.

From requirements determination, you discovered the following: An Evergreen Nurseries customer places a call to the nursery. A sales representative takes the order, verifies the customer's credit standing, determines whether the items are in stock, notifies the customer of the product's status, informs the customer if any special discounts are in effect, and communicates the total payment due. Once an order is entered into the system, the customer's account is updated, product inventory is adjusted, and ordered items are pulled from stock. Ordered items are then packed and shipped to the customer. Once each month, a billing statement is generated and sent to the customer. The customer has 30 days to remit payment in full; otherwise, a 15 percent penalty is applied to the customer's account.

a. Create a use-case diagram for the Evergreen Nurseries' wholesale system. How many use cases should you include? How many actors should there be?

b. Using the template in Figure 6.9, create a written use-case description for at least one of the use cases in the diagram you created for part a.

c. Exchange your use-case diagram and written use-case description with a classmate. Compare and contrast your work with your classmate's. Focus on areas where your work differs and try to figure out why.

CASE: BROADWAY ENTERTAINMENT COMPANY, INC.

Use-Case Modeling for the Web-Based Customer Relationship Management System

Case Introduction

The BEC student team of Tracey Wesley, John Whitman, Missi Davies, and Aaron Sharp left the first meeting with Carrie Douglass, manager of the BEC store in Centerville, Ohio, eager to begin investigating the requirements for the customer relationship management system. Before they began requirements determination, they structured what they had learned already. Based on the Systems Service Request and the initial meeting with Carrie, the team developed a first draft of a use-case diagram for the system (see BEC Figure 6.1). This use-case diagram, using Microsoft Visio, shows the system in the middle, the actors (Customer, Employee, and the Entertainment Tracker BEC in-store information system) that interact with the system on the outside, and the connections among the actors and use cases. While using Visio, the students were reminded that Visio does not comply with all of the standard Unified Modeling Language (UML) notation. For example, in BEC Figure 6.1, the connection from the "Identify rental status" use case to the "Request rental extension" use case is labeled <<extends>> rather than <<extend>>, and the "Display comments on product" use case shows <<uses>> rather than <<include>> in the connections to the two related use cases.

Not too surprisingly, most of the connections are between the system and customers. The use-case diagram helped the team organize for requirements determination. The data collection part of the analysis phase would be used to verify this overview model of the customer relationship management system and to gather details for each connection, detailed actions for each use case, and a data storage component inside the system.

The team needed one more result before beginning the detailed work of analysis and design—a catchy name for the system it was designing. The BEC Customer Relationship Management System was too long and dull. With the cooperation of Carrie Douglass, team members ran a contest among the other teams in their class to give each member of the team with the best name suggestion (as selected by Carrie) a free movie rental at the Centerville BEC store. Some teams tried to create acronyms using the words and acronyms BEC, Broadway Entertainment Company, and customer relationship management, but most of these were not pronounceable or meaningful. Other teams created phrases that conveyed the Web technology to be used to build the system (e.g., one team suggested VideosByBEC, similar to AutoByTel for automobile sales and information on the Web). However, Carrie

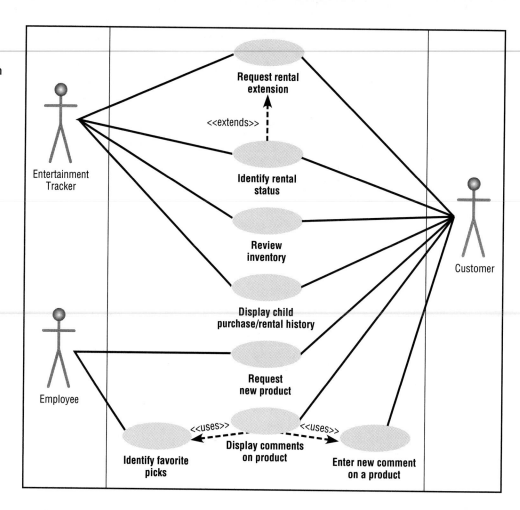

wanted a name that would convey the personal relationship the system will create with the customer. Thus, one suggested name stood out from the rest. The winner was MyBroadway.

Structuring the High-Level Process Findings from Requirements Determination

The BEC student team used various methods to understand the requirements for MyBroadway. The following sections explain how they approached studying each use case on the use-case diagram and what they discovered from their analysis.

Request Rental Extension

The team studied documentation of the Entertainment Tracker system provided to store employees and the manager. From this documentation, the team understood the data about products and product sales and rentals maintained in store records. This was a necessary step to determine what data the "Request rental extension" use case would need from the customer and Entertainment Tracker. It was clear that MyBroadway would not be the system of record to operate the store; Entertainment Tracker was this official record. For example, the official record of when a rented product was due to be returned would be recorded in the Entertainment Tracker database. Thus, product inventory, sales, and rental

data needed by MyBroadway would be extracted periodically from Entertainment Tracker to be stored in MyBroadway for faster access and to keep the two systems as decoupled as possible. Because of the role of Entertainment Tracker, any activity in MyBroadway that changed data in Entertainment Tracker would have to submit a transaction to Entertainment Tracker that Entertainment Tracker understood. The only instance of this the team discovered related to the "Request rental extension" use case. This use case finds the due date in the MyBroadway database and then interacts with Entertainment Tracker to request the extension and to inform the customer whether the extension was accepted. Entertainment Tracker, however, would make the decision, based on its own rules, whether or not to accept the extension. Fortunately, requesting an extension is a transaction in Entertainment Tracker handled from a point-of-sale terminal in the store, so MyBroadway would simply need to simulate this transaction.

Identify Favorite Picks

The team also surveyed employees and customers to understand what would be useful related to the employee "Identify favorite picks" use case. Employees and customers agreed that there are only two broad groups of items for favorite picks: new releases and classics. Each week, a different store employee will select one or two newly released or classic products in a given product category. For example, each week one employee will select one or two newly released children's videos, another employee will select one or two newly released jazz and new age CDs, and yet another employee will select one or two classic romance DVDs. It is not possible to cover every category of videotape, DVD, and CD each week, but over time most categories will be selected. Selections will be retained for 2 years. Each week, five store employees will make selections each in a different product category. An employee will be given a list of those 10 product categories for which favorite picks have not been made for the longest time. Each employee will be matched with the category with which he or she is most familiar and given a list of those newly released and classic products in that category. A classic product is one that continues to be rented or sold at least 10 years after its initial release. An employee selects one or two products on this list and provides a quality grade for each (A, A–, B, . . . F), a description of its contents relevant to language and sexually explicit references, and a few sentences of personal comments about the product that a parent might want to know. The date of the entry would be recorded with the rest of the data.

Request New Product

The team used interviews with customers, Carrie Douglass, and the assistant store manager as well as observations of people using similar Web-based systems from major online bookstores and other shopping enterprises to determine the nature of the other use cases on the use-case diagram. For "Request new product," MyBroadway will collect all the requests and Carrie will trigger printing a list, in decreasing order of frequency of request, of each requested product. Carrie will then use this report to send a letter to the BEC purchasing department requesting the acquisition of these items. New product requests will be kept for 2 months and then purged.

Enter New Comment on a Product

For the "Enter new comment on a product" use case, MyBroadway will show a parent or child basic information about the product (such as title, publisher, artist, and date released) and then allow him or her to enter an unstructured comment about that product. The length of the comment will not be limited. Each comment will be stored separately, and the same person may comment on the same item many times. The date and time of the comment will be stored with the comment. An issue that required some discussion with Carrie was whether people will have to identify themselves for their comments to be recorded. Carrie was unsure what to do, so the team convened a focus group of a few parents to explore this issue. The team discovered that the parents would not consider a comment valid unless it were attributed, and that the parents thought they and their children would enter a more helpful comment if it were attributed. Carrie, however, saw no need to retain data about customers in MyBroadway, but she wondered how bogus customer names could be identified. Entertainment Tracker maintains data about each customer, including each child with a mem-

bership card. Thus, it was decided that customers will have to enter their membership number along with the comment. This number will be sent to Entertainment Tracker for matching with its record of customer numbers after the comment is entered but before it is available to be reported to other customers. Whether the comment is entered by a parent or a child also will be recorded with the comment. If the number does not match a membership number for a BEC customer, the comment will be dropped. When the comment is displayed, the name of the member entering the comment as well as whether that person is a parent or child will be shown.

Review Inventory

The "Review inventory" use case consolidates several similar actions. A customer can ask to see product data by specific title, or to see data for all the products by artist, category (e.g., new age or jazz CD), publisher, release month, or any combination of these factors. In each case, for each product identified by the search criteria, the product title, artist, publisher, release date, media, description, and sale and rental price will be shown.

Display Comments on Products

The "Display comments on products" use case is triggered when a customer enters the name of the product (and possibly searching through a set of products with approximately that name until the exact product is found). Once the exact product the customer is interested in is identified, then all the comments previously entered by customers and favorite picks entered by employees will be available for display. The customer may ask to see only those comments and picks entered since some date they specify and may ask to see comments only by parents, only by children, only by employees (i.e., only favorite picks), or all comments and picks. Comments and picks will be shown in reverse chronology entry order.

Identify Rental Status

For this use case, the customers enter their membership number, and then MyBroadway displays a list of all the product titles and return due dates for all outstanding rented items. Often, customers are engaged in "Identify rental status" before they engage in "Request rental extension," but the team decided to consider these separate use cases.

Display Child Purchase/Rental History

The team discovered that this is arguably the most complex of the use cases on the context diagram. At a high level, this use case needs access to sales and rental history data, including what products have been bought and rented by whom. Customers indicated that a simple history would not be sufficient. They also wanted to see the customer comments and favorite picks ratings for each item. So, the outcome of this use case is a report that shows for a given child the title of each item he or she has bought or rented in the past 6 months, and for each item the rating entered by each employee who has rated that product, and the five most recent parent comments recorded about that item.

Case Summary

Accurately and thoroughly documenting business processes can be tedious and time-consuming, but insightful. The student team working on the analysis and design of MyBroadway quickly discovered how extensive a system Carrie, the store employees, and customers wanted for this customer relationship management system. The team was unsure whether it could do a thorough analysis and design for all the desired features. However, starting with a use-case diagram allowed the team to show the total scope of the system as desired by the project sponsor and system users and yet focus attention on one piece of the system at a time. If only parts of the system could be built during the course project, at least the team would be able to show how those pieces fit into the complete system. The team members also recognized that structuring use cases was only part of the systems analysis. They would also need to identify all the data stored inside MyBroadway and then structure these data into a database specification. Each use case on the use-case diagram would have to be specified in sufficient detail for a programmer to build that functionality into the information system.

The BEC student team made the decision to use automated tools to draw use cases (and other system diagrams) and to record project dictionary data about system objects, such as data objects, activities, and user interfaces. (Because you will use whatever tools your instructor recommends, we do not refer to any specific tools by name in this or subsequent cases.) These automated tools are critical for making it easy to change diagrams, to produce clean documentation about the system requirements, and to make each aspect of the documentation consistent with each other aspect. Drawing the initial diagrams and recording all the dictionary entries is time-consuming. These automated data, however, can be changed by any team member, and team members can prepare new diagrams and dictionary reports at any time with minimal effort.

CASE QUESTIONS

1. Notice in BEC Figure 6.1 how many of the use cases are connected with Entertainment Tracker. Do you agree that this figure shows the nature of the interaction between these use cases and Entertainment Tracker? If not, redraw the use-case diagram to show the proper interaction. Explain why you redrew the diagram as you did. In answering this question, explicitly consider whether there should be an additional use case to extract data from Entertainment Tracker for use in MyBroadway, and then other use cases can use this extract use case.

2. Besides your answer to Question 1, does the use-case diagram in BEC Figure 6.1 represent an accurate and complete overview of the system as described in this case for requirements collected during the analysis phase? If not, what is wrong or missing? If necessary, draw a new use-case diagram in light of what is explained in this case. Why might a use-case diagram initially drawn at the end of project initiation and planning need to be redrawn during the analysis phase?

3. The store manager is not shown as an actor in the use-case diagram in BEC Figure 6.1, except implicitly as an employee who enters favorite picks and sees summaries of requested products. Based on the descriptions in this case, does it make sense that store manager does not appear on the use-case diagram? If not on the use-case diagram, where might the store manager appear or be described? Based on the description in this case, are there any actors missing on the use-case diagram of BEC Figure 6.1?

4. Based on the descriptions of each use case, write templates (as in Figures 6.11, 6.12, and 6.13 in this chapter) for each use case. If this case does not provide all the details you need for each template, propose what analysis activities you would conduct to determine the missing contents of the use case templates.

5. Review your answer to Question 4 for the "Request new product" use case. Was it difficult to write the template for this use case? Did you consider several alternative explanations for this use case? If so, explain the alternatives and why you chose the template you wrote.

6. Look at your answer to Question 4 and focus attention on the "Request rental extension" use case. Modify your template for this use case based on the following explanation. A customer provides his or her customer number or name and a product number or title, and then MyBroadway finds in its records the rental information for this customer's outstanding rental of this product, including the due date. Then the customer may decide that he or she can return the item by the due date, in which case no request for extension is made. If the customer decides to extend the due date, the customer can request a 1-day or 2-day extension, each with a different fee, which will be due when the product is returned. MyBroadway will then send a rental extension request transaction to Entertainment Tracker as if it were a point-of-sale terminal from which the same request was being made. Entertainment Tracker may reject the request if the customer has delinquent fees. Once Entertainment Tracker makes its decision, it returns a code to MyBroadway indicating a yes or the reason for a no to the request. If the decision is no, the customer is given a message to explain rejection. If yes, MyBroadway rental data are updated to reflect the extension, and the user is given a confirmation message.

7. Investigate the capabilities of Microsoft Visio to store and report templates or explanations for use cases on a use-case diagram. Write a report about your findings, and reformulate at least one of your use-case templates from Question 4 into Visio as an example.

Chapter

7

Conceptual Data Modeling

Chapter Objectives

After studying this chapter, you should be able to:

➤ Determine how to develop conceptual data models from use cases and other narratives.

➤ Understand UML notations for conceptual data modeling.

➤ Explain relationship characteristics such as degree and multiplicity.

➤ Describe data relationships such as association, aggregation, and generalization.

➤ Describe different kinds of attributes such as identifier, multivalued, and derived.

Chapter Contents

➤ Chapter Preview
➤ Conceptual Data Modeling
➤ Gathering Information for Conceptual Data Modeling
➤ Introduction to UML Data Modeling
➤ An Example of Conceptual Data Modeling for PVF WebStore

Chapter Preview

Chapter 6 explained how to write a detailed description of a use case from user requirements. This chapter will describe how to structure requirements and develop models to represent the requirements (Figure 7.1). Specifically, this chapter will discuss conceptual data modeling, which examines the structure of organizational data from user requirements while staying independent of implementation considerations. Note that a use case does not capture all the user requirements. However, CASE tools allow the remaining requirements to be attached as documents to the use-case description. After the user requirements are documented, other systems analysis activities can be undertaken, such as developing class diagrams. A significant portion of a UML class diagram is composed of data elements. Thus, for business applications conceptual data modeling is one of the most important analysis activities and is the subject of this chapter.

For business applications, the entity relationship (ER) diagram is still a popular conceptual data modeling choice among data modelers. ER diagramming often is taught in a database course. OOSAD data modeling, however, uses the UML notation, which bears resemblance to the ER notation but can be used to model behavioral aspects of the system. Note that the goal of analysis is to come up with an analysis class diagram. Data modeling is an intermediate step, which provides entity classes that are then used to develop analysis classes.

Figure 7.1 Systems Analysis Has Three Parts: Requirements Determination, Requirements Structuring, and Alternative Generation and Selection

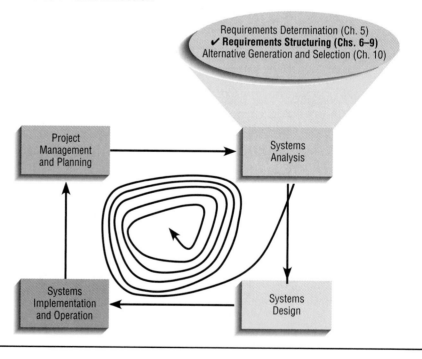

CONCEPTUAL DATA MODELING

Conceptual data model
A detailed model that shows the overall structure of organizational data; it is independent of any database management system or other implementation considerations.

Entity relationship (ER) data model
A graphical representation for depicting a conceptual data model using the notions of entity, attribute, and relationship among entities.

A conceptual data model is a representation of organizational data that shows the structure of, and the interrelationships among, data in an implementation independent manner. A conceptual data model is usually graphical. Data modeling is key to OOSAD projects for business applications because the UML class diagram bears strong resemblance to the data model drawn using UML constructs. Data models provide entity classes, which are used in sequence diagrams to model system behavior.

For about three decades, the entity relationship (ER) data model (Chen, 1976) has been used to show how data are organized in an information system. Data analysts are familiar with ER modeling, and database courses generally include ER modeling. The transition to the UML mode of data modeling should be relatively easy given that the underlying concepts are similar. It is wise to learn both modes of data modeling. The focus of this chapter is on UML data modeling, which is more expressive than ER modeling because a UML data model can be extended later to a class diagram, which includes the structure of objects as well as their behavior. This chapter also introduces the composite structure diagram, which is used to show how an object is made up from its parts.

Systems analysts typically do conceptual data modeling at the same time as other requirements analysis and structuring steps during systems analysis. They can use methods such as interviewing, questionnaires, and JAD sessions to collect information for conceptual data modeling. On larger systems development teams, a subset of the project team concentrates on data modeling while other team members focus their attention on writing use cases or developing class and other UML diagrams. The systems analyst develops (or uses from prior systems development) a conceptual data model for the current system and builds a conceptual data model that supports the scope and requirements for the proposed or enhanced system. The work of all team members is coordinated and shared through the project dictionary or repository. A CASE tool can be used to maintain this repository.

The Process of Conceptual Data Modeling

Typically, conceptual data modeling begins with the development of a data model for the system being replaced, if a system exists. This is essential for planning the conversion of the current files or database into the database of the new system. Further, this is a good, but not a perfect, starting point for understanding the new system's data requirements. Then, a new conceptual data model is built that consists of all of the data requirement, including use cases for the new system. These requirements should have been discovered from the fact-finding methods used during requirements determination. Then a checklist needs to be reviewed to make sure the model is complete. This might require further meetings with the user to obtain missing information or to clarify existing facts. Today, given the popularity of iterative methodologies, these requirements often evolve through various iterations (Figure 7.2).

What is the role of conceptual data modeling in systems analysis and design? The role is illustrated in Figure 7.3, and although some of the stages might be unfamiliar, the eventual goal is to develop an analysis class diagram. Conceptual data modeling is followed by logical data modeling, which involves the translation into an object-relational data model. In OOSAD, object relations need to be identified early so that entity classes can be used to develop sequence diagrams, which can then be used to generate analysis classes. A diagram showing the analysis classes and the relationships among the classes is called an analysis class diagram. Details (e.g., data formats and access methods) are added during the design phase, which follows the analysis phase.

Figure 7.2
Process of Conceptual
Data Modeling

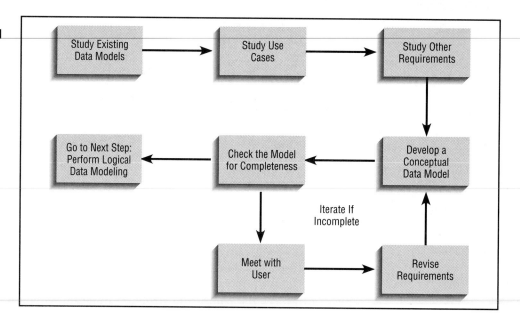

Figure 7.3
Role of Conceptual
Data Modeling in
Systems Analysis

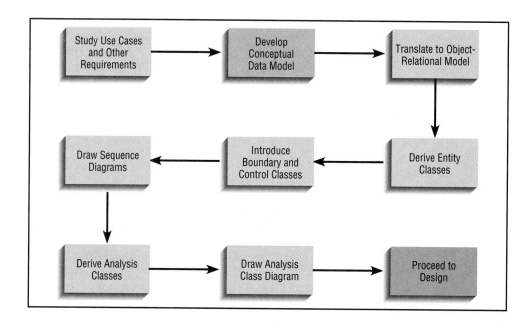

GATHERING INFORMATION FOR CONCEPTUAL DATA MODELING

Requirements determination methods for conceptual data modeling must include questions and investigations that take a data focus rather than a process, logic, or user interface focus. During interviews with potential system users, specific questions must be asked to gain the perspective on data needed to develop a data model. Later in this chapter, some specific terminology and constructs used in data modeling are introduced. However, even without this specific data modeling language, one can begin to understand the kinds of data-related questions that must be answered during requirements determination. Note that users might find it difficult to separate the structure and behavior of objects. A data model essentially represents the structure of objects, so we recommend modeling first. This prevents ignoring the notion of an object; each data object also will have operations. Later on, the behavior of data objects will be incorporated along with other kinds of objects.

Table 7-1 Questions to Consider to Develop Accurate and Complete Data Models.

CATEGORY OF QUESTIONS	INFORMATION TO DERIVE FROM SYSTEM USERS AND BUSINESS MANAGERS
Classes	What are the subjects/objects of the business? What types of people, places, things, and materials are used or interact in this business? How many instances of each object may exist?
Attributes	What data needs to be maintained about the objects? What characteristics describe each object? On what basis are objects referenced selected, qualified, sorted, and categorized? Can a property of an object have multiple values? Is the property mandatory or optional for a given object?
Identifier	What unique characteristic(s) distinguishes each object from other objects of the same type? Could this distinguishing feature change over time or is it permanent? Could this characteristic of an object be missing even though we know the object exists? Can the objects be identified by using a sequence of numbers?
Association, Aggregation, and Composition	What relationships exist between objects? Is a relationship of kind part-whole? If yes, can one exist without the other? How many objects are involved in a relationship? Is the relationship between objects of the same class? What is the cardinality of an object participating in a relationship?
Generalization	Is one object 'a kind' or "a kind" of another? do objects form a hierarchy from more general to more specialized?
Time Dimensions	Over what period of time are you interested in these data? If characteristics of an object change over time, must you know the obsolete values? Do you need historical trends of snapshot values? What is the unit of time?
Integrity Rules	Are values for data characteristics limited in any way? Can the data characteristics take non-null values only?
Security Controls	Who can create data? Who can retrieve data? Who can update data? Who can delete data? Are there time intervals when data cannot be accessed?

Although use cases provide adequate information for an initial data model, further investigation might be needed to develop a complete data model. By using a CASE tool, supplemental information can be attached to the use case. The supplemental information can include reports and screen layouts.

Data modeling typically is done from a combination of perspectives. The first perspective is called the *top-down approach*. It derives the data model from an intimate understanding of the nature of the business, rather than from any specific information requirements in computer displays, reports, or business forms. Table 7-1 summarizes key questions to ask systems users and business managers so that an accurate and complete data model can be developed. Some of these questions are top-down; others follow the middle-of-the-road approach. The questions should be posed in business terms. Technical terms do not mean much to a business manager, so it is essential to learn how to frame questions in business terms. A user typically will not know the differences among association, aggregation, and generalization, so the questions need to be formulated in a way that can be understood and answered by the user. Analysis is as much about communication skills as it is about technical know-how.

Alternatively, the information for data modeling can be gathered by reviewing specific business documents—computer displays, reports, and business forms—handled within the system. These displays, reports, and forms can be attached to the relevant use case. The analyst examines the fields in these documents, and thus starts at a detailed level. This second perspective of gaining an understanding of data is often called a *bottom-up approach*. Consider, for example, Figure 7.4, which shows a customer order form used at Pine Valley Furniture.

From the form in Figure 7.4, it can be determined that the following data must be kept in the database: customer number, name, address, city, state, zip code, order number, order date, promised date, product number, description, quantity ordered, and unit price.

Each order is from one customer, and an order can have multiple line items, each for one product. This kind of understanding of an organization's policies can be used to develop data models.

Chapter 5 introduced some general methods of obtaining requirements. This section has discussed questions that specifically address data modeling. However, it might not be evident how these questions relate to use cases described in Chapter 6. It

```
                    PVF CUSTOMER ORDER
    ORDER NO: 61384                    CUSTOMER NO: 1273

         NAME:            Contemporary Designs
         ADDRESS:         123 Oak St.
         CITY-STATE-ZIP:  Austin, TX 28384

    ORDER DATE: 11/04/2004   PROMISED DATE:  11/21/2004


    PRODUCT                  QUANTITY    UNIT
    NO        DESCRIPTION    ORDERED     PRICE

    M128      Bookcase       4           200.00
    B381      Cabinet        2           150.00
    R210      Table          1           500.00
```

is true that some of these questions also are asked so that use cases can be described. However, as mentioned earlier, use cases do not describe all the user requirements; they probably describe about one- third of the user requirements. A use case probably will not delve into describing each and every data attribute or capture all the integrity constraints pertaining to data; it is text-based, unlike reports and screens, which are visual. Gathering user requirements is an iterative process; as one proceeds, the details can be examined. A use case, in general, is neither top-down nor bottom-up, but more middle of the road. A use case is for communication with the users, who usually are not interested in all the requirements details. An analyst does need to obtain all the requirements, although this might be accomplished over a few iterations.

INTRODUCTION TO UML DATA MODELING

As mentioned in the first two chapters, the UML language is designed to express the static as well as the dynamic aspects of a system. The static part is represented mainly by the class diagram and defined by the classes, attributes of classes, and the relationships among classes. This chapter focuses on the data modeling aspect of the class diagram (i.e., the attributes of the classes and the relationships among classes). Several CASE tools support UML. We will use IBM's Rational Rose, a popular UML CASE tool, in this chapter.

Class

Class
A set of objects that share the same attributes, operations, relationships, and semantics (Booch, Rumbaugh, & Jacobson, 1999).

In data modeling terms, a class is a person, place, thing, event, or concept in the user environment about which the organization wishes to maintain data. This definition is derived from the notion of an entity type in the entity-relationship model. Thus, a data-intensive class also is called an entity class, and its instances are called entity objects. As noted in Table 7-1, the first requirements determination question an analyst should ask concerns entity classes. Some examples of classes follow:

Person: Employee, Student, Patient
Place: State, Region, Country, Branch
Thing: Machine, Building, Automobile, Product
Event: Sale, Registration, Renewal
Concept: Account, Course

Figure 7.5a Class Student

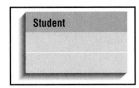

Figure 7.5b
Objects Maria and David of the Same Class Student

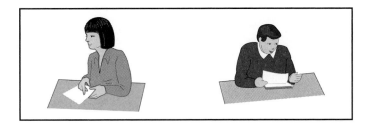

The notation for a class is a rectangle, which is partitioned further into three rectangles: one for the name of the class, the second for the attributes, and the third for the operations (Figure 7.5a). This chapter will not consider the third rectangle, which is for the operations of a class.

Object

Object
An entity that encapsulates data and behavior, and is a single occurrence of a class.

An object is an instance of a class; it encapsulates data and behavior. As mentioned earlier, this chapter will focus on the data part of objects. Thus, Maria and David may be objects of the class Student and have data characteristics such as name and address (Figure 7.5b). The class might have thousands of student objects. A generic object of the class Student can be expressed as :Student.

Attributes

Attribute
A named property of a class that describes a range of values that instances of the attribute might hold (Booch, Rumbaugh, & Jacobson, 1999).

A class has a set of attributes associated with it. An attribute is a property or characteristic of a class that is of interest to the organization (relationships also can have attributes, as we will see in the section on relationships). Asking about attributes is the second question noted in Table 7-1. Following are some typical classes and associated attributes:

Student: studentId, studentName, address, phoneNumber, major
Automobile: vehicleId, color, weight, horsepower
Employee: employeeId, employeeName, address, skill

We use nouns with lowercase letters in naming an attribute (e.g., address); if an attribute is composed of two words, the second word starts with the first letter in uppercase (e.g., studentName). See Figure 7.6, composed using Rational Rose, which shows the attributes of the class Student.

Figure 7.6
The Class Student with Its Attributes

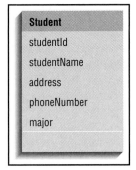

Figure 7.7 The
Identifier Shown by
the Stereotype <<PK>>

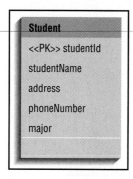

Identifiers

Identifier
An attribute or a combination of attributes that has been selected to be used as the unique characteristic for a class.

Candidate key
An attribute (or combination of attributes) that uniquely identifies each object of a class.

Primary key
A candidate key that has been selected as the unique, identifying characteristic for a class.

Stereotype
A construct that allows an extension of the UML vocabulary.

An *identifier* is an attribute or a combination of attributes that has been selected to be used as the unique characteristic for a class. The values of the identifier allow objects to be distinguished from one another. In a given class, more than one attribute or combination of attributes might distinguish one object from other objects of the same class. A *candidate key* is an attribute (or combination of attributes) that uniquely identifies each object of a data class. Some entities might have more than one candidate key. One candidate key for Student is the studentId provided by a university; a second could be the Social Security number. If more than one candidate key exists, the designer must choose one of the candidate keys as the identifier. Thus, an identifier is a candidate key that has been designated explicitly as the distinguishing characteristic(s). An identifier also is called a *primary key*. In Figure 7.7, we show the identifier of Student as studentId by using the stereotype <<PK>>, where PK stands for primary key. A *stereotype* is a construct that extends the UML vocabulary. Because primary key has no standard UML symbol, the designer can create one using a stereotype.

A DBMS can provide several mechanisms to create an identifier. For example, it can create object identifiers for objects of a class. In many cases (e.g., events, transactions), an attribute can be created and uniqueness ensured by using a sequence of numbers. The sequences generally are managed by the DBMS. A new object gets a number one higher than the previous object, and this ensures uniqueness.

Sometimes more than one attribute is required to identify an object. For example, consider the class Game for a basketball league. The attribute teamName is clearly not a candidate key, because each team plays several games. If each team plays exactly one home game against every other team, then the combination of the attributes homeTeam and visitingTeam is a candidate key for Game. If each team can play several home games against another team, but can play no more than one game on a given date, then the combination of the attributes homeTeam and gameDate is a candidate key for Game; if the home team can play several games in a day, then it might be necessary to use the combination of homeTeam, visitingTeam, and gameDate. Even this might not be adequate though, and an attribute like gameId might have to be created.

Important Considerations for Selecting Primary Keys (Identifiers)

Primary keys should be selected carefully because they are critical for the integrity of data. The following identifier selection rules should be applied:

1. Choose a primary key that will not change its value over the life of each object of the class. For example, the combination of employeeName and address probably would be a poor choice as a primary key for Employee because the value of an employee's name or address could easily change during an employee's term of employment.

2. Choose a primary key such that, for each object of the class, the attribute is guaranteed to have valid values and not be null. Thus, phone number may not be a good choice since some people do not have phones. To ensure valid values,

it might be necessary to include special controls in data entry and maintenance routines to eliminate the possibility of errors. If the primary key is a combination of two or more attributes, then all parts of the key must have valid values.

3. Avoid the use of so-called intelligent keys, whose structure indicates classifications, locations, and other properties. For example, the first two digits of a key for a part class might indicate the warehouse location. Such codes often are modified as conditions change, which renders the primary key values invalid.

4. Consider substituting single-attribute surrogate keys for large composite keys. For example, an attribute called gameId could be used for the entity Game instead of the combination of homeTeam, visitingTeam, and gameDate.

Chapter 2 introduced the notion of object identity and object identifiers. When are object identifiers employed? The term *object identifier* originates from object-oriented programming and applies to a variety of applications such as graphics, windows objects, and so on. If a rectangle is drawn on a screen and a copy of the rectangle is made, the two rectangles appear exactly alike. Yet, each has its own identity. One rectangle can be placed on top of another identical one, and still, each maintains its identity. Because size, coordinates, or any other attribute cannot be used, system-generated identifiers called object identifiers are utilized. In database applications, however, it is common to create an attribute and populate it using a sequence, which takes considerably less space than system-generated object identifiers.

Should object identifiers now be employed instead of conventional identifiers in business applications? Business applications do not appear ready to employ the system-generated object identifier for databases. First, commercial and popular DBMSs have just started offering the object identifier facility, and the usage is yet to mature. Second, analysts, designers, and programmers who work with business applications are familiar with the conventional identifier approach. Working with object identifiers does alter the programming style and SQL statements because identifiers are commonly the attributes used to retrieve data. Third, hundreds of thousands of existing applications use the conventional identifier approach, and organizations do not have the resources to alter these applications unless there is a significant benefit over cost in doing so. Fourth, the object identifier generally takes more space than a designer-created identifier. Fifth, if a copy of a table is made, new object identifiers are created, and this might not be desirable in many situations. Having said that, using object identifiers has some advantages even in business applications, and the analysts, designers, and programmers should be aware of the facility and its usage, especially for maintaining relationships among objects by using references. Usage of object identifiers will be demonstrated in Chapter 11, which covers physical database design issues.

Multivalued Attributes

Multivalued attribute
An attribute that can take on more than one value for each object.

A multivalued attribute can take on more than one value for each object. Suppose that a student can have several phone numbers. Say, for example, the student Rick has six phone numbers, Laurel has four phone numbers, Kalpana has one phone number, and David has none. A student can have none, one, or several phone numbers. The attribute phone number is multivalued because for a given object, the attribute can have more than one value.

During conceptual design, there are two common approaches to handle multivalued attributes. The first approach is to use a symbol for multivalued attributes. Although this can be done using an icon, UML has no standard icon for multivalued attributes. Therefore, the easiest approach is to use the stereotype <<Multivalued>> before the attribute (see Figure 7.8). Note that object-relational DBMSs can implement multivalued attributes directly.

The second approach is to create a separate class for the multivalued attribute and use an association relationship to link it with the main class. Relationships will be introduced soon. The approach also handles several attributes that repeat together, called a repeating group. For example, dependent name, age, and relation

Figure 7.8
Attribute
phoneNumber Shown
as Multivalued

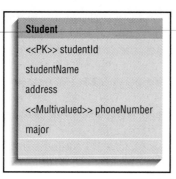

to employee (spouse, child, parent, etc.) are multivalued attributes about an employee, and these attributes repeat together. We can show this using a class called Dependent and a relationship between Dependent and Employee.

Composite Attributes

The attribute address in the class Student can be designed as an atomic, meaning one, attribute; however, it will make querying difficult on a part of the address like City. The address typically has a value such as "11200 SW 8th Street, Miami, FL 33199," where the value of City is embedded in a larger string. Address can be split into four attributes: Street, City, State, and Zip code. However, because the four attributes almost always go together, it is better to design it as a composite attribute consisting of Street, City, State, and Zip code. To accomplish this, the composite needs to be defined as a class. Thus, we define a class Address (Figure 7.9a), which can then be shown as a type in the definition of class Student (Figure 7.9b).

Relationships

Relationship
A semantic connection between objects of one or more classes.

Relationships are the glue that holds together the elements of a class diagram. A relationship is a semantic connection between objects of one or more classes. A relationship can result because of an event that has occurred or because of some natural linkage between entity instances. Relationships generally are labeled with verb phrases. For example, we might be interested in knowing which employees belong to a certain department. This leads to a relationship (called works) between the Employee and the Department classes, as shown in Figure 7.10.

Figure 7.9a
Composite Attribute
Address Shown as a
Class

Figure 7.9b
Attribute Address
Shown as a Type
Address

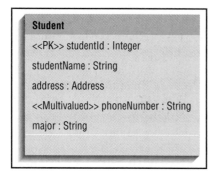

Figure 7.10
Relationship between
Classes

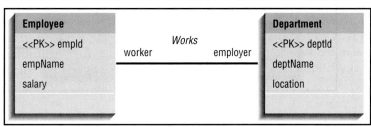

Figure 7.11
Relationship Works
Shown with Roles

The *works* relationship can be used to determine the department of a given employee. Conversely, employees who belong to a particular department also can be determined. The relationship can be optionally qualified by the roles of each class in the relationship. A role provides a name to identify a relationship end within a relationship. For example, the class Department can be qualified by the role Employer, and the class Employee by the role Worker (Figure 7.11). However, this can clutter the class diagram. The exact standards to be followed will vary from company to company.

Role
A name to identify a relationship end within a relationship.

A relationship generally is described by its name, degree, and multiplicity (which is comprised of minimum and maximum cardinality). These three characteristics are adequate for most applications. Next, the degree and multiplicity characteristics will be detailed.

Degree of a Relationship

Degree
The number of classes that participate in a relationship.

The degree of a relationship is the number of classes that participate in that relationship. Thus, the relationship works illustrated previously is of degree two, because it has two classes: Employee and Department. Relationships of degree two (binary) are the most common. Relationships of degree one (unary) and degree three (ternary) are encountered occasionally. Higher-degree relationships are possible, but they rarely are encountered in practice, so this discussion is restricted to these three cases.

Unary Relationship

Unary
A relationship between the objects of one class.

Also called a recursive relationship, a unary relationship is a relationship between the objects of one class. An example is shown in Figure 7.12. The relationship *marriedTo* is between objects of the class Person.

Binary Relationship

Binary
A relationship between objects of two classes.

A binary relationship is a relationship between objects of two classes and is the most common type of relationship encountered in data modeling. Figure 7.10 shows the *works* relationship between Employee and Department.

Figure 7.12
Unary Relationship

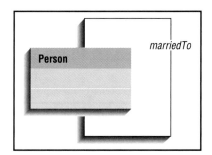

Figure 7.18
Multiplicity in a
Ternary Relationship

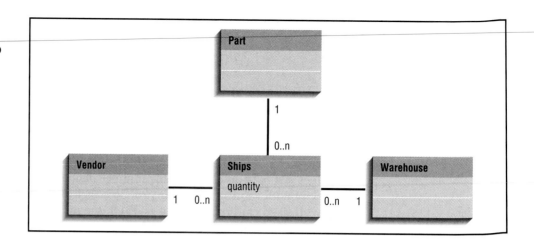

in Figure 7.18 by including the multiplicities. For a detailed treatment of the ternary relationship, please refer to the book by Teorey (1990) or the paper by Ram (1995).

Association

Association
A relationship or link between instances (or objects) of classes.

An association is a relationship where no object is subordinate to others. The association is the most common type of relationship. For example, the relationship between a movie and a videotape (Figure 7.14) and the relationship between an employee and a department (Figure 7.11) are associations. These two relationships are one to many, also denoted as 1:m. Figure 7.12 shows an association, which is unary 1:1. One-to-many relationships normally do not have attributes; if they do, the attribute is shown with the "many" side. An association can be m:n, which sometimes has attributes.

As seen in the examples of the ships ternary relationship, attributes may be associated with a many-to-many relationship, as well as with a class. A many-to-many relationship (which is sometimes shown as m:n or M:N) has the maximum cardinality "many" on each side of the relationship. For example, suppose that the organization wishes to record the date (month and year) when an employee completes each course. Some sample data are shown in Table 7-2.

From these limited data it can be concluded that the attribute dateCompleted is not a property of the class Employee (because a given employee such as 549–23–1948 has completed courses on different dates). Nor is dateCompleted a property of Course because a particular course (such as Software Quality) may be completed on different dates. Instead, dateCompleted is a property of the relationship *completes* between Employee and Course. In this way, an m:n relationship behaves like a class; that is, it has attributes.

Associate Class
A many-to-many association that the data modeler chooses to model as a class.

An associative class is a many-to-many association that the data modeler chooses to model as a class. Several UML CASE tools provide a notation for the associate class. It is a recommended practice to use nouns for classes and verbs for relationships. Thus, the associative class can be renamed from a verb to a noun. Figure 7.19 illustrates the employee-course example using Rational Rose. Note that the relationship *completes* has been renamed as an associative class Certificate.

It is not necessary to clarify the multiplicity. Because Certificate is an associative class, the m:n relationship is implicit. This scenario is similar to that of cardinalities

Table 7-2 Sample Data.

EMPLOYEE_ID	COURSE_NAME	DATE_COMPLETED
549-23-1948	Basic Algebra	March 2006
629-16-8407	Software Quality	June 2006
816-30-0458	Software Quality	Feb 2006
549-23-1948	C Programming	May 2006

Figure 7.19
Example of an
Associative Class

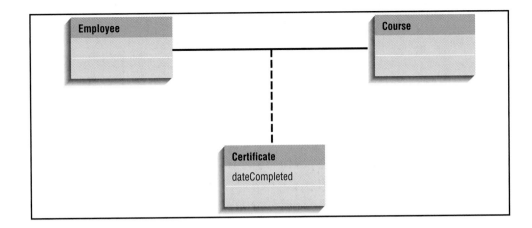

of a ternary relationship. The minimum cardinality on the Employee and Course side is "1" because a Certificate object is based on one employee and one course. The minimum cardinality of Certificate with respect to each of the two classes is "0." The primary key of Certificate will be formed by the concatenation of the primary keys of Employee and Course. If Certificate has its own primary key like certificateId, then you should treat Certificate as an entity, and define its relationships with Employee and Course.

What happens when an associative class is related to another class? Figure 7.20 shows an associative class Work, which results from a relationship between Employee and Project. In order to find out the skills used by an employee in a project, the relationship *useSkills* can be created between Work and Skill. Although *useSkills* is not shown as a ternary relationship, it does have the characteristics of a ternary relationship: The primary key of useSkills is formed by concatenating the primary keys of the three classes Employee, Project, and Skill. However, the ternary relationship by itself would not allow storage of attributes of Work. Hence, the representation shown in Figure 7.20 is better.

Why is useSkills not shown as an associative class even though it is an m:n relationship? This situation has no hard-and-fast rule. Here it is not shown as an associative class because it does not have attributes and because the multiplicity has been specified. One will arrive at the same entity class by following either approach.

Figure 7.20
Relationship between
an Associative Class
and a Class

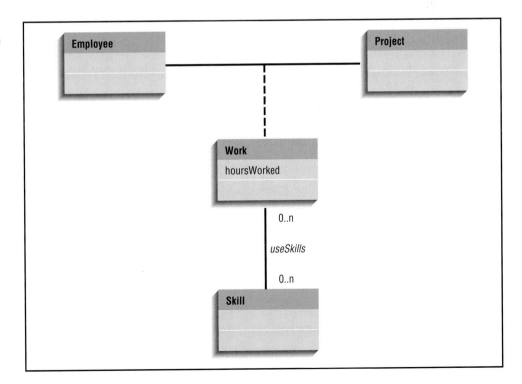

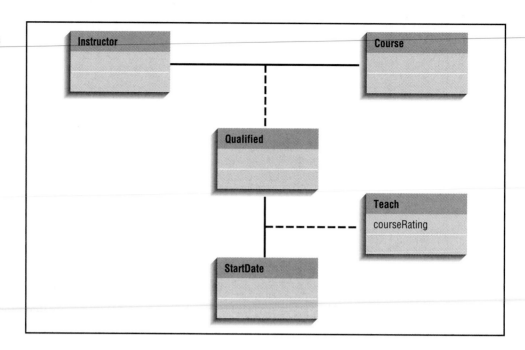

One situation in which a relationship must be turned into an associative class is when it has other relationships with classes besides the relationship that caused its creation. For example, consider Figure 7.21, which represents courses taught by instructors. Although the class Qualified does not have attributes, it needs to be shown as an associative class if it is important which instructor is qualified to teach which courses. Based on this information, users might need to create the teaching schedule called Teach and to store courseRating when available. If it does not matter which instructors are qualified to teach which courses, Teach can be shown as a ternary relationship among Instructor, Course, and StartDate.

Aggregation Relationship

Aggregation
An association that models a whole-part relationship between an aggregate, which is called whole, and its parts. It is a strong form of association in which the aggregate has no meaning without parts.

If two classes are bound by a whole-part relationship, the association is called an aggregation. Hence, aggregation is known as a "part-of" relationship. For example, a car is made up of parts, a computer is made up of parts, and a chair is made up of parts. However, are there examples that are more businesslike? For example, is an order made up of line items, or is a team made up of players? To determine whether a relationship is an aggregation, Quatrani (1999) suggests the following three guidelines:

a. Is the phrase *part of* used to describe the relationships? For example, is a player part of a team?
b. Are some operations on the whole automatically applied to its parts? For example, if a course is deleted, it automatically leads to deletion of all course offerings (or sections) pertaining to the course.
c. Is there an intrinsic asymmetry to the relationships where one class is subordinate to others?

The systems analyst also should consider the phrases *made up of, consists of,* or *element of* in case *part of* does not seem to be a natural way to describe the relationship. Consider how the two objects are retrieved. If one is retrieved, is it likely that the other will be retrieved, too? When you retrieve an order, you typically retrieve its line items, too. In order to add a new object, is it necessary to ensure that an object of the related class already has been created? Before you add a part on a bike, you need to ensure that the bike object has been created. Is one object dependent on another, or can it exist independently of the other? A subassembly for a bike can exist independently of the bike for a while, but eventually it becomes part of a bike. Does the primary key of one class depend on the other class's primary key? The primary key of order line items depends on the primary key of the order.

The answers to these questions determine whether a relationship can be considered an aggregation. The aggregation is strongly bound or loosely bound, depending on the number of criteria satisfied by the relationship. The recognition of a relationship at the analysis stage alerts the designer to consider the storage, addition, deletion, modification, and retrieval of related objects.

Composition
A strong form of aggregation in which the aggregate is meaningless without parts, and the parts meaningless without the aggregate.

A type of strong aggregation is a relationship called composition. In this case, the part is strongly owned by the composite and might not be part of any other composite. Thus, composition is a form of aggregation with strong ownership and a coincident lifetime of part with the whole. Typically, the parts exist only as long as the whole exists. If the whole is deleted, the parts are deleted as well.

A few examples will help illustrate different kinds of aggregation. The most common example of aggregation is the bill of materials, which is a "part-of" or "composed-of" unary relationship. A part can be composed of subparts, which themselves can be decomposed into subparts (see Figure 7.22). Note that the aggregate side has a small diamond at the end. If a part is deleted, the components may or may not be deleted. If the parts are identified by generic part codes, then the aggregation is somewhat loosely bound, and the deletion of the part might not lead to deletion of subparts. A generic part code refers to a family of objects. For example, one of the Cannondale bike models is Jekyll 400. This is a generic part code. Several persons might own a Jekyll 400. (However, the individual Jekyll 400 bikes have separate identities because each is identified by a serial number.) If the Jekyll model is retired, many of its standard parts, such as hub and wheels, may be retained. This is an aggregation relationship.

When parts are identified by serial numbers, a subpart can be part of only one composite. This would be an example of composition and is shown in Figure 7.23. Note that the diamond in the case of aggregation is hollow, and the diamond in the case of composition is filled. In this case, the deletion of a part will cascade deletion

Figure 7.22 Bill of Materials Aggregation

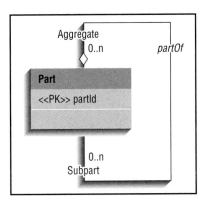

Figure 7.23 Bill of Materials Composition

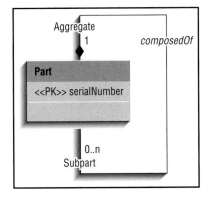

Figure 7.24
Transaction and Line
Items as Composition

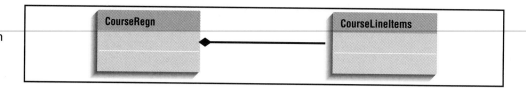

of subparts, which may further cascade deletions. For example, a notebook computer may have the serial number CN-OG5152-48643-42J-1538. Suppose it has a hard drive that has the serial number H123456789. If the notebook is lost, the hard drive is also considered lost. If the notebook is destroyed, the hard drive is likely to be considered destroyed. This is a composition relationship.

Another common example of composition is the relationship between a transaction and its line items. For example, course registration and the list of courses enrolled in by a student are strongly coupled. One cannot have CourseLineItems if a CourseRegn is not created first, and it is meaningless to have a CourseRegn if there are no CourseLineItems; that is, the student has not registered in at least one course (see Figure 7.24). Similarly, an order cannot exist by itself; it needs line items.

An aggregation may be loosely bound: Consider a team that is made up of (or composed of or consists of) players (see Figure 7.25). If the team is dissolved, information about players might or might not be maintained. If the players leave, a team might or might not be dissolved. The deletion semantics will depend on the situation. An analyst may even choose to use association instead of aggregation here.

By treating a relationship as an aggregation, the issues regarding object deletion and creation semantics can be considered more closely. Thus, the information collected at the analysis stage can be helpful to a designer at a later stage. Aggregation not only focuses attention on object creation and deletion issues from querying and programming aspects, but it is also useful during physical design. Later, physical structures can be chosen that provide proximity between an aggregate and its parts, because it is likely that the two are retrieved, inserted, or deleted together.

Usually, it is easy to determine if a relationship is an aggregation or an association. If the aggregation is loosely bound, it might be difficult to distinguish the relationship from an association. If one exercises careful judgment and is consistent, the imprecise distinction between aggregation and ordinary association does not cause problems in practice.

Composite Structure Diagram

Generally, the composition construct is found in engineering applications, where the whole has a number of parts. In such cases, showing the traditional composition relationship can result in a number of links between the class that represents the whole and the classes that represent the parts. Further, there will be relationships among the parts. This leads to a diagram with a lot of clutter. By using a composite structure diagram, the relationships can be shown more clearly.

The composite structure diagram has been introduced in UML 2. Figure 7.26 shows a bicycle as a whole and several interrelated parts such as frame, hub, and wheels. If the multiplicity of a part is more than 1, it can be shown. For example, a bicycle may have no or many [0..n], suspensions, but has only two, [2], wheels. The relationships among the parts can be named if required, although Figure 7.26 keeps the diagram at a high level and does not provide these names. The links among the

Figure 7.25
Loosely Bound
Aggregation

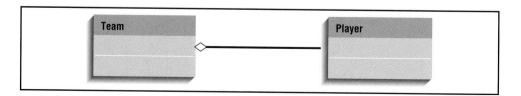

Figure 7.26
Bicycle and Its Parts
Shown in a Composite
Structure Diagram

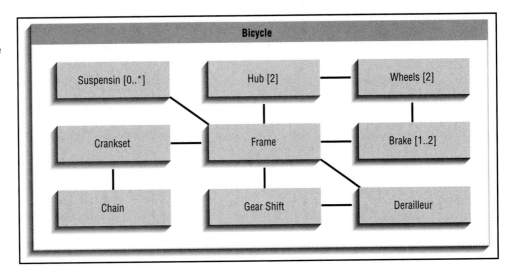

Figure 7.27 Order
and Its Parts Shown in
a Composite Structure
Diagram

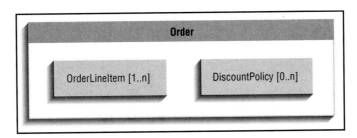

parts are called *connectors*. The composite structure diagram may be less used in tra-ditional transaction-oriented business applications. Figure 7.27 shows the class Order with two parts OrderLineItem and Discount Policy.

Generalization Relationship

Generalization
A superclass/subclass
relationship based on
inheritance.

The generalization relationship also is called a supertype/subtype (or superclass/subclass) relationship and is based on the inheritance concept. Inheritance defines a relationship among classes where one class shares the structure or behavior of another class. This relationship allows one to model a general class (called the super-type) and then to subdivide it into several specialized classes (called subtypes). The subtype (or the subclass) inherits from one (or in some cases more than one) super-type (or superclass). Inheritance is called an "is-a" relationship. The converse of gen-eralization is called specialization. The generalization relationship abstracts structure and behavior common to several classes to create a superclass. The specialization relationship provides the ability to create subclasses that represent refinements to a superclass by adding or modifying structure and behavior.

One of the best examples of generalization/specialization comes from biology. The system for the classification of living things was introduced by Carolus Linnaeus in 1735. In his classification system, animals are classified into invertebrates and ver-tebrates based on the absence or presence of a backbone. The vertebrates are further classified into amphibians, reptiles, mammals, and so on. These are further classified by family type. Eventually, this specialization breaks down to genus and species. As one goes down in the hierarchy of the classification scheme, new attributes and behaviors are added. (For the purist, the scientific classification scheme from general to special is as follows: kingdom, phylum, subphylum, superclass, class, subclass, infraclass, order, family, genus, and species.)

As illustrated in Figure 7.28, a car "is-a" vehicle and a truck "is-a" vehicle. Note that the subclass Car inherits all attributes of Vehicle and has an additional attribute numPassengers. The subclass Truck inherits all attributes of Vehicle and has two

Figure 7.28
Generalization
Applied to Vehicle
Supertype

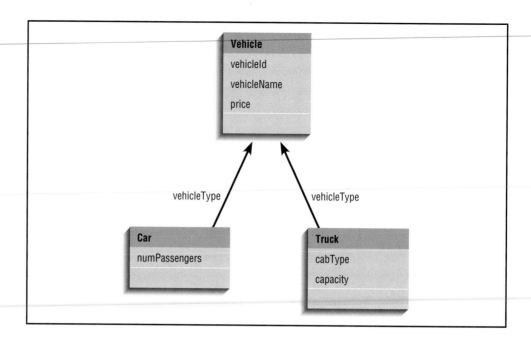

additional attributes: cabType and capacity. Vehicle is the more general type, and Car and Truck are the more specialized types distinguished by vehicleType.

Business applications have several examples of generalization. An employee can be a salaried employee or an hourly employee; a student can be an undergraduate, a master's, or a doctoral student; a member can be an author, reviewer, attendee, and track chair for a conference; and so on.

Let's consider the employee example shown in Figure 7.29. Again, one can clearly see the benefits of generalization; employee attributes need not be repeated in the classes HourlyEmp and SalariedEmp. However, caution must be exercised when using generalization. Generalization should be used only when there is a distinct advantage in doing so. Consider another characteristic—jobType—that can be used to create subtypes of Employee. Suppose there are two subtypes, Engineer and Secretary, based on jobType.

Figure 7.29
Generalization
Applied to Employee
Supertype

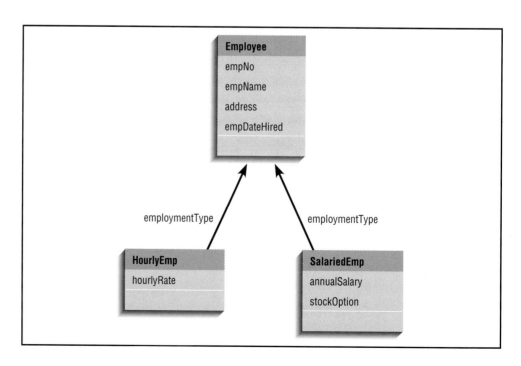

Figure 7.30
Generalization Based
on Two Characteristics

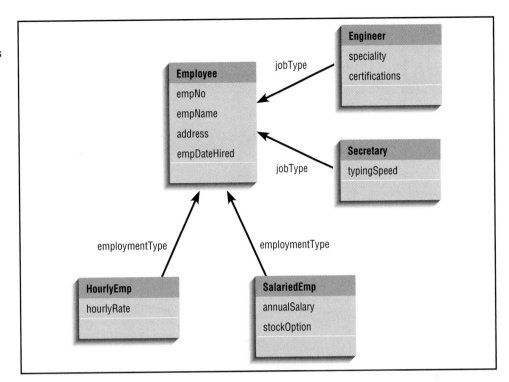

The revised diagram is shown in Figure 7.30. Suppose that James is an engineer who is an hourly employee, and Sally is another engineer who is a salaried employee. This diagram has not considered these possibilities. Four classes are now required—HourlyEmpSecretary, SalariedEmpSecretary, HourlyEmpEngineer, and SalariedEmpEngineer—to represent all possible combinations, and multiple inheritance must be used so the attributes can be inherited from both kinds of subtypes. This not only gets complicated, but some software do not support multiple inheritance. A detailed discussion of this problem is beyond the scope of this book.

Another scenario that can make implementation of generalization difficult is the overlap between subclasses. In other words, an object might belong to more than one subclass for the same generalization characteristics. For example, LandVehicles and WaterVehicles might not have mutually exclusive objects because there are amphibian vehicles. Thus, although generalization seems intuitive, is easy to understand, and is a useful abstraction; when used indiscriminately it can create problems.

AN EXAMPLE OF CONCEPTUAL DATA MODELING FOR PVF WEBSTORE

This section will develop the conceptual data model of the Place Order use case detailed in Figure 6.9 of the previous chapter. The first task is to recognize the classes in the use case. The two obvious classes are Customer and Product. In addition, Order is also a class because it holds transaction data and is identified by order number.

Next, the systems analyst takes a first cut at the attributes. The use case does not provide all the details about the attributes, so the analyst will need to examine documents related to the Place Order use case. Based on these documents, attributes can be assigned to the classes. Certain attributes of the classes have been assumed. Figure 7.31 shows a class diagram, which displays the three classes Customer, Product, and Order along with their attributes. Further, there is an associative class Lineitem, which represents an m:n relationship between Order and Product. Note that Customer has a multi-valued attribute Phone, and Order has three derived attributes: SubTotal, Tax, and TotalAmount. The values of derived attributes can be determined from other data in the model. The relationship buy between Customer and Order is one-to-many.

Derived attribute
An attribute whose value can be determined from other data in the model.

Figure 7.31 PVF WebStore Conceptual Data Model for Place Order Use Case

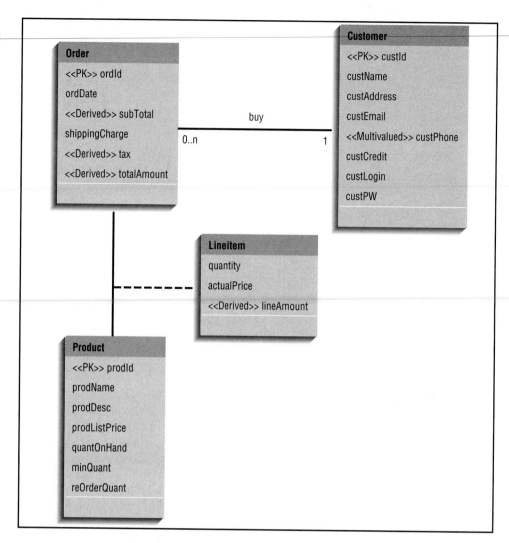

KEY POINTS REVIEW

1. **What is conceptual data modeling? What steps are involved in conceptual data modeling?**
A conceptual data model shows the overall structure of organizational data, but is independent of any database management system or other implementation considerations. To develop a conceptual data model, the use cases and any related documents such as forms and reports must be examined. The systems analyst might need to meet several times with users to enhance and complete the model.

2. **What is the role of conceptual data modeling in the overall systems analysis and design?**
A conceptual data model is used to develop an analysis class diagram. A conceptual data model is mapped into an object-relational data model, which provides entity classes that are then used along with other kinds of classes to capture system behavior. The resulting diagram is called an analysis class diagram.

3. **Define each of the following: object, class, attribute, candidate key, identifier, multivalued attribute, derived attribute, relationship, degree, cardinality, multiplicity, association, associative class, aggregation, composition, and generalization.**
An object is an entity that encapsulates data and behavior. A class is a set of objects that share the same attributes, operations, relationships, and semantics. An attribute is a named property or characteristic of a class that is of interest to the organization. A candidate key is an attribute (or combination of attributes) that uniquely identifies each object of a class. An identifier or primary key is a candidate key that has been selected as the unique, identifying characteristic for a class. A multivalued attribute is an attribute that

may take on more than one value for each object. A derived attribute is one whose value can be determined from other data in the model. A relationship is a semantic connection between objects of one or more classes. The degree is the number of classes that participate in a relationship. The cardinality of an object A is the number of objects of class A that can (or must) be associated with each object of class B. The multiplicity of an object A is the range of the number of objects of class A that can (or must) be associated with each object of class B. An association is a relationship where no object is subordinate to others. An associative class is a many-to-many association that the data modeler chooses to model as a class. An aggregation is a whole-part relationship with the part class subordinate to the whole. A composition is a strongly bound aggregation relationship. A generalization is a superclass/subclass relationship based on inheritance.

4. **Draw a conceptual data model using the UML notation.**

   A conceptual data model uses symbols for class, various kinds of relationships, identifier, attribute, multivalued attribute, and derived attribute. A relationship can be an association, aggregation, or generalization, and is detailed by showing its degree and multiplicity. The diagrams in this chapter use the UML notation to illustrate these concepts. Figure 7.31 shows the conceptual data model of the PVF WebStore case.

5. **Distinguish among unary, binary, and ternary relationships, and give an example of each.**

   A unary relationship is a relationship between the objects of one class (e.g., marriedTo between objects of the class Person, and manages between objects of the class Employee). A binary relationship is a relationship between objects of two classes and is the most common type of relationship encountered in data modeling. Figure 7.10 shows the works relationship between Employee and Department. A ternary relationship is a simultaneous relationship among objects of three classes. The most convenient representation of a ternary (or higher-degree) relationship is to show it as a class and relate it to the involved classes. In the example shown in Figure 7.13, the relationship ships tracks the quantity of a given part shipped by a particular vendor to a selected warehouse.

KEY TERMS CHECKPOINT

Here are the key terms from the chapter. The page where each term is first explained is in parentheses after the term.

a. Aggregation (p. 202)
b. Association (p. 200)
c. Associative class (p. 200)
d. Attribute (p. 193)
e. Binary relationship (p. 197)
f. Candidate key (p. 194)
g. Cardinality (p. 198)
h. Class (p. 192)
i. Composite structure diagram (p. 204)

j. Composition (p. 203)
k. Conceptual data model (p. 189)
l. Degree (p. 197)
m. Derived attribute (p. 207)
n. Entity relationship (ER) data model (p. 189)
o. Generalization (p. 205)
p. Identifier (p. 194)
q. Multiplicity (p. 198)

r. Multivalued attribute (p. 195)
s. Object (p. 193)
t. Primary key (p. 194)
u. Relationship (p. 196)
v. Role (p. 197)
w. Stereotype (p. 194)
x. Ternary relationship (p. 198)
y. Unary relationship (recursive relationship) (p. 197)

Match each of the key terms above with the definition that best fits it.

1. A strong form of aggregation in which the aggregate is meaningless without parts, and the parts are meaningless without the aggregate.
2. A single occurrence of a class.
3. An attribute that can take on more than one value for each object.
4. A simultaneous relationship among objects of three classes.
5. A collection of objects that share common properties and behavior.
6. A relationship between objects of two classes.
7. A many-to-many association that the data modeler chooses to model as a class.
8. A name property of a class that describes a range of values that instances of the attribute might hold.

9. The number of objects of class A that can (or must) be associated with each object of class B.
10. An association that models a whole-part relationship between an aggregate, which is called whole, and its parts. It is a strong form of association in which the aggregate has no meaning without parts.
11. A candidate key that has been selected as the unique, identifying characteristic for a class.
12. A semantic connection between objects of one or more classes.
13. The range of the number of objects of class A that can (or must) be associated with each object of class B.
14. An attribute (or combination of attributes) that uniquely identifies each object of a class.

15. A relationship or link between instances (or objects) of classes.
16. The number of classes that participate in a relationship.
17. A relationship between the objects of one class.
18. A superclass/subclass relationship based on inheritance.
19. A detailed model that shows the overall structure of organizational data while being independent of any database management system or other implementation considerations.
20. An attribute whose value can be determined from other data in the model.

21. A graphical representation for depicting a conceptual data model using the notions of entity, attribute, and relationship among entities.
22. A name to identify a relationship end within a relationship.
23. A construct that allows extension of the UML vocabulary.
24. An attribute or a combination of attributes that has been selected to be used as the unique characteristic for a class.
25. A diagram that shows how a whole is made up of parts, especially in cases where the whole has a number of interacting parts.

REVIEW QUESTIONS

1. List any five categories of questions that you should ask system users and business managers about data modeling.
2. Explain why a ternary relationship is not the same as three binary relationships.
3. When must a many-to-many relationship be modeled as an associative class?
4. Which of the following types of relationships can have attributes associated with them: one-to-one, one-to-many, many-to-many?
5. What is the degree of a relationship? Give an example of each of the relationship degrees illustrated in this chapter.

6. Give an example of a ternary, an aggregation, and a generalization relationship (different from any example in this chapter).
7. What is the difference between cardinality and multiplicity?
8. List the ideal characteristics of an identifier (primary key).
9. Explain the difference between a candidate key and the identifier of a class.

PROBLEMS AND EXERCISES

1. Assume that at Pine Valley Furniture each product (described by Product No., Description, and Cost) is comprised of at least three components (described by Component No., Description, and Unit of Measure) and components are used to make one or many products (i.e., must be used in at least one product). In addition, assume that components are used to make other components and that raw materials are also considered to be components. In both cases of components being used to make products and components being used to make other components, we need to keep track of how many components go into making something else. Draw a conceptual data model for this situation.
2. A software training program is identified by a code and has a short description that explains its goals. Each software training program is divided into training modules, and each module is described by module name and the approximate practice time. Each module sometimes has prerequisite modules. Model this situation of training programs and modules with a conceptual data model.
3. Each semester, a student must be assigned an advisor who counsels students about degree requirements and helps them register for classes. Students must register for classes with the help of an advisor, but if their assigned advisor is not available, they may register

with any advisor. Assume student and advisor are classes. We must keep track of students, their assigned advisors, and with whom the student registered for the current term. Represent this situation of students and advisors with a conceptual data model.
4. An airline reservation is an association between a passenger, a flight, and a seat. (You may visit an airline Web site to become familiar with the reservation details.) Select a few pertinent attributes for each of these classes and represent the scenario using a conceptual data model.
5. In a real estate database, there are properties for sale by the agency. A property is identified by a code. Other data recorded for a property include its description and listed price. Each time a potential property buyer makes a purchase offer on a property, the agency records the date, offering price, and name of the person making the offer. The agency keeps data about potential buyers, including their names, addresses, and phone numbers. Prepare a conceptual data model.
6. Consider the marriedTO unary relationship in Figure 7.16.
   a. Assume we wanted to know the date on which a marriage occurred. Augment this diagram to include a Datemarried attribute.

b. Because persons sometimes remarry after the death of a spouse or divorce, redraw this diagram to show the whole history of marriages (not just the current marriage) for Persons. Show the Datemaried attribute on this diagram.

(If you would like additional practice, we recommend the conceptual data modeling exercises in the book *Modern Database Management*, 7th edition, by Hoffer, Prescott, and McFadden. Chapter 3 has 17 high-quality exercises.)

DISCUSSION QUESTIONS

1. Discuss the role of conceptual data modeling in the overall systems analysis and design process.
2. Using Table 7-1 as a guide, develop a script of at least 10 questions you would ask during an interview of the customer order processing department manager at Pine Valley Furniture. Assume the focus is on analyzing the requirements for a new order entry system. The purpose of the interview is to develop a preliminary class diagram for this system.
3. If possible, contact a systems analyst in a local organization. Discuss with this systems analyst the role of conceptual data modeling in the overall systems analysis and design of information systems at his or her company. How, and by whom, is conceptual data modeling performed? What training in this technique is given? At what point(s) is this done in the development process?

4. Talk to MIS professionals at a variety of organizations and determine the extent to which CASE tools are used in the creation and editing of class diagrams. Try to determine whether or not they use CASE tools for this purpose; which CASE tools are used; and why, when, and how they are used. In companies that do not use CASE tools for this purpose, determine why not and what would have to change in order to use them.

5. Ask a systems analyst to give you a copy of the standard notation he or she uses to draw data modeling diagrams. In what ways is this notation different from notation in this text? Which notation do you prefer and why? What is the meaning of any additional notation?

CASE PROBLEMS

The following are case problems spread over several paragraphs. You may attempt each case one paragraph at a time and then integrate the solutions.

GuardTech Training, Inc.

In 1993, Richard (Rick) Dobrow and his wife Sherrie founded GuardTech Training in Cooper City, Florida. It was the first computer security training business in the area and was immediately successful. Over the decade since its inception, GuardTech has grown steadily and is still the market leader in computer security training in the area. However, the growth of the company has caused bookkeeping problems for the Dobrows who, up to the present, have been keeping all their business records in a series of Microsoft Excel spreadsheets and Access databases. The Dobrows have decided to address the inadequacy of the current system by developing a completely new system that uses Oracle. The Dobrows also have decided that they are too busy running the day-to-day operations of their business to design a database system themselves, so they have requested that you and your consulting team prepare a proposal and prototype for a database system for GuardTech.

GuardTech occupies a suite of large office spaces in a modern office building. Some of the office space is used for administrative purposes and storage, but most of it has been renovated into eight computer-training classrooms (numbered 1 through 8). Each classroom contains computer workstations and chairs for students, as well as a trainer workstation at the front of the room that includes a computer, printer, and projection system for displaying the output of the trainer's computer onto a screen on the front wall of the classroom. The capacity, in students, of the rooms ranges from 10 for the smallest room up to 18 for the largest of the rooms. The rooms also vary in the type of computers and operating systems installed in them. One of the medium-sized classrooms contains Linux machines. Some rooms have Windows 2000, and the remaining have Unix-based systems.

GuardTech currently employs 10 full-time trainers. To encourage retention, the company records the seniority of trainers, who are granted precedence in teaching preferred classes and selecting vacation days based on their seniority. When hired, each trainer is issued an employee number. This number is a nine-digit code comprised of eight digits specifying the year, month, and day an employee was hired, followed by one additional digit to allow for coding multiple hires on the same date. (For example, the first employee hired on December 1, 1998, would have the employee number 199812011.) As with the other information currently recorded by GuardTech, all employee numbers, names, addresses, phone numbers, and e-mail addresses currently are stored in an Excel spreadsheet.

As expected, trainers must learn a course's material before they can teach a class in that course. Rick always attempts to have at least two trainers qualified to teach every course. This provides flexibility in scheduling classes and trainers. When Rick believes that a trainer is familiar enough with the course material to teach a class in a given course, he notes the trainer, the course, and the date in one of his spreadsheets. From this list he can determine which trainers are qualified to teach which classes. Further, he notes the competency level: 0 for under trained, 1 for qualified, and 2 for advanced.

The courses are identified by a 10-character mnemonic code specified by Rick for each course (e.g., INTRUDETEC for the course, Intrusion Detection). Most courses are 2 to 3 days in length, although some are 5 days, and a few are 1 day. The fee charged to attend a class varies, depending on the course. It is also important to note the hardware requirements for a course. GuardTech strictly enforces prerequisites. In other words, before a client may enroll for some of GuardTech's offerings, the client might have to complete one or more prerequisite courses. (Some courses with prerequisites are themselves prerequisites for one or more other courses.)

The specific software requirements for a course also vary. Some courses (e.g., Introduction to Information Security) utilize several programs (e.g., Sonicwall, Netscreen, Cisco, etc.), and others (e.g., Advanced ISS) require only one. Each software program has been given a five-character program code to identify it (e.g., NETSC). The program name and vendor are recorded. The number of licenses that GuardTech owns for each software program is also important to track. (This number represents the maximum number of copies of a particular program that can be in use by GuardTech at any given moment in time.)

Another important component of the courses offered by GuardTech is the course books/company training manuals that are selected by Sherrie for use in each course. The fee charged each client for each course includes one set of the course books/manuals. She keeps records of the books she selects that include the ISBN, book title, author name(s), publisher, and catalog price. Similar information is maintained for training manuals, except that these are identified by internally generated codes. She orders these books from a variety of book vendors. Some orders she places by phone; others she places by e-mail or the Web, and the rest are placed by mail. For each order she places, Sherrie assigns an order number and records the date that the order was placed. A typical book order will contain anywhere from 1 to 10 different titles. Because she attempts to keep GuardTech's on-hand inventory of books to a minimum, she orders specific titles in small quantities frequently. Due to variations in vendor stock levels, the orders that are placed occasionally arrive in multiple shipments. Sherrie keeps track of which books from which orders arrive in what quantity on what date. Because of occasional discrepancies in the price charged by a vendor for a book compared to the publisher's catalog price, she also records the actual price charged.

The core of GuardTech's business is the enrollment of clients for classes offered by the company. It publishes a schedule of class offerings each month that it e-mails to clients who have attended at least one class in the last 6 months. GuardTech also maintains a Web site on which it can post its offerings. A listing for a specific class offering includes the course, trainer, room, and date. For identification purposes, each scheduled class also is assigned a unique, sequential reference number. Sherrie is in charge of marketing efforts and, thus, carefully records information on GuardTech's clients. Each new client is assigned a unique, sequential client number. The client's name, address, and phone number are recorded. Because enrollment requests for some of GuardTech classes might exceed the capacity of the class, Sherrie records the date and time that a client enrolls in a particular class. She knows how many students can be accommodated for a given class, so she is able to inform clients immediately if they are confirmed for the class or if they must be placed on a waiting list. If they are placed on a waiting list, then they may be accepted for a class if other clients cancel their enrollment. The date and time of enrollment determine the order in which clients on the waiting list are promoted to accepted status.

Although each course has a predetermined fee, the amount that a client pays for attending a class offering of a particular course varies. When clients first enroll in a GuardTech course, they are assigned a fee code. The fee code assigned depends on what type of membership the client desires with GuardTech. For example, clients who choose the annual discount plan pay $500 a year for membership but then receive a 30 percent discount off the regular price they would otherwise pay for any class for an entire year. A similar semiannual plan costs $300. Other discounts also are identified by client fee codes. They range from the standard membership with no annual fee and no discounts to the 40 percent discount offered to the clients with most favored status.

a. List the entities in the case. What criteria did you employ to recognize these entities?

b. For each entity, specify the identifier (i.e., primary key). Do your identifiers meet the considerations for identifiers listed in the book?

c. Define the relationships among the entities. Specify the multiplicity of each relationship.

New Tampa Junior Women's Club (NTJWC)

The New Tampa Junior Women's Club (NTJWC) is a volunteer organization located in Tampa, Florida. It draws its membership from citizens in the city who enjoy volunteer work, and provides financial assistance to a variety of charitable organizations. The club currently has approximately 150 women members. The club would like to be able to produce a membership list to act as a club phone book. This list would also facilitate the printing of mailing labels for the newsletters sent to members. Information necessary for the membership list includes each member's number, name (first and last), address (street, city, state, and zip), phone number, fax number, e-mail address, and membership status (provisional or full). A member may be assigned as mentor of another member.

The club would also like to keep track of a member's husband and children (if she has any) using names. Since this is an all-women's organization, it decided not to worry about members being married to one another or being the parent of the same child. Because it does many different family events it would like to also know the ages of each member's children.

In addition to the member information to be included in the membership list, the club wants to record specific skills that the members possess that might be useful to the organization. The names of skills currently held by club members include typist, accountant, electrician, artist, and many others. A member may have many such skills.

The club periodically elects four officers: president, vice president, treasurer, and secretary. It is possible that more officer positions may be created in the future. Recorded for each office, in addition to its name, is its term of office in years (president and vice president are 2-year terms while the others are 1-year terms) and a brief list of the responsibilities associated with the office. A club member may be, for example, the VP one year and the president another. Thus, club members can hold different offices over the years, and each office has been held by a number of different club members. NTJWC wishes to maintain a record of which club members have held which offices during what time periods.

The club's membership is divided into several committees. Each member is assigned to one and only one committee. Although a member may periodically change the committee she works on, only the current assignment is of interest to the club. (That is, historic records of previous committee assignments are not important.) The committees all have a unique name and a specific mission. The minimum number of members needed for each committee is also recorded. Each committee also has a member who has the role of its chairperson. There is no set term of office for committee chairs. Only the current chair of each committee is of interest.

NTJWC sponsors a number of fund-raising events each year. Each event is assigned a sequential number (Event ID) and is given a name. Also recorded for each event is its location, date, and starting and ending times. Additionally, a brief description of each event (e.g., Get out the vote session, 2002 Book Drive, etc.) and the monetary proceeds earned by each event are tracked. A member can work on many events. All events require specific skills in order to be put on. The club wants to be able to match an event's skill needs with the skills the club members possess. NTJWC wishes to record skills used by a member in a given project.

In addition to the money raised by the event activities themselves, some events also receive donations. A specific donation is always allocated to a single event. Each donation is assigned a Donation ID. In addition to the ID, also recorded for each donation is a description of the donation (e.g., cash, artwork, automobile, etc.), what the donation will be used for (door prize, live auction, or silent auction), the club member who is assigned as the contact person for the specific donation, and the monetary value of the donation. All donations come from one and only one donor. Each recorded donor has donated one or more times. Most donors are business entities, although some are individuals. Information tracked on each donor includes a Donor ID; the name of the business (where applicable); the contact person's name (first and last); (for nonbusiness donors, this would be the individual donor's name); and the donor's address (street, city, state, and zip), phone number, and e-mail.

a. List the entities in the case. What criteria did you employ to recognize these entities?
b. For each entity, specify the identifier (i.e., primary key). Do your identifiers meet the considerations for identifiers listed in the book?
c. Define the relationships among the entities. Specify the multiplicity of each relationship.

CASE: BROADWAY ENTERTAINMENT COMPANY, INC.

Conceptual Data Modeling for the Web-Based Customer Relationship Management System

Case Introduction

Requirements determination activities for the MyBroadway project yielded what at times seemed to the student team to be an overwhelming amount of data. The team of students from St. Claire Community College has several hundred pages of notes from various data collection activities including 12 interviews with employees and customers, 6 hours of observation of employees using online shopping services, a 1-hour focus group session with customers, and investigations of Broadway Entertainment documents. Structuring these require-

ments for the analysis of the MyBroadway information system is a much bigger effort than any class exercise the team members had ever encountered.

Also adding to the complexity of requirements structuring activities in the analysis phase of the project is that work is not compartmentalized easily. It seems to the team members that while they are documenting requirements in use cases and associated descriptions, they also have to find ways to understand the meaning of the data the system will handle. Object-oriented conceptual data modeling techniques, primarily data class diagramming, help, but changes are frequent, and the steps are repetitive. As the team digs into the details of each use case, members need to redesign the data model for MyBroadway. When they change the data model, they gain new insights about the data and suggest issues of data-handling processes for validation, special cases, and capturing relationships to be documented within use-case templates.

Structuring the High-Level Data Modeling Findings from Requirements Determination

The various BEC student team members have taken responsibility for different requirements collection activities and for developing the detailed explanations of each use case on the use-case diagram. As a result, no one team member has a complete picture of all the data needs. This is not uncommon on real development projects. The team has yet to appoint someone to be the data administrator for the project. To gain a shared understanding of the database needs for MyBroadway, the team members read all of their notes carefully in preparation for a team meeting.

At the team meeting, all members suggest the data classes they think are needed in their parts of the system. The use cases are described in Chapter 6. Data requirements of the use cases required to formulate a conceptual data model are listed below.

Request Rental Extension. Rental data, sales, and product inventory data are extracted periodically from Entertainment Tracker (ET) to be stored in MyBroadway. Rental transactions, which list products rented to customers, may be updated if there is a request for rental extension. For each rental, the system records due dates. Sales data has historical transactions and also involves products sold to customers. Each product is a CD, DVD, or videocassette title. For example, a product is the movie *Million Dollar Baby* on DVD. Although the Entertainment Tracker operational system must keep track of each copy of a movie available for rent at a store, MyBroadway simply needs to track titles, not individual copies. For items that are for sale, a product is the generic title, not an individual copy, of the product for sale.

The team needs to make a decision whether to keep the rental transactions separate from sales transactions. Since only rental transactions can be updated from the WebStore, one idea is to separate these from the sales transactions when the data are moved from ET to MyBroadway. Alternatively, the transactions can simply be copied from ET to MyBroadway given that an ET transaction involves both sales and rental line items. The sales line items and rental line items can be highlighted in different colors when the customer wishes to make an extension. The sales line items can be prevented from updates. If an extension is granted, the system records the new due date and the charges for the extension.

Another issue to be resolved is that in case the customer is denied an extension for a rental line item, should the reason for denial be recorded in the database? They feel that if the customer feels unhappy with a denial, he or she is likely to call BEC to seek a clarification. For now, the team decided not to do so, although they will confirm it with the users.

The team decides that the rental extension be considered a separate transaction. They wonder if they can allow a customer to pool rental extensions made from different transactions. They decide this scenario would be infrequent, and it would make tracking of the extensions more cumbersome. So they decide that an extension can pertain to only one rental transaction. A rental transaction may result in several extensions.

Identify Favorite Picks. A pick is an unstructured comment and rating by an employee about a specified product (by title) in a given product category. Several picks are made each week and the data is retained for 2 years. Since each employee is matched with the category with which he or she is most familiar, data need to be maintained about which employees are familiar with a given category.

The team decides that product category will be modeled as an entity, and they will have a short code as an identifier for each category. They assume that being an employee can be associated with several categories and that an employee can make picks for categories for which he or she is listed. In other words, "most familiar" can mean more than one. The users have confirmed the team's assertion.

Request New Product. MyBroadway collects all inquiries from customers asking BEC to stock new products. An inquiry is a list of new products requested by an existing customer. BEC may choose never to stock that product, yet if enough requests for the same product are submitted, it is likely that the item eventually will appear on the store shelves. New product requests are kept for 2 months and then purged.

The team is concerned about how there can be consistency in the manner that customers specify products. Since these products are new, there is no BEC product code to identify a product. There is always a problem when customers specify product titles since there can be spelling mistakes. Even when the title is correct, the movie may be another version of an earlier movie, thus causing ambiguity. The team decides that the inquiry should have an unstructured statement where a customer can specify as much information that is available about the product. Someone at BEC would eventually identify the product based on the statement. An inquiry involves only one product request.

Enter New Comment on a Product. A comment is an unstructured statement by a customer about a specified product (by title). The same person may comment on a given item several times. A customer is identified by a member-

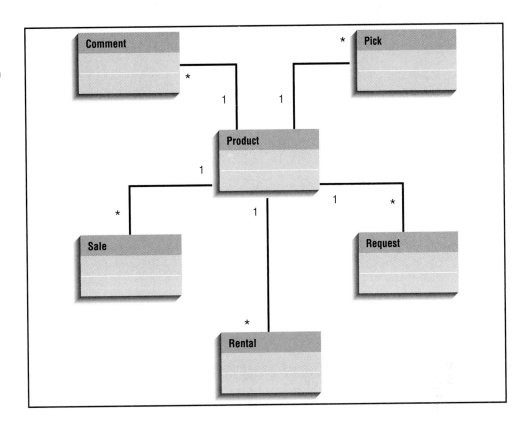

ship number, which is required to enter comments. MyBroadway records whether the comment is entered by a parent or by a child.

Review Inventory. For each product, the title, category, description, artist, publisher, release date, media, sale, and rental price are recorded.

CASE QUESTIONS

1. List the entities in the case. What criteria did you employ to recognize these entities?
2. For each entity, specify the identifier (i.e., primary key). Do your identifiers meet the considerations for identifiers listed in the book?

Case Summary

The MyBroadway team found that the remaining use cases depended on these use cases for obtaining the reports. The team is going over the use cases (listed in Chapter 6) to ensure that the data requirements for MyBroadway are complete.

3. Define the relationships among the entities. Specify the multiplicity of each relationship. Did you encounter a ternary relationship?

Chapter

8

Object-Relational Modeling

Chapter Objectives

After studying this chapter, you should be able to:

➤ Understand the relational data model.

➤ Normalize data to the third normal form.

➤ Understand the object-oriented extensions to the relational model.

➤ Realize the role of object relations in systems analysis.

➤ Be able to translate a conceptual data model into object relations.

➤ Be able to integrate object relations obtained from different use cases.

Chapter Contents

➤ Chapter Preview

➤ Object-Relational Data Modeling

➤ Relational Data Model (RDM)

➤ Object Extensions to Relational Data Model

➤ Translating Conceptual Data Models into Object Relations

➤ Logical Design of PVF WebStore

Chapter Preview

This chapter will continue coverage of how to structure requirements into models (see Figure 8.1). Specifically, students will be taught how to translate a conceptual data model into object relations. The previous chapter mentioned that the goal of analysis is to come up with an analysis class diagram. Data modeling is an intermediate step that provides entity classes, which are then used to develop analysis classes. This chapter will explain how to obtain entity classes, which in the object-oriented language are also called persistent classes. These entity classes will contain data characteristics only. Incorporating behavioral characteristics will be covered in the next chapter.

The entity classes are generated from object relations. An object relation has the features of the relational data model, as well as certain object-oriented extensions. To understand an object relation, one needs to first understand the relational data model, which uses several normalization steps. Normalization is a process of obtaining database structures that have minimum redundancy and allow users to insert, modify, and delete the rows in a table without errors or inconsistencies. The normalization steps are illustrated in the earlier part of this chapter. This is followed by a discussion of the object-oriented features that are available in contemporary database management systems (DBMSs). The chapter then addresses the translation of a conceptual data model into object relations. Finally, the chapter shows how to integrate object relations obtained from different use cases.

Figure 8.1 Systems Analysis Has Three Parts: Requirements Determination, Requirements Structuring, and Alternative Generation and Selection

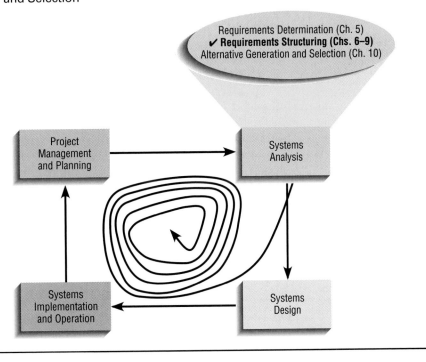

Figure 8.2
Process of Object-
Relational Data
Modeling

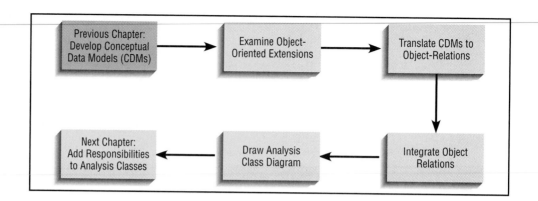

OBJECT-RELATIONAL DATA MODELING

The previous chapter explained how to develop a conceptual data model from a use case. The next step is to learn how to develop an object-relational data model (ORDM) from a conceptual data model. The main steps of this process are captured in Figure 8.2. Object-relational data modeling has three main purposes: produce database structures that are ready for physical database design and implementation by a DBMS, provide entity classes that are then used in sequence diagrams and other diagrams that capture the behavior of objects, and enhance and finalize the attributes in the data model.

A conceptual data model is translated into object relations based on some but not all of the normalization rules of the relational data model. The next section covers the important topic of normalization. If you have studied normalization earlier, this section should serve to refresh the concepts. If you have not studied normalization, then you will need to study this section thoroughly and perhaps refer to another database book to enhance your knowledge.

Object relations include object-oriented features offered by contemporary DBMSs, which are detailed in a separate section. Before translating a conceptual data model into object relations, one needs to examine the available features in order to take advantage, if the application being used so allows. This chapter provides the rules governing the translation from a conceptual data model into object relations only after normalization and object-oriented features have been covered.

The object relations obtained by the different conceptual data models can then be integrated. Note that as conceptual data models are developed for use cases, it is possible to have as many conceptual data models as there are use cases. Thus, if one has 20 use cases, one also will have 20 conceptual data models. These models need to be integrated into one model. This can be done during the conceptual data-modeling phase, or they can be translated individually into object relations and then integrated.

During this process, note that a given object relation can be employed by several use cases. The integrated object relations constitute the entity classes of the system. For now, these entity classes have attributes only. The next chapter discusses how these can be used along with other kinds of classes to capture the behavior of the system.

RELATIONAL DATA MODEL (RDM)

Relational data model (RDM)
Data represented as a set of related tables or relations.

Relation
A named, two-dimensional table of data.

The relational data model (RDM) represents data in the form of related tables or relations. A relation is a named, two-dimensional table of data. Each relation (or table) consists of a set of named columns and an arbitrary number of unnamed rows. Each column in a relation corresponds to an attribute of that relation. Each row of a relation corresponds to a record that contains data values for a class.

Figure 8.3 shows an example of a relation named EMPLOYEE1. This relation contains the following attributes describing employees: Emp_ID, Name, Dept, and Salary. The table has five sample rows corresponding to five employees.

Figure 8.3
A Relation Named
EMPLOYEE1

EMPLOYEE1

Emp_ID	Name	Dept	Salary
100	Margaret Simpson	Marketing	$42,000
140	Allen Beeton	Accounting	$39,000
110	Chris Lucero	Info Systems	$41,500
190	Lorenzo Davis	Finance	$38,000
150	Susan Martin	Marketing	$38,500

The structure of a relation can be expressed by a shorthand notation in which the name of the relation is followed (in parentheses) by the names of the attributes in the relation. The identifier attribute (also called the primary key of the relation) is underlined. For example, EMPLOYEE1 would be expressed as follows:

EMPLOYEE1 (Emp_ID, Name, Dept, Salary)

Not all tables are relations. Relations have several properties that distinguish them from nonrelational tables:

1. Entries in cells are simple (also called atomic). An entry at the intersection of each row and column has a single value. This property also is called the first normal form.
2. Entries in columns are from the same set of values.
3. Each row is unique. Uniqueness is guaranteed because the relation has a nonempty primary key value.
4. The sequence of columns can be interchanged without changing the meaning or use of the relation.
5. The rows can be interchanged or stored in any sequence.

Well-Structured Relations

Well-structured relation/ table

A relation that contains a minimum amount of redundancy and allows users to insert, modify, and delete the rows in a table without errors or inconsistencies.

What constitutes a well-structured relation (or table)? Intuitively, a well-structured relation contains a minimum amount of redundancy and allows users to insert, modify, and delete the rows in a table without errors or inconsistencies. EMPLOYEE1 (Figure 8.3) is such a relation. Each row of the table contains data describing one employee, and any modification to an employee's data (such as a change in salary) is confined to one row of the table.

In contrast, EMPLOYEE2 (Figure 8.4) contains data about employees and the courses they have completed. Each row in this table is unique for the combination of Emp_ID and Course, which becomes the primary key for the table. However, this is not a well-structured relation, because there is a considerable amount of redundancy

Figure 8.4 A Relation That Has Redundant Data

EMPLOYEE2

Emp_ID	Name	Dept	Salary	Course	Date_Completed
100	Margaret Simpson	Marketing	$42,000	SPSS	6/19/2004
100	Margaret Simpson	Marketing	$42,000	Surveys	10/7/2004
140	Alan Beeton	Accounting	$39,000	Tax Acc	12/8/2004
110	Chris Lucero	Info Systems	$41,500	SPSS	1/12/2004
110	Chris Lucero	Info Systems	$41,500	C++	4/22/2004
190	Lorenzo Davis	Finance	$38,000	Investments	5/7/2004
150	Susan Martin	Marketing	$38,500	SPSS	6/19/2004
150	Susan Martin	Marketing	$38,500	TQM	8/12/2004

Figure 8.5 The
Relation EMP_COURSE

EMP COURSE		
Emp_ID	Course	Date_Completed
100	SPSS	6/19/2004
100	Surveys	10/7/2004
140	Tax Acc	12/8/2004
110	SPSS	1/22/2004
110	C++	4/22/2004
190	Investments	5/7/2004
150	SPSS	6/19/2004
150	TQM	8/12/2004

in the sample data in the table. For example, the Emp_ID, Name, Dept, and Salary values appear in two separate rows for employees 100, 110, and 150. Consequently, if the salary for employee 100 changes, this fact must be recorded in two rows (or more, for some employees).

The problem with this relation is that it contains data about two separate things: employees and employees taking courses. Because the relation contains data about two separate things, it is difficult to insert, modify, or delete data in the rows of the table without introducing errors or inconsistencies. EMPLOYEE2 is not a well-structured relation. In order to convert EMPLOYEE2 into a set of well-structured relations, the data in EMPLOYEE2 will have to be normalized. As a result of normalization, two separate relations will result, EMPLOYEE1 (Figure 8.3) and EMP_COURSE, which appears with sample data in Figure 8.5. The primary key of EMP_COURSE is the combination of Emp_ID and Course (we emphasize this by underlining the column names for these attributes). Each resulting relation is about only one thing. EMPLOYEE2 is only about employees. EMP_COURSE is only about the courses that employees have taken.

Normalization

Normalization
A process for converting complex data structures into well-structured relations.

Although an intuitive discussion of well-structured relations has been presented, rules and a process for designing them are needed. Normalization is the process for converting complex data structures into well-structured relations. For example, the principles of normalization were used to convert the EMPLOYEE2 table with its redundancy to EMPLOYEE1 (Figure 8.3) and EMP_COURSE (Figure 8.5). Although normalization is associated with the relational data model, its redundancy control characteristics make it extremely useful to any data model.

Rules of Normalization

Normalization is based on well-accepted principles and rules. Many more normalization rules exist than can be covered in this text (see Hoffer, Prescott, and McFadden's *Modern Database Management* for a more complete coverage). Besides the five properties of relations outlined previously, there are two other frequently used rules:

1. Second normal form (2NF). Each nonprimary key attribute is identified by the whole key (what we call full functional dependency or no partial dependency).
2. Third normal form (3NF). Nonprimary key attributes do not depend on each other (what we call no transitive dependencies).

The result of normalization is that every nonprimary key attribute depends upon the whole primary key and nothing but the primary key. Second and third normal form are discussed in more detail next. What is the first normal form (1NF)? As mentioned earlier, the first property of a relation, "Entries in cells are simple (also called atomic)," constitutes the first normal form. (Object relations do not subscribe to this property and do allow multiple values in a cell.)

Figure 8.6
EXAMPLE Relation

EXAMPLE

A	B	C	D
X	U	X	Y
Y	X	Z	X
Z	Y	Y	Y
Y	Z	W	Z

Functional Dependency and Primary Keys

Functional dependency
The functional dependence of B on A is represented by an arrow (A→B) and implies that every valid value of A uniquely determines the value of B.

Normalization is based on the analysis of functional dependencies. A functional dependency is a particular relationship between two attributes. In a given relation, attribute B is functionally dependent on attribute A if every valid value of A uniquely determines the value of B. The functional dependence of B on A is represented by an arrow, as follows: A → B (e.g., Emp_ID→Name in the relation of Figure 8.3). Functional dependence does not imply mathematical dependence—that the value of one attribute may be computed from the value of another attribute. Instead, functional dependence of B on A means that there can be only one value of B for each value of A. Thus, for a given Emp_ID value, there can be only one Name value associated with it, but the value of Name cannot be derived from the value of Emp_ID. Similarly, functional dependencies such as the following are possible: Order_Number→ Order_Date; Invoice_Number→ Invoice_Date; and Invoice_Number→ Order_Number.

An attribute can be functionally dependent on two (or more) attributes, rather than on a single attribute. For example, consider the relation EMP_COURSE (Emp_ID, Course, Date_Completed) shown in Figure 8.5. The functional dependency in this relation is represented as follows: Emp_ID, Course→ Date_Completed. In this case, Date_Completed cannot be determined by either Emp_ID or Course alone. Date_Completed is a characteristic of an employee taking a course. The employee ID and the course name are needed to determine when a particular employee completed a particular course.

The instances (or sample data) in a relation do not prove that a functional dependency exists. Only knowledge of the problem domain, obtained from a thorough requirements analysis, is a reliable method for identifying a functional dependency. However, sample data can be used to demonstrate that a functional dependency does not exist between two or more attributes. For example, consider the sample data in the relation EXAMPLE (A, B, C, D), shown in Figure 8.6. The sample data in this relation prove that attribute B is not functionally dependent on attribute A because A does not uniquely determine B (two rows with the same value of A have different values of B).

Second Normal Form

Second normal form (2NF)
A relation for which every nonprimary key attribute is functionally dependent on the whole primary key.

A relation is in second normal form (2NF) if every nonprimary key attribute is functionally dependent on the whole primary key and not on part of the primary key. A functional dependency between a nonprimary key attribute and part of a primary key also is called a partial dependency. Second normal form is satisfied if the relation is in 1NF and any one of the following conditions apply:

1. The primary key consists of only one attribute (such as the attribute Emp_ID in relation EMPLOYEE1).
2. No nonprimary key attributes exist in the relation. The relation SERVE (Emp_ID, CommitteeName) is in 2NF.
3. Every nonprimary key attribute is functionally dependent on the full set of primary key attributes. The relation EMP_COURSE is in 2NF.

EMPLOYEE2 (Figure 8.4) is an example of a relation that is not in second normal form. For example, there is a partial dependency, Emp_ID→ Name. Name does not depend in any way on the name of a course an employee takes, yet the attribute Course is also part of the primary key for this relation. The relation can be analyzed to discover all of the functional dependencies it contains and to determine which, if any, are partial dependencies.

The shorthand notation for this relation is:

EMPLOYEE2 (Emp_ID, Name, Dept, Salary, <u>Course,</u> Date_Completed)

The functional dependencies in this relation are:

Emp_ID→ Name, Dept, Salary
Emp_ID, Course→ Date_Completed

The primary key for this relation is the composite key Emp_ID, Course. The non-primary key attributes Name, Dept, and Salary are functionally dependent on only Emp_ID and not on Course. EMPLOYEE2 has redundancy, which results in problems when the table is updated.

To convert a relation to second normal form, the relation is decomposed into new relations using the attributes from the primary key that determine other attributes. An attribute or combination of attributes that determines other attributes is called a determinant. The determinants become the primary keys of these relations. EMPLOYEE2 is thus decomposed into the following two relations shown in Figures 8.3 and 8.5:

Determinant
An attribute or combination of attributes that determines other attributes.

1. EMPLOYEE(<u>Emp_ID,</u> Name, Dept, Salary)
2. EMP_COURSE(<u>Emp_ID, Course,</u> Date_Completed)

Third Normal Form

Third normal form (3NF)
A relation that is in second normal form and that has no transitive dependencies between two (or more) non-primary key attributes.

A relation is in third normal form (3NF) if it is in second normal form and no functional dependencies exist between two (or more) nonprimary key attributes (a functional dependency between nonprimary key attributes also is called a *transitive dependency*). For example, consider the relation:

SALES (<u>Customer_ID,</u> Customer_Name, Salesperson, Region) (sample data shown in Figure 8.7).

The following functional dependencies exist in the SALES relation:

1. Customer_ID→Customer_Name, Salesperson, Region (Customer_ID is the primary key.)
2. Salesperson→Region (Each salesperson is assigned to a unique region.)

Notice that SALES is in second normal form because the primary key consists of a single attribute (Customer_ID). However, Region is functionally dependent on Salesperson, and Salesperson is functionally dependent on Customer_ID. As a result, SALES has data maintenance problems.

1. A new salesperson (Robinson) assigned to the North region cannot be entered until a customer has been assigned to that salesperson (because a value for Customer_ID must be provided to insert a row in the table).

Figure 8.7
A Relation That Has Transitive Dependency

SALES

Customer_ID	Customer_Name	Salesperson	Region
8023	Anderson	Smith	South
9167	Bancroft	Hicks	West
7924	Hobbs	Smith	South
6837	Tucker	Hernandez	East
8596	Eckersley	Hicks	West
7018	Arnold	Faulb	North

Figure 8.8
Relations in 3NF

SALES1

Customer_ID	Customer_Name	Salesperson
8023	Anderson	Smith
9167	Bancroft	Hicks
7924	Hobbs	Smith
6837	Tucker	Hernandez
8596	Eckersley	Hicks
7018	Arnold	Faulb

SPERSON

Salesperson	Region
Smith	South
Hicks	West
Hernandez	East
Faulb	North

2. If customer number 6837 is deleted from the table, the information that salesperson Hernandez is assigned to in the East region is lost.
3. If salesperson Smith is reassigned to the East region, several rows must be changed to reflect that fact (two rows are shown in sample data shown in Figure 8.7).

These problems can be avoided by decomposing SALES into the two relations, based on the two determinants (see Figure 8.8). These relations are the following:

SALES1(Customer_ID, Customer_Name, Salesperson)
SPERSON(Salesperson, Region)

Foreign key
An attribute that appears as a nonprimary key attribute or part of a primary key in one relation and as a primary key attribute in another relation.

Note that Salesperson is the primary key in SPERSON. Salesperson is also a foreign key in SALES1. A foreign key is an attribute that appears as a nonprimary key attribute in one relation (like SALES1) and as a primary key attribute or part of a primary key in another relation. Since Salesperson is not the primary key in SALES1, but is a primary key in another relation, it is dotted underlined in SALES1. Similarly, Emp_ID in EMP_COURSE is a foreign key because Emp_ID by itself is not a primary key in EMP_COURSE, but is a primary key in another relation.

Referential integrity
The presence of each value of an attribute, called a foreign key, in the values of another attribute.

A foreign key must satisfy referential integrity, which specifies that the value of an attribute in one relation depends on the value of the same attribute in another relation. Thus, in Figure 8.8, the value of Salesperson in each row of table SALES1 is limited to only the current values of Salesperson in the SPERSON table. Earlier, in Figures 8.3 and 8.5, the value of Emp_ID in each row of EMP_COURSE is limited to the current values of Emp_ID in EMPLOYEE. Referential integrity is one of the most important principles of the relational model.

The Fourth, the BCNF, and the Other Normal Forms

More can be learned about the normal forms from a database textbook that covers the fourth and some additional normal forms; however, most applications can be addressed by the first three normal forms. Only rarely is the fourth normal form applied. Note that the fourth normal form is applied implicitly at the conceptual modeling stage whenever a ternary relationship situation is encountered. Since the coverage of the fourth normal form is somewhat technical, it is easier to address it at the conceptual model stage. When there are three entities, a ternary relationship can only exist if there is no 1:n relationship among them, that is, all binary relationships are multivalued; then, a ternary relationship exists when there is a constraint binding the three entities. If there is no such constraint, there are two independent binary m:n relationships. For example, if we wish to record what skills are used by an employee in a given project, the relationship is ternary. If we only wish to record what skills are used by an employee, and what projects an employee works in, there are two binary relationships. Since a ternary relationship can be mapped into a relation using translation rules, there is no pressing need to learn the technical details of the fourth normal form.

It is unlikely that a situation that requires the fifth normal form or some of the other normal forms that have been of some theoretical interest but seem to have almost no practical application ever will be encountered. However, there is an interesting normal form called the Boyce Codd normal form (BCNF), which simply states that each determinant must be a candidate key. It can be shown that BCNF addresses the first three normal forms. BCNF can be referenced in a database textbook; however, it might be simpler to learn the first three normal forms. Further, if conceptual data modeling is done right, little or no tweaking might be needed to the resulting relations to bring them to the third normal form.

Where Does the Relational Data Model (RDM) Fall Short?

Before discussing the shortcomings of the relational data model, be aware that the database market is dominated by relational DBMSs (RDBMSs). Even if an object-oriented development methodology is followed, the systems analyst is likely to design a relational database, given the realities of the market. However, it is well known that the relational data model (RDM) has some shortcomings, and RDBMS vendors are slowly incorporating new features, either standard or by installing additional components that are object-oriented.

RDMs fall short in several respects. Although the generalization concept has been popular for more than two decades, it has not been a formal part of the RDM. The first normal form sometimes can lead to unnatural database structures and performance problems. Aggregation has not been formally recognized in RDM. The primary key approach of identifying rows might be inadequate in certain applications. RDM does not address complex types like geographical points. These shortcomings have led to the gradual incorporation of new features in RDBMSs, which are now called object-relational DBMSs (ORDBMSs).

OBJECT EXTENSIONS TO RELATIONAL DATA MODEL

Object-relational data model (ORDM)
A relational data model with object-oriented extensions.

The relational data model has a formal basis, and researchers and practitioners agree on the theory and practice of the model. Although several authors have attempted to formalize the basis of the object-relational data model (e.g., Date & Darwen, 1998) and others have explained its practice (e.g., Brown, 2001; Loney & Koch, 2004), no clear standards have been established yet in this arena (Muller, 1999). Despite the lack of standards, certain features from the object-relational data model are now being incorporated in RDBMS (Rahayu, Taniar, & Pardede, 2006). A broad definition of object-relational data model (ORDM) is that it is essentially "a relational data model with object-oriented extensions." This chapter will include the essentials of these features. Design details of these features will be covered in Chapter 11 (Physical Database Design).

Earlier chapters of this book discussed that OOSAD projects are iterative and incremental. Because implementation of the critical aspects of a project starts early, the DBMS decision also needs to be made by the elaboration phase at the latest. By the time the use cases are fully documented, one should have made the decision to use a particular DBMS. Therefore, when data modeling commences, an analyst is likely to have a good idea about the object-oriented capabilities provided by the DBMS. The analyst need not be concerned with the implementation details of these extensions but should work with the project manager and the designers to select the features that will be employed. This will alert the designers, who might do some preliminary testing to ensure that these features will not lead to problems in data access.

The common object-oriented extensions that generally are available in the popular RDBMSs (such as Oracle, Informix, DB2, and SQL Server) are as follows:

1. Generalization.
2. Multivalued attributes (thus accepting violation to the first normal form).
3. Mechanisms that support aggregation (e.g., nested tables, clusters).
4. Object identifiers.
5. Relationships by references (i.e., pointers) in addition to relationships by foreign keys.
6. Incorporation of methods in a relation.
7. A richer set of types such as geographic points, documents, and large objects.

Perhaps it seems odd that this chapter does not cover pure object-oriented DBMSs (OODBMSs). It is unlikely that OODBMSs will dominate the database market in the near and possibly distant future. A lesson can be learned from the longevity of COBOL. Hundreds of thousands of relational systems are not going to be replaced by object-oriented databases overnight. In any case, it is unlikely that the relational philosophy will be sacrificed given the large productivity gains attained by the use of a declarative language like SQL. Further, relational DBMSs are being extended to incorporate object-oriented concepts. Systems that are able to combine the strengths of the relational approach and the object-oriented approach, and yet provide data access from a variety of sources, eventually will triumph. The following is a brief description of each of the object-oriented features in popular RDBMSs listed previously.

Generalization/Specialization

Object-relational DBMSs are beginning to support generalization, a much-needed feature based on the notion of inheritance. To study examples of generalization, refer to Figures 7.26 and 7.27 in the previous chapter. Chapter 11 will introduce the code required to define generalization/specialization classes.

Multivalued Attributes

The first normal form requires that values of an attribute be atomic, meaning single valued. However, as illustrated in Figure 7.8 in the previous chapter, objects sometimes have multivalued attributes. Figure 7.8 indicated that a student could have several phone numbers. If the first normal form is enforced, the following relations are obtained:

STUDENT(<u>Student id</u>, Name, Address)
STUDENT_PHONES(<u>Student id, Phone Number</u>)

Although this can be implemented in any RDBMS, it is not a natural representation because one of the attributes of STUDENT has been separated from its other attributes. A join needs to be performed to obtain all the attributes of a student. By allowing multivalued attributes, a natural representation can be obtained:

STUDENT(<u>Student id</u>, Name, Address, {Phone_Number})

The notation {} denotes multivalued, although an alternative representation can be used. Multivalued attribute values are implemented by using arrays.

Mechanisms to Support Aggregation

Relational tables, even when tightly bound as in the case of aggregation, are separate. The relationship between these tables is maintained through foreign keys. Mechanisms to support aggregation provide more natural and efficient ways of maintaining the relationship. Two such mechanisms are nested tables and clusters.

Nested Tables

In nested tables, which are like arrays, one table (the nested table) is defined inside another table (the master table). For example, the LINEITEM table can be defined within the ORDER table. This means that corresponding to a row of ORDER, the associated line items are stored as a table and linked to the row. Physically, the nested table records are stored separately from the master table records. Thus, the row in a table like ORDER must have a link field that has the address of the related LINEITEM rows. The link between the rows of the master table to those of the nested table is maintained by using pointers. Nested table data can be accessed only via the master table.

Clusters

Clustering is another mechanism to support aggregation. This requires the aggregate and parts to be stored together physically for ease of retrieval and for other operations. If ORDER and LINEITEM are to be clustered, then a cluster name needs to be defined when the table is created, and the attribute on which the clustering is to be done needs to be specified. In the example, this attribute is OrderNo, which is the attribute that links the two tables. Note the difference between clusters and nested tables: In clusters, the records of related tables are physically placed together; in nested tables, the records are physically separated and linked by a pointer.

Object Identifiers

ORDBMSs allow for the creation of object tables. An object table is slightly different from a relational table. Each row within the object table has an OID, a system that is assigned an object identifier value, which is assigned when the row is created. OIDs can be used as references for establishing relationships. OIDs are not supposed to serve as identifiers in business applications in the traditional sense. For example, OIDs will not replace traditional means of identifying people using a Social Security number or identifying events such as order by using order number.

Relationship by References

The reference mode of establishing relationships uses pointers to link the related rows. This is an alternative method to foreign keys for establishing relationships. Although it is a more efficient way of linking rows and allows one row to obtain data directly from the other, it also requires a new syntax for writing queries. This is a new feature in ORDBMS, and whether it will gain popularity remains to be seen.

Incorporation of Methods in an Object Relation

Because the behavioral aspects of an object have not been discussed, they will be covered in a later chapter.

Richer Set of Types

ORDBMSs now support a large number of types including binary large objects (BLOBs) for pictures and drawings, large character sets for manuscripts, and binary files for movies. Further, extensions like geographic points are available for specialized applications, and user-defined types also are available. This increased vocabulary necessitates the use of stereotypes until a standard emerges. However, the use of stereotypes depends on the organization's practice. The following representation uses the stereotype <<Blob>>:

STUDENT(Student_id, Name, Address, {Phone_Number}, <<Blob>> Photograph)

User-defined types (UDTs) also are supported in ORDBMSs. For example, an object type NAME_T can be defined as a string of size 40. Then attributes can be defined such as First_Name, Last_name as of type NAME_T in an object PERSON_T. The PERSON_T object might also use another type, say, ADDRESS_T, along with standard types such as numbers, strings, and dates for other attributes. Then tables can be defined such as EMPLOYEE, STUDENT, INSTRUCTOR, CUSTOMER, and SALESPERSON that are of type PERSON_T.

TRANSLATING CONCEPTUAL DATA MODELS INTO OBJECT RELATIONS

Transforming a conceptual data model into object relations and then merging all the relations into one final, consolidated set of relations can be accomplished in four steps. These steps are summarized briefly here, and then Steps 1, 2, and 4 are discussed in detail in the remainder of this chapter. Step 3 has already been covered.

1. **Translate classes.** Each class becomes an object relation. The identifier of the class becomes the primary key of the object relation, and other attributes of the class become nonprimary key attributes of the object relation.
2. **Translate relationships.** A relationship in a class diagram can be represented in the relational database design by using a foreign key or by using references (i.e., pointers). This chapter will follow the foreign key approach. In Chapter 11, the implementation of the relationship will be illustrated by reference approach, although this has not gained popularity in relational databases.
3. **Normalize the object relations.** The object relations created in Steps 1 and 2 might have unnecessary redundancy. If so, these object relations need to be normalized to make them well structured. Note that an object relation will likely follow the general principles of the second and the third normal form but can deviate from the first normal form.
4. **Merge the object relations.** Across different sets of object relations, redundant object relations (two or more object relations that describe the same class) might occur that must be merged and renormalized to remove the redundancy.

Note that if an object-oriented extension is not involved, the term *relation* may be used at times instead of *object relation*. The critical difference between a well-structured relation and an object relation is that a well-structured relation follows the first normal form, and an object relation might or might not follow the first normal form. However, from now on, the focus will be on object relations. Accordingly, the notation will be changed slightly. Thus, if the name of a class is Student, then the object relation will be called Student, not STUDENT. Similarly, if there is an attribute studentName in the class Student, it will map to studentName in the object relation, not to Student_Name. The change in notation is to move away from what is popular in the relational database world to what is popular in the UML world. However, the identifier will continue to be shown by an underlined attribute.

Translating Classes

Consider the class STUDENT shown in Figure 8.9. The object-relational translation is:

Student(<u>studentId,</u> name, address, {phoneNumber})

Note that the first normal form is allowed to be violated by accepting multivalued attributes. Thus, Student is not a well-structured relation but an object relation. If the class needs to be mapped to a pure relational representation, then the result, as illustrated earlier, is:

Student(<u>studentId,</u> name, address)
Student Phones(<u>studentId, phoneNumber</u>)

Figure 8.9 The
Class Student

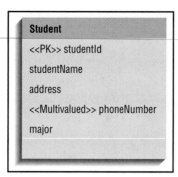

Translating Relationships

The procedure for representing relationships depends on the degree of the relation-ship—unary, binary, ternary—and the multiplicity of the relationship. Within multi-plicity, the maximum cardinality usually dictates the structure of the resulting object relation.

Binary 1:N and 1:1 Relationships

A binary one-to-many (1:n) relationship is represented by adding the primary key attribute (or attributes) of the entity on the one side of the relationship as a foreign key in the relation that is on the many side of the relationship.

Figure 8.10, an example of this rule, shows the places relationship (1:N) linking Customer and Order. Two object relations, Customer and Order, are formed from the respective classes, and customerId, which is the primary key of Customer (on the one side of the relationship), is added as a foreign key to Order (on the many side of the relationship):

Customer (customerId, name, address)
Order (orderNo, orderDate, promisedDate, customerId)

For a binary or unary one-to-one (1:1) relationship between two classes A and B (for a unary relationship, A and B would be the same class), the relationship can be represented by any of the following choices:

1. Adding the primary key of A as a foreign key of B.
2. Adding the primary key of B as a foreign key of A.
3. Both 1 and 2.

The preferred choice is based on how the object relations are accessed while con-sidering the need to minimize redundancy.

Binary and Higher-Degree M:N Relationships

Suppose that there is a binary many-to-many (m:n) relationship (or associative class) between two classes A and B. For such a relationship, a separate object relation C can be created. The primary key of this relation is a composite key consisting of the pri-mary key for each of the two entities in the relationship. Any nonkey attributes that are associated with the m:n relationship are included with the object relation C.

Figure 8.10
One–Many
Relationship

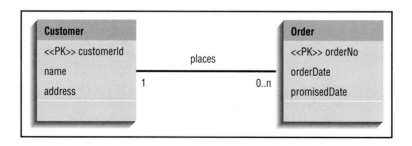

Figure 8.11
Binary and Higher-
Degree Relationships

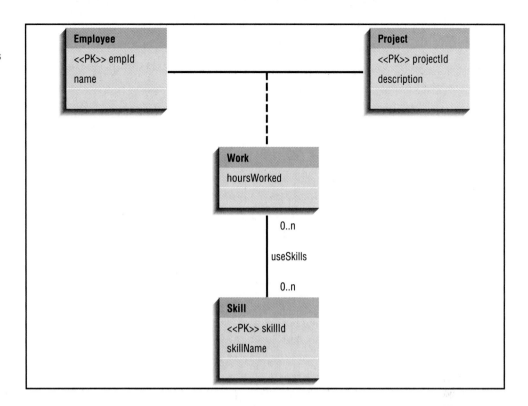

Figure 8.11 shows three classes: Employee, Project, and Skill. There is an associative class work between Employee and Project, and an m:n relationship between Work and Skill. The classes map into object relations. The associative class Work also maps into an object relation and uses a combination of the primary keys empId and projId of the two classes for its primary key.

Employee (empId, name)
Project (projId, description)
Work (empId, projId, hoursWorked)

Similarly, the m:n relationship UseSkills between Work and Skill uses a combination of primary keys empId, projId, and skillId. The object relations for Skill and UseSkills are:

Skill (skillId, skillName)
UseSkills (empId, projId, skillId)

Note that UseSkills does not have nonkey attributes and is not shown as an associative class. However, it can be shown as an associative class. The object-relational representation is the same in either case. Also, note that it involves primary keys of three classes. Thus, it represents a ternary relationship that is formed by an m:n relationship, which in turn has an m:n relationship with a class. The previous chapter featured a ternary relationship represented explicitly as an associative class among three classes. In Figure 7.18, assuming that VendorId, PartNo, and WarehouseId are the primary keys of the three classes, the associative class for the ternary relationship Ships is:

Ships (vendorId, partNo, warehouseId, quantity)

Unary Relationships

A unary relationship, also called a recursive relationship, is a relationship between the objects of a single class. Figure 8.12 shows two common examples. Figure 8.12a shows a 1:n relationship named manages, which associates employees with another employee who is their manager. Figure 8.12b shows an m:n relationship

Figure 8.12a
Employee with
Manages Relationship

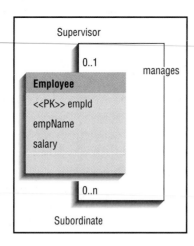

Figure 8.12b
Course with
Prerequisite
Relationship

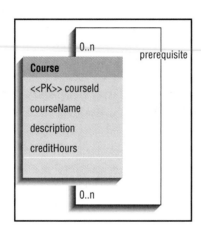

Recursive foreign key
A foreign key in an object relation that references the primary key values of that same relation.

that associates courses with their prerequisite courses. For a unary 1:n relationship, the class (such as Employee) is modeled as an object relation. The primary key of the object relation is the same as for the class. Then a foreign key is added to the object relation that references the primary key values. A recursive foreign key is a foreign key in an object relation that references the primary key values of that same relation. We can represent the relationship in Figure 8.12a as follows:

Employee(empId, empName, salary, managerId)

In this relation, managerId is a recursive foreign key that takes its values from the same set of worker identification numbers as empId.

For a unary m:n relationship, the class Course is modeled as an object relation. Then a separate object relation is created to represent the m:n relationship. The primary key of this new relation is a composite key that consists of two attributes (which should not have the same name) that take their values from the same primary key. We can express the result for Figure 8.12b as follows:

Course(courseId, courseName, description, creditHours)
Prerequisite(courseId, prerequisiteId)

Aggregation and Composition
When translating a class diagram into object relations, the rules that apply to association also apply to aggregation and composition. The difference between association and aggregation surfaces during the design stage (see Chapter 11). Also, note that composition invariably involves a 1:m relationship, while the aggregation involves an m:n relationship.

Generalization

No generally accepted object-relational representation exists for generalization. Until a standard emerges, a stereotype or some kind of annotation should be used. Note that a subclass is just like a class; all one needs to do is name its superclass and use a stereotype like under. Thus, the subclasses HourlyEmp and SalariedEmp can be represented under a class Employee.

Employee (empNo, empName, address, empDateHired)
HourlyEmp << under Employee >> (empNo, hourlyRate)
SalariedEmp << under Employee >> (empNo, annualSalary, stockOption)

Merging Object Relations

A system can have several use cases. Each use case can be used to develop a conceptual data model, and each conceptual data model maps to object relations. Some of the object relations might be similar or redundant; they might refer to the same classes, which are employed in separate use cases. If so, those object relations should be merged to remove the redundancy. This section describes merging object relations, which is the step prior to developing analysis classes.

An Example of Merging Object Relations

Suppose that a conceptual data model results in the following object relation:

Employee1 (EmpId, name, address, {phone})

Another conceptual data model might result in the following relation:

Employee2 (empId, name, address, jobCode, numberOfYears)

Because these two relations have the same primary key (empId) and describe the same entity, they should be merged into one relation. The result of merging the relations is the following relation:

Employee (empId, name, address, {phone}, jobCode, numberOfYears)

Notice that an attribute that appears in both relations (such as name in this example) appears only once in the merged relation.

Problems in Merging Object Relations

When integrating object relations, one must understand the meaning of the data and be prepared to resolve any problems that arise in that process. In this section, three problems that arise in view integration are described and illustrated: synonyms, homonyms, and dependencies between nonkey attributes.

Synonyms. In some situations, two or more attributes may have different names but the same meaning, as when they describe the same characteristic of an entity. Such attributes are called synonyms. For example, empId and employeeNumber may be synonyms.

When merging the relations that contain synonyms, if possible, agreement should be obtained from users and/or other analysts on a single standardized name for the attribute and the other synonym should be eliminated. Another alternative is to choose a third name to replace the synonyms.

For example, consider the following object relations:

Student1 (studentId, name)
Student2 (matriculationNumber, name, address)

In this case, the analyst might discover that the studentId and the matriculation Number are both synonyms for a person's Social Security number and are identical attributes. The analyst could select one of the two primary key names or use a third name like SSN.

Synonyms
Two different names that are used for the same attribute.

Homonym.   In other situations, a single attribute name, called a homonym, might have more than one meaning or describe more than one characteristic. For example, the term *account* might refer to a bank's checking account, savings account, loan account, or other type of account; therefore, account refers to different data, depending on how it is used.

The systems analyst should be on the lookout for homonyms when merging relations. Consider the following example:

Student1(studentId, name, address)
Student2(studentId, name, phoneNo, address)

In discussions with users and after reading the use cases, the systems analyst might discover that the attribute address in Student1 refers to a student's campus address, whereas in Student2 the same attribute refers to a student's home address. To resolve this conflict, new attribute names probably will need to be created, and the merged relation would become:

Student (studentId, name, phoneNo, campusAddress, permanentAddress)

Dependencies between Nonkey Attributes.   When two 3NF relations are merged to form a single relation, dependencies between nonkey attributes may result. For example, consider the following two relations:

Student1 (studentId, major)
Student2 (studentId, advisor)

Because Student1 and Student2 have the same primary key, the two relations may be merged:

Student (studentId, major, advisor)

However, suppose that each major has exactly one advisor. In this case, advisor is functionally dependent on major:

major→ advisor

If the above dependency exists, then Student is in 2NF but not 3NF, because it contains a functional dependency between nonkey attributes. The analyst can create 3NF relations by creating two relations with major as a foreign key in Student:

Student (studentId, major)
MajorAdvisor (major, advisor)

LOGICAL DESIGN OF PVF WEBSTORE

Finally, we show the object-relational representation of the Place Order use case of the PVF WebStore case. Let's revisit the conceptual representation of the use case as captured in Figure 7.30.

Here are the steps to derive the object-relational representation:

1. Translate classes into object relations:
   Customer (custId, custName, custAddress, custEmail, <<Multivalued>> custPhone, custCredit, custLogin, custPW)
   Order (ordId, ordDate, <<Derived>> subTotal, shippingCharge, <<Derived>> tax, <<Derived>> totalAmount)
   Product (prodId, prodName, prodDesc, prodListPrice)
2. Place foreign keys for 1:m relationships. In this case, the Order relation will be altered to include custId as a foreign key:
   Order (ordId, ordDate, <<Derived>> subTotal, shippingCharge, <<Derived>> tax, <<Derived>> totalAmount, custId)

3. Finally, the associative class is translated:
   Lineitem (<u>ordId,prodId</u>, quantity, actualPrice, <<Derived>> lineAmount)

This results in four object relations: Customer, Order, Product, and Lineitem. Note that the resulting solution is based on certain assumptions about the DBMS that will be used in the project. Suppose the project team decides to go with a pure relational model. Thus, the Customer object relation will have to be split into two relations. To account for the multivalued attribute custPhone, one of these relations will be Customer (<u>custId, custPhone</u>). Further, if derived attributes cannot be supported directly, then these must be removed from the representation.

KEY POINTS REVIEW

1. **What is the role of object relations in systems analysis and design?**
   Object-relational data modeling has three main purposes: produce database structures that are ready for physical database design and implementation by a DBMS, provide entity classes that are then used in sequence diagrams and other diagrams that capture the behavior of objects, and enhance and finalize the attributes in the data model.

2. **Briefly explain the following terms:** *relation, well-structured relation, normalization, and relational data model.*
   A relation is a named, two-dimensional table of data. Each relation (or table) consists of a set of named columns and an arbitrary number of unnamed rows. However, not all tables are relations. Relations have several properties that distinguish them from nonrelational tables. A well-structured relation contains a minimum amount of redundancy and allows users to insert, modify, and delete the rows in a table without errors or inconsistencies. Normalization is a process for converting complex data structures into well-structured relations. The relational data model (RDM) represents data in the form of related tables or relations. It is desirable that relations be normalized.

3. **Define the first three normal forms.**
   The first normal form (1NF) requires that cell entries in a relation be atomic. Multiple values in a cell are not permitted. A relation is in second normal form (2NF) if every non-primary key attribute is functionally dependent on the whole primary key and not on part of the primary key. A functional dependency between a nonprimary key attribute and part of a primary key also is called a partial dependency. The functional dependence of B on A is represented by an arrow (A →B) and implies that every valid value of A uniquely determines the value of B. A relation is in third normal form (3NF) if it is in second normal form and there are no functional dependencies between two (or more) nonprimary key attributes. A functional dependency between nonprimary key attributes also is called a transitive dependency.

4. **What are the main shortcomings of the relational data model?**
   The relational data model does not recognize generalization and aggregation, two important modeling concepts. RDM's adherence to the first normal form sometimes leads to unnatural database structures. Its primary key approach of identifying rows might be inadequate in certain applications. It does not address user-defined types and complex types like geographical points.

5. **List the main object-oriented extensions to contemporary RDBMSs.**
   The main object-oriented extensions are generalization; multivalued attributes; mechanisms that support aggregation (e.g., nested tables, clusters); object identifiers; relationships by references (i.e., pointers) and relationships by foreign keys; incorporation of methods in a relation; and a richer set of types such as geographic points, documents, and large objects.

6. **What are the four steps in translating a conceptual data model into object relations?**
   The four steps are translate classes, translate relationships, normalize the object relations obtained, and merge the object relations. Figures 8.9 to 8.12 provide several examples of conceptual data models whose translation is detailed in this chapter.

7. **Briefly explain the main problems in merging object relations.**

The main problems in merging object relations are synonyms, homonyms, and dependencies between nonkey attributes. In some situations, two or more attributes might have different names but the same meaning, as when they describe the same characteristic of an entity. Such attributes are called synonyms. In other situations, a single attribute name, called a homonym, might have more than one meaning or describe more than one characteristic. When two 3NF relations are merged to form a single relation, dependencies between nonkey attributes might result.

KEY TERMS CHECKPOINT

Here are the key terms from the chapter. The page where each term is first explained is in parentheses after the term.

a. Determinant (p. 222)
b. Foreign key (p. 223)
c. Functional dependency (p. 221)
d. Homonym (p. 232)
e. Normalization (p. 220)
f. Object-relational data model (ORDM) (p. 224)
g. Pointer (p. 226)
h. Recursive foreign key (p. 230)
i. Referential integrity (p. 223)
j. Relation (p. 218)
k. Relational data model (RDM) (p. 218)
l. Second normal form (2NF) (p. 221)
m. Synonym (p. 231)
n. Third normal form (3NF) (p. 222)
o. Well-structured relation/table (p. 219)

Match each of the key terms above with the definition that best fits it.

1. A relation for which every nonprimary key attribute is functionally dependent on the whole primary key.
2. A value that stores the address of a row object for the purpose of linking.
3. A named, two-dimensional table of data.
4. Two different names that are used for the same attribute.
5. A process for converting complex data structures into well-structured relations.
6. A relation that contains a minimum amount of redundancy and allows users to insert, modify, and delete the rows in a table without errors or inconsistencies.
7. Two different characteristics that are defined using the same name.
8. An attribute that appears as a nonprimary key attribute or part of a primary key in one relation and as a primary key attribute in another relation.

9. A relational data model with object-oriented extensions.
10. A relation that is in second normal form and that has no functional (transitive) dependencies between two (or more) nonprimary key attributes.
11. An attribute or combination of attributes that determines other attributes.
12. Data represented as a set of related tables or relations.
13. The functional dependence of B on A is represented by an arrow ($A \rightarrow B$) and implies that every valid value of A uniquely determines the value of B.
14. The presence of each value of an attribute, called a foreign key, in the values of another attribute.
15. A foreign key in an object relation that references the primary key values of that same relation.

REVIEW QUESTIONS

1. In what ways is a relation different from a nonrelational table?
2. Give one example of each of the three normal forms (other than those included in the chapter).
3. Create a table that violates all three normal forms.
4. If referential integrity is violated, what problems will result?
5. Create a relation that has several multivalued attributes.
6. Consider a conceptual data model with an m:n relationship and apply the 1:n translation rule to obtain

object relations. What are the problems with this representation?
7. Consider a conceptual data model with a 1:n relationship and apply the m:n translation rule to obtain object relations. What are the problems with this representation?
8. How are relationships between classes represented in the relational data model?
9. How is a foreign key represented in relational notation?
10. Can instances of a relation (sample data) prove the existence of a functional dependency? Why or why not?

1–6. Consider the six problems and exercises in the previous chapter. In each case, translate the conceptual data model into object relations. Note, especially, if there are occurrences of generalization, aggregation, and multivalued attributes.

7. Consider the following list of individual 3NF relations. These relations were developed from several separate normalization activities.

PATIENT (Patient_ID, Room_Number, Admit_Date, Address)

ROOM (Room_Number, Phone, Daily_Rate)

PATIENT (Patient_Number, Treatment_Description, Address)

TREATMENT (Treatment_ID, Description, Cost)

PHYSICIAN (Physician_ID, Name, Department)

PHYSICIAN (Physician_ID, Name, Supervisor_ID)

   a. Merge these relations into a consolidated set of 3NF relations. Make and state whatever assumptions you consider necessary to resolve any potential problems you identify in the merging process.

   b. Draw a class diagram for your answer to Part a.

8. Consider the following well-structured object relations about a sorority or fraternity:

MEMBER (Member_ID, Name, Address, {Phone Number}, Dues_Owed)

OFFICE (Office_Name, Officer_ID, Term_Start_Date, Budget)

EXPENSE (Ledger_Number, Office_Name, Expense_Date, Amt_Owed)

PAYMENT (Check_Number, Expense_Ledger_Number, Amt_Paid)

RECEIPT (Member_ID, Receipt_Date, Dues_Received)

COMMITTEE (Committee_ID, Officer_in_Charge)

WORKERS (Committee_ID, Member_ID)

   a. Foreign keys are not indicated in these relations. Decide which attributes are foreign keys and justify your decisions.

   b. Draw a class diagram for these relations, using your answer to Part a. Employ aggregation and generalization concepts, if applicable. List the assumptions you made about multiplicities in your answer to Part b.

9. Normalize the report shown in Figure 8.13. You may first develop a conceptual data model. A customer order is a transaction involving a list of specific quantities of products to be delivered at an agreed price. An order is processed by one salesperson for one customer.

10. Normalize the reports shown in Figures 8.14a and 8.14b. You may first develop a conceptual data model. Integrate the object relations with those obtained in Problem and Exercise 9. Note that products can be assembled into packages to make other products. For example, the animal photography package is made up of eight items. In addition, some packages become part of much larger packages. All of the various items are considered products, and each has its own product code. In addition, each item is classified into a particular product line, such as clothing, equipment, or recreation.

Figure 8.13 A Report for Problem and Exercise Question 9

Customer Orders

Customer Number	C11
Customer Name	Jones, Indiana

Customer Order Number	1006
Order Date	5/15/04
SalespersonName	Baker
Region	North America

	ItemId	ItemName	Quantity	Price	Item Total
	1000	Animal photography kit	1	$725	$ 725
	121	Compass	1	$ 40	$ 40
	123	Pocket knife - Avon	2	$ 45	$ 90
	125	Tent - 2 person	1	$150	$ 150
			Order Total		$1,005

Customer Order Number	1012
Order Date	2/25/04
SalespersonName	Garcia
Region	South America

	ItemId	ItemName	Quantity	Price	Item Total
	120	Boots - snakeproof	1	$150	$150
	121	Compass	3	$ 40	$120
			Order Total		$270

Figure 8.14a
A Report for Problem
and Exercise
Question 10

Package Assembly

Package ID	1000
Package Name	Animal photography kit

Component ID	Component Name	Qty
101	35-mm camera	1
102	Camera case	1
103	70–210 zoom lens	1
104	28–85 zoom lens	1
105	Photographer's vest	1
106	Lens cleaning cloth	1
107	Tripod	1
108	24 exp. 100ASA 35-mm c	10

Figure 8.14b
A Report for Problem
and Exercise
Question 10

ItemId	ItemName	ItemColor	ProductlineCode	Productline
105	Photographer's vest	Khaki	C	Clothes
120	Boots—snakeproof	Green	C	Clothes
101	35-mm camera		E	Equipment
102	Camera case	Black	E	Equipment
103	70–210 zoom lens		E	Equipment
104	28–85 zoom lens		E	Equipment
106	Lens cleaning cloth	Yellow	E	Equipment
107	Tripod		E	Equipment
123	Pocket knife—Avon	Brown	E	Equipment
124	Pocket knife—Nile	Brown	E	Equipment
122	Hammock	Khaki	F	Furniture
125	Tent—2 person	Khaki	F	Furniture
126	Tent—8 person	Green	F	Furniture
121	Compass		N	Navigation
1000	Animal photography kit		P	Package
10000	East African Safari Package		P	Package

11. Normalize the report shown in Figure 8.15. You may first develop a conceptual data model. Each course can have many sections, but each section refers to only one course. A student registers for a particular section of a course. A course section has a unique Section_Code that identifies the particular section number of a particular course; for example, Section_Code 2366 refers to section 1 of course ISM4210.

Figure 8.15
A Report for Problem
and Exercise
Question 11

Student Registration

Student Number:	999-99-9999		Registration Number:	27734
Student Name:	Alan Alda		Registration Date:	January 5th, 2004
Local Address:	571 Alden Coral Gables, FL 33122			

Section Code	Course Number	Course Name	Section Number	Units
2366	ISM4210	Database Applications	01	3
2455	ISM4220	Data Communication	02	3
4566	MGT4201	Entrepreneurship	01	3
			Total Credits	9

1. Talk to MIS professionals at a variety of organizations and elicit their definition of object-relational data modeling. Determine to what extent these professionals are using object-oriented features mentioned in this chapter for data modeling. Does the use of object-oriented features create any problems?
2. Talk to MIS professionals at a variety of organizations and find out if they strictly follow normalization. Do they adhere to the first normal form? Do they adhere to normal forms beyond the third normal form?
3. Find out what database management systems are available at your university for student use. Investigate which data types these DBMSs support. Compare these DBMSs based upon data types supported, and suggest which types of applications each DBMS is best suited for based on this comparison.
4. From your library, borrow recently published books on popular DBMSs such as Oracle, DB2, Informix, and SQL Server. Compare and contrast the object-relational features.

CASE PROBLEMS

1. Translate the conceptual data model of the case GuardTech Training, Inc. from the previous chapter into object relations.
   a. Translate each entity into a relation. Did you have any multivalued attribute? If yes, how did you handle it in the relational model? Did you encounter composite attributes?
   b. Consider each 1:m relationship. How did you translate such relationships? Did you have a 1:1 relationship? If yes, how did you handle it in the relational model?
   c. Consider each m:n relationship. How did you translate such relationships? Did any of the m:n relationships have attributes?
   d. Do you encounter a unary relationship? If yes, how did you handle it in the relational model?
   e. Do you encounter a ternary relationship? If yes, how did you handle it in the relational model?
   f. Is your solution normalized after translation? Did you have to go through any explicit normalization step?
2. Translate the conceptual data model of the case New Tampa Junior Women's Club from the previous chapter into object relations. Carry out tasks a through f as in Question 1.

CASE: BROADWAY ENTERTAINMENT COMPANY, INC.

Designing the Object-Relational Data Model for the Customer Relationship Management System

Case Introduction

The students from St. Claire Community College are making good progress in the design of MyBroadway, the Web-based customer relationship management system for Broadway Entertainment Company stores. They recently completed the conceptual data model and reviewed this with Carrie Douglass, their client at the BEC store in Centerville, Ohio.

Mapping Relations

Based on the description provided in Chapter 7, the students developed the conceptual data model for the MyBroadway database. When talking with Carrie about this data model, the students made the classes more concrete so Carrie could understand what they had in mind. To make the diagram clearer, they suggested example

attributes for each entity class. The attributes included the primary key of each class and other nonkey attributes as appropriate.

The meanings of a few of the attributes were not obvious to Carrie. For example, the students had to explain that the Type attribute specifies whether the product is music, video, or a game, whereas the Media attribute specifies whether the product is a CD, DVD, or videocassette. In the COMMENT class, the Parent/Child? attribute indicates whether the comment comes from a parent or a child, and the Refund? attribute in the RENTAL class indicates whether the rental yielded a refund for the customer (if they returned the rented item early). The students decided that they will have to prepare a data dictionary for the attributes, that is, list the attributes and explain their meaning in a dictionary format.

As the students discussed the translation of this diagram into normalized relations, they concluded that the task seems somewhat straightforward. Based on procedures they have been taught in courses at St. Claire, each entity becomes a relational table. The identifier of each class can be used at the primary key of the associated relation, and the other attributes of a class become the nonkey attributes of the associated relation. The relationships are represented as foreign keys. For a 1:n relationship, the primary key of the class on the one side of a relationship becomes a foreign key in the relation for the class on the many side of the relationship. For a m:n relationship, the primary keys of the two entities are combined into a composite or concatenated primary key. For a ternary relationship, the primary keys of the three entities are placed in a relation, and the primary key is based on the cardinality of the relationship. For the generalization relationship, the <<under >> notation was used to show the specialized classes.

After the mapping, the students checked if the resulting relations were normalized. They did not use normalization for coming up with the relations, but only for ensuring that the relations obtained from the mapping obeyed the normal forms.

Case Summary

The students are pleased with the progress, but they understand that they have only modeled the data requirements of the system. The classes pertaining to the interface and the business rules are yet to be modeled. Further, the data classes include mainly the attributes, but the operations of these classes have not been specified. They also note the use cases that deal with reports from the system have not been addressed. They look forward to the next milestone in their project, which will accomplish the specification of analysis classes, that is, classes that include the interface and business rules, and specify both data and behavior.

CASE QUESTIONS

1. Verify that the relations you say represent the MyBroadway database are in third normal form. If they are not, change them so that they are.
2. Did you show minimum cardinalities on both ends of each relationship when preparing the conceptual data model for Chapter 7? Are minimum cardinalities represented in some way in the relations in your answer to Question 1? If not, how are minimum cardinalities enforced in the database?
3. Did you notice that transactions typically have a certain pattern in conceptual data modeling, as well as when mapped into relations? Verify this for the transactions, sale/rental, extension, and inquiry. Did you find any differences among the three in their structure?
4. Did you come across any example of a synonym or homonym?

Chapter

9

Analysis Classes

Chapter Objectives

After studying this chapter, you should be able to:

➤ Stereotype classes into entity, boundary, and control classes.

➤ Draw a sequence diagram based on a use-case description.

➤ Translate a sequence diagram into a communication diagram.

➤ Convert a communication diagram into analysis classes.

➤ Draw an activity diagram and a state diagram.

➤ Document business rules using Object Constraint Language (OCL).

➤ Develop decision tables of complex rules.

Chapter Contents

➤ Chapter Preview
➤ Analysis Classes
➤ Stereotyping Classes
➤ Drawing Sequence Diagrams
➤ Robustness Analysis of Sequence Diagrams
➤ Drawing Communication Diagrams
➤ Analysis Class Diagram
➤ Activity Diagram
➤ State (or Statechart) Diagram
➤ Modeling Business Rules in Analysis Classes

Chapter 5 discussed various methods that systems analysts use to collect the information they need to determine systems requirements. Chapter 6 covered how to identify use cases to develop a use-case diagram, and how a use case is described using functional and nonfunctional requirements. Chapters 7 and 8 explained how the use cases and the associated detailed requirements are modeled to come up with the conceptual data model and object relations, which capture the data requirements of the application.

This chapter continues the focus on the requirements structuring step of systems analysis (see Figure 9.1). Object relations will be employed in sequence diagrams, which capture the behavior of the system. A sequence diagram can be translated into a communication diagram, which in turn can be converted into an analysis class diagram, which captures the data and behavior of the application. Sequence and communication diagrams capture behavior by specifying messages among objects. Analysis classes depict behavior as responsibilities of a class.

There are three types of analysis classes: entity, boundary, and control. An entity class is an object relation that is extended to include responsibilities. A boundary class provides the interface between an actor and a use case; the actor can be a human or an external system like a legacy system. A control class coordinates the tasks and captures the main logic in a use case, although portions of the logic also can be captured in an entity or an interface class. Some of the logic aspects of a use case are captured using business rules. Business rules will be introduced, and we will discuss how the rules are captured in the three types of classes. Many rules can be captured by Object Constraint Language, a vendor and platform independent language. The diagram that shows the analysis classes and their interrelationships is called the analysis class diagram. An analysis class diagram resembles the class diagram corresponding to an object-relational diagram. In addition to analysis class diagrams, activity and state diagrams will be presented; these also capture the behavioral aspects of the system.

Figure 9.1 Systems Analysis Has Three Parts: Requirements Determination, Requirements Structuring, and Alternative Generation and Selection

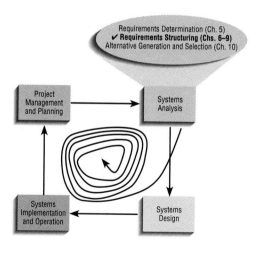

ANALYSIS CLASSES

Analysis class
A class that represents initial data and behavior requirements, and whose software- and hardware-oriented details have not been specified.

Analysis class diagram
A diagram showing analysis classes and the relationships between the classes.

The main purpose of this chapter is to present a technique for determining analysis classes and developing an analysis class diagram of an application. This is achieved by developing an analysis class diagram for each use case and then integrating the diagrams into one or a few diagrams. The previous chapter showed how to come up with object relations for each use case. The object relations constitute the entity classes, which represent the data characteristics of a use case. Next, behavior will be incorporated into entity classes. However, because an entity class is not the only kind of analysis class, other kinds of analysis classes will be presented.

This chapter prescribes a systematic technique, as shown by an activity diagram in Figure 9.2, to come up with the analysis class diagram of a use case. This activity diagram is drawn using UML notations, and it shows the starting point, activities, and ending point of the technique. The first two activities were covered earlier. Chapter 6 covered how to describe a use case. Chapters 7 and 8 detailed an approach to developing object relations. This chapter will cover the remaining four steps featured in Figure 9.2: stereotype classes, draw a sequence diagram, translate the sequence diagram into a communication diagram, and derive an analysis class diagram.

An analysis class is a first cut at defining data and behavior, and can be classified as belonging to one of the following three types: entity, boundary, or control. These three types also are called stereotypes of an analysis class. For each use case, a sequence diagram is drawn depicting the interactions between objects of these classes. The interactions include messages passed between objects. Messages become the responsibilities of the objects that receive them. From the sequence and communication diagrams, the analysis classes can be derived automatically. An analysis class diagram shows the relationships between these classes.

Figure 9.2 A Stepwise Technique to Drawing Analysis Class Diagrams

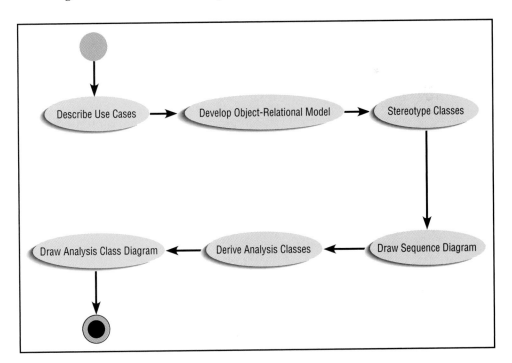

STEREOTYPING CLASSES

As mentioned previously, an analysis class can be classified into one of the following three stereotypes: entity, boundary, or control. We define each type now and use the PVF WebStore use case for illustration.

Entity Class

Entity class
A class whose primary focus is to hold data.

Responsibility
An obligation of a class. It is invoked when an object of a class receives a message.

The distinguishing characteristic of an entity class is that its objects hold most of the data of an application. To obtain an entity class, supplement an object relation's attributes with responsibilities. Objects of entity classes are persistent; that is, they exist beyond the life of a session and sometimes for the life of the system.

The object-relational diagrams defined in the WebStore installment at the end of Chapter 8 have already provided a template structure for the analysis class diagrams to be developed. The four object relations in the diagram—Customer, Order, LineItem, and Product—will become entity classes once responsibilities are specified. This will be done during the construction of sequence diagrams. Figure 9.3a shows the entity class Order. Note the special notation for the entity class stereotype: a horizontal line as a tangent on the bottom of a circle.

Boundary Class

Boundary class
A class whose objects are used by actors to interact with the system.

Objects of a boundary class are used by actors to interact with the system. Examples of boundary classes are forms, dialog boxes, menus, and other screens. However, a boundary class also can serve to establish communication with another system, for example, a legacy system. A boundary class insulates the system from changes outside the system. Although the look and feel of a form might need to be changed occasionally, entity classes generally remain unaffected. Actors are permitted to communicate with the system through boundary classes only.

At the analysis stage, one boundary class per actor/use-case pair generally is recommended. Figure 9.3b shows the OrderForm class, which can be used between the actor :Customer and the use case PlaceOrder from the WebStore system. An analysis boundary class can be decomposed to multiple design boundary classes, if necessary. It is important to identify responsibilities at this stage and not get enmeshed in user interface details and issues regarding the number of boundary classes. If there are preliminary screen layouts from a prototype, these can be associated with the class. A sophisticated CASE tool like Rational Rose allows such additional information to be associated with an analysis class.

Control Class

Control class
A class that provides coordinating behavior in the system.

A control class coordinates the tasks and captures the main application logic in a use case. It can insulate entity classes from frequently changing business rules and policies, making the entity classes more reusable. However, the entity classes and bound-

Figure 9.3a
Entity Class Order

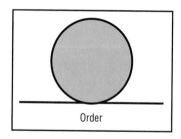

Order

Figure 9.3b
Boundary Class OrderForm

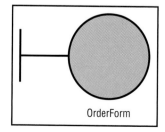

OrderForm

Figure 9.3c
Control Class
OrderControl

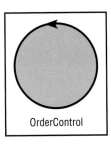

OrderControl

ary classes will also include some of the business rules. A business rule is a statement that defines or constrains some aspect of business. A policy is a guiding principle or procedure, and also in a way, a business rule. Examples of business rules are algorithms, derivations, permitted values, and inferences. Examples of policies are discount policy, grading policy, and so on. Thus, a control class can act as the controller for the sequencing of events like transactions, as well as the enforcer of business rules and policies.

At the analysis stage, it is recommended that each use case have one control class. You may choose to have more than one control class if your case is lengthy. The control classes are also holders of rules at the analysis stage. If you are sure about where you want to place the rule, place it in the appropriate class; otherwise, place it in the control class. During the design stage, you can decide where each rule is to be placed. Such decisions can be made once all the responsibilities are recognized and documented.

Figure 9.3c shows the control class OrderControl for the use case PlaceOrder of the WebStore system. Note the notation for a control class: a circular arrow that points back to its beginning. For transactions, OrderControl is a transaction manager for the use case. It controls the activities in the transaction, directs messages, enforces business rules, implements decision tables, and makes calculations. A sequence diagram in the next section will derive its responsibilities.

DRAWING SEQUENCE DIAGRAMS

The previous section discussed the three stereotypes of analysis classes: entity, boundary, and control. This section will cover how to distribute responsibilities among the analysis classes of a use case. The responsibilities are determined based on the flow of messages among objects. Diagrams that assist in distributing the responsibilities into classes and show the interactions between objects of classes are called interaction diagrams. The common type of interaction diagram is the sequence diagram, which shows the interactions among objects of classes in a time-ordered manner.

In developing a sequence diagram, and consequently distributing the responsibilities, the following guidelines need to be considered:

Sequence diagram
A diagram that shows the interactions between objects to perform critical pieces of use-case behavior in a time-ordered manner.

1. Employ the use-case diagram to determine the use cases (see Figure 9.4 for instance). Determine the actors that interact with the use case. Do not model interactions among actors. Actors are outside the scope of the system.
2. Consider one use case at a time. Obtain the text-based, detailed description of each use case.
3. For a given use case, specify an analysis boundary class between the use case and each actor. Thus, if there are two actors, there will be two boundary classes.
4. For a given use case, specify one control class.
5. Derive the entity classes from object relations for the use case.
6. Interactions in a sequence diagram are among objects of the classes, not among the classes themselves. You should use the notation :Customer to indicate an object of the class Customer.

Figure 9.4 The Use-Case Diagram of the WebStore System

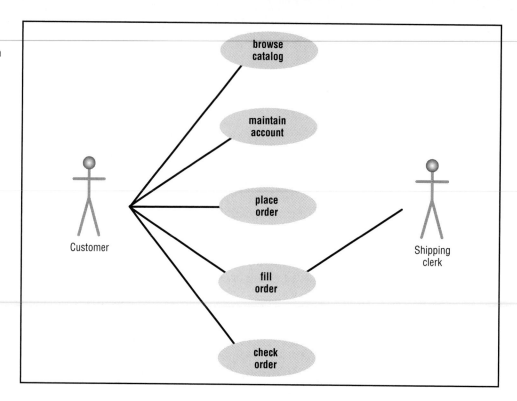

To elaborate on the last guideline, let's study a unit of a sequence diagram, which is a message passed from one object to another. However, consider a familiar situation shown in Figure 9.5. Here a child, say Evan Ann, is playing basketball and is hungry. She asks her mom Karen for a snack. A sumptuous message is passed from the sender (Evan Ann) to the receiver (Karen). The message might include a parameter value like ice cream. It is Karen's responsibility to carry out this request. Evan Ann does not exactly care how the snack is obtained; Karen may have it in the house, get it from a grocery store, or further pass the message to Dad Joey.

Objects of classes exchanging messages work in a similar fashion. This is shown in Figure 9.6, which shows the interaction between a customer and an object of the class OrderForm. Note that the objects :Customer and :OrderForm are represented by vertical dashed lines. A message ConfirmOrder is sent from the sender object :Customer to the receiver object :OrderForm. The receiver object has the responsibility of carrying out the request conveyed by the message, or it can pass the responsibility to another object. Focus of control shows the period of time during which an object is performing some actions. In the figure, this is shown by thin rectangles, one each for the two objects.

Figure 9.5
Message Passing

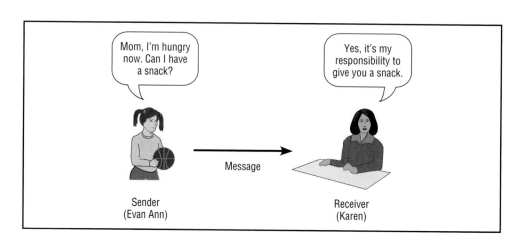

Figure 9.6
Message Passing in
a Sequence Diagram

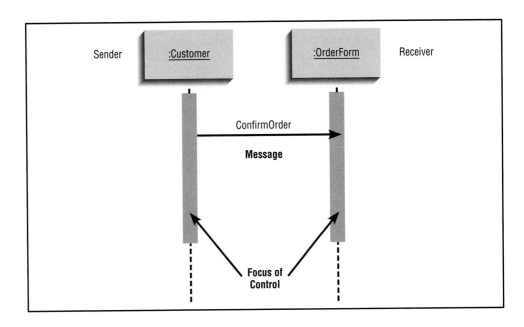

Sequence Diagram for the Place Order Use Case

Let's apply these concepts to the Place Order use case, which was detailed in Chapter 6, to create a sequence diagram. Before employing a CASE tool to draw the sequence diagram, a paper and a pencil can be used to sketch the message interactions. With experience, it might be possible to use the CASE tool directly. If the use case has been written clearly, the corresponding sequence diagram should be easy to construct. Unless the sequence diagram becomes overly complex, you should model the main success scenario together with its extensions.

The use case Place Order is invoked by the actor :Customer. The boundary object between the actor :Customer and the use case Place Order can be called :OrderForm. The control object for Place Order can be called :OrderControl. Finally, the entity objects that are required by the use case are needed. These are :Customer, :Order, :LineItem, and :Product. Although the actor :Customer and the entity object :Customer use the same name, you can observe that the two are different because of the added notation in the diagram. If you are confused, you can adopt a naming convention to distinguish the two. For example, for an actor, you can append the object by adding the letter *A* or the word *Actor*—in this case, the object for the actor :Customer can be written as :CustomerActor.

Now it is time to model the interactions among objects of these classes by spelling out the messages using the format shown in Figure 9.6. The messages are inferred by the actions stipulated in the use-case description. Refer to the description of the Place Order use case included in Chapter 6. Placing an order involves selecting furniture items, loading them to a shopping cart, and checking out by making payment. Assume that a customer already has browsed the items and is ready to select items and place an order. In a real situation, credit card authorization will be required. To keep the diagram simple, the interaction with the actor Credit Card Bureau is not included. This will, however, be included in another example.

Figure 9.7 captures the sequence diagram. The actor :Customer invokes the use case by selecting one or more items. This is indicated by the message //select item, which is conveyed to :OrderForm. Even when a customer wishes to purchase more than one item, the selections will be made one at a time. The form passes the message to the control object :OrderControl, which coordinates two actions—the creation of an order and the addition of line items to the shopping cart. The control object passes on the responsibility of creating a new order to the :Order, which creates a new order (actually, in OO programming languages, the new object is created by the constructor method; in SQL-based implementations, the insert operation creates a new row).

Figure 9.7   Sequence Diagram of the Use Case Place Order

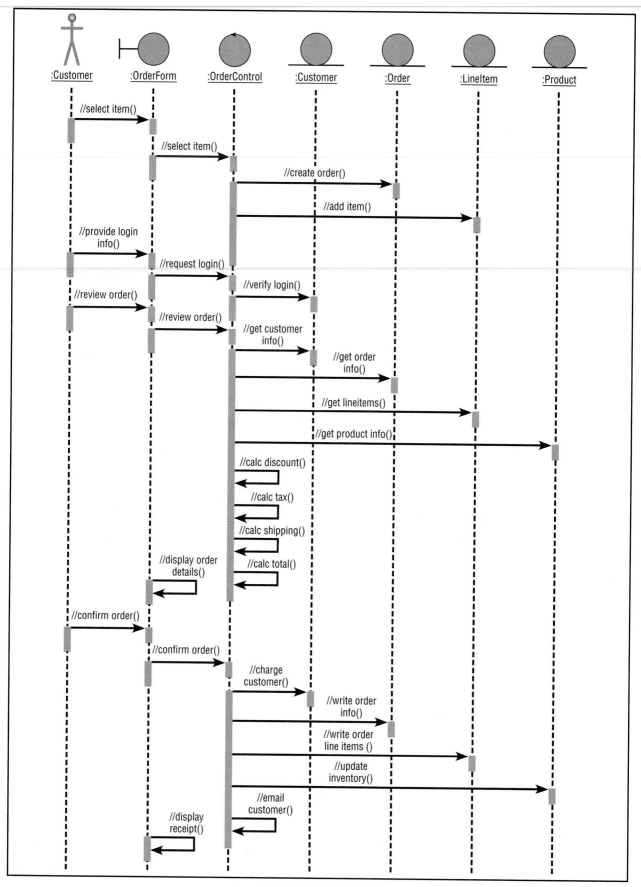

Similarly, the control passes on the responsibility of adding a line item to the :LineItem, which creates a new line item. Alternatively, the :Order object can be responsible for additions of the :LineItem objects, given that their classes have an aggregation relationship and are, therefore, closely related. However, such adjustments can be made at the design stage. At the analysis stage, the main objective is to capture the responsibilities; the optimum allocation can be decided at the design stage.

The customer needs to log in to be able to place the order. The :OrderForm captures log-in information. The request is passed to :OrderControl, which asks the :Customer object to verify log-in information.

Before confirming the order, the customer would like to review order details. The message is passed to :OrderControl, which assembles information from the entity objects :Customer, :Order, :LineItem, and :Product. The control object :OrderControl might provide a discount based on volume or amount, and might apply a tax based on customer address. Further, based on shipping options and customer address, it will calculate the shipping cost.

The calculations of discount, tax, and shipping cost each require a policy, which may be represented by a decision table. The calculation of discount, for instance, might depend on factors such as customer type, volume, amount, and coupon, and also might involve a detailed policy requiring an appropriate representation. It is also possible that these policies are so complicated that the control class eventually will be split into several design classes, one for managing the transaction, another one for discount, and still another for shipping cost. At the analysis stage, however, a single control class per use case is adequate. This is so because a good part of the logic in the control class may be moved to some of the entity classes. For example, at the design stage, you may decide that the :Order object knows the total amount and is the appropriate object to calculate the tax. Further, the :Order object knows the product weight and size, and is the appropriate object to calculate shipping costs.

Other issues may arise as you discuss the placement of these responsibilities. For example, the shipping cost may depend on a number of factors and you may have a table that is looked up; in this case, there may be a Shipping entity class. You can see that you may be distracted if, initially, you focus on where to place the responsibility rather than what the responsibility is in the first place. Focus on the "what" first and on the "where" later. But if you have enough information for the right decision in your first pass, go ahead. Note that your analysis phase will be conducted in several iterations, so an amendment, if necessary, can be made in a later iteration.

To commit the transaction, the customer is prompted for final confirmation. The form passes this message to the control object :OrderControl, which now commits the order information into the appropriate entity objects. For example, the inventory will need to be updated. The customer is charged for the order. If the updates are successful, the form will present a receipt to the customer. Further, the control object will e-mail a message along with the receipt to the actor :Customer.

The actual scenario will be more complex than what was described. Here, only the main success scenario is considered; for a complete diagram, you will need to consider the extensions, too. Nevertheless, the "analysis" sequence diagram shown in Figure 9.7 does illustrate how to capture the main behavioral aspects of the system. The diagram might not be helpful to facilitate discussion between the analyst and the user, but it can facilitate discussion among analysts, who can then query the users appropriately. Further, it provides the analyst with a first glimpse of the responsibilities of the objects of a class.

Although it might sound simple, students sometimes do not understand which object obtains responsibility when a message is passed from the sending to the receiving object. It is evident from the child-mom example that it is the *receiving* object that has the responsibility. The same applies in the case of objects in a sequence diagram.

Consider the case of the message //update inventory() from :OrderControl to :Product. The message is being sent from :OrderControl and received at :Product. We will not create a method update_Inventory() in the class OrderControl. The method update_Inventory() will be in the class Product. The call is made from some method in

Figure 9.8   Sequence Diagram of the Use Case Make Reservation

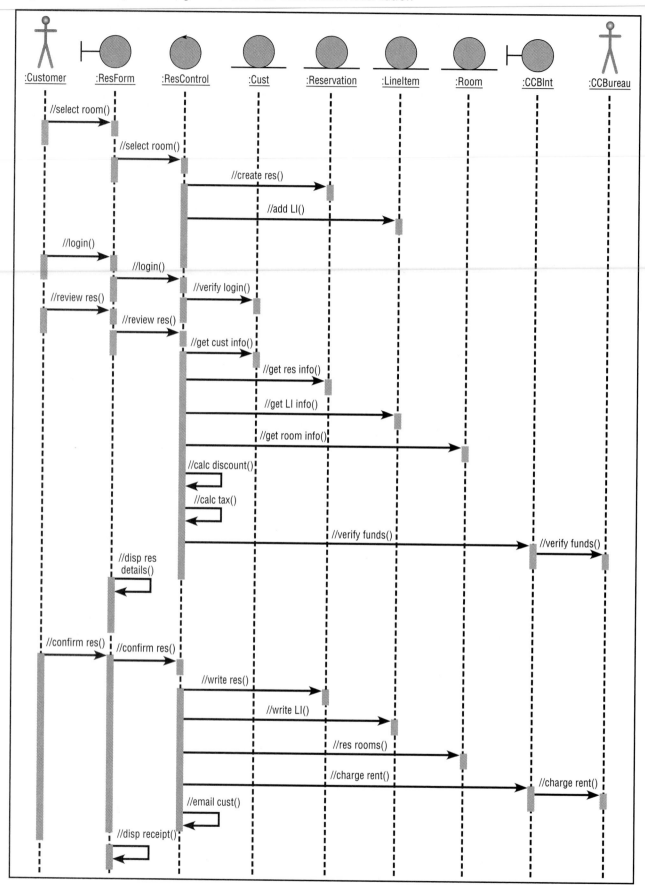

the class OrderControl. In this case, the method is confirm_order(), which is in OrderControl. To summarize, it is the receiving object that has the responsibility of implementing the message. A responsibility at the analysis stage will become one or more operations at the design stage.

Note that the sequence diagram of a transaction will usually have a pattern: there is some browsing/searching, a transaction is initiated (e.g., create order), line items are added, a security check is made (e.g., log in), the transaction is summarized, auxiliary information is added (e.g., calculate tax), and the transaction is committed or rolled back. Let's see if the sequence diagrams for the Place Order use case and the Make Reservation use case bear resemblance.

Sequence Diagram for the Make Reservation Use Case

The sequence diagram for the Make Reservation use case will be slightly more complex than that for the Place Order use case because the Credit Card Bureau will also be included. As you read about the Make Reservation use case in Chapter 6, the hotel charges a per-room nonrefundable rent for the first day. Subsequent charges are handled when the customer checks out, which is a separate use case. A customer can make reservations for more than one room.

Notice the similarity between the Make reservation and Place Order use cases. The transaction is Reservation instead of Order, and the item/service being sold is Room instead of Product. In other respects, the use cases and their sequence diagrams are similar. As mentioned earlier, we do bring in the Credit Card Bureau, which is external to the use case, and is, therefore, an actor. Consequently, you need a boundary class between the use case and this actor. Note that Figure 9.8 has two extra objects.

Assume that the customer has browsed the room types and is ready to reserve one or more rooms. The customer will enter room data and submit the request on :ResForm, which will pass the request to the control object :ResControl. The latter will pass a message for the creation of a new reservation object. Further, one or more new line items will be created.

Before checking out, the customer will need to log in so that the customer information can be retrieved. If the customer does not have an account, she will have to create a new one. If the customer does have an account but has forgotten the password, she may be able to obtain the password upon answering certain questions. These scenarios are extensions, which also follow a pattern. Only the main success scenario is shown in the diagram.

The customer will review the information before checking out. Reviewing the information involves retrieving information from the entity objects :Customer, :Reservation, :LineItem, and :Room to present the customer with a receipt-like document for approval. However, a check is also made to verify that the customer has the funds to pay for the reservation. The processing that happens at the Credit Card Bureau is external to the use case. Hence, :CCBureau is shown as an actor. Thus, a boundary class :CCBInt is required to interface with the bureau.

When the customer confirms the transaction, the controller object :ResControl will ensure that the transaction is committed, which means that the entity objects are updated, and the first night's rent is charged to the customer.

Robustness analysis
Involves analyzing the narrative text of each of the use cases and identifying a first-guess set of objects into entity, boundary, and control objects. It also involves completeness checks and diagramming rules.

Robustness Analysis of Sequence Diagrams

During the structuring system requirements step of systems analysis, robustness analysis can be conducted. Rosenberg and Scott (2001) credit Jacobson with the development of robustness analysis, and they note that this analysis is not a part of Unified Modeling Language (UML) proper. Yet, robustness analysis is a worthwhile step to take before moving on in the analysis process because it allows one to check use cases for correctness and completeness, and it starts the process of identifying the objects and the operations needed in the system. It also helps bridge the gap between analysis and design. For example, stereotyping classes into entity, boundary, and control, which was performed in the previous section, is part of robustness analysis. For a detailed and advanced coverage of robustness analysis, please refer to Rosenberg and Scott's (2001) book *Applying Use Case Driven Object Modeling with UML*, which explains four key roles of robustness analysis: sanity check, completeness check, ongoing discovery of objects, and preliminary design.

In this section, we will list certain robustness diagram rules pertaining to sequence diagrams, which are illustrated in Figure 9.9. According to Rosenberg and Scott (2001), these rules are recommended:

1. Actors can talk only to boundary objects.
2. Boundary objects can talk only to controllers and actors.
3. Entity objects can talk only to controllers.
4. Controllers can talk to boundary objects and entity objects, but not to actors. Controllers also can talk to other controllers.

These rules were followed in the development of the sequence diagram for the Place Order and the Make Reservation use cases. Note that the actor :Customer talks only via the :OrderForm, and the :OrderForm talks only to the control object :OrderControl and returns answers to the actor :Customer. The four entity objects talk only to :OrderControl, which talks to these entity objects and to :OrderForm.

In practice, these rules are occasionally violated. Specifically, entity objects do talk directly to other entity objects, and boundary objects do talk directly to entity objects. So what is the value of robustness analysis? Robustness analysis is most useful if employed at the analysis stage, especially at the beginning of the analysis phase. The amount of logic and coordination required is not clear at the beginning of analysis and sometimes not until the end of analysis. Simple rules that focus on what is to be modeled rather than where the messages are to be placed are invaluable. Hence, it is recommended that these robustness rules be followed at the analysis stage.

Consider the Calculate Discount message and operation. At the initial analysis stage, it is not clear if the operation will be housed in a control class or in an entity class. But for completeness sake, you can capture it in the control class. In a subse-

Figure 9.9
Sequence Diagram
Rules

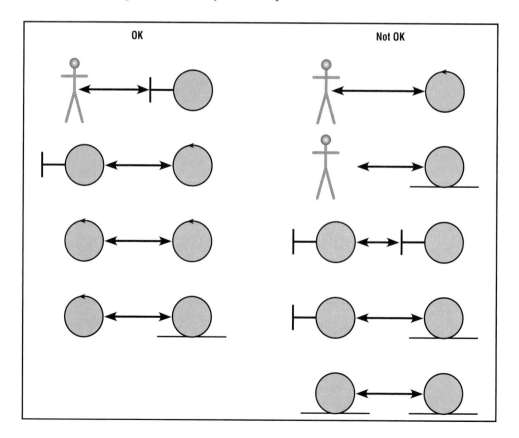

quent iteration, you may note that the requirements indicate that the discount can be calculated by looking at a table and applying a factor. Or, you may discover that there are a number of rules that interplay to come up with the discount amount; in this case, you may keep it in the control class. In the latter case, at the design stage, you may dedicate a separate control class for calculating discount.

So here is a guideline: Use robustness rules to translate the written use case into an initial sequence diagram. Later, consider the best object to conduct an operation and adjust the initial sequence diagram accordingly. The sequence diagram is one of the two interaction diagrams. We now turn our attention to drawing communication diagrams, which is the other, but lesser-used, interaction diagram.

DRAWING COMMUNICATION DIAGRAMS

Communication diagram
A diagram that shows the interactions among objects to perform critical pieces of the use-case behavior. A communication diagram does not show the time element.

A communication diagram (formerly called collaboration diagram) is another kind of interaction diagram. It can be used to come up with analysis classes. The information in a communication diagram is similar to that in a sequence diagram, but a sequence diagram is organized in chronological sequence, and a communication diagram is not. In a communication diagram, the time element is removed. The emphasis is on how objects collaborate with each other instead of on their sequence. A use-case description, which is generally written as a sequence of actions, can be mapped easily into a sequence diagram, so it is preferable to draw the sequence diagram first and then translate it automatically into a communication diagram using a CASE tool.

The communication diagram shown in Figure 9.10 is semantically equivalent to the sequence diagram shown in Figure 9.7. The communication among objects

Figure 9.10
Communication Diagram of the WebStore Case

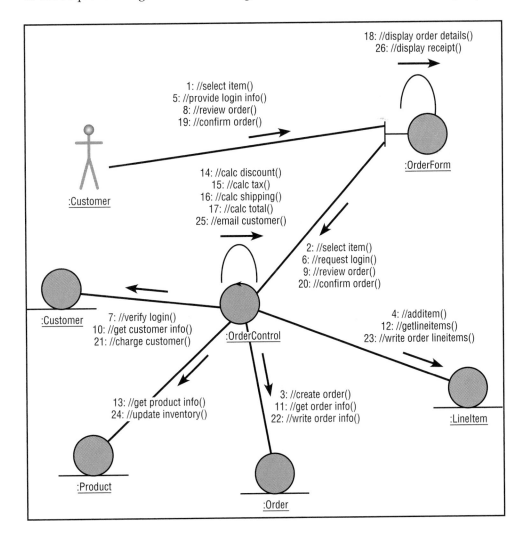

is better represented (hence the name communication diagram), but the time element is missing, although CASE tools can provide the message sequence number from the sequence diagram. Because use cases generally provide time-ordered steps, a communication diagram cannot represent a use case as accurately as a sequence diagram does. However, the communication diagram does indicate what object sends what messages to other objects. Since an object is responsible for carrying out the operations of the messages it receives from other objects, the communication diagram can be used to list all the operations to be carried out by an object. This is very useful in coming up with analysis classes that go into an analysis class diagram.

A common question that is asked is: Which is the more useful diagram—the sequence diagram or the communication diagram? Both diagrams are useful. From a given use case, it would be difficult to draw a communication diagram; a sequence diagram is much easier, and so most analysts consider it as the more important diagram. A CASE tool can easily translate a sequence diagram into a communication diagram. However, a communication diagram is closer to the behavioral aspect of a class diagram, which is what an analyst is eventually trying to model.

ANALYSIS CLASS DIAGRAM

An analysis class diagram shows the analysis classes and the relationships among these classes. By now you have come across two kinds of relationships—structural relationships and behavioral relationships. The structural aspects are available from data modeling. The behavioral aspects of an analysis class diagram can be derived from a sequence diagram or a communication diagram. So which relationship should be shown in an analysis class diagram? There is no hard-and-fast rule here. We recommend that you model the structural relationship in the analysis class diagram, given that there is no explicit support of data modeling in UML. When you wish to look up a behavioral relationship, you can refer to a communication diagram. Using both, you can get the structural as well as the behavioral picture of relationships. You can include both kinds of relationships in a diagram if you use different notations for the two types of relationships, but your diagram will appear cluttered.

Individual class diagrams from different use cases can be integrated in ways similar to how data models are integrated. Thus, attributes as well as operations of the same class Product from different use cases are collated. During integration, you also need to be careful about synonyms and homonyms.

An analysis class diagram of the Place Order use case is shown in Figure 9.11. The attributes were added to the entity classes, and the structural relationships were defined in Chapters 7 and 8. In this chapter, we developed the communication diagram, which showed the messages received by an object of a class. These messages are essentially the operations to be performed by the receiving object. The translation from an interaction diagram to an analysis class diagram is, therefore, somewhat mechanical given that a message from a sender to a receiver becomes a responsibility of the receiver. The addition of responsibilities completes the analysis class diagram for a use case.

Note that the entities classes—Customer, Order, LineItem, and Product—still are related the same way. The boundary class OrderForm and the control class OrderControl have been added. Interaction relationships are not shown. In theory, the relationships between OrderControl and the four entity classes also could be shown. However, this will clutter the diagram. The communication diagram captures this relationship, so it is not necessary to show the relationship here.

Figure 9.11
Analysis Class
Diagram Showing
Structure and
Behavior of Classes

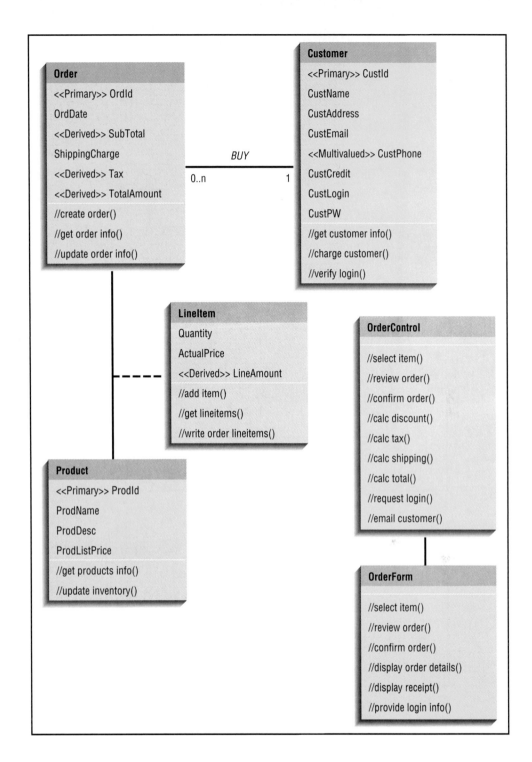

ACTIVITY DIAGRAM

Activity diagram
A diagram that emphasizes the flow of control from activity to activity.

An activity diagram shows the workflow of a system. In other words, an activity diagram shows the flow of control from activity to activity in the system, what activities can be done in parallel, and any alternate paths through the flow (Quatrani, 1999). Activity diagrams are similar to the conventional flowcharts, although the latter have been employed primarily to show flow of control in a program. Incidentally, Figure 9.2 in this chapter is a simple activity diagram that shows the activities involved in the development of an analysis class diagram. Figure 9.12 shows a preliminary activity diagram for the Make Reservation use case. The diagram does not cover all the extensions.

Figure 9.12 An Activity Diagram

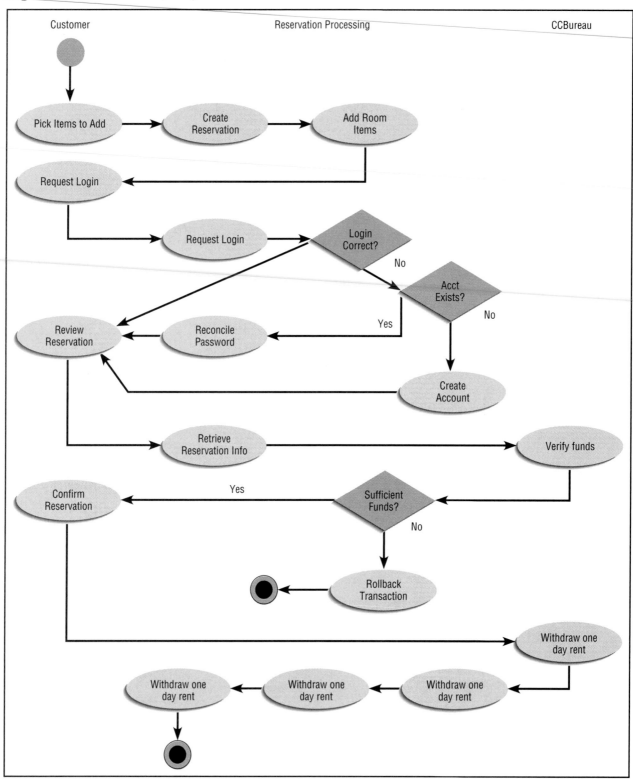

Activity
An activity is some behavior that an object carries out while it is in a particular state.

Transition
A movement from one activity to another or from one state to another.

Decision point
A diamond symbol containing a condition whose responses provide transitions to different paths for activities.

Swimlanes
Lanes used to partition an activity diagram to show who does what activities.

Synchronization bars
Thick horizontal or vertical lines denoting concurrent or parallel processing of activities. The separate set of activities starts at a fork and ends at a join. The entire set of activities needs to be complete before further activities can ensue.

An activity diagram mainly makes use of the following elements: activity, transition, decision point, swimlanes, and synchronization bars. Note that activities are represented by rectangles with rounded sides, transitions by arrows, decision points by diamonds, swimlanes by lanes, synchronization by thick lines, start state by a dot or filled circle, and stop state by a bull's-eye.

Let's examine the activity diagram shown in Figure 9.12. To some extent, the diagram covers similar information when compared to the sequence diagram shown in Figure 9.8. This is not surprising given that both diagrams model the use case Make Reservation. The focus of the activity diagram, however, is different. The sequence diagram does not consider decision points. If you examine the extensions, these are variations from the normal flow. In other words, the extensions occur because there are decision points along the normal route, and you proceed on the normal route so long as the decision results denote success. Along this route, there are a number of exceptions, which are not captured properly either by the sequence diagram or by the written use case. In the case of the sequence diagram, it captures messages only. The written use case captures the extensions, but these are listed at the end, and when they originate is not very clear.

The activity diagram can capture the extensions graphically. This is shown in Figure 9.12 although it must be admitted that even the diagram in Figure 9.12 is somewhat simple. But the diagram does illustrate exactly when in the sequence of activities an extension occurs.

An activity diagram may be derived from a use case. Conversely, an activity diagram can help improve the written use case. Specifically, it can be used to determine the extensions. You can examine an activity in the diagram, and ask if the activity will go as planned; if not, you have an extension. For example, examine the activity "Reconcile Password." What would happen if the password is not reconciled? Is it possible? Sure. The customer may not remember the answer to the password hint. Is it possible that the activity "Create Account" is not successful? Sure. The suggested customer user name may have already been used, or the customer may not enter a strong password.

You may find that an activity diagram is a versatile tool. However, you will need to exercise judgment and caution in using it. If the use case is complete and easily understood, don't draw an activity diagram. Employ it only when it clarifies the requirements. In the next section, we will discuss some situations that warrant its use.

An activity diagram may involve activities that need to be done in parallel. This is shown by synchronization bars. For example, a store might sell items that are mostly manufactured in-house; however, certain items are purchased from vendors and included in the order. In fulfilling an order, the store will have to ensure that in-house items are manufactured and outsourced items are purchased. These two sub-flows will occur in parallel, and the order cannot be dispatched until both activities are complete. Figure 9.13 diagrammatically shows the parallel subflows.

When to Use an Activity Diagram

An activity diagram is a flexible tool that can be used in a variety of situations. It can be used at a high level as well as a low level of abstraction. Remember, it should be used only when it adds value to the project. Drawing an activity diagram for every possible scenario is likely to lead to "analysis paralysis" for the writer and the reader. Our recommendation is to use it sparingly. Ask the question: Does it add value, or is it redundant? Specifically, an activity diagram can be used to:

1. Depict the flow of control from activity to activity.
2. Help in use-case analysis to understand what actions need to take place.
3. Help in identifying extensions in a use case.
4. Model workflow and business processes.
5. Model the sequential and concurrent steps in a computation process.

The interpretation of the term *activity* depends on the perspective from which one is drawing the diagram. At a conceptual level, an activity is some task that needs

Figure 9.13 An Activity Diagram Showing Synchronization of Subflows

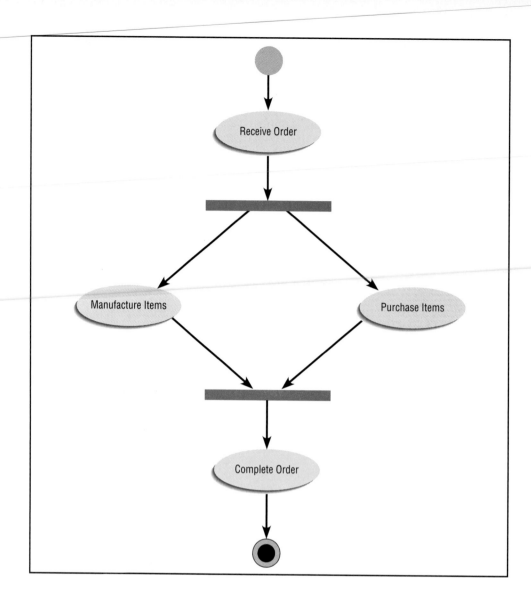

State diagram
A diagram that captures the behavior of an object by specifying the sequences of states it goes through during its lifetime in response to events, together with responses to those events.

State
A condition or situation during the life of an object at which time it satisfies some condition, performs some activity, or waits for some event.

to be done, whether by a human or a computer (Fowler & Scott, 1999). At an implementation level, an activity is a method or a class.

When Not to Use an Activity Diagram

An activity diagram should be avoided if:

1. The use case is simple, and a graphical representation will not be helpful.
2. The purpose is to examine how objects collaborate. An interaction diagram should be used instead (Fowler & Scott, 1999).
3. The purpose is to see how an object behaves over its lifetime. Use a state diagram instead. Activity diagrams and state diagrams are similar; however, the focus in an activity diagram is on the activities, and the focus in a state diagram is on the states of an object.

STATE (OR STATECHART) DIAGRAM

A state diagram captures the behavior of an object by specifying the sequences of states it goes through during its lifetime in response to events, together with responses to those events (Booch, Rumbaugh, & Jacobson, 1999). The state of an

Figure 9.14 State Diagram of the Object: <u>Order</u>

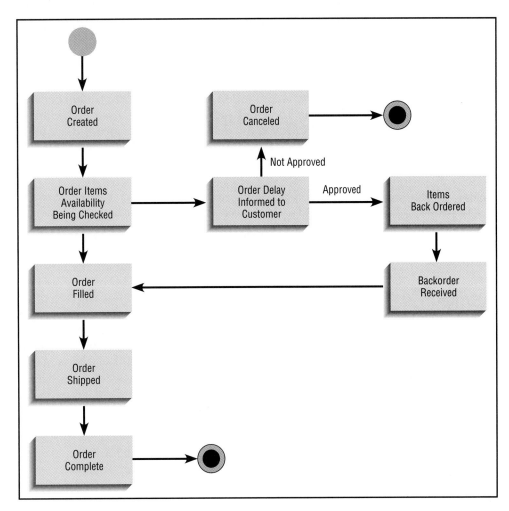

object is a condition or situation during the life of an object at which time it satisfies some condition, performs some activity, or waits for some event.

Because performing an activity also constitutes a state, an activity diagram of an object can be considered a special case of a state diagram. In an activity diagram, all states are activities. A state diagram captures the states of an object during its lifetime. For example, the object :<u>Order</u> goes through creation, filling, shipping, and closing. Before filling an order, the physical inventory will be checked, and this might invoke events such as getting approval of the customer regarding a delay in shipment (see Figure 9.14). For the sake of understanding, the diagram has been kept simple; it will get complicated if partial orders can be shipped, and an order can be split into various shipments, either because some items are backordered or because the items are at different warehouses.

When to Use State Diagrams

Each object in a system has a life cycle, so should a state diagram be drawn for each object? Most objects have a simple life cycle with few states, and modeling such cases certainly will lead to "analysis paralysis." Unless an object can exhibit a number of states, a state diagram need not be drawn. Fowler and Scott (1999) have provided some useful recommendations:

1. State diagrams are useful for describing the behavior of an object across several use cases.
2. State diagrams are not useful for describing behavior that involves a number of objects collaborating together.

3. Some people find state diagrams helpful; others find them unnatural. The systems analyst should find the preferences of those he or she works with.

A number of diagrams have been presented in this chapter. Just knowing how to draw these diagrams should not lead one to draw a large number of diagrams for a limited-size application. A diagram must provide benefits beyond the costs of producing it. Therefore, judgment must be used in deciding when a diagram provides value. However, the data model, the sequence diagram, and the analysis class diagram of a use case probably always will be needed for all but trivial cases.

MODELING BUSINESS RULES IN ANALYSIS CLASSES

The previous chapters discussed at length how to model data using object relations and class diagrams. As a result of data modeling, we came up with entity classes that house application data. However, where are the business rules stored? Before this question can be answered, we need to know about business rules.

From a business perspective, a business rule is a directive, which is intended to influence or guide business behavior, in support of business policy that is formulated in response to an opportunity or threat. From an information systems perspective, a business rule pertains to the facts of the system that are recorded as data and to the constraints on changes to the values of those facts (www.businessrulesgroup.org). A comprehensive treatise of the topic can be found in Barbara von Halle's book (2002) *Business Rules Applied*. We will address key issues pertaining to the topic.

Business rules can be classified as:

Business rule
A directive, which is intended to influence or guide business behavior, in support of business policy that is formulated in response to an opportunity or threat.

Constraints: A constraint is a restriction and can be mandatory or suggested.
Calculations: A calculation is an algorithm that employs operators such as sum, difference, product, quotient, or a similar operation.
Value Inferences: A value inference is based on test conditions and upon finding them true, establishes the value of a new attribute.
Action Enablers: An action enabler is based on test conditions and upon finding them true, implies a new action.

The following list of key words can be learned (from Halle's book) to determine rules in the use cases: *check, qualify, compute, calculate, estimate, evaluate, determine, assess, compare, verify, validate, confirm, decide, diagnose,* and *process*. These words suggest that rules or decisions are behind them.

The traditional approach to modeling business rules was to code them. Before relational model-based DBMSs became popular, even primary key checks had to be hard coded. Contemporary approaches attempt to define business rules declaratively instead of procedurally. However, this is not always possible, especially when the rule is a complex combination of conditions.

Where are the business rules stored? Unlike data, which are stored in entity classes only, business rules can be stored in entity, boundary, and control classes. The astute analyst can start assigning rules to the different classes at the analysis stage rather than relegate it to the design or implementation stage. In general, the rules related to data (entity classes) are more stable, and the rules related to business logic (control classes) and presentation (boundary classes) are less stable. Examples of each are provided in the following section. At the end of this section, Object Constraint Language (OCL)—a language to model business rules—is introduced.

Constraints

The most common examples of constraints are permissible values, validation rules, and multiplicity constraints. Constraints generally are associated with entity classes and can be defined declaratively. An example of a permissible value constraint is a restriction on an attribute to be nonnegative (i.e., zero or positive) or to have a specified range (e.g., between 1 and 10). This can be done by defining the attribute to be of a certain type or belonging to a domain. Sometimes, attributes are initialized at the time of creation of an object, so that they have permissible values. Typically, permissible values will be handled in an entity or a boundary class. If exam scores cannot be more than 100, then they can be constrained in an entity class by choosing the field to be of a certain type or belonging to a domain. Also, they can be handled on the form that accepts the entries. Such value constraints can be documented in a text file attached to the analysis class or modeled using OCL. In Rational Rose, for example, if there is an analysis class Customer, text files can be attached to provide details pertaining to customer requirements. Thus, any business rule related to Customer can be listed there. A constraint on a calculated value that is not stored in an entity class need to be assigned to a control, or boundary class.

An example of a validation rule is the referential integrity rule. Such rules can be derived implicitly from the analysis class model that shows the relationships between entity classes, and further clarified by attaching a text document to the analysis class. Note that the violations of the validation rules need to be handled. The validation rule can be defined in an entity class, but the method that handled the violation might be in a control class.

Multiplicity constraints can be shown on the relationships in the analysis class diagram. For example, if a student can enroll in no more than five courses in a semester, the multiplicity constraint (0..5) can clearly capture this constraint.

Constraints that are flexible and require human judgment to make the final decision are called guidelines. For example, a student may not be allowed to enroll in a course if course prerequisites are not met. However, honor students may be allowed to enroll in a course subject to instructor approval even if course prerequisites are not met. Such decisions generally are governed by policies. If the policies are complex, then formal techniques like decision tables (which are covered in a later section) are needed.

Calculations

A calculation can be as simple as a derived value like calculating sales tax based on a flat percentage of sales, or it can be an algorithm like calculating payroll deduction for federal income tax. Because a calculated value generally is held in an attribute, a calculation is a responsibility (which eventually becomes a method) attached to an attribute. Thus, calculations generally belong to entity classes. However, a complex algorithm that captures complex logic is better assigned to a control class because this logic is likely to change over time and it is preferred to keep volatile elements away from entity classes.

Many business rules are based on calculated values, which, by definition, are also business rules. Thus, one business rule might indicate how a value is to be calculated, and another might indicate how the calculated value is to be used in a rule. Thus, a rule states that the total order amount is the sum of line item amounts less customer discount based on the customer status, where the customer status has been assigned based on their past sales volume. The amount so calculated might then be subject to discounts based on the discount policy on individual order amounts. Such business rules are likely to reside in entity and control classes.

Value Inferences

Although inference is a broad term, a common inference mechanism is the conditional statement. For example, an inference might state that if a donor has donated more than $10,000, then he or she is a high-priority donor. Complex business logic of the type "if-then-else" needs suitable representation mechanisms to minimize ambiguity.

Three popular mechanisms to model complex business logic are decision tables, decision trees, and structured English. Detailed coverage of the topic can be found in the book *Essentials of Systems Analysis and Design* (3rd Edition) by Valacich, George, and Hoffer. Only decision tables are covered in this book. A decision table is

Decision table
A matrix representation of the logic of decisions, which specifies the possible conditions for the decisions and the resulting actions.

Figure 9.15
Complete Decision
Table for Payroll
System Example

Conditions/ Courses of Action		Rules					
		1	2	3	4	5	6
Condition Stubs	Employee type	S	H	S	H	S	H
	Hours worked	<40	<40	40	40	>40	>40
Action Stubs	Pay base salary	X		X		X	
	Calculate hourly wage		X		X		X
	Calculate overtime						X
	Produce Absence Report		X				

a diagram of process logic where the logic is reasonably complicated. (In theory, a decision table can be made for simple logic, but it is not useful in such cases.) Although decision tables are employed for value inference business rules, they also can be used for action enabler rules, which are covered in the next subsection. The only difference is that in the first case the result is a value, whereas in the second it is an action. All of the possible choices and the conditions the choices depend upon are represented in tabular form.

The decision table in Figure 9.15 models the logic of a generic payroll system. The table has three parts: the condition stubs, the action stubs, and the rules. The condition stubs contain the various conditions that apply in the situation the table is modeling. Figure 9.15 shows two condition stubs for employee type and hours worked. Employee type has two values: S, which stands for "salaried," and H, which stands for "hourly." Hours worked has three values: less than 40, exactly 40, and more than 40. The action stubs contain all the possible courses of action that result from combining values of the condition stubs. This table has four possible courses of action: pay base salary, calculate hourly wage, calculate overtime, and produce Absence Report. Not all actions are triggered by all combinations of conditions. Instead, specific combinations trigger specific actions. The part of the table that links conditions to actions is the section that contains the rules.

To read the rules, start by reading the values of the conditions as specified in the first column: Employee type is S, or salaried, and hours worked are less than 40. When both of these conditions occur, the payroll system is to pay the base salary. In the next column, the values are H and > 40, meaning an hourly worker who worked less than 40 hours. In such a situation, the payroll system calculates the hourly wage and makes an entry in the Absence Report. Rule 3 addresses the situation when a salaried employee works exactly 40 hours. The system pays the base salary, as was the case for rule 1. For an hourly worker who has worked exactly 40 hours, rule 4 calculates the hourly wage. Rule 5 pays the base salary for salaried employees who work more than 40 hours. Rule 5 has the same action as rules 1 and 3, and governs behavior with regard to salaried employees. The number of hours worked does not affect the outcome for rules 1, 3, or 5. For these rules, hours worked is an indifferent condition in that its value does not affect the action taken. Rule 6 calculates hourly pay and overtime for an hourly worker who has worked more than 40 hours.

Because of the indifferent condition for rules 1, 3, and 5, the number of rules can be reduced by condensing rules 1, 3, and 5 into one rule, as shown in Figure 9.16. The indifferent condition is represented with a dash. The decision table that started with six rules has now been simplified to a table that conveys the same information with only four rules.

A decision table can be created as a document and attached to a control class. In the WebStore case, for example, the discount, the tax, and the delivery charge can be calculated based on decision tables. The control class can calculate these charges and update entity objects such as :Order. Because discount, tax, and delivery charge

Condition stub
That part of a decision table that lists the conditions relevant to the decision.

Action stub
That part of a decision table that lists the values or actions that result for a given set of conditions.

Rule
That part of a decision table that specifies which values or actions are to be followed for a given set of conditions.

Figure 9.16
Reduced Decision
Table for Payroll
System Example

Conditions/	Rules			
Courses of Action	1	2	3	4
Employee type	S	H	H	H
Hours worked	–	<40	40	>40
Pay base salary	X			
Calculate hourly wage		X	X	X
Calculate overtime				X
Produce Absence Report		X		

determination rules can change frequently, it might be better to put these policies in a control class rather than in an entity class.

Action Enablers

An action enabler rule is a statement that tests conditions and upon finding them true, initiates another business event, message, or activity (Halle, 2002). A common kind of action enabler is a triggering operation, or a trigger. A triggering operation is an assertion or rule that governs the validation of data manipulations such as insert, update, and delete. The scope of triggering operations can span to attributes belonging to more than one class. In the case of value inferences, rules result in values. In the case of triggers, rules result in operations.

A trigger normally includes the following items:

1. User rule: A concise statement of the business rule to be enforced by the trigger.
2. Event: The data manipulation operation (insert, delete, or update) that initiates the operation.
3. Entity Class Name: The name of the entity class being accessed and/or modified.
4. Condition: Condition that causes the operation to be triggered.
5. Action: Action taken when the operation is triggered.

For example, one can create a trigger that prevents insertions into the Employee entity class if the hours are not between 8:00 A.M. and 6:00 P.M., or if the day is Saturday or Sunday. One can create a trigger that rejects transactions if the condition (Withdrawal Amount > Account Balance) is met. If an object is deleted, a trigger may cascade deletes to other objects. Every time the inventory of an item is depleted, a trigger can check if the item needs to be placed on the purchase order list. Triggers generally belong to entity classes. For analysis, one can write the triggers requirements in a document, which can be attached to the appropriate entity class.

Action enablers can belong to control classes. For example, if the Place Order use case is a success, the customer is a frequent buyer, and the delivery mode is selected as overnight delivery, a high-priority message needs to be fired so that Fill Order use case can be initiated immediately. Conversely, if the Place Order use case is successful but the customer has not paid the last two invoices, the delivery date may be delayed or kept on hold based on an algorithm, with a message sent to the customer requesting immediate payment of past invoices.

The Object Constraint Language (OCL)

Object Constraint Language (OCL)
An add-on to UML to write expressions that specify business rules in an unambiguous manner.

Although the word *Constraint* in the Object Constraint Language (OCL) suggests that the language is limited to specifying constraints, OCL can also be used to define business rules, in general. OCL is an add-on to UML used to write expressions that specify business rules in an unambiguous manner. Since UML is dominated by diagrams that cannot express business rules in an unambiguous manner, and since procedural code is too detailed for modeling, there is the need for a formal, declarative language

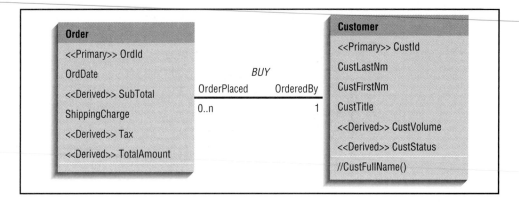

to capture constraint and other business rules. OCL is a declarative language that can express business rules at a high level of abstraction.

This section provides a brief introduction to the language. Comprehensive coverage is available on OMG's site www.omg.org/docs/ptc/03-10-14.pdf. Although OCL can be used to model business rules such as constraints, initial values, derivation rules, query operations, invariants, preconditions, and postconditions, we consider only a subset of the rules.

To illustrate some of these rules, we have adapted a class diagram from the Place Order use case (see Figure 9.17). In the Customer class, the attributes CustTitle, CustVolume, and CustStatus, and the responsibility //CustFullName have been added. CustVolume indicates the grand total amount of orders, and CustStatus is an integer value from 1 to 4 that is determined based on CustVolume, with 1 as the default, and 4 as the elite status. Let's take an example to illustrate the structure of an OCL expression:

context Customer::CustStatus
init: 1

Context
The element for which the OCL expression is defined.

The initial value for CustStatus is specified as 1. The context is that element for which the OCL expression is defined. It can be a class, attribute, responsibility, or data type. Customer::CustStatus stands for the attribute CustStatus in the class Customer.

Suppose that orders are accepted only if the subtotal exceeds 10 dollars. In this case, you need to employ the notion of an invariant, which is a constraint that should be true for an object during its lifetime. In OCL, the term *inv* stands for *invariant*. In this case, the invariant has been named ofSubTotal.

Invariant
A constraint that should be true for an object during its lifetime.

context Order::subTotal
inv ofSubTotal: SubTotal = 10.00

Next, we illustrate how a calculated value is to be shown. For the sake of simplicity, assume that the Tax value is calculated by taking 6.5 percent of the SubTotal value. The attribute Tax has already been stereotyped as derived in the class diagram. So we use the term *derive* to calculate Tax.

context Order::Tax
derive: Tax = SubTotal * 0.065

By using *define*, attributes not shown in the UML diagram can also be defined. Some analysts do not like to show derived attributes in the UML diagram. They need some place to show the derived attributes. This can be done by using OCL. Suppose the attribute Tax were not shown in the class diagram. You can use the term *def*, which stands for *define*, to show the new attribute. Note that *derive* is used for an existing attribute, and *define* is used for a new attribute.

context Order::Tax
def: Tax: Real = SubTotal* 0.065

A responsibility (or operation) can also be derived. For example, to obtain the //CustFullName, you need to concatenate the title with the first and then the last name.

context Customer::CustFullName
derive: title.concat(' ').concat(CustFName).concat(' ').concat(custLName)

When using OCL to navigate from one class to another, the class diagram needs to provide role names on the relationships. Thus, if the context is the class Customer, and you need to navigate to the class Order, you would use the role name OrderPlaced. Conversely, if the context is the class Order, and you need to navigate to the class Customer, you would use the role name OrderedBy. For example, if you need to sum up the total amounts of orders for a given customer, you need to navigate from Customer to Order, and you need to use OrderPlaced. Here you also need to use the function sum().

context Customer::CustVolume
derive: OrderPlaced.TotalAmount $->$ sum

The examples provided in this section provide a very brief introduction to OCL. If you need to learn more, you may refer to OMG's Web site or read a book like *The Object Constraint Language* by Warmer and Kleppe. Even if you don't use OCL, you need to list the business rules using structured English and attach the file to the class diagram.

KEY POINTS REVIEW

This chapter describes how to develop analysis classes from use cases. The previous chapters covered how to develop a data model and generate object relations from a use case. In this chapter, the data model was extended to include the behavioral aspects of use cases. The steps required to develop analysis classes are as follows:

1. **Describe the use case.**
   The use case is written in a stepwise fashion. It captures the key functional requirements. User requirements not captured by a use case can be appended as supplementary requirements. This topic was covered in Chapter 6.
2. **Develop the data model.**
   Because a class diagram resembles a data model in most business applications, developing the data model provides a skeleton class diagram. A data model can be used to derive object relations, which later become entity classes. These topics were covered in Chapters 7 and 8.
3. **Stereotype classes into entity, boundary, and control.**
   The entity classes are obtained from the object-relational data model from the previous step. For each use case, a control class is specified. For each combination of actor and use case, a boundary class is specified. These classes enable the development of the sequence diagram.
4. **Develop the sequence diagram.**
   From the use-case description, the messages between the different objects of classes are mapped in a time sequence fashion. The resulting diagram is called a sequence diagram.
5. **Translate the sequence diagram into the communication diagram.**
   The sequence diagram can be translated into a communication diagram that does not model the time element but instead focuses on the collaboration between objects. The communication diagram indicates what messages are received by a given object.
6. **Draw the analysis class diagram.**
   If a message is passed from a sender to a receiver, then it becomes the responsibility of the receiver to implement the message. By using this rule, the communication diagram can be used to discover the responsibilities of each class. When the attributes of the entity classes are added, the analysis classes are obtained.
7. **Use activity diagrams and state diagrams whenever essential to analysis.**
   Activity and state diagrams can provide a graphical view of certain aspects of use cases and can help analysts better understand the application. These diagrams should be used sparingly and only when there is a real benefit.

8. **Document business rules.**

   Business rules should be listed and documented systematically. Rules are broadly classi-fied into four categories: constraints, calculation, inferences, and action enablers. Rules that are not expressed in some form in the analysis class diagram should be written in a text document and attached to the appropriate classes. The Object Constraint Language (OCL) can be used to formally express these rules.

9. **Develop decision tables of complex rules.**

   Rules for complex policies should be modeled systematically and comprehensively in decision tables, which should then be attached to the appropriate analysis class.

KEY TERMS CHECKPOINT

Here are the key terms from the chapter.

a. Action stub (p. 259)
b. Activity (p. 255)
c. Activity diagram (p. 253)
d. Analysis class (p. 241)
e. Analysis class diagram (p. 241)
f. Boundary class (p. 242)
g. Business rule (p. 258)
h. Communication diagram (p. 251)
i. Condition stub (p. 260)

i. Context (p. 262)
j. Control class (p. 242)
k. Decision point (p. 255)
l. Decision table (p. 259)
m. Entity class (p. 242)
n. Invariant (p. 262)
o. Object Constraint Language OCL (p. 261)
p. Responsibility (p. 242)

q. Robustness analysis (p. 249)
r. Rule (p. 260)
s. Sequence diagram (p. 243)
t. State (p. 256)
u. State diagram (p. 256)
v. Swimlanes (p. 255)
w. Synchronization bars (p. 255)
x. Transition (p. 255)

Match each of the key terms above with the definition that best fits it.

1. That part of a decision table that lists the conditions relevant to the decision.
2. A diamond symbol containing a condition whose responses provide transitions to different paths for activities.
3. A data entity with responsibilities.
4. A matrix representation of the logic of decisions, which specifies the possible conditions for the deci-sions and the resulting actions.
5. A diagram that emphasizes the flow of control from activity to activity.
6. Intermediary class between the interface and actors.
7. That part of a decision table that lists the values or actions that result for a given set of conditions.
8. A diagram that shows the interactions between objects to perform critical pieces of the use-case behavior in a time-ordered manner.
9. A class that represents initial data and behavior requirements, and whose software- and hardware-oriented details have not been specified.
10. A directive, which is intended to influence or guide business behavior, in support of business policy that is formulated in response to an opportunity or threat.
11. A diagram showing analysis classes and the relation-ships among the classes.
12. A diagram that captures the behavior of an object by specifying the sequences of states it goes through dur-ing its lifetime in response to events, together with responses to those events.
13. A class that provides coordinating behavior in the system.
14. Some behavior that an object carries out while it is in a particular state.

15. A diagram that shows the interactions between objects to perform critical pieces of the use-case behavior. It does not show the time element.
16. An obligation of a class. It is invoked when an object of a class receives a message.
17. A movement from one activity to another or from one state to another.
18. Involves analyzing the narrative text of each of the use cases and identifying a first-guess set of objects into entity, boundary, and control objects. It also involves completeness checks and diagramming rules.
19. That part of a decision table that specifies which values or actions are to be followed for a given set of conditions.
20. A condition or situation during the life of an object at which time it satisfies some condition, performs some activity, or waits for some event.
21. Thick horizontal or vertical lines denoting concurrent or parallel processing of activities. The separate set of activities starts at a fork and ends at a join. The entire set of activities needs to be complete before further activities can ensue.
22. An add-on to UML to write expressions that specify business rules in an unambiguous manner.
23. Lanes used to partition an activity diagram to show who does what activities.
24. A constraint that should be true for an object during its lifetime.

REVIEW QUESTIONS

1. What is an analysis class? What is the purpose of an analysis class diagram?
2. What is a sequence diagram? Why do systems analysts use sequence diagrams?
3. Explain the rules for drawing good sequence diagrams.
4. Why is a clearly written use case essential to developing a good analysis class diagram?
5. Do the use cases capture all the requirements of an application?
6. What is the main advantage of drawing a data model before drawing the sequence diagram of a use case?
7. What is a communication diagram? What role does it play in coming up with good analysis classes?
8. What is "analysis paralysis"? How can it be prevented?
9. A message is passed from object A to object B. Which object has the responsibility?
10. What are the steps in creating a decision table? How can the size and complexity of a decision table be reduced?
11. Provide one example of each type of business rule. Do not use the examples provided in this chapter.
12. When should an activity diagram be used? When should an activity diagram not be used?

PROBLEMS AND EXERCISES

1. Using the example of a retail clothing store in a mall, write a use case and draw the sequence diagram. Map the sequence diagram into a communication and an analysis class diagram.
2. Using the example of a loan management system, write a high-level use case and draw the sequence diagram. Map the sequence diagram into an analysis class diagram.
3. Write a use case for the course registration system in your university. Draw the sequence diagram and translate it to a communication diagram. Map the sequence diagram into a communication and an analysis class diagram.
4. Write a use case for typical car maintenance and repair service. Note that a car repair involves servicing as well as replacing parts. Consider parts vendors as actors outside your system. The customer may request the history of maintenance and repairs on a vehicle before ordering service. Draw the sequence diagram and translate it to a communication diagram. Map the sequence diagram into an analysis class diagram.
5. Draw a sequence diagram of the use case "Cancel Unshipped Product" as described by its Flow of Events. What entity classes are needed for the diagram? Use the sequence diagram to assign responsibilities to classes.

Cancel Unshipped Product

The use case describes how an unshipped product can be returned to the company by the customer.

Flow of Events

a. The use case starts when the customer logs in to her customer account.
b. The customer selects Display Pending Orders.
c. The system displays pending orders by order numbers and order dates.
d. The customer selects an order number.
e. The system displays the details of the order including whether or not each product has been shipped.

f. The customer selects a line item for an unshipped product and changes the quantity.
g. The system calculates the revised discount and shipping costs, and the amount refunded to the customer.
h. The system sends an e-mail to the customer.
i. The system sends an e-mail to the shipping department. The use case ends.

6. Draw a sequence diagram of the use case "Provide Feedback" as described by its Flow of Events. Which entity classes are needed for the diagram? Use the sequence diagram to assign responsibilities to classes.

Provide Feedback

The use case describes how a customer can provide feedback to the company. The feedback can be a complaint, suggestion, compliment, or general.

Flow of Events

a. The use case starts when the customer logs in to his customer account.
b. The customer selects "Feedback" from the screen.
c. The system displays four choices: complaint, suggestion, compliment, or general; provides space for order number; and provides space for feedback.
d. The user fills in the options and the feedback text.
e. The user clicks on the button Submit.
f. The system thanks the customer.
g. The system sends the message to the customer service department.
h. The system records the entries in the appropriate file(s).

7. Draw an activity diagram for the following case.

Maximum Software develops and supplies software products to individuals and businesses. As part of its operations, Maximum provides an 800 telephone number help desk for clients with questions about software purchased from Maximum. When a call comes in, an operator inquires about the nature of the call. For calls that are not truly help desk functions, the operator redirects the call to another unit of the company (such as order processing or billing). Because many customer questions require in-depth knowledge of a product, help desk consultants are organized by product. The operator directs the call to a consultant skilled on the software that the caller needs help with. Because a consultant is not always immediately available, some calls must be put into a queue for the next available consultant.

Once a consultant answers the call, he or she determines whether this is the first call from this customer about this problem. If so, a new call report is created to keep track of all information about the problem. If not, the customer is asked for a call report number so the consultant can retrieve the open call report to determine the status of the inquiry. If the caller does not know the call report number, the consultant collects other identifying information such as the caller's name, the software involved, or the name of the consultant who has handled the previous calls on the problem in order to conduct a search for the appropriate call report. If a resolution of the customer's problem has been found, the consultant informs the client what that resolution is, indicates on the report that the customer has been notified, and closes out the report. If resolution has not been discovered, the consultant finds out whether the consultant handling this problem is on duty. If so, the call is transferred to the other consultant (or the call is put into the queue of calls waiting to be handled by that consultant).

Once the proper consultant receives the call, any new details the customer may have are recorded. For continuing problems and for new call reports, the consultant tries to discover an answer to the problem by using the relevant software and looking up information in reference manuals. If the problem can be resolved, the customer is told how to deal with the problem, and the call report is closed. Otherwise, the consultant files the report for continued research and tells the customer that someone at Maximum will be in touch, or if the customer discovers new information about the problem, he or she can call back identifying the problem with a specified call report number.

8. Draw a state diagram of the following case:

At the Sunbelt University, student registration for courses occurs at certain designated times. When the registration period starts, courses are initialized, which implies that the courses are entered into the system along with their maximum allowed enrollments, commonly called caps. Students enroll in the courses. However, when a course reaches its cap, the course is closed. A student can enroll in a closed course only by obtaining written permission from the instructor teaching the course. If a course exceeds its cap, it is called overfull. A student can drop a course, which can lead to the opening of a capped course. Courses that have enrollments of less than 25 percent of the cap are dropped automatically. Courses that have enrollments between 25 percent and 40 percent are listed by department, and the lists are sent to the respective department heads. These courses are called contingent because the approval is dependent on the decision of the department head. A chairperson must decide within 1 week of the receipt of the list whether or not a contingent course will be offered; otherwise, the course is dropped. Courses that have enrollment greater than 40 percent and the ones specifically approved by a chairperson are offered.

9. Draw decision tables for the following cases:

(a) In one company, the rules for buying personal computers are that any purchase of more than $15,000 has to go out for bid, and the Request for Proposals (RFPs) must be approved by the purchasing department. If the purchase is less than $15,000, the personal computers can simply be bought from any approved vendor; however, the purchase order still must be approved by the purchasing department. If the purchase goes out for bid, at least three proposals must be received for the bid. If not, the RFP must go out again. If enough proposals still are not received, then the process can continue with the one or two vendors that have submitted proposals. The winner of the bid must be on an approved list of vendors for the company and, in addition, must not have any violations against it for affirmative action or environmental matters. At this point, if the proposal is complete, the purchasing department can issue a purchase order.

(b) A minimum of 5 percent discount applies for all purchases. If the retailer maintains an average monthly purchase volume of at least $100,000, a 15 percent discount applies, provided the retailer is an elite member. When the retailer's purchase volume is under $100,000, the discount rate is 12 percent for elite members and 7 pecent for nonmembers. Retailers who are not elite members, but who maintain a $100,000 monthly purchase volume, qualify for a 10 percent discount, unless the purchase totals less than $35,000.

(c) Professor Lee has a comprehensive grading policy. The three conditions are average exam score, individual project, and homework assignments. The five actions are the assignment of A, B, C, D, or F as grades. The grading scale for average exam score is as follows: 90–100 = A, 80–89 = B, 70–79 = C, 60–69 = D, and below 60 = F. To receive the grade in the range corresponding to the average exam score, a student must pass the individual project as well as the homework assignments. If the student receives a "fail" in the individual project, the student receives one letter lower than for the average exam score. If the student receives a "fail" in the homework assignments, the student fails the class, regardless of other conditions.

(d) Jessica, a counselor at Less is More, explains the charge system for the first visit of a client. "When clients come into Less is More, we check to see if they have used our service before. New clients are normally charged $200 for the first visit. They get a 10 percent discount (i.e, charge of $180) if they pay cash. A new client gets a $50 rebate (i.e., charge of $150) if a coupon from our advertisements is presented. However, there are no discounts for cash payments if a coupon is presented. Repeat clients are normally charged $100. They, too, get a 10 percent discount (i.e., charge of $90) for cash payments. However, coupons are not valid for repeat clients."

10. Draw the sequence diagram for the following; then translate it to a communication diagram; and finally, map it to an analysis class diagram.

Evergreen Nurseries offers a wide range of lawn and garden products to its customers; it conducts wholesale and retail operations. Although the company serves as a wholesaler to nurseries all over the United States, its founder and president has restricted its retail operations to California, the company's home state. The company is situated on 150 acres and wholesales its bulbs, perennials, roses, trees, shrubs, and Evergreen Accessory products. Evergreen Accessory products include a variety of fertilizers, plant foods, pesticides, and gardening supplies.

In the past 5 years, the company has seen phenomenal sales growth. Unfortunately, its information systems have been left behind. Although many of Evergreen Nurseries' processing activities are computerized, these activities require reengineering. You are part of the project team hired by Seymour Davis, the company's president, to renovate its wholesale division. Your project team was hired to renovate the billing, order taking, and inventory control systems.

From requirements determination, you discovered the following. An Evergreen Nurseries customer places a call to the nursery. A sales representative takes the order, verifies the customer's credit standing, determines whether the items are in stock, notifies the customer of the product's status, informs the customer if any special discounts are in effect, and communicates the total payment due. Once an order is entered into the system, the customer's account is updated, product inventory is adjusted, and ordered items are pulled from stock. Ordered items are then packed and shipped to the customer. Once each month, a billing statement is generated and sent to the customer. The customer has 30 days to remit payment in full; otherwise, a 15 percent penalty is applied to the customer's account.

DISCUSSION QUESTIONS

1. In this chapter, we stereotyped classes into entity, boundary, and control. Do you think this is an appropriate classification? Are control classes needed?
2. In your opinion, are communication diagrams useful? Are activity diagrams useful? Are state diagrams useful? How will you employ these diagrams so that they provide value and do not lead you to analysis paralysis?
3. If you are familiar with the structured analysis approach, compare and contrast the analysis class diagram with data flow diagrams.
4. We modeled entity classes before drawing sequence diagrams. Discuss the pros and cons of this approach.
5. Does robustness analysis provide value? Discuss.

CASE PROBLEMS

Develop the sequence diagram and derive the analysis classes of the following use cases from the GuardTech Training, Inc., case, which was described in Chapter 7. The case description includes the basic path of Flow of Events only. Make suitable assumptions for any missing information. Your instructor may ask you to develop other diagrams, integrate the analysis classes, and draw the resulting analysis class diagram.

Send Catalog

The use case describes the procedure for sending e-mail describing a list of courses being offered. By default, the customers selected have taken at least one class in the last 6 months. However, Sherrie can change the parameters Number of classes taken and Time period. She can send a generic catalog or a customized catalog based on previous courses taken by the customer.

Flow of Events

1. The use case starts when Sherrie selects the Send Catalog button.

2. The screen Send Catalog opens. It includes a text box that shows the number of customers who have taken a class in the last 6 months.
3. Sherrie changes the number of classes taken and the time period, if necessary.
4. Sherrie clicks on the button Generic Catalog or Customized Catalog.
5. The system generates the list of customers and the catalog description to be sent.
6. The e-mails are sent to the customers and the use case ends.

Enroll in Class

The use case describes the process followed by a customer to enroll in a class.

Flow of Events

1. The use case starts when a customer selects Enroll in Class.
2. The screen displays a list of courses offered at GuardTech.
3. The customer clicks on the button Dates Offered next to the desired course.

4. The screen displays the dates offered for a course during the next 6 months.
5. When a customer is ready to enroll in a course, he or she clicks on the Register button.
6. The system informs the customer if the course is capped and asks if the customer wants to be placed on a waiting list. If the customer chooses the waiting list option, the use case ends.
7. If the course is open, the system asks the customer to log in.
8. If the customer does not have a log-in account, it can be opened by filling out a form.
9. The system lists the customer information including any credit amount from canceled classes.
10. The customer provides the credit card information.
11. If the credit application is approved, the system lists the conditions pertaining to enrollment. This includes the right of the company to cancel a class 1 week before the start of the class if the enrollment is lower than 50 percent of the class capacity.
12. If the customer agrees to the conditions, the system charges the credit card; enrolls the customer; and sends a confirmation e-mail with a registration number, dates and times of the class, venue, and the agreed-upon conditions. The use case ends.

Drop a Class

The use case describes the process followed by a customer to drop a class.

Flow of Events

1. The use case starts when a customer selects Drop a Class.
2. The screen displays a form with a text box for entering the registration number. If the registration number has been lost, then the customer needs to call Sherrie; this is a separate use case called Find Lost Registration.
3. The system checks whether the registration number is valid. If it's not valid, then the system displays a message and prompts the customer to enter the number again. The customer may quit at this point.

4. If the registration number is valid, the system normally presents the customer with two choices: take a 100 percent credit to be spent in 6 months, or have 80 percent of the amount refunded to the credit card used to enroll in the class. However, if the cancellation is done within 1 week before the class starts, the corresponding amounts are 75 percent and 50 percent. If the cancellation is done within 48 hours before the class starts, no credit or refund is provided.
5. After the customer makes the choice, the customer enrollment is canceled.
6. The system checks if the current enrollment has dropped below the cap because of the cancellation. If yes, the system performs the Accept Waiting Customer use case. Otherwise, the use case ends.

Accept Waiting Customer

The use case accepts customers who have been placed on the wait list.

Flow of Events

1. The use case starts when a customer drops a class and the enrollment falls below the cap.
2. The system sends an e-mail to the first customer on the waiting list. If the class will not start for 1 month or more, the customer has 72 hours to respond. If the class will start in less than 1 month but more than 1 week, the customer has 48 hours to respond. If the class will start in less than 1 week, then the customer has 24 hours to respond; however, in this case, an e-mail also is sent to Sherrie, who might call the customer to remind him or her about the chance to enroll. If the class will begin in only 2 days, no action is taken.
3. The customer has the option to select Accept Class or Decline Class.
4. If a customer selects Decline Class or does not respond within the stipulated period, the system sends an e-mail to the next customer in line.
5. If the customer selects Accept Class, the system conducts steps 7 through 12 of the Enroll in Class use case. The use case ends.

CASE: BROADWAY ENTERTAINMENT COMPANY, INC.

Designing the Analysis Classes for the Customer Relationship Management System

Case Introduction

The students from St. Claire Community College have done some important analysis and design work for MyBroadway, the Web-based customer relationship management system for Broadway Entertainment Company stores. They have developed use cases for all of the system functions, created a conceptual data model using a class diagram for all the data requirements, and detailed the attributes of this data model with normalized object relations. Now they will attempt to come up with analysis classes. Specifically, the team needs to develop an appropriate set of analysis class specifications (e.g., sequence diagrams, communication diagrams, activity diagrams, state charts, and business rules) for the behavior of data entity classes, as well as for all the processing logic in boundary and control classes needed to show how the system must work to accomplish its user functions. After all of these specifications are developed, they will be reviewed in overview sessions with Carrie Douglass, the BEC store manager for whom the team is working.

Designing Analysis Classes

The student team feels somewhat overwhelmed by the task of developing analysis classes. First, analysis classes are critical in object-oriented systems development. They must be done correctly, and they need to be explicit so programming and database development can occur. Second, the work is detailed and extensive. The specifications need to be clear, not only for development work, but also to provide the documentation to allow subsequent modifications and improvements to be made quickly. Finally, there are so many choices for the different types of diagrams that need to be developed. The team members know they must end up with an analysis class diagram that shows the attributes and behaviors of all data, and boundary and control classes. However, the team has considerable discretion on which supporting diagrams are needed.

BEC Figure 6.1 (use-case diagram) and the data models (developed in Chapters 7 and 8) are important resources for the student team as they begin developing the analysis class diagram. Essentially, they know their analysis class diagram will look much like the conceptual data model, with behavior included in each data entity class, and control and boundary classes also on the chart.

The team makes some key decisions to come up with analysis classes:

a. They will make sequence and communication diagrams for each use case.
b. They will use a CASE tool. Without a CASE tool, it will be practically impossible to seamlessly move from one representation to another.
c. They will follow robustness analysis rules for now, and revisit the diagrams at the design stage.
d. They will complete analysis diagrams for two or three use cases in the first iteration. Based on the experience gained, they will develop, then revise these, as well as complete the remaining use cases in the next iteration.

To get started, the students develop one sequence diagram for what appears to be a critical use case, Request Rental Extension. The use case interfaces with two actors—Customer and Entertainment Tracker (ET). So, two boundary classes are required: a form RentalExtForm, and an interface ETInt. They employ one control class, RentalExtControl.

Next, they recount the key steps in the Request Rental Extension use case. The customer will initiate the use case by opening a :RentalExtForm interface. But he or she would have to know his or her rental information. This means getting the information from :ETActor using the :ETInt interface. This information needs to be provided for scrutiny even before the :RentalExtForm is used. Since the

Identify Rental Status is not being used with other use cases, the team is wondering if the two use cases can be merged. Otherwise, the sequence diagram for the Request Rental Extension use case may be difficult to read. The only pertinent piece of the Identify Rental Status is the member log-in process.

To a fair extent, the pattern of the rental extension begins to resemble the Place Order, and Make Reservation sequence diagrams. There is the log-in part, the line items to be updated, the authorization obtained from :ETActor, the review of the information, the commit, the display of the receipt, and the e-mailing of the receipt. There is some difference—the Rental Extension is predominantly an update process while the Place Order is a new transaction.

They next review the Request New Product use case since a different actor, Employee, is involved. They know that a boundary class will be required between the use case and the Employee actor. However, unlike the Rental Extension sequence diagram, which has the ET actor on the extreme right-hand side, they are unable to place Employee in a similar position. It seems that the Employee and the Customer actors will both be on the left side. At this point, they realize that it seems there are two use cases embedded in the Request New Product. It is evident now that the request of new products may have to be separated from the processing of the requests, which happens at a much later time.

The students have a good start on the sequence diagram for three use cases. Now, they wonder what other diagrams they will need, and how they will handle business rules. They will draw some preliminary activity diagrams to identify possible extensions that they might have missed when writing the use cases. They understand that this is about the last time they will be looking at requirements before the design stage begins, and they would like the requirements and analysis to be complete.

The team knows that state charts can be useful when an object is used by several use cases that change the status of that object. For example, a videotape might be ordered, in inventory, reserved for a customer, or on loan to a customer. Each of these states of a videotape is handled by different use cases. However, these are functions of Entertainment Tracker, not MyBroadway.

As the team reviewed each use case, they also considered whether there were significant business rules or logic (constraints, calculations, value inferences, or action enablers) that needed to be documented. They found some simple ones. For the Request new product use case, it is not necessary to include a requested product on the list to Carrie if, in fact, the product is already in the store. They also addressed documentation of another business rule stating that individual requests are purged once they are 2 months old. The team will consider whether certain class behaviors need documented business rules, or whether the text-based descriptions will be sufficient for development.

Case Summary

The student team is eager to begin prototyping MyBroadway, so they do not plan to spend a lot of time completing the analysis class diagram all at once. They will select a few important, central, or illustrative use cases for developing the first version of the analysis class diagram. Refinements can be made as subsequent use cases are studied as part of the iterative development of MyBroadway.

CASE QUESTIONS

1. Develop sequence and communication diagrams of all BEC use cases shown in BEC Figure 6.1.
2. Do you agree that Identify Rental Status and Request Rental Status should be merged? Justify your answer.
3. Do you agree that Request New Product should be split into two or more use cases so that the diagrams are more meaningful? Justify your answer.
4. Do you think the team should draw activity diagrams for MyBroadway? Justify your answer.
5. What other diagrams, if any, would be useful to document the use cases? Do you see any need to develop a state diagram for any object in MyBroadway? Justify your answer.
6. List at least 10 business rules for the use cases.

Chapter 10

Selecting the Best Alternative Design Strategy

Chapter Objectives

After studying this chapter, you should be able to:

➤ Describe the different sources of software.

➤ Assemble the various pieces of an alternative design strategy.

➤ Generate at least three alternative design strategies for an information system.

➤ Select the best design strategy using qualitative and quantitative methods.

➤ Update a Baseline Project Plan based on the results of the analysis phase.

Chapter Contents

➤ Chapter Preview

➤ Selecting the Best Alternative Design Strategy

➤ The Process of Selecting the Best Alternative Design Strategy

➤ Generating Alternative Design Strategies

➤ Issues to Consider in Generating Alternatives

➤ Selecting the Best Alternative Design Strategy for Pine Valley Furniture's WebStore

➤ Updating the Baseline Project Plan

➤ Before and after Baseline Project Plans for PVF's WebStore

Chapter Preview

This is the point in the analysis phase when all of the information that has been gathered and structured can be transformed into some concrete ideas about the design for the new or replacement information system. This is called the design strategy. Requirements determination has revealed what the current system does. Other research has clarified what the users would like the replacement system to do. From requirements structuring, the systems analyst knows at a logical level independent of any physical implementation what forms the replacement system's functions and data should take. However, some uncertainty still might exist about the capabilities of a new system due to the number of competing alternatives for an implementation environment for any new system. As Figure 10.1 shows, there are three parts to systems analysis: determining requirements, structuring requirements, and selecting the best alternative design strategy. To bring analysis to a conclusion, the systems analyst must take these structured requirements and transform them into several alternative design strategies. One of these strategies will be pursued in the design phase of the life cycle.

Part of generating a design strategy involves tapping into sources inside and outside an organization to determine the best way that organization can acquire the replacement system. If the systems analyst advises the organization to proceed with development inside the organization, the analyst and the team will have to answer general questions about software: Will software be built in-house, purchased off the shelf, or contracted to software-development companies? Is a legacy system written in a third-generation programming language or a new version written in an object-oriented language? The systems analyst also will have to answer general questions about hardware and system software: Will the new system run on a mainframe platform, with stand-alone personal computers, or on a client/server platform? Can the system run on existing hardware? What about the existing corporate data-base management system?

It is also not too early to begin thinking about data conversion issues and how much training users will need. Can the system be built and implemented given the funding and management support that is available? These concerns must be addressed for each alternative generated in order to update the Baseline Project Plan with detailed activities and resource requirements for the next life cycle phase—systems design. In this step of the analysis phase, the current phase is brought to a close, a report and presentation to management concerning continuation of the project are prepared, and the project is ready to move into design.

This chapter discusses why alternative design strategies and guidelines for generating alternatives must be created. The different issues that must be addressed for each alternative also are covered. Once alternatives have been generated, it is time to choose the best design strategy to pursue. We include a discussion of one technique that analysts and users often utilize to help them agree on the best approach for the new information system.

Throughout this chapter, we emphasize the need for sound project management. Now that the various techniques and steps of the analysis phase have been presented, we outline what a typical analysis phase project schedule might look like. We also discuss the execution of the analysis phase and the transition from analysis to design.

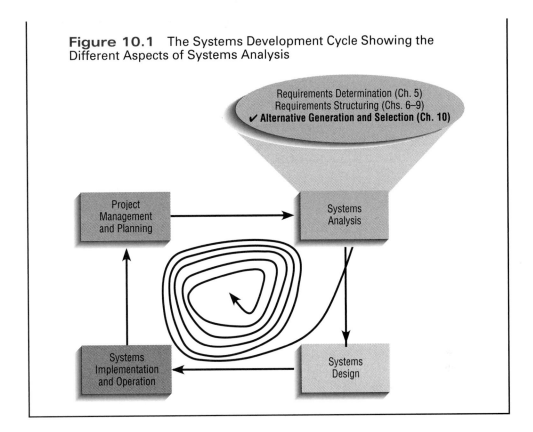

Figure 10.1 The Systems Development Cycle Showing the Different Aspects of Systems Analysis

Requirements Determination (Ch. 5)
Requirements Structuring (Chs. 6–9)
✔ **Alternative Generation and Selection (Ch. 10)**

Project Management and Planning

Systems Analysis

Systems Implementation and Operation

Systems Design

SELECTING THE BEST ALTERNATIVE DESIGN STRATEGY

Design strategy
A particular approach to developing an information system. It includes statements on the system's functionality, hardware and system software platform, and method for acquisition.

Selecting the best alternative design strategy involves at least two basic steps: (1) generating a comprehensive set of alternative design strategies; and (2) selecting the one that is most likely to result in the desired information system, given all of the organizational, economic, and technical constraints that limit what can be done. A system design strategy represents a particular approach to developing the system. Selecting a strategy requires answers to questions about the system's functionality, hardware and system software platform, and method for acquisition. The overall process of selecting the best system strategy and the deliverables from this step in the analysis process are discussed next.

THE PROCESS OF SELECTING THE BEST ALTERNATIVE DESIGN STRATEGY

The three parts to systems analysis are determining requirements, structuring requirements, and selecting the best alternative design strategy. After the system requirements have been structured, analysts again work with users to package the requirements into different system configurations. Shaping alternative system design strategies involves the following processes:

- Dividing requirements into different sets of capabilities, ranging from the bare minimum that users would accept (the required features) to the most elaborate and advanced system the company could afford to develop (which includes all the features desired across all users). Alternatively, different sets of capabilities may represent the position of different organizational units with conflicting notions about what the system should do.

- Enumerating different potential implementation environments (hardware, system software, and network platforms) that could be used to deliver the different sets of capabilities. (Choices on the implementation environment might place technical limitations on the subsequent design phase activities.)
- Proposing different ways to source or acquire the various sets of capabilities for the different implementation environments.

In theory, if there are 3 sets of requirements, 2 implementation environments, and 4 sources of application software, 24 design strategies are possible. In practice, some combinations are usually infeasible, and only a small number—typically 3—can be considered easily. Selecting the best alternative usually is done with the help of a quantitative procedure, an example of which comes later in this chapter. Analysts will recommend what they believe to be the best alternative, but management (a combination of the steering committee and those who will fund the rest of the project) will make the ultimate decision about which system design strategy to follow. At this point in the life cycle, it also is possible for management to end a project before the more expensive phases of design, implementation, and operation begin. A project might end because the costs or risks outweigh the benefits, the needs of the organization have changed since the project began, or other competing projects have become more important but development resources remain limited.

Deliverables and Outcomes

The primary deliverables from generating alternative design strategies and selecting the best one are outlined in Table 10-1. The primary deliverable that is carried forward into design is an updated baseline project plan detailing the work necessary to turn the selected design strategy into the desired replacement information system. That plan cannot be assembled until a strategy has been selected, and no strategy can be selected until alternative strategies have been generated and compared. Therefore, all three objects—the alternatives, the selected alternative, and the plan—are listed as deliverables in Table 10-1. Further, these three deliverables plus the supporting deliverables from requirements determination and structuring steps are necessary to conduct systems design. This information is stored in the project dictionary or CASE repository for reference in later phases.

GENERATING ALTERNATIVE DESIGN STRATEGIES

The solution to an organizational problem might seem obvious to an analyst. Typically, the analyst is familiar with the problem, having conducted an extensive analysis of it and how it has been solved in the past. On the other hand, the analyst might be familiar with a particular solution that he or she attempts to apply to all organizational problems encountered. For example, if an analyst is an expert at using advanced database technology to solve problems, then that analyst might tend to recommend advanced database technology as a solution to every possible problem. As another example, if the analyst designed a similar system for another customer or business unit, the "natural" design strategy would be the one used before. Because of the role of experience in the solutions that analysts suggest, analysis teams typically generate at least two alternative solutions for every problem they work on.

A good number of alternatives for analysts to generate is three. Why three? Three alternatives can represent low, middle, and high ranges of potential solutions. One

Table 10-1

Deliverables for Generating Alternatives and Selecting the Best One.

1. At least three substantively different system design strategies for building the replacement information system.
2. A design strategy judged most likely to lead to the most desirable information system.
3. A Baseline Project Plan for turning the most likely design strategy into a working information system.

alternative typically represents the low end of the range. Low-end alternatives are the most conservative in terms of the effort, cost, and technology involved in developing a new system. Some low-end solutions might not involve computer technology at all, focusing instead on making paper flows more efficient or reducing redundancies in current processes. A low-end strategy provides all the required functionality users demand with a system that is minimally different from the current system.

Another alternative represents the high end of the range. High-end alternatives go beyond simply solving the problem in question and focus instead on systems that contain many extra features users might desire. Functionality, not cost, is the primary focus of high-end alternatives. A high-end alternative will provide all desired features using advanced technologies that often allow the system to expand to meet future requirements.

Finally, the third alternative lies between the extremes of the low-end and high-end systems. Such alternatives combine the frugality of low-end alternatives with the focus on functionality of high-end alternatives. Mid-range alternatives represent compromise solutions. Other possible solutions do exist outside of these three alternatives, but defining the low, middle, and high possibilities allows the analyst to draw bounds around what can be done reasonably.

How does the analyst know where to draw bounds around the potential solution space? The analysis team has gathered the information it needs to identify the solution already, but first that information must be organized systematically. There are two major considerations. The first is determining the minimum requirements for the new system. These are the mandatory features, and if any of them are missing, the design strategy is useless. Mandatory features are those that everyone agrees are necessary to solve the problem or meet the opportunity. Which features are mandatory can be determined from a survey of users and others who have been involved in requirements determination. This survey would be conducted near the end of the analysis phase after all requirements have been structured and analyzed. In this survey, users rate features discovered during requirements determination or categorize features on some scale, and an arbitrary breakpoint is used to divide mandatory from desired features. Some organizations will break the features into three categories: mandatory, essential, and desired. Whereas mandatory features screen out possible solutions, essential features are the important capabilities of a system that serve as the primary basis for comparison of different design strategies. Desired features are those that users could live without but that are used to select between design strategies that are of almost equal value in terms of essential features. Features can take many different forms, as illustrated in Figure 10.2, and might include the following:

- Data kept in system files (for example, multiple customer addresses so that bills can be sent to different addresses from where goods are shipped).

Figure 10.2
Types of System Features and System Constraints

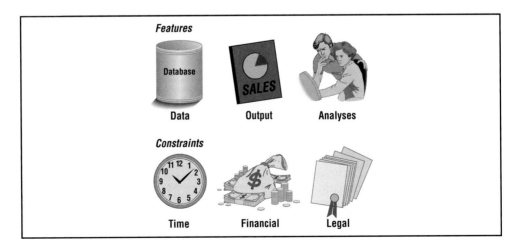

- System outputs, which include printed reports, online displays, and transaction documents such as a paycheck or sales summary graph.
- Analyses to generate the information in system outputs (for example, a sales forecasting module or an installment billing routine).
- Expectations on accessibility, response time, or turnaround time for system functions (for example, online, real-time updating of inventory files).

The second consideration in drawing bounds around alternative design strategies is determining the constraints on system development. Constraints, some of which also appear in Figure 10.2, may exist on such factors as the following:

- A date when the replacement system is needed.
- Available financial and human resources.
- Elements of the current system that cannot change.
- Legal and contractual restrictions (for example, a software package bought off the shelf cannot be modified legally, or a license to use a particular software package might limit the number of concurrent users to 25).
- The importance or dynamics of the problem that might limit how the system can be acquired (for example, a strategically important system that uses highly proprietary data probably cannot be outsourced or purchased).

Remember, be impertinent and question whether stated constraints are firm. The analyst might want to consider some design alternatives that violate constraints that were considered flexible or inflexible.

Requirements and constraints must be identified and ranked in order of importance. The reason behind such a ranking should be clear. Whereas the analyst can design a high-end alternative to fulfill every wish users have for a new system, low-end alternatives are designed to fulfill only the most important wishes. The same is true of constraints. Low-end alternatives will meet every constraint; high-end alternatives will ignore all but the most daunting constraints.

ISSUES TO CONSIDER IN GENERATING ALTERNATIVES

The requirements and constraints of the replacement system raise many issues that analysts must consider when they develop alternative design strategies. Most of the substantive debate about alternative design strategies hinges on the relative importance of system features. Issues of functionality help determine software and hardware selection, implementation, organizational limitations such as available funding levels, and whether the system should be developed and run in-house. This list is not complete, but it does serve as a reminder that an information system is more than just software. We now discuss each issue, beginning with outsourcing.

Outsourcing

Outsourcing
The practice of turning over responsibility of some to all of an organization's information systems applications and operations to an outside firm.

If another organization develops or runs a computer application for an organization, that practice is called outsourcing. Outsourcing includes a spectrum of working arrangements. At one extreme is having an outsourcing firm develop and run a company's application on the outsourcing company's computers—the company that hires the outsourcing company supplies only input and takes output. A common example is a company that runs payroll applications for clients so that clients don't have to develop an independent, in-house payroll system. Instead, they simply provide employee payroll information to the company and, for a fee, the company returns completed paychecks, payroll accounting reports, and tax and other statements for employees. For many organizations, payroll is a cost-effective operation when outsourced in this way. In another example of outsourcing arrangements, company A might hire company B to run company A's applications at company A's site on company A's computers. In some cases, an organization employing such an arrangement will dissolve some or all of its information systems unit and fire all of its information systems employees. Often the company brought in to run the organization's computing will hire many of the information systems unit's employees.

Why would an organization outsource its information systems operations? As shown in the payroll example, outsourcing can be cost-effective. If a company specializes in running payroll for other companies, it can leverage the economies of scale it achieves from running one stable computer application for many organizations into low prices. Why would an organization dissolve its entire information processing unit and bring in an outside firm to manage its computer applications? One reason might be to overcome operating problems the organization faces in its information systems unit. For example, the city of Grand Rapids, Michigan, hired an outside firm to run its computing more than 30 years ago in order to manage its computing center employees better. Union contracts and civil service constraints then in force made it difficult to fire people, so the city brought in a facilities management organization to run its computing operations, and it was able to get rid of problem employees at the same time. Another reason for total outsourcing is that an organization's management might feel its core mission does not involve managing an information systems unit and that it might achieve more effective computing by turning over all of its operations to a more experienced, computer-oriented company. Kodak decided in the late 1980s that it was not in the computer applications business and turned over management of its mainframes to IBM and management of its personal computers to Businessland.

Outsourcing is big business. Some organizations outsource the IT development and many of their IT functions, at a cost of billions of dollars. For example, the 20 largest U.S. government IT contracts awarded in fiscal 2006 were estimated to be worth a total of $250 billion. The Department of Homeland Security contract for outsourced IT services alone was worth $45 billion. Individual outsourcing vendors also sign large contracts for their services. IBM and EDS are two of the biggest, best-known outsourcing firms. Both companies have multiple outsourcing contracts in place with many different firms. IBM's clients include American Express, with a contract worth $4 billion, and Qwest Communications, with a contract worth $2 billion. Outsourcing is not risk-free, however. JP Morgan, the giant financial firm, cancelled a $5 billion outsourcing contract with IBM, and EDS has had well-publicized problems with its $7 billion outsourcing contract with the U.S. Navy.

Analysts need to be aware of outsourcing as an alternative. When generating alternative system development strategies for a system, the analyst should consult organizations in the area that provide outsourcing services. It may well be that at least one such organization already has developed and is running an application that is close to what the analyst's users are asking for. Perhaps outsourcing the replacement system should be one alternative to consider. Knowing what system requirements are desired before considering outsourcing means the systems analyst can assess carefully how well the suppliers of outsourcing services can respond to the company's needs. However, if outsourcing is not the option selected, the analyst can consider whether some software components of the replacement system should be purchased and not built.

Sources of Software

We can group organizations that produce software into five major categories: (1) information technology services firms, (2) packaged software providers, (3) vendors of enterprise-wide solution software, (4) open source software, and (5) in-house development.

Table 10-2
Top 10 Global
Software/Services
Companies in
2005.

RANK	COMPANY	2005 SOFTWARE/SERVICES REVENUE (MILLION USD)	SOFTWARE BUSINESS SECTOR
1	IBM	$61,307	Middleware/Application Server/Web Server/Systems Integration Services/IT Consulting
2	Microsoft	$33,969	Operating Systems
3	EDS	$20,669	IT Sourcing
4	Computer Sciences Corp.	$15,188	Systems Integration Services/IT Consulting
5	Accenture	$15,114	Systems Integration Services/IT Consulting
6	HP	$13,778	Systems Integration Services/IT Consulting
7	Oracle	$10,156	Database/Business Process Management
8	Hitachi	$9,491	Telecommunication Services
9	SAP America	$9,313	Business Process Management
10	Capgemini	$8,581	Systems Integration Services/IT Consulting

Source: www.softwaremag.com

Information Technology Services Firms

If a company needs an information system but does not have the expertise or the personnel to develop the system in-house, and a suitable off-the-shelf system is not available, the company will likely consult an information technology (IT) services firm. IT services firms help companies develop custom information systems for internal use, or they develop, host, and run applications for customers, or they provide other services. Note in Table 10.2, a list of the top 10 global software firms, that 5 out of 10 specialize in services, which includes custom systems development. These firms employ people with expertise in the development of information systems. Their consultants may also have expertise in a given business area. For example, consultants who work with banks understand financial institutions as well as information systems. Consultants use many of the same methodologies, techniques, and tools that companies use to develop systems in-house.

It may surprise you to see IBM listed as the top global software producer. You may think of IBM as primarily a hardware company. Yet IBM has been moving away from a reliance on hardware development for many years. The purchase of the IT consulting arm of PricewaterhouseCoopers by IBM in 2002 solidified its move into services and consulting. IBM is also well known for its development of Web server and middleware software. Other leading IT services firms include traditional consulting firms, such as Computer Sciences Corp., Accenture, and Capgemini. The list also includes HP, another company formerly focused on hardware that has made the transition to an IT services firm.

Packaged Software Producers

The growth of the software industry has been phenomenal since its beginnings in the mid-1960s. Now, some of the largest computer companies in the world, as measured by *Software Magazine*, are companies that produce software exclusively, such as Microsoft (see Table 10.2). Software companies develop what are sometimes called prepackaged or off-the-shelf systems. Microsoft's Project and Intuit's Quicken, QuickPay, and QuickBooks are popular examples of such software. The packaged software development industry serves many market segments. Its software offerings range from general, broad-based packages, such as general ledger, to very narrow, niche packages, such as software to help manage a day care center. Software companies develop software to run on many different computer platforms, from microcomputers to large mainframes. The companies range in size from just a few people to thousands of employees. Software companies consult with system users after the initial software design has been completed and an early version of the system has been built. The systems are then tested in actual organizations to determine whether there are any problems or if any improvements can be made. Until testing is completed, the system is not offered for sale to the public.

Some off-the-shelf software systems cannot be modified to meet the specific, individual needs of a particular organization. Such application systems are sometimes called turnkey systems. The producer of a turnkey system will make changes to the software only when a substantial number of users ask for a specific change. Other off-the-shelf application software can be modified or extended, however, by the producer or the user to fit the needs of the organization more closely. Even though many organizations perform similar functions, no two organizations do the same thing in quite the same way. A turnkey system may be good enough for a certain level of performance, but it will never perfectly match the way a given organization does business. A reasonable estimate is that off-the-shelf software can, at best, meet 70 percent of an organization's needs. Thus, even in the best case, 30 percent of the software system doesn't match the organization's specifications.

Custom Software Producers

If a company needs an information system but does not have the expertise or the personnel to develop the system in-house and a suitable off-the-shelf system is not available, the company will likely consult a custom software company. Consulting firms, such as Accenture (number 5 in Table 10.2) or Capgemini (number 10), will help a firm develop custom information systems for internal use. These firms employ people with expertise in the development of information systems. Their consultants also might have expertise in a given business area. For example, consultants who work with banks understand financial institutions as well as information systems. Consultants use many of the same methodologies, techniques, and tools that companies use to develop systems in-house.

Enterprise Solutions Software

Enterprise resource planning (ERP) system
A system that integrates individual traditional business functions into a series of modules so that a single transaction occurs seamlessly within a single information system rather than several separate systems.

As mentioned in Chapter 1, more and more organizations are choosing complete software solutions, called enterprise solutions or enterprise resource planning (ERP) systems, to support their operations and business processes. These ERP software solutions consist of a series of integrated modules. Each module supports an individual traditional business function, such as accounting, distribution, manufacturing, and human resources. The difference between the modules and traditional approaches is that the modules are integrated to focus on business processes rather than on business functional areas. For example, a series of modules will support the entire order entry process, from receiving an order to adjusting inventory to shipping to billing to after-the-sale service. The traditional approach would use different systems in different functional areas of the business, such as a billing system in accounting and an inventory system in the warehouse. Using enterprise software solutions, a firm can integrate all parts of a business process in a unified information system. All aspects of a single transaction occur seamlessly within a single information system, rather than in a series of disjointed, separate systems focused on business functional areas.

The benefits of the enterprise solutions approach include a single repository of data for all aspects of a business process and the flexibility of the modules. A single repository ensures more consistent and accurate data, as well as less maintenance. The modules are flexible because additional modules can be added as needed once the basic system is in place. Added modules are integrated immediately into the existing system.

Enterprise solutions software also has disadvantages. The systems are complex, so implementation can take a long time to complete. Organizations typically do not have the necessary expertise in-house to implement the systems, so they must rely on consultants or employees of the software vendor, which can be expensive. In some cases, organizations must change how they do business in order to benefit from a shift toward enterprise solutions.

There used to be several major vendors of ERP systems, but now there are only two. The best known is probably SAP AG, a German firm, known for its flagship product R/3. SAP stands for Systems, Applications, and Products in Data Processing. SAP AG was founded in 1972, but most of its growth has occurred since 1992. In 2005, SAP America was the ninth-largest supplier of software in the world (see Table 10.2). The other major vendor of enterprise solutions is Oracle Corp., also a U.S.-based firm, perhaps better known for its database software. Oracle is seventh on the list of the top 10 software companies for 2005 (Table 10.2). Oracle captured a large share of the ERP market through its own financial systems and through the acquisition of other ERP vendors. At the end of 2004, Oracle acquired PeopleSoft, Inc., a U.S. firm founded in 1987. PeopleSoft began with enterprise solutions that focused on human resources management and expanded to cover financials, materials management, distribution, and manufacturing before Oracle acquired them. Just before being purchased by Oracle, PeopleSoft had boosted its corporate strength in 2003 through acquiring another ERP vendor, J.D. Edwards. Together, SAP and Oracle control about 60 percent of the ERP market, which was estimated at around $24 billion in revenues for 2005. The market for ERP is predicted to grow in the range of 6 to 7 percent per year through 2009. As the higher end of the market has become saturated with ERP systems, most ERP vendors are looking to medium and small businesses for growth.

Open Source Software

Open source software is unlike the other types of software you have read about so far. Open source software is different because it is freely available, not just the final product but the source code itself. It is also different because it is developed by a community of interested people instead of by employees of a particular company. Open source software performs the same functions as commercial software, such as operating systems, e-mail, database systems, Web browsers, and so on. Some of the most well-known and popular open source software names are Linux, the operating system; mySQL, a database system; and Firefox, a Web browser. Open source also applies to software components and objects. Open source is developed and maintained by communities of people, and sometimes these communities can be very large. Developers often use common Web resources, such as SourceForge.net to organize their activities. In October 2005, SourceForge.net hosted over 105,000 projects and had over 1.1 million registered users. There is no question that the open source movement would not be having the success it enjoys without the availability of the Internet for providing access and organizing development activities.

If the software is free, you might wonder how anybody makes any money by developing open source software. There are two primary ways companies and individuals can make money with open source: (1) by providing maintenance and other services, or (2) by providing one version of the software free and selling a more fully featured version. Some open source solutions have more of an impact on the software industry than others. Linux, for example, has been very successful in the server software market, where it is estimated to have 24 percent of the market share now, a number that is projected to grow to 33 percent by 2007. In the desktop operating systems, Linux has a 3 percent market share now, projected to double to 6 percent by 2007. These market shares together translate into a market value of $11 billion for Linux currently, with the potential of the market value to grow to $35.7 billion by 2008. Other open source software products, such as mySQL, have also been successful, and open source's share of the software industry seems destined to continue to grow.

Producers	When to go to this type of organization for software	Internal staffing requirements
IT services firms	When task requires custom support and system can't be built internally or system needs to be sourced	Internal staff may be needed, depending on application
Packaged software producers	When supported task is generic	Some IS and user staff to define requirements and evaluate packages
Enterprise-wide solutions	For complete systems that cross functional boundaries	Some internal staff necessary but mostly need consultants
Open source software	When supported task is generic but cost is an issue	Some IS and user staff to define requirements and evaluate packages
In-house developers	When resources and staff are available and system must be built from scratch	Internal staff necessary though staff size may vary

In-House Development

We have talked about four different types of external organizations that serve as sources of software, but in-house development remains an option. In-house development need not entail development of all of the software that will comprise the total system. Hybrid solutions involving some purchased and some in-house software components are common. Table 10.3 compares the five different software sources.

If the decision is made to acquire software from outside sources, this choice is made at the end of the analysis phase. Choosing between a package and an external supplier will be determined by needs, not by what the supplier has to sell. As discussed, the results of the analysis study will define the type of product to buy and will make working with an external supplier much easier, productive, and worthwhile.

Choosing Off-the-Shelf Software

Once the decision is made to purchase off-the-shelf software rather than write some or all of the software for the new system in-house, how does the analyst decide what to buy? Several criteria need to be considered, and special ones may arise with each potential software purchase. For each standard, an explicit comparison should be made between the software package and the process of developing the same application in-house. The most common criteria, highlighted in Figure 10.3, are as follows:

- Cost
- Functionality
- Vendor support
- Viability of vendor
- Flexibility
- Documentation
- Response time
- Ease of installation

The relative importance of these standards will vary from project to project and from organization to organization. If it were necessary to choose two criteria that would always be among the most important, those two probably would be vendor support and vendor viability. It is not wise to license software from a vendor with a reputation for poor support or to get involved with a vendor that might not be in business tomorrow. How the importance of the remaining criteria is ranked depends very much on each specific situation.

Cost involves comparing the cost of developing the same system in-house to the cost of purchasing or licensing the software package. Be sure to include a comparison of the cost of purchasing vendor upgrades or annual license fees with the costs that would be incurred to maintain the company's own software. Costs for purchasing

Figure 10.3
Some of the Common
Criteria for Evaluating
Off-the-Shelf Software

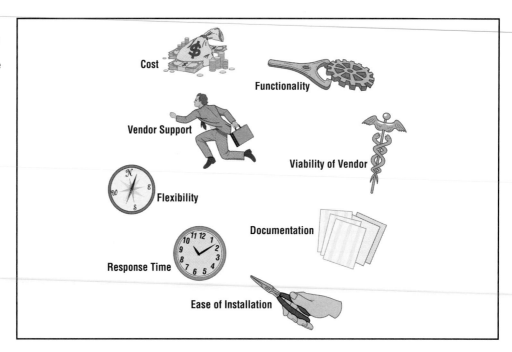

and developing in-house can be compared based on the economic feasibility measures. Functionality refers to the tasks the software can perform and the mandatory, essential, and desired system features. Can the software package perform all or just some of the tasks the company's users need? If some, can it perform the necessary core tasks? Note that meeting user requirements occurs at the end of the analysis phase because packaged software cannot be evaluated until user requirements have been gathered and structured. Purchasing application software is not a substitute for conducting the systems analysis phase.

As stated earlier, vendor support refers to whether and how much support the vendor can provide. Support includes assistance to install the software, to train user and systems staff on the software, and to provide help as problems arise after installation. Recently, many software companies have significantly reduced the amount of free support they provide customers, so the cost to use telephone, on-site, fax, or computer bulletin board support facilities should be considered. Related to support is the vendor's viability. This latter point should not be minimized. The software industry is dynamic, and innovative application software often is created by entrepreneurs working from home offices—the classic cottage industry. Such organizations, even with outstanding software, often do not have the resources or business management ability to stay in business for long. Further, competitive moves by major software firms can render the products of smaller firms outdated or incompatible with operating systems. One software firm we talked to while developing this book was struggling to survive just trying to make its software work on any supposedly IBM-compatible PC (given the infinite combination of video boards, monitors, BIOS chips, and other components). Keeping up with hardware and systems software changes might be more than a small firm can handle, and good, off-the-shelf application software is lost.

Flexibility refers to how easy it is for the systems analyst or the vendor to customize the software. If the software is not flexible, users might have to adapt the way they work to fit the software. Are they likely to adapt in this manner? Purchased software can be modified in several ways. Sometimes the vendor will make custom changes if the company is willing to pay for the redesign and programming. Some vendors design the software for customization. For example, the software might include several different ways of processing data and, at installation time, the customer chooses which to initiate. Also, displays and reports might be easily redesigned if these modules are written in a fourth-generation language. Reports, forms, and displays can be customized easily using a process whereby the company name and chosen titles for reports, displays, forms, and column headings are selected from a table of parameters provided by the user. Some of these same customization techniques can be employed for in-house-developed systems so that the software can be adapted easily for different business units, product lines, or departments.

Documentation includes the user's manual as well as technical documentation. How understandable and up to date is the documentation? What is the cost for multiple copies, if required? Response time refers to how long it takes the software package to respond to the user's requests in an interactive session. Another measure of time would be how long it takes the software to complete running a job. Finally, ease of installation is a measure of the difficulty of loading the software and making it operational.

Validating Purchased Software Information

One way to get all of the information the analyst wants about a software package is to collect it from the vendor. Some of this information might be contained in the software documentation and technical marketing literature. Other information can be provided upon request. For example, the systems analyst can send prospective vendors a questionnaire asking specific questions about their packages. This might be part of a request for proposal (RFP) or request for quote (RFQ) process the organization requires when major purchases are made (see next section for more).

However, there is no replacement for using the software and running it through a series of tests based on the criteria for selecting software. Remember to test not only the software but also the documentation, the training materials, and even the technical support facilities. One requirement that can be placed on prospective software vendors as part of the bidding process is that they install (free or at an agreed-upon cost) their software for a limited amount of time on the company's computers. This way it can be determined how their software works in the company's environment, not in some optimized environment the vendor has.

One of the most reliable and insightful sources of feedback is other users of the software. Vendors usually will provide a list of customers (remember, they will tell the analyst about satisfied customers, so it might be necessary to probe for a cross section of customers) and people who are willing to be contacted by prospective customers. Here is where a personal network of contacts, developed through professional groups, college friends, trade associations, or local business clubs, can be a resource; the analyst should not hesitate to find some contacts personally. Such current or former customers can provide a depth of insight on the use of a package at their organizations.

To gain a range of opinions about possible packages, the analyst can consult with independent software-testing services that periodically evaluate software and collect user opinions. Such surveys are available for a fee either as subscription services or on demand. Occasionally, unbiased surveys appear in trade publications. Often, however, articles in trade publications, even software reviews, are seeded by the software manufacturer and are not unbiased.

In comparing several software packages, assign scores for each package on each criterion and compare the scores using the quantitative method that is demonstrated at the end of this chapter for comparing alternative system design strategies.

Hardware and System Software Issues

The first question to ask about hardware and system software is whether the new system that follows a particular design strategy can be run on the firm's existing hardware and software platform. System software refers to such key components as operating systems, database management systems, programming languages, code generators, and network software. To determine whether current hardware and system software are sufficient, the analyst should consider such factors as the age and capacity of the current hardware and system software, the fit between the hardware and software and the new application's goals and proposed functionality, and, if some of the system components are off-the-shelf software, whether the software can run on the existing hardware and system software. The advantages to running the new system on the existing platform are persuasive:

1. Costs will be lower because little, if any, new hardware and system software have to be purchased and installed.
2. The information systems staff is familiar with the existing platform and how to operate and maintain it.
3. The odds of integrating the new application system with existing applications are enhanced.
4. No added costs are incurred for converting old systems to a new platform, if necessary, or for translating existing data between current technology and the new hardware and system software that must be acquired for the system.

On the other hand, persuasive reasons can be given for acquiring new hardware or system software:

1. Some software components of the new system will run only on particular platforms with particular operating systems. Moving to object orientation might require a new database management system.
2. Developing the system for a new platform gives the organization the opportunity to upgrade or expand its current technology holdings.
3. New platform requirements might allow the organization to change its computing operations radically, as in moving from mainframe-centered processing to a database machine or a client/server architecture.

Because the determination of whether or not to acquire new hardware and system software is so context-dependent, it is essential to provide platform options as part of the design strategy alternatives.

Request for proposal (RFP)
A document provided to vendors to ask them to propose hardware and system software that will meet the requirements of a new system.

If it is decided that new hardware or system software is a strong possibility, the analyst might want to issue a request for proposal (RFP) to vendors. The RFP will ask the vendors to propose hardware and system software that will meet the requirements of the new system. Issuing an RFP gives the analyst the opportunity to have vendors conduct the research needed in order to decide among various options. The analyst can request that each bid submitted by a vendor contain certain information essential for a decision on what best fits the company's needs. For example, performance information related to speed and number of operations per second can be requested. Information can be obtained about machine reliability and service availability, and whether an installation is located nearby that can provide more information. The analyst can even ask to take part in a demonstration of the hardware. The bid also will include information on cost. The information collected can then be used in generating alternative design strategies.

Implementation Issues

As Chapter 14 will explain, implementing a new information system is just as much an organizational change process as it is a technical process. Implementation involves more than installing a piece of software, turning it on, and moving to the next software project. New systems often entail new ways of performing the same work, new working relationships, and new skills. Users have to be trained. Disruptions in work procedures have to be found and addressed. In addition, system implementation may be phased in over many weeks or even months. The technical and social aspects of implementation must be addressed as part of any alternative design strategy. Management and users will want to know how long the implementation will take, how much training will be required, and how disruptive the process will be.

SELECTING THE BEST ALTERNATIVE DESIGN STRATEGY FOR PINE VALLEY FURNITURE'S WEBSTORE

As Jim Woo began to evaluate the possible design options for the WebStore, he quickly realized that he and PVF's technical group had a limited understanding of Internet application development. Consequently, he recommended to PVF management that a consulting firm be hired to assist in setting the WebStore design options. Management quickly approved this recommendation, and Jim retained a small consulting organization that had a strong reputation for designing and developing high-quality electronic commerce solutions. Once under contract, Jim worked with the consulting firm to solidify the system requirements and constraints. During this process, they organized the requirements into three categories: mandatory system requirements, essential system requirements, and desired system requirements, summarized in Table 10.4. In addition to the system requirements, they also identified four significant constraints that any design must address, also summarized in Table 10.4.

Next, Jim and the consultants defined three alternative system designs, with advantages and disadvantages for each. PVF management requested that three alternative designs be defined so that clear comparisons could be made between low-end (low cost and limited features), high-end (high cost and extensive features), and mid-level designs (moderate cost and features). Table 10.5 summarizes the results of this analysis. After the system requirements and constraints, as well as the alternative system designs, had been defined, a meeting would be held with PVF management to select a design strategy for the WebStore.

Selecting the Most Likely Alternative

One method that Jim and PVF management can use to decide among the alternative design strategies for WebStore is illustrated in Figure 10.4. On the left, Jim listed all six system requirements and all four constraints from Table 10.4. These are the decision criteria. Jim has assigned a weight of 10 for each of the six requirements and each of the four constraints, so requirements are weighted more heavily than constraints. Jim did not have to do this for any reason other than his own preference. Using this method of comparing alternatives, weights can be arrived at during discussions among the analysis team, users, and sometimes managers. Weights tend to be fairly subjective, and for that reason should be determined through a process of open discussion to reveal underlying assumptions, followed by an attempt to reach consensus among stakeholders. The only real requirement is that the total of all the weights must be 100.

Table 10-4

WebStore System Requirements and Constraints.

REQUIREMENTS	CONSTRAINTS
Mandatory System Requirements	Christmas season rollout.
Full integration with current inventory, sales, and customer tracking systems.	Small development/support staff.
99.9% uptime and availability.	Transaction-style interaction with current systems.
Essential System Requirements	Limited external consultation budget.
Flexibility and scalability for future systems integration.	
Efficient and cost-effective system management.	
Desired System Requirements	
Available support and/or emergency response.	
Documentation.	

1. Outsource Application Service Provider (low end)	
Advantages	**Disadvantages**
All hardware located off-site	Inflexible
Application developed and professionally managed off-site	Difficult to integrate with current systems
Excellent emergency response	Shared resources with other clients

2. Enterprise Resource Planning System (high end)	
Advantages	**Disadvantages**
Stability	Requires skilled internal staff
Available documentation	Expensive hardware and software
	Big learning curve

3. Application Server/Object Framework (moderate)	
Advantages	**Disadvantages**
Excellent integration with current system	Requires internal development (and/or a professional consultation)
Scalability	Proprietary
Flexible	Documentation crucial during planning and development

Figure 10.4 Weighted Approach for Comparing Three Alternative Design Strategies for PVF's WebStore

Criteria	Weight	Alt A: Outsource		Alt B: ERP		Alt C: Server/Object	
		Rating	Score	Rating	Score	Rating	Score
Requirements							
1) Integration with existing systems	10	2	20	3	30	5	50
2) 99.9% uptime	10	5	50	5	50	5	50
3) Flexibility and scalability	10	2	20	3	30	5	50
4) Efficient system management	10	5	50	5	50	5	50
5) Available support	10	5	50	5	50	4	40
6) Documentation	10	4	40	5	50	4	40
	60		230		260		260
Constraints							
1) Timing: Christmas season rollout	10	5	50	4	40	3	30
2) Small internal staff	10	5	50	2	20	3	30
3) Transaction style interaction with current systems	10	2	20	5	50	5	50
4) Limited external consultation budget	10	2	20	2	20	2	20
	40		140		130		130
TOTAL	100		370		390		410

Jim's next step was to rate each requirement and constraint for each alternative on a scale of 1 to 5. A rating of 1 indicates that the alternative does not meet the requirement well or that the alternative violates the constraint. A rating of 5 indicates that the alternative meets or exceeds the requirement or clearly abides by the constraint. Ratings are even more subjective than weights and also should be determined through open discussion among users, analysts, and managers. The next step is to multiply the rating for each requirement and each constraint by its weight, and follow this procedure for each alternative. The final step is to add up the weighted scores for each alternative. Notice that three sets of totals result: for requirements, for constraints, and overall totals. According to the totals for requirements, alternative C is the best choice (score of 280), because it meets or exceeds all requirements. However, if only constraints are considered, alternatives B and C are tied (scores of 130). When Jim combined the totals for requirements and constraints, he found that the best choice is alternative C (score of 410), because it has the highest overall score.

Alternative C, then, appears to be the best choice for PVF's WebStore. However, whether alternative C is chosen for development is another issue. Management at PVF might have some reservations about the alternative, or other considerations might be important from the management perspective that are not apparent to Jim and his staff. These considerations would not show up in Jim's spreadsheet. Another possibility is that management has found other investments, either internal or external to PVF, that it believes would offer a better return on investment. What might appear to be the best choice for a systems development project might not always be the one that ends up being developed. However, if PVF management did have other concerns, they did not voice them in the meeting they had with Jim. At the meeting Jim held with PVF management, it was unanimously agreed upon that alternative C in Figure 10.4, Application Server/Object Framework, best suited PVF's current needs and future growth initiatives.

A Description of the Chosen Alternative

Scalable
The ability to upgrade the capabilities of the system seamlessly through hardware upgrades, software upgrades, or both.

Web server
A computer that is connected to the Internet and that stores files written in Hypertext Markup Language (HTML); these files are available publicly through an Internet connection.

Application server
A middle-tier software and hardware combination that lies between the Web server and the corporate network and systems.

The proposed system would incorporate a scalable, three-tier architecture to integrate the WebStore with the current systems. A scalable system has the ability to upgrade the capabilities of the system seamlessly through hardware upgrades, software upgrades, or both. As Figure 10.5 shows, tier 1, the Web server layer, processes incoming Internet requests. For example, a scalable electronic commerce system would be one that could effectively handle 6 requests per second with one server; by adding a second server, 12 requests per second could be handled effectively. The Web server is a computer that is connected to the Internet and stores files written in hypertext markup language (HTML); these files are available publicly through an Internet connection. As shown in Figure 10.5, the Web server layer communicates with tier 2, the application server layer. The application server is a middle-tier software and hardware combination that lies between the Web server and the corporate network and systems such as the Customer Tracking System, Inventory Control System, and Order Fulfillment System. In other words, the Web server manages the client interaction and broker requests to the middle-tier application server. The application server manages the data specific to running the WebStore (shopping carts, promotions, site logs, etc.) and also oversees all interactions with existing PVF systems for managing customers, inventory, and orders. A third server, the fail-over server, is an emergency backup system on standby, ready to take the place of either server should one fail. Each of these separate components—Web server, application server, fail-over server—can be thought of as an object, each with a well-defined role that can be defined, designed, implemented, and modified easily. For this reason, option 3 is referred to as an Application Server/Object Framework architecture.

Now that the basic architecture of the WebStore has been defined, Jim needs to meet with the consultants to refine further the specifications of the system. The PVF development staff will use these specifications as a blueprint in their development efforts. They will implement all six system requirements and, to the extent possible, comply with each of the four constraints listed in Table 10.4.

UPDATING THE BASELINE PROJECT PLAN

The Baseline Project Plan was developed during systems planning and selection (see Chapter 4) to explain the nature of the requested system and the project to develop it. The plan originally was presented in Figure 4.14; it is reproduced here

Figure 10.5
WebStore Multitier
System Architecture

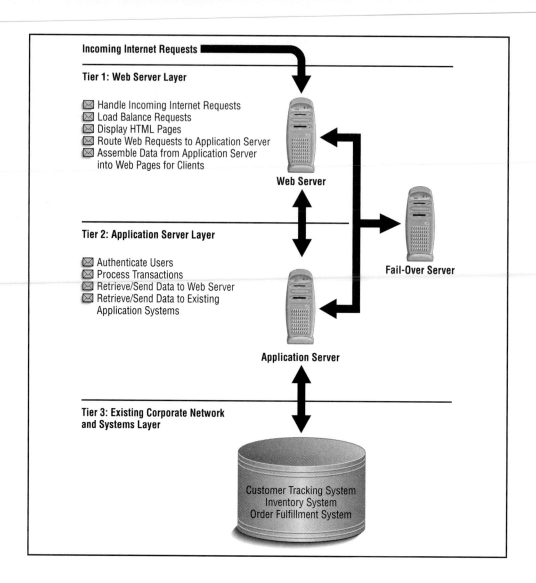

Incoming Internet Requests

Tier 1: Web Server Layer

- ☒ Handle Incoming Internet Requests
- ☒ Load Balance Requests
- ☒ Display HTML Pages
- ☒ Route Web Requests to Application Server
- ☒ Assemble Data from Application Server
  into Web Pages for Clients

Web Server

Fail-Over Server

Tier 2: Application Server Layer

- ☒ Authenticate Users
- ☒ Process Transactions
- ☒ Retrieve/Send Data to Web Server
- ☒ Retrieve/Send Data to Existing
  Application Systems

Application Server

**Tier 3: Existing Corporate Network
and Systems Layer**

Customer Tracking System
Inventory System
Order Fulfillment System

as Figure 10.6. The plan includes a preliminary description of the system as requested, an assessment of the feasibility or justification for the system (the business case), and an overview of management issues for the system and project. This plan was presented to a steering committee or other body, which approved the commitment of funds to conduct the analysis phase just completed. Thus, it is time to report back (in written and oral form) to this group on the project's progress and to update the group on the findings from the analysis. This group will make the final decision on the design strategy to be followed and approve the commitment of resources outlined from the logical (and possibly physical) design steps. This group could determine that the business case has not developed as originally thought and either stop or drastically redirect the project.

The outline of the Baseline Project Plan still can be used for the analysis phase status report. The updated plan typically will be longer as more is known on each topic. Further, the various process, logic, and data models often are included to make the system description more specific. Usually only high-level versions of the diagrams are included within section 2.0, and more detailed versions are provided as appendices.

Every section of the Baseline Project Plan Report is updated at this point. For example, section 1.0.B will now contain the recommendation for the design strategy chosen by the analysis team. Section 2.0.A provides the descriptions of the competing strategies studied during alternative generation and selection, often including the types of comparison charts shown earlier in this chapter. Section 3.0 typically is

Figure 10.6 Outline of Baseline Project

Baseline Project Plan Report

1.0 *Introduction*
  A. Project Overview—Provides an executive summary that specifies the project's scope, feasibility, justification, resource requirements, and schedules. Additionally, a brief statement of the problem, the environment in which the system is to be implemented, and constraints that affect the project are provided.
  B. Recommendation—Provides a summary of important findings from the planning process and recommendations for subsequent activities.

2.0 *System Description*
  A. Alternatives—Provides a brief presentation of alternative system configurations.
  B. System Description—Provides a description of the selected configuration and a narrative of input information, tasks performed, and resultant information.

3.0 *Feasibility Assessment*
  A. Economic Analysis—Provides an economic justification for the system using cost-benefit analysis.
  B. Technical Analysis—Provides a discussion of relevant technical risk factors and an overall risk rating of the project.
  C. Operational Analysis—Provides an analysis of how the proposed system solves business problems or takes advantage of business opportunities in addition to an assessment of how current day-to-day activities will be changed by the system.
  D. Legal and Contractual Analysis—Provides a description of any legal or contractual risks related to the project (e.g., copyright or nondisclosure issues, data capture or transferring, and so on).
  E. Political Analysis—Provides a description of how key stakeholders within the organization view the proposed system.
  F. Schedules, Time Line, and Resource Analysis—Provides a description of potential time frame and completion date scenarios using various resource allocation schemes.

4.0 *Management Issues*
  A. Team Configuration and Management—Provides a description of the team member roles and reporting relationships.
  B. Communication Plan—Provides a description of the communication procedures to be followed by management, team members, and the customer.
  C. Project Standards and Procedures—Provides a description of how deliverables will be evaluated and accepted by the customer.
  D. Other Project-Specific Topics—Provides a description of any other relevant issues related to the project uncovered during planning.

---

changed significantly because the needs of the organization are now known much better than they were during project initiation and planning. For example, economic benefits that were intangible before might now be tangible. Risks, especially operational ones, are likely better understood.

Section 3.0.F will now show the actual activities and their durations during the analysis phase, as well as include a detailed schedule for the activities in the design phases and whatever additional details can be anticipated for later phases. Many Gantt charting packages can show actual progress versus planned activities. It is important to show in this section how well the actual conduct of the analysis phase matched the planned activities. This helps the systems analyst and management understand how well the project is understood and how likely it is that the stated future schedule will occur. Knowing those activities for which actual durations differed significantly from planned durations might be useful in estimating future activity durations.

Often, the design phase activities will be driven by the capabilities chosen for the recommended design strategy. For example, specific design activities are placed on the schedule for such design deliverables as the following:

- Layout of each report, and data input and display screens.
- Structuring of data into logical tables or files.
- Programs and program modules that need to be described.
- Training on new technologies to be used in implementing the system.

Many design phase activities result in developing design specifications for one or more examples of the types of design deliverables listed previously.

Section 4.0 also is updated. It is likely that the project team needs to change as new skills are needed in the next and subsequent project phases. Also, because project team members often are evaluated after each phase, the project leader may request the reassignment of a team member who has not performed as required. Reassessing the communication plan shows whether other communication methods are necessary. New standards and procedures will be needed as the team discovers that some current procedures are inadequate for the new tasks. Section 4.0.D is often used to outline issues for management that have been discovered during analysis. Recall, for example, that Chapter 5 discussed how redundancies and inconsistencies might be found in job descriptions and the way people actually do their jobs. Because these issues must be resolved by management and addressed before detailed system design can be started, now is the last time to call them to the attention of management.

The project leader and other analysts also must ensure that the project workbook and CASE repository are completely up to date as the analysis phase is finalized. Because the project team composition will likely change and, as time passes, facts learned in earlier stages are forgotten, the workbook and repository are necessary to transfer information between phases. This is also a good time for the project leader to do a final check that all elements of project execution have been handled properly.

Besides the written Baseline Project Plan Report update, an oral presentation typically is made, and it might be at this meeting that a decision to approve the analyst's recommendations, redirect those recommendations, or kill the project is made. It is not uncommon for the analysis team to follow this project review meeting with a suitable celebration for reaching an important project milestone.

BEFORE AND AFTER BASELINE PROJECT PLANS FOR PVF's WEBSTORE

Jim Woo and his staff had developed a Baseline Project Plan for PVF's WebStore. The plan included information for each area listed in Figure 10.6. Now that the analysis phase of the life cycle has ended, the plan must be updated. Updated sections are reproduced in the following section. The first item considered is the cost-benefit analysis, Section 3.0.A (economic analysis) of the Baseline Project Plan. The initial cost-benefit analysis for the WebStore project is shown in Figure 10.7, which was first shown in Figure 4.11.

The sources of the numbers in Figure 10.7 were all provided in Chapter 4, where Jim and his staff determined that WebStore would have up-front costs of $42,500 and that there would be annual operational costs of $28,500. It also was explained in Chapter 4 how Jim determined, using the time value of money, that the overall net present value of WebStore would be $35,003. The rate of return on the project was projected to be 24 percent.

Figure 10.8 shows the cost-benefit analysis at the end of analysis. This information appears in the updated Baseline Project Plan. Notice that developing the new

Figure 10.7 Initial Cost-Benefit Analysis for PVF's WebStore

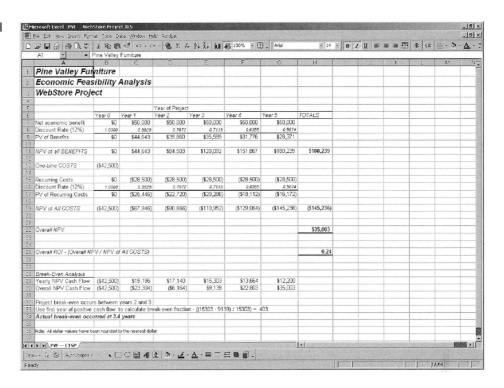

Figure 10.8 Revised Cost-Benefit Analysis for PVF's WebStore Project

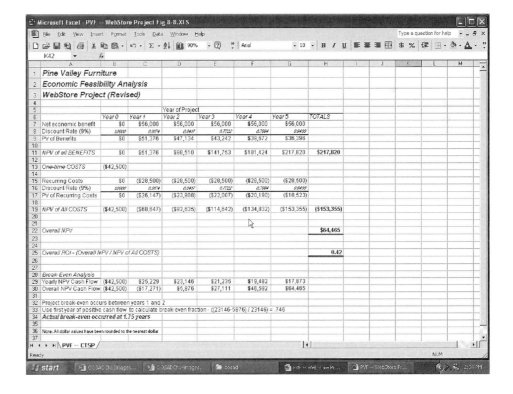

system, represented by alternative C in Figure 10.4, is now a better investment, with a 42 percent return. Yet the overall costs of alternative C exceed the costs of the original estimation of the system. What happened?

Much of Figure 10.8 is the same as Figure 10.7. Recurring costs are the same, as are one-time costs. There are two major changes, though. First, the discount rate has changed. Given the current economic climate, projects can have a lower discount rate,

Figure 10.9
Original PVF
WebStore Project
Schedule

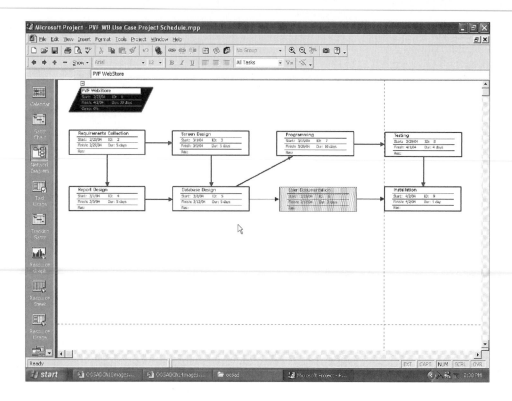

so 9 percent has been substituted for the 12 percent in Figure 10.7. Second, net benefits are now estimated to be larger than in Figure 10.7. Recent research purchased by PVF shows that almost 93 percent of Web users in the United States have now made at least one online purchase. Given the potential size of the online shopping market, and after further analysis, Jim's staff estimated that their earlier sales estimates were too pessimistic. In Figure 10.8, expected benefits from WebStore have been increased by 12 percent per year, to $56,000. Both of these changes have made a big difference in the attractiveness of the project. Even if Jim is wrong about the projected benefits, the adjustment in the discount rate alone has made the WebStore project more attractive.

Figure 10.9 shows the project schedule from the initial version of the Baseline Project Plan. Notice that the schedule covers the entire development process, from requirements determination through installation. Jim originally projected that the entire development effort would take 30 days, with task 7, programming, taking the most time at 10 days. Note from the diagram how user documentation is being written at the same time programming is being completed. As this is a preliminary schedule, the estimates of how long each task should take to complete are all rough.

Compare Figure 10.9 to Figure 10.10, the revised schedule that goes in the updated Baseline Project Plan. The schedule in Figure 10.10 more closely reflects the development time necessary for alternative C. Note that the project dates have been changed so that the system can be rolled out in time for the big Christmas holiday retail season. Development has been pushed up from February and March to August and September. WebStore can be up and running by the end of September if development begins by August 27. Because the chosen alternative is easier to integrate with existing systems than the other alternatives, and because of its flexibility and scalability, 3 fewer days are scheduled for programming and 1 less day is planned for testing. The fact that alternative C is proprietary also results in less development time for screen and report design. Jim has decided to use existing screens and reports for the initial rollout. Given how flexible alternative C is, he and his staff can make changes easily after the initial live test of the system during the holiday retail season. Overall, the project time has been reduced from 30 days to 23 days. Even though the schedule for development is shorter after deciding on alternative C, the start-up costs remain the same.

Figure 10.10
Revised PVF
WebStore Project
Schedule

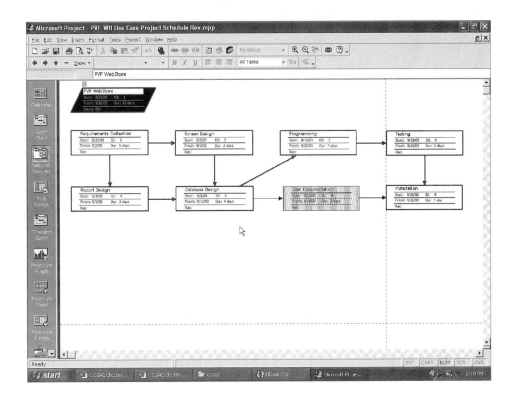

We have shown only two parts to the Baseline Project Plan for Pine Valley Furniture's WebStore project. Even for a project this small, a complete Baseline Project Plan would be too much to include in this book. These examples, though, should provide a good general idea of what an initial Baseline Project Plan contains and how it changes when a major life cycle phase, like analysis, ends.

KEY POINTS REVIEW

In selecting the best alternative design strategy, the systems analyst develops alternative solutions to the organization's information system problem. A design strategy is a combination of system features, a hardware and system software platform, and an acquisition method that characterizes the nature of the system and how it will be developed. A good number of alternative design strategies to develop is three, as three alternatives can represent the high end, middle, and low end of the spectrum of possible systems that can be built.

1. **Describe the different sources of software.**

   Application (and system) software can be obtained from hardware vendors, packaged software vendors, custom software developers, and enterprise-wide solution vendors, as well as from internal systems development resources. An organization can be hired to handle all of the company's systems development needs; this is called outsourcing. It also is important to know which criteria to use to be able to choose among off-the-shelf software products. These criteria include cost, functionality, vendor support, vendor viability, flexibility, documentation, response time, and ease of installation. The systems analyst also must determine whether new hardware and system software are needed. Requests for proposals are one way to collect more information about hardware and system software, their performance, and costs. In addition to hardware and software issues, implementation issues must be considered, as well as broader organizational concerns, such as the availability of funding and management support.

2. **Assemble the various pieces of an alternative design strategy.**

   Alternative design strategies are developed after a system's requirements and constraints have been identified and prioritized. The systems analyst can start initially with a simple list of features and obstacles for each alternative being considered. From there, numerical weights can be assigned to each of the system requirements and constraints. Finally, each alternative can be rated on each attribute, and these numbers can be used to determine numerical rankings of the alternatives.

3. **Generate at least three alternative design strategies for an information system.**
Generating different alternatives is something the analyst would do in actual systems analysis or as part of a class project. Three is not a magic number. It represents, instead, the end points and midpoints of a series of alternatives, such as the most expensive, the least expensive, and an alternative somewhere in the middle.

4. **Select the best design strategy using qualitative and quantitative methods.**
Once developed, alternatives can be compared to each other through quantitative methods, but the actual decision might depend on other criteria, such as organizational politics. This chapter introduced one way to compare alternative design strategies quantitatively.

5. **Update a Baseline Project Plan based on the results of the analysis phase.**
Because generating and selecting alternative design strategies completes analysis, the systems development project has reached a major milestone. Once an analysis of alternative design strategies is completed, the systems analyst and other members of the analysis team present their findings to a management steering committee or the client requesting the system change. In this presentation (written and oral), the requirements discovered are summarized, alternative design strategies are evaluated, and the recommended alternative is justified; in addition, an updated Baseline Project Plan is presented for the project to follow if the committee decides to fund the next development phase.

KEY TERMS CHECKPOINT

Here are the key terms from the chapter. The page where each term is first explained is in parentheses after the term.

a. Application server (p. 287)
b. Design strategy (p. 273)
c. Enterprise resource planning (ERP) system (p. 279)
d. Outsourcing (p. 276)
e. Request for proposal (RFP) (p. 284)
f. Scalable (p. 287)
g. Web server (p. 287)

Match each of the key terms with the definition that best fits it.

1. A computer that is connected to the Internet and stores files written in hypertext markup language (HTML); the files are publicly available through an Internet connection.
2. A particular approach to developing an information system. It includes statements on the system's functionality, hardware and system software platform, and method for acquisition.
3. The ability to upgrade the capabilities of the system seamlessly through either hardware upgrades, software upgrades, or both.
4. A system that integrates individual traditional business functions into a series of modules so that a single transaction occurs seamlessly within a single information system rather than several separate systems.
5. The practice of turning over responsibility of some to all of an organization's information systems applications and operations to an outside firm.
6. A document provided to vendors to ask them to propose hardware and system software that will meet the requirements of the new system.
7. A middle-tier software and hardware combination that lies between the Web server and the corporate network and systems.

REVIEW QUESTIONS

1. What are the deliverables from selecting the best alternative design strategy?
2. Why should at least three alternative design strategies be generated?
3. Describe five sources of software.
4. How do analysts decide among various off-the-shelf software options? What criteria should be used?
5. What issues are considered when analysts try to determine whether new hardware or system software is necessary?
6. What is an RFP, and how do analysts use one to gather information on hardware and system software?
7. What issues other than hardware and software must analysts consider in preparing alternative system design strategies?

8. How do analysts generate alternative solutions to information systems problems?
9. How do managers decide which alternative design strategy to develop?
10. Which elements of a Baseline Project Plan might be updated during the alternative generation and selection step of analysis?
11. What methods can a systems analyst employ to verify vendor claims about a software package?
12. What are enterprise resource planning systems? What are the benefits and disadvantages of such systems as a design strategy?

PROBLEMS AND EXERCISES

1. Find the most current Software 500 list from *Software Magazine*. How much has the rank order of the top software companies changed compared to the list in Table 10.2? Try to determine why your list is different from that of Table 10.2. What changes are occurring in the computer industry that might affect this list?

2. Research how to prepare a request for proposal. Prepare an outline of an RFP for Pine Valley Furniture to use in collecting information on hardware for WebStore.

3. Re-create the spreadsheet in Figure 10.4 in your spreadsheet package. Change the weights and compare the outcome to Figure 10.4. Change the rankings. Add criteria. What additional information does this "what if" analysis provide for you as a decision maker? What insight do you gain into the decision-making process involved in choosing the best alternative system design?

4. Prepare a list for evaluating computer hardware and system software that is comparable to the list of criteria for selecting off-the-shelf application software presented earlier.

5. The method for evaluating alternatives used in Figure 10.4 is called weighting and scoring. This method implies that the total utility of an alternative is the product of the weights of each criterion times the weight of the criterion for the alternative. What assumptions are characteristic of this method for evaluating alternatives? That is, what conditions must be true for this to be a valid method of evaluation alternatives?

6. Weighting and scoring (see Problem and Exercise 5) is only one method for comparing alternative solutions to a problem. Go to the library, find a book or articles on qualitative and quantitative decision making and voting methods, and outline two other methods for evaluating alternative solutions to a problem. What are the pros and cons of these methods compared to the weighting and scoring method? Under weighting and scoring and the other alternatives you find, how would you incorporate the opinions of multiple decision makers?

7. Prepare an agenda for a meeting at which you would present the findings from analysis to the CEO of Pine Valley Furniture about WebStore. Use information provided in Chapters 5 through 10 as background in preparing this agenda. Concentrate on which topics to cover, not the content of each topic.

8. Review the criteria for selecting off-the-shelf software presented in this chapter. Use your experience and imagination, and describe other criteria that are or might be used to select off-the-shelf software in the real world. For each new criterion, explain how its use might be functional (i.e., it is useful to use this criterion), dysfunctional, or both.

9. The owner of two pizza parlors located in adjacent towns wants to computerize and integrate sales transactions and inventory management within and between both stores. The point-of-sale component must be easy to use and flexible enough to accommodate a variety of pricing strategies and coupons. The inventory management, which will be linked to the point-of-sale component, also must be easy to use and fast. The systems at each store need to be linked so that sales and inventory levels can be determined instantly for each store and for both stores combined. The owner can allocate $40,000 for hardware and $20,000 for software, and must have the new system operational in 3 months. Training must be short and easy. Briefly describe three alternative systems for this situation, and explain how each would meet the requirements and constraints. Are the requirements and constraints realistic? Why or why not?

10. Compare the alternative systems from Problem and Exercise 9 using the weighted approach demonstrated in Figure 10.4. Which system would you recommend? Why? Was the approach taken in this and Problem and Exercise 9 useful even for this relatively small system? Why or why not?

11. Suppose that an analysis team did not generate alternative design strategies for consideration by a project steering committee or client. What might be the consequences of having only one design strategy? What might happen during the oral presentation of project progress if only one design strategy is offered?

12. In the section on choosing off-the-shelf software, eight criteria are proposed for evaluating alternative packages. Suppose the choice were between alternative custom software developers rather than prewritten packages. What criteria would be appropriate to select and compare among competing bidders for custom development of an application? Define each of these criteria.

13. How might the project team recommending an enterprise resource planning design strategy justify its recommendation as compared to other types of design strategies?

1. Consider the purchase of a new PC to be used by you at your work (or by you at a job that you would like to have). Describe, in detail, three alternatives for this new PC that represent the low, middle, and high points of a continuum of potential solutions. Be sure that the low-end PC meets at least your mandatory requirements and the high-end PC is at least within a reasonable budget. At this point, without quantitative analysis, which alternative would you choose?

2. For the new PC just described, develop ranked lists of your requirements and constraints as displayed in Figure 10.4. Display the requirements and constraints, along with the three alternatives, as done in Figure 10.4, and note how each alternative is rated on each requirement and constraint. Calculate scores for each alternative on each criterion and compute total scores. Which alternative has the highest score? Why? Does this choice fit with your selection in the previous question? Why or why not?

3. One of the most competitive software markets today is electronic spreadsheets. Pick three packages (e.g., Microsoft Excel, Lotus 1-2-3, and Quattro Pro, but any three spreadsheet packages would do). Study how to use spreadsheet packages for school, work, and personal financial management. Develop a list of criteria that are important to you for comparing alternative packages. Then contact each vendor and ask for the information you need to evaluate its package and company. Request a demonstration copy or trial use of its software. If the company cannot provide a sample copy, then try to find a computer software dealer or club where you can test the software and documentation. Based on the information you receive and the software you use, rate each package using your chosen criteria. Which package is best for you? Why? Talk to other students to find out which package they rated as best. Why are there differences between what different students determined as best?

4. Obtain copies of actual requests for proposals used for information systems developments and/or purchases. If possible, obtain RFPs from public and private organizations. Find out how they are used. What are the major components of these proposals? Do these proposals seem to be useful? Why or why not? How and why are the RFPs different for the public versus the private organizations?

CASE PROBLEMS

Pine Valley Furniture

During your time as a Pine Valley Furniture intern, you have learned much about the systems analysis and design process. You have been able to observe Jim Woo as he serves as the lead analyst on the WebStore project, and you also have read about PVF's Customer Tracking System project. The requirements determination and requirements structuring activities for the Customer Tracking System are now complete, and it is time to begin generating alternative design strategies.

On Monday afternoon, Jim Woo stops by your desk and requests that you attend a meeting scheduled for tomorrow morning. He mentions that during tomorrow's meeting, the Customer Tracking System's requirements and constraints, weighting criteria, and alternative design strategy ratings will be discussed. He also mentions that during the previously conducted systems planning and selection phase, Jackie Judson and he prepared a Baseline Project Plan. When the initial Baseline Project Plan was prepared, the in-house development option was the preferred design strategy. The marketing group's unique information needs seemed to indicate that in-house development was the best option. However, other alternative design strategies have since been investigated.

During Tuesday's meeting, several end users, managers, and systems development team members meet, discuss, and rank the requirements and constraints for the new Customer Tracking System. Also, weights and rankings are assigned to the three alternative design strategies. At the end of the meeting, Jim Woo assigns you the task of arranging this information into a table and calculating the overall scores for each alternative. He would like to review this information later in the afternoon. Tables 10.6 and 10.7 summarize the information obtained from Tuesday's meeting.

a. Generally speaking, what alternative design strategies were available to Pine Valley Furniture?

b. Of the alternative design strategies available to Pine Valley Furniture, which were the most viable? Why?

c. Using the information provided in Table 10.7, calculate the scores for each alternative.

d. Based on the information provided in Tables 10.6 and 10.7, which alternative do you recommend?

Table 10-6 Comparison of Alternative Design Strategies for PVF's Customer Tracking System.

CRITERIA	ALTERNATIVE A	ALTERNATIVE B	ALTERNATIVE C
New Requirements			
Ease of use	Acceptable	Fair	Good
Easy real-time updating of customer profiles	Yes	Yes	Yes
Tracks customer purchasing activity	No	Yes	Yes
Supports sales forecasting	Some forecasting models are supported	Some forecasting models are supported	Provides support for all necessary forecasting models
Ad hoc report generation	No	Yes	Yes
Constraints			
Must interface with existing systems	Requires significant modifications	Minor modifications	Minor modifications
Costs to develop	$150,000	$200,000	$350,000
Cost of hardware	$80,000	$80,000	$100,000
Time to operation	6 months	7 months	9 months
Must interface with existing systems	Requires significant modifications	Minor modifications	Minor modifications
Ease of training	3 weeks of training	3 weeks of training	2 weeks of training
Legal restrictions	Cannot be modified	Allows for customization	None

Table 10-7 Weighting and Scoring Data for PVF's Customer Tracking System.

CRITERIA	WEIGHT	ALTERNATIVE A		ALTERNATIVE B		ALTERNATIVE C	
REQUIREMENTS		RATING	SCORE	RATING	SCORE	RATING	SCORE
Ease of use	15	2		3		5	
Real-time customer profile updating	12	3		3		4	
Tracks customer purchasing activity	12	1		3		3	
Sales forecasting	8	2		2		3	
Ad hoc report generation	3	1		2		3	
Total	50						
Constraints							
Interfaces with existing systems	15	3		4		2	
Development costs	10	5		4		2	
Hardware costs	10	5		4		2	
Time of operation	5	4		1		2	
Ease of training	5	2		2		4	
Legal restrictions	5	1		2		5	
Total	50						

CASE: BROADWAY ENTERTAINMENT COMPANY, INC.

Formulating a Design Strategy for the Web-Based Customer Relationship Management System

Case Introduction

Defining a design strategy for a systems development project is typically a crucial step for a project team. The team must select the scope of functionality, the implementation platform, and the method of acquisition for the system. Many alternatives might be possible, and different sets of users might support different design strategies. The design strategy, chosen near the end of the analysis phase, is also crucial because it sets the direction for the rest of the project. In contrast, a prototyping or iterative development approach, used to prove the concept for the value of a system, need not be perfect. Further, the prototype does not need to take the exact form of the final system. For these reasons, some choices can be made to meet shorter-term rather than longer-term objectives. This is the case with MyBroadway, the customer relationship information system being developed by a team of students from St. Claire Community College for Carrie Douglass, manager of the Broadway Entertainment Company store in Centerville, Ohio. The object-oriented development methodology the students are employing is an iterative approach, and the system at each iteration, even the final one, is meant to be an illustration of what eventually could be developed by the information technology (IT) professionals at BEC.

Determining the System Functionality

The activities of systems analysis for the MyBroadway project have identified possible system requirements. The object-oriented methodology follows a repetitive development process of building, testing, and refining system features one or a few at a time until the user agrees that the system functions as desired. In the case of MyBroadway, the prototype will be used more during the design and implementation (rather than analysis) phases to refine system requirements (as documented during analysis) and user interfaces, and to test customer acceptance. The student team developed a diagram, using Microsoft Visio, to explain their process (see BEC Figure 10.1). So far, the students have concentrated only on analysis activities, documenting initial system requirements via use cases, class diagrams, object-relational data structures, and sequence diagrams and analysis classes. The team took this approach of doing considerable analysis work up front, before doing any design and implementation, because they are still learning the object-oriented methodology. The BEC environment is new to them so they wanted to analyze many system features before design and implementation; and Carrie Douglass is still formulating her system requirements. Even with this somewhat atypical concentration on

BEC Figure 10.1
Design and Implementation Process for MyBroadway System

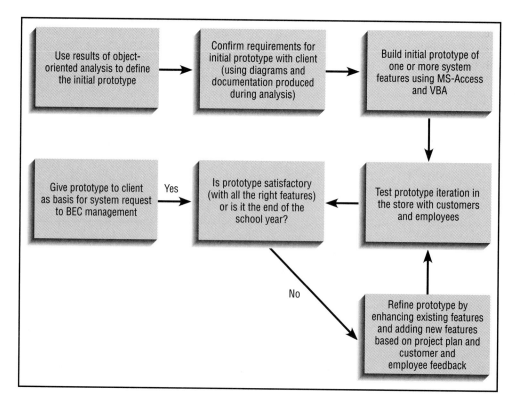

PHYSICAL DATABASE DESIGN

Physical database design Part of database design that deals with the efficiency considerations for access of data.

The first step in coming up with design classes is to conduct physical database design, which considers not only functional requirements, but also focuses on non-functional requirements such as response time and transaction throughput. Efficient physical database design ensures that users do not have to wait for unreasonable periods when running queries and can, therefore, perform their tasks efficiently. For physical database design of most business applications, a designer will consider the object-relational model. Techniques like indexing are the most common mechanisms for efficient access. It is common to combine two or more entity classes into one for efficient access. Rarely, a class may be split. Because the operations might have to follow this combination or split, physical database design needs to precede finalization of operations of entity classes. During physical database design, one also defines the data types of the fields and specifies constraints, if any. Finally, the analyst considers the design of object-relational features pertinent to the application.

Before designing physical files and databases, certain information needs to be collected from analysts and users, although it might have been collected during prior phases. In addition, certain information needs to be determined about the technology to be deployed (see Figure 11.2). This information includes the following:

- A list of analysis classes including volume estimates.
- Characteristics of each attribute.
- Descriptions of where and when data are used, entered, retrieved, deleted, and updated (including frequencies).
- Expectations or requirements for response time and throughput.
- Descriptions of the technologies used for implementing the database.

Figure 11.2 Factors That Influence Physical Database Design

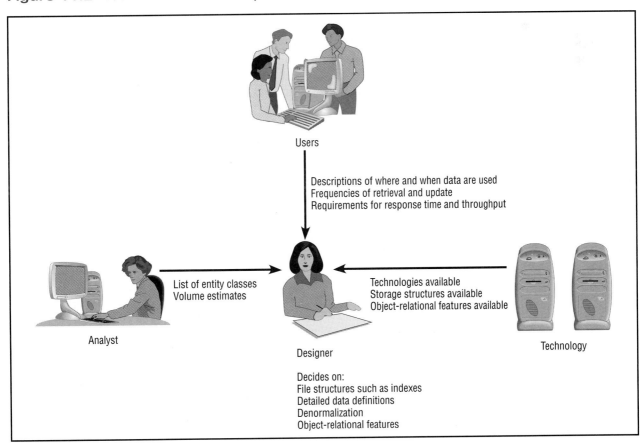

- Storage structures available in the database software selected.
- Object-oriented features available in the database software selected.

Statistics on the number of objects in each class sometimes are collected during requirements determination in systems analysis. If not, these statistics need to be gathered in order to proceed with database design. Similarly, frequencies of updates and retrievals, as well as response times and throughputs, need to be collected from users. Entity classes are obtained from the analysis phase, and the numbers of objects in entity classes are estimated. A detailed definition of each attribute (or field) is specified so that the length of a row in each object relation can be determined. Storage structures and features available in the object-relational DBMS (ORDBMS) selected will guide physical database design.

A designer begins the physical design phase by addressing the design of physical fields corresponding to each attribute in a logical data model. Next, the designer can proceed to assess the analysis classes for opportunities for denormalization, conduct file organization, and evaluate the use of object-relational features (Figure 11.3). This chapter will detail these techniques without emphasizing a vendor-specific syntax, although Oracle 9i/Oracle 10g occasionally is employed as the ORDBMS for illustration purposes.

Because the sections in this chapter use Structured Query Language (SQL), we begin with a brief description of the essential SQL commands. Several books offer detailed background material on SQL, such as Hoffer, Prescott, and McFadden (2004) or Bordoloi and Bock (2003).

Structured Query Language (SQL)
The standard language used for creating and querying tables in relational databases.

STRUCTURED QUERY LANGUAGE (SQL)

SQL (pronounced sometimes as "sequel") is the standard language used for creating and querying tables in relational databases. The latest standard from American National Standards Institute (ANSI) is called SQL-99, and RDBMSs are working to become SQL-99 compliant. The previous ANSI standard was SQL-92. Contemporary DBMSs are SQL-92 compliant.

SQL is the most widely used language for retrieving, inserting, updating, and deleting data in relational databases. Designers with a heavy programming background in an object-oriented language such as Java or C++ may sometimes argue that using relational databases implies moving away from the object-oriented approach. This is not true. What is termed as *persistence* in the object-oriented environment is called *database* in the business environment. Today, most business systems like the elec-

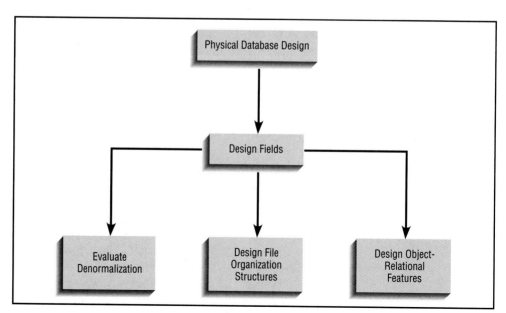

Figure 11.3 Steps in Physical Database Design

EMP TABLE

EMPNO	ENAME	JOB	MGR	HIREDATE	SAL	COMM	DEPTNO
7369	SMITH	CLERK	7902	17-Dec-80	800		20
7499	ALLEN	SALESMAN	7698	20-Feb-81	1600	300	30
7521	WARD	SALESMAN	7698	22-Feb-81	500	30	
7566	JONES	MANAGER	7839	2-Apr-81	2975		20
7654	MARTIN	SALESMAN	7698	28-Sep-81	1250	1400	30
7698	BLAKE	MANAGER	7839	1-May-81	2850		30
7782	CLARK	MANAGER	7839	9-Jun-81	2450		10
7788	SCOTT	ANALYST	7566	19-Apr-87	3000		20
7839	KING	PRESIDENT		17-Nov-81	5000	10	
7844	TURNER	SALESMAN	7698	8-Sep-81	1500	0	30
7876	ADAMS	CLERK	7788	23-May-87	1100		20
7900	JAMES	CLERK	7698	3-Dec-81	950		30
7902	FORD	ANALYST	7566	3-Dec-81	3000	20	
7934	MILLER	CLERK	7782	23-Jan-82	1300		10

DEPT TABLE

DEPTNO	DNAME	LOC
10	ACCOUNTING	NEW YORK
20	RESEARCH	DALLAS
30	SALES	CHICAGO
40	OPERATIONS	BOSTON

tronic commerce systems you encounter when making online purchases use relational databases at the back end, which is the end that stores and processes data.

This section provides a brief description of some of the more important SQL commands. It employs the two tables Emp and Dept, which are created under the schema SCOTT during a default Oracle installation. The tables stand for entities employee and department with the constraint that an employee works for one department. To test the commands, Oracle software can be downloaded and installed, subject to a licensing agreement, from the Web site http://www.oracle.com/technology/software/products/database/oracle10g/index.html. Tables 11-1a and 11-1b show the rows in the two tables. Five SQL commands are illustrated: Create Table, Insert, Select, Update, and Delete.

1. **Create Table command:** The Create Table command is used to create a table, list the names and types of fields, define any constraints on the fields, and provide any additional attributes of the table. For example, to create the DEPT table, the following command is used:

   ```
   Create Table DEPT
   (DEPTNO NUMBER(2) not null,
   DNAME VARCHAR2(14),
   LOC VARCHAR2 (13),
   constraint DEPT_PK Primary Key(DEPTNO))
   ```

   Note that if the schema SCOTT in Oracle is being used, the table DEPT should already have been created during installation. The table DEPT has the field DEPTNO, defined as the primary key of type NUMBER, and the fields DNAME and LOC (for location) as of type variable characters. A specification VARCHAR2(14) means that a value in the field should not exceed 14 characters; if the value has fewer than 14 characters, then the actual space used is adjusted accordingly.

2. **Insert command:** The Insert command is used to add a row object into a table by providing values of the fields. For an insert command to be successful, the values provided should meet all constraints specified when creating the

table. For example, to insert a new row in the table DEPT, the following command can be used:

Insert into DEPT
Values (50, 'DESIGN', 'MIAMI');

3. **Select command:** The Select command is used to retrieve row objects from one or more tables. The Select command is the most frequently used and the most important in SQL. This command has resulted in such a dramatic improvement in developer productivity that it is inconceivable to think of any contemporary business information system that does not use it for data retrieval purposes. The structure of a Select command with the essential keywords is provided below:

Select <enter *columns and functions on columns here*>
From <enter *tables here*>
Where <enter *restrict and join conditions here*>
Order By <enter *sort conditions here*>
Group by <enter *group by fields here*>
Having <enter *aggregate conditions here*>

Let's illustrate SQL commands using examples:
Select * from DEPT;

Deptno	Dname	Loc
10	ACCOUNTING	NEW YORK
20	RESEARCH	DALLAS
30	SALES	CHICAGO
40	OPERATIONS	BOSTON

The command lists all the rows and all the fields.
Select * From EMP Where ENAME = 'SMITH';

Empno	Ename	Job	Mgr	Hiredate	Sal	Comm	Deptno
7369	SMITH	CLERK	7902	17-DEC-80	800		20

The aforementioned command lists all the field values of the employee whose name is SMITH. Note that SQL commands can be written in one or several lines.

Select EMPNO, ENAME, JOB
From EMP
Where JOB = 'SALESMAN'
Order By ENAME;

Empno	Ename	Job
7499	ALLEN	SALESMAN
7654	MARTIN	SALESMAN
7844	TURNER	SALESMAN
7521	WARD	SALESMAN

This query shows rows projected to three fields—EMPNO, ENAME, and JOB—for the job SALESMAN. The answer is sorted by ENAME values.

The Select command is tremendously powerful due to its ability to perform join operations, which involve the comparison of values of a field (or fields) from one table to a field (or fields) from another table. One of the fields is usually a primary key and the other a foreign key. A foreign key is a field (or fields) in a table that is the primary key in another table. This definition of join can be extended to several tables. The following shows an example of a join:

Select EMPNO, ENAME, DNAME from EMP, DEPT
Where EMP.DEPTNO = DEPT.DEPTNO and DEPT.LOC = 'CHICAGO';

Empno	Ename	Dname
7499	ALLEN	SALES
7521	WARD	SALES
7654	MARTIN	SALES
7698	BLAKE	SALES
7844	TURNER	SALES
7900	JAMES	SALES

This example joins EMP.DEPTNO, which is the foreign key of EMP, with DEPT. DEPTNO, which is the primary key of DEPT. The value of DEPTNO corresponding to LOC CHICAGO is 30, which is then matched up with the corresponding values in the foreign key EMP.DEPTNO.

Aggregation operations such as sum and average frequently require the use of Group By and Having keywords:

Select JOB, Avg(SAL) from EMP
Group by JOB
Having Avg(SAL) >= 3,000

JOB	AVG(SAL)
ANALYST	3,000
PRESIDENT	5,000

The aforementioned query calculates the average salary by JOB and lists the averages that are greater than or equal to $3,000. The condition Avg(SAL) >= 3000, shown with the Having keyword, is an example of an aggregate condition because it is based on a group of values instead of one value.

4. **Update command:** The Update command is used to modify one or more values in data. Suppose one wants to modify employee Blake's (EMPNO 7698) salary to $3,000. The SQL command is:

Update EMP
Set SAL = 3,000
Where EMPNO = 7698;

5. **Delete command:** The Delete command is used to delete one or more values. Suppose one wants to delete the employee Turner's (EMPNO 7844) row object.

Delete from EMP
Where EMPNO = 7844;

DESIGNING FIELDS

Field
The smallest unit of named application data recognized by system software.

Composite attribute
An attribute composed of multiple fields.

A field is the smallest unit of application data recognized by system software, such as a programming language or database management system. The term *attribute* generally is used during logical database design, and the term *field* generally is used during physical database design. An attribute normally maps to a field, and the design for a simple attribute is straightforward. However, a composite attribute from a logical database model maps to several fields. For example, the EMPNAME attribute in an EMPLOYEE relation may be represented as three fields: LASTNAME, FIRSTNAME, and MIDDLEINIT. Similarly, the attribute Address can be composed of four fields: STREET, CITY, STATE, and ZIP. In object-relational databases, the composite attributes are represented by types. For example, NAME and ADDRESS each can be defined as types.

Create or replace type NAME_TYPE as object (

LASTNAME VARCHAR2(25),
FIRSTNAME VARCHAR2(25),
MIDDLEINIT CHAR(1));

Table 11-2

Common Oracle
9i/10g Data Types.

Data Type	Description
VARCHAR2	Stores variable length character data. Maximum length is 4,000 bytes.
CHAR	Stores fixed length character data. If the value has fewer characters than specified, the remaining characters are padded with blanks. Maximum length is 2,000 bytes.
NUMBER (PRECISION, SCALE)	Stores fixed on floating-point numbers. Precision is the total number of digits. Scale determines where rounding occurs. Maximum precision is 38.
DATE	Date values ranging from 4712 B.C. to 9999 A.D.
TIMESTAMP	Date values with precision down to a fraction of a second with up to nine places after the decimal.
LONG	Stores variable length character data, is like VARCHAR2, but maximum length is 2 GB.
LOB	There are four types: Binary LOB (BLOB), Character LOB (CLOB), National Character LOB (NCLOB), and Binary file (BFILE). The data type is used to store large objects such as images, video files, and character data in a number of languages.

Create or replace type ADDRESS_TYPE as object (

STREET VARCHAR2(50),
CITY VARCHAR2(25),
STATE CHAR(2),
ZIP CHAR(5));

Common field types available in Oracle 9i/10g are listed in Table 11-2. VAR-CHAR2 allows field values of variable length; CHAR requires field values to be fixed in length.

Object types NAME_TYPE and ADDRESS_TYPE can now be used to define a PERSON_TYPE, which also includes simple fields such as PHONE and DATEBIRTH (see Figure 11.4).

Create or replace type PERSON_TYPE as object (
NAME NAME_TYPE,
ADDRESS ADDRESS_TYPE,
DATEBIRTH DATE,
PHONE VARCHAR2(12));

The type PERSON_TYPE can be used (and reused) in numerous object-relational tables such as STUDENT, EMPLOYEE, PERSON, INSTRUCTOR, CUSTOMER, SALESPERSON, and VENDOR.

Figure 11.4
Composite Attributes
Defined Using Types

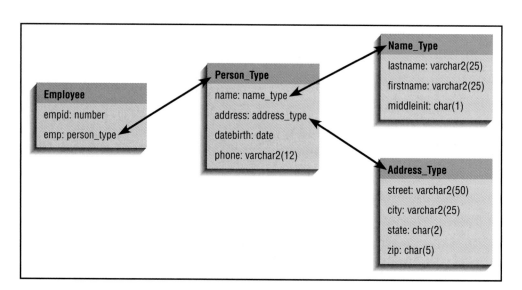

For example, EMPLOYEE can be created by using PERSON_TYPE.

Create table EMPLOYEE (
EMPID NUMBER(8) not null primary key,
EMP PERSON_TYPE);

Note how this approach affects insertion of values. To insert a row object, the types are used as constructors, which are similar to the constructors you may have encountered in an object-oriented language like Java.

Insert into EMPLOYEE
values (1000, PERSON_TYPE (NAME_TYPE ('Brown', 'David', 'M'),
ADDRESS_TYPE ('Columbia Pike', 'Arlington', 'VA', '22201'),
to_date ('16-Apr-1956', 'dd-mm-yyyy'), '703-111-2222'))

The abstract data types PERSON_TYPE, NAME_TYPE, and ADDRESS_TYPE are object types and have constructor methods. A constructor is an operation that creates and initializes an instance of a class.

Choosing Data Types

A data type is a coding scheme recognized by system software for representing organizational data. The bit pattern of the coding scheme is usually immaterial to the systems analyst, but the space to store data and the speed required to access data are of consequence in the physical file and database design. The specific file or database management software used with the system will dictate which choices are available. The systems analyst needs to be familiar with the available data types of the software that will be deployed in the system. For example, if Java interacts with Oracle, the data types available in the two differ and can result in mismatch errors unless explicitly addressed.

Selecting a data type balances the following four objectives, which will vary in degree of importance depending on the application:

1. Minimize storage space.
2. Represent all possible values of the field.
3. Improve data integrity for the field.
4. Support all data manipulations desired on the field.

The analyst wants to choose a data type for a field that minimizes space, represents every possible legitimate value for the associated attribute, and allows the data to be manipulated as needed. For example, suppose a Quantity sold field can be represented by a Number data type. The analyst would select a length for this field that would handle the maximum value plus some room for growth of the business. However, systems analysts must be careful: The data type must be suitable for the life of the application; otherwise, maintenance will be required. Most people remember the costs incurred to fix the Y2K problem. Choose data types for future needs by anticipating growth. The analyst should be familiar with the operations provided for a data type (e.g., date arithmetic can be done so that dates can be subtracted or time periods can be added to or subtracted from a date). Avoid character types of fixed length; if a field like Last_Name is defined as being of variable length with a maximum of 50 characters and the last name is McCool, then space for only about 6 characters plus a small overhead is actually allocated. In this case, a data type of variable character length is appropriate.

Typically, a field is related mathematically to other data. For example, an invoice can include a total due field, which represents the sum of the amount due on each item on the invoice. A field that can be derived from other database fields is called a computed or derived field. Some database technologies allow the analyst to define computed fields explicitly along with other raw data fields. If a field is specified as computed, the analyst usually will be prompted to enter the formula for the calculation; the formula can involve other fields from the same row object and possibly fields

Constructor
An operation that creates and initializes an instance of a class.

Data type
A coding scheme recognized by system software for representing organizational data.

Computed or derived field
A field that can be arithmetically calculated, or derived from other database fields from one or multiple tables.

from row objects in related files. The database technology either will store the calculated value or compute it when requested. Computed fields also can be defined using functions, which are then detailed as methods during design and implementation.

Controlling Data Integrity

Data typing helps control data integrity by limiting the possible range of values for a field. Additional physical file and database design options can be used to ensure higher-quality data. Although these controls can be imposed within application programs, it is better to include these as part of the file and database definitions so that the controls are guaranteed to be applied all the time as well as uniformly for all programs. The five popular data integrity control methods, which are explained next, are default value, format control, range control, referential integrity, and null value control.

1. *Default value.* A default value is the value a field will assume unless an explicit value is entered for the field. For example, the city and state of most customers for a particular retail store will likely be the same as the store's city and state. Assigning a default value to a field can reduce data entry time (the field can be skipped during data entry) and data entry errors, such as typing IM instead of IN for Indiana.

2. *Format control.* Some data must follow a specified pattern. A format (or input mask or picture) is a pattern of codes that restricts the width and possible values for each position within a field. For example, a product number at Pine Valley Furniture is four alphanumeric characters—the first is alphabetic and the next three are numeric—defined by a format of A999, where A means that only alphabetic characters are accepted and 9 means that only numeric digits are accepted. M128 is an acceptable value, but 3128 or M12H would be unacceptable. Other types of format controls can be used to format currency values, indicate how to show negative numbers, suppress showing leading zeros, or justify the value within the space for the field display.

3. *Range control.* Numeric and alphabetic data may have a limited set of permissible values. For example, a field for the number of product units sold might have a lower bound of 0, and a field that represents the month of a product sale might be limited to the values JAN, FEB, and so forth. Oracle 10g allows a CHECK clause, and Microsoft Access has a VALIDATION RULE for range control and some other conditions.

4. *Referential integrity.* As noted earlier in this chapter, the most common example of referential integrity is cross-referencing between object relations when relationships are maintained by foreign keys. For example, consider the pair of relations in Figure 11.5a. In this case, the values for the foreign key Customer_ID field within a customer order must be limited to the set of Customer_ID values from the customer relation; no one wants to accept an order for a nonexistent or unknown customer. Referential integrity might be useful in other instances. Consider the employee relation example in Figure 11.5b. In this example, the employee relation has a field of

Figure 11.5
Examples of Referential Integrity Field Controls

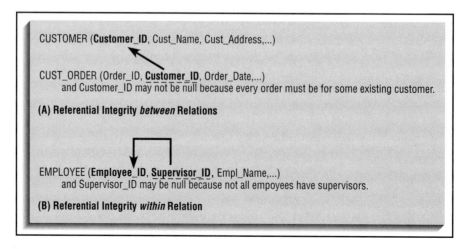

CUSTOMER (**Customer_ID**, Cust_Name, Cust_Address,...)

CUST_ORDER (Order_ID, **Customer_ID**, Order_Date,...)
and Customer_ID may not be null because every order must be for some existing customer.

(A) Referential Integrity *between* Relations

EMPLOYEE (**Employee_ID**, **Supervisor_ID**, Empl_Name,...)
and Supervisor_ID may be null because not all empoyees have supervisors.

(B) Referential Integrity *within* Relation

Supervisor_ID. This field refers to the Employee_ID of the employee's supervisor and should have referential integrity on the Employee_ID field within the same relation.

Null value
A special field value, distinct from 0, blank, or any other value, that indicates that the value for the field is missing or otherwise unknown.

5. *Null value control.* A null value is a special field value, distinct from 0, blank, or any other value, that indicates that the value for the field is missing or otherwise unknown. Sometimes when it is time to enter data—for example, information about a new customer—the customer's fax number is unknown and can have a null value. On the other hand, a value for the Customer_ID field must always be provided. Using a "not null" clause can enforce that Customer_ID not have null values. In fact, DBMSs automatically enforce the "not null" constraint when a primary key is defined. In other cases, the clause must be specified explicitly. For example, because of referential integrity, a customer order should not be entered without knowing an existing Customer_ID value. This constraint can be enforced by using a "not null" clause for the foreign key Customer_ID. SQL queries ignore null values when performing counts or averages. Also, most SQL implementations allow a null value to be replaced by a discrete value at query run time by using a function like the NVL function in Oracle.

DESIGNING PHYSICAL TABLES AND DENORMALIZATION

An object-relational database is a set of related tables. A table can represent the data portion of an entity class. If the relational approach is used, tables are related by foreign keys referencing primary keys. However, if the object-relational approach is used, tables can also be related using references (or pointers). The latter approach is commonly used in object-oriented programming languages like Java, but it is just beginning to find acceptance in the database world. The foreign key approach dominates how tables are related, and is, therefore, the main subject of physical database design.

Earlier, you grouped into a relation those attributes that concern some unifying business concept, such as customer, product, or employee. In contrast, a physical table is a named set of rows and columns that specifies the fields in each row of the table. A physical table might or might not correspond to one relation. Whereas normalized relations possess properties of well-structured relations, the design of a physical table has two goals different from those of normalization: efficient use of primary (main memory) and secondary storage (hard disk), and data processing speed.

The primary storage has far greater speed than the secondary storage; thus, a DBMS attempts to keep data in primary storage whenever possible. In addition, data are processed most efficiently when they are stored close to one another, thereby minimizing the number of operations that must be performed. Typically, the data in one physical table (all the rows and fields in those rows) are stored close together on a disk. If data from separate relations need to be joined, combining them is expensive in terms of primary and secondary storage and central processing unit (CPU) operations, because the tables are likely placed apart.

Denormalization
The process of combining normalized relations into physical tables based on affinity of use of rows and fields, and on retrieval and update frequencies on the tables.

Denormalization is the process of combining normalized relations into physical tables based on affinity of use of rows and fields and based on retrieval and update frequencies on the tables. On the negative side, denormalization increases the chance of errors and inconsistencies that normalization tries to avoid. It optimizes certain data processing functions at the expense of other functions, so if the frequencies of different processing activities change, the benefits of denormalization may no longer exist. In combining different tables, denormalization is most useful when retrievals considerably exceed updates in the table.

Consider the denormalized table shown in Table 11-3. The table combines the data from the tables EMP and DEPT shown in Table 11-1. A query that involves data from both tables now can be answered from one table. Thus, a query to find out employee and department information for the employee WARD can get the information more

Table 11-3 Denormalized Relation.

EMPNO	ENAME	JOB	MGR	HIREDATE	SAL	COKM	DEPTNO	DNAME	LOC
7369	SMITH	CLERK	7902	17-DEC-80	800		20	RESEARCH	DALLAS
7499	ALLEN	SALESMAN	7698	20-FEB-81	1,600	800	30	SALES	CHICAGO
7521	WARD	SALESMAN	7698	22-FEB-81	1,250	500	30	SALES	CHICAGO
7566	JONES	MANAGER	7839	02-APR-81	2,975		20	RESEARCH	DALLAS
7654	MARTIN	SALESMAN	7698	28-SEP-81	1,250	1,600	30	SALES	CHICAGO
7698	BLAKE	MANAGER	7839	01-MAY-81	2,850		30	SALES	CHICAGO
7782	CLARK	MANAGER	7839	09-JUN-81	2,450		20	ACCOUNTING	NEW YORK
7788	SCOTT	ANALYST	7566	19-APR-87	3,000		20	RESEARCH	DALLAS
7839	KING	PRESIDENT		17-NOV-81	5,000	10		ACCOUNTING	NEW YORK
7844	TURNER	SALESMAN	7698	08-SEP-81	1,500	0	30	SALES	CHICAGO
7876	ADAMS	CLERK	7788	23-MAY-87	1,100		20	RESEARCH	DALLAS
7900	JAMES	CLERK	7698	03-DEC-81	950		30	SALES	CHICAGO
7902	FORD	ANALYST	7566	03-DEC-81	3,000		20	RESEARCH	DALLAS
7934	MILLER	CLERK	7782	23-JAN-82	1,300		10	ACCOUNTING	NEW YORK

directly from Table 11-3 than from EMP and DEPT in Table 11-1, where it would first search information in EMP, find Ward's department, and then look up the DEPT table. However, the denormalized table has some problems: It violates the third normal form, there is redundancy in the fields DNAME and LOC, information of department 40 cannot be represented, and there can be update anomalies. Thus, denormalization needs to be considered with an eye on compromise between ease of access, and redundancy and anomalies. Here are three common situations in which denormalization may make sense:

1. **Two entities with a one-to-one relationship.** Figure 11.6 shows student data with optional data from a standard scholarship application a student might complete. In this case, one row object could be formed with five fields from the Student and ScholarshipApplication relations.

   Normalized relations:
   Student(<u>studentId</u>, stuName, application_Id)
   ScholarshipApplication(<u>application_Id</u>, applicationDate, qualifications)
   Denormalized relation:
   Student(<u>student_Id</u>, stuName, application_Id, applicationDate, qualifications)

   The only problem is that fields from the optional entity might have null values in the denormalized relation; in this case, note that each student may not apply for a scholarship. Some wasted space might result from these null values. However, no redundancy or anomaly problems arise because of the merger, and the one-to-one relationship is the ideal scenario for denormalization.

2. **A many-to-many relationship (associative entity class) with nonkey attributes.** Figure 11.7 shows best price quotes for different items from different vendors. In this case, fields from Item and CanSupply relations might be combined into one

Figure 11.6
Denormalization Situation: Two Entity Classes with a One-to-One Relationship

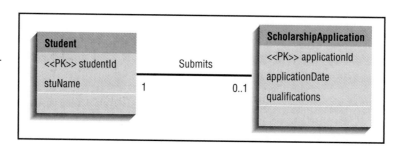

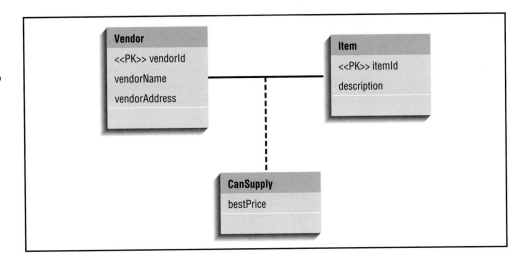

physical table CanSupplyDR. The reason for combining might be that these two tables frequently are accessed together and the join could be avoided.

Normalized relations:
Vendor(<u>vendorId</u>, vendorName, vendorAddress)
Item(<u>itemId</u>, description)
CanSupply(<u>vendorId, itemId</u>, bestPrice)
Denormalized relations:
Vendor(<u>vendorId</u>, vendorName, vendorAddress)
CanSupplyDR(<u>vendorId, itemId</u>, description, bestPrice)

In the denormalized relation CanSupplyDR, the second normal form is violated. (Note that the DR in CanSupplyDR is to distinguish it from CanSupply and is for illustration only; DR stands for "denormalized relation.") This will create duplication of data; the Item fields, such as description, will repeat for each best price quote. Integrity problems can crop up during insertions, updates, and deletions. For example, items that are not supplied by a vendor cannot be listed. In this case, denormalization will be beneficial only if the retrievals far outnumber insertions and updates, and each item is supplied by at least one vendor. Otherwise, denormalization should be avoided in a scenario involving many-to-many relationships with nonkey attributes.

3. **A one-to-many relationship.** Figure 11.8 shows that a customer belongs to a region, and a region can have several customers. In this case, the Region data can be stored in the Customer table. Again, a designer must have an explicit reason based on retrieval and update statistics to denormalize in this situation.

Normalized relations:
Customer(<u>custId</u>, custName, custAddress, custPhone, regionName)
Region(<u>regionName</u>, regionManager)
Denormalized relation:
Customer(<u>custId</u>, custName, custAddress, custPhone, regionName, regionManager)

Figure 11.8
Denormalization
Situation: Two
Entity Classes
with a One-to-
Many Relationship

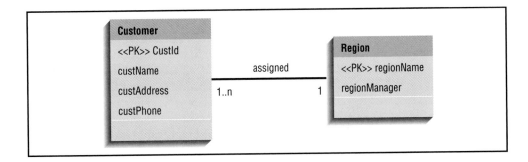

The obvious advantage in combining the tables is that the join is avoided. The disadvantage is that the third normal form is violated, which means that integrity problems can result from insertions and updates. In this case, the value of regionName will repeat if several customers are in a region, and the systems analyst needs to ensure that RegionManager has the same value for a given RegionName. If region managers do not change often, the denormalization might be advantageous. Further, in this case, each region has at least one customer, so all regions are shown in the denormalized relation; if the multiplicity indicated (0..n) suggesting that a region may not have a customer, the denormalized relation will not include regions that have no customers. If this is not a problem, denormalization will be beneficial if the retrievals far outnumber insertions and updates; otherwise, denormalization should be avoided in a scenario involving one-to-many relationships.

FILE ORGANIZATION

File organization
A technique for physically arranging the row objects of a file.

The result of normalization versus denormalization is the definition of one or more physical files. A computer operating system stores data in physical files. A physical file is a named set of table rows kept in secondary storage. Establishing relational terminology, we will use the term *row object* synonymously with table row; when operations capability is added to a row object, we will use the term *object*.

To the operating system such as Windows, Linux, or UNIX, each table may be one file, several tables may be in one file, or the whole database may be in one file, depending on how the database technology and database designer organize the data. The way the operating system arranges table rows in a file is called a file organization. With most database technologies, the systems designer can choose among several organizations for a file. If database designers have a choice, they will choose an organization system for a specific file to provide the following:

1. Fast data retrieval.
2. High throughput for processing transactions.
3. Efficient use of storage space.
4. Minimal need for reorganization.
5. Accommodation of growth.

It is no surprise, therefore, that sophisticated DBMSs provide a number of features so that these multiple requirements can be met. In fact, the file organization topic is so important that several DBMS vendors provide certification in performance and tuning for their software. It becomes especially important when a new system is tested and users find that it runs painfully slow.

It is impossible to provide a detailed description of all the file organization features for performance and tuning provided by a DBMS. In the next several sections, we will provide a summary of the issues to be considered. First, let's study the road map of file organization shown in Figure 11.9. File organization involves the following general steps, some of which are detailed in the following sections:

1. **Estimate row sizes and numbers:** The larger the table is, the more acute the need is to define file organization structures.
2. **Calculate blocking factor and number of blocks:** This step provides the size of tables in terms of number of blocks, which allows a calculation of scan times. A block is a storage size that is a unit of data retrieval.
3. **Calculate scan time of each table:** The scan time of a table is like a benchmark that can be used to determine whether file organization structures are required. If a file organization structure results in query times longer than the scan time, the structure is not required.
4. **Estimate frequencies of Select and Update queries:** The cost of a file organization structure is mainly incurred during update operations, and the benefit is

Figure 11.9
Overview of File
Organization

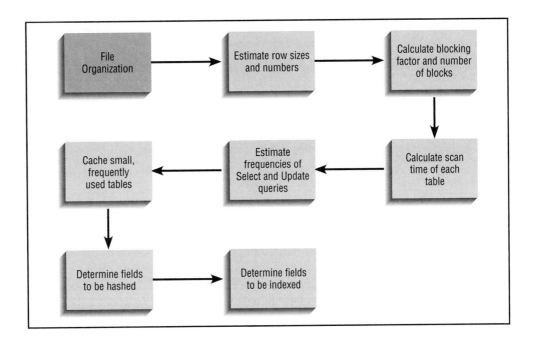

accrued during searches of records. However, note that updates also can involve searches.

5. **Cache small, frequently used tables:** The better DBMSs provide this option, and it is an inexpensive way to speed up queries.

6. **Determine fields to be hashed:** The hashing option, if available, can be used for primary keys that do not need sequential access.

7. **Determine fields to be indexed:** This is the most commonly available option to speed up queries. Indexes allow random and sequential access.

Steps 1 and 4 are to be completed by obtaining requirements input from users. Steps 2 and 3 are covered in the next section after providing an introduction to secondary storage concepts. Step 5 is self-explanatory and is not detailed in subsequent sections. Step 6, because of its limited usage, is covered briefly. Step 7 is covered in detail because contemporary DBMSs depend mainly on indexing to speed up queries. Realistically, one needs to determine use of other file organization structures; these structures include clusters and nested tables, topics that will not be covered in detail in this book.

Secondary Storage Concepts

Database files are stored in secondary storage like a hard disk, which is an electromechanical device. For processing, data are brought into primary storage (main memory), which is an electronic device. The speed differential between primary storage and secondary storage is at least the order of 10^5:1. The hard disk performance is measured in milliseconds (ms). This is considerably slower than main memory performance, which is measured in nanoseconds. Database files are stored in secondary storage because it offers a nonvolatile medium. Primary storage is volatile and susceptible to data loss for several reasons, including power outages, operating system failures, and process failures. Detailed coverage of secondary storage characteristics is available in the textbook *Fundamentals of Database Systems* by Elmasri and Navathe (2003).

How slow is the performance of a hard disk? To estimate this, we have to understand how a hard disk works. In some respects, a hard disk is similar to a CD-ROM. A hard disk is divided into concentric storage areas called tracks. A track is divided into blocks. A block is a unit of data retrieval, which is retrieved under the supervision of the operating system. Based on the block address, a controller mechanism needs to align itself with the right track. The controller then waits until the right

Block
A unit of data retrieval from secondary storage. A block contains row objects.

block on the track on the rotating disk arrives under it and then the block is transferred. Transfer time has three components:

1. **Average seek time:** Depends on the drive and is about 5 ms.
2. **Average rotational delay:** Depends on the rotational speed. If the drive rotates at 7,200 revolutions per minute (i.e., 7,200/60 or 120 revolutions per second), this implies that it takes 8.3 ms for one rotation. The average rotational delay then is 4.15 ms.
3. **Transfer time:** Usually negligible.

The average total time to fetch a block is, therefore, about 10 ms. Note that this is the time if the block is to be fetched at random. If the next block to be retrieved is placed adjoining the previous one and the fetch is thus not random, the fetch time may be approximately zero. This happens if a table needs to be completely scanned. In fact, in DBMSs such as Oracle and DB2, multiple blocks are read together; the number of blocks that can be read together depends on the operating system buffer size. This concept is called sequential prefetch. In such DBMSs, tables are placed in contiguous blocks called extents. If four blocks are read together, the average scan time per block is reduced to approximately (10ms/4) or 2.5 ms. In fact, up to 16 blocks can be read together. We will assume a value of 2.5 ms as the average scan time/block in this and the next sections of this chapter.

The time to scan a table depends on row object size, number of row objects, block size, and average scan time per block. A scan is a complete read of a table. To search a row object for a given value using the scan approach, each row object is checked separately for the value. This is usually an inefficient approach. It is similar to searching for one particular attendee at a large conference by asking each attendee whether that is his or her name (see Figure 11.10). This could take a long time. Scans work well only when all or a large number of row objects need to be looked up to answer the query.

To determine the scan time, the blocking factor is determined first, as well as the total number of blocks in the table. For example, if a table has only 100 row objects, the length of the row object is 400 bytes, and space available in a block is 2,000 bytes; the blocking factor, which is the number of row objects/block, is 2,000/400 or 5, and the number of blocks is (100/5) or 20. The scan time will be 20 × 2.5 ms or 50 ms, a relatively small period. A database, however, has a number of large-sized tables, and the scan times of such tables can be significant.

Suppose a table Person has 1 million row objects, the length of each row object is 100 bytes, block size is 2,000 bytes, the blocking factor is 2,000/100 or 20, and the number of blocks is 1 million/20, or 50,000. The scan time is 50,000 × 2.5 ms, or 125 seconds, a relatively large period and inefficient if a query is searching for only one or a few row objects. However, this scan time is quite reasonable for a query that will use all or a large number of the 1 million objects.

Because a response time of 125 seconds is unacceptable, scanning is generally an unacceptable strategy for online applications. The relational model does not require

Extent
A set of contiguous blocks.

Scan
A complete read of a file block by block, regardless of the number of row objects in the answer to a query.

Blocking factor
The number of row objects that can fit in one block.

Figure 11.10
Scanning Approach of Finding a Person (Joyce Elam) at a Conference

Heap
A file whose row objects are placed in no organized structure.

a storage structure, so row objects can be stored in the order in which they arrive. This structure is called a heap; it means that there is no organized structure. Thus, the heap structure is not acceptable for online applications if a table is large. Consider the following SQL query:

Select PersonName from Person where SSNo = '111-22-3333';

Even though we need only one row object to provide the answer, it will take 125 seconds, or about 2 minutes, without a storage structure. This is not practical. If someone has to wait 2 minutes while another person pulls up his or her record or a Web site performs an authentication, the person waiting will not be happy. Hence, storage structures are needed to speed up such queries.

Although several storage structures are available, the two most common structures are indexing and hashing. Indexing requires a structure that is stored in secondary storage, and hashing is an algorithm to determine a storage address from a search value, which also is called a key. The advantages of indexing are that it provides fast random access, as well as fast sequential address. Hashing provides even faster random access and does not require physical storage; however, it does not provide sequential addresses. Because applications typically require random as well as sequential access, hashing is not as popular as indexing, and some DBMSs do not even provide hashing.

Hashed File Organizations

Hashed file organization
A technique that uses an algorithm to convert a key value into a row address.

In a hashed file organization, the address of each row is determined using an algorithm that converts a key value into a logical row address, which is then translated to a physical row address so that it can be accessed under the supervision of the operating system (see Figure 11.11). Although there are several variations of hashed files, in most cases the rows are located nonsequentially as dictated by the hashing algorithm. Thus, sequential data processing is impractical. On the other hand, random retrieval of rows is fast. Issues arise in the design of hashing file organizations, such as how to handle two primary keys that translate into the same address, but again, these issues are beyond our scope. (See Elmasri and Navathe [2003] for a thorough discussion.)

Indexed File Organizations

Indexed file organization
A storage structure that can enable fast, random, and sequential access.

Database index
A key value and a pointer.

Key
A field or a combination of fields whose values are used for searching row objects.

Pointer
A value that stores the address of a row object for the purpose of linking.

Primary key
A key that has unique values.

How do patrons locate a book in a library? The person can scan through each book, but that would take a long time. A more effective way is to look up the book location in a computerized (or manual) catalog (see Figure 11.12). The catalog search is based on author name, book name, ISBN number, or some other attribute. The catalog uses structures called indexes and provides the location number of a book. The patron then finds the correct floor and the aisle that has the book. This search will take only minutes instead of days.

In an indexed file organization, an index is created that allows the application software to locate individual rows quickly. The table rows generally are stored nonsequentially, although certain storage structures allow rows to be stored sequentially. The index file is stored in secondary storage. A database index is similar to a book index; a book index has a topic and a page number, and a database index has a key and a pointer. A pointer stores the address of a row object. Each entry matches a key value with one or more rows. An index can point to unique rows (a primary key index, such as on the productId field of a Product table) or to more than one row. An index that allows each entry to point to more than one row

Figure 11.11
Hashed File Organization

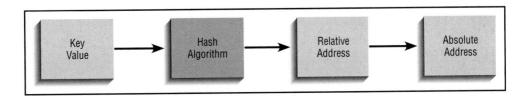

Figure 11.12 Use of Index to Locate a Library Book

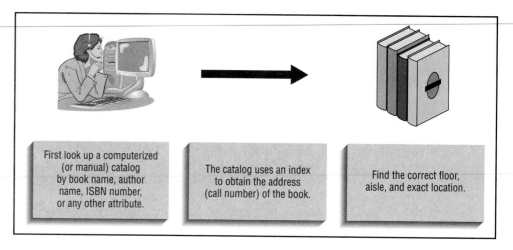

First look up a computerized (or manual) catalog by book name, author name, ISBN number, or any other attribute.

The catalog uses an index to obtain the address (call number) of the book.

Find the correct floor, aisle, and exact location.

Secondary key
A key that is not primary. The values of a secondary key may or may not be unique.

object is called a secondary key index. An example would be an index on the field LastName of Student table. For example, the last name Hernandez can correspond to several students.

Although a book index and a database index are similar in some respects, there is an important difference. A book index is linear; however, a database index usually has the shape of a B+ tree. The B in "B+" stands for balanced, and + indicates that additional properties are associated with the tree data structure. A tree data structure is hierarchical and uses pointers to enable links between one tree node and another.

Random Access Processing Using B+ Tree Indexes

Figure 11.13 shows an example of a B+ tree. Suppose you want to access the row object with the key value 1,600. The root level of the index is checked first. Because 1,600 is greater than 1,250, the right pointer is used to get to the block with entries 1,425 and 2,000. Because 1,600 is between these two values, the middle pointer is used, which takes us to the leaf level block. This block has the key value 1,600. The associated pointer is the address of the row object with the key value 1,600 in the data file, which can now be retrieved. Note that the index scheme ensures that the leaf-level key values are sorted, thus enabling sequential access.

The figure depicts a rather simple representation of the tree because it shows only one or two indexes in a node. A real B+ tree usually will have about 50 to 200

Figure 11.13 Example of a B+ Tree

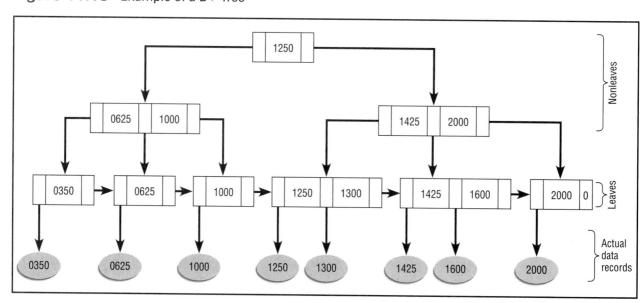

indexes in a node. A node is a block and is generally of the size 2K, 4K, 8K, 16K, or 32K bytes. This allows the tree to fan out quickly and have hundreds of thousands to millions of entries at the leaf level of a three-level index structure. The first level of the tree is called the root. Each entry at the leaf level provides a pointer, which can enable the operating system to retrieve the block that has the desired row object.

Although one can calculate the exact number of accesses required in the case of a database index to retrieve a row object based on a primary key value, the number is generally about three (about 3×10 ms or 30 ms/random access a in time period, given a 10-ms random access time per block). Because of the fan-out property of a B+ tree, the number of levels of a B+ tree rarely exceeds three. Assuming a three-level B+ tree, fetching a row object entails traversing the three levels, getting the pointer from the last level, and using the pointer address to obtain the required block. This requires four accesses in a three-level B+ tree; however, it is safe to assume that the root level of an index usually lies in the database cache in the memory. Therefore, the secondary storage accesses are restricted to two in the index and one in the data files; hence, the number of accesses is practically (2+1), or 3, and the time is 30 ms. In practice, the access time is likely to be even less than 30 ms because modern databases allocate a lot of space to database cache, which minimizes disk accesses.

Note that the scan time of a file is proportional to the size of the file. However, the time to access a row object based on an index is practically independent of the size of the file. Let's revisit the query that searches for one row object in a file of 1 million row objects:

Select PersonName from PERSON where SSNo = '111-22-3333';

If the storage structure is heap, the DBMS needs to scan the table. This takes 125 seconds as calculated earlier. Contrast it with the indexed approach. If the block size is 4K, the size of a value of SSNo is 9 bytes, and the pointer size is 6 bytes, the index size is (9 + 6), or 15 bytes, and the number of indexes in a block is (4,000/15), or 266.

Fan-out ratio
The number of indexes in a block.

Assuming a fill factor of 75 percent (index blocks in a B+ tree vary from 50 percent full to 100 percent full), the effective fan-out ratio is (0.75 × 266), or approximately 200. The fan-out ratio is the number of indexes in a block. Assuming 200 indexes in each block, the maximum number of row objects that can be accessed in a three-level index can be calculated. The root level has 200 index entries. The second level will have 200 blocks, each with 200 index entries; in total, there will be 200 × 200, or 40,000 index entries. The third level will have 40,000 × 200, or 8 million entries. Thus, if the number of row objects in the PERSON table is between 40,001 and 8 million, the B+ tree needs three levels. (Extrapolating, if the number of row objects is between 8,000,001 and 1.6 billion, the B+ tree needs four levels.) With three levels, the estimated retrieval time is three accesses, or 30 ms. With four levels, the estimated retrieval time is 40 ms. It is evident that the time to access one row object based on an index is robust to changes in the number of row objects in the table. To summarize, assume that for practically all large tables, a random access for a row object will take about three accesses.

Sequential Processing Using Indexes

Because the leaf level of a B+ tree is sorted based on key values, indexing facilitates sequential access. Sequential access is required in two kinds of queries: queries based on a secondary key, and queries based on a range. The most common query based on a secondary query has the condition *<field name = value>*. (Calculations are shown for the time associated with secondary storage access only. This is the dominant portion of the total query time. For the sake of simplicity, the CPU and the main memory portion of the query time are ignored.) For example, consider the following query:

Select * from EMPLOYEE where empLName = 'Chawla';

If only one row object matches the last name Chawla, what is the time taken assuming that there are three levels of B+ tree based on empLName index? As has been discussed, the retrieval time requires three accesses, and the time is 30 ms (i.e., 20 ms to find the entry in the index file and 10 ms to fetch the row object from the file). Note that the access time for the root level is not considered. You can consider

Figure 11.14
Sequential Processing
for Equality Condition
Using Indexes

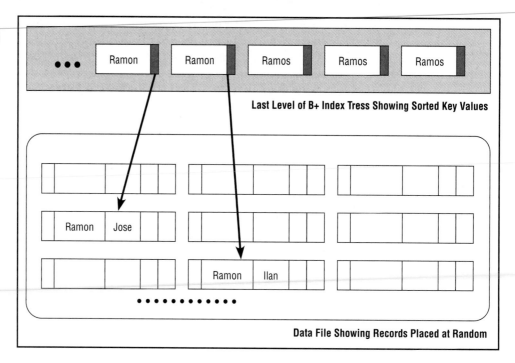

Last Level of B+ Index Tress Showing Sorted Key Values

Data File Showing Records Placed at Random

the time as $(2 + 1) \times 10$ ms, where the 2 is the number of levels in the B+ tree less 1, and 1 is the number of row objects retrieved. Now consider the following query:

Select * from EMPLOYEE where EmpLName = 'Ramon';

Suppose two row objects qualify this condition. Is the retrieval time 2×30 ms? No. Because an index sorts the values at the leaf level of the B+ tree, the key value entries for the two row objects will be next to each other, and in all probability, in the same index block. This is shown pictorially in Figure 11.14. Having found the first index entry in two accesses, the additional access time is based on the two fetches from the data file. Note that the index entries for "Ramon" are adjacent, but the row objects can be anywhere in the data file. Therefore, the total time is 40 ms.

Now consider the following query:

Select * from EMPLOYEE where EmpLName = 'Brown';

The first index entry, as usual, is found in two accesses. Let's assume that 10 employees have the last name Brown. There is a good likelihood that all 10 index entries are in the same leaf-level index block. The 10 row objects can be retrieved from the data file using the 10 associated pointers. Therefore, the total access time is 20 ms + $(10 \times 10$ ms), or 120 ms.

A pattern is emerging: To retrieve n row objects, the total time is 20 ms + $n \times 10$ ms, or $(n + 2) \times 10$ ms. If n is large, the formula approximates to $n \times 10$ ms, or $n/100$ seconds. Can n become very large, thereby deteriorating the time taken to complete a query? Yes, n, the number of row objects retrieved to satisfy a query, can become large if the number of distinct values of a field is small. The number of distinct values of a primary key is equal to the number of row objects and is the largest possible number of distinct values in a given table. Last names (say, in an Employee table) also have a large number of distinct values, but because several employees might have the same last name, this number is smaller than the number of row objects in a table. However, a field like gender has only two distinct values— male and female. Consider the following query:

Select avg(Salary) from EMPLOYEE where Gender = 'Female';

Assuming a company has 100,000 employees and an equal split between males and females, the number of row objects required to satisfy the query is 100,000/2, or 50,000. The time taken will be $n/100$, or 50,000/100, or 500 seconds. However, the scan time for the table is less than 500 seconds. Assuming a blocking factor of 20, the number of blocks is 100,000/20, or 5,000 blocks. The scan time is $5,000 \times 2.5$ ms, or 12.5 seconds. In this case, it's better to scan (time = 12.5 seconds) than to use the index (time = 500 seconds).

Because the Gender index does not provide any benefit, it should not be defined. A sophisticated DBMS has the intelligence to estimate such costs (in terms of time and resources) and not to use an index even though it has been defined. This does not imply that designers need not put in the effort to determine which fields should not be indexed. There is another reason an index should be avoided if it is unlikely to yield a query processing time lower than is offered by a simple scan. When using indexes, there is a trade-off between improved performance due to retrievals and degrading performance due to inserts, deletions, and updates to the rows in a file. Each time a row object is added to a table, the index segments for the table need to be updated. This overhead can be significant if many indexes are defined. Thus, an index should not be defined for a field that has a small number of distinct values.

Processing Range Queries Using Indexes

A range query is of the form <attribute between value1 and value2>, where value1 and value2 define the lower and upper limit (or upper limit and lower limit). Because the leaf level of an index is sorted, sequential processing can be performed. Consider the following query:

Select * from STUDENT where GPA between 3.90 and 4.00;

Figure 11.15 illustrates how the query can be processed using an index based on grade point average (GPA). On the last level of the B+ tree, GPA entries will be in ascending order. The figure shows a block that has three entries between 3.90 and 4.00: 3.93, 3.93, and 3.97. The row objects corresponding to these entries may be randomly distributed in the data file. However, sequential processing on the range is possible because of the index.

Is an index always beneficial in range queries? To answer this, let's consider an example from the EMPLOYEE table.

Select * from EMPLOYEE where Salary between 50000 and 60000;

Assuming salary is uniformly distributed and the range is $10,000 to $210,000, the proportion of row objects satisfying the condition is $(60,000 - 50,000)/(210,000 - 10,000)$, or $10,000/200,000$, or 5 percent. This proportion also is called selectivity. With 100,000 row objects, the number of row objects satisfying the condition is $100,000 \times 5$ percent, or 5,000, and the resulting time is $5,000 \times (10/1,000)$, or 50 seconds when using an index. With a scan time of 12.5 seconds, the query can be answered faster by scanning.

Figure 11.15
Sequential Processing for Range Queries Using Indexes

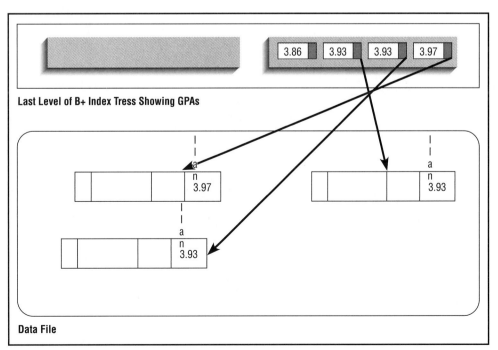

Last Level of B+ Index Tress Showing GPAs

Data File

However, if the salary range in the query is $50,000 to $51,000, the selectivity is (51,000 − 50,000)/(210,000 − 10,000), or 1,000/200,000, or 0.5 percent. With 100,000 row objects, the number of row objects satisfying the condition is 100,000 × 0.5 percent, or 500, and the query processing time when using the Salary index is 500 × (10/1,000), or 5 seconds, which is better than the 12.5 seconds from scanning the table. Thus, as the range decreases, the time taken for the query decreases proportionately if an index is used. Thus, indexing becomes more attractive as the range span specified in the query becomes smaller. A DBMS can estimate the time when using an index, and make a decision on whether an index is to be used or not.

The aforementioned analysis assumes that the attribute Salary is distributed uniformly. This assumption might not hold in practice. Many DBMSs can provide better estimates by recording the distribution of values. Such detailed analysis is beyond the scope of this book.

Heuristics for Using Indexes

Certain heuristics determine whether or not an index needs to be defined for a given attribute or combinations of attributes. The heuristics are represented using the diagram in Figure 11.16. We list these heuristics, but the savvy analyst should consider performing a detailed cost analysis in order to make accurate decisions.

1. **Specify a unique index for the primary key of each table (file).** This selection ensures the uniqueness of primary key values and speeds retrieval based on those values. Random retrieval based on primary key value is common for answering multitable queries and for simple data maintenance tasks such as inserting, deleting, and updating.
2. **Don't index an attribute other than the primary key for small, frequently used tables.** Preferably, place these tables in database cache, that is, the main memory allocated for data.
3. **Don't index an attribute other than the primary key for remaining small tables.** The scan times of these tables are small.

Figure 11.16 Heuristics for Indexing

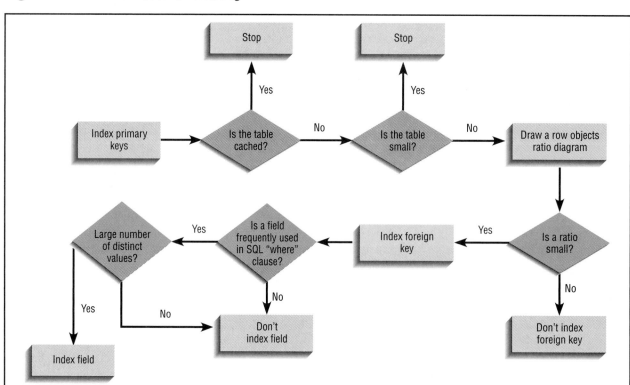

Figure 11.17
Row Objects Ratio
Diagram

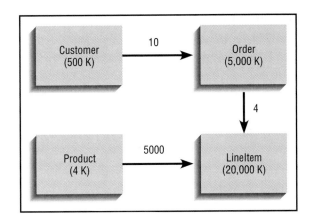

4. **Specify an index for a foreign key if a restriction on a value of the key results in a small number of row objects.** This can be determined easily by drawing a row objects ratio diagram, which shows the number of row objects of a many-side entity class that, on average, join with one row object of the one-side entity class. Foreign keys are the sites of joins, and indexes can potentially increase the processing of multitable queries if the ratios are small. Later, Figure 11.17 shows such a diagram for the PVF WebStore case.

5. **Specify an index for a nonkey field if it is used frequently to retrieve data and if the number of distinct values is high.** The latter condition ensures that a small number of row objects is retrieved. For example, last names usually have high distinct values, and the field is a good candidate for indexing. If range queries are used frequently, index the attribute if the range is likely to be small. For example, salary is a good candidate if the queries using salary as a range condition are frequent, and the salary range is small.

The heuristics presented previously pertain to relational query processing. Some of the strategies and heuristics discussed will be modified slightly when we consider object-relational features. However, you should have gained enough knowledge to make an initial attempt at the physical database design of any business application. Calculations will be based on parameters obtained from the vendors of the hardware and software. Further, increasing main memory can reduce retrievals from secondary storage considerably, thereby reducing response times. The decisions made in this initial attempt need to be examined again after conducting test runs. Several tools can provide assistance in tuning an application. These tools will continue to help the systems analyst make alterations after the system has gone into production.

DESIGN OF OBJECT-RELATIONAL FEATURES

Generalization
A relationship between a more general (or a parent) class and a more specific (or a child) class, where the more specific class has additional attributes or operations.

Object-relational DBMSs support features such as generalization, aggregation, multivalued attributes, object identifiers, relationship by reference, and support of large objects. Further, extensions, which are sometimes called cartridges, can be installed to handle special applications like spatial data. The object-oriented features gradually are being incorporated in relational DBMSs, and this section provides a brief discussion and illustration of some of these features from a design perspective. It also examines how these design features can affect query-processing efficiency.

Inheritance
The mechanism by which the more specific class includes the attributes and operations of the more general class.

Generalization

Generalization, based on inheritance, is supported in Oracle, Informix, and some other object-relational DBMSs. We use Oracle 9i/10g syntax for designing supertype/subtype relationships.

```
create type EMP_TYPE as object (
empNo number,
empName varchar2(50),
empAddress varchar2(100)
)
not final;
create type HOURLY_EMP_TYPE under EMP_TYPE (
hourlyRate number
);
create table HOURLY_EMP of HOURLY_EMP_TYPE;
insert into HOURLY_EMP values
(100,'Rick Husband','100 Memorial Drive',70);
```

In this case, HOURLY_EMP_TYPE is a subtype of EMP_TYPE, which is defined as "not final" because subtypes will be created under it. The HOURLY_EMP table inherits the attributes from EMP_TYPE, and an object can thus be inserted in the table. The implementation of generalization is done by the ORDBMS using pointers. If a specialized object needs to be built and it uses data from the generalized object or objects, the DBMS will look up the database cache first, and if the data are not found, it will use the pointers. Each time a pointer is used, it translates to one random access.

Aggregation

Aggregation
An association that models a whole-part relationship between an aggregate, which is called whole, and its parts. It is a strong form of association in which the aggregate has no meaning without parts.

Aggregation is a strongly bound association. If two objects are strongly bound and an operation is performed on one, it is likely that the same operation is applied to the other. For example, if an ORDER object is retrieved, chances are that LINEITEMs are likely to be retrieved, too. One option is to cluster the objects (i.e., place them in close physical proximity).

```
create table ORDER_Table
(OrderNo varchar2(10),
OrderDate Date)
Cluster ORDERLINEITEM(OrderNo);
create table LINEITEM_Table
(OrderNo varchar2(10),
ProdNo varchar2(6),
ActualPrice Number,
Quantity Number)
Cluster ORDERLINEITEM(OrderNo);
create index ORDERLINEITEMndx
on cluster ORDERLINEITEM;
```

In this case, the two tables are clustered by the field OrderNo. Also, a clustered index is created to facilitate rapid access. This can improve significantly the time taken to process the following kind of query, which is required to display information about an order:

```
Select O.OrderNo, O.OrderDate, L.ProdNo, L.ActualPrice, L.Quantity
From ORDER_Table O, LINEITEM_Table L
Where O.OrderNo = L.OrderNo and O.Orderno=12345678;
```

Note that once the order object is accessed, the line items are likely to be found in the same block and will not require extra time. This implies that the query can be completed in the time required for random access of one object (i.e., 30 ms). How will the time change if information such as Description is needed from the PRODUCT table? Because PRODUCT is not clustered with ORDER and LINEITEM, individual products will have to be looked up using indexes, each taking 30 ms. If there are 10 line items, this look-up time will be 10×30 ms, or another 300 ms. Several solutions will reduce this time. One option is to permanently cache the PRODUCT table if it is not unusually large. If the table is large, the analyst might need to denormalize and redundantly store the most frequently used PRODUCT fields such as Description and ListPrice in LINEITEM. An alternative would be to simply live with the slightly longer retrieval time, which would be less than 1 second in almost all cases.

Aggregation also can be designed by creating a nested table. It is possible to create the LINEITEM table as a kind of varying array of rows within the ORDER table. The nested table is defined as a column within the main table. The data for LINEITEM will be stored separately from ORDER, and the relationship will be maintained by using pointers. This organization also provides convenient access from an order object to the joining line item objects; specifically, it will take just one access using the pointer. However, LINEITEM is also related to PRODUCT, and it might not be convenient to link the two. A nested table is a reasonable aggregation option when the nested table is not related to other tables. For a detailed discussion and illustration of nested tables, refer to Loney and Koch (2005).

Multivalued Attributes

In the case of a nested table approach, multiple rows of the nested table correspond to one row of the main table. In the case of multivalued attributes, multiple values of an attribute correspond to one row of a table. Multivalued attributes are not allowed in the traditional relational model, so implementation of this feature represents a significant move away from pure relational systems and toward object-relational systems. However, multivalued attributes can be handled in the traditional relational way (i.e., creating an additional table) if a significant number of queries are based on the multivalued attribute. In this way, object-relational systems can provide a choice between the best relational and the object-oriented features.

In Oracle, multivalued attributes are handled by varying arrays defined by using the VARRAY type:

```
create type PHONE_VA as varray(10) of VARCHAR2(12);
create table CONTACT
(name varchar2(50),
phones PHONE_VA);
```

```
insert into CONTACT VALUES
('Ilan Ramon', PHONE_VA('505-555-1234','684-555-8901','788-555-2222'));
```

However, the syntax can be confusing if queries are based on phone values. For example, to list the phone numbers, the following SQL command is required:

```
select c.name, n.*
from contact c, table(c.phones) n
```

Name	Column_Value
Ilan Ramon	505-555-1234
Ilan Ramon	684-555-8901
Ilan Ramon	788-555-2222

Similarly, conditions can be specified:

```
select c.name, n.*
from contact c, table(c.phones) n
where n.column_value = '505-555-1234'
```

Name	Column_Value
Ilan Ramon	505-555-1234

However, this SQL syntax might be unfamiliar to developers, and if frequent queries are made based on a multivalued attribute, the designer needs to make a choice between creating a separate table for the attribute, which is the traditional relational approach, and the object-relational approach, which is presented here. Further, the designer needs to ensure that such queries will work in the implementation environment. For example, if client-server architecture is being used and the technologies at the client and at the server belong to different vendors, the designer needs to consider the issue of connectivity using the available middleware, which is the software that enables client software from one vendor to communicate with server software from a different vendor.

The performance benefit in the case of multivalued attributes is obvious. The multivalued attribute is part of the table, and a join is not needed between the original table and a separate table created because of a multivalued attribute. When the object is retrieved, so is the multivalued attribute. This results in efficient query processing. Having said this, until this implementation matures, the analyst might want to consider other ways of handling multivalued attributes. For example, in the case of customer phone numbers, if three fields—office phone, home phone, and cell phone—are created, a multivalued attribute does not need to be defined. The analyst can model this scenario by using three fields.

Object Identifier

Object identifier
A unique value assigned for identity purposes by a software such as an ORDBMS or a programming language when an object is first created. Identity is the property of an object that makes it distinct even if the state is the same as that of another object.

A conventional relational table has rows and columns. A table that is based on an object type has row objects. Each row object has an object identifier, which is assigned by the ORDBMS when the row is created and cannot be altered during the life of the row.

Earlier in this section, we created a table HOURLY_EMP based on an object. Its object identifier can be obtained by using the REF function:

select REF(E), EmpName from HOURLY_EMP E

Ref(E)	Empname
00002802099E6D3A80CB784A859308C4BA9205822A567E6C5B5C3F4 F10AD3D1A40B22742AE0040C92A00	Rick Husband

One will immediately observe the length of the reference, which consists of 86 characters. Although identity and uniqueness are guaranteed, developers who are used to primary keys (which are usually numbers) fewer than 10 or 15 bytes in length might find this reference unwieldy and inefficient. Imagine a customer reading out 86 characters on the phone so that the row object can be fetched! What does this mean for real applications?

The object identifier is actually used only for maintaining relationships by using references. You will never use the actual value of the identifier in a query. You will thus have two primary keys—one an object identifier, and the second a traditional primary key likely generated by using a sequence. Most business applications will employ the traditional mode for providing values for most queries. The object identifier can be used for establishing relationships. Just as relational systems establish relationships by using primary and foreign keys, object-oriented systems establish relationships by using references.

Relationship by Reference

Relationship can be established by using references (i.e., pointers). Before defining such a relationship, the referred table needs to be defined as an object so that it has object identifiers for its row objects. In this example, we choose CUSTOMER as the table to which references will be made from the ORDER table. Because CUSTOMER is based on the CUSTOMER_TY object, the rows inserted in CUSTOMER will have object identifiers.

```
create type CUSTOMER_TY as object
(lastName varchar2(25),
```

```
firstName varchar2(25),
creditLimit Number);
```

create table CUSTOMER of CUSTOMER_TY;

```
insert into CUSTOMER values
(CUSTOMER_TY('Scobee','Francis',20000));
insert into CUSTOMER values
(CUSTOMER_TY('Smith','Michael',15000));
insert into CUSTOMER values
(CUSTOMER_TY('McNair','Ronald',18000));
```

```
create table ORDER
(ordNo Number,
cust REF CUSTOMER_TY);
```

A reference can now be inserted into ORDER for the CUSTOMER who placed this order by using the function REF. This allows us later to retrieve CUSTOMER row objects directly from ORDER by using the DEREF function. Note that a join is not required. Also, the retrieval will be faster than an index because the pointer to the customer row object is available in the ORDER row.

```
insert into ORDER
select 1000, REF(C)
from CUSTOMER C
where LastName = 'Smith';
select * from ORDER;
```

Ordno	Cust
1000	000022020879565D86CF3D42BF9B70845D571395944FA65D9854A0452DA4D 10FB5DA24CB6B

```
select DEREF(O.CUST) from ORD O
where Ordno = 1000;
```

Lastname	Firstname	Creditlimit
'Smith'	'Michael'	15,000

The relationship by reference method provides a fast way to access, for example, a CUSTOMER object from an ORDER object; it takes one access instead of the three accesses required by an index. But what about getting to the ORDER object or objects determined by the restrict condition (e.g., OrdNo = 1000)? The latter access entails access via index.

PHYSICAL DATABASE DESIGN OF PVF WEBSTORE

In Chapter 8, we obtained the following object relations for the PVF WebStore case:
  Customer(custId, custName, custAddress, custEmail, <<Multivalued>>custPhone, custCredit, custLogin, custPW)
  Order(ordId, ordDate, <<Derived>> subTotal, shippingCharge, <<Derived>>tax, <<Derived>> totalAmount, custId)
  Lineitem(ordId, prodId, quantity, actualPrice, <<Derived>> lineAmount)
  Product(prodId, prodName, prodDesc, prodListPrice)
Suppose the following information is given for each table:

Table Name	No. of Row Objects	Size of Each Row Object in Bytes
Customer	500,000	200
Order	5,000,000	100
Lineitem	20,000,000	40
Product	4,000	200

Table 11-4
PVF WebStore Table Characteristics.

TABLE NAME	NO. OF ROWS	SIZE OF EACH ROW IN BYTES	BLOCKING FACTOR (BF)	NO. OF BLOCKS	SCAN TIME (SECONDS)	INDEXES REQUIRED?
CUSTOMER	500,000	200	20	25,000	62.5	Yes
ORDER	5,000,000	100	40	125,000	312.5	Yes
LINEITEM	20,000,000	40	100	200,000	500	Yes
PRODUCT	4,000	200	20	200	0.5	No

Let's assume that the analyst has selected a block size of 4 K (4,096 bytes) with available space of 4,000 bytes. In the case of the Customer table, the blocking factor will be 4,000/200, or 20. The size of the Customer table in blocks is 500,000/20, or 25,000. The scan time of Customer is 2,500 * 2.5 ms, or 62,500 ms, or 62.5 seconds. Similarly, calculations can be performed for the three remaining tables (see Table 11-4).

The aforementioned calculations indicate that Customer, Order, and Lineitem are large tables and will need indexes to speed up queries. Product, which requires only 200 blocks, can be cached in the buffers of the database server. Even if is not cached, the scan time is only 0.5 seconds, and it is not necessary to index any attribute other than the primary key. Table 11-4 can thus help the analyst make some broad design decisions. Figure 11.17 can offer guidance in determining indexes on foreign keys. The figure shows the ratio of number of rows in the "many" side to the "one side." This ratio is the *average* number of row objects of the "many" side that join with one row of the "one side." For example, on an average, a customer has 10 orders, and with such a low value, Order.custId is a good candidate for indexing.

The following are some design recommendations:

1. Index the four primary keys—custId, ordId, (ordId, prodId), and prodId—of the four tables. A primary key is usually the most frequently accessed attribute. When any value is entered in a primary key field, we need to check whether the same value already exists. Also, a referential integrity check requires looking up the primary key. A primary key can contain more than one attribute, for example (ordId, prodId). In this case, the corresponding index is also joint.
2. Cache the table Product.
3. Index foreign keys that have a large number of distinct values. Foreign keys are sites for joins and are used frequently for retrieval. It is obvious that Order.custId and Lineitem.ordId are good candidates for indexing because of high distinct values and low ratios. For example, if custId needs to be looked up in Order, it will lead to 10 orders since the ratio is 10. However, for Lineitem.prodId, the ratio, 5,000, is relatively high. Should we index on this foreign key? The scan time for Lineitem is 500 seconds. Indexing results in a retrieval time of (5,000 + 2) *10 ms, or about 50 seconds. Therefore, indexing still provides much faster time. The decision will depend on whether enough queries require a join of Product.prodId with Lineitem.prodId, because indexing incurs the overhead cost of maintaining the B+ tree during insert, updates, and deletions.
4. Index nonkey attributes that are accessed frequently and have a relatively large number of distinct values. CustName and CustLogin are obvious choices.

The issue of joins is not covered in detail. However, the heuristics described in this section also should help in efficient processing of joins. For detailed coverage of this topic, refer to the book by Elmasri and Navathe (2003).

The calculations shown in this chapter are conservative because the general assumption is that main memory is limited. We recommend that, given the affordable prices, systems analysts canvass for a large amount of main memory in order to have a large database cache. Consider testing of the physical database design as a priority item. Finally, analysts should use tools to monitor and tune the various characteristics of the database.

KEY POINTS REVIEW

1. **Before designing physical files and databases, what information is needed and from whom?**

   From the users, you need to know the following: descriptions of where and when data are used, frequencies of retrieval and update, and requirements for response time and throughput. From the analysts, you need to obtain the list of entity classes along with their estimates. From the DBMS vendor, you need to obtain the documentation that lists the storage structures and object-oriented features available.

2. **What are the main objectives when selecting a data type?**

   The four objectives are as follows: minimize storage space, represent all possible values of the field, improve data integrity for the field, and support all data manipulations desired on the field.

3. **How can you control data integrity?**

   The five popular data-integrity control methods are default value, format control, range control, referential integrity, and null value control.

4. **What is denormalization? What are the main advantages and disadvantages of denormalization?**

   Denormalization is the process of combining normalized relations into physical tables based on affinity of use of rows and fields, and on retrieval and update frequencies on the tables. Denormalization can result in better response times and throughput. On the negative side, denormalization increases the chance of errors and inconsistencies that normalization tries to avoid.

5. **What objectives does a designer try to achieve in choosing file organization structures?**

   A designer tries to achieve the following objectives: fast data retrieval, high throughput for processing transactions, efficient use of storage space, minimum need for reorganization, and accommodation of growth in the size of the tables.

6. **What is a table scan? When is a scan useful? When does it fail? When is hashing useful? When does it fail? When is indexing useful? When does it fail?**

   A scan is a complete read of a table. Scanning works for small tables, but it is not useful for large tables. Structures such as indexes and hash schemes need to be defined. Hashing provides fast random access but fails when sequential access is required. Indexing provides fast random, and fast or reasonably fast, sequential access in certain cases.

7. **List the heuristics for using indexes to provide better response times and throughput.**

   The main heuristics for using indexes to provide better response times and throughput are: Specify a unique index for the primary key of each table (file); don't index an attribute other than the primary key for small, frequently used tables; don't index an attribute other than the primary key for the remaining small tables; specify an index for a foreign key if a restriction on a value of the key results in a small number of row objects; and specify an index for a non-key field if it is used frequently to retrieve data and if the number of distinct values is high.

8. **What is aggregation? What options do you have to implement aggregation?**

   Aggregation is a strongly bound association. If two objects are strongly bound and an operation is performed on one, it is likely that the same operation is applied to the other. One option is to cluster the objects (i.e., place them physically in close proximity). Another option is to create a nested table.

KEY TERMS CHECKPOINT

Here are the key terms from the chapter. The page where each term is first explained is in parentheses after the term.

a. Aggregation (p. 324)
b. Block (p. 315)
c. Blocking factor (p. 316)
d. Computer or derived field (p. 309)
e. Composite attribute (p. 307)
f. Constructor (p. 309)
g. Data type (p. 309)
h. Database index (p. 317)
i. Default value (p. 310)
j. Denormalization (p. 311)
k. Extent (p. 316)
l. Fan-out ratio (p. 319)
m. Field (p. 307)
n. File organization (p. 314)
o. Format (or input mask or picture) (p. 310)
p. Generalization (p. 323)
q. Hashed file organization (p. 317)
r. Heap (p. 317)
s. Indexed file organization (p. 317)

t. Inheritance (p. 323)	x. Physical database design (p. 303)	bb. Secondary key (p. 318)
u. Key (p. 317)	y. Pointer (p. 317)	cc. Structured query language
v. Null value (p. 311)	z. Primary key (p. 317)	(SQL) (p. 304)
w. Object identifier (p. 326)	aa. Scan (p. 316)	

Match each of the key terms above with the definition that best fits it.

1. A key that has unique values.
2. A technique that uses an algorithm to convert a key value into a row address.
3. A complete read of a file block by block regardless of the number of row objects required to answer a query.
4. The process of splitting or combining normalized relations into physical tables based on affinity of use of rows and fields and based on retrieval and update frequencies on the tables.
5. The value a field will assume unless an explicit value is entered for the field.
6. The smallest unit of named application data recognized by system software.
7. A file whose row objects are placed in no organized structure.
8. A unit of data retrieval from secondary storage.
9. A field or a combination of fields whose values are used for searching row objects.
10. A unique value assigned for identity purposes by software such as an ORDBMS or a programming language when an object is first created.
11. A value that stores the address of a row object for the purpose of linking.
12. A field that can be derived from other database fields.
13. An attribute composed of multiple fields.
14. The number of row objects that can fit in one block.
15. A special field value, distinct from zero, blank, or any other value, that indicates that the value for the field is missing or otherwise unknown.

16. A key that is not primary.
17. A technique for physically arranging the row objects of a file.
18. A set of contiguous blocks.
19. A storage structure that can enable fast, random, and sequential access.
20. An operation that creates and initializes an instance of a class.
21. A coding scheme recognized by system software for representing organizational data.
22. A pattern of codes that restricts the width and possible values for each position within a field.
23. The standard language used for creating and querying tables in relational databases.
24. An association that models a whole-part relationship between an aggregate, which is called whole, and its parts. It is a strong form of association in which the aggregate has no meaning without parts.
25. A key and a pointer.
26. The number of indexes in a block.
27. A relationship between a more general (or a parent) class and a more specific (or a child) class, where the more specific class has additional attributes or operations.
28. The mechanism by which the more specific class includes the attributes and operations of the more general class.
29. Part of database design that deals with efficiency considerations for access of data.

REVIEW QUESTIONS

1. What is the purpose of denormalization?
2. What factors influence the decision to create an index on a field?
3. What are the factors that should be considered in selecting a file organization?
4. What information is needed to perform physical database design?
5. Describe a situation where denormalization would be beneficial. Conversely, describe another situation where denormalization would be harmful.
6. When is a heap structure preferred? When should the heap structure be avoided?
7. Compare a book index and a B+ tree database index.
8. Why should primary keys be indexed?
9. When should foreign keys be indexed?
10. When should keys that are nonprimary and nonforeign be indexed?
11. What are the various ways to address multivalued attributes?

PROBLEMS AND EXERCISES

1. Consider the following database. Assume that sequential access time is 3 ms and random access time is 10 ms. The size of a block is 4 K, 4,000 bytes are available for data. Response time greater than 2 seconds is considered undesirable for online applications. A database has the following number of row objects and the size of a row object in each table:

Table	Rows	Length
Customer:	20,000	200 bytes
Order:	500,000	100 bytes
Ordline:	4,000,000	40 bytes
Product:	1,000	100 bytes
PurchOrd:	4,000	200 bytes
POrdLine:	100,000	40 bytes
Vendor:	100	200 bytes

Assume all primary keys are indexed. Ignoring primary key considerations, which tables need to be considered for indexing nonkey attributes? Assume attributes for each table. Which attributes are good candidates for indexing?

2. Consider the following database. The row objects' count and size are provided after the structure.

Inst(inst#, iName, iDept)	4,000; 100 bytes
Student(stu#, stuName, sMajor, sGpa)	100,000; 400 bytes
Course(ref#, cCode, cTitle, cLevel, cHrs)	1,000; 100 bytes
Teach(ref#, semCode, inst#, cap, count1)	10,000; 100 bytes
Enroll(stu#, ref#, semCode, grade, points)	4,000,000; 100 bytes

The block size has 4,000 bytes available. Consider query times longer than 1 second as undesirable for online processing. Assume the following as the number of average distinct values: iDept has 200 values; stuName: has 50,000; semCode: has 10 values

The time to read a block is 10 ms for random access when using an index and 3 ms when performing a scan. Consider access through the following five attributes in a single-table query with restrict condition of type attribute = value:
(e.g., Select * from Inst where idept = 'DSIS')
Show calculations for each field, and decide whether you need to have an index on each of the following five fields:
a. iDept
b. stuName
c. Enroll.stu#
d. Enroll.ref#
e. Teach.semCode

3. Consider the following database:
Patient(patNo, patLastname, patFirstName, patDtBirth, patCity, patState, patInsCo)
Item(itemNo, itemName, standardCharge, itemAccount)
Usage(transactionNum, patNo, itemNo, actCharge, dtUsage, timeUsage)
Number of row objects are: Patient: 1,000,000; Item: 10,000; Usage: 10,000,000
Size of row objects in bytes are: Patient: 200; Item: 100; Usage: 40
Block size is 4 K. Available space for join in memory is 250 blocks. There are 500 insurance companies (patInsCo), 100 item accounts, and 100 date usages (i.e., distinct values).
Consider each attribute and determine whether it needs an index. Make suitable assumptions, if required.

4. Consider the following database:
Student(stuId, stuName, stuMajor, stuAddress, status)
Enroll(stuId, classId, grade)
Class(classId, classCode, className, instNo, Term, Year, cap, creditHours)
Instructor(instNo, instName, officeAddr, officePhone)
Major(stuMajor, advisor, contactNo)
Assume block size is 2,000 bytes, scan time for a block is 3 ms, and random access time is 10 ms.

Assume the following count and size of row objects:

Student: 200,000; 200 bytes
Class: 4,000; 100 bytes
Enroll: 2,000,000; 40 bytes
Instructor: 1,000; 100 bytes
Major: 100; 40 bytes

Status has 10 distinct values. No other information is provided. Ignore the primary keys. Which fields need to be indexed? Make suitable assumptions, if required.

DISCUSSION QUESTIONS

1. Talk to MIS professionals at a variety of organizations to find out how they conduct physical database design. What structures do they employ? Who is responsible for physical database design? Determine to what extent these professionals are using object-oriented features mentioned in this chapter for data modeling. Does the use of object-oriented features create any problems?

2. Talk to MIS professionals at a variety of organizations to find out whether they conduct denormalization. Do they violate normal forms? What factors impact their decisions?

3. Perform a Web search for tools that help conduct physical database design.

CASE: BROADWAY ENTERTAINMENT COMPANY, INC.

Designing the Physical Database for the Customer Relationship Management System

Case Introduction

The students from St. Claire Community College are beginning the technical design steps for MyBroadway, the Web-based customer relationship management system for Broadway Entertainment Company stores. They have the object relations from a previous step. In an earlier iteration, they had developed a small prototype of the MyBroadway system using Microsoft Access. They will continue to enhance the prototype in another iteration, which they hope to complete in about two weeks. The design strategy uses prototyping, which means that Carrie Douglass, their client at the BEC store in Centerville, Ohio, will have frequent opportunities to see a working version of the design as the system evolves. By using simple forms and reports, which will be translated into queries, the team would like to have a better idea of the fields required as well as the nature of database processing involved. Also, as a prototype, with limited data in the database and few simultaneous users, performance (in terms of speed and resource utilization) will not be a main concern for the team. However, Professor Tann, the instructor of the course at St. Claire through which they are doing this project, expects a thorough physical database design. So the team is split in two—one will work on enhancing the prototype using Access while the other will go through the first iteration of the physical database design assuming that a DBMS, such as Oracle, will eventually be used to implement the back end. The first iteration will consider the critical object relations and assume row sizes. After Professor Tann approves the first design, the second iteration will be conducted for all the object relations using the fields obtained from the Access prototype. Before the teams split up and perform their respective iterations, they will sit down and jointly resolve some issues.

Designing the Physical Object-Relational Database

Two important inputs for the students to consider are the object-relational data model and the analysis class diagram, with the associated analysis diagrams they already have developed. In terms of the database, the object-relational data model will be the most useful, whereas the analysis class diagram adds behaviors, which will be implemented primarily in VBA code on forms and in application modules. The Access prototype will consider all the object relations. This case will mainly detail decisions made for the first iteration of the physical database design, which considers a subset of the object relations.

When the students designed the object-relational data model for MyBroadway, they deferred dealing with the issue of using generalization in representing transaction relations. Although Sale and Rental, and SaleLineItem and RentalLineItem relations have similar structures and are candidates for generalization of, say, Transaction and TransactionLineItem, the students did not see a substantial benefit in creating these structures. The rental extension will simply refer to the rental, and specify the revised due date. If the project had several other transactions, they believed that it might be useful to define generalization structures.

For the physical database design, the team selects a subset of the object-relational solution as shown:

> Customer (<u>membershipId</u>, cLastName, cFName, custPhone, address, email, pw)
>
> Employee (<u>empId</u>, empLName, empFName,{empPhone}, address, Active?)
>
> Product (<u>productId</u>, title, artist, type, publisher, category, media, description, releaseDate, salePrice, rentalPrice)
>
> Rental (<u>rentalId</u>, rentalDate, dueDate, membershipId, empId)
>
> RentalLineItem (<u>rentalId, productId</u>, actualRentalPrice)
>
> CustComment (<u>commentId</u>, commentDate, membershipId, productId, prodComment)

They reckon that since Sale will have similar counts as compared to Rental, the Sale and SaleLineItem can be considered in the next iteration. The team is not as concerned with the employee picks because they don't expect that the counts will be large. The inventory count is likely to be similar to the product count, and its design will be taken up later. New product requests are maintained for only two months, and the counts are likely to be low, making the design less critical.

The following object relations will be considered for physical database design: Customer, Employee, Product, Rental, RentalLineItem, and CustComment. The students decide to create nonintelligent keys to be used as the primary and foreign product keys for most of these relations. A nonintelligent key is a system-assigned value that has no business meaning. Each DBMS provides a mechanism (e.g., sequence) to create such keys for entity identifiers. Thus, the Product table is assigned a primary key: productId.

The team decided to maintain only one phone number for the customer, since contact by phone should be rare. However, for employees, the company should maintain as many phone numbers as possible, so this will be shown as a multivalued attribute. Most of this information is available through the existing BEC system. The database will maintain employee information even if the employee leaves, otherwise the Employee Picks relations will be affected because of referential integrity. A field *active?* will maintain if the employee is still with the company. The team notes that the company policy prohibits more than one rental of the same product in a given transaction, so there is no need to maintain LineItem quantity in a given rental. They also note that prodComment will be a memo or long kind of field, but there needs to be a limit to the length of the comment, and about 3,000 characters should be enough. Otherwise, readers could get bored reading long evaluations. This will also enable them to define prodComment as varchar2 type, which limits a field to 4,000 characters. Consequently, they also decide that the block size should be 4K.

To conduct the physical database design, the team needs row sizes and counts. After discussing with Carrie, they come up with the following estimates:

TableName	Row Size (bytes)	Row Count
Customer	200	100,000
Employee	200	50
Product	400	10,000
Rental	100	5,000,000
RentalLineItem	50	20,000,000
CustComment	3,500	100,000

Case Summary

The student team has many specific decisions to make in order to finalize the design of the database for MyBroadway. They plan to take the time to use all the power of a DBMS to create an efficient and reliable database. They view defining indexes as the most important task. Professor Tann will help them define advanced structures like clusters and nested table to enhance rapid navigation from Rental to RentalLineItem. Note that the coverage of advanced structures is beyond the scope of this book.

CASE QUESTIONS

1. This BEC case indicated the data types chosen for only a few of the fields of the listed tables. Suggest data types, formats, and lengths for each attribute of each relation. Specify additional fields if required. Use the data types and formats supported by Oracle. What data type should be used for the nonintelligent primary keys? Estimate row sizes and compare them with the ones provided in the case.

2. Calculate blocking factors and scan times for the tables provided. Which tables are large, and which are small for indexing criterion? In the large tables, which fields are good candidates for defining indexes?

3. Draw a diagram showing the ratios between tables that can be joined based on a primary and a foreign key? Which ratios are small enough so that an index on the foreign key can be recommended?

4. Do you agree with the decision not to implement generalization for the transactions?

5. Complete all table and field definitions for the MyBroadway database. Determine indexing requirements of the fields.

6. Another important physical database design decision is denormalizaton of the object relations. Do you recommend any specific denormalization for the MyBroadway database?

Chapter 12

Design Elements

Chapter Preview

If analysis pertains to determining what needs to be done, design relates to how to do what needs to be done. Analysis focuses on specifying requirements, spotlighting problems, re-engineering tasks for maximizing effectiveness, and considering alternatives. Design focuses on detailing the solution, finalizing on a systems architecture, selecting components, finalizing design classes, aiming for efficiency, selecting technology, and adding details so that coding and implementation can be done (see Figure 12.1). During design, the systems analyst first decides on systems architecture, considering the need to balance simplicity with flexibility to manage growth. Analysis classes are adjusted after tuning the sequence diagram and are then mapped into design elements, which comprise design classes and components. The design classes and components are grouped into logical chunks called packages, although this step may have been initiated at the analysis stage. The operations of the classes are detailed by specifying parameters. The design classes include the entity, the control, and the boundary classes. Physical database design considerations result in redefining entity classes (see Chapter 11). The amount of logic in a use case will determine if there are none, one, or several control classes; usually, you will have one or a few classes. Interface design helps detail boundary classes (see Chapter 13). Design also involves identifying areas where the functionality of classes can be provided by using components. Systems development is becoming more dependent on the use of components, which generally are purchased from third-party vendors. Standards are needed in order for components from different vendors to work together. Therefore, systems analysts must understand the existing and emerging component standards, and learn about the technologies associated with these standards.

Figure 12.1 Systems Design Has Three Parts: Physical Database Design, Creating Design Elements, and Designing the Human Interface

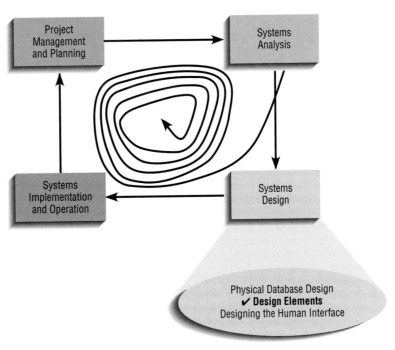

We begin this chapter by defining design elements and by providing an overview of design architecture. Current thinking about design architectures is to look at architecture in terms of tiers or layers. We define single-tier, two-tier, three-tier, and n-tier architectures. The next major section of the chapter is devoted to mapping analysis classes to design classes. In simple cases, an analysis class will map directly to a single design class. In other cases, however, one analysis class might map into multiple design classes, a part of a design class, a component, or a package. Given the growing popularity of component-based development, we next focus on components and on the many competing component standards and design frameworks. The four popular component standards that we cover are Microsoft's Component Object Model (COM), Object Management Group's Common Object Request Broker Architecture (CORBA), Sun's Enterprise Java Beans (EJB), and the popular Extensible Markup Language, with a transport protocol such as Simple Object Access Protocol (XML/SOAP). We also cover two competing design frameworks: Microsoft's .NET and Sun's Java 2 Enterprise Edition (J2EE). We end this section of the chapter with a discussion of package diagrams. The section of the chapter on components, frameworks, and packages contains plenty of information, much of which may be new to you. It is important that prospective object-oriented developers are at least familiar with the different technological choices that are available. The next-to-last section of this chapter is about design class diagrams. In developing design class diagrams, the analyst assigns data types to attributes and converts responsibilities to operations. Finally, we end the chapter with the latest developments in the Pine Valley Furniture WebStore example.

DESIGN ELEMENTS

Design element
A design class or a component.

Component
A replaceable part of a system that provides a clearly defined function through a set of interfaces.

A design element is either a design class or a component. Design not only involves the detailed specifications of classes, but also the use of components, and the standards and technologies that enable components to work together in a system. During design, the system is prepared for coding and implementation.

Chapter 11 introduced the first step in design and provided guidelines to finalize entity classes. Entity classes were addressed first because they constitute the dominant proportion of all the classes in a typical business system. Note that every system need not have a large database piece, and in such a case, the systems analyst does not need to devote much attention to the database step. If the system is a game like FreeCell or Chess, it is better to ignore the formal database steps because such systems write minimally to the disk and use programs that work mostly in the main memory. In these cases, one can follow pure object-oriented techniques. However, business applications typically have a significant database piece and generally are implemented in the conventional way (e.g., relational or object-relational). You need to employ techniques that take advantage of the relational or object-relational manner of handling data, and embed in the object-oriented manner of handling a system.

After entity classes are finalized, the system can be examined from an overall design perspective by including the other two kinds of classes: control and boundary. Issues regarding the user interface are covered in Chapter 13. Detailed design includes the specifications, such as the parameters and types for the operations of the classes of the entity, boundary, and control classes. It also includes identification of subsystems that can be implemented by using components.

At the design stage, the system also should be examined for reuse opportunities. Classes or subsystems (i.e., a group of related classes) that provide similar functionalities or interfaces can be compared. It is possible that two subsystems have similar but not exactly the same interfaces. In this case, the analyst might have to find the common denominator and modify the interfaces so both subsystems can reuse a piece of the system.

At an early stage of design, the design architecture of the system needs to be defined, which provides an overall blueprint of the system design. The design architecture usually is specified in terms of its tiers, as explained in more detail in the next section. A design architecture needs to balance simplicity with flexibility. Then the technological choices of the system must be finalized. These technological pieces will implement the detailed design classes and components.

DESIGN ARCHITECTURE

Design architecture
An overall blueprint of the design of the system.

A design architecture is an overall blueprint of the system. The design architecture is decided based on factors such as the complexity of the application, its ability to embrace change, and the skill level of the project team. Decisions relating to the systems architecture can be made at the analysis stage or at the design stage. In general, there is a fair idea about the architecture at the analysis stage. The idea is then explicated at the design stage.

Applications are not stagnant—they evolve over time. An application has an immediate goal, but as time passes, new requirements emerge, perhaps in unanticipated ways. It is possible that the application that was designed and implemented has been so successful that the demand for the system has skyrocketed. A side effect of this success may be that users are demanding considerably more functionality. Enterprise Application Design (EAD) is the process of designing applications that embrace change. EAD emphasizes building applications that integrate smoothly with internal and external processes, can be extended to reflect the constant state of change found within a business, and have high availability. EAD is affected by the design architecture of the system.

Enterprise Application Design (EAD)
The process of designing applications that embrace change.

Consider a simple architecture that shows a mainframe connected by dumb terminals. Assume that the complete system is written only in the programming language COBOL, as was the case for systems developed several decades ago. If the system is large and is evolving constantly, as it happens in today's environment, the resulting change management will be a significant task. For example, simply adding another field on a form affects the whole system. If an index is defined on a field, the coding of the procedures that use this field will be changed significantly. Such a system does not embrace change. To accept change, the systems architecture needs to be tiered.

Tiered Architecture

Tiered or layered architecture
The partitioning of a system into layers such that each layer performs a specific type of functionality and communicates with the layers that adjoin it.

In a tiered or layered architecture, the system is partitioned into layers such that each layer performs a specific type of functionality and communicates with the layers that adjoin it. This logical partitioning invariably translates to physical partitioning, whereby different computers house different layers. A given computer, however, can house more than one layer.

The notion of layers entails reliance on object-oriented concepts. Each layer needs interfaces to communicate with adjoining layers. A given layer needs to care only about its own implementation but not the implementation of the others. The interfaces of the other layers guarantee their functionality.

The example provided earlier of a mainframe connected to dumb terminals is an illustration of the single-tier architecture. The single machine, single-tier architecture is now rare for new systems, and it is seen only for simple applications on a personal computer or legacy applications on mainframes from the past. The two-tier architecture and the n-tier architecture (that is, three-tier and higher) are the more common designs.

Figure 12.2 Two-Tier Structure

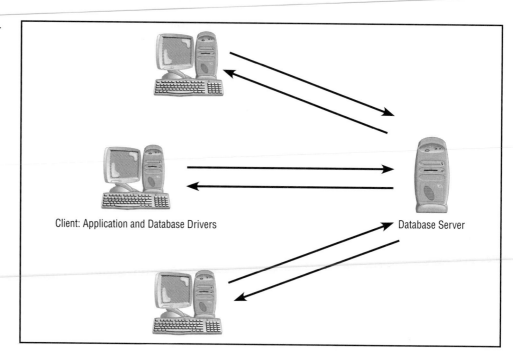

Client: Application and Database Drivers   Database Server

Two-Tier Architecture

Two-tier architecture
A design architecture that involves two layers: application and data.

Middleware
Software that provides one set of interfaces for connection to a client and another set of interfaces for connection to a server, thereby providing the possibility of connections between one of several clients and one of several servers.

The two-tier architecture, or the client-server architecture, involves two layers: an application layer (sometimes called the front end) and a data layer (sometimes called the back end). The application layer has the graphical user interface (GUI) and the application logic; it communicates with a database using native drivers, or middleware that supports data access (Figure 12.2). The database is installed on a server and is shared; however, the application needs to be installed individually on client workstations. This architecture is adequate for simple applications, but for complex applications, it has the following problems:

- The client end is thick because it has a large piece of the overall application. This large piece has to be installed on each client workstation. However, if several programs can share a piece of logic, it can be placed in the database as a stored procedure with the load reduced on the front end.
- Any changes in the application need to be installed on each client workstation.
- Two-tier applications usually are implemented with proprietary technologies. When applications need to be integrated, this weakness is exposed, because proprietary technologies don't integrate well. The problem is exacerbated because the applications have to be integrated on individual thick clients.

As an example, consider an order-taking application for entering customer orders. The user interface and the business logic will need to be installed on individual workstations. Using middleware, the application layer can be linked to a database on, say, Microsoft's SQL Server. It will not require major changes in the application if the DBMS is changed to Oracle. In this sense, the two layers—application and database—are loosely coupled. However, if the order application needs to be enhanced (e.g., a form is altered), it must be updated on each workstation. Similarly, if a discount policy is changed, this change in business rules and the resulting revised code need to be updated on each workstation.

Three-tier architecture
A design architecture that involves three layers: presentation, business rules, and data.

Three-Tier Architecture

The application layer of a two-tier architecture has two parts: presentation and business rules. In a three-tier architecture, these are separated explicitly in logical and, usually, in physical terms. Thus, a three-tier architecture has the following layers:

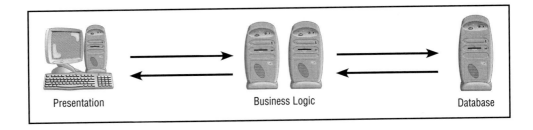

Figure 12.3
Three-Tier
Architecture

Presentation   Business Logic   Database

Presentation layer
The front tier, which addresses the presentation of information to users and acceptance of commands from the users. It may embed some rules such as formatting, calculations, and constraint checking.

Business rules layer
The middle tier, which addresses the rules, decisions, and logic embedded in a system. This layer is sometimes called the application layer; note that the meaning of the application layer depends on the architecture.

Data layer
The back tier, which addresses the storage and access to data. It may embed some rules such as constraint checking and calculations.

presentation, business rules, and data (Figure 12.3). Since a large number of systems allow Web access, the presentation layer is usually browser-based.

The presentation layer addresses the user interface, which is usually graphical. This includes the text boxes, combo and list boxes, labels, grids, and pictures. It also includes data entry checks and rules. The presentation layer can be developed using a programming language such as Visual Basic (VB) or Java, or it can be embedded in a Web browser with nothing more than HTML and a scripting language like JavaScript.

The business rules layer contains the business logic; it also contains classes and components that interact with the presentation layer on one end and the database layer on the other. These classes and components should, but might not, subscribe to some component architecture such as Enterprise Java Beans (EJB), Component Object Model (COM/COM+), or Common Object Request Broker Architecture (CORBA), or they might employ a nonproprietary standard like the Extensible Markup Language/Simple Object Access Protocol (XML/ SOAP)–based architecture. These terms will be explained in a later section.

The data layer of a three-tier architecture is somewhat similar to that of a two-tier architecture. However, in a three-tier architecture, some of the logic embedded in stored procedures may be transferred to the middle tier and still be shared, and can be written in a nonproprietary language so that dependence on a specific technology is minimized.

The three-tier architecture has the following advantages:

- The architecture is loosely coupled. Changes can be made to one layer, and if the interfaces are not changed, the changes should result in minimum alteration to other layers in the system.
- The architecture leads to reuse of not only data but also business rules.
- The processing load is spread over more machines; therefore, the system is more scalable.

The main problem with the three-tier architecture is that its implementation in practice may still be based on proprietary technologies, which can permeate any and all of the three layers. Further, the three-tier structure is more complex, and if there is a stable, well-configured two-tier system with an optimized network, then there is no compelling need to move to a three-tier system. Note that a three-tier architecture may have reduced traffic to the database, but the network will have to be adequately designed for the traffic between the presentation and the business rules layer. Also, application changes can be tested from one workstation before mirroring them to other workstations in the two-tier architecture. The changes affect all the clients immediately in the three-tier architecture. In today's business environment with the need of Web presence for a transaction system, the three-tier architecture is becoming the standard.

N-Tier Architecture

The three-tier principles can be extended to design an even more loosely coupled application in an n-tier architecture. This is especially pertinent now because the Web browser is usually the first layer, and the widespread availability of this thin layer can provide access to a system at any time and from anywhere. If there are two layers between the browser and the database, it will result in a four-tier architecture. More layers, in general, will provide a more scalable application and minimize the

Figure 12.4
N-Tier Architecture
Example

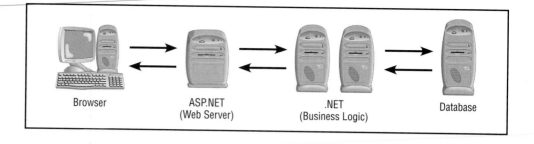

| Browser | ASP.NET
(Web Server) | .NET
(Business Logic) | Database |

N-tier architecture
A design architecture based on multiple layers that address presentation, business logic, and data.

cascading effects of changes in one part of the system. However, great skill is needed to implement an n-tier architecture successfully.

For example, Figure 12.4 provides an example of a four-tier architecture. A Web browser (layer 1) may be invoked from a browser on a workstation or even from a personal digital assistant (PDA). The presentation logic (layer 2) can be captured on Active Server Pages (ASP) stored on a Web server. The business rules logic (layer 3) can be captured in any language supported by the .NET framework, which includes a transaction facility. The framework also has embedded functionality to provide data access to a DBMS (layer 4) such as Oracle, DB2, Informix, or SQL Server.

Some of the terms used in explaining these architectures might be unfamiliar, but they will be clarified in subsequent sections.

MAPPING FROM ANALYSIS CLASSES TO DESIGN ELEMENTS

A design element is either a design class or a component. When analysis classes are detailed, areas that can be served by components should be identified. Although a component can be constructed in-house, it invariably is bought from a third party. Design classes will have to be written in-house or may be outsourced. So during the transition from analysis to design, areas that can be designed using components need to be examined. For example, except for some core areas, an e-commerce site is likely to be developed using components. The sequence diagrams and the resulting class diagrams need to then be modified. Further, if the object-oriented methodology is being used in the company already, it might be possible to reuse existing design elements.

An analysis class can map to a design class if it is simple and represents one logical thing. For example, an entity class like LineItem will map directly from analysis to design. In fact, many entity classes map directly from analysis to design, because the main purpose of an entity class is to store data and provide it to other objects upon request.

An analysis class can map to:

- *A single design class:* An entity class typically maps directly from analysis to design.
- *Multiple design classes:* This can happen for a number of reasons. For example, in detailing the analysis class Employee, it might be discovered that two categories really exist—FullTimeEmp and PartTimeEmp. Further, objects of FullTimeEmp can be administrators or general employees, necessitating more categories. It is possible that these decisions were not made earlier and are being made at this stage in a subsequent iteration. New classes also might come up because one class has too much information. Thus, it might be convenient to detail the Product class into Product and ProductPrice, where the latter provides the price of a product during an interval of time. A control class with a large number of business rules can be split into two or more control classes, or into a control class and an entity class.
- *A part of a design class:* Conversely, if specialization classes were shown during analysis and no good reason exists for keeping them as separate classes,

they can be combined. If a specialization class has only a few extra attributes or methods and these can be handled in its generalization class, then the two can be merged. As mentioned earlier, denormalization concerns may lead to combining classes. Control classes that contain simple logic can be eliminated, and the logic can be made part of the boundary and entity classes.

- *A component:* Several analysis classes can be addressed using commercially available components. A department store that also sells through its Web site might have an analysis class DealerLocater, which provides customers with the option of picking up merchandise from a store located close to their residence. It is not necessary to build this class in-house because the functionality can be provided by a component.

- *A package:* An analysis class may represent a group of classes that have similar and interrelated functionality. This grouping is logical and is called a package. For example, during analysis, a class Customer might be identified. However, because customer relations management is important, the systems analyst decides to keep track not only of the basic customer data, but also the products purchased in the past and any suggestions obtained from customers, whether solicited or unsolicited. Thus, CustomerRelations could be a package that contains classes and components that maintain and manipulate customer-related data. A package diagram shows the packages and the relationships among them.

Package
A general-purpose mechanism for organizing elements into groups.

Package diagram
A diagram that shows the packages and the relationships among them.

Let's distinguish the terms *package* and *component*. A package is a logical grouping of classes and components. However, a component has a well-defined interface and functionality, is usually purchased from a third party, and its source code is not provided to the buyer. In today's system development environment, components play a significant role.

COMPONENTS

Software component
A software element with a well-defined interface and functionality for a specific purpose that can be deployed in a variety of applications using plug-and-play capability; invariably purchased from a third party.

The four most common reasons for using software components are code reuse, assembly of new business applications, support for heterogeneous computing infrastructures, and ability of an application to scale (PricewaterhouseCoopers, 2001). A software component (also simply called a component) has the following characteristics:

a. A specific purpose; not for a specific application.
b. A collection of classes and interfaces.
c. Hidden implementation details.
d. Plug-and-play capability.
e. Usually distributed in binary code, that is, in executable form.
f. Invariably purchased from a third party.
g. Can be reused in a variety of applications.
h. More expensive to develop in-house.
i. Usually well tested and relatively error-free.
j. Can be written in any language as long as the language supports the particular component standard's interface conventions.

A software component is not much different than a daily-use component such as an audio-video receiver, a universal power supply (UPS), a cellular phone, or a car oil filter. The focus is placed on the functionality and interface of a component rather than its internals. When an improved version of a component is available, it almost always can be replaced without affecting the overall working of the system. By using components, a workable system can be put together in a relatively short period of time at a low cost.

Let's consider a component from everyday life. A DVD player has a specific purpose—to play movies and other recordings on a DVD videodisc. Its front and rear panels provide interfaces for interaction and connection to other components, such as an audio-video receiver or a television. The interfaces need to subscribe to certain standards that allow plug-and-play capability. The receiver, which connects to a DVD player, can be replaced with another receiver. The parts that do the work are inside a box; these implementation details are hidden from a user. A DVD player, which is developed by a company specializing in such components, can be purchased from a store. Even though the technology to build a DVD player is extremely complex, the price is low because the manufacturer can build and distribute millions of players and thus spread the development costs. In general, such components are reliable because of the extensive testing undertaken before their release.

Software components show similar characteristics. In today's development environment, thousands of components are available. The following are some examples of functionality provided by components:

1. Use customized screen for address and telephone formats based on a customer's country.
2. Create and print industry-standard bar codes.
3. Add biometric security to desktop applications.
4. Generate a rule set using a data-mining component that explains and predicts selected values in an input data set, based on other user-selected values.
5. Add sophisticated time management capability to handle time blocks in applications using a collection of user interface components.
6. Validate credit card before sending for authorization.
7. Add compression and encryption.
8. Employ charting facilities on a mobile device.
9. Run queries and produce reports using drag and drop without the need to understand SQL.
10. Provide shopping cart Web service and credit card gateway.
11. Build a complete Internet commerce kit including order processing, database management, and payment processing.
12. Perform loan functions for finance, loan, installment credit, and repayment of credit.
13. Add dictionary and thesaurus capabilities to any application.
14. Add flexible sliding gauges and meters to an application.
15. Add search functionality to a Web site.

If a Web search is conducted on component providers and functionality, it can be seen that each component is qualified by several component types, such as .NET object, COM object, ActiveX DLL, ASP, ASP.NET Server Control, ADO, EJB, JSP, Applet, Servlet, Java Class, Web Control, CORBA, and so on. In order to make good choices among available components, the systems analyst needs to understand some of these terminologies, which will be encountered when reading about the functionality and documentation of components. This understanding will enhance considerably one's ability to design software elements. The next sections provide a brief introduction to these technologies; however, detailed illustrations and examples are beyond the scope of this book. First, let's study the component standards that are popular in today's market.

Component Object Model (COM)
Microsoft's component standard, which supports transaction, security, and identity services, and allows components following the standard to call each other locally or remotely by a messaging service.

Run-time environment
The classes and components required to support the services like handling secure transactions at run time.

COMPONENT STANDARDS

If components need to communicate with a system or among each other, they need to adhere to a standard. The four most popular component standards are Microsoft's Component Object Model (COM), Object Management Group's Common Object Request Broker Architecture (CORBA), Sun's Enterprise Java Beans (EJB), and the increasingly popular Extensible Markup Language, with a transport protocol such as Simple Object Access Protocol (XML/SOAP).

Middle tier
Application layer sandwiched between presentation and data layers.

Run time
The period of time during which a computer program executes.

COM, COM+, and Distributed COM (DCOM)

When an application is developed using the Microsoft Windows platform, several pieces of software are needed. Visual Basic (or Java or C++) can be selected as the primary language to write the modules that bring together the components supplied

Transaction

An all-or-nothing unit of business work. In terms of information systems, a transaction is a sequence of computer operations, all of which must be completed successfully to leave the database in a consistent state. A system that provides transactional integrity must guarantee four properties: atomicity, consistency, isolation, and durability (ACID).

Common Object Request Broker Architecture (CORBA)

A component standard published by the Object Management Group for a distributed and heterogeneous network.

Object Management Group (OMG)

An open-membership, not-for-profit consortium that produces and maintains computer industry specifications for interoperable enterprise applications (http://www.omg.org).

Interface Definition Language (IDL)

A language that defines interfaces so that client-side and server-side elements, written in different programming languages, can interoperate.

Object Request Broker (ORB)

A software unit that mediates and directs communication requests from CORBA clients to CORBA server objects.

Enterprise Java Beans (EJB)

An architecture proposed by Sun for component-based distributed computing. EJB is a server-sided component model that addresses issues that involve the management of distributed objects in a multitier architecture and requires CORBA to connect to clients.

by Microsoft or by a third party to support services such as transactions, security, and identity. The Component Object Model (COM) is the bond that brings these pieces together. COM+ is an extended version of COM, which provides a run-time environment for components that run in the middle tier (Pattison, 2000). Run time is the period of time during which a program executes. COM+ includes the best features of Microsoft Transaction Server (MTS), which allows business objects running on Windows to run and control distributed transactions from the middle tier. To develop a large, multitier application, other services, such as Internet Information Services (IIS) and Active Server Pages (ASP), might be needed. The COM standard has now largely been replaced by the more open XML/SOAP standard.

COM defines an environment that allows a developer to create interfaces for code modules, which then allows any code modules to send messages and obtain results from other COM modules on the same machine. To pass messages on networked Windows platforms, developers use distributed COM (DCOM), which allows remote procedure calls (RPC) among distributed COM components. DCOM and COM+ usually are called by the generic term *COM*.

Common Object Request Broker Architecture (CORBA)

Common Object Request Broker Architecture (CORBA) is a standard, published by the Object Management Group (OMG), for a distributed (i.e., objects can exist on different computers) and heterogeneous network (i.e., the computers can be on different platforms) of objects. The interfaces for the objects are defined in Interface Definition Language (IDL), which is independent of any programming language. An IDL compiler is used to map the IDL to a specific language. The Object Request Broker (ORB) is a software element that mediates and directs requests from CORBA clients to CORBA server objects. Thus, a method invocation on a remote server object appears as a local method invocation. This means that the developer does not need to know where the target object is located.

The code that implements a CORBA environment can be written in an object-oriented language like Java, or in a nonobject-oriented language like C or even COBOL. For example, COBOL modules can be "wrapped" in IDL interfaces; that is, these interfaces can specify the input and outputs to and from the COBOL modules. Thus, a legacy system written in COBOL can be integrated with a new system.

IDL is similar to Java or C++ (other than the use of in and out for function parameters). For example, here is an IDL interface declaration (adapted from the book *Pure CORBA* by Fintan Bolton):

```
//IDL
interface CustomerAccount {
        string get_name();
        long get_account_no();
        boolean deposit_money (in float amount);
        boolean tranfer_money (
                in float amount,
                in long destination_account_no,
                out long confirmation_no
        );
```

Enterprise Java Beans (EJB)

Enterprise Java Beans (EJB) is an architecture proposed by Sun for component-based distributed computing. EJB is a server-sided component model that addresses issues that involve the management of distributed objects in a multitier architecture (Morisseau-Leroy, Solomon, & Basu, 2000). EJB components have interfaces written in Java, which can run and execute in any environment that has a Java Virtual Machine (JVM) and an EJB container. An EJB container provides a set of services, such as transaction management, security, naming, and database connectivity. EJBs allow applications to communicate across multitier client-server environments, and across Internet and Intranet structures. EJB requires CORBA to connect to clients. To understand EJB, one also needs to understand Java, JavaBeans, and JDBC, all of which are explained in the next two subsections.

Java and JavaBeans

Java was released in 1995 and has gained acceptance rapidly. It is an object-oriented development language and can be deployed on any computing platform. It is a simple yet powerful language with a small set of keywords. Java's popularity is largely due to platform independence and the widespread availability of a library of classes, which provide extensive functionality. To compile Java source code, the Java Development Kit (JDK) must be installed on the computer. The JDK includes the compiler, the Java Virtual Machine (JVM), and a large number of packages, which are collections of classes. JavaBean is a Java class that follows certain design rules for naming conventions. For example, the default names for the access methods of a property named Address are getAddress() and setAddress(string newValue). To enable a Java program to access the objects and methods of another Java program running on a different computer, Java provides remote method invocation (RMI).

Java is a versatile language that can be used to create applets, servlets, front-end GUIs, application procedures, and database-driven applications. An applet is a Java program that is sent to the user via HTTP and executed by the JVM embedded in a Web browser. A servlet is a Java program that is executed by the JVM on a Web server. Java Server Pages (JSPs) can be used to create dynamic Web pages using HTML, XML, and Java. JSPs are transformed into Java servlets, which are processed at the Web server. Java uses JDBC, which is explained in the next section and illustrated with a simple program, for access to databases.

JDBC

Although JDBC is technically not an abbreviation of Java Database Connectivity, its purpose is to allow Java applications to connect to any DBMS. To run a Java application that can access a DBMS like Oracle, the JDK, the DBMS, and the JDBC, drivers are needed at a minimum; further, these three pieces of software must be compatible. A statement containing the SQL code is created and passed to the DBMS, which returns a result set for processing. We provide a simple example to demonstrate JDBC programming in particular and access to databases in general. The example creates a class JDBCProg1 that connects to an Oracle database and executes a query that lists employee names, which are then loaded into a result set. Using a while loop, the results are displayed. The following program was compiled and executed using Jcreator, and the results are shown in Figure 12.5. A similar program can be run using VB.NET and ADO.NET to connect to Oracle.

```
/*
JDBCProg1.java connects to an Oracle database
as user "scott" and password "tiger".
The program lists each employee name and prefixes Hello,
e.g., "Hello Smith", "Hello Allen"
*/

// import the standard JDBC package
// java.sql, which has DriverManager, Connection, Statement,
// and ResultSet classes

import java.sql.*;
public class JDBCProg1 {
public static void main (String args []) {
// initialize Connection and Statement objects
Connection myConnection = null;
Statement myStatement = null;
// Place code in a try block so an exception can be caught
```

Java Virtual Machine (JVM)
An interpreter designed specifically for each type of computing platform to execute Java bytecode, which is produced during the compilation of a Java program.

JavaBean
A Java class that follows certain design rules for naming conventions.

Remote method invocation (RMI)
A middleware that enables a Java program to access the objects and methods of another Java program running on a different computer.

Applet
A Java program that is sent to the user via HTTP and executed by the Java Virtual Machine (JVM) embedded in a Web browser.

Servlet
A Java program that is executed by the JVM on a Web server.

Java Server Pages (JSPs)
A technology that mixes Java code with HTML and XML to generate dynamic Web pages.

JDBC
A middleware to connect a Java application with a database in a DBMS-independent manner.

Figure 12.5 An Example of JDBC Programming for Accessing an Oracle Database

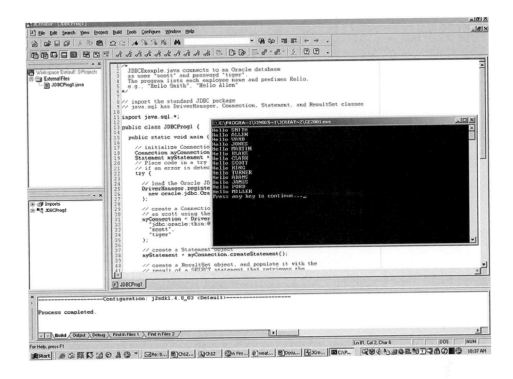

```
// if an error is detected
try {
        // load the Oracle JDBC drivers
        DriverManager.registerDriver(
                new oracle.jdbc.OracleDriver()
        );
        // create a Connection object, and connect to the database
        // as scott using the Oracle JDBC Thin driver
        myConnection = DriverManager.getConnection(
                "jdbc:oracle:thin:@localhost:1521:ORCL",
                "scott","tiger"
        );
        // create a Statement object
        myStatement = myConnection.createStatement();
        // create a ResultSet object, and populate it with the
        // result of a SELECT statement that retrieves the
        // employee names - the executeQuery() method of the
        // Statement object is used to perform the SELECT
        ResultSet myResultSet = myStatement.executeQuery(
                "SELECT ename " +
                "FROM emp "
        );
        // start a while loop to retrieve the rows from the ResultSet
        // one at a time using the next() method
        while (myResultSet.next()) {
                // extract the data using the getString() method
                String ename = myResultSet.getString("ename");
                // retrieve the employee names
                System.out.println("Hello " + ename);
        }
        // close this ResultSet object using the close() method
        myResultSet.close();
```

```
            }
    // catch any exception
    catch (SQLException e) {
            System.out.println(e);
    }
    finally {
            try {
            // close the Statement and Connection objects
            myStatement.close();
            myConnection.close();
            }
            catch (SQLException e) {
            System.out.println(e);
            }

    }
} // end of main()
    }
```

COM, CORBA, and EJB: Comparisons and Problems

COM, CORBA, and EJB provide transaction, security, and interconnection services, and are thus quite popular. Table 12-1 provides a comparison of the important middleware services from OMG, Microsoft, and Sun. Note the new term, *CCM*, which stands for CORBA Component Model, usually referred to as CORBA.

The three component standards do have problems. These proprietary and binary technologies are tightly coupled and lock data transfer into underlying networks and object infrastructures (Coyle, 2002). None supports Transmission Control Protocol/Internet Protocol (TCP/IP), the standard Web protocol. A component based on one standard cannot communicate easily with a component based on another standard. A standard is needed that employs the open-Web protocols and integrates systems regardless of the platform, the operating system, or the language used. The new standard that addresses this need is XML/SOAP, discussed next.

XML/SOAP: An Integration Solution

Systems coupled by the use of Extensible Markup Language with a transport protocol, such as Simple Object Access Protocol (XML/SOAP), hold considerable promise. Currently, frameworks that employ XML/SOAP and that provide services such as transaction and security are increasingly popular. Transaction management in a distributed system is an especially difficult task.

HyperText Markup Language (HTML) has been successful, but it lacks certain features. HTML is not suitable for data interchange and is semantically impoverished, providing only a limited set of tags. On the other hand, Extensible Markup Language (XML) provides a method for putting structured data into an ASCII-based text file. XML is an important method for interchanging data between computers and computer applications. It is, therefore, a simple and reliable method for business-to-business (B2B) data exchange. For example, self-describing XML tags can show an instance of ReviewerAllocation data:

Transmission Control Protocol/Internet Protocol (TCP/IP)
The networking protocol used on the Internet.

HyperText Markup Language (HTML)
A tag-based language used widely across the Web to render documents in browsers.

Extensible Markup Language (XML)
A method for putting structured data into a text file to facilitate data communication among computers and computer applications.

Business-to-business (B2B)
Electronic commerce among businesses.

Table 12-1
Important Middleware Services: A Comparison of OMG, Microsoft, and Sun.

SERVICE	OMG	MICROSOFT	SUN
Object Model	CORBA	COM	Java
Component Model	CCM	COM, COM+	JavaBeans, EJB
Distributed Middleware	CORBA	DCOM	RMI, CORBA
Advanced Component Model	CCM	COM+	EJB
Data Access	Not Available	ODBC, OLE DB, ADO	JDBC

Source: Adopted from Technology Forecast 2001–2003 by PricewaterhouseCoopers. Used by permission.

Simple Object Access Protocol (SOAP)

An XML-based protocol for exchanging information in a distributed environment. SOAP defines an XML envelope for delivering XML contents across HTTP, FTP, or SMTP protocol.

HyperText Transfer Protocol (HTTP)

A protocol for initiating requests and moving data over the Web.

File Transfer Protocol (FTP)

A protocol allowing a user on one computer to transfer files to and from another computer over a TCP/IP network.

Simple Mail Transfer Protocol (SMTP)

A protocol for the reliable and efficient delivery of mail for the Internet.

Web services

A process and protocols for discovering software as a service across the Web.

.NET

A Microsoft development framework that integrates COM+ and Active Server Pages (ASP) technologies but builds it around XML/SOAP to deliver software as Web services.

```
<?xml version="1.0" encoding="UTF-8" ?>
<dataroot xmlns:od="urn:schemas-microsoft-com:officedata"
xmlns:xsi="http://www.w3.org/2001/XMLSchema-instance"
xsi:noNamespaceSchemaLocation="ReviewerAllocationXML.xsd"
generated="2005-11-22T14:22:11">
        <ReviewerAllocation>
                <AuthorLast>Dutta</AuthorLast>
                <AuthorFirst>Kaushik</AuthorFirst>
                <Title>OPTIMIZING CACHING OF WEB OBJECTS</Title>
                <Rev1>Meer</Rev1>
                <Rev1Email>debra.vandermeer@abc.edu</Rev1Email>
                <Rev2>Koulamas</Rev2>
                <Rev2Email>christos.koulamas@xyz.edu</Rev2Email>
        </ReviewerAllocation>
</dataroot>
```

Note that only one object is included here. Obviously, an XML document will typically have thousands or millions of objects. Also, there are some interesting extensions to the aforementioned basic structure. A free tutorial on XML is available at http://www.w3schools.com/xml/default.asp.

XML intentionally separates data content from presentation. Several technologies allow XML data to be extracted and manipulated. Unlike the binary protocols used by COM, CORBA, and EJB, the Simple Object Access Protocol (SOAP) is a text-based transport protocol, which can be used by HyperText Transfer Protocol (HTTP), File Transfer Protocol (FTP), and Simple Mail Transfer Protocol (SMTP). SOAP messages have a common format that includes a SOAP envelope, an optional header, and a body section that contains the message content. The body holds the transported XML data.

A promising area of XML/SOAP is the area of Web services, which describes a process and protocols for discovering software as a service across the Web. A software component or application can be exposed as a Web service so that it can be discovered and used by another component or application. Because SOAP is an open-Web protocol, it allows a component to be available globally. This can lead to innovative business-to-business (B2B) solutions. For detailed coverage of Web services, please refer to the book by Tabor (2002).

FRAMEWORKS

Framework

A collection of components, consisting of code and interfaces written in a specific language, that solves or helps build applications.

Java 2 Enterprise Edition (J2EE)

A Sun development framework that provides a specification of architectural components designed to work together to define a complete enterprise architecture. It also includes XML, SOAP, and Web services.

The success of XML/SOAP, a simple open mechanism to provide Web services, depends on the ability to at least guarantee transactions, security, and identity. XML/SOAP by itself does not provide these critical underlying services. To provide a complete set of services, the industry has come up with frameworks. A framework is any collection of components, consisting of code and interfaces written in a specific language, that solves or helps build applications. The two leading frameworks are .NET from Microsoft and Java 2 Enterprise Edition (J2EE) from Sun. Microsoft's .NET represents the implementation of a complete architecture. J2EE, however, is a specification of architectural components designed to work together to define a complete enterprise architecture. Sun, BEA, IBM, Oracle, and HP have provided implementations of the J2EE specification.

.NET Framework and Visual Studio .NET

Microsoft's .NET framework is based on a strategy intended to deliver software as Web services (Reynolds et al., 2001). The framework integrates COM+ and Active Server Pages (ASP) technologies but builds it around XML/SOAP. The implementation of .NET is available as Visual Studio .NET, and its characteristics are discussed briefly.

Visual Basic has been considered an easy-to-learn and easy-to-use language. However, it was considered a language with limited enterprise appeal until the release of the .NET framework changed that perception. Visual Basic (VB) .NET, which is part of Visual Studio .NET, is a powerful development tool. The Studio also includes a Java-like language, C# (pronounced C-sharp). Further, the Studio includes Visual C++ .NET, ADO.NET, Active Server Pages (ASP) .NET, Web forms, XML creation facilities, and Web services. The underlying theme of the framework is to provide a powerful yet easy development environment for Web-based applications.

The power of the .NET framework is its ability to decouple the application from a subsystem to be accessed. The application accesses subsystems through objects. Thus, if the application needs to access a file on a Linux subsystem instead of a Windows subsystem, the same object can open either file. The .NET framework illustrates that the power does not belong to a language but to the application development environment, which needs to be open and service-oriented, and which provides the library of components and classes to offer rich functionality.

In the .NET framework, the application is compiled into Microsoft Intermediate Language (MSIL) instead of native x86 instructions. The intermediate language is not dependent on any processor, and it allows applications to run on any execution platform. The run-time environment of .NET is called Common Language Runtime (CLR). The environment manages a number of functions, such as loading and executing code, application isolation, memory management, security, exception handling, and interoperation.

To understand the .NET framework, one must understand the underlying technologies such as ADO and ASP. A brief description of some of the important technologies follows.

ActiveX

The ActiveX technology has its roots in object linking and embedding (OLE), which provided a way for making an application accessible from external code. This allowed a program to link to compiled binary code like dynamic link library (DDL) and to use the functionality provided by the functions and procedures in the DLL. These technologies led to ActiveX controls and ActiveX DLLs. To work with any graphical user interface (GUI) language like VB, form controls must be used. An ActiveX DLL is actually a component based on COM. A Visual Basic book should provide instructions on how to create a custom control or DLL.

Open Database Connectivity (ODBC)

The Open Database Connectivity (ODBC) interface was developed by Microsoft to allow an application program to make SQL calls in a DBMS-independent manner. ODBC is rarely used now because better options are available today. In other words, an application program using ODBC to connect to an Oracle DBMS requires no or minimum alteration to work with Microsoft's SQL server. Introduced by Microsoft, ODBC has been overtaken by OLE DB and ADO, which in turn have been overtaken by ADO.NET.

ActiveX Data Objects (ADO)

VB version 6.0 gave us a new way to access databases with the integration of ActiveX Data Objects (ADO). This new method not only allowed access from development environments such as VB, Java, and C++, but it also allowed Web developers to call databases from Active Server Pages (ASP) and from scripting languages such as JScript and VBScript. ADO is an improvement over OLE DB, which is a COM-based component to support query operations, such as select, insert, update, create tables, create indexes, and other functions like record locking.

ActiveX Data Objects (ADO)
An improvement over OLE DB that provides a consistent-language, independent means to access data from almost any source. ADO also allows Web developers to call databases.

ADO.NET
An extension of the ADO middleware that uses a disconnected architecture.

By using the functionality provided by ADO, a client like VB can retrieve data from Oracle and place it in recordsets, which can be manipulated and displayed using the controls provided by the client. Note that ADO itself is a component and provides the interface for query manipulation. Its implementation is hidden from the user. For detailed coverage of ADO, refer to Chapter 12 of Kroenke's book *Database Processing* (2004).

ADO.NET

Since it is a disconnected architecture, ADO.NET is an improvement over ADO. An application is connected to a database long enough to retrieve or update and then is disconnected. Once data are retrieved from a database, the connection is disengaged. This allows a large number of users to access a database because each application is connected for only a limited time. This facilitates scalable applications because the impact of the system is minimal even if the number of users increases appreciably. The .NET framework supports the Dataset class, which stores the data retrieved on the client memory. The data are disconnected from the data store and can be manipulated on the client. These changes can then be applied back to the data store. The data in a Dataset are formatted as XML, which allows the data to be exchanged easily among objects.

Active Server Pages (ASP)
Microsoft's server-side technology, which embeds the functionality of a programming language to build Web documents dynamically.

Active Server Pages (ASP) and ASP.NET.

Active Server Pages (ASP) is a server-side technology that embeds the functionality of a programming language to build Web documents dynamically. Active server pages are processed on a Web server by an ActiveX component called a scripting engine. This engine generates HTML code. The dynamically generated code can be viewed on any computer with any modern Web browser. The scripting engine is bundled with Microsoft's Internet Information Server (IIS) and Personal Web Server (PWS). However, ASP can run on other Web servers directly or through products from third-party vendors. ASP.NET is an improvement over ASP and includes features such as Web forms, Web Services, and better caching.

ASP.NET
An improvement over ASP that includes features such as Web forms and Web Services.

Java 2 Enterprise Edition (J2EE)

An alternative to Microsoft's .NET is the Java 2 Enterprise Edition (J2EE), which is Sun's standard for building enterprise applications. Table 12-1 lists Sun's middleware services, including Java, EJB, and JDBC. J2EE extends these services by including XML, SOAP, and Web services. Note that .NET is a product, and J2EE is a specification. This means that various vendors implement J2EE. Sun provides an implementation, but so do IBM, BEA, HP, and Oracle.

Application programming interfaces (APIs)
A calling convention by which an application accesses the services of a software library.

J2EE provides its Web services standards by specifying application programming interfaces (APIs) for services that several vendors can implement. An API is a calling convention by which an application accesses the services of a software library. This ensures a reasonable degree of code portability when switching from one vendor to another. Complete portability is not achieved because vendors usually supply implementation in excess of API specifications listed in a standard.

J2EE's Web services pack includes Java API for a number of services. Note that a number of vendors support J2EE; therefore, we do not provide descriptions of products from the leading vendors.

LOGIC AT THE BROWSER: SCRIPTING LANGUAGES

So far this chapter has covered logic embedded at the middle tier. However, logic can be executed at the browser by using scripting languages such as JavaScript and VBScript. A scripting language is like a programming language, except it has fewer

Figure 12.6
JavaScript Example
with Code, Data Entry,
and Result All Shown

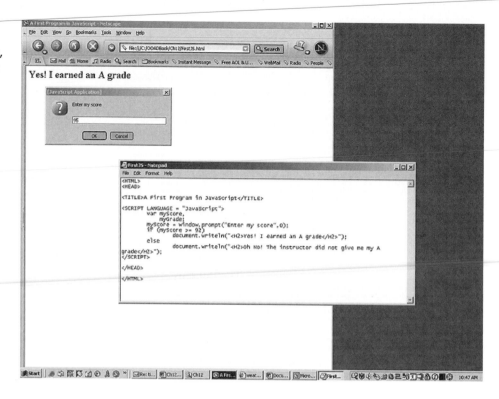

rules. Here is a self-explanatory example of JavaScript code. The result, data entry, and the code are overlaid on Figure 12.6:

```
<HTML>
<HEAD>
<TITLE>A First Program in JavaScript</TITLE>
<SCRIPT LANGUAGE = "JavaScript">
        var myScore,
myGrade;
myScore = window.prompt("Enter my score",0);
if (myScore >= 92)
        document.writeln("<H2>Yes! I earned my A grade</H2>");
else
        document.writeln("<H2>No! The instructor did not give me my A
grade</H2>");
</SCRIPT>
</HEAD>
</HTML>
```

JavaScript
A scripting language created by Netscape to enhance the functionality and appearance of Web pages. JavaScript is not Java. The Microsoft version is called Jscript.

VBScript
A scripting language created by Microsoft to enhance the functionality and appearance of Web pages. VBScript is a subset of VB, but it is not popular because many browsers do not support it directly. It is used more in the server-side ASP.

JavaScript and VBScript are client-side technologies in contrast to ASP and JSP, which are server-side technologies. Client-side technologies reduce the workload on the server, because they are processed on the client. However, client-side technologies have disadvantages, because the code is exposed and the Web application is browser-dependent. For more details on these technologies, please refer to Deitel, Deitel, and Nieto (2001).

ENCAPSULATION AT THE DATABASE END

DBMS packages now provide features that enable operations definitions to be included along with the attribute definitions, thus enabling encapsulation at the database end. For example, in Oracle 10g, you can define procedures and functions along with the attributes. A procedure can take zero, one, or more input parameters, and can return zero, one, or more output parameters. A function can take zero, one, or more input parameters but returns one parameter. Procedures and functions implement operations in Oracle. You can see detailed examples in the book *Object-Oriented Oracle* by Rahayu, Taniar, and Pardede (2006). The following code shows a procedure Give_Bonus written in PL/SQL.

```
create or replace type Employee_T as object
(Empno number(4),
Ename varchar2(30),
Job varchar2(20),
Sal number(7,2),
member procedure
Give_Bonus
)
/
— The implementation follows
— Note the use of the word body
create or replace type body Employee_T as

member procedure
Give_Bonus is
        v_bonus number;
        v_total number;

begin
— determine the bonus as a percentage
        v_bonus :=
        case
                when Sal > 100000 then 10
                when Sal > 50000 then 20
                when Sal > 20000 then 30
                else 40
        end;
— calculate total salary
        v_total := Sal*(1+v_bonus/100);
— print the bonus percentage and the total salary
        dbms_output.put_line('The bonus is '||v_bonus||' percent');
        dbms_output.put_line('The total is '||v_total);
end give_bonus;
end;
/
```

First, the class Employee_T is defined. Note that the procedure Give_Bonus is included somewhat similar to an attribute. In this case, there is no input parameter because a bonus is calculated based on an employee's salary, and the salary value is obtained from the attribute *sal* of the object. However, if the bonus were explicitly specified, and added to the salary to get the total, then the procedure give_bonus would be defined like give_bonus(v_bonus number).

Note that the procedure is detailed in a separate part by using the word *body*. Thus, encapsulation and information hiding is achieved because the details of the code need not be made public, while the definition of the class is made public. Both the definition and the implementation are compiled. The class Employee_T then can be instantiated and used just like in an object-oriented language such as Java or C#. A brief example coded in PL/SQL follows:

```
declare
— Construct an Employee object my_emp
        my_emp Employee_T := Employee_T(1234, 'Faisal Kaleem',
'Analyst', 90000);
```

```
begin
        my_emp.Give_Bonus;
end;
/
```

When run, the following output will appear:

The bonus is 20 percent
The total is 108000

PL/SQL procedure successfully completed.

PACKAGES

A package is a logical grouping of classes and can include specifications and implementations of these classes. The purpose of a package is to organize the classes. Think about how you organize shelf space or how you organize files in a directory—the notion of package is similar. A package also can include source or program code, collaborations, requirements, diagrams, and other (nested) packages, narrative documentation, tests or verifications documents, and other documents (D'Souza & Wills, 2002). A package diagram shows the packages and the relationships among them.

Packages should have some desirable characteristics. Packages can be based on several criteria:

a. **Cohesiveness:** Classes in a package should pertain to the same business subsystem. For example, a math class would not be placed in a sales package. However, Order and LineItem should go together in a sales package.
b. **Allocation of resources among development teams:** For project management reasons, a project can be divided into units, which are assigned to different groups and different sites. For example, a package related to the core business might be developed in-house, and another related to utilities might be outsourced or purchased.
c. **User types:** For example, knowledge workers like engineers might use a system in a considerably different manner compared to order-taking clerks.
d. **Propensity to change:** If the boundary classes are likely to experience considerable change in the future, they should be placed in a separate package. Otherwise, packages should be demarcated based on functional grounds.
e. **Development phase:** A package created for the analysis phase may have a corresponding package for the design phase.
f. **Separate utilities from system-specific components:** This allows the development team to focus on the critical development pieces in a system.

To determine whether the classes in a package are functionally related, use the following criteria:

a. Does the change in one class affect the other class?
b. If one class is removed, does it impact the other class?
c. Do objects of classes exchange several messages?
d. Is the purpose of a boundary class to present information from an entity class?
e. Do the classes relate to each other by foreign keys or references?
f. Do objects of one class create objects of another?

Dependency
A relationship that denotes that one element from a package needs data, information, or functionality from an element from another package.

A package diagram shows the relationships among packages. An important relationship shown is the dependency relationship. In business terms, a dependency relationship means that one package has an element that depends on another element in another package. In design terms, a dependency relationship means that an element from one package needs data, information, or functionality from an element from another package (Pender, 2003). The dependency relationship is represented by a dashed arrow.

Figure 12.7
Packages CRM
and Sale

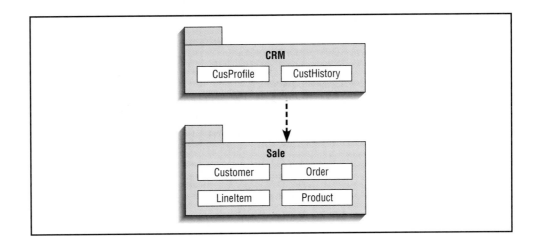

Consider the package diagram in Figure 12.7. It shows a package Sale, which has four classes: Customer, Order, LineItem, and Product. Suppose that the company would like to emphasize customer relations (CRM), which needs two additional classes: CustProfile and CustHistory. The class CustHistory will store historical information about a customer's purchases, and the class CustProfile will store customer preferences, information obtained from solicited contacts, and buying behavior. Since CRM obtains its data and information from the four classes of the Sale Package, there is a dependency between CRM and Sale.

DESIGN CLASS DIAGRAMS

Design class diagram
A class diagram that shows the visibility and types of attributes, and the signature of the operations.

An analysis class diagram lists the attributes and the responsibilities of each class, and the relationships among classes. At this stage, it is time to ensure that the appropriate class has a given responsibility. During design, each class is detailed so that the attributes are qualified by data types and the responsibilities are transformed into operations. The detailed diagram is called a design class diagram. Sample data types were listed in the previous chapter. Each attribute is qualified by its type. Further, the visibility of each attribute is stated explicitly. In an analysis diagram, the visibility is not specified, or it defaults to private for attributes and public for operations. The operations are detailed to reveal their signatures, that is, the list of arguments with types, and the return type of the operation, if applicable.

Signature
The list of arguments with types, and the return type of the operation, if applicable.

Verifying Responsibility Allocation

The chapter on analysis classes discussed how to assign responsibilities using sequence diagrams. Before mapping the responsibilities to operations, certain checks should be performed to ensure that a given responsibility indeed belongs to the appropriate class. Larman (2001) provides guidelines in this regard using the notion of pattern. A pattern is a named description of a problem and solution that can be applied to new contexts.

Pattern
A named description of a problem and solution that can be applied to new contexts.

1. Assign a responsibility to the information expert—the class that has the information necessary to fulfill the responsibility. For example, the class OrderControl has the responsibility //calcTotal to calculate totalAmount. However, the class Order, which is related to LineItem, has all the information necessary to calculate totalAmount, so this responsibility can be allocated to Order. Similarly, the class LineItem has all the information to calculate lineAmount. This solution is called the *expert* pattern and is the most commonly used pattern.

2. Assign class B the responsibility to create an object of class A if B aggregates A, B contains A, B closely uses A, or B has the initializing data that will be passed to A when it is created. Thus, the class Order may take the responsibility for sending messages for creating LineItem objects. This solution is called the *creator* pattern.

3. Assign a responsibility so that coupling remains low and cohesion remains high. Coupling is a measure of how strongly one class is connected to, has knowledge of, or relies upon other classes. Cohesion measures the strength and focus among the responsibilities of a class. In other words, cohesion is high if the responsibilities of a class do related work. If a class is assigned too many responsibilities, it is likely that the class is bloated and not cohesive. This can happen in a control class if it does not delegate work. These solutions are called *loose coupling* and *strong cohesion*. For example, the transaction Order is quite central and is closely associated with customer, lineitem, and product, and can, thus, be assigned the responsibility to collate order-related information from the entity classes.

Let's examine how an analysis sequence diagram changes if the aforementioned patterns are applied to the Pine Valley Furniture Webstore case. The resulting design sequence diagram is illustrated in Figure 12.8. Note that the object :Order can create the object :LineItem because the order aggregates the line items. The object :Order is also the information expert and can be used to collect information necessary to review order as well as to confirm order.

Visibility

Let's consider the design class Product as shown in Figure 12.9. The name of the class is shown along with its package name—Inventory. Each attribute name (or field name) is preceded by its visibility sign and followed by its type. The operations of the class have been detailed.

Visibility implies whether other objects can access an attribute or an operation directly. The + sign denotes that the visibility is public and that other objects can access the attribute or the operation directly. The − sign denotes that the visibility is private and that the attributes and operations are meant to be used only by the owning object; other objects cannot access the attribute or operation directly. To preserve encapsulation, it is recommended that attributes have private visibility. Other objects can obtain a value of an attribute by requesting a method of the class. Such methods are called the Get methods. CASE tools can generate a basic code for these methods automatically. If an attribute called ProdName exists, then a corresponding method, getProdName(), will allow access to the value of the attribute. During the Get operation, the method can display the value in a specific way. For example, a data value may be stored as a number and displayed in one of the several popular ways. The Get methods are sometimes considered implicit and may not be shown in a design class.

Similar to Get methods are Set methods, which provide the initial values of attributes when an object is created. Thus, for the attribute ProdName, there will also be a method setProdName(string vProdName), where vProdName is a new value for the ProdName attribute of the object. The Get methods and the Set methods are popular in the object-oriented approach and are meant to protect the visibility of the data as well as perform any action while getting or setting values of attributes. Although the relational approach does not follow this convention, it can be implemented by using object wrappers. An object wrapper is basically a layer on top of a conventional RDB engine that simulates object-oriented features. Using object wrappers, the system appears object-oriented although the back end is relational.

Protected visibility is in between public and private, and it implies visibility to the owning object, other objects of the same class, and objects of that class's subclass.

Visibility
The characteristics of an attribute or an operation that reveal whether it can be accessed directly.

Public
Visible to any requesting object (i.e., client).

Private
Visible to the owning object only.

Protected visibility
Visible to the owning object, other objects of the same class, and objects of that class's subclass.

Figure 12.8 Design Sequence Diagram for the Use Case Place Order

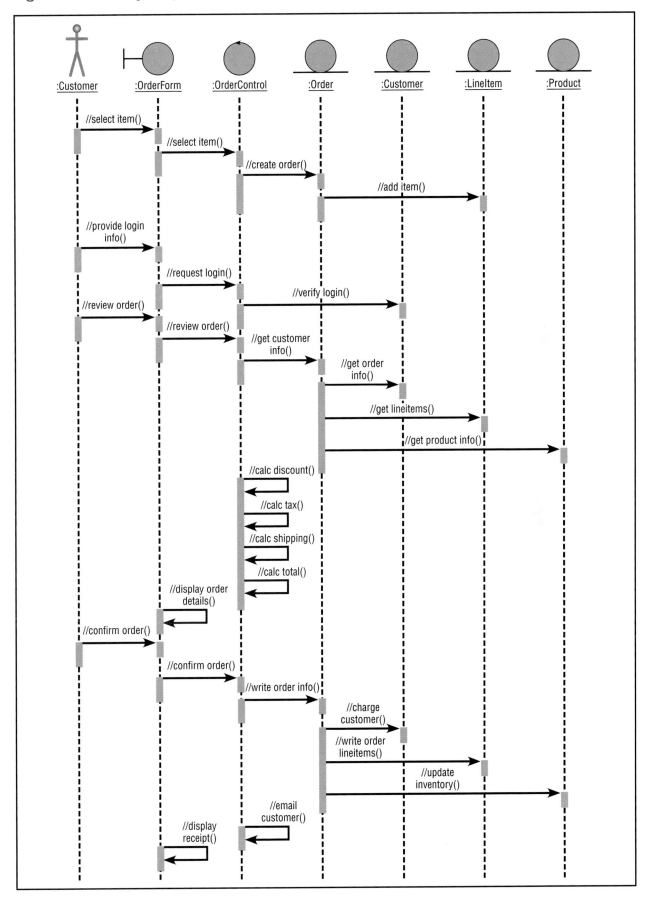

Figure 12.9
Design Class Product

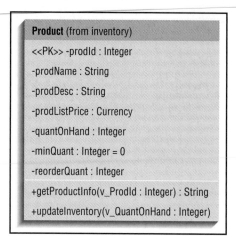

Product (from inventory)
<<PK>> -prodId : Integer
-prodName : String
-prodDesc : String
-prodListPrice : Currency
-quantOnHand : Integer
-minQuant : Integer = 0
-reorderQuant : Integer
+getProductInfo(v_ProdId : Integer) : String
+updateInventory(v_QuantOnHand : Integer)

In Figure 7.29, the classes HourlyEmp and SalariedEmp are subclasses of Employee. Thus, an object of the subclass SalariedEmp will have direct access to the attribute empDateHired, and it can retrieve or update it.

Attribute Types

Each attribute is qualified by its type. Further, if any attribute value needs to be defaulted during creation of an object, it is specified after the type. For example, in Figure 12.9, the attribute minQuant will get a value of 0 if not explicitly specified during the creation of a PRODUCT row object.

The responsibilities //get product info and //update inventory of the analysis Product class are now transformed to operations getProductInfo and updateInventory. An operation typically will take arguments and return one or more values. The operation getProductInfo takes in an argument v_ProdId of type integer and returns a string that contains values from attributes such as ProdName, ProdDesc, and ListPrice.

Next, consider the design class Order (Figure 12.10). Note that the class has several derived attributes. A common notation for derived attribute is /. Thus, subtotal is shown as /-subTotal, the prefix /- implying that the attribute is derived and private. The class also shows the foreign key custId, but instead of a simple type like Integer, it is qualified as of type Customer. This is the foreign key method of showing a relationship. If the relationship between Order and Customer is to be shown using references, then CustId will not be included in the class Order. Instead, the line showing the link between the two design classes will suggest that the relationship should be implemented using references.

Figure 12.10
Design Class Order

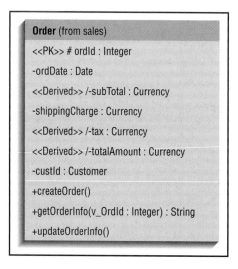

Order (from sales)
<<PK>> # ordId : Integer
-ordDate : Date
<<Derived>> /-subTotal : Currency
-shippingCharge : Currency
<<Derived>> /-tax : Currency
<<Derived>> /-totalAmount : Currency
-custId : Customer
+createOrder()
+getOrderInfo(v_OrdId : Integer) : String
+updateOrderInfo()

52. A technology that mixes Java code with HTML and XML to generate dynamic Web pages.
53. A scripting language created by Netscape to enhance the functionality and appearance of Web pages. JavaScript is not Java. The Microsoft version is called Jscript.
54. A low-level, platform-independent language that is created as an intermediate step when a language is compiled in .NET.
55. Application layer sandwiched between presentation and data layers.
56. A design architecture based on multiple layers that address presentation, business logic, and data.
57. An open-membership, not-for-profit consortium that produces and maintains computer industry specifications for interoperable enterprise applications.
58. A middleware based on COM objects that allows connection between an application program and a database in a DBMS-independent manner. OLE DB allows access to relational and other kinds of databases.
59. The front tier, which addresses the presentation of information to users and acceptance of commands from the users. It may embed some rules such as formatting, calculations, and constraint checking.
60. Visible to the owning object only.

61. Visible to the owning object, other objects of the same class, and objects of that class's subclass.
62. Visible to any requesting object (i.e., client).
63. The classes and components required to support the services at run time.
64. A software element with a well-defined interface and functionality for a specific purpose that can be deployed in a variety of applications using plug-and-play capability; invariably purchased from a third party.
65. The partitioning of a system into layers such that each layer performs a specific type of functionality and communicates with the layers that adjoin it.
66. A scripting language created by Microsoft to enhance the functionality and appearance of Web pages. It is a subset of VB, but it is not popular because many browsers do not support it directly. It is used more in the server-side ASP.
67. A language that helps individuals write programs to create applications for the Microsoft Windows operating system and for use over the Internet.
68. A tool kit that uses C++ and is supported by Microsoft foundation classes.
69. Software that contains a suite of tools and languages, which includes VB .NET, C#, ADO.NET, ASP.NET, and XML creation facilities.

REVIEW QUESTIONS

1. How is design different from analysis?
2. What is a design architecture? What factors impact the choice of a design architecture?
3. What is enterprise application design? How can scalability be achieved in a large project?
4. What is middleware? What is the main advantage of using middleware?
5. What is a component? What are the advantages of using components?
6. What are the key advantages of using a SOAP/XML standard over COM, EJB, and CORBA? What is the main disadvantage?
7. What is a framework?
8. What is a Web service?
9. What are the advantages and disadvantages of using scripting languages at the browser?
10. What does the term *dynamic* in dynamic link library (DLL) suggest?
11. How is a package different from a component?
12. What is a transaction? What is the ACID test? Give examples of transactions.

PROBLEMS AND EXERCISES

1. Conduct a Web search using terms like *component.* Who is supplying components? List examples of functionality that can be provided by using components.
2. Compare and contrast the popular tiered design architectures.
3. If you are familiar with the structured approach, compare and contrast the design class diagram approach with structured charts.
4. Consider a payroll application. Make suitable assumptions to come up with an analysis class diagram. Translate it to a design class diagram.
5. Consider a student enrollment application. Make suitable assumptions to come up with an analysis class diagram. Translate it to a design class diagram.
6. Consider a hotel reservation example. Make suitable assumptions to come up with an analysis class diagram. Translate it to a design class diagram.

1. Discuss the pros and cons of a component-based design modeling approach.
2. How can the mismatch between an object-oriented application tier and an object-relational database tier be reconciled?
3. How can legacy systems be incorporated within an object-oriented framework?
4. If possible, contact a designer in a local organization. Discuss how design is addressed at his or her company. Who, other than designers, are involved in the design? What design training is given? Do they use components?

5. If you are a designer and the coding in your company typically is outsourced offshore, do you need to take any additional steps in the design?
6. Talk to MIS professionals at a variety of organizations and determine the extent to which CASE tools are used in design. Try to determine whether or not they use CASE tools for this purpose; which CASE tools are used; and why, when, and how they are used. In companies that do not use CASE tools for this purpose, determine why not and what would have to change in order for them to use them.
7. To what degree will you conduct design for an enterprise resource planning (ERP) system?

CASE: BROADWAY ENTERTAINMENT COMPANY, INC.

Developing Design Elements for the Customer Relationship Management System

Case Introduction

The students from St. Claire Community College have developed some specifications for data entity design classes, but much more design work needs to be done for MyBroadway, the Web-based, customer relationship management system for Broadway Entertainment Company stores. They need to decide on an architecture for their prototype as well as propose an architecture for the real system. They need to decide on the use of components. Finally, they need to convert the sequence diagrams from the analysis phase into sequence diagrams at the design stage.

Design Architecture

The students need to make two decisions here on the design architecture—one for the prototype, and the second for the proposed system. They discuss the latter first. It is evident that customers will use a Web interface, so a three-tier architecture is the natural conclusion for the proposed system. But they also have to demonstrate a prototype. They are working on a limited budget, so the purchase of components or expensive software is ruled out. They will have to work with the academic software available in the college for their class project. If a component is required, they will include it in the proposal, but for their prototype, they will simulate the functionality or simplify it. For example, they will not perform credit card checks, but will assume that the customer has the capability to pay for a transaction, or simulate the functionality from a class.

Yet, they would like it to be realistic and use state-of-the-art technology. Fortunately, their college has academic

licenses with Oracle and Microsoft, and so they can build a class project without incurring extra expenses. Since most students on the team have taken courses that employed Oracle and VB.NET, the team feels that they can build a prototype on a stand-alone first in an initial iteration, and then modify the code to show it as a two-tier application. In the second iteration, they will also add some error-handling capabilities. They will not go to a three-tier application for the prototype.

Project Management Plan of Detailed Design and Implementation

The student team begins its work by reviewing the results of prior steps, especially the development of analysis classes and the object relations. The analysis class diagram they developed includes earlier inventories of all the data entity, boundary, and control classes they think they need for MyBroadway. The object relations show the attributes of each relation, and the associated documentation identifies data types, data integrity controls, and primary and secondary keys. The sequence diagrams and other documentation related to analysis classes provide further background information. The team won't design all of the classes at once. They will divide the design into two high-level packages—those that are related to the transaction of rental extension, and the remaining ones. If necessary, they will divide the packages further. Each package will be handled in a separate iteration. However, they have also made an earlier decision to iteratively expand the prototype from single-tier to two-tier architecture. They will hold a meeting with Carrie and their instructor in attendance to finalize the management of the detailed design and implementation. The team members have agreed to keep the prototype simple, but functionally accurate.

Developing Design Classes

At the analysis stage, the team had employed robustness analysis to come up with sequence diagrams. The team calls these diagrams "analysis sequence diagrams," and needs to convert them into "design analysis diagrams." When using robustness analysis, the business logic was concentrated into control classes. Entity objects, for example, were relegated simple responsibilities, such as providing the value of an attribute. The students decide to use Larman's patterns to distribute the business logic among the three classes.

CASE QUESTIONS

1. Consider each sequence diagram you developed at the analysis stage and translate it into a design sequence diagram.
2. Select the class diagram corresponding to a sequence diagram. Detail the signature for each operation.
3. Write a short report that presents the design and implementation plan. How many iterations are involved? Do packages help with the planning?

The students first consider the transaction-oriented use cases. They assess that the transaction entity object is central to a transaction-oriented use case, and has the knowledge about other objects. A transaction also has an aggregate relationship with respect to its line items. Hence, some of the logic associated with control classes will shift to the transaction entity classes (such as rental extension).

Case Summary

The students complete the design of each sequence diagram. They are now ready to add the parameters and visibility of the attributes and operations. The student team is eager to begin prototyping. Soon they will also have to design specific human interfaces for each boundary class, but first they must make sure that the logic of the operations for each boundary class is right.

4. Choose a development environment (e.g., VB.NET and Oracle), and based on the scope defined by your instructor, develop your own prototype.
5. Do you agree that the transaction entity class in a transaction-oriented use case, such as placing an order or making a reservation, is the "expert" class and needs to handle and coordinate the logic?

Chapter 13

Designing the Human Interface

Chapter Objectives

After studying this chapter, you should be able to:

➤ Explain the process of designing forms and reports and the deliverables for their creation.

➤ Apply the general guidelines for formatting forms and reports.

➤ Describe how to format text, tables, and lists effectively, and explain common errors when designing Web layouts.

➤ Explain the process of designing interfaces and dialogues, and the deliverables for their creation.

➤ Describe and apply the general guidelines for interface design, including guidelines for layout design, structuring data entry fields, providing feedback, and system help.

➤ Explain the common errors when designing Web interfaces.

➤ Design human–computer dialogues, including the use of dialogue diagramming.

Chapter Contents

➤ Chapter Preview
➤ Designing Forms and Reports
➤ Formatting Forms and Reports
➤ Designing Interfaces and Dialogues
➤ Designing Interfaces
➤ Designing Dialogues

Analysts must complete three important activities during system design, as illustrated in Figure 13.1: designing the physical database, developing design classes, and designing the human interface. This chapter focuses on guidelines for designing the human–computer interface. This discussion is divided into two major areas: the design of forms and reports, and the design of dialogues. The next section describes the process of designing forms and reports, and provides guidance on the deliverables produced during this process. This is followed by a general discussion of guidelines for formatting information. Next, guidelines are provided for designing interfaces and human–computer dialogues. Finally, a method for representing human–computer dialogues, called dialogue diagrams, is presented.

Figure 13.1 Systems Design Has Three Parts: Physical Database Design, Creating Design Elements, and Designing the Human Interface

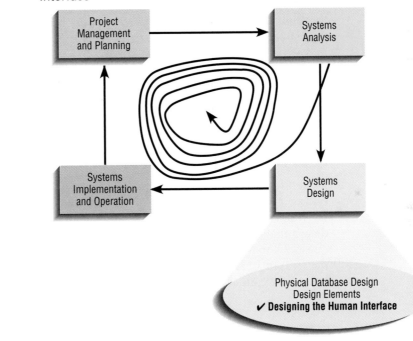

DESIGNING FORMS AND REPORTS

System inputs and outputs—forms and reports—are the way in which humans exchange information with a computer-based system. During systems analysis, the focus is on identifying system requirements, developing use cases, modeling data, and creating class diagrams. Through this analysis, one gains an understanding of which forms and reports need to exist and the content they need to contain. However, during analysis, the designer should not be concerned with the precise appearance of these forms and reports. Prototypes of forms and reports that emerged during analysis might have been distributed to users as a way to confirm requirements. Forms and reports are closely related to use-case diagrams developed during requirements structuring.

For those who are unfamiliar with computer-based information systems, it will be helpful to clarify exactly what a form or report is in this context. A form is a business document containing some predefined data; it often includes some areas where additional data are to be filled in. Most forms have a stylized format and usually are not arranged in simple rows and columns. Examples of business forms are product order forms, employment applications, and class registration sheets. Traditionally, forms have been displayed on a paper medium, but today video display technology allows the layout of almost any printed form to be duplicated, including an organizational logo or any graphic, on a video display terminal. Forms on a video display can be used for data display or data entry. Additional examples of forms are an electronic spreadsheet, computer sign-on or menu, and an automated teller machine (ATM) transaction layout. On the Internet, form interaction is the standard method of gathering and displaying information when consumers order products, request product information, or query account status.

A report is a business document containing only predefined data; it is a passive document used solely for reading or viewing. Examples of reports are invoices, weekly sales summaries by region and salesperson, and a pie chart of population by age categories (see Table 13-1). Typically, one thinks of a report as printed on paper, but a report can be printed to a computer file, a visual display screen, or some other medium such as microfilm. Often, a report has rows and columns of data, but a report can be in any format, such as mailing labels. Frequently, the differences between a form and a report are subtle. A report is only for reading and often contains data about multiple unrelated records in a computer file. On the other hand, a form typically contains data from only one record or is, at least, based on one record, such as data about one customer, one order, or one student. The guidelines for the design of forms and reports are similar.

The Process of Designing Forms and Reports

Designing forms and reports is a user-focused activity that typically follows a prototyping approach (see Figure 5.7 to review the prototyping method). First, the intended user and task objectives must be understood during the requirements determination process. During this process, the intended user must answer several questions that attempt to answer the who, what, when, where, and how related to the creation of all forms or reports, as listed in Table 13-2. Understanding these questions is a required first step in the creation of any form or report.

Table 13-1
Common Type of Business Reports.

REPORT NAME	DESCRIPTION
Scheduled Reports	Reports produced at predefined intervals—daily, weekly, or monthly—to support the routine informational needs of an organization.
Key-Indicator Reports	Reports that provide a summary of critical information on recurring basis.
Exception Reports	Reports that highlight data that are out of the normal operating range.
Dull Down Reports	Reports that provide details behind the summary values on a key-indicator or exception report.
Ad Hoc Report	Unplanned information requests in which information is gathered to support a nonroutine decision.

Table 13-2
Fundamental Questions When Designing Forms and Reports.

1. Who will use the form or report?
2. What is the purpose of the form or report?
3. When is the form or report needed and used?
4. Where does the form or report need to be delivered and used?
5. How many people need to use or view the form or report?

Understanding the skills and abilities of users helps in the creation of an effective design. Are the system's anticipated users experienced computer users or novices? What are their educational levels business backgrounds and task-relevant knowledge? Answers to these questions provide guidance for the format and the content of the designs. Also, what is the purpose of the form or report? What task will users be performing, and what information is needed to complete this task? Other questions also are important to consider. Where will the users be when performing this task? Will users have access to online systems, or will they be in the field? How many people will need to use this form or report? If, for example, a report is being produced for a single user, the design requirements and usability assessment will be relatively simple. A design for a larger audience, however, might need to go through a more extensive requirements collection and usability assessment process.

After collecting the initial requirements, this information is structured and refined into an initial prototype. Structuring and refining the requirements are completed without assistance from the users, although users might need to be contacted occasionally to clarify some issue that was overlooked during analysis. Finally, users are asked to review and evaluate the prototype; then they can accept the design or request that changes be made. If changes are needed, the construction-evaluate-refinement cycle is repeated until the design is accepted. Usually, several repetitions of this cycle occur during the design of a single form or report. As with any prototyping process, these iterations should occur rapidly in order to gain the greatest benefits from this design approach.

The initial prototype can be constructed in numerous environments, including Windows, Linux, Apple, or HTML. The obvious choice is to employ standard development tools used within the organization. Often, initial prototypes are simply mock screens that are not working modules or systems. Mock screens also can be produced from a word processor, computer graphics design package, electronic spreadsheet, or even paper (Snyder, 2003). It is important to remember that although the focus of this activity is on the design—content and layout—the way that specific forms or reports are implemented must be considered. It is fortunate that tools for designing forms and reports are evolving rapidly, making development faster and easier. In the past, inputs and outputs of all types typically were designed by hand on a coding or layout sheet. For example, Figure 13.2 shows the layout of a data input form using a coding sheet.

Although coding sheets are still used, their importance has diminished due to significant changes in system operating environments and the evolution of automated design tools. Prior to the creation of graphical operating environments, for example, analysts designed many inputs and outputs that were 80 columns (characters) by 25 rows, the standard dimensions for most video displays. These limits in screen dimensions are radically different in graphical operating environments such as Microsoft's Windows or the Web, where font sizes and screen dimensions often can be changed from user to user. Consequently, the creation of new tools and development environments was needed to help analysts and programmers develop these graphical and flexible designs. Figure 13.3 shows an example of the same data input form as designed in Microsoft's Visual Basic. Note the variety of fonts, sizes, and highlighting that was used. Given the need for rapid, iterative development in OOSAD, tools that seamlessly move prototype designs to functional systems are rapidly becoming the standard in most professional development organizations.

Deliverables and Outcomes

When designing forms and reports, design specifications are the major deliverables and are inputs to the system implementation and operation activities. Design specifications have three sections:

1. Narrative overview with a use-case diagram.
2. Sample design.
3. Testing and usability assessment.

Figure 13.2 The Layout of a Data Input Form Using a Coding Sheet

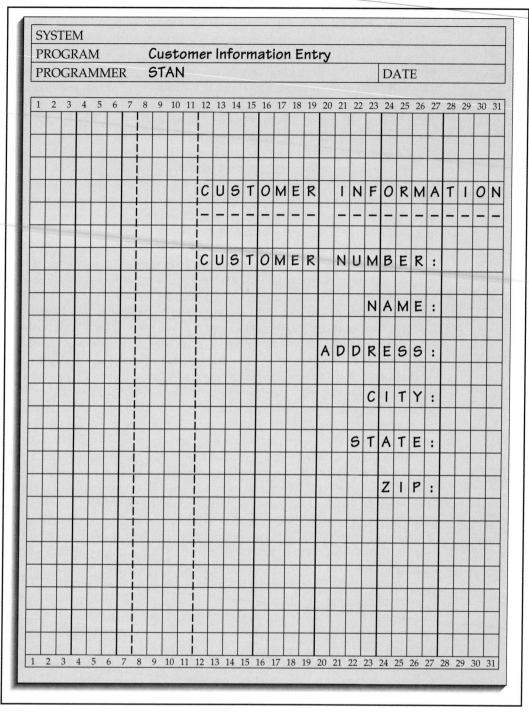

Figure 13.3
A Data Input Screen
Designed in
Microsoft's Visual
Basic

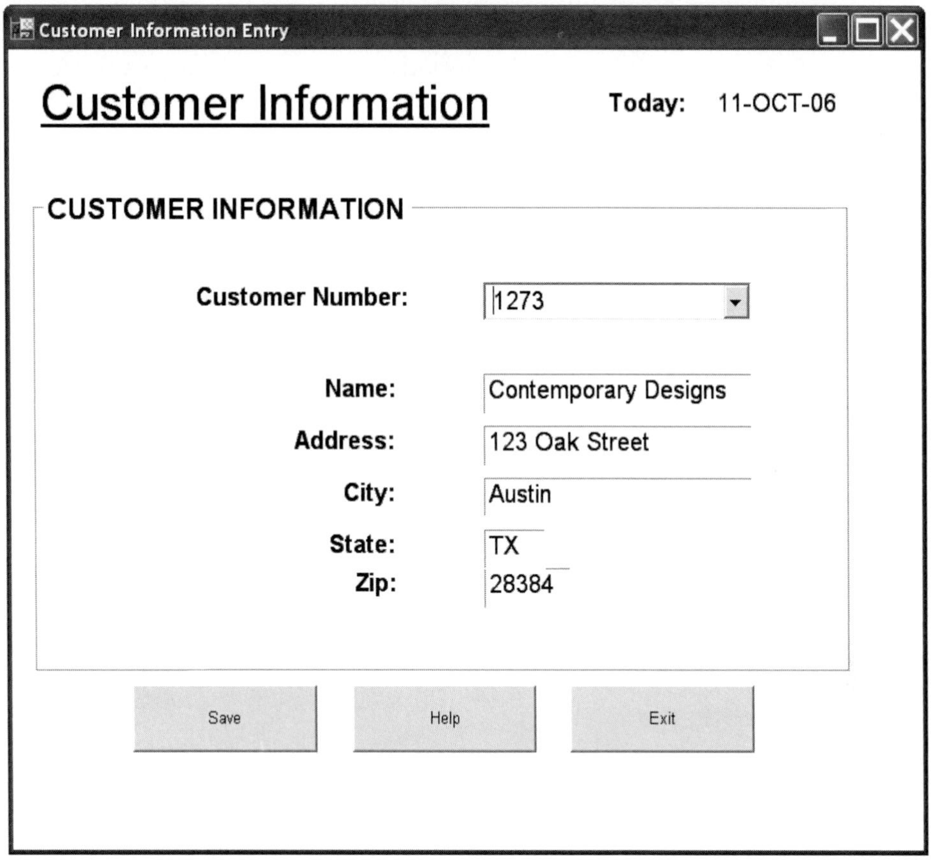

The narrative overview provides a general overview of the characteristics of the target users, tasks, system, and environmental factors in which the form or report will be used. Its purpose is to explain to those who actually will develop the final screen why it exists and how it will be used so that they can make the appropriate implementation decisions. This section includes a list of general information and the assumptions that helped shape the design. For example, Figure 13.4 shows an excerpt of a design specification for a Customer Account Status checking screen for the Pine Valley Furniture WebStore system. The first section of the specification, Figure 13.4a, provides a narrative overview containing the relevant information for developing and using the screen. The overview explains the tasks supported by the screen, where and when the form is used, characteristics of the people using the form, the technology delivering the form, and other pertinent information. For example, if the form is delivered on a visual display terminal, this section describes the capabilities of this device, such as whether it has a touch screen, and whether color and a mouse are available. In addition, a complete use-case diagram is included in this overview.

The second section of the specification, Figure 13.4b, shows a sample design of the screen. This design may be drawn by hand using a coding sheet although, in most instances, it is developed using CASE or standard development tools. Using actual development tools allows the design to be more thoroughly tested and assessed. The final section of the specification, Figure 13.4c, provides all testing and usability assessment information. Some specification information might be irrelevant when designing certain forms and reports. For example, the design of a simple yes/no selection form might be so straightforward that no usability assessment is needed. Also, much of the narrative overview might be unnecessary unless intended to highlight some exception that must be considered during implementation.

Figure 13.4 A Design Specification for a Customer Account Status Form for Pine Valley Furniture: (a) the Narrative Overview Containing the Relevant Information to Developing and Using the Form within PVF; (b) a Sample Design of the PVF Form; (c) Testing and Usability Assessment Information

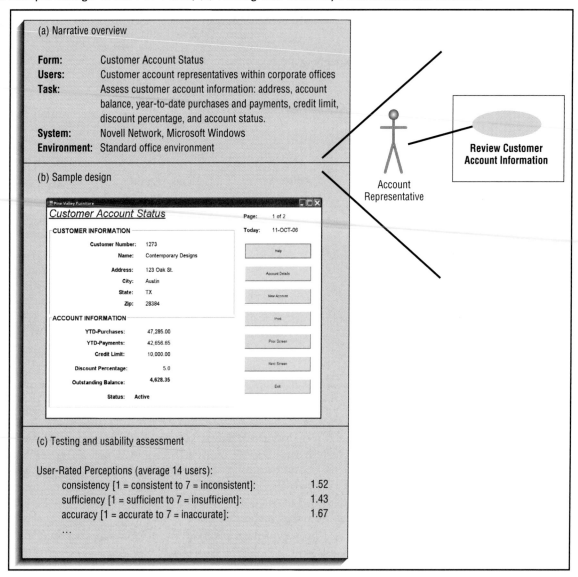

FORMATTING FORMS AND REPORTS

A wide variety of information can be provided to users of information systems using a wide variety of formats ranging from text to video to audio. As technology continues to evolve, a greater variety of data types will be used. A definitive set of rules for delivering every type of information to users has yet to be defined because these rules are evolving continuously along with the rapid changes in technology. Research on human–computer interaction has provided numerous general guidelines for formatting information. Many of these guidelines undoubtedly will apply to the formatting of all evolving information types on yet-to-be-determined devices. Keep in mind that designing usable forms and reports requires active interaction with users. If this single and fundamental activity occurs, the designer will likely create effective designs.

For example, personal digital assistants (PDAs) like the Palm Pilot or Pocket PC are becoming increasingly popular. PDAs are used to manage personal schedules, send and receive electronic mail, and browse the Web. One of the greatest challenges of handheld computing is in the design of the human–computer interface because the video display is significantly smaller than full-size displays, and many devices do not always have a color display. These two characteristics represent significant challenges for application designers. For example, surfing the Web on a PDA is difficult because most Internet sites still assume that users will have a full-size, color display. To address this problem, the Web browser on a Pocket PC is "smart" and automatically shrinks images so that the user's viewing experience is adequate. Alternatively, a growing number of Web sites are designed with the PDA user specifically in mind. For example, these sites provide a vast array of information preformatted for smaller screens. As these and other computing devices evolve and gain in popularity, standard guidelines will emerge to make the process of designing interfaces for them much less challenging.

General Formatting Guidelines

Over the past several years, industry and academic researchers have investigated how information formatting influences individual task performance and perceptions of usability. Through this work, several guidelines for formatting information have emerged, as highlighted in Table 13-3. These guidelines reflect some of the general truths of formatting most types of information. The differences between a well-designed form or report and a poorly designed one often will be obvious. For example, Figure 13.5a shows a poorly designed form for viewing a current account balance for a PVF WebStore customer. Figure 13.5b (only page 2 of 2 is shown) is a better design, incorporating several general guidelines from Table 13-3.

The first major difference between the two forms has to do with the title. The title in Figure 13.5a (Customer Information) is ambiguous, whereas the title in Figure 13.5b (Detail Customer Account Information) clearly and specifically describes the contents of the form. The form in Figure 13.5b also includes the date (October 11, 2006). The form was generated so that, if printed, it will be clear to the reader when this occurred. Figure 13.5a displays information that is extraneous to the intent of the form—viewing the current account balance—and provides information that is not in the most useful format for the user. For example, Figure 13.5a provides all customer data as well as account transactions and a summary of year-to-date purchases and payments. The form does not, however, provide the current outstanding balance of the account, leaving the reader to perform a manual calculation. The layout of information between the two forms also varies in balance and information density. Gaining an understanding of the skills of the intended system users and the tasks they will be performing is invaluable when constructing a form or report. By following these general guidelines, the designer's chances of creating effective forms and

Table 13-3
Guidelines for Designing Forms and Reports.

GUIDELINE	DESCRIPTION
Use meaningful titles	Clear and specific titles describing content and use of form or report.
	Revision date or code to distinguish a form or report from prior versions.
	Current date that identifies when the form or report was generated.
	Valid date that identifies on what date (or time) the data in the form or report were accurate.
Include meaningful information	Only needed information displayed.
	Information provided in a usable manner without modification.
Balance the layout	Information balanced on the screen or page.
	Adequate spacing and margins used.
	All data and entry fields clearly labeled.
Design an easy navigation system	Clearly show how to move forward and backward.
	Clearly show where you are (e.g., page 1 of 3). Notify user of the last page of a multipage sequence.

Figure 13.5 Contrast of a Poorly Designed and a Well-Designed Form: (a) A Poorly Designed Form for Viewing a Current Account Balance for a PVF WebStore Customer; (b) a Better Design, which Incorporates Several General Guidelines from Table 13-3

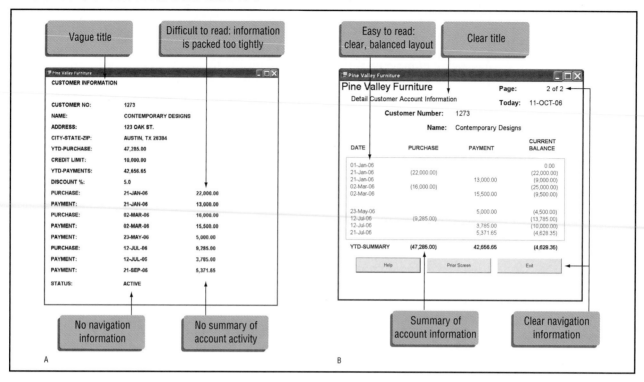

reports will be enhanced. The next sections discuss specific guidelines for highlighting information, displaying text, and presenting numeric tables and lists.

Highlighting Information

As display technologies continue to improve, a greater variety of methods will be available to highlight information. Table 13-4 lists the most commonly used methods for highlighting information. Given this vast array of options, it is important to consider how highlighting can be used to enhance an output without being a distraction. In general, highlighting should be used sparingly to draw the user to or away from certain information and to group together related information. In several situations, highlighting can be a valuable technique for conveying special information:

- Notifying users of errors in data entry or processing.
- Providing warnings to users regarding possible problems such as unusual data values or an unavailable device.
- Drawing attention to keywords, commands, high-priority messages, and data that have changed or gone outside normal operating ranges.

Table 13-4
Methods of
Highlighting.

Blinking and audible tones
Color differences
Intensity differences
Size differences
Font differences
Reverse video
Boxing
Underlining
All capital letters
Offsetting the position of nonstandard information

Figure 13.6
A Form in Which
Several Types of
Highlighting Are Used

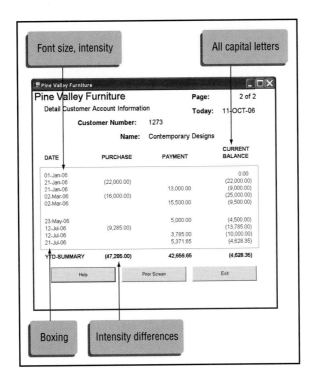

Highlighting techniques can be used singularly or in tandem, depending upon the level of emphasis desired by the designer. Figure 13.6 shows a form where several types of highlighting are used. In this example, boxes clarify different categories of data, capital letters and different fonts distinguish labels from actual data, and bolding is used to draw attention to important data.

Highlighting should be used conservatively. For example, blinking and audible tones should be used only to highlight critical information requiring the user's immediate response. Once a response is made, these highlights should be turned off. In addition, highlighting methods should be selected consistently and used based upon the level of importance of the emphasized information. It is also important to examine how a particular highlighting method appears on all possible output devices that could be used with the system. For example, some color combinations might convey appropriate information on one display configuration but wash out and reduce legibility on another.

Recent advances in the development of graphical operating environments such as Windows, Macintosh, or the Web have provided designers with some standard highlighting guidelines. However, because these guidelines are evolving continuously, they are often vague and leave a great deal of control in the hands of the systems developer. To realize the benefits of using standard graphical operating environments—such as reduced user training time and interoperability among systems—one must be disciplined in how highlighting is used.

Displaying Text

In business-related systems, textual output is becoming increasingly important as text-based applications such as electronic mail, bulletin boards, and information services (e.g., Dow Jones Industrial Average stock index) are more widely used. The display and formatting of system help screens, which often contain lengthy textual descriptions and examples, is one example of textual data that can benefit from following the simple guidelines that have emerged from systems design research. These guidelines appear in Table 13-5. The first one is simple: Text should be displayed using common writing conventions such as mixed uppercase and lowercase and appropriate punctuation. For large blocks of text, and if space permits, text should be double-spaced. However, if the text is short or rarely used, it might make sense to use single spacing and place a blank

Table 13-5
Guidelines for
Displaying Text.

Case	Display text in mixed upper- and lowercase and use conventional punctuation.
Spacing	Use double-spacing if space permits. If not, place a blank line between paragraphs.
Justification	Left-justify text and leave a ragged-right margin.
Hyphenation	Do not hyphenate words between lines.
Abbreviations	Use abbreviations and acronyms only when they are widely understood by users and are significantly shorter than the full text.

line between each paragraph. Text also should be left justified with a ragged-right margin; research shows that a ragged-right margin makes it easier to find the next line of text when reading than when text is left and right justified.

When displaying textual information, the designer also should be careful not to hyphenate words between lines or use obscure abbreviations and acronyms. Users might not know whether the hyphen is a significant character if it is used to continue words across lines. Information and terminology that are not widely understood by the intended users could influence the usability of the system significantly. Thus, abbreviations and acronyms should be used only if they are significantly shorter than the full text and are commonly known by the intended system users. Figure 13.7 shows two versions of a help screen from an application system at PVF. Figure 13.7a shows many violations of the general guidelines for displaying text, whereas Figure 13.7b shows the same information following the general guidelines. Formatting guidelines for the entry of text and alphanumeric data are also important and will be discussed later in this chapter.

Designing Tables and Lists

Unlike textual information, where context and meaning are derived through reading, the context and meaning of tables and lists are derived from the format of the information. Consequently, the usability of information displayed in tables and alphanumeric lists is likely to be much more influenced by effective layout than most other types of information display. As with the display of textual information, tables and lists also can be enhanced greatly by following a few simple guidelines that are sum-

Figure 13.7 Contrasting Two Help Screens from an Application System at PVF: (a) A Poorly Designed Help Screen with Many Violations of the General Guidelines for Displaying Text; (b) an Improved Design for a Help Screen

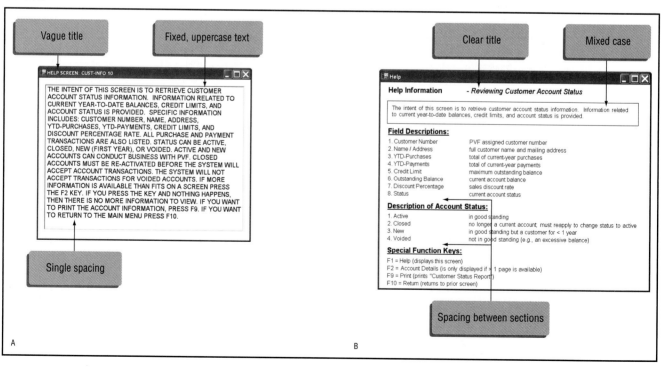

Table 13-6 General Guidelines for Displaying Tables and Lists.

GUIDELINE	DESCRIPTION
Use meaningful labels	All columns and rows should have meaningful labels.
	Labels should be separated from other information by using highlighting.
	Redisplay labels when the data extend beyond a single screen or page.
Formatting columns, rows, and text	Sort in a meaningful order (e.g., ascending, descending, or alphabetic).
	Place a blank line between every five rows in long columns.
	Similar information displayed in multiple columns should be sorted vertically (i.e., read from top to bottom, not left to right).
	Columns should have at least two spaces between them.
	Allow white space on printed reports for user to write notes.
	Use a single typeface, except for emphasis.
	Use same family of typefaces within and across displays and reports.
	Avoid overly fancy fonts.
Formatting numeric, textual, and alphanumeric data	Right-justify *numeric data* and align columns by decimal points or other delimiter.
	Left-justify *textual data*. Use short line length, usually 30 to 40 characters per line (this is what newspapers use, and it is easy to speed-read).
	Break long sequences of *alphanumeric data* into small groups of three to four characters each.

marized in Table 13-6. These guidelines should be reviewed and applied carefully to assure that tables and lists are highly usable.

Figure 13.8 shows two versions of a form design from a Pine Valley Furniture application system that displays customer year-to-date transaction information in a table format. Figure 13.8a displays the information without consideration of the guidelines presented in Table 13.6, and Figure 13.8b (only page 2 of 2 is shown) displays this information after consideration of these guidelines.

One key distinction between these two display forms relates to labeling. The information reported in Figure 13.8b has meaningful labels that stand out more clearly compared to the display in Figure 13.8a. Transactions are sorted by date, and numeric data are right justified and aligned by decimal point in Figure 13.8b, which

Figure 13.8 Contrasting Two Pine Valley Furniture Forms: (a) A Poorly Designed Form; (b) an Improved Design Form

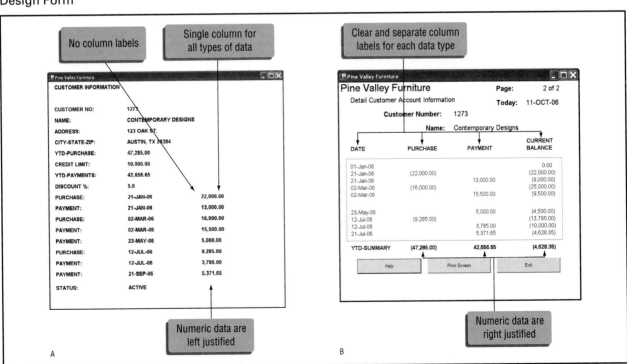

helps to facilitate scanning. Adequate space is left between columns, and blank lines are inserted after every five rows in Figure 13.8b to make finding and reading the information easier. Such spacing also provides room for users to annotate data that catch their attention. Using the guidelines presented in Table 13-6 helps create an easy-to-read layout of the information for the user.

Most of the guidelines in Table 13-6 are rather obvious, but this and other tables serve as a quick reference to validate that the designer's form and report designs will be usable. It is beyond our scope here to discuss each of these guidelines, but each should be read carefully with consideration given to why it is appropriate. For example, why should labels be repeated on subsequent screens and pages (the third guideline in Table 13-6)? One explanation is that pages can be separated or copied and the original labels no longer will be readily accessible to the reader of the data. Why should long alphanumeric data (see the last guideline) be broken into small groups? (Look at a credit card or bank check to see how the account number is displayed.) Two reasons are that the characters will be easier to remember as they are read and typed, and there will be a natural and consistent place to pause when speaking them over the phone, for example, when placing a phone order for products in a catalog.

When the display of numeric information is designed, one must determine whether a table or a graph should be used. In general, tables are best when the user's task involves finding an individual data value from a larger data set, whereas line and bar graphs are more appropriate for analyzing data changes over time. For example, if the marketing manager for Pine Valley Furniture needed to review the actual sales of a particular salesperson for a particular quarter, a tabular report like the one shown in Figure 13.9 would be most useful. This report has been annotated to emphasize good report design practices. The report has a printed date as well as a clear indication, as part of the report title, of the period over which the data apply. The amount of white space is sufficient to provide some room for users to add personal comments and observations. Often, to provide such white space, a report must be printed in landscape, rather than portrait, orientation. Alternatively, if the marketing manager wants to compare the overall sales performance of each sales region, a line or bar graph would be more appropriate, as illustrated in Figure 13.10.

Paper versus Electronic Reports

When a report is produced on paper rather than on a computer display, some additional things need to be considered. For example, laser printers (especially color laser printers) and ink-jet printers allow the production of a report that looks exactly as it does on the display screen. Thus, when using these types of printers, the general design guidelines offered here can be followed to create a report with high usability. However, other types of printers cannot closely reproduce the display screen image onto paper. For example, many business reports are produced using high-speed impact printers that produce characters and a limited range of graphics by printing a fine pattern of dots. The advantages of impact printers are that they are fast, reliable, and relatively inexpensive. They are also the only viable option for printing multipart forms. Their drawbacks are that they have a limited ability to produce graphics and have a somewhat lower print quality. In other words, they are good at producing reports that contain primarily alphanumeric information rapidly but cannot exactly replicate a screen report onto paper. Because of this, impact printers are used mostly for producing large batches of reports, like a batch of phone bills for the telephone company, on a wide range of paper widths and types. When designing reports for impact printers, a coding sheet like that displayed in Figure 13.2 is used, although coding sheets for designing printer reports typically can have up to 132 columns. Like the process for designing all forms and reports, a prototyping process is followed and the spacing of characters is carefully controlled in order to produce a high-quality report. However, unlike other form and report designs, the range of formatting, text types, and highlighting options might be limited. Nonetheless, a highly usable report of any type can be produced easily if the available formatting options are used carefully and creatively.

Figure 13.9 Tabular Report Illustrating Good Report Design Guidelines

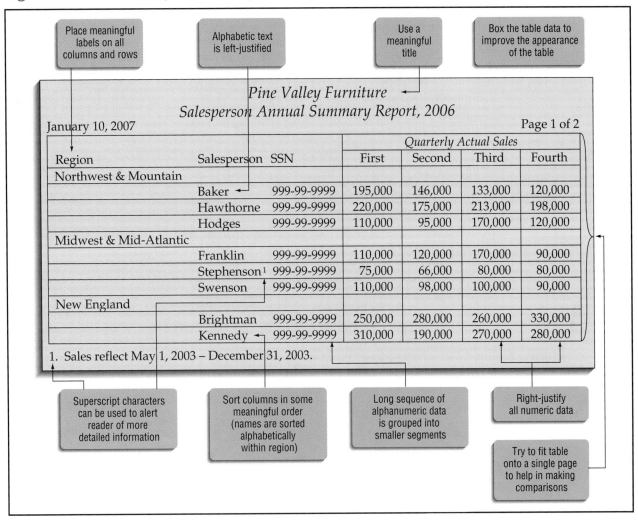

Place meaningful labels on all columns and rows

Alphabetic text is left-justified

Use a meaningful title

Box the table data to improve the appearance of the table

Pine Valley Furniture
Salesperson Annual Summary Report, 2006

January 10, 2007   Page 1 of 2

Region	Salesperson	SSN	Quarterly Actual Sales			
			First	Second	Third	Fourth
Northwest & Mountain						
	Baker	999-99-9999	195,000	146,000	133,000	120,000
	Hawthorne	999-99-9999	220,000	175,000	213,000	198,000
	Hodges	999-99-9999	110,000	95,000	170,000	120,000
Midwest & Mid-Atlantic						
	Franklin	999-99-9999	110,000	120,000	170,000	90,000
	Stephenson[1]	999-99-9999	75,000	66,000	80,000	80,000
	Swenson	999-99-9999	110,000	98,000	100,000	90,000
New England						
	Brightman	999-99-9999	250,000	280,000	260,000	330,000
	Kennedy	999-99-9999	310,000	190,000	270,000	280,000

1. Sales reflect May 1, 2003 – December 31, 2003.

Superscript characters can be used to alert reader of more detailed information

Sort columns in some meaningful order (names are sorted alphabetically within region)

Long sequence of alphanumeric data is grouped into smaller segments

Right-justify all numeric data

Try to fit table onto a single page to help in making comparisons

Figure 13.10 Graphs Showing Quarterly Sales at Pine Valley Furniture: (a) Line Graph; (b) Bar Graph

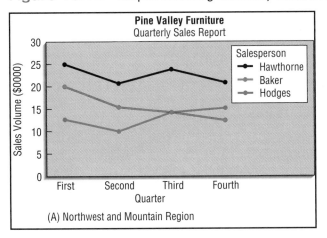

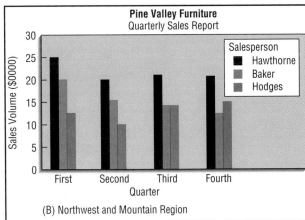

Designing Web Layouts

Designing the forms and reports for an Internet-based electronic commerce application is a central and critical activity. Because this is where a customer will interact with a company, much care must be put into its design. Like the process followed when designing the forms and reports for other types of systems, a prototyping

Table 13-7 Common Errors in Designing the Layout of Web Pages.

ERROR	RECOMMENDATION
Nonstandard Use of GUI Widgets	Make sure that when using standard design items, they behave in accordance to major interface design standards for example, the rules for radio buttons state that they are used to select one item among a set of items, that is, not confirmed until "OK'ed" by a user. In many Web sites, radio buttons are used as both selection and action.
Anything That Looks Like Advertising	Since research on Web traffic has shown that many users have learned to stop paying attention to Web advertisement, make sure that you avoid designing any legitimate information in a manner that resembles advertising (e.g., banners, animations, pop-ups).
Bleeding-Edge Technology	Make sure that users don't need the latest browsers or plug-ins to view your site.
Scrolling Test and Looping Animations	Avoid scrolling text and animations since they are both hard to read and users often equate such content as advertising.
Nonstandard Link Colors	Avoid using nonstandard colors to show links and for showing links that users have already used; nonstandard colors will confuse the user and reduce ease of use.
Outdated Information	Make sure your site is continuously updated so that users "feel" that the site is regularly maintained and updated. Outdated content is a sure way to lose credibility.
Slow Download Times	Avoid using large images, lots of images, unnecessary animations, or other time-consuming content that will slow the downloading time of a page.
Fixed-Formatted Text	Avoid fixed-formatted text that requires users to scroll horizontally to view content or links.
Displaying Long Lists as Long Pages	Avoid requiring users to scroll down a page to view information, especially navigational controls. Manage information by showing only N items at a time, using multiple pages, or by using a scrolling container within the window.

design process is most appropriate. The rapid deployment of Internet Web sites has resulted in countless people designing sites who, arguably, have limited ability to do so. To put this into perspective, consider the following quote from Web design guru Jakob Nielsen (1999, pp. 65–66):

> If the [Web's] growth rate does not slow down, the Web will reach 200 million sites sometime during 2003 . . . . The world has about 20,000 user interface professionals. If all sites were to be professionally designed by a single UI professional, we can conclude that every UI professional in the world would need to design one Web site every working hour from now on to meet demand. This is obviously not going to happen. . . .

> There are three possible solutions to the problem:

> - Make it possible to design reasonably usable sites without having UI expertise.
> - Train more people in good Web design.
> - Live with poorly designed sites that are hard to use.

When designing forms and reports, several errors are specific to Web site design. It is beyond the scope of this book to examine critically all possible design problems with contemporary Web sites. Here, we will simply summarize those errors that commonly occur and are particularly detrimental to the user's experience (see Table 13-7). Numerous excellent sources are available for learning more about designing useful Web sites (Flanders and Willis, 1998; Johnson, 2000; Nielson, 1999, 2000; www.useit.com; www.webpagesthatsuck.com).

DESIGNING INTERFACES AND DIALOGUES

Interface and dialogue design focus on how information is provided to and captured from users. Dialogues are analogous to a conversation between two people. The grammatical rules followed by each person during a conversation are analogous to the human–computer interface. The design of interfaces and dialogues involves defining the manner in which humans and computers exchange information. A good human–computer interface provides a uniform structure for finding, viewing, and invoking the different components of a system. This section describes how to design interfaces and dialogues.

The Process of Designing Interfaces and Dialogues

Similar to designing forms and reports, the process of designing interfaces and dialogues is a user-focused activity. A prototyping methodology is followed that consists of iteratively collecting information, constructing a prototype, assessing usability, and making refinements. To design usable interfaces and dialogues, the same who, what, when, where, and how questions used to guide the design of forms and reports must be answered (see Table 13-2). Thus, this process parallels that of designing forms and reports.

Deliverables and Outcomes

The deliverables and outcomes from system interface and dialogue design are the creation of a design specification. This specification is similar to the specification produced for form and report designs with one exception. Recall that the design specification for forms and reports had three sections (see Figure 13.4):

1. Narrative overview with a use-case diagram.
2. Sample design.
3. Testing and usability assessment.

For interface and dialogue designs, one additional subsection is included: a section outlining the dialogue sequence—the ways a user can move from one display to another. Later in this chapter we will cover how to design a dialogue sequence by using dialogue diagramming. An outline for a design specification for interfaces and dialogues is shown in Figure 13.11.

Figure 13.11
An Outline for a Design Specification for Interfaces and Dialogues

Design Specification

1. Narrative Overview
   a. Interface/Dialogue Name
   b. User Characteristics
   c. Task Characteristics
   d. System Characteristics
   e. Environmental Characteristics

2. Interface/Dialogue Designs
   a. Form/Report Designs
   b. Dialogue Sequence Diagram(s) and Narrative Description

3. Testing and Usability Assessment
   a. Testing Objectives
   b. Testing Procedures
   c. Testing Results
      i) Time to Learn
      ii) Speed of Performance
      iii) Rate of Errors
      iv) Retention over Time
      v) User Satisfaction and Other Perceptions

This section covers the design of interface layouts. It provides guidelines for structuring and controlling data entry fields, providing feedback, and designing online help. Effective interface design requires a thorough understanding of each of these concepts.

Designing Layouts

To ease the processes of user training and data recording, standard formats can be used for computer-based forms and reports; this is similar to the use of paper-based forms and reports for recording or reporting information. A typical paper-based form for reporting customer sales activity is shown in Figure 13.12. This form has several general areas common to most forms:

- Header information.
- Sequence and time-related information.
- Instruction or formatting information.
- Body or data details.
- Totals or data summary.

Figure 13.12
Paper-Based Form for Reporting Customer Sales Activity at Pine Valley Furniture

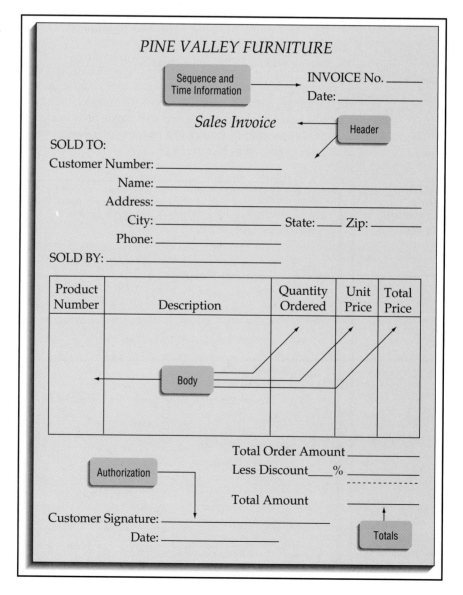

- Authorization or signatures.
- Comments.

In many organizations, data are often recorded first on paper-based forms and then later recorded within application systems. When designing layouts to record or display information on paper-based forms, try to make both as similar as possible. In addition, data entry displays should be formatted consistently across applications to speed data entry and reduce errors. Figure 13.13 shows a computer-based form that is equivalent to the paper-based form shown in Figure 13.12.

The design of between-field navigation is another item to consider when planning the layout of computer-based forms. Because the sequence for users to move between fields can be controlled, standard screen navigation should flow from left to right and top to bottom just as when working on paper-based forms. For example, Figure 13.14 contrasts the flow between fields on a form used to record business contacts. Figure 13.14a uses a consistent left-to-right, top-to-bottom flow. Figure 13.14b uses a flow that is nonintuitive. When appropriate, data fields should be grouped into logical categories with labels describing the contents of the category. Areas of the screen not used for data entry or commands should be inaccessible to the user.

When designing the navigation procedures within the system, flexibility and consistency are primary concerns. Users should be able to move freely forward and backward or to any desired data entry fields. Users should be able to navigate each

Figure 13.13
Computer-Based Form for Reporting Customer Sales Activity at Pine Valley Furniture

Figure 13.14
Contrasting the Navigation Flow within a Data Entry Form: (a) Proper Flow between Data Entry Fields with a Consistent Left-to-Right, Top-to-Bottom Flow; (b) Poor Flow between Data Entry Fields with Inconsistent Flow

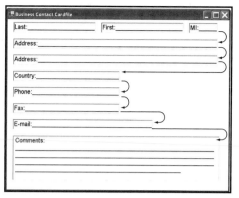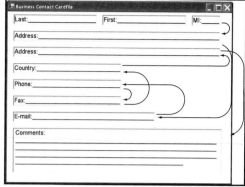

form in the same way or in as similar a manner as possible. In addition, data usually should not be saved permanently by the system until the user makes an explicit request to do so. This allows the user to abandon a data entry screen, back up, or move forward without adversely impacting the contents of the permanent data.

Consistency extends to the selection of keys and commands. Each key or command should be assigned only one function. This assignment should be consistent throughout the entire system and across systems, if possible. Depending upon the application, various types of functional capabilities will be required to provide smooth navigation and data entry. Table 13-8 provides a checklist for testing the functional capabilities for providing smooth and easy navigation within a form. For example, a good interface design provides a consistent way for moving the cursor to different places on the form, editing characters and fields, moving among form displays, and obtaining help. These functions can be provided by keystrokes, the mouse, the menu, or function keys. It is possible that for a single application, not all capabilities listed in Table 13-8 will be needed in order to create a good user interface. Yet, the capabilities that are used should be applied consistently to provide an optimal user environment. Table 13-8 provides a checklist for validating the usability of user interface designs.

Table 13-8
Checklist for Validating the Usability of User Interface.

CHECKLIST FOR VALIDATING THE USABILITY OF USER INTERFACE

Cursor-Control Capabilities

Move the cursor forward to the next data field.

Move the cursor backward to the previous data field.

Move the cursor to the first, last, or some other designated data field.

Move the cursor forward one character in a field.

Move the cursor backward one character in a field.

Editing Capabilities

Delete the character to the left of the cursor.

Delete the character under the cursor.

Delete the whole field.

Delete data from the whole form (empty the form).

Exit Capabilities

Transmit the screen to the application program.

Move to another screen/form.

Confirm the saving of edits or go to another screen/form.

Help Capabilities

Get help on a data field.

Get help on a full screen/form.

Source: Adapted from J. S. Dumas (1988). *Designing User Interfaces for Software.* Upper Saddle River. NJ: Prentice Hall.

Table 13-9 Guidelines for Structuring Data Entry Fields.

Entry	Never request data that are already online or that can be computed; for example, do not request customer data on an order form if those data can be retrieved from the database, and do not request extended prices that can be computed from quantity sold and unit prices.
Defaults	Always provide default values when appropriate; for example, assume today's date for a new sales invoice, or use the standard product price unless overridden.
Units	Make clear the type of data units requested for entry; for example, indicate quantity in tons, dozens, pounds, etc.
Replacement	Use character replacement when appropriate; for example, allow the user to look up the value in a table or automatically fill in the value once the user enters enough significant characters.
Captioning	Always place a caption adjacent to fields; see Table 8-8 for caption options.
Format	Provide formatting examples when appropriate; for example, automatically show standard embedded symbols, decimal points, credit symbol, or dollar sign.
Justify	Automatically justify data entries; numbers should be right justified and aligned on decimal points, and text should be left justified.
Help	Provide context-sensitive help when appropriate; for example, provide a hot key, such as the F1 key, that opens the help system on an entry that is most closely related to where the cursor is on the display.

Structuring Data Entry

Several guidelines should be considered when structuring data entry fields on a form. These guidelines are listed in Table 13-9. The first is simple, yet is often violated by designers. To minimize data entry errors and user frustration, the user never should be required to enter information that already is available within the system or information that can be computed easily by the system. For example, the user should not have to enter the current date and time, because each of these values can be retrieved easily from the computer system's internal calendar and clock. By allowing the system to do this, the user simply confirms that the calendar and clock are working properly.

Other guidelines are equally important. For example, suppose that a bank customer is repaying a loan on a fixed schedule with equal monthly payments. Each month when a payment is sent to the bank, a clerk needs to record that the payment has been received into a loan-processing system. Within such a system, default values for fields should be provided whenever appropriate. This means that the clerk has to enter data into the system only when the customer pays more or less than the scheduled amount. In all other cases, the clerk simply verifies that the check is for the default amount provided by the system and presses a single key to confirm the receipt of payment.

When entering data, the user should not be required to specify the dimensional units of a particular value, for example, whether an amount is in dollars or a weight is in tons. Use field formatting and the data entry prompt to make clear the type of data being requested. In other words, place a caption describing the data to be entered adjacent to each data field so that the user knows what type of data is being requested. As with the display of information, all data entered onto a form should justify automatically in a standard format (e.g., date, time, money). Table 13-10 illustrates display design options for printed forms. For data entry on video display terminals, the area in which text is entered should be highlighted so that the exact number of characters per line and number of lines are clearly shown. Check-off boxes or radio buttons also can be used to allow users to choose standard textual responses. Use data entry controls to ensure that the proper type of data (alphabetic or numeric, as required) are entered. Data entry controls are discussed next.

Controlling Data Input

One objective of interface design is to reduce data entry errors. As data are entered into an information system, steps must be taken to ensure that the input is valid. The systems analyst must anticipate the types of errors users might make and design features into the

Table 13-10
Display Design
Options for Entering
Text.

OPTIONS	EXAMPLE
Line caption	Phone Number (___) - ___
Drop caption	(___) - ___
	Phone Number
Boxed caption	Phone Number
Delimited characters	(___) - ___
	Phone Number
Check-off boxes	Method of payment (check one)
	☐ Check
	☐ Cash
	☐ Credit Card: Type

system's interfaces to avoid, detect, and correct data entry mistakes. Several types of data errors are summarized in Table 13-11. Data errors can occur from appending extra data onto a field, truncating characters off a field, transcripting the wrong characters into a field, or transposing one or more characters within a field. Systems designers have developed numerous tests and techniques for detecting invalid data before saving or transmission, thus improving the likelihood that data will be valid. Table 13-12 summarizes these techniques. These tests and techniques often are incorporated into data entry screens and when data are transferred from one computer to another.

It is much easier to correct erroneous data before it is stored permanently in a system. Online systems can notify a user of input problems as data are being entered. When data are processed online as events occur, it is much less likely that data validity errors will occur and not be caught. In an online system, most problems can be identified and resolved easily before permanently saving data to a storage device, by using many of the techniques described in Table 13-12. However, in systems where data inputs are stored and entered (or transferred) in batches, the identification and notification of errors is more difficult. However, batch processing systems can reject invalid inputs and store them in a log file for later resolution.

Table 13-11
Types of Data Errors.

DATA ERROR	DESCRIPTION
Appending	Adding additional characters to a field
Truncating	Losing characters from a field
Transcripting	Entering invalid data into a field
Transposing	Reversing the sequence of one or more characters in a field

Table 13-12 Techniques Used by Systems Designers to Detect Data Errors before Saving or Transmission.

VALIDATION TEST	DESCRIPTION
Class or composition	Test to assure that data are of proper type (e.g., all numeric, all alphabetic, alphanumeric).
Combinations	Test to see if the value combinations of two or more data fields are appropriate or make sense (e.g., does the quantity sold make sense given the type of product?).
Expected values	Test to see if data are what is expected (e.g., match with existing customer names, payment amount, etc).
Missing data	Test for existence of data items in all fields of a record (e.g., is there a quantity field on each line item of a customer order?).
Pictures/templates	Test to assure that data conform to a standard format (e.g., are hyphens in the right places for a student ID number?).
Range	Test to assure data are within a proper range of values (e.g., is a student's grade-point average between 0 and 4.0?).
Reasonableness	Test to assure data are reasonable for situation (e.g., pay rate for a specific type of employee).
Self-checking digits	Test where an extra digit is added to a numeric field in which its value is derived using a standard formula (see Figure 8.15).
Size	Test for too few or too many characters (e.g., is Social Security number exactly nine digits?).
Values	Test to make sure values come from a set of standard values (e.g., two-letter state codes).

Figure 13.15
How a Check Digit
Is Calculated

Description	Techniques where extra digits are added to a field to assist in verifying its accuracy
Method	1. Multiply each digit of a numeric field by weighting factor (e.g., 1, 2, 1, 2,...). 2. Sum the results of weighted digits. 3. Divide sum by modulus number (e.g., 10). 4. Subtract remainder of division from modulus number to determine check digit. 5. Append check digits to field.
Example	Assume a numeric part number of: 12473 1–2. Multiply each digit of part number by weighting factor from right to left and sum the results of weighted digits: $\begin{array}{ccccc} 1 & 2 & 4 & 7 & 3 \\ \times 1 & \times 2 & \times 1 & \times 2 & \times 1 \\ \hline 1 + & 4 + & 4 + & 14 + & 3 \end{array} = 26$ 3. Divide sum by modulus number. $\quad$ 26/10 = 2, remainder 6 4. Subtract remainder from modulus number to determine check digit. $\quad$ check digit = 10 − 6 = 4 5. Append check digits to field. $\quad$ Field value with appended check digit = 124734

Most of the straightforward tests and techniques shown in Table 13-12 are widely used. Some can be handled by data management technologies, such as a database management system (DBMS), to ensure that they are applied for all data maintenance operations. If a DBMS cannot perform these tests, then the tests must be designed into program modules. Self-checking digits, shown in Figure 13.15, are an example of a sophisticated program. The figure provides a description and an outline of how to apply the technique. A short example then shows how a check digit is added to a field before data entry or transfer. Once entered or transferred, the check digit algorithm is applied again to the field to check whether the check digit received obeys the calculation. If it does, it is likely (but not guaranteed, because two different values could yield the same check digit) that no data transmission or entry error occurred. If not equal, then some type of error occurred.

In addition to validating the data values entered into a system, controls must be established to verify that all input records are entered correctly and processed only once. A common method used to enhance the validity of entering batches of data records is to create an audit trail of the entire sequence of data entry, processing, and storage. In such an audit trail, the actual sequence, count, time, source location, and human operator are recorded in a separate transaction log in the event of a data input or processing error. If an error occurs, corrections can be made by reviewing the contents of the log. Detailed logs of data inputs are not only useful for resolving batch data entry errors and system audits, but also serve as a powerful method for performing backup and recovery operations in the case of a catastrophic system failure.

Audit trail
A record of the sequence of data entries and the date of those entries.

Providing Feedback

When people talk with friends, they expect their friends to give feedback by nodding and replying to questions and comments. Without feedback, people would be concerned that their friends were not listening. Similarly, when designing system interfaces, providing appropriate feedback is an easy way to make a user's interaction more enjoyable; not providing feedback is a sure way to frustrate and confuse. System feedback can consist of three types:

1. Status information.
2. Prompting cues.
3. Error and warning messages.

Status Information

Providing status information is a simple technique for keeping users informed of what is going on within a system. For example, relevant status information such as displaying the current customer name or time, placing appropriate titles on a menu or screen, and identifying the number of screens following the current one (e.g., Screen 1 of 3) all provide needed feedback to the user. Providing status information during processing operations is especially important if the operation takes longer than a second or two. For example, when opening a file, the screen might display, "Please wait while I open the file," or when performing a large calculation, the message "Working ..." could be flashed to the user. Further, it is important to tell the user that besides working, the system has accepted the user's input and the input was in the correct form. Sometimes it is important to give the user a chance to obtain more feedback. For example, a function key could toggle between showing a "Working ..." message and giving more specific information as each intermediate step is accomplished. Providing status information reassures users that nothing is wrong and makes them feel in command of the system, not vice versa.

Prompting Cues

A second feedback method is to display prompting cues. When prompting the user for information or action, it is useful to be specific in the request. For example, suppose a system prompts users with the following request:

READY FOR INPUT: _____

With such a prompt, the designer assumes that the user knows exactly what to enter. A better design would be specific in its request, possibly providing an example, default values, or formatting information. An improved prompting request might be as follows:

Enter the customer account number (123-456-7):_____.

Errors and Warning Messages

A final method available for providing system feedback is using error and warning messages. Following a few simple guidelines can greatly improve the usefulness of these messages. First, messages should be specific and free of error codes and jargon. In addition, messages should never scold the user but rather should attempt to guide the user toward a resolution. For example, a message might say, "No customer record found for that customer ID. Please verify that digits were not transposed." Messages should be in user, not computer, terms. Terms such as *end of file*, *disk I/O error*, or *write protected* might be too technical and not helpful for many users. Multiple messages can be useful so that a user can get more detailed explanations if wanted or needed. Also, error messages should appear in roughly the same format and placement each time so that they are recognized as error messages and not as some other information. Examples of bad and good messages are provided in Table 13-13. These guidelines can be used to provide useful feedback in designs. A special type of feedback is answering help requests from users. This important topic is described next.

Table 13-13
Examples of Poor and
Improved Error
Messages.

POOR ERROR MESSAGES	IMPROVED ERROR MESSAGES
ERROR 56 OPENING FILE	The file name you typed was not found. Press F2 to list valid file names.
WRONG CHOICE	Please enter an option from the menu.
DATA ENTRY ERROR	The prior entry contains a value outside the range of acceptable values. Press F9 for list of acceptable values.
FILE CREATION ERROR	The file name you entered already exists. Press F10 if you want to overwrite it. Press F2 if you want to save it with a new name.

Providing Help

Designing a help system is one of the most important interface design issues the systems analyst will face. When designing a help system, it is important to think like a user. When accessing help, the user likely does not know what to do next, does not understand what is being requested, or does not know how the requested information needs to be formatted. A user requesting help is much like a ship in distress, sending an SOS. Table 13-14 shows our SOS guidelines for the design of system help: Simplicity, Organize, and Show. The first guideline, *simplicity*, suggests that help messages should be short, to the point, and use words that users can understand. This leads to the second guideline, *organize*, which means the information in help messages can be absorbed easily by users. Long paragraphs of text are often difficult for people to understand. A better design organizes lengthy information in a manner that is easier for users to digest through the use of bulleted and ordered lists. Finally, it is often useful to explicitly *show* users how to perform an operation and the outcome of procedural steps. Figure 13.16 contrasts the designs of two help screens: one that employs our guidelines and one that does not.

Many commercially available systems provide extensive system help. For example, Table 13-15 lists the range of help available in a popular electronic spreadsheet. Many systems also are designed so that users can vary the level of detail provided. Help can be provided at the system level, screen or form level, or individual field level. The ability to provide field-level help often is referred to as context-sensitive help. For some applications, providing context-sensitive help for all system options is a tremendous undertaking that is virtually a project in itself. If an extensive help system is designed with many levels of detail, the systems analyst must be sure that he or she knows exactly what the user needs help with, or all those efforts might confuse users more than help them. After leaving a help screen, users should always

Table 13-14
Guidelines for
Designing System
Help.

GUIDELINE	EXPLANATION
Simplify	Use short, simple wording, common spelling, and complete sentences. Give users only what they need to know, with the ability to find additional information.
Organize	Use lists to break information into manageable pieces.
Show	Provide examples of proper use and the outcomes of such use.

Table 13-15
Types of Help.

TYPE OF HELP	EXAMPLE OF QUESTION
Help on help	How do I get help?
Help on concepts	What is a customer record?
Help on procedures	How do I update a record?
Help on messages	What does "Invalid File Name" mean?
Help on menus	What does "Graphics" mean?
Help on function keys	What does each function key do?
Help on commands	How do I use the "Cut" and "Paste" commands?
Help on words	What do "merge" and "sort" mean?

Figure 13.16
Contrasting Help
Screens: (a) A Poorly
Designed Help Screen;
(b) an Improved
Design for a Help
Screen

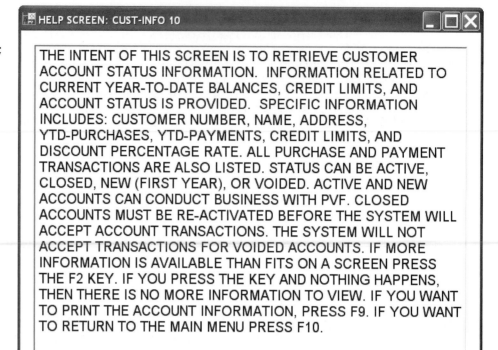

HELP SCREEN: CUST-INFO 10

THE INTENT OF THIS SCREEN IS TO RETRIEVE CUSTOMER
ACCOUNT STATUS INFORMATION. INFORMATION RELATED TO
CURRENT YEAR-TO-DATE BALANCES, CREDIT LIMITS, AND
ACCOUNT STATUS IS PROVIDED. SPECIFIC INFORMATION
INCLUDES: CUSTOMER NUMBER, NAME, ADDRESS,
YTD-PURCHASES, YTD-PAYMENTS, CREDIT LIMITS, AND
DISCOUNT PERCENTAGE RATE. ALL PURCHASE AND PAYMENT
TRANSACTIONS ARE ALSO LISTED. STATUS CAN BE ACTIVE,
CLOSED, NEW (FIRST YEAR), OR VOIDED. ACTIVE AND NEW
ACCOUNTS CAN CONDUCT BUSINESS WITH PVF. CLOSED
ACCOUNTS MUST BE RE-ACTIVATED BEFORE THE SYSTEM WILL
ACCEPT ACCOUNT TRANSACTIONS. THE SYSTEM WILL NOT
ACCEPT TRANSACTIONS FOR VOIDED ACCOUNTS. IF MORE
INFORMATION IS AVAILABLE THAN FITS ON A SCREEN PRESS
THE F2 KEY. IF YOU PRESS THE KEY AND NOTHING HAPPENS,
THEN THERE IS NO MORE INFORMATION TO VIEW. IF YOU WANT
TO PRINT THE ACCOUNT INFORMATION, PRESS F9. IF YOU WANT
TO RETURN TO THE MAIN MENU PRESS F10.

return to where they were prior to requesting help. If these simple guidelines are followed, a highly usable help system should be the result.

As with the construction of menus, many programming environments provide powerful tools for designing system help. For example, Microsoft's Help Compiler allows the fast construction of hypertext-based help systems. In this environment, a text editor is used to construct help pages that can be linked easily to other pages containing related or more specific information. Linkages are created by embedding

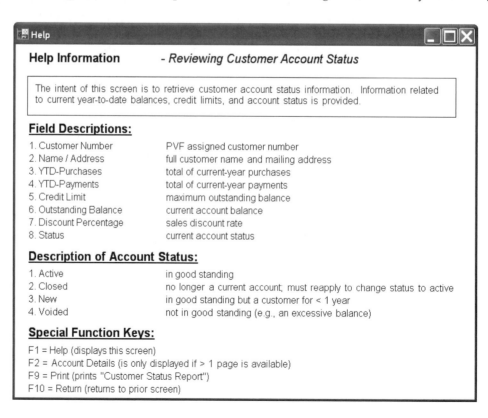

Help

Help Information   – *Reviewing Customer Account Status*

The intent of this screen is to retrieve customer account status information. Information related to current year-to-date balances, credit limits, and account status is provided.

Field Descriptions:

1. Customer Number   PVF assigned customer number
2. Name / Address   full customer name and mailing address
3. YTD-Purchases   total of current-year purchases
4. YTD-Payments   total of current-year payments
5. Credit Limit   maximum outstanding balance
6. Outstanding Balance   current account balance
7. Discount Percentage   sales discount rate
8. Status   current account status

Description of Account Status:

1. Active   in good standing
2. Closed   no longer a current account; must reapply to change status to active
3. New   in good standing but a customer for < 1 year
4. Voided   not in good standing (e.g., an excessive balance)

Special Function Keys:

F1 = Help (displays this screen)
F2 = Account Details (is only displayed if > 1 page is available)
F9 = Print (prints "Customer Status Report")
F10 = Return (returns to prior screen)

Figure 13.17   Hypertext-Based Help System from Microsoft

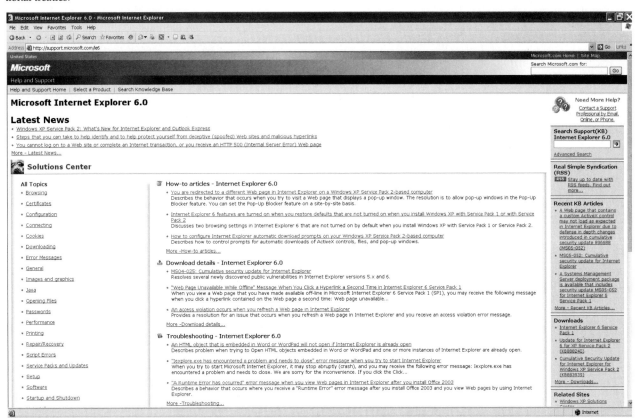

special characters into the text document that make words hypertext buttons—that is, direct linkages—to additional information. The Help Compiler transforms the text document into a hypertext document. For example, Figure 13.17 shows a hypertext-based help screen from Microsoft. Hypertext-based help systems have become the standard environment for most commercial operating environments. This has occurred for two primary reasons. First, standardizing system help across applications eases user training. Second, hypertext allows users to access the level of help they need selectively, making it easier to provide effective help for novices and experienced users within the same system.

Designing Web Interfaces

Over the years, interaction standards have emerged for virtually all of the commonly used desktop computing environments such as Windows or Macintosh. However, some interface design experts believe that the growth of the Web has resulted in a big step backwards for interface design. One problem is that countless nonprofessional developers are designing commercial Web applications. In addition to this, four other important contributing factors can be cited (Johnson, 2000):

- Web's single click-to-act method of loading static hypertext documents (i.e., most buttons on the Web do not provide click feedback).
- Limited capabilities of most Web browsers to support finely grained user interactivity.
- Limited agreed-upon standards for encoding Web content and control mechanisms.
- Lack of maturity of Web scripting and programming languages as well as limitations in commonly used Web GUI component libraries.

Table 13-16 Common Errors When Designing the Interface and Dialogues of Web Sites.

ERROR	DESCRIPTION
Opening New Browser Window	Avoid opening a new browser window when a user clicks on a link unless it is clearly marked that a new window will be opened; users may not see that a new window has been opened, which will complicate navigation, especially moving backwards.
Breaking or Slowing Down the Back Button	Make sure users can use the back button to return to prior pages. Avoid opening new browser windows, using an immediate redirect where, when a user clicks the back button, they are pushed forward to an undesired location, or prevent caching such that each click of the back button requires a new trip to the server.
Complex URLs	Avoid overly long and complex URLs since it makes it more difficult for users to understand where they are and can cause problems if users want to e-mail page locations to colleagues.
Orphan Pages	Avoid having pages with no "parent" that can be reached by using a back button; requires users to "hack" the end of the URL to get back to some other prior page.
Scrolling Navigation Pages	Avoid placing navigational links below where a page opens, since many users may miss these important options that are below the opening window.
Lack of Navigation Support	Make sure your pages conform to user's expectation by providing commonly used icon links such as a site logo at the top or other major elements. Also place these elements on pages in a consistant manner.
Hidden Links	Make sure you leave a border around images that are links, don't change link colors from normal defaults, and avoid embedding links within long blocks of text.
Links That Don't Provide Enough Information	Avoid not turning off link marking borders so that links clearly show which links users have clicked and which they have not. Make sure users know which links are internal anchor points versus external links and indicate if a link brings up a separate browser window from those that do not. Finally, make sure link images and text provide enough information to users so that they understand the meaning of the link.
Buttons That Provide No Click Feedback	Avoid using image buttons that don't clearly change when being clicked; use Web GUI toolkit buttons, HTML form submit buttons, or simple textual links.

In addition to these contributing factors, designers of Web interfaces and dialogues are often guilty of many design errors. Although not inclusive of all possible errors, Table 13-16 summarizes those errors that are particularly troublesome.

DESIGNING DIALOGUES

Dialogue
The sequence of interactions between a user and a system.

The process of designing the overall sequences that users follow to interact with an information system is called dialogue design. A dialogue is the sequence in which information is displayed to, and obtained from, a user. As with other design processes, designing dialogues is a three-step process:

1. Designing the dialogue sequence.
2. Building a prototype.
3. Assessing usability.

The primary design guideline for designing dialogues is consistency; dialogues need to be consistent in sequence of actions, keystrokes, and terminology. In other words, designers should use the same labels for the same operations on all screens and the same location of the same information on all displays.

One example of these guidelines concerns removing data from a database or file (see the Reversal entry in Table 13-17). It is good practice to display the information that will be deleted before making a permanent change to the file. For example, if the customer service representative wants to remove a customer from the database, the system should ask only for the customer ID in order to retrieve the correct customer account. Once found, and before allowing the confirmation of the deletion, the system should display the account information. For actions making permanent changes to system data files and when the action is not performed often, many systems designers use the double-confirmation technique whereby the users must confirm their intention twice before being allowed to proceed.

Table 13-17

Guidelines for the Design of Human-Computer Dialogues.

GUIDELINE	EXPLANATION
Consistency	Dialogues should be consistent in sequence of actions, keystrokes, and terminology (e.g., use the same labels for the same operations on all screens and the same location of the same information on all displays).
Shortcuts and sequence	Allow advanced users to take shortcuts using special keys (e.g., CTRL-C to copy highlighted text). A natural sequence of steps should be followed (e.g., enter first name before last name, if appropriate).
Feedback	Feedback should be provided for every user action (e.g., confirm that a record has been added, rather than simply putting another blank form on the screen).
Closure	Dialogues should be logically grouped and have a beginning, middle, and end (e.g., the last in the sequence of screens should indicate that there are no more screens).
Error handling	All errors should be detected and reported; suggestions on how to proceed should be made (e.g., suggest why such errors occur and what the user can do to correct the error). Synonyms for certain responses should be accepted (e.g., accept either "**t**," "T," or "TRUE").
Reversal	Dialogues should, when possible, allow the user to reverse actions (e.g., undo a deletion); data should not be deleted without confirmation (e.g., display all the data for a record the user has indicated is to be deleted).
Control	Dialogues should make the user (especially an experienced user) feel in control of the system (e.g., provide a consistent response time at a pace acceptable to the user).
Ease	Dialogues should provide simple means for users to enter information and navigate between screens (e.g., provide means to move forward, backward, and to specific screens, such as first and last).

Source: Adopted from B. Shneiderman (2002). Designing the User Interface: Strategies for Effective Human Computer Interaction, Third Edition. Reading, MA: Addison-Wesley.

Designing the Dialogue Sequence

The first step in dialogue design is to define the sequence. In other words, the designer must have a clear understanding of the user, task, and technological and environmental characteristics when designing dialogues. Suppose that the marketing manager at Pine Valley Furniture (PVF) wants sales and marketing personnel to be able to review the year-to-date transaction activity for any PVF customer from the WebStore. After talking with the manager, you both agree that a typical dialogue between a user and the Customer Information System for obtaining this information might proceed as follows:

1. Request to view individual customer information.
2. Specify the customer of interest.
3. Select the year-to-date transaction summary display.
4. Review customer information.
5. Leave system.

Once a designer understands how a user wants to use a system, these activities can be transformed into a formal dialogue specification.

Dialogue diagramming
A formal method for designing and representing human–computer dialogues using box and line diagrams.

A method for designing and representing dialogues is dialogue diagramming. Dialogue diagrams, illustrated in Figure 13.18, have only one symbol—a box with three sections; each box represents one display (which might be a full screen or a specific form or window) within a dialogue. The three sections of the box are used as follows:

1. **Top:** Contains a unique display reference number used by other displays for referencing it.
2. **Middle:** Contains the name or description of the display.
3. **Bottom:** Contains display reference numbers that can be accessed from the current display.

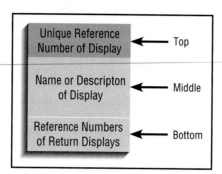

Figure 13.18
A Dialogue
Diagramming Box Has
Three Sections

Unique Reference Number of Display	← Top
Name or Descripton of Display	← Middle
Reference Numbers of Return Displays	← Bottom

All lines connecting the boxes within dialogue diagrams are assumed to be bidirectional and thus do not need arrowheads to indicate direction. This means that users are always allowed to move forward and backward between adjacent displays. If only unidirectional flows are desired within a dialogue, arrowheads should be placed on one end of the line. Within a dialogue diagram, the sequencing of displays, the selection of one display over another, or the repeated use of a single display (e.g., a data entry display) can be represented easily. These three concepts—sequence, selection, and iteration—are illustrated in Figure 13.19.

Continuing with the PVF example, Figure 13.20 shows a partial dialogue diagram for processing the marketing manager's request. In this diagram, the analyst placed the request to view year-to-date customer information within the context of the overall Customer Information System. The user must first gain access to the system through a log-on procedure (item 0). If log-on is successful, a main menu is displayed that has four items (item 1). Once the user selects the Individual Customer Information (item 2), control is transferred to the Select Customer display (item 2.1). After a customer is selected, the user is presented with an option to view customer information four different ways (item 2.1.1). Once the user views the customer's year-

Figure 13.19
Dialogue Diagram
Illustrating Sequence,
Selection, and
Iteration

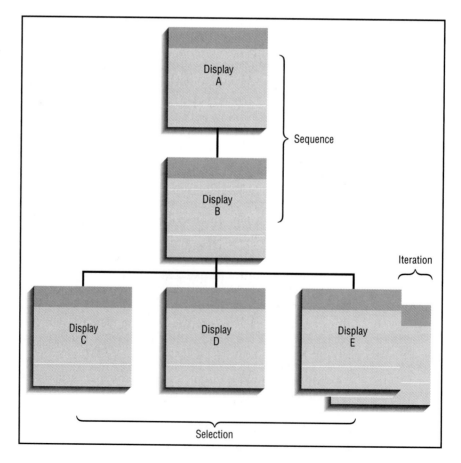

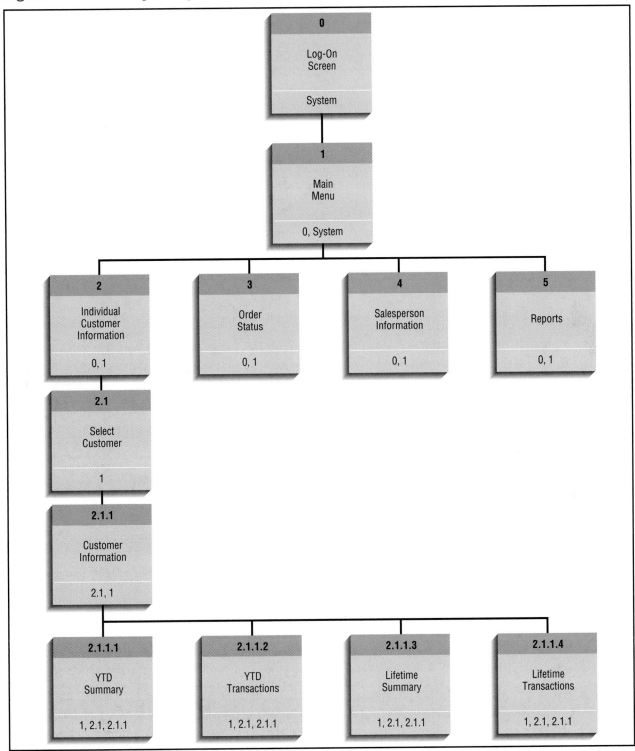

to-date transaction activity (item 2.1.1.2), the system will allow the user to back up to select a different customer or back up to the main menu (see bottom of item 2.1.1.2).

Building Prototypes and Assessing Usability

Building dialogue prototypes and assessing usability are often optional activities. Some systems might be simple and straightforward. Others might be more complex, but are extensions to existing systems where dialogue and display standards already have been established. In either case, building prototypes and doing a formal assessment might not be required. However, for many other systems, it is critical that prototype displays are built and then the dialogue is assessed; this can pay numerous dividends later in the systems development life cycle (e.g., it might be easier to implement a system or train users on a system they already have seen and used).

Building prototype displays is often a relatively easy activity if graphical development environments such as Microsoft's Visual Basic are used. Some systems development environments include easy-to-use input and output (form, report, or window) design utilities. Also, several tools called "Prototypers" or "Demo Builders" allow displays to be designed quickly and show how an interface will work within a full system. These demo systems allow users to enter data and move through displays as if they were using the actual system. Such activities are useful not only for showing how an interface will look and feel, but also for assessing usability and performing user training long before actual systems are completed.

KEY POINTS REVIEW

1. **Explain the process of designing forms and reports and the deliverables for their creation.**
   Forms and reports are created through a prototyping process. Once created, designs can be stand-alone or integrated into actual working systems. The purpose of the prototyping process, however, is to show users what a form or report will look like when the system is implemented. The outcome of this activity is the creation of a specification document where characteristics of the users, tasks, system, and environment are outlined along with each form and report design. Performance testing and usability assessments also can be included in the design specification.

2. **Apply the general guidelines for formatting forms and reports.**
   Guidelines should be followed when designing forms and reports. These guidelines, proven over years of experience with human–computer interaction, help designers create professional, usable systems. Guidelines have been created for the use of titles, layout of fields, navigation between pages or screens, highlighting information, format of text, and the appropriate use and layout of tables and lists.

3. **Describe how to format text, tables, and lists effectively, and explain common errors when designing Web layouts**
   Textual output is becoming increasingly important as text-based applications such as electronic mail, bulletin boards, and information services become more popular. Text should be displayed using common writing conventions such as mixed uppercase and lowercase lettering, appropriate punctuation, left justification, and a minimal number of obscure abbreviations. Words should not be hyphenated between lines, and blocks of text should be double-spaced or, minimally, a blank line should be placed between each paragraph. Tables and lists should have meaningful labels that clearly stand out. Information should be sorted and arranged in a meaningful way. Numeric data should be right justified. Care should be taken when designing Web layouts to make page maintenance efficient and user navigation and viewing acceptable on a variety of devices. Complex graphics, nonstandard link colors, and other errors can frustrate users and make pages harder to maintain.

4. **Explain the process of designing interfaces and dialogues, and the deliverables for their creation.**
   Designing interfaces and dialogues is a user-focused activity that follows a prototyping methodology of iteratively collecting information, constructing a prototype, assessing usability, and making refinements. The deliverable and outcome from interface and dialogue design are the creation of a specification that can be used to implement the design.

5. **Describe and apply the general guidelines for interface design, including guidelines for layout design, structuring data entry fields, providing feedback, and system help. Also explain common errors that can result when designing Web interfaces.**

To have a usable interface, users must be able to move the cursor position, edit data, exit with different consequences, and obtain help. Numerous techniques for structuring and controlling data entry as well as providing feedback, prompting, error messages, and a well-organized help function can be used to enhance usability. When designing Web interfaces, care must be taken to assure that users can navigate easily and understand where they are in the site. Hidden links, complex URLs, and errors can frustrate users and make sites difficult to utilize.

6. **Design human–computer dialogues, including the use of dialogue diagramming.**

Human–computer dialogues should be consistent in design, allow for shortcuts, provide feedback and closure on tasks, handle errors, allow for operations reversal, and give the user a sense of control and ease of navigation. Dialogue diagramming is a technique for representing human–computer dialogues. The technique uses boxes to represent screens, forms, or reports and lines to show the flow between each.

KEY TERMS CHECKPOINT

Here are the key terms from this chapter. The page where each term is first explained is in parentheses after the term.

a. Audit trail (p. 385)
b. Dialogue (p. 390)
c. Dialogue diagramming (p. 391)
d. Form (p. 366)
e. Report (p. 366)

Match each of the key terms above with the definition that best fits it.

1. A formal method for designing and representing human–computer dialogues using box and line diagrams.
2. A business document that contains only predefined data; it is a passive document used only for reading or viewing, and typically contains data from many unrelated records or transactions.
3. The sequence of interactions between a user and a system.
4. A business document that contains some predefined data and may include some areas where additional data are to be filled in. An instance of a form typically is based on one database record.
5. A record of the sequence of data entries and the date of those entries.

REVIEW QUESTIONS

1. Describe the prototyping process of designing forms and reports. What deliverables are produced from this process? Are these deliverables the same for all types of system projects? Why or why not?
2. To which initial questions must the analyst gain answers in order to build an initial prototype of a system output?
3. How should textual information be formatted on a help screen?
4. What type of labeling can be used in a table or list to improve its usability?
5. What column, row, and text formatting issues are important when designing tables and lists?
6. Describe how numeric, textual, and alphanumeric data should be formatted in a table or list.
7. Provide some examples where variations in user, task, system, and environmental characteristics might impact the design of system forms and reports.
8. List and describe the common errors that are made when designing the layouts of Web sites.
9. Describe the process of designing interfaces and dialogues. What deliverables are produced from this process? Are these deliverables the same for all types of system projects? Why or why not?
10. List and describe the functional capabilities needed in an interface for effective entry and navigation. Which capabilities are most important? Why? Will this be the same for all systems? Why or why not?
11. Describe the general guidelines for structuring data entry fields. Can you think of any instances when it would be appropriate to violate these guidelines?
12. Describe four types of data errors.
13. Describe the types of system feedback. Is any form of feedback more important than the others? Why or why not?
14. Describe the general guidelines for designing usable help. Can you think of any instances when it would be appropriate to violate these guidelines?
15. List and describe the common interface and dialogue design errors found on Web sites.
16. What steps do you need to follow when designing a dialogue? Of the guidelines for designing a dialogue, which is most important? Why?

PROBLEMS AND EXERCISES

1. Imagine that you are to design a budget report for a colleague at work using a spreadsheet package. Following the prototyping discussed in this chapter (see also Figure 5.7), describe the steps you would take to design a prototype of this report.

2. Consider a system that produces budget reports for your department at work. Alternatively, consider a registration system that produces enrollment reports for a department at a university. For whichever system you choose, answer the following design questions: Who will use the output? What is the purpose of the output? When is the output needed, and when is the information that will be used within the output available? Where does the output need to be delivered? How many people need to view the output?

3. Imagine the worst possible reports from a system. What is wrong with them? List as many problems as you can. What are the consequences of such reports? What could go wrong as a result? How does the prototyping process help guard against each problem?

4. Given the guidelines presented in this chapter, identify flaws in the design of the Report of Customers shown below. What assumptions about users and tasks did you make in order to assess this design? Redesign this report to correct these flaws.

REPORT OF CUSTOMERS—26-OCT-06

Cust-ID	Organization
AC-4	A.C. Nielson Co.
ADTRA-20799	Adran
ALEXA-15812	Alexander & Alexander, Inc.
AMERI-1277	American Family Insurance
AMERI-28157	American Residential Mortgage
ANTAL-28215	Antalys
ATT-234	AT&T Residential Services
ATT-534	AT&T Consumer Service
. . .	. . .
DOLE-89453	Dole United, Inc.

Cust-ID	Organization
DOME-5621	
DO-67	DO-67
Doodle Dandies	
. . .	...
ZNDS-22267	Zenith Data System

5. Consider the design of a registration system for a hotel. Following design specification items in Figure 13.11, briefly describe the relevant users, tasks, and displays involved in such a system.

6. Examine the help systems for some software applications that you use. Evaluate each using the general guidelines provided in Table 13-14.

7. Design one sample data entry screen for a hotel registration system using the data entry guidelines provided in this chapter (see Table 13-9). Support your design with arguments for each of the design choices you made.

8. Describe some typical dialogue scenarios between users and a hotel registration system. For hints, reread the section in this chapter that provides sample dialogue between users and the WebStore Customer Information System at Pine Valley Furniture.

9. Represent the dialogues from the previous question through the use of dialogue diagrams.

10. When developing an Internet-based electronic commerce system, why is the design of the human–computer interface one of the most critical elements? What makes the interface for an Internet-based electronic commerce system good? What makes it bad?

11. Use the Internet to find commercial Web sites that demonstrate each of the common errors listed in Table 13-7.

12. Use the Internet to find commercial Web sites that demonstrate each of the common errors listed in Table 13-16.

13. List four contributing factors that have acted to impede the design of high-quality interfaces and dialogues on Internet-based applications.

DISCUSSION QUESTIONS

1. Discuss the differences between a form and a report. What characteristics make a form or report good (bad) and effective (ineffective)?

2. Discuss the various ways that information can be highlighted on a computer display. Which methods are most effective? Are some methods better than others? If so, why and when?

3. What problems can occur if a system fails to provide clear feedback and error messages to users?

4. How would you assess a system's usability? How do you know when a system is usable?

CASE PROBLEMS

Pine Valley Furniture

Assume you are a systems analyst working on Pine Valley Furniture's Customer Tracking System for its WebStore. Several iterations on this project have been concluded, and you have been given the task of designing some additional forms and reports for this system that are described in the following section.

During the requirements determination phase, Jackie Judson requested that a customer profile be created for each customer. The customer profile is established when new customers place their first order. Customers will have the option of not completing a profile; however, to encourage customer participation, a 10 percent discount on the customer's total order will be given to each customer who completes a profile. In the beginning, existing customers also will be given the opportunity to participate in the customer profiling process. Customer profile information will be collected via a Customer Profile Form.

Gracie Breshers, a marketing executive, has requested that the Customer Tracking System generate a Products by Demographics Summary Report. This summary report should identify Pine Valley Furniture's major furniture categories, such as business furniture, living room, dining room, home office, and kitchen. Within each furniture category, she would like the total sales by region and customer age reported. She also has requested that several detailed reports be prepared; these reports will associate customer demographics with specific furniture category items.

Thi Hwang, a Pine Valley Furniture sales executive, would like to know, in terms of percentages, how many of Pine Valley Furniture's customers are repeat customers and how often they make purchases. Additionally, he would like to have this information categorized by customer type. For each customer type, he would like to know the frequency of the purchases. For instance, does this type of customer place an order at least once a month, at least every 6 months, at least once a year, or less often than once per year? To be considered a repeat customer, the customer must have made two separate purchases within a 2-year period.

a. What data will the Customer Profile Form need to collect? Using the guidelines presented in this chapter, design the Customer Profile Form.
b. Using the guidelines presented in this chapter, design the Products by Demographics Summary Report.
c. Using the guidelines presented in this chapter, design the Customer Purchasing Frequency Report.
d. Modify the dialogue diagram presented in Figure 13.20 to reflect the addition of the Customer Profile Form, Products by Demographics Summary Report, and the Customer Purchasing Frequency Report.

Hoosier Burger

Assume that you are a systems analyst for the Hoosier Burger project, which is automating all aspects of customer sales, inventory management, and order delivery. As the lead analyst on this project, you are responsible for overseeing the design of all forms and reports required by the new system. Because the inventory system is being automated and a new delivery system is being implemented, the Hoosier Burger system requires the development of several forms and reports.

Using use-case diagrams and other OOSAD diagrams, you begin the task of identifying all the necessary forms and reports. You readily identify the need for a Delivery Customer Order Form, a Customer Account Balance Form, a Low-in-Stock Report, and a Daily Delivery Summary Report. The Delivery Customer Order Form will capture order details for those customers placing delivery orders. Bob will use the Customer Account Balance Form to look up a customer's current account balance. The Low-in-Stock Report will be generated daily to identify all food items or supplies that are low in stock. The Daily Delivery Summary Report will summarize each day's delivery sales by menu item sold.

a. What data will the Delivery Customer Order Form need to collect? Using the design guidelines presented in this chapter, design the Delivery Customer Order Form.
b. What data will the Customer Account Balance Form need to show? Using the design guidelines presented in this chapter, design the Customer Account Balance Form.
c. Using the design guidelines presented in this chapter, design the Daily Delivery Summary Report.
d. Using the design guidelines presented in this chapter, design the Low-in-Stock Report.

Pet Nanny

Pet owners often have difficulty locating pet sitters for their pets, boarding their pets, or just getting the pets to the veterinarian. Recognizing these needs, Gladys Murphy decided to open Pet Nanny, a business that provides specialized pet-care services to busy pet owners. The company provides a multitude of services, including pet grooming, massage, day care, home care, aroma therapy, boarding, and pickup and delivery. The company has been experiencing a steady increase in demand for its services.

Initially, when the company was founded, all pet-care records were kept manually. However, Gladys recognizes the need to renovate Pet Nanny's existing systems and hired your consulting firm to perform the renovation. Your analysis team currently is working on the design of the system's forms and reports.

During analysis, you determined that several forms and reports were necessary, including a Pet Enrollment Form, Pet Service Form, Pickup and Delivery Schedule Report, and Daily Boarding Report. When a customer wants to use Pet Nanny's services for a new pet, the customer must provide basic information about the pet. For instance, the customer is asked to provide his or her name, address, phone number, the pet's name, birth date (if known), and special care instructions. When a customer requests a special service for the pet, such as grooming or a massage, a service record is created. Because the pickup and delivery service is one of the most popular services offered by Pet Nanny, Gladys wants to make sure that no pets are forgotten. Each morning, a report listing the pet pickups and deliveries is created. She also needs a report listing the pets being boarded, their special needs, and their length of stay.

a. What data should the Pet Enrollment Form collect? Using the guidelines provided in this chapter, design the Pet Enrollment Form.

b. What data should the Pet Service Form collect? Using the guidelines provided in this chapter, design the Pet Service Form.

c. Using the guidelines provided in this chapter, design the Pickup and Delivery Schedule Report.

d. Using the guidelines provided in this chapter, design the Daily Boarding Report.

CASE: BROADWAY ENTERTAINMENT COMPANY, INC.

Designing the Human Interface for the Customer Relationship Management System

Case Introduction

The students from St. Claire Community College are eager to begin building a prototype of MyBroadway, the Web-based customer relationship management system for Carrie Douglass, manager of the Broadway Entertainment Company (BEC) store in Centerville, Ohio. Prototyping seems like an ideal design approach for this system, because the final project product is not intended to be a production system. Rather, the student team is producing a proof-of-concept, initial system version to be used to justify full development by BEC. Before building the prototype in Microsoft Access, the team is ready to plan the structure for the human interface of the system. For a Web-based system, the human interface is, to the customer, the system. Although the MyBroadway prototype system is not meant to be extensive, the prototype will be effective only if the human interface delights BEC customers. The students first decide to do a pencil-and-paper prototype before development in Access. This initial prototype will be used primarily for discussion among the team and for sharing with other teams in their information systems projects class at St. Claire. Professor Tann, their instructor, encourages collaborative learning, and the members of other teams will be valued, impartial evaluators of the usability of the system's human interface design.

Identifying the Human Interfaces

The human interfaces for MyBroadway are clearly visible from boundary classes identified in sequence diagrams and the analysis class diagram (see the BEC case at the end of Chapter 9). The main human interfaces are the forms and reports to and from each human external entity—customers and employees. The team decided to concentrate on the customer interfaces for the purpose of the pencil-and-paper prototype. BEC Table 13-1 lists the seven customer-related boundary classes.

The team quickly realized that each boundary class is often several Web pages and part of a dialogue with a user. Any Web page that is needed to implement the boundary class is also a human interface. For example, to produce the result of the review inventory use case, the customer must enter criteria for selecting which inventory items to display.

The student team decided that when customers log on to MyBroadway, they first should see a home or welcome

BEC Table 13-1
Customer Human Interfaces (Boundary Classes) for MyBroadway.

Enter new comment on a product (see pages 1.1 and 1.1.1).
Display comments on products (see pages 1.1 and 1.1.2).
Review inventory (see pages 1.2 and 1.2.1 and :ReviewForm boundary class).
Request new product (see page 1.3).
Identify rental status (see page 2.1).
Rental request extension (see pages 2.1.1 and 2.1.1.1).
Display child purchase/rental history (see page 2.2).
Note: Page references refer to dialogue diagram Web page numbers in BEC Figure 13.1.

page, with a catchy graphic and menu selections for accessing different parts of the system. One logical way to categorize system functions would be to group all inputs, or data entry pages, together and all system outputs, or form and report display pages, together into a second group. The team decided, however, that this is a system-centric view, not a user-centric view of the system's functionality. After some brainstorming, the team decided that it would be more logical for users to understand and use the system if pages were grouped by the type of data the users want to use. Two natural data groupings are evident: product and purchase/rental data.

Designing the Dialogue between MyBroadway and Users

BEC Figure 13.1 is a dialogue diagram that represents the relationships between customer-oriented Web pages developed by the student team using a type-of-data orientation for human interfaces. Each page is an implemented boundary class, whereas the boundary classes identified on sequence diagrams and the analysis diagram are implemented as one or more Web pages. For example, when the students designed the sequence diagram for the Review inventory use case (see the BEC case at the end of Chapter 9), they identified a boundary class, :ReviewForm, for the interface with

BEC Figure 13.1   Dialogue Diagram of Customer Interfaces for MyBroadway

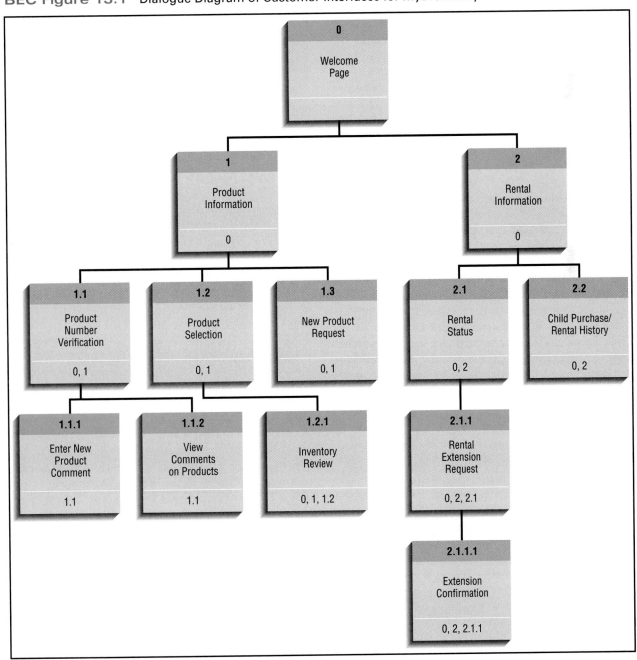

the :Customer actor. The :ReviewForm as described there is implemented in several boundary classes that appear as at least Web pages 1.2 and 1.2.1 (and possibly Web page 1). That is, :ReviewForm, as used on the Review inventory sequence diagram, was a logical, not a physical, boundary class.

Page 0 is the welcome page. Besides information to introduce MyBroadway to customers, this page provides menu options or buttons for users to indicate which data group they want to use. For example, if a customer wants to work with product data, then the user navigates to page 1, which provides the interface and methods to enter the request for a new product on page 1.3. Page 1.3 is part of the implementation of the boundary class associated with the Request new product use case. Page 1.1 guides the user to the pages that implement use case Enter a new comment on a product (page 1.1.1) or use case Display comments on product (page 1.1.2). Thus, page 1.1 must provide a way for the user to select or enter data to identify the product for use in subordinate pages.

As the students visualize it, each boundary class has a terminal (or leaf) node of the dialogue diagram. Each superior node above a leaf is a step for guiding the user to a system input or output; these guiding steps also appeared in the sequence diagram for the use cases when the students developed them earlier in the project. Sometimes a system output can be the basis for a customer to create a system input. For example, consider pages 2.1, 2.1.1, and 2.1.1.1. Page 2.1 is the human interface for the Identify rental status use case. The team decided that users will want to invoke this use case before requesting an extension to a particular rental (the Request rental extension use case), which is done on page 2.1.1, with the confirmation message to the :Customer actor on page 2.1.1.1. Thus, page 2.1 not only displays the output of the Identify rental status use case; it also provides a way for a user to select a particular outstanding rental for which to request an extension in page 2.1.1. Page 2.1.1.1 is a message page (possibly not a totally separate page but rather a message window to overlay on top of page 2.1.1) that will say whether or not the extension request is accepted.

Designing Forms and Reports for MyBroadway

Each of the 13 pages identified in BEC Figure 13.1 needs to be designed for customer usability. The team realized that usability means that the page is easy to understand, helps the customer perform a given task, and is efficient for the customer to use. From their courses at St. Claire Community College, the students are familiar with many usability guidelines for human–computer interfaces. Also from their education, the students know that usability is improved if the proposed human interfaces are reviewed frequently. This is another reason why prototyping will be an effective development strategy for MyBroadway. Initial designs for each page will be reviewed by the team's classmates from St. Claire, and then working prototype iterations will be evaluated by customers in the Centerville store.

BEC Figure 13.2 Interface Design for Page 1.2

Two of the pencil-and-paper page prototypes appear in BEC Figures 13.2 and 13.3. Page 1.2 (BEC Figure 13.2) is an intermediate page that helps the user formulate the criteria to specify which items from inventory to include in the Inventory Review system output, output 1 from BEC Table 13.1. Page 1.2 has a title and an explanation of its purpose. Because the page is not too full of data, the team decided to include an explanation of its purpose and content. Alternatively, the team considered excluding this explanation, instead making it accessible via a help button. The user clicks in a check box to indicate that a value will be entered or selected for each type of product selection criteria. Because a BEC store's inventory includes thousands of titles, the team decided not to use a drop-down menu for entering a title, but rather the user enters the approximate title of the product. The team realized that in many cases, the title entered will not match exactly the title stored in the database. The logic that processes a title will have to search for the best match.

All other criteria, if checked by the user, have a more limited set of options, so drop-down selection boxes are used. The team decided that the user should be able to exit the page in four different ways, the first three of which are shown in the dialogue diagram in BEC Figure 13.1. The first option is to submit the product selection, which will take the user to page 1.2.1 (BEC Figure 13.3), the Inventory Review, or output 1. The second option is to return to the welcome page (page 0). The third option is to go back to page 1 to consider other product data tasks. Although not shown in BEC Figure 13.1, a fourth option is to clear the values in page 1.2 to consider another selection. This might occur because the user changes his or her mind after indicating some selections, or upon returning from page 1.2.1, the user might want to enter another selection starting with no selection values.

Page 1.2.1 (BEC Figure 13.3) is the Inventory Review system output, thus the title of the page. The team decided to show the selection criteria in a top frame on the page to

INVENTORY REVIEW

These are the criteria you selected:	Title: Category: Publisher: Release Date:		Return to Product Information	Return to Welcome Page
			Back	Print

Title: Artist:

Category: Publisher: Release Date:

Description:

Price—Sale: Rental:

remind the user of the selections. Because many items might satisfy a selection, the team allowed for scrolling through all results in the bottom frame. Besides the three exit options from this page shown on the dialogue diagram of BEC Figure 13.1—go back to page 1.2, return to the Product Information page (page 1), and return to the Welcome Page—a fourth user action is to print the query results. The students had not even considered the need for printing until designing this screen. The team noted this new platform requirement and will ask Carrie about this at their next meeting. The cost of the printer would not be that great, but the team is more concerned about paper costs; keeping a supply of paper in the printer; and the extra effort to keep the printer free of paper jams, full of ink cartridges, and otherwise in working order. The use of a printer would require more active involvement of store staff than the team had previously explained to Carrie would be necessary.

Case Summary

The student team believes that the design of the user dialogue and two system pages represents a suitable project deliverable that should be reviewed by someone outside the team. Fortunately, Professor Tann has scheduled project status report presentations for the next session of the team's project class. The MyBroadway student team will present the pencil-and-paper prototype shown in BEC Figures 13.1, 13.2, and 13.3 to obtain an initial reaction to the design. Because the team has not invested a great deal of time in the initial design, the team members believe they can be open to, not defensive in response to, constructive suggestions. Because other teams also will likely walk through human interface designs, the BEC team will see some other creative designs, which will give them additional ideas for improvement.

CASE QUESTIONS

1. Using guidelines from this chapter and other sources, evaluate the usability of the dialogue design depicted in BEC Figure 13.1. Specifically, consider the overall organization, grouping of pages, navigation paths between pages, and depth of the dialogue diagram and how this depth might affect user efficiency.

2. Are any pages missing in BEC Figure 13.1? Can you anticipate the need for additional pages in the customer interface for MyBroadway? If so, where do these pages come from if not from the list of system inputs and outputs in BEC Table 13.1?

3. Using guidelines from this chapter and other sources, evaluate the usability of the two pages shown in BEC Figures 13.2 and 13.3.

4. This chapter encourages the design of a help system early in the design of the human interface. How would you incorporate help into the interface as designed by the St. Claire students?

5. Given the designs for pages 1.2 and 1.2.1, design pages 1.1.2 and 1.3. Assume that the designs for pages 1.2 and 1.2.1 represent the look and feel desired for MyBroadway.

6. The designs for pages 1.2 and 1.2.1 include a Back button. Is this button necessary or desirable?

7. Is the use of drop-down selection lists a good feature of the design of page 1.2? Can you think of a better way to provide these selections?

8. The design for page 1.2.1 includes a Print button. Design the printed version of this page.

9. Are any other navigation paths exiting page 1.2 possible that are not shown in BEC Figure 13.1? Is page 1.2.1 the only possible result of searching on the selection criteria? If not, design pages for other results.

10. In Case Questions in the BEC case at the end of Chapter 9, you developed several sequence diagrams. Match your sequence diagrams to the Web pages in BEC Figure 13.1. In particular for all the sequence diagrams, map the messages to each Web page, rather than to what you may have designed as one logical boundary class for each sequence diagram. Also, redo all the sequence diagrams showing all the physical boundary classes rather than just the logical ones you may have drawn. This also will show clearly which messages are associated with each physical boundary class.

Chapter 14

OOSAD Implementation and Operation

Chapter Objectives

After studying this chapter, you should be able to:

➤ Describe the process of coding, testing, and converting an organizational information system, and outline the deliverables and outcomes of the process.

➤ Apply four installation strategies: direct, parallel, single location, and phased installation.

➤ List the deliverables for documenting the system and for training and supporting users.

➤ Compare the many modes available for organizational information system training, including self-training and electronic performance support systems.

➤ Discuss the issues of providing support for end users.

➤ Explain why systems implementation sometimes fails.

➤ Explain and contrast four types of maintenance.

➤ Describe several factors that influence the cost of maintaining an information system.

Chapter Contents

Chapter Preview

The implementation and operation phase of the systems development cycle is the most expensive and time-consuming. This phase is expensive because so many people are involved in the process. It is time-consuming because of all the work that has to be completed throughout the entire life of the system. During implementation and operation, physical design specifications must be turned into working computer code. As the code is written, it is tested until most of the errors have been detected and corrected. Then the system is installed, user sites are prepared for the new system, and users must come to rely on the new system rather than the existing one to get their work done. Even once the system is installed, new features are added to the system, new business requirements and regulations demand system improvements, and corrections are made as flaws are identified from use of the system in new circumstances. These changes will have ripple effects, causing rework in much of the system.

The seven major activities covered in this chapter are coding, testing, installation, documentation, training, support, and maintenance. These and other activities are highlighted in Figure 14.1. Our intent is not to explain how to program and test systems; rather, this chapter shows where coding and testing fit in the overall scheme of implementation, and it stresses the view of implementation as an organizational change process that is not always successful.

Figure 14.1 Systems Implementation and Operation Involves Several Different Activities, Including Coding, Testing, Installation, Documentation, Training, Support, and Maintenance

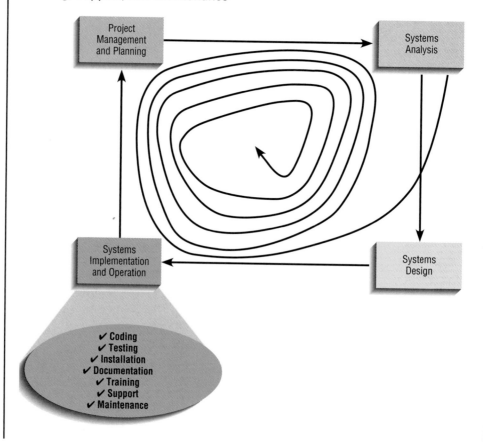

In addition, this chapter covers providing documentation about the new system for the information systems personnel who will maintain the system, and providing documentation and conducting training for the system's users. Once training has ended and the system has become institutionalized, users must have a means for getting answers to their additional questions and for identifying areas in which further training is needed.

It is not uncommon for new college graduates in this general field to begin their careers as maintenance programmers/analysts. Maintenance can begin soon after the system is installed. A question many people have about maintenance relates to how long organizations should maintain a system. Five years? Ten years? Longer? This question has no simple answer, but it is most often an issue of economics. In other words, at what point does it make financial sense to discontinue updating an older system and build or purchase a new one? The focus of a great deal of upper IS management attention is devoted to assessing the trade-offs between maintenance and new development. This chapter describes the maintenance process and the issues that must be considered when maintaining systems. The end of the chapter covers the process of implementing the WebStore system at Pine Valley Furniture.

SYSTEMS IMPLEMENTATION AND OPERATION

Systems implementation and operation is made up of seven major activities:

- Coding
- Testing
- Installation
- Documentation
- Training
- Support
- Maintenance

The purpose of these steps is to convert the final physical system specifications into working and reliable software and hardware, document the work that has been done, and provide help for current and future users and caretakers of the system. Usage of the system leads to changes, so during maintenance, users and others submit maintenance requests, requests are transformed into specific changes to the system, the system is redesigned to accept the changes, and the changes are implemented.

These steps often are handled by other project team members besides analysts, although analysts might do some programming and other steps. Often, the analyst and developer team who are responsible for testing, documenting, training, and maintenance activities are different from those who developed the original system. In any case, analysts are responsible for ensuring that all of these various activities are planned and executed properly. These activities are discussed briefly in three groups:

1. Activities that lead to the system going into operation—coding, testing, and installation.
2. Activities that are necessary for successful system operation—documenting the system and training and supporting users.
3. Activities that are ongoing and needed to keep the system working, and up-to-date-maintenance.

Coding, as mentioned before, is the process whereby the physical design specifications created by the design team are turned into working computer code by the programming team. Depending on the size and complexity of the system, coding can be an involved, intensive activity. Once coding has begun, the testing process can begin and proceed in parallel. As each program module is produced, it can be tested individually, then as part of a larger program, and then as part of a larger system. The different strategies for testing will be discussed later in this chapter. Although testing is done during implementation, the systems analyst must begin planning for testing earlier in the project. Planning involves determining what needs to be tested and collecting test data. This often is done during the analysis phase because testing requirements are related to system requirements.

Installation is the process during which the current system is replaced by the new system. This includes conversion of existing data, software, documentation, and work procedures to those consistent with the new system. Users must give up the old ways of doing their jobs, whether manual or automated, and adjust to accomplishing the same tasks with the new system. Users sometimes will resist these changes, and the systems analyst must help them adjust. However, one cannot control all of the dynamics of user–system interaction involved in the installation process.

Deliverables and Outcomes from Program Development, Testing, and Installation

Table 14-1 shows the deliverables from the coding, testing, and installation processes. The most obvious outcome is the code itself, but just as important as the code is documentation of the code. Some object-oriented languages, such as Eiffel, provide for documentation to be extracted automatically from software developed in Eiffel. Other languages, such as Java, employ specially designed utilities, such as JavaDocs, to generate documentation from the source code. Other languages will require more effort on the part of the coder to establish good documentation. However, even well-documented code can be mysterious to maintenance programmers who must maintain the system for years after the original system was written and the original programmers have moved to other jobs. Therefore, clear, complete documentation for all individual modules and programs is crucial to the system's continued smooth operation.

CASE tools can be used to maintain the documentation needed by systems professionals. Documentation is even more important for object-oriented systems than for traditionally developed systems, because objects written for one system might be used in many others. This important concept of reuse will be addressed in more detail later in this chapter.

The results of program and system testing are important deliverables from the testing process because they document the tests as well as the test results. For example, what type of test was conducted? What test data were used? How did the system

Table 14-1
Deliverables from Coding, Testing, and Installation.

ACTION	DELIVERABLE
Coding	Code
	Program documentation
Testing	Test scenarios (test plan) and test data
	Results of program and system testing
Installation	User guides
	User training plan
	Installation and conversion plan
	Hardware and software installation schedule
	Data conversion plan
	Site and facility remodeling plan

handle the test? The answers to these questions can provide important information for system maintenance because changes will require retesting, and similar testing procedures will be used during the maintenance process.

The next two deliverables, user guides and the user training plan, result from the installation process. User guides provide information on how to use the new system, and the training plan is a strategy for training users so they can learn the new system quickly. The development of the training plan probably began earlier in the project, and some training on the concepts behind the new system might have taken place already. During the early stages of implementation, the training plans are finalized and training on the use of the system begins. Similarly, the installation plan lays out a strategy for moving from the old system to the new. Installation includes installing the system (hardware and software) at central and user sites. The installation plan answers such questions as when and where the new system will be installed, which people and resources are required, which data will be converted and cleansed, and how long the installation process will take. It is not enough that the system is installed; users must actually use it.

The job of an analyst is to ensure that all of these deliverables are produced and done well, whether by the analyst or by others. Coding, testing, and installation work can be done by IS professionals in the organization, contractors, hardware designers, and, increasingly, users. The extent of the analyst's responsibilities will vary according to the size and standards of the organization, but the analyst's ultimate role includes ensuring that all the coding, testing, and installation work leads to a system that meets the specifications developed in earlier project phases.

The Processes of Documenting the System, Training Users, and Supporting Users

Although the process of documentation proceeds throughout the development cycle, it receives formal attention now because once the system is installed, the analysis team's involvement in system development usually ceases. As the team is getting ready to move on to new projects, the analysts need to prepare documents that reveal all of the important information they learned about this system during its development and implementation. This final documentation has at least three audiences: (1) the information systems personnel who will maintain the system throughout its productive life, (2) the information systems personnel who will reuse the objects in other systems, and (3) the people who will use the system as part of their daily lives.

Larger organizations also tend to provide training and support to computer users throughout the organization, sometimes as part of a corporate university. Some of the training and support is directed to off-the-shelf software packages. For example, it is common to find courses on Microsoft Windows and WordPerfect in organization-wide training facilities. Analysts typically work with corporate trainers to provide training and support tailored to particular computer applications they have helped develop. Centralized information system training facilities tend to have specialized staff who can help with training and support issues. In smaller organizations that cannot afford to have well-staffed, centralized training and support facilities, fellow users are the best source of training and support users have, whether the software is customized or off the shelf.

Deliverables and Outcomes from Documenting the System, Training Users, and Supporting Users

Table 14-2 shows the deliverables from documenting the system, training users, and supporting users. For languages like Eiffel and Java, from which documentation can be derived from the source code, the documentation itself can be generated in many formats, from Word documents to HTML. For training, the development team should think through the user training process: Who should be trained? How much training is

Documentation	User training modules
System documentation	Training materials
User documentation	Computer-based training aids
User training plan	User support plan
Classes	Help desk
Tutorials	Online help
	Bulletin boards and other support mechanisms

adequate for each training audience? What do different types of users need to learn during training? The training plan should be supplemented by actual training modules, or at least outlines of such modules, that at a minimum address the three questions stated previously. Finally, the development team also should deliver a user support plan that addresses such issues as how users will be able to find help once the information system has become integrated into the organization. The development team should consider a multitude of support mechanisms and modes of delivery. Each deliverable is addressed in more detail later in this chapter.

The Process of Maintaining Information Systems

Throughout this book, the systems development cycle has been drawn as a circle where one phase leads to the next, with overlap and feedback loops. This means that the process of maintaining an information system is the process of returning to the beginning of the SDC and repeating development steps, focusing on the needs for system change, until the change is implemented.

Four major activities occur within maintenance:

1. Obtaining maintenance requests.
2. Transforming requests into changes.
3. Designing changes.
4. Implementing changes.

Obtaining maintenance requests requires that a formal process be established whereby users can submit system change requests. In Chapter 4, a user request document called a Systems Service Request (SSR) was presented. Most companies have some sort of document like an SSR to request new development, to report problems, or to request new system features with an existing system. When developing the procedures for obtaining maintenance requests, organizations also must specify an individual within the organization to collect these requests and manage their dispersal to maintenance personnel. The process of collecting and dispersing maintenance requests is described in much greater detail later in this chapter.

Once a request is received, analysis must be conducted to gain an understanding of the scope of the request. It must be determined how the request will affect the current system and the duration of such a project. As with the initial development of a system, the size of a maintenance request can be analyzed for risk and feasibility (see Chapter 4). Next, a change request can be transformed into a formal design change, which can then be fed into the maintenance implementation phase. Thus, many similarities exist between the SDC and the activities within the maintenance process. Figure 14.2 equates SDC phases to the maintenance activities described previously. The figure shows that the first step of the SDC—project management and planning—is analogous to the maintenance process of obtaining a maintenance request (step 1). The SDC step systems analysis is analogous to the maintenance process of transforming requests into a specific system change (step 2). The systems design step of the SDC equates to the designing changes process (step 3). Finally, the SDC step system implementation and operation equates to implementing changes (step 4). This similarity between the maintenance process and the SDC is no accident. The concepts and techniques used to develop a system initially also are used to maintain it.

Figure 14.2
Maintenance Activities in Relation to the Systems Development Cycle

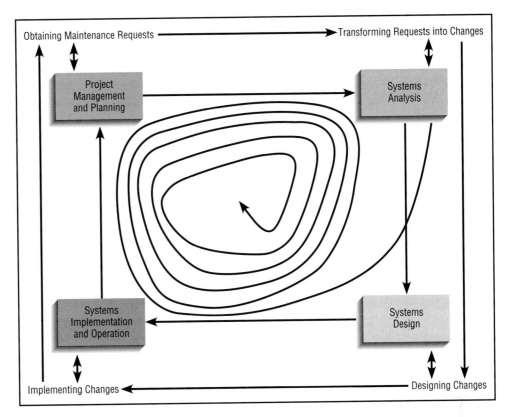

Obtaining Maintenance Requests ──────────→ Transforming Requests into Changes

Project Management and Planning

Systems Analysis

Systems Implementation and Operation

Systems Design

Implementing Changes ←────────── Designing Changes

Deliverables and Outcomes from Maintaining Information Systems

Because maintenance is basically a subset of the activities of the entire development process, the deliverables and outcomes from the process are the development of a new version of the software and new versions of all design documents developed or modified during the maintenance process. This means that all documents created or modified during the maintenance effort, including the system itself, represent the deliverables and outcomes of the process. Those programs and documents that did not change also might be part of the new system. Because most organizations archive prior versions of systems, all prior programs and documents must be kept to ensure the proper versioning of the system. This enables prior versions of the system to be re-created if needed. A more detailed discussion of configuration management and change control is presented later in this chapter.

Because of the similarities between the steps, deliverables, and outcomes of new development and maintenance, the question might arise of how to distinguish between these two processes. One difference is that maintenance reuses much of the existing system in producing the new system version. Other distinctions are that a new system is developed when there is a change in the hardware or software platform or when fundamental assumptions and properties of the data, logic, or process models change.

CODING

Expectations about coding have changed dramatically over the past couple of decades. Whereas it was once typical to expect systems to be developed and written from scratch, such an approach today would be overly expensive and, in large part, a waste of time and effort. This is true whether the system is being developed using traditional programming languages and techniques or using object-oriented techniques. From an OOSAD perspective, many of the parts and pieces of a proposed system already have been written in the form of preexisting objects and components. The key issue is finding those pieces and making them work together. Therefore, coding remains an important systems development activity, because code must be written to make the pieces work together. Coding is also essential for taking existing objects and components and modifying them to work as needed in the system being developed. However, teaching how to write and modify objects and components is beyond the scope of this book; these things will be covered in object-oriented language courses. Here, only three ideas related to coding object-oriented software are mentioned: combining coding and testing, reuse, and object frameworks.

Combining Coding and Testing

You read about agile methodologies in Chapters 1 and 5. You also read there about eXtreme programming, an approach to software development put together by Kent Beck (2000). eXtreme programming is distinguished by short cycles, an incremental planning approach, a focus on automated tests written by programmers and customers to monitor the process of development, and a reliance on an evolutionary approach to development that lasts throughout the lifetime of the system. One of the key emphases of eXtreme programming is its use of two-person programming teams and having a customer on-site during the development process.

Although coding and testing are in many ways part of the same process, it is not uncommon in large and complicated systems development environments to find the two practices separated from each other. Big companies and big projects often have dedicated testing staffs who develop test plans and then use the plans to test software after it has been written. We will show shortly how many different types of testing there are, and one can deduce from that how elaborate and extensive testing can be. A different approach has been developed as part of eXtreme programming (Beck, 2000). Under this approach, coding and testing are intimately related parts of the same process. The programmers who write the code also write the tests. The emphasis is on testing those things that can break or go wrong, not on testing everything. Code is tested soon after it is written. The overall philosophy behind eXtreme programming is that code will be integrated into the system it is being developed for and tested within a few hours after it has been written. Code is written, integrated into the system, and then tested. If all the tests run successfully, then development proceeds. If not, the code is reworked until the tests are successful.

Another part of eXtreme programming that makes the code-and-test process work more smoothly is the practice of pair programming. All coding and testing is done by two people working together, writing code and writing tests. Pair programming is not one person typing while the other one watches. Rather, the two programmers work together on the problem they are trying to solve, exchanging information and insight and sharing skills. Compared to traditional coding practices, the advantages of pair programming include: (1) more (and better) communication among developers, (2) higher levels of productivity, (3) higher-quality code, and (4) reinforcement of the other practices in eXtreme programming, such as the code-and-test discipline (Beck, 2000). Although the eXtreme programming process has its advantages, just as with any other approach to systems development, it is not for everyone and not for every project.

Reuse

Reuse
The use of previously written software resources, especially objects and components, in new applications.

Reuse is the use of previously written software resources in new applications. As so many bits and pieces of applications are relatively generic across applications, it seems intuitive that great savings can be achieved in many areas if those generic bits and pieces do not have to be written anew each time they are needed. Reuse should increase programmer productivity, because being able to use existing software for some functions means they can perform more work in the same amount of time. Reuse also should decrease development time, minimizing schedule overruns.

Because existing pieces of software already have been tested, reusing them also should result in higher-quality software with lower defect rates, ultimately making it easier to maintain.

Although reuse can conceivably apply to many different aspects of software, it is applied most commonly to object-orientation and component-based development. For example, an employee object class would contain the data about employees and the instructions necessary for calculating payroll for a variety of job types. The class could be used in any application that dealt with employees, but if changes had to be made in calculating payroll for different types of employees, the changes would have to be made only to the class and not to the various applications that used it. By definition, using the employee object class in more than one application constitutes reuse.

Some evidence shows that reuse can be effective, especially for object classes. For example, one laboratory study found reuse of class libraries to result in increased productivity, reduced defect density, and reduced rework (Basili, Briand, & Melo, 1996). For HP, a reuse program resulted in cutting time-to-market for certain products by a factor of three or more, from 18 months to less than 5 months (Griss, 2003). However, for reuse to work in an organizational setting, many different issues must be addressed. Technical issues include the current lack of a methodology for creating and clearly defining and labeling reusable objects for placement in a library, and the small number of reusable and reliable software resources currently available. Key organizational issues include the lack of commitment to reuse, as well as the lack of proper training and rewards needed to promote it; the lack of organizational support for institutionalizing reuse, and the difficulty in measuring the economic gains from reuse. Key legal and contractual issues focus on reusing objects and components originally used in other programs and systems (Kim & Stohr, 1998).

To get the most out of reuse, it is important for a company to match its approach to reuse with its strategic business goals (Griss, 2003). The benefits of reuse grow as more corporate experience is gained from it, but so do the costs and the amount of resources necessary for reuse to work well. Software reuse has three basic steps: abstraction, storage, and recontextualization (Grinter, 2001). Abstraction involves the design of a reusable piece of software, starting from existing software assets or from scratch. Storage involves making software assets available for others to use. Although it sounds like a simple problem to solve, storage can be challenging. The problem is not simply putting software assets on a shelf—the problem is labeling and cataloging assets correctly so that others can find the ones they want to use. Once an asset has been found, recontexualization becomes important; this involves making the reusable asset understandable to developers who want to use it in their systems. Software is complex, and a software asset developed for a particular system under system-specific circumstances might not be at all what it appears to be. For example, what appears to be a generic asset called "Customer" might be something quite different, depending on the context in which it was developed. It often might appear to be easier to simply build new assets rather than invest the time and energy it takes to establish a good understanding of software someone else has developed. A key part of a reuse strategy, as mentioned previously, is establishing rewards, incentives, and organizational support for reuse to help make reuse more worthwhile than developing new assets.

Organizations can choose from four basic approaches to reuse (Table 14-3). The ad hoc approach to reuse is not really an approach at all, at least from an official organizational perspective. Individuals are free to find or develop reusable assets on their own, and few if any organizational rewards are offered for reusing assets. Storage is not an issue, as individuals keep track of and distribute their own software assets. For such an ad hoc, individually driven approach, it is difficult to measure any potential benefits to the company. Another approach is called facilitated reuse. Under this approach, developers are not required to practice reuse, but they are encouraged to do so. The organization makes available some tools and techniques that enable the development and sharing of reusable assets, and one or more employees may be assigned the role of evangelist to publicize and promote the program. However, little is done to track the quality and use of reusable assets, and the

Table 14-3 Four Approaches to Reuse.

	Ad Hoc Reuse	Facilitated Reuse	Managed Reuse	Designed Reuse
Theme	Individuals find assets on their own, sharing with colleagues as they choose.	Organization encourages and supports reuse with limited resources, infrastructure, and policies to make reuse easier.	Organization enforces reuse practice through policies, resources, tools, and people.	Organization invests in carefully designing assets for reuse, choosing assets for domain or product line. Assets are architected or reengineered to fit together.
Typical Reuse Level	Varies, usually unknown	5–15%	15–50%	40–90%
Relative Cost	Minimal	Low	Medium	High
People/Roles	Individual effort, no reuse roles.	Evangelist, reuse facilitation, Web master/librarian.	Facilitated roles plus librarians/registrars, certifiers/reviewers, process engineers.	Managed roles plus architect(s), domain analyst(s), component developers, component support specialists.
Process and Policies	None	Incentives, asset check-in process, limited review before publication.	Reuse-adapted process, mandated with specific goals. Reuse reviews and asset documentation, packaging, and certification guidelines; specified metrics to be collected.	Some domain analysis, reuse-oriented architecture; specific steps to design for and with reuse.
Tools and Technology	File system or minimal Web site, e-mail.	Self-use repository or Web site, submitters may add some metadata to improve search and evaluation.	Registrar-monitored repository, extensive metadata, multiproject source code control, asset quality assurance, change notification, utilization measurements.	Requirements and portfolio management tools, frameworks, standards, generators, change management tools.

Source: Adapted from Griss, 2003. Used by permission.

overall corporate investment is small. Managed reuse is a more structured and more expensive mode of managing software reuse. Under managed reuse, the development, sharing, and adoption of reusable assets are mandated. The organization establishes processes and policies for ensuring that reuse is practiced and that the results are measured. The organization also establishes policies and procedures for ensuring the quality of its reusable assets. The focus is on identifying existing assets that potentially can be reused from various sources including utility asset libraries that come with operating systems, from companies that sell assets, from the open source community, from internal repositories, from scouring existing legacy code, and so on. The most expensive and extensive approach to reuse is designed reuse. In addition to mandating reuse and to measuring its effectiveness, the designed reuse approach takes the extra step of mandating that assets be designed for reuse as they are being designed for specific applications. The focus is more on developing reusable assets than on finding existing assets that might be candidates for reuse. A corporate reuse office might be established to monitor and manage the overall methodology. Under such an approach, as much as 90 percent of software assets can be reused across different applications.

Each approach to reuse has its advantages and disadvantages. No single approach is a silver bullet that will solve the reuse puzzle for all organizations and for all situations. Successful reuse requires an understanding of how reuse fits within larger organizational goals and strategies, as well as an understanding of the social and technical world into which the reusable assets must fit.

Object Frameworks

Object framework
A collection of cooperating objects that provide an integrated solution for a particular problem.

Object frameworks are collections of cooperating objects that provide an integrated solution for a particular problem (Bichler, Segev, & Zhao, 1998; Fayad & Schmidt, 1997). Frameworks are targeted to particular business units or application domains, such as user interfaces, real-time avionics, manufacturing, and telecommunications. Frameworks can be specialized to produce custom applications. Object frameworks have been used successfully for many years in specific areas of development, such as graphical user interfaces. Examples include MacApp, Interviews, and Microsoft's Microsoft Foundation Classes, the de facto industry standard for creating graphical user interfaces for the PC platform. Frameworks for more complex domains are just now being developed, made possible by object-request broker standards, such as CORBA, which was discussed in Chapter 12. Embedded in the idea of object frameworks is the reuse of entire application designs, not just specific classes or components. Design reuse leverages all of the advantages of reuse discussed earlier, but the added complexity inherent in a complete design makes object frameworks risky, as well. Frameworks provide many challenges and much potential for future systems development efforts.

SOFTWARE APPLICATION TESTING

Testing software begins early in the systems development cycle, even though many of the actual testing activities are carried out during implementation. During analysis, an overall test plan is developed. During design, the systems analyst develops a unit test plan, an integration test plan, and a system test plan. During implementation, these various plans are put into effect and the actual testing is performed.

The purpose of these written test plans is to improve communication among all the people involved in testing the application software. The plan specifies what each person's role will be during testing. The test plans also serve as checklists that can be used to determine whether all testing steps have been completed. The overall test plan is not just a single document but a collection of documents. Each of the component documents represents a complete test plan for one part of the system or for a particular type of test.

Some organizations have specially trained personnel who supervise and support testing. Testing managers are responsible for developing test plans, establishing testing standards, integrating testing and development activities in the development cycle, and ensuring that test plans are completed. Testing specialists help develop test plans, create test cases and scenarios, execute the actual tests, and analyze and report test results.

Seven Different Types of Tests

Inspection
A testing technique in which participants examine program code for predictable, language-specific errors.

Software application testing is an umbrella term that covers several types of tests. Tests can be done with or without executing the code, and they can be manual or automated. Using this framework, types of tests can be categorized as shown in Table 14-4.

Let's examine each type of test in turn. Inspections are formal group activities during which participants manually examine code for occurrences of well-known errors. Syntax, grammar, and some other routine errors can be checked by automated inspection software, so manual inspection checks are used for more subtle errors. Code inspection participants compare the code they are examining to a checklist of well-known errors for that particular language. Exactly what the code does is not investigated in an inspection. Code inspections have been used by organizations to

Table 14-4
A Categorization
of Test Types.

	MANUAL	AUTOMATED
Without Code Execution	Inspections	Syntax checking
With Code Execution	Walk-throughs	Unit testing
	Desk checking	Integration testing
		System testing
		Stub testing

detect from 60 percent to 90 percent of all software defects, as well as to provide programmers with feedback that enables them to avoid making the same types of errors in future work. The inspection process also can be used to ensure that design specifications are met.

Unlike in an inspection, what the code does is an important question in a walk-through. Using structured walkthroughs is an effective method of detecting errors in code. As shown in Chapter 4, structured walk-throughs can be used to review many systems development deliverables, including design specifications and code. Whereas specification walk-throughs tend to be formal reviews, code walkthroughs tend to be informal. Informality makes programmers less apprehensive of criticism and thus helps increase the frequency of walk-throughs. Code walk-throughs should be done frequently when the pieces of work reviewed are relatively small and before the work is formally tested. If walk-throughs are not held until the entire program is tested, the programmer already will have spent too much time looking for errors that the programming team could have found much more quickly. Further, the longer a program goes without being subjected to a walk-through, the more defensive the programmer becomes when the code is reviewed. Although each organization that uses walk-throughs conducts them differently, a basic structure can be followed that works well (see Figure 14.3).

It should be stressed that the purpose of a walk-through is to detect errors, not to correct them. It is the programmer's job to correct the errors uncovered in a walk-through. Sometimes it can be difficult for the reviewers to refrain from suggesting ways to fix the problems they find in the code, but increased experience with the process can help change reviewers' behavior.

Desk checking
A manual testing technique in which the program code is executed sequentially by the reviewer.

What the code does is also important in desk checking, an informal process during which the programmer or someone else who understands the logic of the program works through the code with paper and pencil. The programmer executes each instruction, using test cases that might or might not be written down. In one sense, the reviewer acts as the computer, mentally checking each step and its results for the entire set of computer instructions.

Syntax checking typically is done by a compiler. Errors in syntax are uncovered, but the code is not executed. For the other three automated techniques, the code is executed.

Figure 14.3
Guidelines for
Conducting a Code
Walkthrough

GUIDELINES FOR CONDUCTING A CODE WALK-THROUGH

1. Have the review meeting chaired by the project manager or chief programmer, who is also responsible for scheduling the meeting, reserving a room, setting the agenda, inviting participants, and so on.
2. The programmer presents his or her work to the reviewers. Discussion should be general during the presentation.
3. Following the general discussion, the programmer walks through the code in detail, focusing on the logic of the code rather than on specific test cases.
4. Reviewers ask to walk through specific test cases.
5. The chair resolves disagreements if the review team cannot reach agreement among themselves and assigns duties, usually to the programmer, for making specific changes.
6. A second walk-through is then scheduled, if needed.

Unit testing
Each module is tested alone in an attempt to discover any errors in its code.

Integration testing
The process of bringing together all of the objects and components that a program comprises for testing purposes.

System testing
The bringing together of all the programs that a system comprises for testing purposes. Programs typically are integrated in a top-down, incremental fashion.

The first such technique is unit testing. In unit testing, each object or component is tested alone in an attempt to discover any errors that exist in its code. Yet, because objects and components coexist and work with other objects and components in systems, they must be tested together in larger groups. Combining objects and components and testing them is called integration testing. Integration testing is gradual. Modules and components are tested in pairs and in larger combinations. System testing is a similar process, but programs are tested instead of objects and components. System testing follows the same incremental logic that integration testing does. Under integration and system testing, not only do individual objects, components, and programs get tested many times, so do the interfaces between them.

System testing is more than simply expanded integration testing in which the systems analyst is testing the interfaces between programs in a system rather than testing the interfaces between objects and components in a program. System testing also is intended to demonstrate whether or not a system meets its objectives. The system test typically is conducted by information systems personnel led by the project team leader, although it also can be conducted by users under the guidance of information systems personnel.

The Testing Process

Up to this point, this chapter has covered an overall test plan and seven different types of tests for software applications. Little has been said about the process of testing itself. Two important things to remember about testing information systems are:

1. The purpose of testing is to confirm that the system satisfies requirements.
2. Testing must be planned.

Testing is not haphazard. Many different aspects of a system must be observed, such as response time, response to boundary data, response to no input, response to heavy volumes of input, and so on. Anything (within resource constraints) that could go wrong or be wrong with a system must be tested. At a minimum, the most frequently used parts of the system should be tested, as well as many other paths through the system as time permits. Planning gives analysts and programmers an opportunity to think through all of the potential problem areas, list these areas, and develop ways to test for problems. As indicated previously, one part of a test plan is creating a set of test cases, each of which must be documented carefully. See Figure 14.4 for an outline of a test case description and summary.

A test case is a specific scenario of transactions, queries, or navigation paths that represent a typical, critical, or abnormal use of the system. A test case should be repeatable so that it can be rerun as new versions of the software are tested. This is important for all code, whether written in-house, developed by a contractor, or purchased. Test cases need to determine that new software works with other existing software with which it must share data. Even though analysts often do not do the testing, systems analysts, because of their intimate knowledge of applications, often make up or find test data. The people who create the test cases typically are not the same people who coded and tested the system. In addition to a description of each test case, a summary of the test results must be generated, with an emphasis on how the actual results differed from the expected results. The testing summary will indicate why the results were different and what, if anything, should be done to change the software. Further, this summary will suggest the need for retesting, possibly introducing new tests necessary to discover the source of the differences.

One important reason to keep such a thorough description of test cases and results is so that testing can be repeated for each revision of an application. Although new versions of a system might necessitate new test data to validate new features of the application, previous test data usually can and should be reused. Results from use of the test data with prior versions are compared to new versions to show that changes have not introduced new errors and that the behavior of the system, including response time, is no worse.

Figure 14.4
Test Case Description
and Summary

Pine Valley Furniture Company
Test Case Description and Summary

Test Case Number: Date:
Test Case Description:

Program/Module Name:
Testing State:
Test Case Prepared By:
Test Administrator:
Description of Test Data:

Expected Results:

Actual Results:

Explanation of Differences between Actual and Expected Results:

Suggestions for Next Steps:

Acceptance Testing by Users

Acceptance testing
The process whereby actual
users test a completed
information system, the end
result of which is the users'
acceptance of it.

Alpha testing
User testing of a completed
information system using
simulated data.

Beta testing
User testing of a completed
information system using
real data in the real user
environment.

Once the system tests have been completed satisfactorily, the system is ready for acceptance testing, which is testing the system in the environment where it eventually will be used. Acceptance refers to the fact that users typically sign off on the system and accept it once they are satisfied with it. The purpose of acceptance testing is for users to determine whether the system meets their requirements. The extent of acceptance testing will vary with the organization and with the system in question. The most complete acceptance testing will include alpha testing, where simulated but typical data are used for system testing; beta testing, in which live data are used in the users' real working environment; and a system audit conducted by the organization's internal auditors or by members of the quality assurance group.

During alpha testing, the entire system is implemented in a test environment to discover whether or not the system is overtly destructive to itself or to the rest of the environment. The types of tests performed during alpha testing include the following:

- *Recovery testing:* Forces the software (or environment) to fail in order to verify that recovery is performed properly.
- *Security testing:* Verifies that protection mechanisms built into the system will protect it from improper penetration.
- *Stress testing:* Tries to break the system (e.g., what happens when a record is written to the database with incomplete information or what happens under extreme online transaction loads or with a large number of concurrent users).
- *Performance testing:* Determines how the system performs in the range of possible environments in which it might be used (e.g., different hardware configurations, networks, operating systems, and so on); often the goal is to have the system perform with similar response time and other performance measures in each environment.

In beta testing, a subset of the intended users runs the system in their own environments using their own data. The intent of the beta test is to determine whether the software, documentation, technical support, and training activities work as intended. In essence, beta testing can be viewed as a rehearsal of the installation phase. Problems uncovered in alpha and beta testing in any of these areas must be corrected before users can accept the system.

INSTALLATION

Installation
The organizational process of changing over from the current information system to a new one.

Direct installation
Changing from the old information system to a new one by turning off the old system when the new one is turned on.

Parallel installation
Running the old information system and the new one at the same time until management decides the old system can be turned off.

Single location installation
Trying out a new information system at one site and using the experience to decide if and how the new system should be deployed throughout the organization.

Phased installation
Changing from the old information system to the new one incrementally, starting with one or a few functional components and then gradually extending the installation to cover the whole new system.

The process of moving from the current information system to the new one is called installation. All employees who use a system, whether they were consulted during the development process or not, must give up their reliance on the current system and begin to rely on the new system. Four different approaches to installation have emerged over the years:

- Direct installation
- Parallel installation
- Single location installation
- Phased installation

These four approaches are highlighted in Figure 14.5 and Table 14-5. The approach (or combination) an organization decides to use will depend on the scope and complexity of the change associated with the new system and the organization's risk aversion. In practice, a single strategy is rarely chosen to the exclusion of all others; most installations will rely on a combination of two or more approaches. For example, if a single location strategy is chosen, the analyst has to decide how installation will proceed there and at subsequent sites. Will it be direct, parallel, or phased?

Planning Installation

Each installation strategy involves converting not only software but also data and (potentially) hardware, documentation, work methods, job descriptions, offices and other facilities, training materials, business forms, and other aspects of the system. For example, it is necessary to recall or replace all of the current system documentation and business forms, which suggests that the IS department must keep track of who has these items so that they can be notified and receive replacement items.

Of special interest in the installation process is the conversion of data. Because existing systems usually contain data required by the new system, current data must be

Figure 14.5
Comparison of Installation Strategies: (a) Direct Installation; (b) Parallel Installation

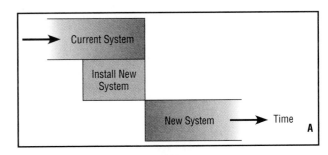

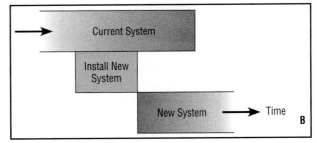

Figure 14.5
(c) Single Location
Installation (with
Direct Installation)
at Each Location; (d)
Phased Installation

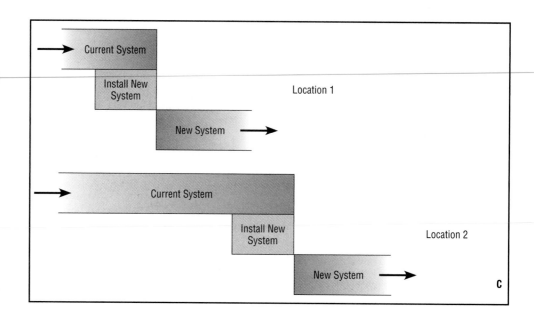

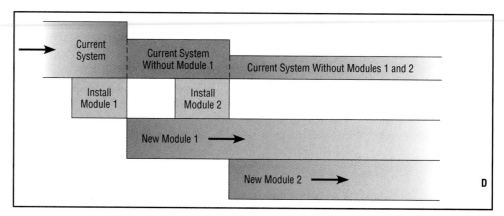

made error free, unloaded from current files, combined with new data, and loaded into new files. Data might need to be reformatted to be consistent with more advanced data types supported by newer technology used to build the new system. New data fields might have to be entered in large quantities so that every record copied from the current system has all the new fields populated. Manual tasks, such as taking a physical inventory, might need to be done in order to validate data before they are transferred to the new files. The total data conversion process can be tedious. Furthermore, this process might require that current systems be shut off while the data are extracted so that updates to old data, which would contaminate the extract process, cannot occur.

Any decision that requires the current system to be shut down, in whole or in part, before the replacement system is in place must be done with care. Typically, off-hours are used for installations that require a lapse in system support. Whether or not a lapse in service is required, the installation schedule should be announced to users well in advance to let them plan their work schedules around outages in service and periods when their system support might be erratic. Successful installation steps also should be announced and special procedures put in place so that users can easily inform the systems analyst of problems they encounter during installation periods. Emergency staff also need to be available in case of system failure so that business operations can be recovered and made operational as quickly as possible. Another consideration is the business cycle of the organization. Most organizations face heavy workloads at particular times of the year and relatively light loads at other times. A well-known example is the retail industry, where the busiest time of year is the fall, right before the year's major gift-giving holidays. It would not be

Table 14-5 Approaches to Information Systems Installation.

CHARACTERISTICS	POSITIVE ASPECTS	HAZARDS/RISKS
Direct Installation • Abrupt • "Cold turkey"	• Low cost • High interest in making installation a success • May be the only possible approach if new and existing systems cannot coexist in some form	• Operational errors have direct impact on users and organization • It may take too long to restore old system, if necessary • Time-consuming, and benefits may be delayed until whole system is installed
Parallel Installation • Old and new systems coexist • Safe	• New systems can be checked against old system • Impact of operational errors are minimized because old system is also processing all data	• Not all aspects of new system can be compared to old system • Very expensive due to duplication of effort to run and maintain two systems • Can be confusing to users • May be a delay until benefits result • May not be feasible due to costs or system size
Single Location Installation • Pilot approach • Middle-of-the-road approach • May involve a series of single location installations • Each location may be branch office, factory, or department	• Learning can occur and problems fixed by concentrating on one site • Limits potential harm and costs from system errors or failure to selected pilot sites • Can use early success to convince others to convert to new system	• Burden on IS staff to maintain old and new systems • If different sites require data sharing, extra programs need to be written to "bridge" the two systems • Some parts of organization get benefits earlier than other parts
Phased Installation • Staged, incremental, gradual; based on system functional components • Similar to bringing system out via multiple releases	• Allows for system development also to be phased • Limits potential harm and costs from system error or failure to certain business activities/functions • Risk spread over time • Some benefits can be achieved early • Each phrase is small and more manageable	• Old and new sytems must be able to work together and share data, which likely will require extra programming to "bridge" the two systems • Conversion is constant and may extend over a long period, causing frustration and confusion for users

wise to schedule installation of a new point-of-sale system to begin December 1 for a department store.

Planning for installation can begin as early as the analysis of the organization supported by the system. Some installation activities, such as buying new hardware, remodeling facilities, validating data to be transferred to the new system, and collecting new data to be loaded into the new system, must be done before the software installation can occur. Often the project team leader is responsible for anticipating all installation tasks and assigns responsibility for each to different analysts.

Each installation process involves getting workers to change the way they work. As such, installation should be looked at not as simply installing a new computer system, but as an organizational change process. More than just a computer system is involved; how people do their jobs and how the organization operates will change as well.

DOCUMENTING THE SYSTEM

In one sense, every information systems development project is unique and will generate its own unique documentation. In another sense, though, systems development projects are probably more alike than they are different. Each project shares a similar systems development cycle, which dictates that certain activities be undertaken and each of those activities documented. Specific documentation will vary depending on the development cycle being followed, and the format and content of the documentation might be mandated by the organization. It is good practice to start developing documentation elements early, as the information needed is captured.

The situation can be simplified by dividing documentation into two basic types, system documentation and user documentation. System documentation records detailed information about a system's design specifications, its internal workings, and its functionality. System documentation can be further divided into internal and external documentation. Internal documentation is part of the program source code or is generated at compile time. Internal documentation for objects is important for anyone who would reuse those objects in other systems. External documentation includes the outcome of all of the diagramming techniques that have been covered in this book, such as use-case diagrams and sequence diagrams. User documentation is written or other visual information is included about an application system, how it works, and how to use it. Although not part of the code itself, external documentation can provide useful information to the primary users of system documentation—maintenance programmers. In the past, external documentation typically was discarded after implementation, primarily because it was considered too costly to keep up to date, but today's CASE environment makes it possible to maintain and update external documentation as long as desired.

Whereas system documentation is intended primarily for maintenance programmers, user documentation is intended mainly for users. An organization might have definitive standards on system documentation, often consistent with CASE tools and the systems development process. These standards can include the outline for the project dictionary and specific pieces of documentation within it. Standards for user documentation are not as explicit.

User Documentation

User documentation consists of written or other visual information about an application system, how it works, and how to use it. An excerpt of user documentation for Adobe Reader appears in Figure 14.6. Each phrase listed under "Contents" is a link to a detailed treatment of that particular topic. Some topics have multiple subparts, indicated by the plus signs. Clicking on the plus sign expands the list so that all of the subparts are visible. These presentation methods have become standard for help files in PC documentation. Many PC help files also contain links to the software vendor's Web site, where more information, and more up-to-date information, can be found.

Figure 14.6 represents the content of a reference guide, which is just one type of user documentation. Other types of user documentation include a quick reference guide, user's guide, release description, system administrator's guide, and accep-

System documentation
Detailed information about a system's design specifications, its internal workings, and its functionality.

User documentation
Written or other visual information about an application system, how it works, and how to use it.

Internal documentation
System documentation that is part of the program source code or is generated at compile time.

External documentation
System documentation that includes the outcome of structured diagramming techniques such as use-case and sequence diagrams.

Figure 14.6
Content from User Documentation for Adobe Reader

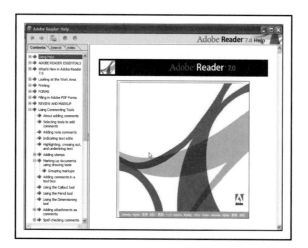

viding the support for free. Most vendors now charge for support, and many have instituted 900 numbers and other automated support mechanisms or sell customers unlimited support for a given monthly or annual charge. Common methods for automating support include online support forums (on private Web sites or public Internet service providers like America Online), bulletin board systems, on-demand fax, and voice-response systems. Online support forums provide users with access to information on new releases, bugs, and tips for more effective usage. On-demand fax allows users to order support information through an 800 number and receive that information instantly over their fax machines. Finally, voice-response systems allow users to navigate option menus that lead to prerecorded messages about usage, problems, and work-arounds. Organizations have established similar support mechanisms for systems developed or purchased by the organization. Internal e-mail, group support systems, and office automation can be used to support such capabilities within an organization.

Providing Support through a Help Desk

Help desk
A single point of contact for all user inquiries and problems about a particular information system or for all users in a particular department.

Whether assisted by vendors or going it alone, the center of support activities for a specific information system in many organizations is the help desk. A help desk is an information systems department function, staffed by IS personnel. The help desk is the first place users should call when they need assistance with an information system. The help desk staff members either deal with the users' questions or refer the users to the most appropriate person.

Today, help desks are very common, as management comes to appreciate the special combination of technical skills and people skills needed to make good help desk staffers. Many software packages exist to automate the recordkeeping for a help desk. Records must be kept on each user contact, the content of the question or problem, and the status and resolution of the problem. Help desk managers use the software to track problems with different information systems, assess help desk personnel efficiency and effectiveness, and identify users who require training.

Help desk personnel need to be good at communicating with users; they must listen to their problems and intelligently communicate potential solutions. These personnel also need to understand the technology they are helping users with. It is crucial, however, that help desk personnel know when new systems and releases are being implemented and when users are being trained for new systems. Help desk personnel themselves should be well trained on new systems. One sure recipe for disaster is to train users on new systems but not train the help desk personnel that these same users will turn to for their support needs.

WHY IMPLEMENTATION SOMETIMES FAILS

Despite the best efforts of the systems development team to design and build a quality system and to manage the change process in the organization, the implementation effort sometimes fails. Sometimes employees will not use the new system that has been developed for them, or if they do use the system, their level of satisfaction with it is low.

The conventional wisdom that has emerged over the years is that at least two conditions are necessary for a successful implementation effort: management support of the system under development and the involvement of users in the development process. Yet, despite the support and active participation of management and users, information systems implementation still sometimes fail.

The following are some insights about the implementation process:

- *Risk:* User involvement in the development process can help reduce the risk of failure when the system is complex, but it also can make failure more likely when the development process has financial and time constraints.

- *Commitment to the project:*   The systems development project should be managed so that the problem being solved is well understood and the system being developed to deal with the problem solves it.
- *Commitment to change:*   Users and managers must be willing to change behaviors, procedures, and other aspects of the organization.
- *Extent of project definition and planning:*   The more extensive the planning effort is, the less likely implementation failure is.
- *Realistic user expectations:*   The more realistic a user's early expectations are about a new system and its capabilities, the more likely it is that the user will be satisfied with the new system and use it.

Whether a system implementation fails or succeeds also depends on your definition of success. Although there are many ways to determine if an implementation has been successful, the two most common and trusted are the extent to which the system is used and the user's satisfaction with the system. Whether a user will use a new system depends on several additional factors not already mentioned:

1. How relevant the system is to the work the user performs.
2. Ease of system use and reliability.
3. User demographics, such as age and degree of computer experience.
4. The more users can do with a system and the more creative ways they can develop to benefit from the system, the more they will use it. Then, the more people use the system, the more likely they are to find even more ways to benefit from it.
5. The more satisfied the users are with the system, the more they will use it. The more they use it, the more satisfied they will be.

It should be clear that, as an analyst and as someone responsible for the successful implementation of an information system, one has more control over some factors than others. For example, the systems analyst has considerable influence over the system's ease of use and reliability, and might have some influence over the levels of support that will be provided for users of the system. The analyst has no direct control over a user's demographics, relevance of the system, management support, or the urgency of the problem to the user. However, these factors cannot be ignored. In fact, these factors need to be understood well, because they will have to be balanced with the factors in the system design and implementation strategy that can be changed. A user's demographics or personal stake in a system cannot be changed, but the system and the implementation strategy can be designed with these factors in mind.

The factors mentioned so far are straightforward. For example, a lack of computer experience can make a user hesitant, inefficient, and ineffective with a system, leading to a system that is not providing its full potential benefit. If top management does not seem to care about the system, why should subordinates care? However, additional factors can be categorized as political and might be more hidden, difficult to effect, and even unrelated to the system that is being implemented, yet instrumental to the system's success.

The basis for political factors is that individuals who work in an organization have their own self-interested goals, which they pursue in addition to the goals of their departments and of their organizations. For example, people might act to increase their own power relative to that of their coworkers; at other times, people will act to prevent coworkers with more power (such as bosses) from using that power or from gaining more. Because information is power, information systems often are seen as instruments of one's ability to influence and exert power. It is helpful to understand the history and politics around an information system, and to deal with negative political factors as well as the more objective and operational ones.

Chapter 3 discussed the various phases of project management, from project initiation to closing down the project. A project manager who has guided a project successfully through all of the phases of the systems development cycle presented so far in this book is now ready to close down the project. Although systems operation is just about to begin, the development project itself is over. As the following sections will show, maintenance can be thought of as a series of smaller development projects, each with its own series of project management phases.

As discussed in Chapter 3, the first task in closing down the project involves many different activities, from dealing with project personnel to planning a celebration of the project's ending. The project manager will likely have to evaluate the team members, reassign most to other projects, and perhaps terminate others. A project manager also will have to notify all of the affected parties that the development project is ending and that the project is now switching to operation and maintenance mode.

The project manager's second task is to conduct post-project reviews with management and customers. In some organizations, these post-project reviews follow formal procedures and may involve internal or electronic data processing (EDP) auditors. The point of a project review is to critique the project, its methods, its deliverables, and its management. Many lessons can be learned from a thorough post-project review that will improve future projects.

The third major task in project closedown is closing out the customer contract. Any contract that has been in effect between the project manager and customers during the project (or as the basis for the project) must be completed. This may involve a formal signing-off by the clients stating that the work is complete and acceptable. Maintenance activities typically are covered under new contractual agreements. If a customer is outside of the organization, a separate support agreement probably will be negotiated.

Some organizations conduct a post-implementation audit of a system shortly after it goes into operation, during or shortly after project closedown. A system audit may be conducted by a member of an internal audit staff, responsible for checking any data-handling procedure change in the organization. Sometimes a system audit is conducted by an outside organization, such as a management consulting firm or public accounting firm. The purpose of a system audit is to verify that a system works properly by itself and in combination with other systems. A system audit is similar to a system test but is done on a system in operation. A system audit not only checks that the operational system works accurately, but the audit also is likely to review the development process for the system. Such a process audit checks that sound practices were used to design, develop, and test the system. For example, a process audit will review the testing plan and summary of results. Errors found during an audit will generate requests for system maintenance, and in an extreme case, could force a system to cease operation.

The job of an analyst member of the development team on a particular project ends during project closedown. Analysts will likely be reassigned to other projects dealing with some other organizational problem. During a career as a systems analyst, many job assignments will be to perform maintenance on existing systems. This important part of the systems implementation and operation phase is covered next.

CONDUCTING SYSTEMS MAINTENANCE

Maintenance
Changes made to a system to fix or enhance its functionality.

A significant portion of an organization's budget for information systems does not go to the development of new systems but to the maintenance of existing systems. We describe various types of maintenance, factors influencing the complexity and cost of maintenance, alternatives for managing maintenance, and the role of CASE

Table 14-7
Types of Maintenance.

TYPE	DESCRIPTION	APPROXIMATE PERCENTAGE OF MAINTENANCE EFFORT
Corrective	Repair design and programming errors	70
Adaptive	Modify system to environmental changes	10
Perfective	Evolve system to solve new problems or take advantage of new opportunities	15
Preventive	Safeguard system from future problems	5

during maintenance. Given that maintenance activities consume the majority of information systems–related expenditures, gaining an understanding of these topics will yield numerous benefits to one's career as an information systems professional.

Types of Maintenance

Several types of maintenance can be performed on an information system, as described in Table 14-7. In this case, maintenance refers to fixing or enhancing an information system. Corrective maintenance refers to changes made to repair defects in the design, coding, or implementation of the system. For example, if a person purchases a new home, corrective maintenance would involve repairs made to things that had never worked as designed, such as a faulty electrical outlet or a misaligned door. Most corrective maintenance problems become apparent soon after installation. When corrective maintenance problems do surface, they are typically urgent and need to be resolved to curtail possible interruptions in normal business activities. Some corrective maintenance is due to incompatibilities between the new system and other information systems with which it must exchange data. Corrective maintenance adds little or no value to the organization; it simply focuses on removing defects from an existing system without adding new functionality.

Adaptive maintenance involves making changes to an information system to evolve its functionality to changing business needs or to migrate it to a different operating environment. Within a home, adaptive maintenance might be adding storm windows to improve the cooling performance of an air conditioner. Adaptive maintenance is usually less urgent than corrective maintenance because business and technical changes typically occur over some period of time. Contrary to corrective maintenance, adaptive maintenance is generally a small part of an organization's maintenance effort but does add value to the organization.

Perfective maintenance involves making enhancements to improve processing performance, to improve interface usability, or to add desired, but not necessarily required, system features ("bells and whistles"). In the home example, perfective maintenance would be adding a new room. Many systems professionals believe that perfective maintenance is not really maintenance but new development.

Preventive maintenance involves changes made to a system to reduce the chance of future system failure. An example of preventive maintenance might be to increase the number of records that a system can process far beyond what is currently needed. In the home example, preventive maintenance could be painting the exterior to better protect the home from severe weather conditions. As with adaptive maintenance, perfective and preventive maintenance are typically a much lower priority than corrective maintenance. Adaptive, perfective, and preventive maintenance activities can lead to corrective maintenance activities if not carefully designed and implemented.

The Cost of Maintenance

Information systems maintenance costs are a significant expenditure. For some organizations, as much as 90 percent of their information systems budget is allocated to maintenance activities (de Souze, Anquetil, & de Oliveira, 2005). This proportion has risen from roughly 50 percent 20 years ago due to the fact that many organizations

Corrective maintenance
Changes made to a system to repair flaws in its design, coding, or implementation.

Adaptive maintenance
Changes made to a system to evolve its functionality to changing business needs or technologies.

Perfective maintenance
Changes made to a system to add new features or to improve performance.

Preventive maintenance
Changes made to a system to avoid possible future problems.

have accumulated more and more older, so-called legacy systems that require more and more maintenance. More maintenance means more maintenance work for programmers. In situations where a company has not developed its systems in-house but instead has licensed software, as in the case of enterprise resource planning (ERP) systems, maintenance costs remain high. In many cases, the annual maintenance fees for ERP systems can be as high as 20 percent of the up-front costs (Worthen, 2003). In addition, about one-third of the costs of establishing and keeping a presence on the Web go to programming maintenance (Legard, 2000). These high costs associated with maintenance mean that the factors influencing the maintainability of systems must be understood. Maintainability is the ease with which software can be understood, corrected, adapted, and enhanced. Systems with low maintainability result in uncontrollable maintenance expenses.

Numerous factors influence the maintainability of a system. These factors, or cost elements, determine the extent to which a system has high or low maintainability. Of these factors, three are most significant: number of latent defects, number of customers, and documentation quality. The others—personnel, tools, and software structure—have noticeable but less influence.

- *Latent defects:* This is the number of unknown errors existing in the system after it is installed. Because corrective maintenance accounts for most maintenance activity, the number of latent defects in a system influences most of the costs associated with maintaining a system.
- *Number of customers for a given system:* In general, the greater the number of customers, the greater the maintenance costs are. For example, if a system has only one customer, problem and change requests will come from only one source. Also, training, reporting errors, and support will be simpler, and maintenance requests are less likely to be contradictory or incompatible.
- *Quality of system documentation:* Without quality documentation, maintenance efforts can increase exponentially. Quality documentation makes it easier to find code that needs to be changed and to understand how the code needs to be changed. Good documentation also explains why a system does what it does and why alternatives were not feasible, which saves wasted maintenance efforts.
- *Maintenance personnel:* In some organizations, the best programmers are assigned to maintenance. Highly skilled programmers are needed because the maintenance programmer is typically not the original programmer and must quickly come to understand and carefully change the software.
- *Tools:* Tools that automatically can produce system documentation where none exists also can lower maintenance costs. In addition, tools that can automatically generate new code based on system specification changes can reduce maintenance time and costs dramatically.
- *Well-structured programs:* Well-designed programs are easier to understand and fix.

Since the mid-1990s, many organizations have taken a new approach to managing maintenance costs. Rather than develop custom systems internally or through contractors, they have chosen to buy packaged application software. Although vendors of packaged software charge an annual maintenance fee for updates, these charges are more predictable and lower than for custom-developed systems. Internal maintenance work still can be needed when using packages. One major maintenance task is to make the packaged software compatible with other packages and internally developed systems with which it must cooperate. When new releases of the purchased package appear, maintenance might be needed to make all the packages continue to share and exchange data. Some companies are minimizing this effort by buying comprehensive packages, such as enterprise resource planning (ERP) packages (see Chapter 10), which provide information services for a wide range of organizational functions (from human resources to accounting, manufacturing, and sales and marketing). Although the initial costs to install such ERP packages can be significant, they promise great potential for drastically reducing system maintenance costs.

Because maintenance can be so costly, it is important to measure its effectiveness. To measure effectiveness, these factors must be considered:

- Number of failures.
- Time between each failure.
- Type of failure.

Mean time between failures (MTBF)
A measurement of error occurrences that can be tracked over time to indicate the quality of a system.

Measuring the number of and time between failures will provide the basis for calculating a widely used measure of system quality. This measure is referred to as the mean time between failures (MTBF). As its name implies, the MTBF measure shows the average length of time between the identification of one system failure until the next. Over time, the MTBF value should be expected to increase rapidly after a few months of use (and corrective maintenance) of the system. If the MTBF does not increase rapidly over time, it will be a signal to management that major problems exist within the system that are not being resolved adequately through the maintenance process.

A more revealing method of measurement is to examine the failures that are occurring. Over time, logging the types of failures provides a clear picture of where, when, and how failures occur. For example, knowing that a system repeatedly fails logging new account information to the database when a particular customer is using the system can provide invaluable information to the maintenance personnel. Were the users adequately trained? Is there something unique about this user? Is there something unique about an installation that is causing the failure? What activities were being performed when the system failed?

Tracking the types of failures also provides important management information for future projects. For example, if a higher frequency of errors occurs when a particular development environment is used, such information can help guide personnel assignments; training courses; or the avoidance of a particular package, language, or environment during future development. The primary lesson here is that without measuring and tracking maintenance activities, the knowledge to improve or know how well the system is doing relative to the past cannot be gained. To manage effectively and to improve continuously, performance must be measured and assessed over time.

Controlling Maintenance Requests

Another maintenance activity is managing maintenance requests. From a management perspective, a key issue is deciding which requests to perform and which to ignore. Because some requests will be more critical than others, some method of prioritizing requests must be determined.

Figure 14.9 shows a flowchart that suggests one possible method for dealing with maintenance change requests. First, the type of request must be determined. If, for example, the request is an error—that is, a corrective maintenance request—then a question related to the error's severity must be asked. If the error is "very severe," then the request has top priority and is placed at the top of a queue of tasks waiting to be performed on the system. If, however, the error is considered "not very severe," then the change request can be categorized and prioritized based upon its type and relative importance. Categorization and prioritization can be done by the same review panel or board that evaluates new system requests.

If the change request is not an error, then the analyst must determine whether the request is to adapt the system to technology changes or business requirements, or to enhance the system with new business functionality. Adaptation requests also will need to be evaluated, categorized, prioritized, and placed in the queue. Enhancement-type requests must be evaluated first for alignment with future business and information systems' plans. If not aligned, the request will be rejected and the requester will be informed. If the enhancement is aligned with business and information systems' plans, it can then be prioritized and placed into the queue of

Figure 14.9   Flowchart Showing How to Control Maintenance Requests

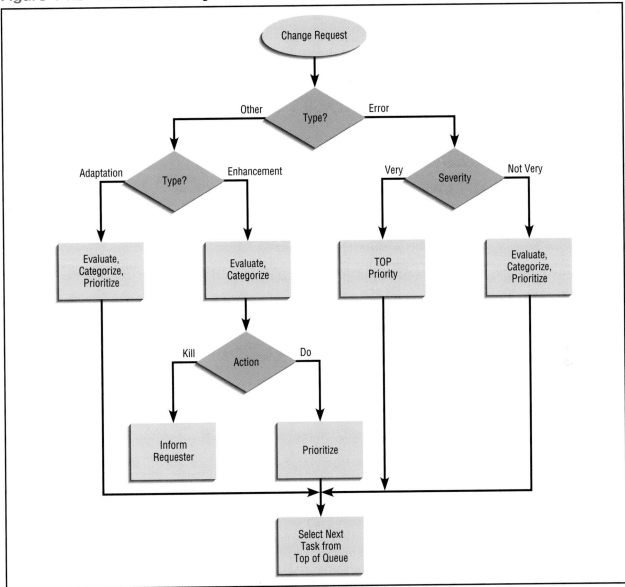

future tasks. Part of the prioritization process includes estimating the scope and feasibility of the change. Techniques used for assessing the scope and feasibility of entire projects should be used when assessing maintenance requests (see Chapter 4).

Managing the queue of pending tasks is an important activity. The queue of maintenance tasks is dynamic; it grows and shrinks based upon business changes and errors. In fact, some lower-priority change requests might never be accomplished, because only a limited number of changes can be accomplished at a given time. In other words, changes in business needs between the time the request was made and when the task finally rises to the top of the queue might result in the request being deemed unnecessary or no longer important given current business directions.

Although each change request goes through an approval process as depicted in Figure 14.9, changes usually are implemented in batches, forming a new release of the software. It is too difficult to manage a lot of small changes. Further, batching changes can reduce maintenance work when several change requests affect the same or highly related modules. Frequent releases of new system versions also may confuse users if the appearance of displays, reports, or data entry screens changes.

Role of CASE and Automated Development Tools in Maintenance

In traditional systems development, much of the time is spent on coding and testing. When software changes are approved, code is changed first and then tested. Once the functionality of the code is assured, the documentation and specification documents are updated to reflect system changes. Over time, the process of keeping all system documentation current can be a tedious and time-consuming activity that often is neglected. This neglect makes future maintenance by the same or different programmers difficult.

A primary objective of using CASE and other automated tools for systems development and maintenance is to change radically how code and documentation are modified and updated. When using an integrated development environment, analysts maintain design documents not source code. In other words, design documents are modified and then code generators automatically create a new version of the system from these updated designs. Also, because the changes are made at the design specification level, most documentation changes already will have been completed during the maintenance process itself. One of the biggest advantages to using CASE, for example, is its benefits during system maintenance.

SYSTEMS IMPLEMENTATION AND OPERATION FOR PINE VALLEY FURNITURE'S WEBSTORE

The programming of all WebStore software is now complete. The programmers tested each component extensively and then performed a system-wide test of the WebStore. In this section, we examine how test cases were developed, how bugs were recorded and fixed, and how alpha and beta testing was conducted.

Developing Test Cases for WebStore

To begin the system-wide testing process, Jim and the PVF development team developed test cases to examine every aspect of the system. Jim knew that system testing, like all other aspects of the SDC, needed to be a structured and planned process. Before opening the WebStore to the general public, every module and component of the system needed to be tested within a controlled environment. Based upon his experience in implementing other systems, Jim believed they would need to develop approximately 150 to 200 separate test cases to fully examine the WebStore. To help focus the development of test cases and to assign primary responsibility for specific areas of the system to certain members of his team, Jim developed the following list of testing categories:

- *Simple functionality:* Add to cart, list section, calculate tax, change personal data.
- *Multiple functionality:* Add item to cart and change quantity, create user account, and change address.
- *Function chains:* Add item to cart, check out, create user account, purchase.
- *Elective functions:* Returned items, lost shipments, item out of stock.
- *Emergency/crisis:* Missing orders, hardware failure, security attacks.

The development group broke into five separate teams, each working to develop an extensive set of cases for each of the testing categories. Each team had 1 day to develop its test cases. Once developed, each team would lead a walk-through so that everyone would know the totality of the testing process and to facilitate extensive feedback to each team so that the testing process would be as comprehensive as possible. To make this point, Jim stated, "What happens when a customer repeatedly enters the same product into the shopping cart? Can we handle that? What happens when the customer repeatedly enters and then removes a single product? Can we handle that? Although some of these things are unlikely to ever occur, we need to be confident that the system is robust to any type of customer interaction. We must develop every test case necessary to give us confidence that the system will operate as intended, 24-7-365!"

A big part of successful system testing is to make sure that no information is lost and that all tests are described in a consistent way. To achieve this, Jim provided all teams with a standard form for documenting each case and for recording the results of each test. This form had the following sections:

- Test Case ID.
- Category/Objective of Test.
- Description.
- System Version.
- Completion Date.
- Participant(s).
- Machine Characteristics (processor, operating system, memory, browser, etc.).
- Test Result.
- Comments.

The teams also developed standard codes for each general type of test, and this was used to create the Test Case ID. For example, all tests related to "simple functionality" were given an ID with SF as a prefix and a number as the suffix—for example, SF001. The teams also developed standards for categorizing, listing objectives, and writing other test form contents. Establishing these standards assured that the testing process would be documented consistently.

Bug Tracking and System Evolution

An outcome of the testing process is the identification of system bugs. Consequently, in addition to setting a standard method for writing and documenting test cases, Jim and the teams established several other rules to assure a smooth testing process. Experienced developers have long known that an accurate bug-tracking process is essential for rapid troubleshooting and repair during the testing process. Bug tracking can be thought of as creating a paper trail that makes it much easier for programmers to find and repair the bug. To make sure that all bugs were documented in a similar way, the team developed a bug-tracking form that had the following categories:

- Bug Number (simple incremental number).
- Test Case ID That Generated the Bug.
- Is the Bug Replicable?
- Effects.
- Description.
- Resolution.
- Resolution Date.
- Comments.

The PVF development team agreed that bug fixes would be made in batches, because all test cases would have to be redone every time the software was changed. Redoing all the test cases each time the software is changed is done to assure that in the process of fixing the bug, no other bugs are introduced into the system. As the system moves along in the testing process—as batches of bugs are fixed—the version number of the software is incremented. During the development and testing phases, the version is typically below the "1.0" first release version.

Alpha and Beta Testing the WebStore

After completing all system test cases and resolving all known bugs, Jim moved the WebStore into the alpha testing phase, during which the entire PVF development team as well as personnel around the company would put the WebStore through its paces. To motivate employees throughout the company to participate actively in testing the

TEST TYPE	SAMPLE OF TESTS PERFORMED
Recovery	Unplug main server to test power backup system.
Security	Switch off main server to test the automatic switching to backup server.
Stress	Try to purchase without being a customer.
Performance	Try to examine server directory files both within the PVF domain and when connecting from an outside Internet service provider.
	Have multiple users simultaneously establish accounts, process purchases, add to shopping cart, remove from shopping cart, etc.
	Examine response time using different connection speeds, processors, memory, browsers, and other system configurations.
	Examine response time when backing up server data.

WebStore, several creative promotions and giveaways were held. All employees were given a T-shirt with the motto "I shop at the WebStore, do you?" In addition, all employees were given $100 to shop at the WebStore and were offered a free lunch for their entire department if they found a system bug while shopping on the system. Also during alpha testing, the development team conducted extensive recovery, security, stress, and performance testing. Table 14-8 provides a sample of the types of tests performed.

After completing alpha testing, PVF recruited several of its established customers to help in beta testing the WebStore. As real-world customers used the system, Jim was able to monitor the system and fine-tune the servers for optimal system performance. As the system moved through the testing process, fewer and fewer bugs were found. After several days of "clean" usage, Jim felt confident that it was now time to open the WebStore for business.

WebStore Installation

Throughout the testing process, Jim kept PVF management aware of each success and failure. Because Jim and the development team followed a structured and disciplined development process, far more successes than failures were recorded. In fact, he was now confident that the WebStore was ready to go online and would recommend to PVF's top management that it was now time to "flip the switch" and let the world enter the WebStore.

KEY POINTS REVIEW

1. **Describe the process of coding, testing, and converting an organizational information system, and outline the deliverables and outcomes of the process.**
   Coding is the process whereby the physical design specifications created by the design team are turned into working computer code by the programming team. Once coding has begun, the testing process can begin and proceed in parallel. As each program module is produced, it can be tested individually, then as part of a larger program, and then as part of a larger system. Installation is the process during which the current system is replaced by the new system. This includes conversion of existing data, software, documentation, and work procedures to those consistent with the new system. The deliverables and outcomes from coding, testing, and conversion are program and system code with associated documentation; testing plans, data, and results; and installation user guides, training plan, and conversion plan for hardware, software, data, and facilities.

2. **Apply four installation strategies: direct, parallel, single location, and phased installation.**
   Direct installation is the changeover from the old information system to a new one by turning off the old system when the new one is turned on. Parallel installation means running the old information system and the new one at the same time until management decides the old system can be turned off. Single location installation is trying out a new information system at one site and using the experience to decide whether and how the

new system should be deployed throughout the organization. Phased installation is changing from the old information system to the new one incrementally, starting with one or a few functional components and then gradually extending the installation to cover the whole new system. Often, a combination or hybrid of these four strategies is employed for a particular information system installation. The approach (or combination) an organization decides to use depends upon the scope and complexity of the change associated with the new system and the organization's risk aversion.

3. **List the deliverables for documenting the system and for training and supporting users.** The deliverables are system and user documentation; a user training plan for classes and tutorials; user training materials including computer-based training aids; and a user support plan including such elements as a help desk, online help materials, and bulletin boards and other support mechanisms.

4. **Compare the many modes available for organizational information system training, including self-training and electronic performance support systems.** The most common delivery mode for corporate training is led by an instructor and takes place in a classroom. Increasingly, though, training is being delivered by e-learning or distance learning methods. Another popular delivery method for training is a combination of instructor-led training and e-learning. Also important are self-training and reliance on a resident expert. An important software help component used for training is called an electronic performance support system (EPSS). EPSS is a component of a software package or application where training and educational information have been embedded. The EPSS can include a tutorial, an expert system shell, or hypertext jumps to context-sensitive reference material.

5. **Discuss the issues of providing support for end users.** Support is more than just answering user questions about how to use a system to perform a particular task or about the system's functionality. Support also consists of such tasks as providing for recovery and backup, disaster recovery, and PC maintenance; writing newsletters and offering other types of proactive information sharing; and setting up user groups. It is the responsibility of analysts for a new system to be sure that all forms of support are in place before the system is installed.

6. **Explain why systems implementation sometimes fails.** Even well-executed systems development projects, in which the right requirements have been identified and a sound system has been designed and installed, can fail. Research and experience have shown that management support of the system under development and the involvement of users in the development process can be important but are not sufficient to achieve success. In addition, users must have a commitment to the project and a commitment to change. Poorly done project definition and planning can set up a project for failure. Users and developers also must have realistic and consistent expectations of the system's capabilities. The system must be relevant to the work the user performs. Also important are the ease of use and reliability of the system and user demographics, such as age and degree of computer experience. The more users can do with a system and the more creative ways they can develop to benefit from the system, the more they will use it. More use leads users to find even more ways to benefit from the system. The more satisfied the users are with the system, the more they will use it. The more they use it, the more satisfied they will be.

7. **Explain and contrast four types of maintenance.** Corrective maintenance means repairing flaws in a system's design, coding, or implementation. Adaptive maintenance means implementing changes to a system to evolve its functionality to changing business needs or technologies. Perfective maintenance means adding new features or improving system performance. Preventive maintenance means avoiding possible future problems. Corrective maintenance is the most frequent, by far, and should primarily occur soon after a system release is installed. Corrective maintenance must be done, usually quickly. Adaptive maintenance also usually must be done. Some adaptive maintenance and all perfective and preventive maintenance are discretionary and must be categorized and prioritized.

8. **Describe several factors that influence the cost of maintaining an information system.** The factors that influence the cost of maintaining an information system are (1) latent defects, which are unknown errors existing in the system after it is installed; (2) number of customers for a given system; (3) quality of system documentation; (4) maintenance personnel; (5) tools

that automatically can produce system documentation where none exists; and (6) well-structured programs. The most influential of these are latent defects, number of customers, and quality of documentation. Also, some companies have adopted a strategy of using packaged application software, especially enterprise resource planning systems, to reduce maintenance costs.

KEY TERMS CHECKPOINT

Here are the key terms from this chapter. The page where each term is first explained is in parentheses after the term.

a. Acceptance testing (p. 416)
b. Adaptive maintenance (p. 428)
c. Alpha testing (p. 416)
d. Beta testing (p. 416)
e. Corrective maintenance (p. 428)
f. Desk checking (p. 414)
g. Direct installation (p. 417)
h. Electronic performance support system (EPSS) (p. 423)
i. External documentation (p. 420)
j. Help desk (p. 425)
k. Inspection (p. 413)
l. Installation (p. 417)
m. Integration testing (p. 415)
n. Internal documentation (p. 420)
o. Maintenance (p. 427)
p. Mean time between failures (MTBF) (p. 430)
q. Object framework (p. 413)
r. Parallel installation (p. 417)
s. Perfective maintenance (p. 428)
t. Phased installation (p. 417)
u. Preventive maintenance (p. 428)
v. Reuse (p. 410)
w. Single location installation (p. 417)
x. Support (p. 424)
y. System documentation (p. 420)
z. System testing (p. 415)
aa. Unit testing (p. 415)
bb. User documentation (p. 420)

Match each of the key terms above with the definition that best fits it.

1. A testing technique in which participants examine program code for predictable, language-specific errors.
2. A testing technique in which the program code is sequentially executed manually by the reviewer.
3. Component of a software package or application in which training and educational information is embedded. It can include a tutorial, expert system, and hypertext jumps to reference material.
4. Written or other visual information about an application system, how it works, and how to use it.
5. Changing over from the old information system to a new one by turning off the old system when the new one is turned on.
6. Changes made to a system to evolve its functionality to changing business needs or technologies.
7. Each module is tested alone in an attempt to discover any errors in its code.
8. The organizational process of changing over from the current information system to a new one.
9. A measurement of error occurrences that can be tracked over time to indicate the quality of a system.
10. System documentation that includes the outcome of structured diagramming techniques such as use-case and sequence diagrams.
11. The process whereby actual users test a completed information system, the end result of which is the users' acceptance of it.
12. The use of previously written software resources, especially objects and components, in new applications.
13. Changes made to a system to avoid possible future problems.
14. Detailed information about a system's design specifications, its internal workings, and its functionality.
15. Running the old information system and the new one at the same time until management decides the old system can be turned off.

16. The process of bringing together all of the objects and components that a program comprises for testing purposes.
17. Changes made to a system to add new features or to improve performance.
18. A collection of cooperating objects that provide an integrated solution for a particular problem.
19. Changing from the old information system to the new one incrementally, starting with one or a few functional components and then gradually extending the installation to cover the whole new system.
20. The bringing together of all the programs that a system comprises for testing purposes. Programs typically are integrated in a top-down, incremental fashion.
21. Changes made to a system to fix or enhance its functionality.
22. System documentation that is part of the program source code or is generated at compile time.
23. Providing ongoing educational and problem-solving assistance to information system users. Support material and jobs must be designed along with the associated information system.
24. User testing of a completed information system using real data in the real user environment.
25. Changes made to a system to repair flaws in its design, coding, or implementation.
26. Trying out a new information system at one site and using the experience to decide whether and how the new system should be deployed throughout the organization.
27. User testing of a completed information system using simulated data.
28. A single point of contact for all user inquiries and problems about a particular information system or for all users in a particular department.

1. What are the deliverables from coding, testing, and installation?
2. What is eXtreme programming?
3. What is reuse? Why would an organization encourage reuse? How is reuse best managed?
4. What is an object framework?
5. Explain the testing process for code.
6. What are the four approaches to installation? Which is the most expensive? Which is the most risky? How does an organization decide which approach to use?
7. List and define the factors that are important to successful implementation efforts.
8. What is the difference between system documentation and user documentation?
9. List and define the various methods of user training.
10. Describe the delivery methods many vendors employ for providing support.
11. List the steps in the maintenance process and contrast them with the phases of the systems development cycle.
12. What are the different types of maintenance and how do they differ?
13. Describe the factors that influence the cost of maintenance. Are any factors more important? Why?
14. What types of measurements must be taken to gain an understanding of the effectiveness of maintenance? Why is tracking mean time between failures an important measurement?
15. Describe the process for controlling maintenance requests. Should all requests be handled in the same way, or are there situations when you should be able to circumvent the process? If so, when and why?

1. One of the difficult aspects of using the single location approach to installation is choosing an appropriate location. What factors should be considered in picking a pilot site?
2. You have been a user of many information systems including, possibly, a class registration system at your school, a bank account system, a word processing system, and an airline reservation system. Pick a system you have used and assume you were involved in the beta testing of that system. What criteria would you apply to judge whether or not this system was ready for general distribution?
3. Why is it important to keep a history of test cases and the results of those test cases even after a system has been revised several times?
4. What is the purpose of electronic performance support systems? How would you design one to support a word processing package? A database package?
5. Discuss the role of a centralized training and support facility in a modern organization. Given advances in technology and the prevalence of self-training and consulting among computing end users, how can such a centralized facility continue to justify its existence?
6. Is it good or bad for corporations to rely on vendors for computing support? List arguments for and against reliance on vendors as part of your answer.
7. Your university or school probably has a help desk for students. What functions does the help desk perform? How do these functions compare to those outlined in this chapter?
8. Suppose you were responsible for organizing the user documentation for Pine Valley Furniture's WebStore. Write an outline that shows the documentation you would suggest creating, and generate the table of contents or an outline for each element of this documentation.
9. In what ways is a request to change an information system handled differently from a request for a new information system?
10. What can a systems analyst do to reduce the frequency of corrective maintenance, the most common form of maintenance?
11. What other information should be collected on a Systems Service Request for maintenance as opposed to a Systems Service Request for a new system?
12. Briefly discuss how a systems analyst can manage each of the six cost elements of maintenance.
13. Figure 14.1 shows an arrow going from systems implementation and operation to systems planning and selection. Explain the meaning of this arrow. What causes the transition from implementation and operation to planning and selection? How do maintenance activities within implementation and operation relate to the whole SDC?

1. If possible, ask a systems analyst you know or have access to about implementation. Ask what the analyst believes is necessary for a successful implementation. Try to determine what the analyst believes in comparison to what is discussed in this chapter as far as which factors influence the success of implementation.

2. Talk with people you know who use computers in their work. Ask them to get copies of the user documentation they rely on for the systems they use. Analyze the documentation. Would you consider it good or bad? Support your answer. Whether good or bad, how might you improve it?

3. Volunteer to work for a shift at a help desk at your school. Keep a journal of your experiences. What kind of users did you have to deal with? What kinds of questions did you get? Do you think help desk work is easy or hard? What skills are needed by someone in this position?

4. Let's say your professor has asked you to help him or her train a new secretary on how to prepare class notes for electronic distribution to class members. Your professor uses word processing software and an e-mail package to prepare and distribute the notes. Assume the secretary knows nothing about either package. Prepare a user task guide that shows the secretary how to complete this task.

5. Study an information systems department with which you are familiar or to which you have access. How does this department measure the effectiveness of systems maintenance? What specific metrics are used, and how are these metrics used to effect changes in maintenance practices? If there is a history of measurements over several years, how can changes in the measurements be explained?

CASE PROBLEMS

 ## Pine Valley Furniture

Pine Valley Furniture's Customer Tracking System is now entering the final phases of the systems development cycle. This is a busy time for the project team; project team members are busy coding, testing, training end users, and finalizing the system's documentation.

To enhance your learning experience, Jim Woo has asked you to participate in the implementation process. As a result of this assignment, you have been attending all meetings concerning coding, testing, installation, end-user training, and documentation. During several of these meetings, the installation strategies, necessary end-user training, and required documentation have been discussed. You recall from your recent systems analysis and design course that several options for each of these areas are available.

  a. Locate a technical writing article on the Web. Briefly summarize this article.

  b. Which installation options are available for the Customer Tracking System? Which would you recommend?

  c. How can you determine if implementation has been successful?

  d. What conditions are necessary for a successful implementation effort?

Kitchen Plus

Kitchen Plus is one of the nation's top kitchenware producers. The company has several product lines, including cookware, small appliances, cutlery, and tableware. Over the last several years, the company has watched its market share begin to slip. Several information system projects were rushed into development, including an MRP project. Kitchen Plus executives believed that the new MRP system would enable the company to reduce escalating costs, especially in the areas of inventory, labor, and shipping.

The new MRP system has just been installed, and it is now time to close down the project. As project manager, one of your tasks is to evaluate project team members. Most of the team members performed well, and their work was exemplary. However, Joe McIntire's performance is a different story. Joe was asked to complete several tasks for this project, such as assisting with interviewing, diagramming, testing, and documentation preparation. Several end users called and complained about Joe's interrogation methods. In addition, his diagrams were incomplete, sloppily done, and not completed by the due date. During the testing phase, Joe took a week off from work; Pauline Applegate was assigned to take over Joe's duties.

  a. Identify the tasks involved in project closedown.

  b. How would you evaluate Joe's performance?

  c. What types of maintenance problems can you expect from this information system?

  d. What factors will influence the maintainability of this system?

CASE: BROADWAY ENTERTAINMENT COMPANY, INC.

Designing a Testing Plan for the Customer Relationship Management System

Case Introduction

The students from St. Claire Community College are eager to get reactions to the initial prototype of MyBroadway, the Web-based customer relationship management system that they are designing for Carrie Douglass, manager of the Broadway Entertainment Company (BEC) store in Centerville, Ohio. Based on the user dialogue design (see BEC Figure 13.1 at the end of Chapter 13), the team divided up the work of building the prototype. Tracey Wesley accepted responsibility for defining the database, starting from the physical database design they developed (see BEC case at the end of Chapter 11), and then populating the portions of the database that in production would come from the BEC store and corporate systems with sample data. She will work closely with the other team members responsible for implementing each use case.

Because both John Whitman and Aaron Sharp have had the most Microsoft Access and VBA experience on the team, they are responsible for developing the menus, forms, and displays for specific subsets of the customer pages. They decided to work on one use case at a time, which will be the iterations of the evolutionary development. The team also decided to look through libraries of VBA components available for free on the Internet as starting points for developing each use case. For example, reviewing the contents of inventory is a fairly common system function for any retail enterprise, and a component might be available, saving them time in developing their prototype.

Missi Davies accepted the role of developing and managing the process of testing the system. The team decided that it would be desirable to have someone who is not directly involved in developing the system take responsibility for all aspects of testing. Testing will include tests conducted by Missi herself as well as the use of the prototypes by BEC store employees and customers. While Tracey, John, and Aaron were developing the prototype, Missi began organizing the testing plan.

Preparing the Testing Plan

Now that the database and human interface elements of the system have been reasonably well outlined, Missi has a general understanding of the likely functionality and operation of MyBroadway. Because MyBroadway has a natural modular design, Missi believes that a top-down, modular approach can be used as a general process for testing.

Missi decided that the testing plan must involve a sequence of related steps, in which separate use-case implementations and then combinations of such implementations are used. Missi will initially test the individual use-case implementations and will test the combinations subsequently. However, once she has tested all the customer pages for one or several use cases and is reasonably sure they work, then it will be time to test the prototype with store employees and customers.

After studying the dialogue design for MyBroadway (BEC Figure 13.1 at the end of Chapter 13), Missi determined that five major groups, or modules, of use cases can be tested independently by employees and customers. These testing modules correspond to the five pages on the third level of the dialogue diagram: pages 1.1, 1.2, 1.3, 2.1, and 2.2. Missi decided, however, that such a piecemeal testing would be too confusing for employees and customers, but these modules can drive the internal testing process.

Before her independent tests of pages and modules can be done, Missi knows that she will have to test Tracey's work on building the database. Missi is considering the list of database tables the team developed for MyBroadway (see BEC Figure 8.2 at the end of Chapter 8). Data for the Comment, Pick, and Request relations will be entered by customers of MyBroadway. Product, Sale, and Rental data will be fed from in-store BEC systems. So, Missi can see the steps of the testing plan emerging.

Missi determined that the first step is to have Tracey build the database and populate it with sample data simulating the feeds from in-store systems. For the prototype, the team won't actually build the feeds. Missi contacted Carrie to request printouts of data on products, and sales and rental history. Missi asked Tracey to be prepared to test the loading of Product data first. She believes that only Product data from the in-store data feeds are needed to test pages 1.1, 1.2, and 1.3. This approach will allow Missi to test Tracey's work on loading Product data before John can develop the Product Information module he is developing as he needs a stable database to work with. Then Missi will test John's work on the Product Information module of MyBroadway. She can test Tracey's work of loading sales and rental history and Aaron's work to build the Rental Information module separately.

Missi will select some of the data Carrie provides to use in Tracey's testing. Once she sees the data, Missi can create some other fictitious data to cover special circumstances (e.g., products that have missing field values or extreme field values). Missi will keep some of the data Carrie sends her for use in her own testing of the procedures Tracey builds for loading data. Missi decided that John and Aaron should do their own testing of pages until they believe that the pages are working properly. She wants them to use their own test data for this purpose, and she

Collect Product, Sales, and Rental data from Carrie
    Select subset for Tracey
    Create extra sample data for Tracey's tests
    Design test documentation format for Tracey
    Give data to Tracey
    Create extra sample data for Missi's tests
Design test documentation format for John and Aaron
Design test documentation format for Missi's testing
Conduct module tests
    Conduct walkthrough with Tracey on Product data entry procedures
    Test Product data entry procedures from Tracey
        Provide Tracey with feedback on testing
    Test Product Information navigation pages from John and Aaron
    Test page 1.1.1
    Test page 1.1.2
    Do integration test of pages 1.1.1 and 1.1.2
    Test page 1.2.1
    Test page 1.3
    Conduct walkthrough with Tracey on Rental and Sales history data entry procedures
    Test Rental and Sales history data entry procedures from Tracey
        Provide Tracey with feedback on testing
    Test Rental Information navigation pages from John and Aaron
    Test pages 2.1.1 and 2.1.1.1
    Test page 2.2
        Provide John and Aaron with feedback on testing
Conduct tests of revisions made from initial module tests
    Cycle revising and retesting until system is ready for client testing
Conduct tests with employees
    Design employee feedback forms to collect test results
    Test pages 1 and below
    Test pages 2 and below
Review employee test results
    Cycle revising and retesting internally until system addresses employee concerns
Conduct tests with customers
    Design customer feedback forms to collect test results
    Test whole system with customers
Review customer test results
    Cycle revising and retesting internally until system addresses customer concerns
Summarize results of testing for inclusion in final report to professor and client

will develop separate test data when she looks at their pages.

Missi has put her ideas for a testing plan into a rough outline (BEC Figure 14.1). At this point, the outline does not show a time line or sequence of steps. Missi knows that she has to develop this time line before she can present the testing plan to her team members. After she reviews this outline and time line with the whole team, Aaron, who is maintaining the project schedule, will use Microsoft Project to enter these activities into the official project schedule that Professor Tann, the instructor of the information systems project course at St. Claire, requires each team to maintain.

Preparing a Test Case

Among all the work Missi must do to manage the testing process, she must develop a detailed test case for each of the testing steps assigned to her in the overall testing plan in BEC Figure 14.1. Never having tested a new system before, Missi believes that she should develop one case so that she can get feedback from Professor Tann before proceeding to develop the rest of the cases. Missi decided to

develop one of the easiest test cases first, and a suitable candidate for this appears to be the test for page 1.1.1, the entry by a customer of a new comment on a product.

Missi reviewed the relations the team developed for the physical database (BEC Figure 8.2 at the end of Chapter 8). Page 1.1.1 deals with entry of data in the Comment table. The Comment table in the database will contain data for:

- *membershipid:*   Indicates who is entering the comment. Missi assumes this datum will be collected in a prior page, so this datum will not be an integral part of testing page 1.1.1.

- *commentTimeStamp:*   Indicates when the comment is entered. John's procedures for the page will have to get this computer system value and store it in the table, but the user won't deal with the data. Whether the time is captured correctly can be tested during the integration testing of pages 1.1.1 and 1.1.2, because comments on a product are reviewed in chronological order.

- *productid:*   Indicates on which product the customer is entering a comment. This value will be entered or selected on page 1.1, so pages 1.1 and 1.1.1 should be tested together. Missi asked John how he is designing page 1.1. John has decided to have users select the product through a series of questions so that only a valid product is used in pages 1.1.1 and 1.1.2. Thus, tests on this field will check that only existing products appear among the values for a customer to select.

- *parent/child?:* Indicates whether the comment is entered by a parent or a child. This field has two values, and John says he will use a pair of radio buttons for entry of this field; the choice of "Parent" will be the default on the page. Thus, this has no meaningful data entry test, but when doing the integration testing with page 1.1.2, Missi will check that the proper value was recorded. Missi makes a note to tell Tracey that John assumes that "Parent" is the default value for this field in the database.
- *memberComment:* Free-form textual comment entered by the customer about the selected product. Special cases of this field are that the customer submits the comment before entering a value for this field or enters a comment that is longer than what can

be stored. Because the team chose to use the Memo data type for this field, a truncated field is unlikely.

Besides making sure MyBroadway can handle alternative values for each field, Missi considered other important tests she learned about in her classes at St. Claire. Because the prototype will be used on only one PC in the store, there are no issues of concurrent use of the Comment data. Also, stress testing is of no concern for the same reason. Because Carrie has never indicated that security is a concern, no security testing will be done. A type of recovery test would be to turn off the power to the PC during the entry of data. Performance testing is also of no concern with the limited usage prototype the team is building.

Case Summary

Missi is fairly confident that she has a good start on detailing the testing plan for MyBroadway. Once she can put her ideas on the example test case into a form for Professor Tann to review along with the testing outline, Missi will be ready to set a time line for testing. She needs to check with her team members to see when they think each module of the system will be ready for testing, and when they will need the instructions from her on how they should do their individual alpha testing.

CASE QUESTIONS

1. Using Figure 14.4 as a guide, develop a test case description and summary form for the test Missi has designed for page 1.1.1.
2. Critically evaluate the outline of a testing plan Missi has developed (BEC Figure 14.1). Can you think of missing steps? Are too many steps included, and should some steps be combined?
3. The testing outline in BEC Figure 14.1 does not show sequencing of steps and what steps could be done in parallel. Develop a testing schedule from this figure, using Microsoft Project or another charting tool that shows how you would suggest sequencing the testing steps. Make assumptions for the length of each testing step.
4. One element of the testing plan outline is cycling the alpha testing of pages as Missi tests and finds problems, and then the other team members have to rewrite the code for the problematic module. What guideline would you use to determine when to stop the alpha testing and release the module for beta testing with employees?

5. Design the test documentation format that Tracey, John, or Aaron is to use to explain how that student tested his or her code and the results of that testing.
6. Design the customer feedback form to be used to capture comments from customers during their use of the MyBroadway prototype. What measures of usability should be established for MyBroadway, and is a customer feedback form a sufficient means to capture all the usability measures you believe should be collected?
7. How would you suggest that the beta testing with customers be conducted? For example, should users use the system directly or through someone else at the keyboard and mouse? Should the customer be observed while using the system, either by a student team member watching or by videotape?
8. Do you think that the reuse of components available free of charge on the Internet will be worthwhile for the students? Justify your answer.

White Paper: TP-173 5/00. www.rational.com, accessed 10/3/2002.

Martin, R. C. 1999. *Iterative and incremental development.* Object Mentor Article. www.objectmentor.com, accessed 8/6/03.

Martin, R. C. 2002. *Agile software development: Principles, patterns, and practices.* Upper Saddle River, NJ: Prentice Hall.

Martin, R. C. 2002. Continuous care vs. initial design. *Object Mentor Article.* Available at www.objectmentor.com, accessed 8/6/03.

Martin, R. C. 2003. *UML for Java programmers.* Upper Saddle River, NJ: Prentice Hall.

McConnell, S. 1996. *Rapid development.* Redmond, WA: Microsoft Press.

Miller, R. W. 1989. *How to plan and control with PERT: Managing projects and programs.* Boston: Harvard Business School Press.

Murch, R. 2001. *Project management: Best practices for IT professionals.* Upper Saddle River, NJ: Prentice Hall.

Nicholas, J. 2001. *Project management for business and technology: Principles and practice.* Upper Saddle River, NJ: Prentice Hall.

Page-Jones, M. 1985. *Practical project management.* New York: Dorset House.

Pressman, R. S. 2001. *Software engineering: A practitioner's approach.* 5th ed. New York: McGraw-Hill.

Rettig, M. 1990. Software teams. *Communications of the ACM 33* (10): 23–27.

Royce, W. 1998. *Software project management.* Boston: Addison-Wesley.

Rumbaugh, J., I. Jacobson, and G. Booch. 1999. *The Unified Modeling Language reference manual.* Reading, MA: Addison-Wesley Longman, Inc.

Schwalbe, K. 2002. *Information technology project management.* 2d ed. Boston: Course Technology.

Thomsett, R. 1985. Foreword to *Practical project management,* by M. Page-Jones. New York: Dorset House.

Zachary, G. P. 1993. Agony and ecstasy of 200 code writers beget Windows NT. *Wall Street Journal* (May 26): A1–A6.

Chapter 4

Applegate, L. M., and F. W. McFarlan. 1999. *Corporate information systems management: The challenges of managing in an information age.* 5th ed. New York: McGraw-Hill.

Atkinson, R. A. 1990. The motivations for strategic planning. *Journal of Information Systems Management 7* (4): 53–56.

Atkinson, R. A., and J. Montgomery. 1990. Reshaping IS strategic planning. *Journal of Information Systems Management 7* (4): 9–15.

Carlson, C. K., E. P. Gardner, and S. R. Ruth. 1989. Technology-driven long-range planning. *Journal of Information Systems Management 6* (3): 24–29.

Dewan, S., S. C. Michael, and C-k. Min. 1998. Firm characteristics and investments in information technology: Scale and scope effects. *Information Systems Research 9* (3): 219–32.

Hasselbring, W. 2000. Information system integration. *Communications of the ACM 43* (6): 33–38.

Hoffer, J. A., J. F. George, and J. S. Valacich. 2005. *Modern systems analysis and design.* 4th ed. Upper Saddle River, NJ: Prentice Hall.

IBM. 1982. Business systems planning. In *Advanced system development/feasibility techniques,* ed. J. D. Couger, M. A. Colter, and R. W. Knapp, 236–314. New York: Wiley.

Kerr, J. 1990. The power of information systems planning. *Database Programming and Design 3* (December): 60–66.

King, J. L., and E. Schrems. 1978. Cost benefit analysis in information systems development and operation. *ACM Computing Surveys 10* (1): 19–34.

Kirsch, L. J. 2000. Software project management: An integrated perspective for an emerging paradigm. In *Framing the domains of IT management: Projecting the future from the past,* ed. R. W. Zmud, chapter 15: 285–304. Cincinnati: Pinnaflex Educational Resources.

Koory, J. L., and D. B. Medley. 1987. *Management information systems: Planning and decision making.* Cincinnati: South-Western.

Lederer, A. L., and J. Prasad. 1992. Nine management guidelines for better cost estimating. *Communications of the ACM 35* (2): 51–59.

Martin, J. 1990. *Information engineering.* Upper Saddle River, NJ: Prentice Hall.

McKeen, J. D., T. Guimaraes, and J. C. Wetherbe. 1994. A comparative analysis of MIS project selection mechanisms. *Data Base 25* (February): 43–59.

Moriarty, T. 1991. Framing your system. *Database Programming and Design 4* (June): 57–59.

Morton, C. 1992. Information competition: Can OLTP and DSS peacefully coexist? *Data Base Management 2* (June): 24–28.

Parker, M. M., and R. J. Benson. 1988. *Information economics.* Upper Saddle River, NJ: Prentice Hall.

Parker, M. M., and R. J. Benson. 1989. Enterprisewide information management: State-of-the-art strategic planning. *Journal of Information Systems Management 6* (Summer): 14–23.

Porter, M. 1980. *Competitive strategy: Techniques for analyzing industries and competitors.* New York: Free Press.

Porter, M. 1985. *Competitive advantage.* New York: Free Press.

Pressman, R. S. 2001. Software engineering: A practitioner's approach. 5th ed. New York: McGraw-Hill.

Radosevich, L. 1996. Can you measure Web ROI? *Datamation* (July): 92–96.

Reifer, D. J. 2002. The business case for development. *Application Development Trends* (August): 32–42.

Reingruber, M. J., and D. L. Spahr. 1992. Putting data back in database design. *Data Base Management 2* (March): 19–21.

Ross, J., and D. Feeny. 2000. The evolving role of the CIO. In *Framing the domains of IT management: Projecting the future from the past,* ed. R. W. Zmud, chapter 19: 385–402. Cincinnati: Pinnaflex Educational Resources.

Segars, A. H., and V. Grover. 1999. Profiles of strategic information systems planning. *Information Systems Planning 10* (3): 199–232.

Shank, J. K., and V. Govindarajan. 1993. *Strategic cost management*. New York: Free Press.

Yourdon, E. 1989. *Structured walkthroughs*. 4th ed. Upper Saddle River, NJ: Prentice Hall.

Chapter 5

Beck, K. 2000. *eXtreme Programming eXplained*. Upper Saddle River, NJ: Addison-Wesley.

Carmel, E., J. F. George, and J. F. Nunamaker, Jr. 1992. *Supporting joint application development (JAD) with electronic meeting systems: A field study*. Proceedings of the thirteenth international conference on information systems. Dallas (December): 223–32.

Carmel, E., R. Whitaker, and J. F. George. 1993. Participatory design and joint application design: A transatlantic comparison. *Communications of the ACM 36* (June): 40–48.

Constantine, L. 2002. Process agility and software usability: Toward lightweight usage-centered design. *Information Age* (August/Sept).

Davenport, T. H. 1993. *Process innovation: Reengineering work through information technology*. Boston: Harvard Business School Press.

Dennis, A. R., J. F. George, L. Jessup, J. F. Nunamaker, Jr., and D. R. Vogel. 1988. Information technology to support electronic meetings. *MIS Quarterly 12* (December): 591–624.

Dobyns, L., and C. Crawford-Mason. 1991. *Quality or else*. Boston: Houghton Mifflin.

Hammer, M., and J. Champy. 1993. *Reengineering the corporation*. New York: Harper Business.

Lucas, M. A. 1993. The way of JAD. *Database Programming and Design 6* (July): 42–49.

Mintzberg, H. 1973. *The nature of managerial work*. New York: Harper & Row.

Moad, J. 1994. After reengineering: Taking care of business. *Datamation 40* (20): 40–44.

Naumann, J. D., and A. M. Jenkins. 1982. Prototyping: The new paradigm for systems development. *MIS Quarterly 6* (3): 29–44.

Patton, J. 2002. Designing requirements: Incorporating usage-centered design into an agile SW development process. In D. Wells and L. Williams (eds), *XP/Agile Universe 2002*, LNCS 2418, 1–12. Berlin: Springer-Verlag.

Wood, J., and D. Silver. 1989. *Joint application design*. New York: Wiley.

Chapter 6

Chonoles, M. J., and J. A. Schardt. 2003. *ULM 2 for Dummies*. NY: Wiley Publishing Inc.

Cockburn, A. 2001. *Writing effective use cases*. Reading, MA: Addison-Wesley.

Cockburn, A. 2002. Use case fundamentals. http://members.aol.com/acockburn/papers/AltIntro.htm, accessed 11/7/02.

Eriksson, H., and M. Penker. 1998. *UMLToolkit*. New York: Wiley.

Jacobson, I., M. Christerson, P. Jonsson, and G. Overgaard. 1992. *Object-oriented software engineering: A use-case driven approach*. Reading, MA: Addison-Wesley.

Kettenis, J. 2005. "Getting Started with Use Case Modeling: An Oracle White Paper." Redwood Shores, CA: Oracle Corp. Available at http://www.oracle.com/technology/products/jdev/collateral/papers/10g/gswUseCaseModeling.pdf. Accessed 10/17/2005.

Rosenburg, D., and K. Scott. 1999. *Use case driven object modeling with UML*. Reading, MA: Addison-Wesley.

Chapter 7

Booch, G., J. Rumbaugh, and I. Jacobson. 1999. *The Unified Modeling Language user guide*. Upper Saddle River, NJ: Addison-Wesley.

Chen, P. P. 1976. The entity-relationship model: Toward a unified view of data. *ACM Transactions on Database Systems 1* (1): 9–36.

Quatrani, T. 1999. *Visual modeling with Rational Rose 2000 and UML*. Upper Saddle River, NJ: Addison-Wesley.

Ram, S. 1995. Deriving functional dependencies from the entity relationship model. *Communications of the ACM 38* (9): 95–107.

Rosenberg, D., and K. Scott. 1999. *Use case driven object modeling*. Upper Saddle River, NJ: Addison-Wesley.

Rumbaugh, J., I. Jacobson, and G. Booch. 1999. *The Unified Modeling Language reference manual*. Upper Saddle River, NJ: Addison-Wesley.

Teorey, T. J. 1990. *Database modeling and design: The entity-relationship approach*. San Mateo, CA: Morgan Kaufmann.

Valacich, J. S., J. F. George, and Jeffrey A. Hoffer. 2006. *Essentials of systems analysis and design*. 3d ed. Upper Saddle River, NJ: Prentice Hall.

Chapter 8

Brown, P. 2001. *Object-relational database development*. Upper Saddle River, NJ: Prentice Hall.

Date, C. J., and H. Darwen. 1998. *Foundation for object/relational databases*. Reading, MA: Addison-Wesley.

Hoffer, J. A., M. B. Prescott, and F. R. McFadden. 2002. *Modern database management*. Upper Saddle River, NJ: Prentice Hall.

Loney, K. 2004. *Oracle Database 10g: The complete reference*. New York: McGraw-Hill.

Muller, R. J. 1999. *Database design for smarties*. San Francisco, CA: Morgan Kaufmann.

Rahayu, J. W., D. Taniar, and E. Pardede. 2006. *Object-Oriented Oracle*. Hershey, PA: Cybertech Publishing.

Chapter 9

Boggs, W., and M. Boggs. 1999. *Mastering UML with Rational Rose*. Alameda, CA: Sybex.

Booch, G., J. Rumbaugh, and I. Jacobson. 1999. *The Unified Modeling Language user guide*. Upper Saddle River, NJ: Addison-Wesley.

Fowler, M., and S. Fowler. 1997. *UML distilled*. Upper Saddle River, NJ: Addison-Wesley.

Fowler, M., and K. Scott. 1999. *UML distilled*. 2nd ed. Reading, MA: Addison-Wesley.

von Halle, B. 2002. *Business rules applied.* New York: John Wiley.

Quatrani, T. 1999. *Visual modeling with Rational Rose 2000 and UML.* Upper Saddle River, NJ: Addison-Wesley.

Rosenberg, D., and K. Scott. 1999. *Use case driven object modeling.* Upper Saddle River, NJ: Addison-Wesley.

Rosenberg, D., and K. Scott. 2001. *Applying use case driven object modeling with UML.* Upper Saddle River, NJ: Pearson Education.

Valacich, J. S., J. F. George, and Jeffrey A. Hoffer. 2006. *Essentials of systems analysis and design.* 3d ed. Upper Saddle River, NJ: Prentice Hall.

Warmer, J. and A. Kleppe. 2003. *The object constraint language.* 2nd ed. Boston, MA: Pearson Education.

Chapter 10

2005. "Software 500." Available at http://www.softwaremag.com, accessed 10/18/2005.

Applegate, L. M., and R. Montealegre. 1991. *Eastman Kodak Company: Managing information systems through strategic alliances.* Harvard Business School case 9-192-030. Cambridge, MA: President and Fellows of Harvard College.

Cowley, S. 2004. "JP Morgan cancels $5bn IBM Outsourcing Deal." ComputerWeekly.com, 9/16/04. Available at http://www.computerweekly.com/Article133359.htm, accessed 10/27/04.

Coy, P. The future of work. *BusinessWeek,* March 22, 2004, pp. 50–52.

Gross, G. 2005. "US Government to Award $250 Billion in IT Contracts." OutSourcingWorld. Available at http://www.oswmag.com/news/viewArticle/ARTICLEID=329, accessed 10/25/2005.

Harper, D. 1994. Seek a partner, not a vendor. *Industrial Distribution 83* (April): 97.

Hartmann, C. R. 1993. How to write a proposal. *D & B Reports 42* (March–April): 62.

King, R. T., Jr., and J. E. Rigdon. 1994. Hewlett prints computer services in big capital letters. *Wall Street Journal* (June 3): B8.

Microcomputer procurement guidelines. 1994. *Public Works 125* (April 15): G23 1.

Mikulski, F. A. 1993. *Managing your vendors: The business of buying technology.* Upper Saddle River, NJ: Prentice Hall.

Moad, J. 1993. Inside an outsourcing deal. *Datamation 39* (February 15): 20–27.

More companies are chucking their computers. 1989. *Business Week* (June 19): 72–74.

Semich, J. W. Is it bye-bye Borland? *Datamation 40* (June 15): 52–53.

Stein, M. 1993. Don't bomb out when preparing RFPs. *Computerworld 27* (February 15): 102.

Woodie, A. 2005. "ERP Market Grew Solidly in 2004, AMR Research Says." *The Windows Observer,* 2(25). Available at http://www.itjungle.com/two/twp062205-story04.html, accessed 10/25/2005.

Zachary, G. P. 1990. How Ashton-Tate lost its leadership in PC software arena. *Wall Street Journal* (April 1): A1–A2.

Zachary, G. P., and W. M. Bulkeley. 1990. Ashton-Tate loses flagship software's copyright shield. *Wall Street Journal* (December 14): B1, B4.

Chapter 11

Bordoloi, B., and D. Bock. 2003. *Oracle SQL.* Upper Saddle River, NJ: Prentice Hall.

Elmasri, R., and S. Navathe. 2000. *Fundamentals of database systems.* Reading, MA: Addison-Wesley.

Hoffer, J. A., M. B. Prescott, and F. R. McFadden. 2002. *Modern database management.* Upper Saddle River, NJ: Prentice Hall.

Loney, K., and G. Koch. 2002. *Oracle9i: The complete reference.* Berkeley, CA: Oracle Press.

Chapter 12

Coyle, F. P. 2002. *XML, web services, and the data revolution.* Boston, MA: Addison-Wesley.

D'Souza, D. F., and A. C. Wills. 2002. *Objects, components, and frameworks with UML.* Reading, MA: Addison-Wesley.

Deitel, H. M., D. J. Deitel, and T. R Nieto. 2001. *e-Business and e-Commerce.* New Jersey: Prentice Hall.

Kroenke, D. 2004. *Database processing: Fundamentals, design, and implementation.* NJ: Pearson Education.

Morisseau-Leroy, N., M. K. Solomon, and J. Basu. 2000. *Oracle 8i Java component programming with EJB, CORBA, and JSP.* Berkeley, CA: McGraw-Hill.

Pattison, T. 2000. *Programming distributed applications with COM+ and VB 6.0.* Redmond, WA: Microsoft Press.

Pender, T. 2003. *UML Bible.* Indianapolis, IN: Wiley Publishing, Inc.

Rayayu, J. W., D. Taniar, and E. Pardede. 2006. *Object-Oriented Oracle.* Hershey, PA: CyberTech Publishing.

Reynolds, M., et al. 2001. *Beginning VisualBasic.NET.* Birmingham, UK: Wrox Press.

Tabor, R. 2002. Microsoft.NET XML Web services. Indianapolis, IN: Sams.

PriceWaterhouseCoopers. 2001. *Technology Forecast: 2001-2003.* Menlo Park, CA: PriceWaterhouseCoopers.

Chapter 13

Flanders, V., and M. Willis. 1998. *Web pages that suck: Learn good design by looking at bad design.* Alameda, CA: Sybex Publishing.

Johnson, J. 2000. *GUI bloopers: Don'ts and do's for software developers and Web designers.* San Diego: Academic Press.

Nielsen, J. 1999. User interface directions for the Web. *Communications of the ACM 42* (1): 65–71.

Nielsen, J. 2000. *Designing Web usability: The practice of simplicity.* Indianapolis: New Riders Publishing.

Snyder, C. 2003. *Paper prototyping: The fast and easy way to design and refine user interfaces.* San Francisco: Morgan Kaufmann Publishers.

www.useit.com

www.webpagesthatsuck.com

Chapter 14

Basili, V. R., L. C. Briand, and W. L. Melo. 1996. How reuse influences productivity in object-oriented systems. *Communications of the ACM 39* (10): 104–16.

Beck, K. 2000. eXtreme programming eXplained. Upper Saddle River, NJ: Addison-Wesley.

Bell, P., and C. Evans. 1989. *Mastering documentation.* New York: Wiley.

Bichler, M., A. Segev, and J. L. Zhao. 1998. Component-based e-commerce: Assessment of current practices and future directions. *SIGMOD Record 27* (4): 7–14.

Brooks, F. P., Jr. 1995. *The mythical man-month.* Anniversary ed. Reading, MA: Addison-Wesley.

Cole, K., O. Fischer, and P. Saltzman. 1997. Just-in-time knowledge delivery. *Communications of the ACM 40* (7): 49–53.

Crowley, A. 1993. The help desk gains respect. *PC Week 10* (November 15): 138.

de Souza, S., N. Anquetil, and K. de Oliveira. 2005. *A study of the documentation essential to software maintenance.* ACM SIGDOC '05, Coventry, UK, 68–75.

Dillon, N. 1997. Internet-based training passes audit. *Computerworld* (November 3): 47–48.

Downes, S. 2005. E-learning 2.0 *E-learn Magazine.* Available at elearnma.org, accessed 11/30/2005.

Eason, K. 1988. *Information technology and organizational change.* London: Taylor & Francis.

Fayad, M. E., and D. C. Schmidt. 1997. Object-oriented application frameworks. *Communications of the ACM 40* (10): 32–38.

Ginzberg, M. J. 1981a. Early diagnosis of MIS implementation failure: Promising results and unanswered questions. *Management Science 27* (4): 459–78.

Ginzberg, M. J. 1981b. Key recurrent issues in the MIS implementation process. *MIS Quarterly 5* (2) (June): 47–59.

Grinter, R. E. 2001. *From local to global coordination: Lessons from software reuse.* Proceedings of Group '01, Boulder, CO: 144–53.

Griss, M. 2003. *Reuse comes in several flavors.* Flashline White Paper. Available at www.flashline.com, accessed 6/9/2003.

Ives, B., and M. H. Olson. 1984. User involvement and MIS success: A review of research. *Management Science 30* (5): 586–603.

Jones, C. 1997. How to measure software costs. *Application Development Trends* (May): 32–36.

Kim, K-J, C. J. Bonk, and T. T. Zeng. 2005. Surveying the future of workplace e-learning: The rise of blending, interactivity, and authentic learning. *E-learn Magazine.* Available at elearning.org. accessed 11/30/2005.

Kim, Y., and E. A. Stohr. 1998. Software reuse: Survey and research directions. *Journal of MIS 14* (4): 113–47.

Legard, D. 2000. Study: Online maintenance costs just keep growing. *InfoWorld* (November 8). Available at http://www.pcworld.com/resource/article/0%2Caid%2C34502%2C00.asp, accessed 8/8/2003.

Lytton, N. 2001. Maintenance dollars at work. (July 16). *Computerworld.* Available at www.computerworld.com, accessed 6/9/2003.

Mosley, D. J. 1993. *The handbook of MIS application software testing.* Upper Saddle River, NJ: Yourdon Press.

United States General Accounting Office. 2003. *Information technology training: Practices of leading private-sector companies.* Available at http://www.gao.gov/getrpt?GAO-03-390, accessed 11/30/2005.

Worthen, B. 2003. No tolerance for high maintenance. *CIO Magazine* (June 1). Available at www.cio.com/archive/060103/vendor.html, accessed 6/9/2003.

Acronym Glossary

1:1	unary	**JVM**	Java Virtual Machine
1:m	one to many	**LF**	late finish
1NF	first normal form	**LLBGC**	Lilly Langley's Baking Goods Company
2NF	second normal form	**M:N**	many-to-many relationship
3NF	third normal form	**MIS**	management information system
ACID	atomicity, consistency, isolation, and durability	**MSIL**	Microsoft Intermediate Language
ADO	ActiveX Data Objects	**MTBF**	mean time between failures
API	application programming interfaces	**MTS**	Microsoft Transaction Server
ASP	Active Server Pages	**NBDS**	Natural Best Delivery Service
ATM	automated teller machine	**NPV**	net present value
B2B	business to business	**OCL**	Object Constraint Language
BBS	Build a Better System	**ODBC**	Open Database Connectivity
BCNF	Boyce Codd normal form	**OMG**	Object Management Group
BLOB	binary large objects	**OODBMS**	object-oriented DBMS
BPP	baseline project plan	**OOSAD**	object-oriented systems analysis and design
CASE	computer-aided software engineering	**ORB**	object request broker
CD	compact disc	**ORDBMS**	object-relational DBMS
CIO	chief information officer	**ORDM**	object-relational data model
CLR	Common Language Runtime	**PDA**	personal digital assistant
COM	Component Object Model	**PERT**	Program Evaluation Review Technique
CORBA	Common Object Request Broker Architecture	**PK**	primary key
DBMS	database management systems	**PVF**	Pine Valley Furniture
DCOM	distributed COM	**RDBMS**	by relational DBMS
DFD	data flow diagram	**RDM**	relational database model
DLL	dynamic link library	**RFP**	request for proposal
DSS	decision support system	**RFQ**	request for quote
EAD	Enterprise Application Design	**RMI**	remote method invocation
EDP	electronic data processing	**ROI**	return on investment
EF	early finish	**RPC**	remote procedure calls
EIP	enterprise information portal	**RUP**	Rational Unified Process
EIS	executive information system	**SDC**	systems development cycle
EJB	Enterprise Java Beans	**SDLC**	systems development life cycle
EPSS	electronic performance support system	**SMTP**	Simple Mail Transfer Protocol
ER	entity relationship	**SOAP**	Simple Object Access Protocol
ERP	enterprise resource planning	**SQL**	Structured Query Language
ET	estimated time	**SSR**	systems service request
FTP	File Transfer Protocol	T_E	earliest expected completion time
GUI	graphical user interface	T_L	latest expected completion time
HTML	HyperText Markup Language	**TCP/IP**	Transmission Control Protocol/Internet Protocol
HTTP	HyperText Transfer Protocol	**TPS**	transaction processing system
IDL	Interface Definition Language	**TVM**	time value of money
IE	information engineering	**UML**	Unified Modeling Language
IIS	Internet Information Services	**UPS**	universal power supply
J2EE	Java 2 Enterprise Edition	**VB**	Visual Basic
JAD	joint application design	**WBS**	work breakdown structure
JDK	Java Development Kit	**XML**	Extensible Markup Language
JSP	Java Server Pages		

Inspection A testing technique in which participants examine a program code for predictable, language-specific errors.

Installation The organizational process of changing over from the current information system to a new one.

Intangible benefit A benefit derived from the creation of an information system that cannot be measured in dollars easily or with certainty.

Intangible cost A cost associated with an information system that cannot be measured in terms of dollars easily or with certainty.

Integration testing The process of bringing together all of the objects and components that a program comprises for testing purposes.

Interface A named set of operations that characterize the behavior of a class or component.

Interface Definition Language (IDL) A language that defines interfaces so that client-side and server-side elements, written in different programming languages, can interoperate.

Internal documentation System documentation that is part of the program source code or is generated at compile time.

Interrelated components Dependence of one part of the system on one or more other system parts.

Invariant A constraint that should be true for an object during its lifetime.

Iteration A time-bound minor milestone within a phase.

Iterative methodology Development of a piece by growing, improving, and refining over several time periods.

JAD session leader The trained individual who plans and leads Joint Application Design sessions.

Java 2 Enterprise Edition (J2EE) A Sun development framework that provides a specification of architectural components designed to work together to define a complete enterprise architecture. It also includes XML, SOAP, and Web services.

Java Server Pages (JSPs) A technology that mixes Java code with HTML and XML to generate dynamic Web pages.

Java Virtual Machine (JVM) An interpreter designed specifically for each type of computing platform to execute Java bytecode, which is produced during the compilation of a Java program.

JavaBean A Java class that follows certain design rules for naming conventions.

JavaScript A scripting language created by Netscape to enhance the functionality and appearance of Web pages. JavaScript is not Java. The Microsoft version is called Jscript.

JDBC A middleware to connect a Java application with a database in a DBMS-independent manner.

Key A field or a combination of fields whose values are used for searching row objects.

Legal and contractual feasibility The process of assessing potential legal and contractual ramifications due to the construction of a system.

Level Perspective from which a use-case description is written, typically ranging from high level to extremely detailed.

Maintenance Changes made to a system to fix or enhance its functionality.

Mean time between failures (MTBF) A measurement of error occurrences that can be tracked over time to indicate the quality of a system.

Message The passing of information from one object to another.

Method The implementation of an operation.

Microsoft Intermediate Language (MSIL) A low-level, platform-independent language that is created as an intermediate step when a language is compiled in .NET.

Middle tier Application layer sandwiched between presentation and data layers.

Middleware Software that provides one set of interfaces for connection to a client and another set of interfaces for connection to a server, thereby providing the possibility of connections between one of several clients and one of several servers.

Minimal guarantee The least amount promised to the stakeholder by a use case.

Modularity Dividing a system into smaller chunks or modules.

Multiplicity The range of the number of objects of class A that can (or must) be associated with each object of class B.

Multivalued attribute An attribute that can take on more than one value for each object.

.NET A Microsoft development framework that integrates COM1 and Active Server Pages (ASP) technologies but builds it around XML/SOAP to deliver software as Web services.

Network Diagram A diagram that depicts project tasks and their interrelationships.

Nonfunctional requirements Desired system characteristics that describe not what the software will do but how it will do it. Nonfunctional requirements include such qualities as cost, maintainability, and security.

Normalization A process for converting complex data structures into well-structured relations.

N-tier architecture A design architecture based on multiple layers that address presentation, business logic, and data.

Null value A special field value, distinct from 0, blank, or any other value, that indicates that the value for the field is missing or otherwise unknown.

Object An entity that encapsulates properties and behavior.

Object Constraint Language (OCL) An add-on to UML to write expressions that specify business rules in an unambiguous manner.

Object framework A collection of cooperating objects that provide an integrated solution for a particular problem.

Object identifier A unique value assigned for identity purposes by a software such as an ORDBMS or a programming language when an object is first created. Identity is the property of an object that makes it distinct even if the state is the same as that of an object that makes it distinct even if the state is the same as that of another object.

Object Management Group (OMG)   An open-membership, not-for-profit consortium that produces and maintains computer industry specifications for interoperable enterprise applications (http://www.omg.org).

Object-oriented systems analysis and design approach (OOSAD)   An analysis and design approach based on notion of an object, which captures the data and processes of a thing in a single construct.

Object-relational data model (ORDM)   A relational data model with object-oriented extensions.

Object Request Broker (ORB)   A software unit that mediates and directs communication requests from CORBA clients to CORBA server objects.

OLE DB   A middleware based on COM objects that allows connection between an application program and a database in a DBMS-independent manner. OLE DB allows access to relational and other kinds of databases.

One-time cost   A cost associated with project start-up and development, or system start-up.

Open Database Connectivity (ODBC)   An interface developed to allow an application program to make SQL calls in a DBMS-independent manner.

Open-ended question   An interview question that has no prespecified answer.

Operation   A specification that can be used to invoke behavior in an object by passing a message.

Operational feasibility   The process of assessing the degree to which a proposed system solves business problems or takes advantage of business opportunities.

Outsourcing   The practice of turning over responsibility of some to all of an organization's information systems applications and operations to an outside firm.

Package   A general-purpose mechanism for organizing elements into groups.

Package diagram   A diagram that shows the packages and the relationships among them.

Parallel installation   Running the old information system and the new one at the same time until management decides the old system can be turned off.

Pattern   A named description of a problem and solution that can be applied to new contexts.

Perfective maintenance   Changes made to a system to add new features or to improve performance.

Phased installation   Changing from the old information system to the new one incrementally, starting with one or a few functional components and then gradually extending the installation to cover the whole new system.

Physical database design   Part of database design that deals with efficiency considerations for access of data.

Plug-and-play   The ability to substitute one class or component with another without affecting the overall functionality of the system.

Pointer   A value that stores the address of a row object for the purpose of linking.

Political feasibility   The process of evaluating how key stakeholders within the organization view the proposed system.

Polymorphic   Different classes or components implementing the same interfaces.

Preconditions   Things that must be true before a use case can start.

Present value   The current value of a future cash flow.

Presentation layer   The front tier, which addresses the presentation of information to users and acceptance of commands from the users. It may embed some rules such as formatting, calculations, and constraint checking.

Preventive maintenance   Changes made to a system to avoid possible future problems.

Primary key   A candidate key that has been selected as the unique, identifying characteristic for a class.

Private   Visible to the owning object only.

Program Evaluation Review Technique (PERT)   A technique that uses optimistic, pessimistic, and realistic time estimates to calculate the expected time for a particular task.

Project   A planned undertaking of related activities to reach an objective that has a beginning and an end.

Project charter   A short, high-level document prepared for both internal and external stakeholders to formally announce the establishment of the project and to briefly describe its objectives, key assumptions, and stakeholders.

Project closedown   The final phase of the project management process that focuses on bringing a project to an end.

Project execution   The third phase of the project management process in which the plans created in the prior phases (project initiation and planning) are put into action.

Project initiation   The first phase of the project management process in which activities are performed to assess the size, scope, and complexity of the project and to establish procedures to support later project activities.

Project management   A controlled process of initiating, planning, executing, and closing down a project.

Project management and planning   The first step in systems development in which an organization's total information systems needs are analyzed and arranged, and in which a potential information systems project is identified and an argument for continuing or not continuing when the project is presented.

Project manager   A systems analyst with a diverse set of skills—management, leadership, technical, conflict management, and customer relations—who is responsible for initiating, planning, executing, and closing down a project.

Project planning   The second phase of the project management process, which focuses on defining clear, discrete activities and the work needed to complete each activity within a single project.

Project scope statement   A document prepared for the customer that describes what the project will deliver